LONDON STORIES

LONDON STORIES

BEING A COLLECTION OF THE LIVES AND ADVENTURES OF LONDONERS IN ALL AGES
EDITED BY JOHN O' LONDON

"HOW LONDON DOTH POUR OUT
HER CITIZENS!"—*SHAKESPEARE*

CRESCENT BOOKS
New York

First published 1882
by T. C. and E. C. Jack, London and Edinburgh.

1985 edition published by Crescent Books.
Distributed in the USA by Crown Publishers, Inc.

ISBN 0-517-494655

Printed and bound in Finland by
Werner Söderström Oy.

CONTENTS

	PAGE
Bow Bells	1
The "Old Cheshire Cheese"	5
Jane Shore	9
The Old London Christmas	12
The King of Bootmakers	16
Back from Agincourt	17
John Baldwin Buckstone	21
The Musical Small-Coal Man	24
The Duke of Wellington in London	26
Ivan Turgenev in London	33
Swearing on the Horns	35
The Charlies	37
Lord Macaulay at Campden Hill	41
Primrose Hill	43
The Great Fire	45
Miss Whitehead, the "Bank Nun"	52
William Hogarth	55
London Catch Phrases	61
An Earl at Tyburn	62
Sam House	66
The Great South Sea Bubble	67
Thomas Carlyle in London	75
"Poodle" Byng	80
Baron D'Aguilar	82
The Sublime Society of Beef Steaks	85
Old Opera Days	89
John Cavanagh, Fives Player	94
The London Omnibus	97
Dr. Johnson in Fleet Street	103
Verlaine in London	105
The Garrotters of the Sixties	107
The Blue-Stockings	111
The Prince at Carlton House	115
The Decline of Hanging	119
A Portrait in the Abbey	124
Jedediah Jones in Search of London	127
How Railways Came to London	133
Disraeli's Golden Youth	138
The Old Cogers	142
The Birth of the National Gallery	144
Evans's Supper Rooms	149
Sally in Our Alley	152
Swiss Cottage	155
The Ghost of Berkeley Square	157
Paul's Cross	160
Sir Walter Raleigh at Islington	163
Almack's Assemblies	165
Coronation Robes and Humours	167
Benjamin Webster at the Adelphi	170
	PAGE
"The Unfortunate Dr. Dodd"	173
A Millbank Myth	177
Dolly's Chop-House	178
The Old Canterbury	179
The Jester Who Built a Hospital	182
The Fleet Marriages	185
Painting the Dome of St. Paul's	188
The Beautiful Gunnings	190
The Beheading of Sir Walter Raleigh	194
Charlotte Brontë in London	197
Major Foubert's Passage	201
Old Tea-Drinking Days in London	203
Lord Erskine at Hampstead	206
Oliver Cromwell's Head	209
How Gas Came to London	211
Where Scots Foregathered	213
How the Chartists Shook London	217
Theodore Hook and the Berners Street Hoax	221
Old Sadler's Wells and its Theatre	225
Tennyson in London	228
The Trial of Henry Fauntleroy	233
The Burning of the Houses of Parliament	237
Crockford's	242
The Londoner who Wrote "Robinson Crusoe"	245
Samuel Rogers at Stoke Newington	247
The Porter and the Dwarf	249
The Leverian Museum	250
The Wild Lord Camelford	252
Georgiana, Duchess of Devonshire	255
Statesmen at Play	260
Louis Napoleon in London	262
Round About Northumberland House	265
A Drury Lane Romance	269
The Lion Comique	273
The Birth of the British Museum	275
Daniel Lambert	278
The Lord Dundreary Mania	280
The Execution of Lord Derwentwater	285
A Shakespearean Character	288
The Old London Dustman	289
An Eccentric Lady	292
Some Early London Highwaymen	293
An Old Duelling Resort	299
Chateaubriand in London	300
An Old London Ferry-boat	304

▼

CONTENTS

	PAGE
John Wilkes	307
"Paris is but a Dog-hole to it"	312
The Writing on the Wall	317
A Queen's Funeral Triumph	311
George Cruikshank in the Hampstead Road	319
The Marble Arch	322
The Empire at Home	323
The Macaronis	325
The Colosseum	329
King and Bankrupt	331
White's	334
A Memorable Party	338
Charles II's Return to London	339
The Story of Christie's	342
A Famous Player at Draughts	346
Glorious Siddons	347
The Old Night Haunts	351
George Morland in London	354
A Debut at Drury Lane	357
Louis Philippe in London	360
The "Spectator's" London	363
Three Poets in One Court Suit	365
The Gold-headed Cane and its Owners	366
The Cockney of Old Time	368
A Nest of Genius at Chelsea	369
Old St. Dunstan's Clock	374
George Augustus Sala	376
The Execution of Lord William Russell	379
Miser and Landlord	382
Voltaire in London	383
The Thames Pirates	386
A Dandy Whip	389
Nelson in London	390
A Famous Dwarf	395
Round the Clock in a London Prison	396
The Last Hours of Monmouth	402
Tattersall's	405
The Bellman of Holborn	408
The Great Storm of 1703	409
London Bridge is Broken Down	411
Sydney Smith in London	414
London's First Balloon and Parachute	417
Henry Fielding at Bow Street	421
The Golden Ball	424
The Clapham Sect	425
The Death of Sir Robert Peel	428
Hazard at Brooks's	431
Old Harry	433
Peter the Great in London	434
The "Boar's Head" in Eastcheap	438
Madame de Staël in London	440
Newcastle House and its Duke	442
Turner in Maiden Lane	445
Benjamin Franklin as a London Compositor	447
The Admiralty Semaphore	448
Garibaldi in London	450
The Crystal Palace	452
"Gentleman Jackson"	455
The O.P. Riots	457
Shooting the Bridge	459
Jean Jacques Rousseau in London	461
A Remarkable Epitaph	463
Don Saltero's Museum	464
George Augustus Selwyn	466
Daniel Defoe in the Pillory	468
An Old House in Pall Mall	469
The Humorist of Craven Street	472
Pierce Egan	474
Wylde's Globe, Leicester Square	475
A Tragedy of London Literary Life	476
London by the Sea	479
Thrice Found "Not Guilty"	486
The Tournament on the Bridge	492
The Nelson Column	494
Index	497

BOW BELLS

IN Old London the ringing of bells was incessant. Sir Walter Besant vividly describes the jinglings and the janglings, the sonorous clang and the melodious peal, the chimings and the strikings, the music and the jarring of London's thousand bells. " They rang all day long," he says; " they rang from the great Cathedral and from the little parish church; from the stately monastery, the nunnery, the College of Priests, the Chapel and the Hermitage. . . . They rang in the baby; they rang out the passing soul; they rang for the bride; they rang in memory of the dead; they rang for work to begin and for work to cease; they rang to exhort, to admonish, to console."

But in most cases the sound of these bells has passed away for ever upon the air, and is forgotten; one bell only out of all the City bells still booms in our nursery rhymes and rings in our fairy-tales, enters into our folk-lore, and is so closely identified with London that it has passed into a proverb—Bow Bells, " the Great Bell of Bow."

The present Bow Church in Cheapside was built by Sir Christopher Wren after the Great Fire of 1666; but it stands on the site of a Norman Church, dating from the time of William the

Conqueror. It is with this earlier church that we are at present concerned.

" The Great Bell of Bow "—for at first there was only one bell in the steeple—must have had a deeper note and one of stronger vibration than any of the other City bells. Four miles away, on Highgate Hill, its sound reached the ears of a poor boy who had run away from the city. Above the tinkle of the sheep-bells and the songs of birds its notes rang out ; and as they rolled over the distance they shaped themselves into words : " Turn again, Whittington, Lord Mayor of London." So runs the story : and it is quite possible that the real Richard Whittington, who was thrice Lord Mayor of London in the fifteenth century, may have been called back to the City by the sound of Bow Bells, with its message of human companionship, and busy toil, and joyful activity. For this Bell, swinging out its music at all hours of the day, came to seem the very voice of London herself, to symbolise her hopes and promises, to be her distinguishing feature ; until at last, if you were born within the sound of Bow Bells you belonged to London, you could claim citizenship of the great city, you were, in fact, a " cockney."

The term " cockney " was not at first a term of reproach ; it meant, one who dwelt in the land of Cocaigne, that is, the Land of Plenty. Cocaigne was an imaginary town in mediæval story, where all the houses were made of cake, and all the streets paved with gold : so London appeared to the rude country-folk a city overflowing with food and riches · therefore they called the townspeople cockneys. It would seem from an old play of Elizabeth's time that " Bow Bell " was actually used as synonymous with cockney :

" He's a Bow Bell," signifying, " He's a cockney." Certain it is that in the following century the connection between Bow Bell and cockney was fully established, for Fuller in his *English Worthies*, published 1662, says that to be born within the sound of Bow Bell is the periphrasis of a Londoner, " the sound of this bell exceeding the extent of the Lord Mayor's mace."

Up to a late date Bow Bell rang out the curfew. By a Statute of 1469 it was decreed " that the Bow Bell should be nightly rung by nine of the clock," but the practice of ringing the curfew at this church had existed long before.

It is possible that the apprentices of " Chepe " (as Cheapside was then called) had to work until the curfew sounded—a terribly long day, according to our modern views—or perhaps they were only sleepy. At any rate we learn from an old rhyme that they complained against the late ringing of the bell.

Clarke of the Bow Bell, with the yellow lockes
For thy late ringing thy head shall have knockes.

To this the obsequious clerk replies

Children of Chepe, hold you all still,
For you shall have Bow Bell rung at your will.

The name *Bow* Bells, *Bow* Church, is derived from the architectural form of the church. Just as Bow in East London takes its name from the arched bridge built by Matilda—the first Norman arched bridge constructed in the kingdom—so Bow Church, the Church of the Arches, was so called because it was built over an arched crypt remaining to this day. The Archbishop's Court, held here before the Fire of 1666, took its name from the same source and was called the Court of Arches.

The ancient silver parish seal of St. Mary-le-Bow, which is still in existence, gives us an excellent idea of the steeple as it was before the Great Fire. The first steeple had fallen down in 1271, killing many people, and its re-erection was not completed till 1512. A few years later " the arches or bows thereupon, with the lanthorns, five in number, to wit, one at each corner, and one on the top in the middle upon the arches, were also finished, of stone brought from Caen in Normandy." It was intended to have these lanterns glazed, and lights placed in them nightly during the winter, to guide travellers to the City : but it is doubtful if this was ever done. Such beacons would have been a valuable boon to wayfarers over the dangerous wastes of Moorfields. Five bells were hung in this completed steeple in 1512.

Although the present steeple is considered one of Wren's masterpieces, we would gladly exchange it for the old steeple, fraught with such historic memories, where the Great Bell of Bow sounded.

Wren, however, had some regard for the historic associations of Bow Church : for he constructed a balcony,

CHEAPSIDE CROSS

repeated to this day, on the north face of the tower, at its second story; beneath the projecting clock. This balcony commands a view of Cheapside, and Charles II. and Queen Anne were visitors to its predecessor to see processions. The balcony was made in memory of the " Shed " on the north side of the old church, which Edward III. caused to be strongly built of stone " for himself, the Queen, and other estates to stand in, there to behold the joustings and other shows at their pleasure," the original wooden gallery, used by Edward I. for this purpose, having fallen down. Much of Cheapside was in old days an open space in which tournaments were held, and Bow Church was the best point of vantage for witnessing these, as well as the Lord Mayor's Show, the May Day festivities, the Marching Watch on Midsummer Eve, and the various processions and pageants of which London was so fond. It is a noticeable fact that the only two street-views of London before the Great Fire represent processions passing through Cheapside by the Chepe Cross ; one depicts the Coronation Procession of Edward VI., 1547 ; the other, the procession of Marie de Medici on her visit to Charles I. and his Queen, 1638.

Chepe Cross was perhaps the most striking feature in Chepe. It stood in the middle of the road facing Wood Street, and was one of the nine crosses put up by Edward I. where the coffin of Eleanor his Queen rested on the way from Nottinghamshire to Westminster Abbey. This cross underwent many more vicissitudes than the one at Charing, and in the time of Elizabeth, the figures in the lower tier were attacked and mutilated by the Puritans as Popish images. A little later, an attempt was made to substitute a pyramid for the crucifix, and the goddess Diana for the Virgin Mary. In a tract dated 1641 we find the following curious conversation :

Charing Cross. Sister of Chepe, crosses are incident to us all, and our children. But what's the greatest cross that hath befallen you ?

Chepe Cross. Nay, Sister, if my cross were fallen, I should live at more heart's ease than I do.

Charing Cross. I believe it is the cross upon your head that hath brought you to this trouble, is it not ?

In 1643 Parliament ordered the destruction of Chepe Cross. " At the fall of the top cross," we read, " drums beat, trumpets blew, and multitudes of caps were thrown into the air, and a great shout of people with joy."

And over all these sounds—above the noise of crowbar and pickaxe, above the tramp and music of processions—the voice of London thundered in the Great Bell of Bow.

Bow Bells still ring out—and there are twelve bells now in the belfry. Only eight were hung at first. In 1758, seven of the bells were re-cast and two trebles added, and the ten thus formed were first rung in honour of King George III.'s birthday. Two bells have since been added, so that the full number of twelve is attained. Though their music cannot fling itself over the vast metropolis that has extended on every side, they yet speak to us more intimately than any other sound of a little vanished London, crowded, incredibly busy, compact within its walls ; they ring up in our imagination the coloured scenes of the past, and call to our hearts—as they called to the Londoners of old—with the music of home.

THE OLD
CHESHIRE CHEESE

MANY a bard with lightsome heart and succulent thought of the joys of dining and wining has sung of the pleasures of the Cheese—the Cheshire Cheese in Wine Office Court, Fleet Street, where are still shown the historic chair that Dr. Johnson made his own ; the corner that Goldsmith occupied.

The " Cheese " has ever been the haunt of those famous in the journalistic field, as well as those who have made reputations on the stage.

One lively poet sang years ago :

From Shakespeare and Ben Jonson,
    And players of the age ;
From authors who to Jonson
    Owe their first printed page !
From Johnson, Lexiconic,
    Goldy and Garrick, seize
From them the Attic tonic
    They scattered at the " Cheese."

It may be a decidedly moot point as to whether Shakespeare on his way to the Globe Theatre, on Bankside, made the Cheshire Cheese a house of call, with his old friend Ben Jonson, though it is more likely that Ben Jonson was a visitor. 'Tis said it was in the old Cheshire Cheese that the dispute arose as to who would most quickly make the best couplet :

    I, Sylvester
    Kiss'd your sister.

when the report was

    I, Ben Jonson,
    Kiss'd your wife.

" But that's not rhyme," said Sylvester. " No," said Jonson, " but it's true." To wipe out this little incident many a tankard was passed to and fro, and the contents went to swell the enjoyment of the evening. The Cheshire Cheese was not only famous for its epigrammatists in the seventeenth century and earlier, but it has managed to keep up its reputation for wit and humour even to the present day. The late Lord Tennyson in his younger days besides being a frequenter of the Cock close to Chancery Lane, was often to be seen at the Cheese, and so was Algernon Charles Swinburne.

It was in the celebrated coffee room, where the pudding on certain days is still served with pomp, that Isaac Bickerstaff composed the well-known epigram :

When late I attempted your pity to move,
What made you so deaf to my prayers ?
Perhaps it was right to dissemble your love,
But—why did you kick me downstairs ?

Dr. Johnson, and Dr. Goldsmith, and Sir Joshua Reynolds with, of course, Boswell tripping at their heels, made the Cheese one of their special houses of call, as well as the Mitre, and it has been recorded that in the enthusiasm of a happy moment Johnson said : " There is nothing which has yet been contrived by man, by which so much happiness is produced as by a good tavern or inn."

Thomas Wilson Reid, who compiled a capital handbook about the jolly old establishment which the management of the hotel still issue, said : " Not the least delightful characteristic of the Cheese, is the persistency of its old customers. Those who have once been admitted to its charmed circle soon become wedded to its ways and remain faithful." George Augustus Sala was a most loyal attendant, and constantly took his chop or steak there. After a long visit to Paris " G.A.S.," returned to London, and when he had done his business with the *Daily Telegraph*, of which he was a special correspondent for many years, went immediately to the Cheshire Cheese for the old English

fare, and said to the head waiter : " William ! Bring me a beef steak, some potatoes in their jackets, and a pint of ale. I've had nothing to eat for six weeks "—which, perhaps, was not altogether complimentary to Parisian cookery.

Oliver Goldsmith lived at No. 6 Wine Office Court, nearly opposite the " Cheese," and there he wrote the " Vicar of Wakefield," which Dr. Johnson took to the publisher, old John Newbery, and sold for sixty pounds. The doctor resided within a minute's walk, in Gough Square, where under many great difficulties, his splendid English Dictionary was compiled and finished. In 1868 Mr. Cyrus Jay produced a little work of considerable interest which was dedicated to " The Lawyers and Gentlemen with whom I have dined for more than half a century at the Old Cheshire Cheese, Wine Office Court, Fleet Street." This delightful but somewhat garrulous old gentleman says in his preface : " During the fifty-three years that I have frequented the Cheshire Cheese Tavern there have been only three landlords. When I first visited the house, I used to meet several very old gentlemen who remembered Dr. Johnson being nightly at the Cheshire Cheese ; and they have told me what is not generally known, that the Doctor, whilst living in the Temple, always went to the Mitre or Essex Head ; but when he removed to Gough Square and Bolt Court, he was a constant visitor at the Cheshire Cheese, because nothing but a hurricane would have induced him to cross Fleet Street." Then again Cyrus Redding in his " Fifty Years' Recollections " says, " I often dined at the Cheshire Cheese. Johnson and his friends, I was informed, used to do the same, and

I was told that I should see individuals that had met them there. This I found to be correct ; the company was more select then than in later times. Johnson had been dead about twenty years, but there were Fleet Street tradesmen who well remembered both Johnson and Goldsmith in this place of entertainment." It should be noted that on going into the Cheshire Cheese the room on the left hand and the table on the extreme right, upon entering the apartment, was the table monopolised by Johnson and his friends. This table and the room are still preserved in all their ancient glory. However, when Dr. Johnson wished to retire from the madding crowd, another room on the next floor, supplied all the privacy which they occasionally desired, and here to this day is to be seen the chair in which the Doctor sat and from which he enunciated his thunderous opinions. Above Dr. Johnson's seat hangs his portrait, painted after one by Sir Joshua Reynolds ; and a brass tablet records the fact of his visits. It is daringly said that the memories of the celebrated men already mentioned, mingle with those of the delightful Devonshire poet Herrick, and perhaps of Christopher Marlowe of " the mighty line " of Greece who was so jealous of Shakespeare's popu-

larity, and of Thomas Middleton who wrote " A Mad World, my Masters," and all the players of the day. When we come to later times we know that

AT THE CHESHIRE CHEESE ; THE OLD STAIRCASE

Charles Dickens, John Forster, W. M. Thackeray, Thomas Hood, and Tom Hood (long associated as editor with *Fun*), Wilkie Collins, and many other writers of light and leading, constantly lunched and dined there. And here also foregathered, on their visits to England, the best of American poets and humorists—Longfellow and Mark Twain.

Of course, the one great feature of

the Cheese is " the Pudding," served regularly on Wednesdays and Saturdays " at one-thirty sharp " ; and then, on Shrove Tuesdays, the Pancakes are a joy to all those who like this particular variation of batter. But every kind of food is served daily, and the wines, spirits, and ales are also a speciality— and all visitors to London from the Continent, from America, the Antipodes and elsewhere, know that they have not done London until they have done the " Cheese." In regard to the pudding it is stated that William, who was for many years the head waiter, and who was at the height of his glory on pudding days, used to consider it his duty to go round to the different tables insisting that the guests should have a second or even third helping. " Any gentleman say Pudden ? " was his constant query ; and this habit of pronunciation was not broken even when a crusty customer growled, " No gentleman says Pudden." William either never saw the point, or, with a loftiness of soul which makes the waiter superior to all amendment, disdained to make any reply.

As to the construction of the pudding itself it is, as " Jeames de La Pluche " says, " wropt in mystery," because up to the present the secret of its composition has never been divulged. But we get a little idea of its capacity when we know that it ranges from fifty to sixty pounds in weight, and that in the interior of a huge basin, finally covered with a light, inviting, suet crust, there are nestling such agreeable things as : juicy beefsteaks, agreeable kidneys, fascinating oysters and larks, and delicious mushrooms, with wondrous spices and other ingredients, all blended together—completing that marvellous pudding that is the wonder and the admiration of all who have

been tempted to partake of its joy. The boiling process takes from sixteen to twenty hours and the ceremony of serving it is quite a solemn matter, as any casual visitor or happy customer may judge by the expectancy depicted on the faces of those who, seated at the tables, begin to fumble nervously with their knives and forks directly the monster is wheeled into the room.

In Brain Street once, as George Augustus Sala happily christened the Street of Fleet, sorrow and dismay seized upon the regular Cheshireites who were assembled to do honour to the desired meal. On that day the Pudding was dropped. Let us pause, because the catastrophe cast a gloom over an expectant army of fifty hungry men. The waiter, bringing in triumph the pudding, appeared on the scene with a smiling countenance. By some mishap his foot slipped, the pudding lost its balance and also slipped on the floor, broke into fragments, and gathered nothing on its perilous way but sawdust as it tumbled and splashed along.

There was a breathless silence. The proprietor, Mr. Beaufrey Moore, dropped the upraised carver, stood speechless for a moment, and then went out and— and the rest is silence. And those who had come to the feast departed in sorrow with hearts too full for words.

There have been many great festivities at the " Cheese," and some of the most eminent men of the day, including Gladstone, Disraeli, and Chamberlain, wishing to see this " storied inn," with its quaint staircases and curious cellars, have relieved the tedium of larger thoughts from Parliament and other spheres of activity, and taken a walk down Fleet Street and there regaled themselves.

JANE SHORE

THERE are many legends in connection with the name of Shoreditch, which was originally a village on the Roman military highway. Stow, who wrote in the year 1598, says that the place was called Soersditch more than four hundred years before his time. The fanciful story of the name Shoreditch being traced to Jane Shore and her dying in a ditch in its neighbourhood arose through a misreading, or rather is traceable to a black letter ballad, in the Pepys collection. This was entitled " The Woful Lamentation of Jane Shore, a Goldsmith's wife in London, some time King Edward the Fourth his Concubine " :

Thus, weary of my life at lengthe,
I yielded up my vital strength
Within a ditch of loathsome scent,
Where carrion dogs did much frequent :
The which now, since my dying daye,
Is Shoreditch call'd, as writers saye.

However, this ballad, which Dr. Percy in his " Reliques " prints in full, dates back only to the middle of the seventeenth century. Jane Shore, a lovely but frail woman, was the daughter of a merchant in Cheapside, and she married, when only sixteen years old, a young and prosperous goldsmith, William Shore, who carried on business in Lombard Street, City. She lived with him for seven years, but her love of finery was her undoing. Unfortunately, and to the distress of her husband, she attracted the attention of Edward the Fourth, who made her his mistress about 1470, and with him she lived in luxury and greatness until his death.

There are many accounts as to her attractiveness. Sir Thomas More for instance says : " Proper she was and faire, nothing in her body that you would have changed, but if you would

have wished her somewhat higher.
Yet delighted not men so much in her
bewty as in her pleasant behaviour.
For a proper wit had she, and could
both rede wel and write; mery in
company, ready and quick of answer,
neither mute nor ful of bable, sometimes taunting without displeasure
and not without disport." He says
that of all the King's favourites: "The
meriest was the Shore's wife, in whom
the King therefore toke special
pleasure." "For many," goes on More,
"he had, but her he loved whose
favour, to sai the trouth (for sinne it
were to belie the devil), she never
abused to any man's hurt, but to
many a man's comfort and relief.
Where the King toke displeasure, she
would mitigate and appease his mind:
where men were out of favour she
would bring them in his grace: for
many that had highly offended shee
obtained pardon."

It is evident that with all her faults
Jane was of a kind and generous spirit,
and was ever charitable. Curiously
enough, Drayton the poet describes
her as being of mean stature, "her haire
of a dark yellow; her face round and
full; her eye grey, delicate harmony
being between each part's proportion
and each proportion's colour; her
body fat, white, and smooth; her
countenance cheerful, and like to her
condition. The picture I have seen
of her was such as she rose out of her
bed in the morning, having nothing
on but a rich mantle cast under one
arme over her shoulder, and sitting on
a chair on which her naked arme did
lie." Shore, her husband, who was a
man of wealth and high character,
entirely abandoned her after she became the favourite of the King, and
eventually went abroad, where he is said
to have died of grief. Drayton further

tells us in the language of the time:
"Richard the Third causing her to do
open penance in St. Paul's Churchyard,
commanded that no man should relieve
her, which the tyrant did not so much
for his hatred to sinne, but that, by
making his brother's life odious, he
might cover his horrible treasons the
more cunningly." Then again the
partiality which Jane Shore entertained
with Lord Hastings—to whom she
became attached after the death of her
royal lover—for the young Princes,
greatly angered Richard the Crook-
back, who took his vengeance by
having Hastings beheaded, and making
Jane suffer in an outrageous manner
in public. In the long metrical
account of her life given by Dr. Percy,
already referred to, every detail of her
life is recounted by some unknown
bard: how that she married Matthew
Shore, how that she attracted to
Lombard Street in a shop of gold
many a gallant of the town with whom
she had intrigues. It is further related how she was led astray by a
mistress Blague, a near neighbour who
persuaded her when the King was
making his advances, to listen to him,
and eventually Jane Shore went from
the City to the Court, where she became acquainted with many secrets of
the King. When the death of the
King occurred and her downfall came,
all her friends deserted her, and though
the old ballad is not correct, as to her
death at any rate, the following lines
are worth quoting:

> Then unto Mrs. Blague I went,
> To whom my jewels I had sent,
> In hope thereby to ease my want,
> When riches fail'd, and love grew scant:
> But she denied to me the same,
> When in my need for them I came;
> To recompense my former love,
> Out of my doors shee did me shove.

*   *   *   *   *

My gowns, beset with pearl and gold,
Were turn'd to simple garments old ;
My chains and gems, and golden rings,
To filthy rags and loathsome things.

Thus was I scorned of maid and wife,
For leading such a wicked life ;
Both sucking babes and children small,
Did make their pastime at my fall.

The statement as to Jane Shore dying in a ditch so repeatedly quoted is erroneous, as Sir Thomas More distinctly mentions her being alive in the reign of Henry the Eighth, and suggests that he himself had seen her. " Richard the Third," adds More, caused " the Bishop of London to put her to ann open penance, going before the cross in procession upon a Sunday, with a taper in her hand ; in which she went in countenance and face demure, so womanly, and albeit she were out of all array save her kirtle only yet she went so fair and lovely, namely while the wondering of the people cast a comely red in her cheeks (of which she had before most miss), that her great shame was her much praise among those who were more amorous of her body than curious of her soul ; and many good folk, also, who hated her living, and were glad to see sin corrected, yet pitied they more her penance than rejoiced therein, when they considered the Protector procured it more of a corrupt intent than any virtuous intention."

After this shameful treatment Jane Shore was lodged and fed in Ludgate, and afterwards, by order of the Duke of Gloucester, in Cheapside. She survived her disgrace nearly half a century and died about 1527 at the computed age of eighty. Naturally the strangeness of her life was capable of much expansion and Jane Shore has been introduced into many a romance. As far back as 1602 a play was produced from the pens of Henry Chettle and John Day. About a hundred years later Nicholas Rowe took the subject in hand, and his drama was given at Drury Lane in 1714. But perhaps the most famous piece of all was written by W. G. Wills for Miss Caroline Heath, the wife of Wilson Barrett, and special elocutionist to Queen Victoria. Miss Heath presented " Jane Shore " at the Princess's Theatre in Oxford Street in 1876, where it ran for nearly twelve months.

JANE SHORE (*From an Old Print*)

CHRISTMAS IN A LONDON MERCHANT'S CITY MANSION, SIXTEENTH CENTURY
(*From Rodwell's "Old London Bridge"*)

THE OLD LONDON CHRISTMAS

CHRISTMAS has always been marked in London by an abundance of good cheer and lavish hospitality, and by a lively indulgence in the amusement we call "dressing-up," namely in masquerade, in pageant and in mumming. Let us first say a word about the great Christmas Banquets of London held by our kings in Westminster Hall. From the days of Edward the Confessor, and for five hundred years onward, the Palace of Westminster was a royal residence, and many of our Sovereigns kept royal state here at Christmas, King John being the first to celebrate the season in Westminster Hall, and Edward VI. the last. Let us, from various sources, try to reconstruct a Christmas Feast in the reign of Richard II., who kept Christmas in Westminster Hall in 1399. This King had already feasted ten thousand persons here, and no doubt at his Christmas banquets he entertained almost as great a number of guests.

The scene was one of dazzling splendour. The King wore his crown and a superb garment of cloth of gold, garnished with pearls and precious stones. The Yule-log, the burning of which was a custom pre-Christian in its antiquity, descending from the days when our ancestors built bonfires in honour of the god Thor, was blazing on the hearth. The love of pageantry and elaborate ritual connected with the garnishing and serving of dishes helped to veil the mere material enjoyment of food : thus the great Christmas dish of ceremony—not then the turkey, but the boar's head—was heralded by a flourish of trumpets and carried in on a dish of gold, while a procession of knights and ladies followed singing, perhaps, the Ancient Boar's Head Carol, the words of which are still extant. Roast peacocks would be borne in to the sound of music. These birds having been cooked, stuffed with spices and sweet herb, and basted with yolk of egg, were sewn up again in their feathers, their beaks gilt, and so served. Sometimes the whole bird was covered with gold leaf, so that the eye was catered for as carefully as the palate.

Richard II.'s master cook was, we know, an expert in his profession, for he has left a very curious and interesting Roll of Cookery, which may still be consulted by the curious. He had two thousand cooks to assist him ! It would be impossible to name in our brief survey the hundreds of various dishes put upon the tables by magnificently attired knights and squires : geese, capons, pheasants, pies of carps' tongues, blancmanges, tarts, jellies in all colours and all figures. Mince-pies (or Christmas pies), however, and plum-pudding are dishes of later date.

So much for the King's Christmas banquet : and banquets, be it remembered, less sumptuous, but elaborate enough, were being held all over London. A word now must be said

THE LORD OF MISRULE
(*From Chambers's "Book of Days"*)

about another almost universal symbol of merriment—masquerade.

The Christmas Season was Old London's Carnival, a hilarious time of disguise, mummery and pageant. Wise men put off their wisdom, and abandoned themselves to fun and folly. The whole spirit of the festivities is summed up in the "Lord of Misrule," an officer appointed in all great houses to organise the games and sports and lead the revels. Stow, writing in the sixteenth century gives the following interesting account of the Lord of Misrule : " In the feast of Christmas, there was in the King's house, wheresoever he lodged, a Lord of Misrule, or Master of Merry Disports, and the like had ye in the house of every noble-man of honour or good worship, were he spiritual or temporal. The Mayor of London, and either of the Sheriffs, had their several Lords of Misrule, ever contending, without quarrel or offence, who should make the rarest pastime to delight the beholders . . . there were fine and subtle disguisings, masks and mummeries, with playing at cards for counters, nails and points, in every house, more for pastimes than for gain."

The London Inns of Court were famous for their Christmas celebrations, their great halls being well adapted to the Christmas revels. The Lord of

Misrule was here a notable figure, and one of these lords in the reign of Charles I. spent no less than two thousand pounds out of his own purse on these Christmas revels. Many grotesque ceremonies accompanied the making of a Lord of Misrule—there was dancing round the fire, and hunting in the hall with nine or ten couples of hounds, a fox and a cat, both tied at the end of a pole, until they were killed beneath the fire. This was no doubt the occasion of much mirth—for mediæval London, with its pits for bull and bear baiting, had no imagination for the sufferings of animals.

Carol-singing entered into the Christmas revels, at first taking its turn with the other performances of the mummers. Afterwards the choirs of the churches went about singing carols from door to door. Carol-singing is only just dying out, and the Waits are still with us. They were originally minstrels who performed the office of watchmen at the King's Court, calling out the hours as did the Night-Watchmen of London —their name and origin is at least as early as the year 1400.

The custom of giving presents at this season was practised in Old London—it is indeed a custom descending from Pagan times, but the origin of the term Christmas-*box* is obscure. It is suggested that priests used to hang up a box for offerings, and that the word is thence derived. The grumbling at the Christmas-box is no new thing, but has about it a flavour of antiquity, as witness the enclosed amusing account of Boxing Day in London from a letter dated 1731 : " By that time I was up, my servants could do nothing but run to the door. Inquiring the meaning, I was answered, the people were come for their Christmas-box ; this was logick

to me ; but I found at last, that, because I had laid out a good deal of ready money with my brewer, baker, and other tradesmen, they kindly thought it my duty to present their servants with some money for the favour of having their goods. This provoked me a little ; but being told it was the custom, I complied. These were followed by the watch, beadles, dustmen, and an innumerable tribe . . ." and the writer goes on to relate how he was obliged to give half a crown to the bellman " for breaking my rest for many nights together."

It was to cure grumblers like the writer of this letter that Dickens gave us " The Christmas Carol " : and in so doing, drew for us an ideal Christmas which exercises a strong influence over Londoners even to this day. It is interesting to observe that the ideal Dickens holds up, is in many respects curiously like the ideal Christmas of Londoners in the Middle Ages.

Let us look at Christmas in London some fifty years ago. The Christmas of Dickens' Christmas books is a cold Christmas, the conventional " Christmas Card " Christmas : it is a foggy Christmas—the conventional London Christmas. The Ghost of the Christmas Present shows Scrooge his own sitting room decked out with the symbols of the ideal Christmas : " The walls and ceiling were so hung with living green that it looked a perfect grove ; from every part of which bright gleaming berries glistened . . . such a mighty blaze went roaring up the chimney, as that dull petrifaction of a hearth had never known in Scrooge's time, or Marley's time, or for many and many a winter season gone. Heaped up on the floor to form a kind of throne, were turkeys, geese, game, poultry, brawn, great joints of meat, sucking-pigs, long wreaths of sausages, mince pies, plum puddings, barrels of oysters, red-hot chestnuts, cherry-cheeked apples, juicy oranges, luscious pears, immense twelfth cakes, and seething bowls of punch, that made the chamber dim with their delicious steam." An abun-

holme (the evergreen oak), ivy, bays, and whatsoever the season of the year afforded to be green. The conduits and standards in the streets were likewise garnished."

Dickens' Christmas is linked with the Christmas of Old London by being a merry Christmas: although there is

GEORGE CRUIKSHANK ENJOYS HIS CHRISTMAS DINNER
(*From Cruikshank's Comic Almanack*)

dance of good cheer: that is the first note struck; and we realise that fifty years ago, as in the Middle Ages, the season is most universally celebrated, both by rich and by poor, in the Christmas dinner. The lavish decoration of green and the blazing fire: these also are survivals of mediæval ideals; for in the Middle Ages, the Londoners decked not only the interior of their houses with green, but the exterior also: the invaluable Stow tells us, "against the feasts of Christmas every man's house, as also their parish churches, were decked with

no mumming or masquerade, it is a time of infectious high spirits. The underpaid clerk "went down a slide on Cornhill, at the end of a lane of boys, twenty times, in honour of its being Christmas Eve, and then ran home to Camden Town as hard as he could pelt, to play at Blindman's Buff." There we have the very spirit of merry Christmas.

But there is a new note in Dickens' description of Christmas—a note peculiarly characteristic of the present age—the note of pity, the note of humanity. From ancient times, it is true, Londoners have endeavoured to share with their less fortunate brethren the good things of the season, and we read of many London feasts to poor men. Henry III. for instance, when he kept Christmas at Eltham, bid his Treasurer fill Westminster Hall from Christmas Day to New Year's Day with poor people and feast them there. Dickens, however, is not dealing with the lavish hospitality of kings, but with very simple and humble Londoners, and in his description of the London Christmas there is a kindness and a tenderness, an all-embracing diffusion of good-will, a radiating geniality, a sympathy with the weak, the helpless and even with the futile, that is unique in London literature.

There are few new features to be recorded in connection with the London celebrations of Christmas. The Christmas Tree, with the Pantomime, is of foreign origin. The first Christmas Tree in London was set up in Buckingham Palace by Queen Charlotte, wife of George III., who thus introduced into England the ancient practice of Germany. Every Christmas, at her command, a tree was decked, either at Buckingham Palace, or at Kew. It was, however, only after the marriage of Queen Victoria with Prince Albert that the Christmas Tree became popular in England.

THE KING OF BOOTMAKERS

HOBY, of St. James's Street, was not only the greatest and most fashionable bootmaker, but a Methodist preacher at Islington. He was said to employ three hundred workmen, and was privileged to say all sorts of things to his customers, whom he sometimes annoyed with his humour. Horace Churchill, an ensign in the Guards, one day entered Hoby's shop in a great passion, saying that his boots were so ill-made that he should never employ Hoby for the future. Hoby gravely called to his shopman, " John, close the shutters. It is all over with us. I must shut up shop. Ensign Churchill withdraws his custom from me."

Calling on the Duke of Kent to try on some boots, the news arrived of Lord Wellington's great victory over the French army at Vittoria. The Duke was kind enough to mention the glorious news to Hoby, who coolly said : " If Lord Wellington had had any other bootmaker than myself, he would never have had his great and constant successes ; for my boots and prayers bring his lordship out of all his difficulties." He was bootmaker to the Duke of Wellington from his boyhood, and received innumerable orders in the Duke's handwriting, both from the Peninsula and France, which he always preserved. On one occasion the late Sir John Shelley came into Hoby's shop to complain that his top-boots had split in several places. Hoby quietly said : " How did that happen, Sir John ? " " Why, in walking to my stables." " Walking to your stables ? " said Hoby, with a sneer ; " I made the boots for riding, not walking."

Hoby was bootmaker to George III., the Prince of Wales, the royal Dukes, and many officers in the Army and Navy. His shop was situated at the top of St. James's Street, at the corner of Piccadilly, next to the old Guards' Club. Hoby was the first man who drove about London in a tilbury. It was painted black, and drawn by a beautiful black cob. He died worth a hundred and twenty thousand pounds.

BACK from AGINCOURT.

HENRY V. returned to London with his army almost immediately after the Battle of Agincourt, for his ranks were too exhausted to pursue the retreating French. In the chorus of the last act of *Henry V.* we can see almost before our eyes the reception that awaited him:

> . . . So let him land,
> And solemnly see him set on to London.
> So swift a pace hath thought, that even now
> You may imagine him upon Blackheath ;
> Where that his lords desire him to have borne
> His bruised helmet and his bended sword,
> Before him, through the city : he forbids it,
> Being free from vainness and self-glorious
> pride:
> Giving trophy, signal, and ostent,
> Quite from himself to God. But now behold,
> In the quick forge and working-house of
> thought,
> How London doth pour out her citizens !
> The mayor, and all his brethren, in best sort,—
> Like to the senators of th' antique Rome,
> With the plebeians swarming at their heels,—
> Go forth, and fetch their conquering Cæsar
> in :

> As, by a lower but by loving likelihood,
> Were now the general of our gracious
> empress
> (As in good time he may) from Ireland
> coming,
> Bringing rebellion broached on his sword,
> How many would the peaceful city quit,
> To welcome him ! much more, and much
> more cause,
> Did they this Harry.

Henry V. had been crowned on April 24, 1413, and on that occasion London had been the scene of a snow-tinged pageant. The flakes had covered the silken canopy above the young King as he passed through the streets attended by his Peers, the Lord Mayor, and the Aldermen of London. But "the pageant of all the pageants of the fifteenth century was," as Richard Davey observes in that admirably well-informed volume, "The Pageant of London," "this gallant King's triumphant entry into his metropolis after Agincourt."

Many weeks before the fateful battle

rumours had spread through England telling of defeat and even of massacre. The suspense had been terrible, and when the news of the great victory arrived the reaction from anxiety to joyful relief was immediate and tumultuous. The Lord Mayor and the Aldermen went in ceremonial procession on foot to the Abbey, where a grateful Te Deum was sung. As soon as the people grasped the full scope of the victory, their excitement knew no bounds, and the crowd on Dover Strand, as the King's ship drew near, plunged into the sea and carried the victor of Agincourt shoulder-high to the shore. All the way from Dover to the capital it was one long procession of victory. The smallest village vied with the township in homage to Henry V., who was hailed at Canterbury with as much enthusiasm as at Rochester.

On Saturday, November 23, 1415, just one week after the landing at Dover, a procession of the Archbishops, Bishops, Abbots, and Peers, together with the Lord Mayor, Sheriffs, and Aldermen, proceeded to Blackheath to greet the King. The vast London crowd was wild with excitement, and there was no little curiosity to behold the famous prisoners that the English King was bringing back with him from France. The scene, indeed, must have been one of almost delirious joy, and as usual there were quaint and picturesque participants in this historic welcome. At the entrance to London Bridge, for example, a giant and a giantess stood impassively. The giant was holding an axe in his right hand, while the keys of the city hung at his girdle. The giantess held only a bouquet of flowers, which she proffered to the King with a smile of welcome upon

her lips. The heads of giant and giantess alike were made of painted leather, and their faces were yet more highly coloured masks.

At the opposite end of the bridge white-robed choristers, representing Cherubim and Seraphim, sang an English hymn. A pavilion had been erected over the conduit in Cornhill, in which "the Fellowship of the Prophets" had their places. There was also a somewhat similar pavilion over "the gret conduyt" at the east end of Cheapside, where the Company of the Apostles took their stand together with twelve kings of England, all "Martyrs and Confessors."

The Cross in Cheapside had been turned into a kind of tower, on each side of which stood an arched gateway. Above, angels chanted a Te Deum, while on a platform beneath a group of maidens hailed the victor with glad cries of "Noel! Noel! Welcome, Henry the Fifte, Kynge of Englond and of Fraunce."

At the west end of Cheapside a broad canopy, as of floating clouds, was spread over the conduit. This represented the Deity in the likeness of a sun enthroned in flaming majesty and surrounded on all sides by archangels. A procession of Bishops and clergy greeted the King at St. Paul's, and having turned aside to "offer" in the customary fashion, he proceeded on his route. "And so the Kyng and his prisoners of Frensshmen reden through London unto Westm' to mete (meat, *i.e.* dinner), and there the Kyng abod stille." "During the procession," notes Sir James H. Ramsay in "A Century of English History," "Henry distinguished himself by his sober demeanour. He forbad all songs of personal panegyric; and even refused to allow the dinted basnet to be exhibited." The King had defended in his own person his brother, Humphrey, whom he had found lying among the wounded at Agincourt. He himself had been struck by a battle-axe, and his helmet had been dinted by the blow, a part of the jewelled crown having been knocked off. There is ample evidence of this historic fact, for the dinted head-piece remained in Westminster Abbey to attest it to future generations.

All along the route from London Bridge the people had surged and swayed in eagerness to catch a glimpse of the impassive conqueror. From Billingsgate to Westminster the proudest ladies of England had waited on balconies to join in this truly national welcome. As the *plante à genet* was not in bloom, they showered gold-paper leaves upon the King, while groups of children stationed at regular intervals along the route of the procession sang hymns in homage to the war-lord of Merrie England.

Henry himself cared little for such pageants of peace, but the people welcomed him with all their hearts, acclaiming the dark conqueror, who has been so often called a blond, as their veritable national hero. "In no other age," writes Richard Davey,

THE TOMB OF HENRY V. IN WESTMINSTER ABBEY

"had King or general more richly deserved the homage paid. Henry looked a very hero. He was tall and graceful beyond the average. His regular features were lighted up by clear grey eyes that glittered between their long black lashes, and contrasted superbly with the swarthy complexion, and long raven locks of the handsomest and bravest leader of the time."

It was Henry's magnanimity no less than his courage that appealed to the

people of England. The victor of Agincourt was hostile to all unnecessary acts of barbarity, to unnecessary sacking of towns and burning of villages. He was merciful, too, to the famous poet, the Duke of Orleans, who held a conspicuous place among the French prisoners, who swelled sadly the gorgeous pageant of their country's humiliation. The Duke was honourably treated, but very closely guarded during his imprisonment of over twenty years in the Tower. A part at least of the record of his household expenses has come down to us, and there is no doubt that he lived, prisoner though he was, with considerable state, and that he spent much of his time in practising on musical instruments.

Only a quite insignificant retinue of his personal household attended the King, but a strong escort guarded the prisoners of war. It must have been pitiable for the widow of Henry IV. to see among these prisoners her younger son, Arthur, parading in this triumph of the English King. But as for the Duke of Orleans, it is improbable that he was in any way perturbed either by the commiseration or the exultation of his enemies. His poetry, as a matter of fact, flourished in England, and many an exquisite French lyric has, by the irony of history, its origin in the defeat of the French arms at Agincourt.

The day drew to a close, but doubtless the enormous structures of canvas and wood that had been arranged at the chief points through the line of march lingered for a little here and there to remind the people of Agincourt. But on the Sunday morning that followed, the tribute to the conquering King took a wholly different form from that of scriptural pageants and hymns of welcome. For, a deputation started on that day from the city, and presented Henry V. with the sum of one thousand pounds, an enormous amount of money reckoned by the standard of those days. The same deputation also presented him with two golden bowls, the value of which was estimated at no less than £500.

In these seemingly more placid days, when flags and bunting are almost affairs of ordinary routine, one is apt perhaps to under-estimate this old time pageant of welcome through the streets of London. In reality the national greeting had a very deep significance. Henry V. had become at once King of the English and master of England at a time when rebellion was almost as normal as loyalty. Out of the nine kings who reigned over England before Henry VII. united the Roses of York and Lancaster, six were deposed, and of these five met their death. Resistance on the part of nobles and people alike was an unknown quantity never negligible, and this triumphant procession, popularly acclaimed through the heart of the capital, was the external evidence of what one may call kingship in a new sense. The central figure of this national festival of thanksgiving was not only Henry V., the conqueror of the French, but also Harry of England.

M E Buckstone

JOHN BALDWIN BUCKSTONE AT THE HAYMARKET THEATRE

FIRST-HAND statements are the best, and so, in a slightly altered form, we present an account of the trials, tribulations, and successes of the career of John Baldwin Buckstone, a great London favourite in his day, as related by himself. Buckstone, who was for so many years the lessee of the " leading comedy house " in London, the Haymarket, was born at Hoxton " near London " in 1802, and died in October 1879.

At the Anniversary dinner of the Royal General Theatrical Fund in 1855, the celebrated comedian, in proposing the toast of the evening, gave a very interesting account of his early struggles as an actor. Amongst many incidents and vicissitudes he said that he walked once from Northampton to London—seventy-two miles—on fourpence halfpenny. He had a fellow player with him, who was in the same dire financial strait. He described his costume on that occasion, which consisted of a threadbare " whitey blue coat, with tarnished metal buttons, secured to the throat," and he wore underneath a flowered waistcoat made of glazed chintz of a very showy pattern which he usually adopted when playing country boys and singing comic songs. Buckstone said : " I will not attempt to describe my hat ; while my trousers must only be delicately alluded to, as they were made of what was originally white duck, but as they had been worn about six weeks, and having myself been much in the fields, there was a refreshing tint of a green-and-clay-colour about them, which imparted to that portion of my attire quite an agricultural appearance."

After many experiences at the Surrey and Adelphi theatres, John Baldwin Buckstone found his career at the Haymarket Theatre, over which he ruled and reigned from about 1844 until the day of his death, which occurred in 1879. Buckstone was what is known as a " broad comedian." In other words, he chiefly relied upon his effects, which were almost invariably comical ; upon his unctuous utterance and his extraordinarily ludicrous facial play. We have a good proof of this from Dr. Westland Marston, who, as a dramatist, was for many years associated with the Haymarket Theatre. Dr. Marston says : " To carry drollery to its furthest point seemed the height of his ambition. It would be untrue to say he cared little for the exhibition of character. His genial people were

ultra genial, his cowards thorough poltroons, his mischief-makers revelled in their sport ; but it is quite true to say that characterisation with him was quite subordinate to mirth."

In Shakespeare, although it must be affirmed that Buckstone took liberties, his comicality, his way of " taking odds " with his face and his own extraordinary visage, almost invariably gave the infection of laughter to the house. He was " sly, devilish sly," as Major Bagstock would say, in all his movements, and he was able to put on that affectation of modesty, in trying circumstances, that no other actor was able to convey.

" It is nevertheless certain that, in almost every part he undertook, he was Buckstone ; it is equally so that the public did not wish him to be any one else. There were good reasons for this. Never was there a face more fitted to excite laughter—there being an expression of astuteness and self-restraint in the upper part of the actor's face, while the lips, and the lines, from the somewhat expansive nose downwards, seemed on the alert for a grin, giving a union of shrewdness and drollery, with their interaction upon each other, that was irresistibly comic."

Tom Taylor sold to Buckstone, after much haggling, the English rights of *Our American Cousin*, which had been a remunerative production in America, for the sum of one hundred and fifty pounds. Buckstone made a clear profit of five thousand. Edward Askew Sothern was of course Lord Dundreary, while Buckstone acted the character of Asa Trenchard. This piece was an enormous success, and drew crowds to the theatre. Then came another big attraction in *David Garrick* which was given after many trials and disappointments. *David*

Garrick was the work of Tom Robertson, and neither Sothern nor Buckstone thought there was any hope for it, although before coming to London it had been tried at Liverpool, with encouraging applause. But Sothern was very nervous over this new part, and was considerably afraid because of the famous love-making scene; however, all went well in the end, and *David Garrick* became a great success with Buckstone as Squire Chivy and Sothern as Garrick.

Queen Victoria was among his warmest admirers. She often came to the Haymarket with Prince Albert, and on such occasions they were personally received by Buckstone. The following picture of such an arrival, drawn by Mr. Cyril Maude in his valuable " Records and Reminiscences " of the Haymarket, is as amusing as it is historically interesting :

In the days of her late Majesty's visits to the Haymarket Theatre far more ceremony was observed in the reception of Royalty than is the custom in this year of grace. The Royal entrance in those days was through the door of Buckstone's London house, adjoining the back of the theatre in Suffolk Street. A passage led to another door opening on to the anteroom of the Royal box. At the street door waited the manager, bearing in either hand a massive silver candlestick with which to light the Royal party to their box, conducting them with much ceremony through the passage until the door of the anteroom was reached. One windy night ' Bucky ' was seated in his office, awaiting the arrival of the Royal party, with the two as yet unlighted candles on a table by his side. Suddenly there came the loud double knock that usually heralded the advent of her late Majesty. It took but a second to light the two candles, and picking them up, ' Bucky ' took his stand at the Royal entrance. The door was opened with a flourish—only to reveal the portly presence of the laundress, bearing a large basket containing the week's washing ! The good lady was hurriedly bidden to take her burden to the stage-door, and ' Bucky ' once

more resumed his seat. Presently there came the sound of wheels, and another loud, impetuous double knock. ' Bucky ' again took up his position, the door was thrown open, and Her Majesty stood upon the threshold. At the same moment a gust of wind extinguished the candles, which so flustered Mr. Buckstone that he ejaculated : ' There, just look at that, now ! ' The Queen, laughing heartily, was conducted to her box by the much-embarrassed manager bearing the candles, whose only effect was to leave a trail of white and extremely odoriferous smoke behind them.

Buckstone's next mishap in connection with the Queen's visits was even more pronounced. Mr. Maude relates that " one night when the late Queen Victoria had commanded her box, ' Bucky ' stood at the door, with a candlestick in either hand, to usher the Royal party, which included the late Prince Consort, among other members of the Royal Family. It so happened that ' Bucky ' was a little ' off colour ' that night, and quite forgetting the two steps at the end of the passage, fell head over heels, candlestick and all, exclaiming in tones of great distress, ' Oh, Lord, ma'am, just look at that ! ' Luckily, ' Bucky ' did himself no serious damage, but the performance had to be postponed at least five minutes to allow the Queen and the Prince Consort to have their laugh out."

In *Box and Cox*, by Maddison Morton, Buckstone was so funny that even Mrs. Fitz William, who played Mrs. Bouncer, burst out into a scream of laughter on the first night, on account of his comical description of having his hair cut—"mowed" he called it. He had a sly look in his eye that was irresistible.

The parts that Buckstone shone in most were Tony Lumpkin in Goldsmith's *She Stoops to Conquer*, Bob Acres, in Sheridan's *The Rivals*, Sir Andrew Aguecheek in *Twelfth Night*, Touchstone, Slender, and nearly all the low comedy parts in the Shakespearean plays. One critic, in 1862, said, "Mr. Buckstone has talents, Mr. Buckstone has humour, and the pit is always ready with a roar. His voice is in perfect keeping with his person : it suggests a distillation ; it seems to flow lazily from a mind charged with full thoughts, unctuous conceits. He has the true low comedy in his walk and gesture. . . . He is the true son of mirth." Although occasionally inclined to be vulgar, Buckstone had a sure sense of character, and in poetic plays such as Gilbert's *Palace of Truth* he usually gave the reading that the author desired. Buckstone belonged to what is known as the old school of acting, and kept almost invariably to the broad path of humour, in all kinds of farces and comedies that demanded a wide expression of manner and a large indulgence of fun, the Haymarket comedian was excellent. Notwithstanding that nearly half his life Buckstone was almost stone deaf, he was always able to pick up his cues, which he did by watching the lips of his brother performers, and very few of the public ever heard of his infirmity.

Off the stage Buckstone was as droll as on it, and he it was who said " that actors could not be too grateful to architects ; for it seems to have been a general plan with them to build every theatre as near as possible to a public house."

THE MUSICAL SMALL-COAL MAN

THIS famous Clerkenwell character died in 1714. It used to be said of him, "There goes the small-coal man, who is a lover of learning, a performer of music, and a companion for gentlemen."

Thomas Britton came to London from Northamptonshire, and after serving his apprenticeship to a small-coal man in John Street, Clerkenwell, he set up business for himself in a stable which he hired in Jerusalem Passage, close to St. John's Gate. Above the stable was a loft, and in this loft the small-coal man organised local and instrumental concerts which became as famous as any in London. It was a triumph of personality. Handel himself played the organ here, and Pepusch, Banister, and Whichello—all musicians of eminence—joined in the harmony, while the audiences were fashionable enough to include, on occasion, a duchess. It was only when he took a better room that the success of his concerts was imperilled, and he promptly returned to the hay loft. Ned Ward thus describes this temple of harmony. " His Hut wherein he dwells, which has long been honoured with such good Company, looks without Side as if some of his Ancestors had happened to be Executors to old snorling Diogenes, and that they had carefully transplanted the Athenian Tub into Clerkenwell ; for his House is not much higher than a Canary Pipe, and the Window of his State Room but very little bigger than the Bunghole of a Cask." From Ned Ward's pen, also, comes this stanza :

Upon Thursdays repair
To my palace, and there
Hobble up stair by stair ;
But I pray ye take care
That you break not your shins by a stumble.

And without e'er a souse,
Paid to me or my spouse,
Sit as still as a mouse,
At the top of the house,
And there you shall hear how we fumble.

In this Clerkenwell loft this extraordinary man kept up his famous concerts for something like forty years. Nor does his fame end here, for to his musical accomplishments he added a fine taste in books and the nose of a book-hunter. At that time many noblemen had a passion for collecting old books and manuscripts, notably the Earls of Oxford, Pembroke, Sunderland, Winchilsea, and the Duke of Devonshire. Wilson relates (" Remarkable Characters ") that these noblemen in the winter season, on Saturdays, the parliament not sitting on that day, used to resort to the city, and dividing themselves, took different routes, some to Little Britain, some to Moorfields, and others to different parts of the town inhabited by booksellers. There they would inquire in the several shops as they passed along for old books and manuscripts ; and some time before noon would assemble at the shop of Christopher Bateman, a bookseller at the corner of Ave Maria Lane, in Paternoster Row, where they were frequently met by other persons engaged in the same pursuits. A conversation on the subject of their inquiries ensued, and while they were thus engaged, and as near as possible to the hour of twelve by St. Paul's

THOMAS BRITTON

clock, Britton, who by that time had finished his round, arrived clad in his blue frock, and pitching his sack of small coal on the bulk of Mr. Bateman's shop window, would go in and join them. After a conversation which generally lasted about an hour, the abovementioned noblemen adjourned to the Mourning Bush at Aldersgate, where they dined and spent the remainder of the day.

Britton, the most peaceful of men, met his death through fright under very remarkable circumstances. One of his musical friends introduced him to a man named Honeyman, who had considerable skill in ventriloquism, an art to which Britton was probably a stranger. There seems to have been a jocular plan to frighten the small-coal man, which succeeded only too well. Honeyman, without moving his lips or seeming to speak, announced, as from a distance, the death of poor Britton within a few hours unless he immediately fell on his knees and said the Lord's Prayer. The old man did as he was bid, but went home to die in a few days. He was buried in the church of St. James's, Clerkenwell. There is no inscription to mark his grave, but the fame of the small-coal man lives in many books, and in Prior's lines :

Tho' doom'd to small coal yet to arts allied ;
Rich without wealth, and famous without
    pride.

THE IRON DUKE AS SEEN BY LONDONERS

THE DUKE OF WELLINGTON IN LONDON

THE Duke of Wellington loved London, and became one of its most familiar human landmarks. There are still a few old Londoners, boys, so to speak, of the "Old Brigade," who remember that "good grey head that all men knew." To these old partisans London has never seemed quite the same since the Iron Duke, in his blue coat, with the striking buttons, white duck trousers, and deliberate stock, was seen taking his rides abroad in the Park—Hyde Park, of course—the most delightful park in London town, and along Piccadilly, to and from Apsley House. As he picked his way, his habit was to acknowledge with a raised forefinger the salutations of all those who bowed.

When Apsley House was ceded to the Duke by a grateful nation, his especial pleasure was to amble down Piccadilly and the Mall, on the "sweet shady side," and St. James's Park, where he delighted to pass remarks with the milk-sellers.

Colonel Gurwood relates that the Duke complained that liberties were taken with him by inconsequent persons. He said, when he went to Court, after William IV.'s death, the Duke of Cambridge said, "Why, Duke, why d'ye have your hair so short?" Directly after, the Duke of Sussex said, "Why are you not in mourning, Duke?" The Duke said, "I ordered black, your Royal Highness." "Ah," said he, "it is not black. It is what the French call *tête-de-nègre*." "The Duke of Marlborough," said the Duke to Gurwood, "because he was an old man, was treated like an old woman. I won't be. And the reason why I have a right never to have a liberty taken with me, is because I never take a liberty with any man." And the Duke was right, for his power of holding his own was one of his strongest characteristics.

THE DUKE OF WELLINGTON AND MRS. ARBUTHNOT IN HYDE PARK

Lord Strangford was staying with the Duke of Wellington at Walmer Castle where his Grace had occasionally to be in attendance, as Warden of the Cinque Ports, when one morning, at breakfast, the Duke informed him that he was obliged to go up to London immediately as all his razors required setting, but he would be back to dinner. Lord Strangford at once offered to lend him razors, or to have his own set in Dover. The Duke replied, "The man who always sharpens my razors has sharpened them for many years; I would not trust them with any one else. He lives in Jermyn Street, and there they must go. So, you see, Strangford, every man has a weak point, and my weak point is about the sharpening of my razors. Perhaps you are not aware that I shave myself, and brush my own clothes. I regret that I cannot clean my own boots; for servants bore me, and the presence of a crowd of idle fellows annoys me more than I can tell you."

Although apparently such an austere man, the Duke was very popular wherever he went, and he was equal on all occasions to saying a graceful thing and also, when it was necessary, something cleverly pungent. Once he was asked by an Army man "If he was ever surprised?" "No," replied his Grace, "but I am now." Sometimes besieging correspondents had the advantage of the gallant Duke. John Timbs relates an anecdote of a Mrs. Dowell who kept a tobacconist's shop at the entrance to Wilton Place, Knightsbridge. She took such a liking to the Duke that she was continually inventing some new plan whereby to express her regard for him. She sent him patties, cakes, and other delicacies; and as it was useless to attempt to defeat the old woman's pertinacity, everything sent was taken in. Her mania for the Duke carried itself to the extent that every day she regularly laid out a knife, fork, and plate, saying "That's for the Duke."

His Grace was particularly fond of children at all times, and whenever they were about he would romp and play with them and allow them to take all sorts of liberties, and he always delighted in their happy ways and childish glee. Once when a party of them had to go to bed his pleasure was to try to catch them, at which, of course, they ran their hardest and screamed their mightiest, until they got into their bedrooms, and then they slyly opened their door to see if he was still after them, and as he was still ready for the fun they ran away crying with that excessive joy only known to children. Gurwood said that the Duke gave away at least a thousand pounds a year in charity, and also he relates that when Alexander's—a famous bank —failed, the Duke helped the unfortunate losers with six thousand pounds by sending off banknotes to all those whom he thought most needed immediate assistance.

One evening at a big reception in London some ladies pressed the Duke for some account of his exploits. After some little time the Duke said : " Well, although so many stories have been told about me, I'll tell you one that has never yet been printed." And here is the gist of it : In the middle of the Battle of Waterloo, he saw a man in plain clothes riding about on a cob in the thickest fire. During a temporary lull the Duke beckoned to him and he asked him what business he had there ? The intruder replied that he was an Englishman accidentally at Brussels, and that as he had never seen a fight, he thought he would like to be in the thick of one. The Duke told him he was in imminent danger of his life, and then the Duke suddenly said to him, " Will you take this order to that Regiment over there ? " The strange little man instantly knowing who it was who was speaking obeyed ; and, having secured the man's card, when he got back to London the Duke remembered the incident, found out that the man was working for a firm of button makers, and installed him in a vacancy that fell to his discretion in the Mint, with a salary of eight hundred a year. There is another story about a firm of wine merchants who sent him a dozen bottles of sherry with their compliments, and with an intimation that sherry was considered good for the gout. They had a reply from his Grace's secretary to the effect that the " Duke of Wellington had tried their sherry and was much obliged— but he preferred the gout ! "

Mr. G. S. Street, in his interesting "Ghosts of Piccadilly," suggests that the most famous of all the ghosts of this delightful thoroughfare who might visit the glimpses of the moon is that of the wonderful Wellington. In 1831 the Iron Duke had his own special political opinions, for which he suffered " Wellington," says Mr. Street. " was honestly opposed to reform, and therefore unpopular with the mob who, while his wife lay on her deathbed in Apsley House, sent stones crashing through the windows, destroying not them only, but also the pictures on the walls. What wonder that he kept the iror shutters closed to the days of his death ? Twelve years later an immense mob followed, cheering him now, up Constitution Hill. The Duke took no notice whatever, but trotted leisurely to Apsley House ; then, stopping at the gate, he pointed to those iron shutters, bowed to the mob, and silently rode into the court."

On June 18, 1832, the seventeenth anniversary of Waterloo, the Duke had a mixed experience of the London crowd. He related it to Samuel Rogers, with whom he was dining a few days later, in the following words :

"I rode to Pistrucci in the Mint. He had made a bust of me, but wished for another sitting. So I went, without giving him notice, on that day at nine o'clock, and mounted my horse at half-past ten to leave him ; when I found a crowd at the gate, and several groaned and hooted. Some cried, ' Buonaparte for ever ! '

"I rode on at a gentle pace, but they followed me. Soon a magistrate [Ballantyne] came and offered his services. I thanked him, but said I thought I should get on very well. The noise increased, and two old soldiers, Chelsea Pensioners, came up to me. One of them said he had served under me for many a day, and I said to him, ' Then keep close to me now '; and I told them to walk on each side ; and whenever we stopt, to place themselves, each with his back to the flank of my horse. Not long afterwards I saw a policeman making off, and I knew it must be to the next station for assistance. I sent one of my pensioners after him ; and presently we got another police-

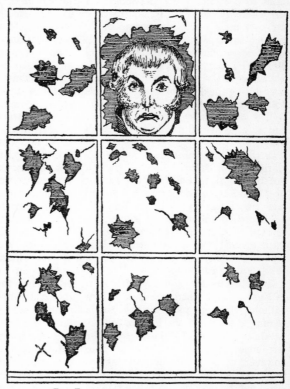

THE BROKEN WINDOWS OF APSLEY HOUSE
From a Contemporary Drawing

man. We did pretty well, till I reached Lincoln's Inn, where I had to call at an attorney's chambers [Maule's]. Sugden and many others came out of the Chancery Court to accompany me, and a large reinforcement of police came from Bow Street. The conduct of the citizens affected me not a little. Many came out of the shops to ask me in. Many ladies in their carriages were in tears, and many waved their handkerchiefs from the windows, and pointed downwards to ask me in. I came up Holborn by the advice of a man with a red cape. At first I thought it might be a snare, but found him to be a City Marshal. I was forty minutes coming from the Mint to Lincoln's Inn. A young man in a buggy did me great service, flanking me for some time, and never looking towards me for any notice."

A correspondent of *Notes and Queries* (May 25, 1895) who had been a witness of the above scene, mentions that during the disturbance in Lincoln's Inn the clerks of the Exchequer Office sallied out, armed with their heavy rulers, and helped to drive the mob away.

In the recently published "Memoirs" of the eighth Duke of Argyll there is a notable description of the great warrior of Waterloo. The Duke of Argyll had an interview with Wellington, in regard to the claims of some Civil servant who thought he had a grievance against the Government. The Duke of Argyll says: "It was a formidable ordeal for me. I felt I had before me the greatest man in Europe, and I had to speak to him without the guidance of one single leading question from him or observation of any kind. There was but one encouragement: the great one, however, of close and absolute attention on the Duke's part. His eyes were not wandering, but fixed upon the ground. It seemed as if he felt it a duty to listen and to listen carefully. And then," continues the Duke of Argyll, "I could not look upon that 'good grey head that all men knew' inclined before me with its massive forehead and brain on the working of which the fate of Europe had so often hung—without need of all the pluck I could command in telling my story." . . . Of Wellington's prominent nose everybody has

heard; it was certainly striking, and gave a very conspicuous suggestion of that forceful character that eventually made him the most important personage in the whole of Europe. We assume from all descriptions that the Duke's eyes were very large; his " eyelids cutting across them very high up, but not leaving them uncovered." They arrested the attention of every one at a moment, and those who saw him knew instantly that he was a man of power. In appearance he was always a soldier, and carried in his manner self-possession, calmness, and determination. His head, presumably his forehead, has been described as not being a high one, but very broad and massive. The Duke of Argyll says: " It was, as it were, a battlemented forehead, 'four square to all the winds that blew,' his voice was powerful, deep-toned, and with a military imperativeness of enunciation."

There are many very good stories told about the Duke, one of which is the well-authenticated tale of a sycophantic person who once piloted him (his eyesight was very bad) from Constitution Hill to Apsley House—merely across the road. Upon reaching the gateway of the Duke's mansion this curious individual said: " I shall always remember this as the proudest day of my life—the day on which I have had the inestimable privilege of rendering a small service to the great Duke of Wellington." Then he bowed profoundly, holding his hat in his hand. The Duke turned away somewhat abruptly, and exclaimed, "Don't be a fool." On one occasion, being dunned by his son's washerwoman for a bill by a Mr. Tomkins, the Duke replied: " Field Marshal the Duke of Wellington has received a letter from Mr. Tomkins stating that the Marquess of Douro is in debt to his mother, Mrs. Tomkins. The Duke of Wellington is not the Marquess of Douro. The Duke regrets to find that his eldest son has not paid his washerwoman's bill. Mrs. Tomkins has no claim upon the Duke of Wellington. The Duke recommends her, failing another application, to place the matter in the hands of a respectable solicitor." The best part of this is that the Marquess did not owe any money to his washerwoman, and that Mr. Tomkins, whoever he was, was simply an autograph hunter, and got exactly what he desired, the signature of the Duke.

Carlyle and Tennyson, by the way, were duped by this same Tomkins, much to their chagrin when they compared notes.

Wellington was always particularly English in his views, and once, speaking of Lord Hertford, and quoting Sir Robert Peel, he observed that he, Hertford, was a man of great comprehension. "In fact, if he had lived in London instead of frittering his time away in Paris, he would have no doubt become Prime Minister of England." Then Wellington, in one of his casual observations, said, "Paris only breeds women and boys"—this was, of course, after he had vanquished Napoleon.

It may not be generally known that the Carlton Club, unquestionably the premier political club of London, was originally founded by the Duke of Wellington and, with the co-operation of a few of his intimate friends, it was established in Charles Street, St. James's, in 1831, and later made a movement into Pall Mall, where it

THE DUKE OF WELLINGTON AT THE ROYAL ACADEMY
A Contemporary Sketch in the "Illustrated London News"

still holds sway as the chief Conservative stronghold of England. At this club he was one of the most familiar figures, jealous of his dignity, and jealous of his authority. Although he was no gambler himself, he was a frequent visitor at Crockford's, and on one occasion, when he saw a youth who had only just entered the Army, likely to get into trouble, he went to the table, pushed the young lieutenant on one side, took up his stakes and won, and then with a wise admonition as to the evils of gambling, presented the budding officer with his gains.

Captain Gronow, writing in 1814, says of Almack's, another fashionable resort: "At the present time one can hardly conceive the importance which is attached to getting admission to Almack's, the seventh heaven of the fashionable world." This temple of the *beau monde* was practically in the hands of certain Society ladies, who held such power and control as the "committee of discretion," that they could refuse admission to even the greatest man or woman in the land, and a very amusing instance of the despotism and caprices of these high and mighty female aristocrats is connected with the Duke of Wellington. The fair, but autocratic ladies, who were supreme and governed this little dancing and gossiping world, sent forth a solemn proclamation that no gentleman would be admitted at any of the assemblies unless he were dressed in knee breeches, white cravat, and *chapeau bras*. The Duke of Wellington on one occasion—this great man—was about to ascend the staircase leading to the ballroom dressed in black trousers, when Willis, the guardian of the establishment, politely went forward and, with many apologies, said, "Your Grace cannot be admitted in trousers."

Whereupon the Duke, who had saved England from, perhaps, one of the greatest disasters that might have happened to Great Britain, through the desperation of that "Corsican," showed his soldierly respect for orders and regulations, bowed his head, and quietly walked away !

The efficiency and sufficiency of the Duke's character are interesting in all their manifestations. When a critical debate was in progress, on which the fate of Peel's Ministry hung, the Duke sat unmoved in Apsley House, entertaining the Austrian Ambassador. Sir Herbert Maxwell relates : " Lord Lyndhurst offered to send early information of the result of the division. 'I am quite satisfied,' said the Duke, 'to have it when the newspapers come in at ten o'clock. If I could do any good by having it earlier, I would ; but as I can't, I'd just as soon wait.' 'You take things coolly,' interposed Lady Salisbury. 'I suppose you never lie awake with anxiety ?' 'No,' replied the Duke, 'I don't like lying awake ; it does no good. I make a point never to lie awake.' "

Of course, Wellington's efficiency and sufficiency did not pervade his career with atmospheric ubiquity. His marriage was not too happy ; he who never lost a gun for England lost much at his own hearth. His wife, whom he married under a chivalrous impulse rather than with considered choice, proved an indifferent companion. As Sir Herbert Maxwell says : " Wellington's life, with all its stir and activity, was a lone one ; his sense of having missed something in the lottery of marriage is revealed by a casual remark in one of his conversations. Lady Salisbury asked him whether Lady Peel had any influence over Sir Robert. 'No,' he replied ; 'she is not a clever woman : Peel had no wish to marry a clever woman.' 'It is very curious,' remarked Lady Salisbury, 'that a man of ability should not care to have a wife capable of entering into subjects in which he takes an interest.' 'Aye,' said the Duke, 'and of anticipating one's meaning ; that is what a clever woman does—she sees what you mean.' "

Two women were clever enough to understand the Duke and to win his confidence : Mrs. Arbuthnot and the second Marchioness of Salisbury. They deserved his trust and affection. Yet no man was ever less influenced by women than Wellington. He treated women "either as agreeable companions or playthings." Even the amiable weakness—one does not know what other name to give it—which led him to correspond for seventeen years with the mysterious "Miss J." scarcely amounts to an exception : the issues of the acquaintance were so trivial. Sir Herbert Maxwell has done well to treat this episode with a wise frankness. Miss J. was a beautiful girl who by her ministrations had brought a hardened murderer, named Cook, to repentance on the eve of his execution. The moment Cook was hanged Miss J. conceived him as "a glorious spirit." Proud of her work, she next turned to the Duke of Wellington, although she did not even know that he was the conqueror of Napoleon. He granted her strange request for an interview, and called on her at the house near Piccadilly, where she lodged with a relative. Miss J. was then

twenty years of age, and the Duke sixty-five. A correspondence began which lasted from 1834 to 1851, and drew from the Duke no fewer than 390 letters. Miss J.'s letters were even more numerous. She besought the Duke to seek eternal salvation, and to make her Duchess of Wellington, in which character she could the more surely direct him in the heavenly way. The Duke's letters taken individually are patient and discreet. But it is clear that he often regretted having written them. "I am very glad," he writes, "that you intend to send back all the letters I ever wrote to you." The genuineness of the Duke's letters is beyond reasonable doubt, both Sir William Fraser and Sir Herbert Maxwell being satisfied that he wrote them. Every life has more of drama and irony than we know. And perhaps the dramatic fitness of things required that a "Miss J." should think of the great Duke only as having a soul to be saved, and that when his august life was closed, and his bier was being borne under "the golden cross," one faithful, fanatical woman should breathe the hope that the leader of men had joined Cook at the Throne.

IVAN TURGENEV IN LONDON

IVAN TURGENEV, the famous Russian novelist whose "Annals of a Sportsman " did for the Russian serf what Mrs. Beecher Stowe's " Uncle Tom's Cabin " did for the American negro, paid more than one visit to London. Lady Ritchie in her fascinating " Blackstick Papers " recalls her first childish remembrance of the great Russian as "a tall figure, standing in the summer twilight, in that familiar green drawing-room in

Onslow Square." Years afterwards, in 1871, she met him again at Mrs. Huth's drawing-rooms in Prince's Gate. Madame Viardot, the scarcely less famous sister of the great Malibran, was singing or rather "almost whispering " the last words of a song. " Just then," writes Thackeray's daughter, "my glance fell upon Tourguénieff leaning against the door-post at the far end of the room, and as I looked I was struck, being shortsighted, by a certain resemblance to my father, which I tried to realise to myself. He was very tall, his hair was grey and abundant, his attitude was quiet and reposeful; I looked again and again while I pictured to myself the likeness. When Tourguénieff came up after the music, he spoke to us with great kindness, spoke of our father and of having dined at our house, and he promised kindly and willingly to come and call next day upon my sister and me in Onslow Gardens."

Lady Ritchie tells another characteristic anecdote of the great Russian, related to her by an old friend, who had called on Madame Viardot in the winter of 1871: "It was in the Wimpole Street region, and as they were reaching the door they saw a figure advancing half hidden by countless white frills rising one above the other. It was no ghost, it was Tourguénieff carrying a clothes-basket full of freshly ironed dresses straight from some foreign laundry. The house was in confusion, he explained, the frocks were absolutely needed by the ladies, and as none else could go, he himself had been to fetch them home; so much for a born gentleman's simplicity and natural dignity."

On the whole Turgenev seems to have been rather puzzled by the English, who struck him as a nation of originals. Thackeray, for example, disconcerted him by bursting out laughing when he repeated a few lines of his national poet, Pushkin, merely because he knew no Russian. Occasionally the distinguished Slav would visit Carlyle, who was a great admirer of one of his shorter stories entitled, "Mumu." Carlyle assured him, among many other curiosities of criticism, that Byron was forgotten and that Dickens had no weight with the English people. "One day," says Turgenev, "I happened to tell him that I suffered occasionally from blurs in the eyes; I saw motes in my eyes. Once when I was out shooting, I thought that I had in front of me a hare; I had already raised my gun to my shoulder and was going to fire, when I was seized with the suspicion that what I took for a hare was perhaps only a black spot which I had before my eyes. Carlyle listened to me attentively, remained for a moment thoughtful, and then burst out into a noisy and inextinguishable laugh. I could not understand what had put him into such a good-humour; I saw nothing comic in the incident that I had just related to him. 'Ha! Ha! ha!' he exclaimed at last, still bursting with laughter: 'To fire at one's own motes in the eyes,—Ha! ha! ha! To fire at a spot—Ha! ha! ha!' Then I understood the cause of his hilarity; a Frenchman or a Russian would have found nothing laughable in my story." The Russian was puzzled and thus mildly sums up his impressions of the English: "For the same reason an actor who makes grimaces, and who in France would be hissed off the stage to the accompaniment of baked apples, will amuse the English public and make them laugh."

SWEARING ON THE HORNS AT HIGHGATE

IN 1826 Hone described the custom of "Swearing on the Horns at Highgate," as more honoured in the breach than the observance. Yet as late as 1865 John Timbs wrote: "The old custom of swearing-in at Highgate continues to this day, and each of the older public houses keeps the horns ready." Nearly half a century has passed, and the horns are still preserved, and are still, on rare occasions, used in the old ritual. Hone enumerates no fewer than nineteen houses, in or about Highgate, where the famous Highgate oath was administered. There is little doubt that the first scene of the ceremony was the Gate House, which still flourishes, though modernised. The most probable explanation of the custom is that Highgate was the

nearest place to London at which drivers and their cattle, bound for Smithfield, put up for the night. As they could not exclude strangers who like themselves were travelling on their business, they instituted this ritual as a test of good-fellowship and to assert their peculiar claim to accommodation. The horns used at the various inns were stag's, bullock's and ram's. Bullock's horns were used at the Red Lion and Sun whose landlord, Mr. Sontho, was long remembered as "a most facetious swearer-in."

So noted was the custom in Highgate that in 1824 a new landlord of the Fox and Crown, who ignored it, found that his custom fell off. He determined to repair his error, and to carry out the ceremony in future with unusual pomp. Robed in a domino, with a wig and mask, and holding a book containing the terms of the oath, he recited his part with much gravity, while an old villager interpolated "Amens" at every pause. His performance is the subject of the drawing by George Cruikshank at the head of this chapter. It only remains to describe the ceremony, and this will be best accomplished in the words of a contemporary. The horns were fixed on a pole about five feet in height and held near the person about to be sworn, who in common with every one present was bidden to take off his hat. The landlord then addressed him as follows :

"Take notice what I now say unto you, for that is the first word of your oath—mind *that !* You must acknowledge me to be your adopted father ; I must acknowledge you to be my adopted son. If you do not call me father, you forfeit a bottle of wine ; if I do not call you son, I forfeit the same. And now, my good son, if you are travelling through this village of Highgate, and you have no money in your pocket, go call for a bottle of wine at any house you think proper to go into, and book it to your father's score. If you have any friends with you, you may treat them as well ; but if you have money of your own, you must pay for it yourself. For you must not say you have no money when you have ; neither must you convey the money out of your own pocket into your friends' pockets, for I shall search you as well as them ; and if it is found that you or they have money, you forfeit a bottle of wine for trying to cozen and cheat your poor old ancient father. You must not eat brown bread while you can get white, except you like the brown the best ; you must not drink small beer while you can get strong, except you like the small the best ; you must not kiss the maid while you can kiss the mistress, except you like the maid the best—but sooner than lose a good chance, you may kiss them both. And now, my good son, for a word or two of advice. Keep from all houses of ill-repute, and every place of public resort for bad company ; beware of false friends, for they will turn to be your foes, and inveigle you into houses where you may lose your money and get no redress ; keep from thieves of every denomination. And now, my good son, I wish you a safe journey through Highgate and this life. I charge you, my good son, that if you know any in this company who have not taken this oath, you must cause them to take it, or make each of them forfeit a bottle of wine ; for if you fail to do so, you will forfeit a bottle of wine yourself. So now, my son, God bless you ! Kiss the horns, or a pretty girl if you see one here, which you like best, and so be free of Highgate."

If a female be in the room, she is usually saluted ; if not, the horns must be kissed—the option was not allowed formerly.

As soon as the salutation is over, the swearer-in commands "Silence ! " and then addressing himself to his new-made son, he says : "I have now to acquaint you with your privilege as a freeman of this place. If at any time you are going through Highgate, and want to rest yourself, and you see a pig lying in a ditch, you have liberty to kick her out and take her place ; but if you see three lying together, you must only kick out the middle one and lie between the other two. God save the king ! "

THE CHARLIES.

WHEN Steele, in No. 376 of the *Spectator* (May 12, 1712), told the tale of a partnership between a watchman or Charlie and a goose, the town smiled, but saw nothing improper in the association. Charlie and goose marched as appropriately together as Dogberry and Verges. It was in the neighbourhood of the Tower, says Steele (whether he jests or not we can no longer affirm), and the watchman, "with a melancholy midnight voice at noonday," was punctually attended by the goose, "who bears the bob of his ditty, and confirms what he says with a Quack, quack." It was to pleasure the goose that the Charlie patrolled the "suburbs" of the Tower by day instead of by night.

"My friend gave me the history," says Steele with admirable gravity; "and interrupted my commendation of the man, by telling me the livelihood of these two animals is purchased rather by the good parts of the goose than of the leader; for it seems the peripatetic who walked before her was a watchman in that neighbourhood; and the goose of herself, by frequent hearing this tone, out of her natural vigilance, not only observed, but answered it very regularly from time to time. The watchman was so affected with it, that he bought her, and has taken her in partner, only altering their hours of duty from night to day. The town has come into it, and they live very comfortably."

In this satirical little tale is summed up for us the situation of the Charlies, and the attitude of society with regard to them. The town had gradually "come into" the Charlies, and the Charlies lived "very comfortably" by neglecting the town. Had Charlie lapsed, the goose might have borne the rattle; the town would have known no difference. Yet the Charlies were, for a period of nearly two centuries, London's chief representatives of law and order.

The first Charlie was a bellman, and we meet with him and his harmless halberd in the reign of Charles II., after whom he was presently nicknamed.

"A CHARLIE"

An Act of Common Council (not of Parliament, be it noted ; Parliament in Charles II.'s time did next to nothing for police) provided a force of a thousand bellmen, who should keep ward in those streets, " dim as Erebus," where a kind of rushlight showed at every tenth door from dusk till mid-

night. But from his earliest days the bellman was a byword. "Unfortunately," says Captain Melville Lee, "these watchmen were allowed to shirk their duties, and were well known to be altogether inefficient, so much so, that when rowdy apprentices and other unruly assemblages gave trouble, as they too often did, no one thought of looking to such weakened officials for the safety of the town. On such occasions companies of soldiers were requisitioned to protect the main thoroughfares, and, as a further precaution, chains were stretched from one side of the street to the other to prevent the free movement of the riotous bands."

As was the bellman of the seventeenth century, such was the Charlie of the eighteenth. We know that inept figure of burlesque, in a great cape and muffled to the ears, with staff and rattle and smoky lantern, "the creature of street-walkers and publicans rather than the servant of the public." "You shall comprehend all vagrom men," ran the charge, even from the days of Shakespeare ; but the Charlie dozed vinously in his box, and the vagrom men did all the comprehending. Those were the fat days of the highwayman, the robber, the footpad, the cut-purse, the Mohocks and all sons of Belial infesting the murky, sunken, and broken thoroughfares of London. At this date (we are still in the much-vaunted eighteenth century) the whole of the metropolis was split up into unwieldy parishes, and the parish policed itself, or not, precisely as it thought fit. Thus, no fewer than twelve parishes were totally unprotected, and this at a period when, after six o'clock of autumn nights, London was but a degree or so less black than Milton's Hell. St. James's and Marylebone relied for their protection upon a handful of Chelsea pensioners. The City (always more shrewdly guarded than London proper) supported 765 watchmen. Kensington — a region almost ultramondane— had a notable police force of three headboroughs: excellent men they may have been, said Peel in introducing his Bill, but were they three angels, instead of three headboroughs, they were useless in Kensington.

Now we might at least suppose that, many or few, the civil guardians of a city weltering in obscurity, and swarming with noxious characters, would at least be picked with some regard to martial quality. Not at all: a stout and sturdy candidate for the staff and lantern was rejected with something like contumely. "You are thought here," says Dogberry to neighbour Seacoal, "to be the most senseless and fit man for the constable of the watch; therefore bear you the lantern;" and this indeed, even in the eighteenth century, was the principle of selection.

It is sufficiently proved by a jocular paragraph in the *Morning Herald* of October 30, 1802 (the nineteenth century !), to this effect : "It is said that a man who presented himself for the office of watchman to a parish at the West End of the Town very much

A SCENE IN A WATCH HOUSE
By Robert Cruikshank

infected by depredators, was lately turned away from the Vestry with this reprimand: 'I am astonished at the impudence of such a great sturdy, strong fellow as you are, being so idle as to apply for a watchman's situation, when you are capable of labour.'" If this is jocular, we have the more serious statement of Fielding (a magistrate when he made it) that the Charlies were "chosen out of those poor old decrepid People, who are from their Want of bodily Strength rendered incapable of getting a Livelihood by Work."

A traditional and peculiar notion of duty the Charlies had. Punctually twice an hour they issued from their watchboxes, announced the time of night and the state of the weather to an audience which, being for the most part asleep, was not concerned on either point—and then withdrew. If by chance they learned that a householder had been robbed, they awoke him, and informed him of the fact.

"BRING ME AN OLD SILVER CANDLESTICK"

Understand you ! well I believe you are an honest man. Do you hear ? bring me an old silver candlestick.

> Then to my box I creep,
> And then fall fast asleep,
> St. Paul's strikes one.
> Thus, after all the mischief's done
> I goes and gives them warning,
>   And loudly bawls
>   As strikes St. Paul's,
> Past one o'clock, and a
>   cloudy morning.

The grotesque incompetency of the Charlies was, indeed, a staple subject with the humorists of two or three generations. They were earnestly advised how to keep themselves warm at night, and how to avoid the sight of dangerous persons. They were adjured to regard themselves as merely " hired by the parish to sleep in the open air." They were told that they might substitute " Shiver and Shake " for their professional motto of " Watch and Ward " ; inasmuch as " they spent half the night shivering with cold and the other half shaking with fright." In the little library of writing that is consecrated to them there is not one word in the Charlie's praise. Lightly damned by Shakespeare as the " most senseless and fit," they have descended to us under the pens of all chroniclers and all historians exactly as he created them for the stage. From the seventeenth century until the close of the second decade of the nineteenth the essential type underwent no essential change.

Waving their lanterns as they went, and thumping with their staves, they admonished the thief of their propinquity, and he had simply to turn about and make for the next parish. It was the popular opinion that the Charlies included black sheep who not only connived at robbing but took their share of its proceeds, and Dibdin's song " The Watchman," illustrated by J. R. Marshall, began as follows :

A watchman I am, and I knows all the round
  The housekeepers, the strays, and the
    lodgers,
Where low devils, rich dons, and high rips,
    may be found,
  Odd dickies, queer kids, and rum codgers ;
Of money and of property, I'm he that takes
    the care,
  And cries, when I see rogues go by, hey !
    what are you doing there ?
  Spoken) Only a little business in that
house ; you understand me ?

One practical purpose the Charlies served unwillingly during all the eighteenth century. They were the *corpus vile* of every practical joker after dark.

The Mohocks and Jerry Hawthorns and Corinthian Toms were never tired of battering them and smothering them under their boxes. In an essay in the *World* (May 30, 1754), one of "this venerable faternity," who "it seems has been lately disciplined by a set of Bucks," complains of this "insult to the sacredness of office";

and Thackeray's readers will remember Bludger, that "brave and athletic man," who "would often give a loose to his spirits of an evening, and mill a *Charlie* or two, as the phrase then was."

The Charlie was the failure and the butt of London until Peel at last disposed of him in 1829.

LORD MACAULAY AT CAMPDEN HILL

IT is the setting of the sun that we have to describe in the story of Lord Macaulay at Campden Hill; the story of a writer, of a statesman, who has given up most of his active work in the world, and who knows that death cannot be very long delayed. Honours crowd upon him, unprecedented success attends his literary ventures; he has friends and loving relatives, books, and in the heart of London, a garden : but he knows that his great work, the "History of England from the reign of James II." must be left unfinished, and that much of the material he has painfully accumulated will never receive life from his pen. Yet it is a sunset full of dignity and mellowness; the affections strong, the brain unclouded, the emotions quick, the hand open and generous to a fault, when claims were made upon its charity.

Holly Lodge (now Airlie Lodge), Campden Hill, where Macaulay lived from 1856 till his death in 1859, was an ideal place of retirement. Situated in London, within easy reach of London friends and London sights, it yet possessed all the quiet of the country. It occupies, to quote Sir George Trevelyan, Macaulay's nephew and biographer, "the most secluded corner of

the little labyrinth of by-roads, which, bounded to the east by Palace Gardens, and to the west by Holland House, constitutes the district known as Campden Hill. The villa—for a villa it is—stands in a long and winding lane, which with its high black paling concealing from the passer-by everything except a mass of dense and varied foliage, presents an appearance as rural as Roehampton and East Sheen present still."

The garden added very greatly to the charm of the house. It was, to give Macaulay's own words, " a little Paradise of shrubs and turf," the lawn " a perfect emerald ": hollies abounded, laurels and hawthorns, roses, lilacs and laburnums. Macaulay was keenly sensitive to these delights; he even enjoyed gardening a little, and waged a vigorous war against the dandelion tribe—the flowers with the "great impudent flaring yellow faces," as he describes them to his little niece Alice. The garden, however, was less a place for physical exercise than for reading and meditation. The library gave directly on the lawn, and Macaulay loved to take one of his beloved classics from the shelf—Cicero or Homer or Aristophanes—and wander out into the open ; or wishing to assure himself that his amazing memory was in no wise impaired—that memory which retained after a single reading many cantos of " The Lay of the Last Minstrel," and which knew " Paradise Lost " and the " Pilgrim's Progress " by heart—he would learn by rote " the noble fourth act of *The Merchant of Venice* " or the entire roll of the House of Lords.

Not only private appreciation but public honours followed Macaulay to Holly Lodge. It was at the time of the Indian Mutiny that he received the offer of a peerage. He writes : " August 28, 1857. A great day in my life. I stayed at home, very sad about India. Not that I have any doubt about the result ; but the news is heartbreaking. I went, very low, to dinner, and had hardly begun to eat when a messenger came with a letter from Palmerston. An offer of a peerage ; the Queen's pleasure already taken. . . . Perhaps no such offer was ever made without the slightest solicitation to a man of humble origin and moderate fortune, who had long quitted public life." His literary success was no doubt an even greater source of gratification to him : 26,500 copies of his " History " were sold in ten weeks, and he writes in 1857 : " I should not wonder if I made £20,000 clear this year by literature."

Still, the " History " remained unfinished, and it is pathetic to think of Macaulay reading over pamphlets of the reign of Queen Anne—a reign which he was so peculiarly fitted to undertake—when he knew it was very doubtful if he would be able to complete even the reign of William III. He did continue to write the " History " at Holly Lodge, as well as several articles for the " Encyclopædia Britan-

nica " : but writing had become a greater effort, and the habit of procrastination was gaining ground. Yet Macaulay was not old ; he was only fifty-nine when he died. In 1853, however, he had had a heart-attack, from the effects of which he never entirely recovered, and from that time he was troubled with asthma and violent fits of coughing, which sapped his vitality.

Although Macaulay never married, he was of a deeply affectionate nature, and in particular his devotion was lavished upon his sister, Lady Trevelyan. The last year of his life was clouded by the fear that he would have to part from her. Her husband had sailed for India as Governor of Madras : she was to follow a little later. " I dread the next four months," writes Macaulay, " more than even the months that will follow the separation. This prolonged parting, this slow sipping of the vinegar and the gall, is terrible." But after all it was not his sister who was to go from Macaulay, but Macaulay who was to go from his sister. On December 28 George Trevelyan found him seated in his library, in a languid and drowsy reverie. Alarmed at his condition, he hastened home to fetch his mother. As she and her son drove up to the house " the maids ran crying out into the darkness to meet us, and we knew that all was over. We found him in the library, seated in his easy chair, and dressed as usual ; with his book on the table beside him. . . . He died as he had wished to die ; without pain ; without any formal farewell ; preceding to the grave all whom he loved ; and leaving behind him a great and honourable name, and the memory of a life every action of which was as clear and transparent as his own sentences."

EIGHTEENTH-CENTURY EVENINGS ON PRIMROSE HILL

PRIMROSE HILL has associations and a history that take us right back to Roman days, when most of the northern part of London was a large forest, filled with wolves and other wild animals. It was not until the beginning of the thirteenth century that Middlesex was disafforested, although in the reign of Elizabeth the woods were sufficiently dense to provide shelter and concealment for Babington the conspirator and his associates. Primrose Hill took its name from the primroses that grew there in vast patches when it was, comparatively speaking, an untrodden hillock in the fields between Tottenham Court and Hampstead.

In the days of good Queen Bess the slopes of the Hill were used as meadowland, and old writers allude to the many "haicockes in July at Pancredge" (St. Pancras), as known to everybody. Walford says in "Old and New London": "This district dates back to very early times, if we may accept the name of Barrow Hill—formerly Greenberry Hill—which lies on its western side, as evidence that it was once the scene of a battle and place

of sepulture for the slain. There was formerly a Barrow Farm . . . and the name survives in Barrow Hill Place and Road."

It is suggested that it was called Green - Berry - Hill from the names of the three persons, named Green, Berry, and Hill, who were executed for the murder of Sir Edmund Berry Godfrey, whose body was found here, October 17, 1678, under circumstances which have never been discovered or satisfactorily cleared up. The affair is the subject of a separate chapter in this work.

Bishop Burnet describes Primrose Hill as "about a mile out of Town, near St. Pancras Church." Such a description was perfectly accurate in Burnet's time, when St. Pancras Church, which stands nearly opposite Euston Station, was the only landmark of importance in the neighbourhood, and the Hill and the church were only separated by hayfields and gardens, where vegetables were cultivated for Covent Garden Market.

Primrose Hill, it may be noted, is a portion of the land bequeathed by "sun ry devout men of London" to

St. James's Hospital; it was then granted by Henry the Sixth to Eton College. Later it was claimed by, and surrendered to, Henry the Eighth; then it was returned to the College once more. About seventy years ago it was transferred to the Government in exchange for a piece of Crown-land at Windsor, and Primrose Hill was then dedicated to the public for ever. A noteworthy point about Primrose Hill is the tunnel of the London and North-Western Railway, which, at the time, was considered a marvellous achievement of engineering skill.

We get a very good idea of the popularity of all the open spaces of London round Regent's Park and Tottenham Court, from the oft-mentioned custom among cockneys to flock to Primrose Hill and to disport themselves by climbing up the various sides of the mount, and by rolling and tumbling down again, to gain that amusement which seemed to please many of the boisterous youths and maids of older London Town—London Town which, then, was so many miles off. In the days of Henry the Eighth his most Royal Majesty was much desirous to have " The Games of hare, partridge, pheasant and heron, preserved in and about His Honour of the Palace of Westminster, for his own disport and pastime." In other words, the King went hunting to Highgate, to Hornsey Park, and round about Primrose Hill, and so home again to Westminster.

In its wild state Primrose Hill drew all sorts of ruffians and robbers, in the early part of the eighteenth century, as a hiding-place, from which they could pounce upon innocent way-farers; and by rapidly riding round from one side of the hill to the other highwaymen made it a vantage-ground to intercept the coaches going north, generally to their own nefarious advantage, but not always.

Since those " good old times," when the law luckily came to the rescue and many adventurous " meetings " took place, Primrose Hill was taken charge of by the English Parliament, which empowered the Local Authorities to have the Hill planted with trees and laid out so as " to convert it into a public garden." The eminence itself is now greatly resorted to as a cricket and football field, and also for the advantage of its gymnasium.

It may be observed that on May 29, 1856, " Fireworks were exhibited on Primrose Hill for the first time," in celebration of the Peace and the end of the Crimean War, as well as in Hyde, Green, and Victoria Parks. In 1864, under the auspices of a committee, an oak was planted by Samuel Phelps, the tragedian, to commemorate the Tercentenary of Shakespeare. Strange to say, Shakespeare's name is inscribed on the plate in brackets ! The summit of Primrose Hill is two hundred and six feet above the Trinity high-water mark of the Thames, and the views to be obtained not only include the whole of London, but also parts of Hampstead and Highgate. The dome of St. Paul's can easily be seen. In another direction the eye may glance over Islington and Holloway, and away to the hills of Kent and Surrey ; and, upon a clear day, the bright roof of the Crystal Palace at Sydenham is easily discernible, as well as that of the Alexandra Palace at Muswell Hill.

THE GREAT FIRE OF LONDON

THE summer of 1666 was of exceptional dryness. In London the timber of the houses—for all the upper and overhanging portions were built of wood—seemed almost ready to kindle in the glare of the sun. Many Londoners had only just returned to their houses from the country, whither they had fled on account of the Great Plague of the year before ; and as the miasma thickened from the refuse of the narrow streets into an almost tangible vapour, the dread of a recurrence of that scourge must have darkened the minds of many. One hundred thousand Londoners had died amid scenes of indescribable horror, and the citizens well knew that the enemy lingered in hidden lanes and byways, ready at the first opportunity to pounce upon them and slay them.

But there was never to be another manifestation of the Plague in London ; it was to be driven from its outposts by a power as fierce, as irresistible as itself. London was to be saved from the Plague by being practically swept out of existence—thirteen thousand of her houses destroyed, four hundred of her streets, ninety of her churches razed to the ground. In four days Old London vanished off the face of the earth, with all its beauty of building, its historic interest, its unthinkable squalor and dirt ; but the fire that burnt her purged her, and the New London that rose on the ashes—preserving happily all the old historic sites and landmarks—rose free from ancient disease and century-old ills.

The story of the fire is terrible, tragic; thrilling ; told by many an eye-witness with graphic touches and minute personal details, so that the scene lives before us in all its wonder and its terror.

Early on Sunday morning, September 2, 1666, Jane, maidservant to Samuel Pepys (Clerk to the Acts of the Navy, who had his house and office in Crutched Friars) called up her master and mistress to tell them of a fire she saw in the City. Pepys looked out of the window, thought it far enough off, and so went to bed again and to sleep. It is what most of us do when we see the glare of a fire at a good distance. But others, whose duty it was to take quick and concerted action, regarded and that fire broke out in houses widely separated from the original conflagration. The Monument, put up to commemorate the fire, had at one time an inscription stating this to be an absolute fact. This column stands two hundred and two feet from the spot where the fire first broke out, and is two hundred

THE FIRE OF LONDON SEEN FROM SOUTHWARK
After Hollar

the fire, like Pepys, as quite unimportant, and so it was allowed to grow into proportions beyond the control of man and to wreak a destruction rarely paralleled in history.

The fire started in the house of a baker in Pudding Lane, near Fish Street Hill, within ten houses of Lower Thames Street. It was a district of narrow lanes and alleys, the buildings being of timber, lath and plaster ; there were many shops with combustible material, and a strong north-east wind was blowing. How the fire started remains a mystery. It was widely believed that certain houses were fired by Papists, and some asserted that they saw men throwing fire-balls into houses,

and two feet high. The inscription asserted that the burning was carried out by the Popish faction, in order to the effecting their horrid plot for extirpating the Protestant religion and English liberties, and to introduce Popery and slavery. Hence the allusion by Pope, himself a Roman Catholic, to the Monument :

Where London's column, pointing to the skies
Like a tall bully, lifts its head and *lies*. . . .

And certainly the case is non-proven, and the inscription has been removed : though one unhappy man confessed his guilt and was hanged on his own confession alone. But neither the judges nor any present at the trial did believe him guilty, writes Lord Clarendon, " but that he was a poor distracted wretch, weary of his life, and chose to part with it this way." The House of Commons was so perplexed that it adopted the extraordinary expedient of summoning before it the astrologer Lilly, and examined him as to his fore-knowledge of the calamity, and his occult finding as to the origin of the fire. Lilly claimed (on very insufficient evidence) that he had foretold both the Fire and the Plague : and asserted that the fire was not of man, but of God.

Another prophet was the enthusiast Solomon Eagles, who ran about London nearly naked in 1665 with a pan of burning brimstone on his head — a terrible object. He is introduced by Harrison Ainsworth into his novel " Old St. Paul's " where he is encountered in Cheapside. " His eyes were large and black, and blazed with insane lustre." He is crying to the mob : " Do you hear this,

SOLOMON EAGLES, THE PROPHET OF PLAGUE AND FIRE IN 1665

utterly burnt with fire—for strong is the Lord who judgeth it."

We will now accompany the Lord Mayor to the spot of the outbreak. It is 3 o'clock on Sunday morning. Fires

O sinners ? God will proceed against you in the day of his wrath, though he hath borne with you in the day of his patience. O, how many hundred years hath he spared this city. But now . . . plagues shall come upon it and desolation ; and it shall be are common in London, and the Lord Mayor is rather annoyed at having been hurried out of his bed for so slight a matter. " A woman might put it out ! " he scornfully exclaimed. But by eight o'clock the fire had got as far as London Bridge ; and there dividing, it burned all the houses left on the bridge since the last great fire of 1633 and pressed on westward along the river-bank. The Lord Mayor was now beside himself; he refused for some time to pull down houses, because he dared not do so "without the consent of the owners"; and he utterly rejected the counsel of some stout seamen, who suggested gunpowder, even at this early stage. About eleven o'clock the same day, Pepys met the Lord Mayor in Cannon Street. The Lord Mayor cried like a fainting woman: "Lord! what can I do? I am spent, and the people will not obey me. I have been pulling down houses, but the fire overtakes us faster than we can do it." He added that he must go home and refresh himself, having been up all night.

The scene of panic, terror and confusion now baffles all description. London was then an inhabited city, not, as the City is to-day, a hive of offices. Citizens lived over their shops and businesses, and it was their very homes that were being devastated. Some lost their heads, and rushed about

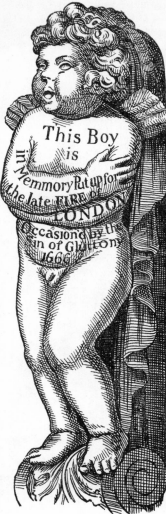

AT PYE CORNER

as if distracted others bent their whole energies in saving their goods from the flames. No organised attempt was made to fight the fire; every one worked for his own personal possessions. In frantic haste the people piled movables upon carts, or got them into boats: the whole Thames was soon covered with lighters and barges laden with furniture—goods were swimming in the water, and showers of fire-drops falling all over the town and river. The rich dug pits in their gardens to store their gold and their wine, and even their cheeses: laden carts were driven out into the fields close by—Moorfields and St. George's Fields: sick people were carried along the streets in their beds. Many of the wretched citizens stayed in their houses till the very fire touched them, and then you might see them rushing for the boats, clambering from one pair of stairs by the waterside to another.

The noise was appalling. To the "fearful cries and howlings of undone people" we must add the horrid roar the flames made, "like a thousand iron chariots beating upon stones," says one ; the thunder and hiss of the fire ; the crashing of the buildings, the houses of whole streets falling down one after another. The heavens themselves seemed on fire, or, as one described it, like the top of a burning oven : rounded by scaffolding : in one moment the structure was a sheet of flame. The stones flew like granados : the lead melted as if it had been snow in the sun. The molten metal of the ironwork, the bells and the plate poured down the street ; the pavements glowed with

THE BURNING OF LUDGATE (*From Wilkinson's Londina Illustrata*)

the light of the flames could be seen for forty miles round. Clouds of smoke (reaching fifty miles in length) formed a canopy over the city, and when the sun looked through, it appeared red as blood. At last the air became so inflamed that no one could approach the fire.

On Sunday the fire got as far as Cannon Street : on Monday it reached Cornhill, burned the Royal Exchange, and four fires joined in a great flame at Cheapside. On Tuesday the Cheapside fire and the riverside fire met, attacked and burned down Old St. Paul's. The Cathedral was at that time undergoing repairs and was surrounded fiery redness. In the intolerable heat great flakes of stone peeled from the building ; and soon St. Paul's was in hopeless ruin. The Guildhall in the fire presented an amazing spectacle. It stood for several hours together red-hot without flames, like a palace of gold or burnished brass : probably because the timber was such solid oak. Pepys watched the fire from the river and from Bankside, and he describes it as " a most horrid malicious bloody flame, not like the fine flame of an ordinary fire." " God grant;" writes Evelyn, " my eyes may never behold the like, who now saw close ten thousand houses all in one flame."

II

D

The fire extended two miles along the waterside, and one mile to the north.

As to the unhappy Londoners, their

THE MONUMENT A HUNDRED YEARS AGO, WITH OLD
LONDON BRIDGE IN THE DISTANCE

several miles in circle; some under tents, some under miserable huts and hovels; many without a rag or any necessary utensils, bed or board, who from delicateness, riches and easy accommodation, in stately and well-furnished houses, were now reduced to extremest poverty and misery." On September 7 he writes: "I then went towards Islington and Highgate, where one might have seen two hundred thousand people, of all ranks and degrees dispersed and lying along by their heaps of what they could save from the fire, deploring their loss: and yet ready to perish for hunger and destitution, yet not asking one penny for relief, which seemed to me a stranger sight than any I had yet beheld."

Dryden's picture in his "Annus Mirabilis" is touching:

Night came, but without darkness or repose,
    A dismal picture of the general doom;
Those who have homes, when homes they do repair,
    To a last lodging call the wandering friends;
Their short uneasy sleeps are broke with care,
    To look how near their own destruction tends.
Those who have none sit round where once it was,
    And with full eyes each wonted room require;
Haunting the yet warm ashes of the place,
    As murdered men walk where they did expire.

plight was pitiable. We quote the account given in Evelyn's diary. "The poor inhabitants," he writes, "were dispersed about St. George's Fields and Moorfields as far as Highgate, and

On Wednesday night there was an alarm that the French were coming against them to cut their throats, and in the fields where the wretched people were assembled, and in the suburbs, the cry was "Arm! arm!" But the alarm proved a false one, and war was not added to the horrors of the situation.

In this crisis King Charles II. and his brother the Duke of York showed energy and determination. It seems to have been by their command that gunpowder was first used, to blow up the houses and form a gap over which the flames could not reach. The king and his brother laboured in person and were present to command, reward and encourage the workmen. By Wednesday the fire had received a check; by Thursday the flames were extinguished. The fire had extended along the river-bank from the Tower to the Temple, indeed, it almost licked the windows of the Temple Church, and the Tower itself was only saved by the timely use of gunpowder. The fire extended north as far as Pie Corner, which stands at the Giltspur Street end of Smithfield; the figure of a fat boy still marks the spot.

In this fire only about six persons lost their lives—and of these, two or three perished in being too venturesome in going over the ruins.

" So fell great London! that ancient city! that populous city! that rich city! that joyous city!" Yet only four years later another London had arisen on the spot, to prove more populous, more rich—though not more joyous—than the London of old.

And again Dryden's great lines come to mind:

Methinks already, from this chymic flame,
  I see a City of more precious mould,
Rich as the town which gives the Indies name,
  With silver paved, and all divine with gold.

More great than human now, and more august,
  Now deified, she from her fires doth rise;
Her widening streets on new foundations trust,
  And, opening, into larger parts she flies.

AN EARLY FIRE ENGINE

THE OLD LADY OF THE BANK

MISS WHITEHEAD, THE "BANK NUN"

IN the first quarter of the last century the Bank of England was haunted by the forlorn lady whose figure is here represented. She was the Miss Flite of the City. Her story is alluded to by many writers. Wilson gives a somewhat over-coloured account of her in his "Wonderful Characters," but the picture of her given in "Real Life in London" is more lively and accurate. When the pilgrims visit the Bank of England the Hon. Tom Dashall greets an official, Mr. M——, in the Rotunda, which was then virtually a Stock Exchange, and the following conversation ensues :

" Pray," said Tallyho, " who is that extraordinary looking Lady with such red lips and cheeks, beneath the garb of sadness ? "

" A constant visitor here," replied Mr. M. " I may say a day scarcely passes without her being present."

" She has a curious appearance," said Bob ; " her dress is all black from head to foot, and yet her cheeks disclose the ruddy glow of uninterrupted health. Is it that her looks belie her garb, or, that her garb belies her looks ? "

" Hush," said Mr. M., " let her pass and I will give you some information relative to her, which, if it does not gratify you, will at least satisfy some of your inquiries. I am half inclined to believe that all is not right in the seat of *government* with her (pointing his finger to his head) ; and she is therefore rather deserving of pity than an object of censure or ridicule ; though I have reason to believe she frequently meets with attacks of the latter, when in search of the sympathy and benefit to be derived from a proper exercise of the former. Her name is Miss W——. Her father was formerly a twopenny postman, who resided at Rockingham Row, Walworth, and was himself somewhat eccentric in his dress and manners, and it was not at all unusual to meet him in the morning in the garb of his office, though decidedly against his inclination, and to see him on 'Change during 'Change hours, in silk stockings and in every other way dressed as a Merchant, attending there according to custom and practice ; and he managed, by some means or other, to keep up a character of respectability, and to give an accomplished education to the younger branches of this family ; so that this lady, though unfortunate in her present circumstances, has been well brought up, and mingled in political society ; and if you were to enter into conversation with her now, you would find her intelligent in the selection of her words and the combination of sentences, to explain to you the most improbable events, and the most unheard of claims that she has upon all the Governments in the known world. This, however, would be done in good temper, unless anything like an insulting observation should be concerned, or intended to be conveyed."

"And, pray, what is supposed to be the cause of her present manners and appearance ? " inquired Bob.

" It is principally attributed," replied Mr. M., " to the circumstance of losing a beloved brother, who she now continually declares is only kept from her by the persons who daily visit the Rotunda, with a view to prevent the recovery of the property she lays claim to, and the particulars of which she generally carries in her pocket. That brother, however, suffered the penalty of the law for a forgery ; but this she cannot be induced to believe. We have reason to think she is frequently much straitened for want of the necessary supplies for sustenance, and she has temporary relief occasionally from those who knew her family and her former circumstances in life, while she boldly perseveres in the pursuit of fancied property, and the restoration of her brother.

" I have heard her make heavy complaints of the difficulties she has had to encounter, and the privations she has been subjected to ; but her own language will best speak the impressions on her mind. Here is a printed letter which was circulated by her some time ago :

' *To the worthy Inhabitants of the Parish of St. Mary, Newington, Surrey.*

' It is with feelings of deep regret I have to deplore the necessity that compels me to adopt a public measure, for the purpose of obtaining my property from those gentlemen that hold it in trust. For a period of ten years I have endured the most cruel and unjustifiable persecution, which has occasioned the premature death of my mother ; a considerable loss of property ; all my personal effects of apparel and valuables ; has exposed me to the most wanton and barbarous attacks, the greatest insults, and the severe and continual deprivation of every common necessary. Having made every appeal for my right, or even a maintenance, without effect, I now take the liberty of adopting the advice of some opulent friends in the parish, and solicit general favour in a loan by subscription for a given time, not doubting the liberal commiseration of many ladies and gentlemen, towards so great a sufferer. As it is not possible to describe the wrongs I have endured, the misery that has been heaped upon me, in so limited a space, I shall be happy to give every explanation upon calling for the result of this entreaty and to those ladies and gentlemen that condescend to favour

'S. WHITEHEAD
'With their presence, at
'The White Hart Inn, Borough.'

"The property alluded to in this letter, is enumerated by her to be as follows :

PROPERTY BELONGING TO MISS WHITEHEAD.

Inscription of French Stock, Nº. 29606 série 5 Somme	Francs-Rentes. 247,000
Prussian Bonds, Nº. 9743 to 10,051, 309 Bonds for £1000 sterl. each	£309,000
Spanish Bonds, Nº. 1400 to 6899, 5500 Bonds, of 100 hard piastres each	Piastres. 550,000
Venezuelan Debentures, —1641, 1642, 1643, 1644, 1645, five Bonds, 10,000 dollars each	Dollars. 50,000
Columbian Ditto; Nº. 10, 23, 29, 31, four Bonds, 15,000 dollars each	Dollars. 60,000
North Pole Obligations, 6701 to 7000, 300 Obligations, valued at £150 each	£45,000
Morocco and Fez Stock, at 6 per cent. payable in cowries	Cowries. 120,000

Abyssinian 3 per cents. Dividend not yet payable, valued at—

Besides Bills to an immense amount, accepted by the Dey of Algiers, and payable by his Grand Plenipotentiary.

Various sums in the English and Irish Funds, in the names of various Trustees : in the 3 per cent. Consols—3 per cent. 1726—3 per cent. South Sea Annuities —3 per cent. Old South Sea Annuities— —4 per cent. 3½ per cent. 5 per cent. Long Annuities.

Besides various Freehold, Copyhold, and Leasehold Estates, Reversions and Annuities, of incalculable value.

One of the Freehold Estates is that known by the name of Ireland's Row, and the Brewhouse adjacent, Mile End ; the Muswell Hill Estate ; a large House in Russell Square, tenanted at present by Mr. B——dd ! ! !

"For the truth of this statement, or the real existence of any property belonging to her, I am not able to vouch. She is well known in all the offices of this great Establishment, is generally peaceable in her conduct, and communicative in her conversation, which at times distinguishes her as a person of good education.

"'Hard is the fortune which your Sex attends,
Women, like princes, find few real friends ;
All who approach them their own ends pursue,
Lovers and ministers are seldom true.
Hence oft from reason heedless beauty strays,
And the most trusted guide the most betrays.'"

Wilson's account of Miss Whitehead adds little to the above narrative. Upon one occasion she attacked Baron Rothschild upon the Stock Exchange, in the midst of his business, and after calling him by some hard names told him he had defrauded her of her fortune, and demanded the £2000 he owed her ; upon which, after casting his eye upon her for a moment, he took half a crown from his waistcoat-pocket, and giving it to her, said : "There, then, take that, and don't bother me now ; I'll give you the other half to-morrow ;" upon which she thanked him and went away.

She might be found every day in the purlieus of the Bank, or at one of the chop-houses in Threadneedle Street, where she generally dropped in to dine, and would not refuse a glass of wine when offered to her.

After more than twenty-five years of this strange life, her appearance, between the age of fifty and sixty, became very much altered. She failed in health, and at last, some time before her death, discontinued altogether her visits to the Bank.

HOGARTH AND HIS DOG

WILLIAM HOGARTH, LONDONER

LONDON was William Hogarth's element. Born in Bartholomew Close ("next doore to Mr. Downinge's the Printer's, November ye 10th, 1697 "), he was as staunch a Londoner as Johnson, or Lamb, or Dickens. His tastes were " essentially metropolitan," and to all hostile critics he proved, in the *Marriage à la Mode* series, that the West was as familiar to him as the slums. Still, though we can scarcely pretend to hobnob with Hogarth, we may take a turn with him in Leicester Fields when he strolls there of an evening, in his scarlet roquelaure, with " his hat cocked and

stuck on one side, much in the manner of the Great Frederick of Prussia." And that " shrewd, sensible, blue-eyed head in its Montero cap," painted by his own hand, which looks out at us from the canvas in the National Gallery, is one of the most familiar portraits in the world. A sturdy little man, " the downright artist of Leicester Fields," not unaware of his genius, and not puffed up about it, abhorring all " picture-mongery and sham connoisseurship " : we admire, esteem, and like him.

When Hogarth was born William III. had still five years to reign, and he lived on into the reign of George III. His father, Richard Hogarth, son of a yeoman-farmer of Westmorland, came to London, and kept a school in Ship Court, Old Bailey; not too successfully, it seems, for he was also a corrector of the press. He had scholarship enough to compile a Latin dictionary, but not means enough to publish it. William, by his own desire, was apprenticed to a silver-plate engraver, Ellis Gamble, at the sign of the Golden Angel, in Cranbourne Street or Alley, Leicester Fields. The shop card he engraved for his master is extant. Of Hogarth's prentice days a slight but pleasing anecdote is told by John Thomas Smith in "Nollekens and his Times." "I have several times," he says, "heard Mr. Nollekens observe that he frequently had seen Hogarth, when a young man, saunter round Leicester Fields, with his master's sickly child hanging its head over his shoulder." Smith adds an anecdote of Hogarth's later life in Leicester Square. Asked whether he had ever seen Hogarth, the painter Barry replied, "Yes, once. I was walking with Joe Nollekens through Cranbourne Alley, when he exclaimed, 'There, there's Hogarth!' 'What!' said I, 'that little man in the sky-blue coat?' Off I ran, and though I lost sight of him for only a moment or two, when I turned the corner into Castle Street he was patting one of two quarrelling boys on the back, and, looking steadfastly at the expression in the coward's face, cried, 'D—n him! if I would take it from him. At him again.'"

Hogarth tells us that at twenty years of age his own utmost ambition was engraving on copper. Pretty soon, however, he showed himself to be no ordinary designer, and stories are told of his "singular power of seizing expression"; but not until 1724 did he publish a plate on his own account. This was Masquerades and Operas, and Hogarth was now twenty-seven years of age. In Masquerades and Operas, says Mr. Dobson, we see "how definitely he had chosen his line from the beginning. Throughout his whole life we shall find him striking vigorously at foreign favourites and dubious exotics—at charlatans and shams of all sorts; and in this little plate he touches the keynote of his future work."

Presently we find him attending Sir James Thornhill's art school in James Street, Covent Garden (where, by the way, most of the artists of George II.'s time got their teaching); and in 1729 he ran away with Sir James's handsome daughter Jane. They were married at Old Paddington Church, and an excellent and devoted wife Jane Hogarth made. Not until A Harlot's Progress was issued did Thornhill become reconciled to his son-in-law. "The man who can furnish representations like these," said he shrewdly, "can also maintain a wife without a portion."

Hogarth had begun to paint while not yet relinquishing the graver, and in 1733 he settled down in Leicester Fields, where, "with occasional absences at the 'villakin' he bought sixteen years later by the Thames at Chiswick, he lived mainly until his death." Here we behold him in his comfortable plain brick house, with its gilt sign of the Golden Head, a bust of Van Dyck carved by himself. The cosy Bedford Arms was near at hand, and among the neighbours were John Leveridge the singer, George Lambert the scene-painter (and future founder of the Beef Steak Club), John Pine the engraver, and probably that benevolent man, Captain Coram, with whom originated the Foundling Hospital.

Although there are no grievous shifts or struggles to record, Hogarth at thirty‑six had not achieved a reputation with the public. There were but few print-shops in London at this era, and an artist of Hogarth's independent habit was not the man to advertise himself by common means. Nevertheless he was beginning to be known for his little "conversation pieces" on canvas, and the day of his renown was not far off.

Soon after his marriage he had begun to work upon the oil paintings for the first of the two great *Progresses*, the *Harlot's*. He has himself aptly furnished us with the notion of the scheme of this earliest extraordinary effort at "pictured morals"—Garrick's happy phrase. "I . . . wished," he says, "to compose pictures on canvas similar to representations on the stage. . . . I have endeavoured to treat my subject as a dramatic writer; my picture is my stage, and men and women my players, who by means of certain actions and gestures are to exhibit *a dumb show*."

Hogarth, it will be observed, here deliberately likens himself to a dramatic author, and we are to remember that

HOGARTH'S TOUR IN KENT
EMBARKING AT THE ISLE OF GRAIN

Hazlitt in his lectures seats him among the "comic writers." Fielding remarks of Hogarth's figures, not that they "seem to breathe," but that they "appear to think."

Lamb says most felicitously that, whereas we "look" at other pictures, we "read" the prints of Hogarth.

Arthur Murphy styles Hogarth "the Cervantes of his art," and elsewhere compares his characters with Molière's

In *A Harlot's Progress* Hogarth shows himself for the first time the realist complete and unflinching, the one painter of genius in an age of mediocrity. Every mature reader knows something of the stages of poor Mary Hackabout, whom Hogarth depicts as vividly and unsparingly upon canvas as, at a later day, Balzac depicted another of the class in a different artistic medium. Some of the characters in the series can be and have been named—among them " the infamous Colonel Francis Charteris and the equally infamous Mother Needham, the latter of whom died after exposure in the pillory in 1731." The six copper-plate engravings of the paintings were immediately successful, and the subscriptions, at a guinea a set, are thought to have realised some £1260. They were ruthlessly pirated.

Hogarth followed with the not less tragical story of *A Rake's Progress*. The reception of this was hardly so favourable. " It flew at higher social game. It attacked the vices of the man instead of the vices of the woman." Undoubtedly, however, the new *Progress* increased the reputation of Hogarth as a satirist ; and the great master of satire in another field, Dean Swift, was now sounding his praises in Dublin :

How I want thee, humorous Hogarth !
Thou, I hear, a pleasant rogue art.
Were but you and I acquainted,
Every monster should be painted, &c.

Thanks to the print-sellers, Hogarth, before he had reached fifty, was a popular man with the public ; and though he had not yet set up the carriage in which at a later date it pleased him to take the air (when first he acquired that vehicle he would sometimes, in sheer absence of mind, leave it at the door of a house he had been visiting, and hail a hackney coach), there could have been no lack of comfort at home, with substantial Georgian cheer. Failing the prints, indeed, the wolf must often have strayed into Leicester Fields, for Hogarth was still, as always, at odds with the dealers, and much of his best work in oil hung upon his hands. In 1745, in the style that proclaimed the man, he sold a number of original paintings by a species of auction for the shockingly inadequate sum of £427 7s. The engraved ticket of admission to the sale contained an inscription, " half-ironic, half-defiant," such as Hogarth's especial public had grown to expect from him : " The Bearer hereof is Entitled (if he thinks proper) to be a Bidder for Mr. Hogarth's Pictures, which are to be Sold on the Last Day of this Month."

Now also were advertised for sale the six paintings of *Marriage à la Mode*, William Hogarth's capital achievement, his master-stroke in art. It is not easy to think of a slack market in connection with work of this quality, " the finest pictorial satire of the century ".; but *Marriage à la Mode* was six years in finding its purchaser. It was altogether a humiliating business, but Hogarth's terms—idiosyncratic enough—were largely to blame. " The bidding . . . was to be by written notes ; no dealers in pictures were to be admitted as bidders ; and the highest bidder at noon on June 6 (1751) was to be the purchaser." This was certainly not very astute on Hogarth's part. The sole bidder to put in an appearance on the date named, at the Golden Head, was a Mr. Lane, " of Hillingdon, near Uxbridge." The highest written offer was declared to be £120. " I'll make it guineas," said Mr. Lane ; " but subsequently (Mr. Dobson tells us), and much to his credit, offered the artist a delay of some hours to find a better purchaser." None came forward, and the mortified Hogarth (who had paid four guineas apiece for the Carlo Maratti frames) surrendered his masterwork to the fortunate gentleman from Hillingdon. In 1797 the splendid set was sold at Christie's for £1050 to Mr. John Julius Angerstein, whose complete collection was secured in 1824 by the directors of the National Gallery.

Upon a mercenary man of Hogarth's genius this warning would have had effect. It had none in his case. A very few years later, for instance, there were the original pictures of the delightful *Election* series to dispose of. Once again Hogarth would sell in his own way or not at all. The pictures "were to be raffled for, two hundred chances, at two guineas the stake." How many names were sent in we know not, but the only subscriber to attend in person was Hogarth's old and tried friend, David Garrick. The story of Garrick's acquisition of these paintings is interesting. When Hogarth had finished them he went to Garrick and said : " It does not appear likely that I shall find a purchaser, as I value them at two hundred guineas ; I therefore intend to dispose of them by a raffle among my friends, and I hope you will put down your name." Garrick told him he would consider it

HOGARTH'S HOUSE AT CHISWICK

and call on him the next day. He faithfully did so, and, putting down his name for five or ten guineas, took his leave. He had scarcely stepped into the street, when (as Mrs. Garrick, from whom the story is derived, stated) he began a soliloquy to the following effect : " What have I been doing ? I have just put down my name for a few guineas at Mr. Hogarth's request, and as his friend ; but now he must still go to another friend, and then to another : to how many must he still apply before he gets a sufficient number ? This is mere begging ; and should such a man as Hogarth be suffered to beg ? Am I not his friend ? " The result was that he turned back, and purchased the four pictures at the price of two hundred guineas.

In 1823, after his widow's death, came the memorable sale of Garrick's art treasures at Christie's. Sir John Soane then had the paintings knocked down to him for £1732 10s. They hang to-day in their original frames in a small room in his house in Lincoln's Inn Fields, now the Soane Museum. Like the *Marriage à la Mode* in the National Gallery, they form a series, their titles being *The Entertainment, The Canvassing, The Polling,* and *The Chairing of the Member.*

The last scene is rendered wildly farcical by the stampede of a sow and its litter, and the antics of a show-

man's monkey seated on a bear's back.
Despite its broad humours, the pictures
are beautiful in their colour and accessories, and ought to be better known to
Londoners. There is an interesting
point in the *Canvassing* picture. With
or without reason, John Ireland, the
author of " Hogarth Illustrated," insists that the voter between the two
bribers gave to Sir Joshua Reynolds
the idea for his famous picture of
Garrick between Tragedy and Comedy,
of which a sketch appears in Part I. of
this work above the chapter on Garrick's
farewell to the Stage. The figures
rather favour this theory.

Hogarth was eminently a " good
fellow " : he loved cakes and ale and
cheerful talk at Old Slaughter's Coffee
House or the Bedford, and he was not
seldom ready for a discreet frolic. In
May 1732 Hogarth made a trip down
the river into Kent with four boon
companions. These were Samuel Scott,
the marine painter; John Thornhill,
who was the son of Sir James Thornhill, the great decorator, and Hogarth's
brother-in-law; William Tothall, a
genial woollen draper of Tavistock
Row and afterwards a smuggler at
Dover; and Ebenezer Forrest, an
attorney, who chronicled the trip in a
pleasant essay which the Rev. William
Gostling, of Canterbury, who was a
friend of several of the company,
turned into Hudibrastic verse. Many
writers, including G. A. Sala, erro-
neously attribute Gostling's lines to
Forrest, whereas they were founded on
Forrest's prose narrative. They begin :

'Twas first of morn on Saturday
The seven-and-twentieth of May,
When Hogarth, Thornhill, Tothall, Scott,
And Forrest, who this journal wrote,
From Covent Garden took departure,
To see the world by land and water.

Hogarth's humours began early, at

Puddle Dock, where they encountered

a porter grim,
Whose portrait Hogarth, in a whim,
Presented him in caricature,
He pasted on the cellar door.

The adventures of the party on their
sailing and walking tour through
Gravesend, Rochester, Strood, Chatham, the Isle of Grain, and Sheppey,
and their return to Billingsgate in a
" mackerel-gale," are faithfully and
amusingly described in Forrest's narrative, which, adorned with sketches,
was read out for the delectation of the
company at the Bedford Head. The
original book containing the story and
its embellishments is now in the British
Museum.

The circumstances of Hogarth's
death, which took place at his house,
the Golden Head, in the south-east
corner of Leicester Square, on October
25, 1764, were pathetic. After his bitter
quarrel with Wilkes and Churchill,
which need not be recounted, Hogarth
went down to his Chiswick cottage to
seek peace in retouching several plates.
Tom Taylor remarks that he was
cheerful but weak, and must have felt
that the end was near. It was now
that he executed the last of all his
prints, preparatory to their publication
in folio. " What is to be the subject ?"
asked a friend. " The end of all
things," was the answer. " In that
case, your business will be finished,
for there will be an end of the painter."
" There will so," said Hogarth with a
sigh, and he went to work. The result
was the famous plate *Bathos*, a jumble
of last acts and things, Old Time with
drooping wings and broken scythe and
shattered hour-glass being the central
figure, and among many other details
may be noticed Hogarth's own print
The Times catching fire from a dying
candle.

In truth the great portrayer and satirist of his time was near his end. Tom Taylor proceeds to tell us how the end came. "On October 25 he ordered his coach—the last coach but one—and left Chiswick, where the autumn leaves were falling fast, for the old home in Leicester Fields. Here he found his faithful friend and housekeeper, Mary Lewis, who looked after the sale of his prints, and probably was left at Leicester Fields for that purpose when the painter and his wife removed to Chiswick. The journey fatigued him, but he was cheerful. He found a letter from Dr. Franklin, and wrote the draft of an answer. This exhausted him, and he retired to bed. Soon after, Mary Lewis heard a violent ringing of her bell, and ran to his room, found him in a paroxysm of angina pectoris, and supported him in her arms till he died."

He was buried at Chiswick under a massive marble tomb on which may still be read Garrick's lines :

Farewell, great painter of mankind !
 Who reach'd the noblest point of art ;
Whose pictured morals charm the eye,
 And through the eye correct the heart !

If genius fire thee, reader, stay :
 If nature touch thee, drop a tear ;
If neither moves thee, turn away,
 For Hogarth's honour'd dust lies here.

LONDON CATCH PHRASES

GEORGE AUGUSTUS SALA said that the earliest street cry that he could remember was "*Flare up*," which was a rallying call about 1832. It signifies too, "Flare up and join the Union," when there was a revolt against the use of machinery and strikes were in the air.

"*Yes, my word !*" and "*It's great !*" may stand alone. But "*Twopence more and up goes the donkey !*" is street acrobat slang, remotely derived from a supposed promise on the part of the posture-master to make a donkey ascend a ladder balanced on the nose of the performer.

"*How are you off for soap ?*" is forgotten, and so is the cry, "*Who shot the dog ?*" with which Volunteers were wont to be greeted, it being supposed that one of their number had the misfortune to shoot a canine by accident. "*Do you see any green in my eye ?*" comes from the far-away times and is never likely to be forgotten.

There are two or three meanings attached to the name "*Walker*," especially "Hookey." Hookey Walker, whose real name was John, was an out-door clerk employed by a firm in Cheapside, and he was noted for his eagle nose, which gained him the nickname of "Old Hookey." Walker's duty was to keep the workmen to their work or report them to the principals. Of course it was in the interest of the employees to throw discredit on Walker's reports, and the poor old man was so badgered and ridiculed that the firm at last abolished the office. But to this day "Hookey Walker" means a tale to be discredited, and when a gentleman puts his finger on one side of his nose and says "Walker," it may be accepted as a fact that he has doubts as to the truthfulness of the other gentleman's recital.

AN EARL AT TYBURN

A GENTLEMANLY condemned criminal, about to set out from Newgate on his way to Tyburn, begged that he might have the shelter of an umbrella. He was very liable, he said, to catch cold, and there were some threatenings of rain. We have not heard that any umbrella was forthcoming on that occasion ; but the Tyburn authorities once did provide a silken rope, or, as was doubtless remarked on the occasion, a silken necktie. This was for the purpose of hanging in a genteel way the Earl Ferrers of that time, who was executed on May 5, 1760, for the crime of shooting a Mr. Johnson, who had been appointed to receive the rents of his estates. There were other indications of deference to his rank. The scaffold was draped in black, and some ingenious person whose name escaped the attention of the contemporary annalist had designed and provided what was thenceforth known as "the New Drop," a raised part of the scaffold which fell out at the hangman's signal. "Part of the platform on which he stood dropped a few minutes before three," it stands recorded of another execution when the same device was first brought into use for common men.

In these days Earl Ferrers would neither have been executed by means of a silken rope, nor otherwise. He would have been sent to Broadmoor for detention "during the King's pleasure " ; for that he was a madman there would not now be the slightest doubt. What seems to have undone him, indeed, was the cunning of mania : he defended himself with such skill that his judges pronounced unhesitatingly in favour of his sanity.

There was madness in the family, which was a very old one, prominent in affairs at least as early as the reign of Edward I. The Earl Ferrers who suffered at Tyburn succeeded his uncle, who died in a lunatic asylum. His aunt was also confined as a maniac. For his own part he dealt so madly with his possessions that, though he had some talents for business, it was found necessary to appoint a receiver of his rents, on whom he would be dependent for his income. His habits were melodramatic, to say the least. He was subject to sudden gusts of outrageous passion. He would stamp about a room, grinning, clenching his fists, biting his lips, and all about nothing, so far as anybody could see. He found a lady to marry him, nevertheless, and treated her with such brutality that she had to be separated from him by Act of Parliament. It was then that Johnson, the receiver of rents, or, as he is sometimes called, the land steward, was appointed. This man had long been in the service of the family, and seems to have been a faithful servant of the Caleb Balderstone type. Lord Ferrers had nothing against him. He had, indeed, nominated him for the new place ; but he appears to have found himself seized upon by uncontrollable passion and deadly hate as soon as he felt the pressure of financial control.

Just an ordinary, honest, firm-minded man, Johnson was determined to deal with Lord Ferrers according to the strict letter of his engagement, which line of conduct was not quite what was expected of him in that quarter. The long-descended peer, who was sometimes the wild country lout, keeping the company which he

LORD FERRERS SHOOTING HIS STEWARD, JOHNSON (*After "Phiz"*)

found at village public-houses, and
sometimes the fine gentleman, begging
others not to be affronted by his
behaviour, was friendly with Johnson
even when he seems to have made up
his mind to murder him. The two
lived near to each other, the peer at
Staunton, close to Ashby-de-la-Zouch,
and Johnson at a farm about a mile
away.

The household of Lord Ferrers consisted of a housekeeper and her four

daughters, and also two men-servants and three maids. There came a day when he sent the housekeeper and her daughters out for a walk, and also got rid of the two men-servants. It was a day on which he expected Mr. Johnson to call.

No time was lost when, according to arrangement, the agent appeared at Staunton. He was at once shown into his lordship's room. Then the door was locked in his face, and he was required to sign a paper which was a confession of villainy in his dealings with the estate. Heated words followed. Johnson firmly refused to sign. The maid servants were listening outside the door, and one of them heard Lord Ferrers shout, "Down on your other knee. Declare what you have done. Your time is come. You must die." A pistol shot followed these words, and Johnson fell, the ball having entered his body just below the last rib. Then the assassin was attacked by remorse. It is said that he was about to fire again ; but that the pleading of Johnson's face restrained him. That cannot be certainly known. What he did was this : First he called in the servant-maids and asked them to find a man to help him to carry Johnson to bed. Then he sent a messenger for a surgeon, and himself went to inquire how the land steward found himself. Then he sent for Johnson's daughter, assisted her to apply styptics to the wound, and finally drunk himself into a state of intoxication. To the surgeon he said that he had intended to shoot Johnson dead, because he was a villain ; "but now that I have spared his life," he added, "I desire you to do all you can for him." Then he prepared to defend himself. He said he would shoot any one who attempted to arrest him.

The surgeon found it necessary to humour him as he sat filling himself with drink. The earl became confidential. He showed in what position he stood when he fired the pistol. He was astonished that the ball had lodged in the body, as the same pistol had sent a bullet through an inch and a half deal plank two or three days before. But Johnson, he thought, was rather frightened than hurt. Full of this notion, and under the influence of further potations, he rushed into the room where the poor man lay dying, pulled off his wig, and threatened to shoot him through the head.

To a suggestion from his housekeeper that Johnson should be taken home, he replied with passion that he should not be removed, and that he would keep him there to kill him. However, the madman was got to bed at last, after promising to provide for Miss Johnson in case of her father's death, and his victim was then carried to his own farmhouse, where he died at nine o'clock the next morning.

And then the neighbours rose. They banded themselves together to hunt Lord Ferrers as they would have hunted a wolf. When, for a long time, they had beset the house, the murderer appeared at a garret window. If the people would disperse, he said, he would surrender. He ordered them into the house to get meat and drink, and then made off, swearing that he would not be taken alive. He had armed himself with a blunderbuss, two or three pistols, and a dagger ; but in spite of this striking armament a sturdy coal miner took him without much trouble. He had killed a villain, he said, and he gloried in the act ; after which he quietly surrendered to his captors.

Peers are tried by their peers. When

a coroner's jury had declared Earl Ferrers to be guilty of wilful murder the House of Lords took the matter in hand, sending a large escort to conduct the murderer to London. That he really did glory in his crime now became evident enough. He proceeded to indulge in fantastic whims. He was removed to London in his own landau, drawn by six horses. This was for dignity's sake ; but as if to mock at that same dignity he dressed himself up like a jockey, in a close riding frock, with jockey boots and cap. On arriving in London he was taken to the House of Lords and committed to the custody of Black Rod, who ordered him to the Tower, where he was a prisoner for two months and a half.

The trial in the House of Lords came on in the middle of April 1760. It would have been a simple and speedy affair if Lord Ferrers, who was defending himself, had not put in the plea of insanity ; but he managed to present this view of his case with such an appearance of saneness that he may be said to have procured his own conviction. The sentence was that he should be hung, and then anatomised, on the following April 21. Then another concession was made to his rank. The execution of the sentence was deferred to May 5, and meanwhile frantic attempts were made by his relatives to obtain a commutation, but without success. There were none but those who desired to preserve the honour of the family from so black a stain who cared to lift a finger to save the life of Earl Ferrers.

The sentence was brutal, according to the fashion of the day. Simple hanging might have been enough. But the fact that he was to be mutilated after his death did not in the least depress the spirits of the noble murderer.

He resumed his fantastic swagger, in fact. For his execution he dressed himself in a suit of light-coloured clothes, embroidered with silver, said to be his wedding suit. His own carriage and six came to convey him to the scaffold. "You may, perhaps, sir," he said to the Sheriff by whom he was accompanied, "think it strange to see me in this dress ; but I have my particular reasons for it."

The very most was made of the procession by way of public show. The condemned peer was accompanied on his way to Tyburn by a large body of constables and many soldiers, on horse and on foot. The carriages of the two Sheriffs of London made part of his retinue. There were mourning coaches, and there was a hearse-and-six. The journey to Tyburn occupied two hours and three-quarters, during which, say the contemporary accounts, his lordship was perfectly resigned, only expressing regret that he was not permitted to suffer at the same spot as his ancestor, the Earl of Essex, for which favour he had petitioned the King. "He thought it hard that he must die at the place appointed for common felons."

The air of genteel comedy was successfully preserved up to the last. At first the titled criminal declined to join in prayers ; but at length he consented to repeat the Lord's Prayer, because he had "always thought it very fine." He presented one of the Sheriffs with his watch, and he meant to give five pounds to the hangman ; but by mistake handed it to the assistant of that official, whereupon there was a difference of opinion which outraged the proprieties. His lordship then extended his pardon to the executioner, and to all mankind, "as," he added, "I hope to be forgiven."

Though Earl Ferrers perished at the same place as common criminals, and by the same means, it was not on the ordinary gallows, " soiled by all ignoble use." A special scaffold had been erected, lower than usual, and furnished with the aforesaid " New Drop."

The body was duly exposed to public view, and, on the third day after the execution, given over to friends for interment. It was found that in his will Earl Ferrers had left £1500 to the children of his victim, and though the document was invalid this bequest was not disputed by the authorities.

SAM HOUSE

SAM HOUSE, known as the " patriotic publican," was a famous London character in the latter half of the eighteenth century. His tavern was in Peter Street, Soho, and he made it a veritable political caucus in the interests of his hero, Charles James Fox. Early in his career he got fame by undertaking for a wager to leap off Westminster Bridge into the Thames, against any Newfoundland dog that should be brought. He performed the feat. It was in 1763 that he commenced politician, taking an active part in support of Mr. Wilkes. During this violent struggle, Sam sold his beer at threepence a pot, in honour of Wilkes, then the champion of freedom ; and at his own expense gave entertainments to his neighbours, and others, who he thought were friends to the same cause. It is said his exertions in the election for Middlesex, on the side of the popular candidate, did not cost him less than £500.

SAM HOUSE

Sam was all for liberty and the rights of the people, in opposition to the influence of the Crown. At the election for Westminster in the year 1780, when the contest was between Lord Lincoln, supported by the Court, and Fox, supported by the people, he exerted every nerve in favour of the latter. During the poll he headed a considerable number of electors every day to the hustings, who gave their suffrages to Fox. His exertions in the cause of his friend were again conspicuous during the memorable contest for Westminster, between Fox, Hood, and Wray. When tendering his vote for Fox, at the hustings, he was asked his trade. " I am," said he, " a publican, and a republican."

Sam House died on April 25, 1785, after being visited by Fox. He was buried in the churchyard of St. Paul's, Covent Garden, amid demonstrations which displayed more good-feeling than dignity.

SOUTH SEA HOUSE DURING "THE BUBBLE"

THE GREAT SOUTH SEA BUBBLE

IN the spring and summer of 1720 all roads of London led to 'Change Alley, which now, as then, lies in the labyrinth of lanes and courts between Lombard Street and Cornhill. The town had been bitten by the tarantula of speculation, and was dancing mad. It was as though Pactolus, the golden river of Lydia, had been magically diverted into the celebrated lane of the brokers. They were the roaring days of the South Sea Company.

For the origin of this, which has been called "the most monstrous commercial folly of modern times," we must travel back into the closing years of Queen Anne's reign. The South Sea Company was practically the creation of Anne's Lord Treasurer, Harley, Earl of Oxford, whose flatterers called it "the Earl's masterpiece." It was not precisely a masterpiece, but neither was the fault precisely Harley's. In 1710 it began to be necessary above everything to restore public credit. There was a floating debt of between nine and ten millions sterling, and for the repayment of this no provision had been made. Harley's scheme was to "incorporate the proprietors of this debt as a chartered company with a monopoly of the trade to Spanish America." An association of merchants, incorporated by Act of Parliament, adopted the name of the South Sea Company, and became responsible for the debt. The privileges of the Company were to be perpetual, but the debt, on which the Government guaranteed an interest of 6 per cent.; was to be redeemable at one year's notice after 1716.

The grandest things were expected

of the South Sea Company. The wealth of the Spanish Indies was considered to be as that of Ophir, and even as the Red Sea fleet of Solomon had sailed to that fabled region, so would the ships of England go to the eastern coast of South America and return laden with ingots of gold and silver. But Philip V. of Spain had his tongue in his cheek. He had no notion of giving the Protestant subjects of Great Britain freedom of trade in his Spanish American ports. As is pointed out by Mr. Benians in the eighteenth-century volume of the "Cambridge Modern History," the South Sea Company never at any time enjoyed the opportunity that the dreams of the English public had created for it. Its fortunes, in consequence, were "chequered and unprosperous . . . It never enjoyed any real prospect of developing commerce with the Spanish possessions, or of planting colonies in South America, and the enlargement of its trading privileges which it was led to expect was 'afterwards refused.'

Joy
From a "Bubble" Caricature

By the Treaty of Utrecht which, as Seeley has observed, gave us a definite place in the abominable slave traffic, certain concessions were secured, but they turned out to be of very slight importance and were hedged about with all sorts of tiresome provisions. "Trouble gathered thick round the American trade in its infancy. Unexpected delays, obstacles, charges and confiscation by Spanish officials, for, which no redress could be obtained, diminished its profits, and, on the outbreak of war in 1718, the Spanish Government seized the effects of the Company; contrary to the original agreement." In fact, the rupture with Spain put an end to the legal trade.

By one venture and another the Company had none the less made a good deal of money; it was still regarded with favour by the public, and considered itself justified in putting forward the gigantic project to which is owing its celebrity in history.

This was nothing less than that the South Sea Company should become the sole public creditors. Such was the proposal advanced in January 1720, by the most prominent of the directors, Sir John Blount. The National Debt at this time amounted to some £49,000,000, and for this, Government paid the lenders 5 per cent. per annum, no trifling sum out of the then yearly revenue of between eight and nine millions. Interest on the irredeemable annuities alone, which had been granted during the last two reigns for ninety-nine years, amounted now to £800,000 a year. This burden, the South Sea

GRIEF
From a "Bubble" Caricature

accepted the scheme for the Government, but the House of Commons was disposed " to set the nation to auction." Let us, said the house in effect, have a bid or two from other companies. A bid was promptly forthcoming from the Bank of England. The Bank, in brief, outbid the Company. The Company, not to be beaten, sprang its offer to £7,500,000. It was a fateful and a fatal leap. In no circumstances could the stock of the Company be worth the extravagant price to which it must inevitably be raised in order to make

Company was ready to take upon itself. It was also prepared " to liquidate the entire National Debt in twenty-six years." Manifestly this offered a large gain to the State. As Mr. Benians says : " An immense debt would be converted into a redeemable form, while the interest upon it was to be reduced from 5 to 4 per cent. after 1727, and, in addition, the Directors offered to pay £3,500,000 as the price of the contract."

Aislabie, Chancellor of the Exchequer;

the transaction a financial success, and as a modern critic observes, " the project should have been still-born." But the directors, headed by Blount, were as astute as they were venturesome, and with amazing success the modern art of unblushing puffery began for the first time to be used on the great scale. It mattered nothing what the South Sea Company was pledged to pay the public ; the more it had to pay, the higher did the stock rise, " and before the South Sea Act had passed through Parliament . . . the price of the stock had risen above 300." Vainly, and almost alone among statesmen, had Walpole opposed the Bill in its every stage. The measure, he insisted, gave countenance to " the dangerous practice of stockjobbing, and would divert the genius of the nation from trade and industry. The great principle of the project was an evil of first-rate magnitude; it was to raise artificially the value of the stock, by exciting and keeping up a general infatuation and by promising dividends out of funds which could never be adequate to the purpose." Nothing could have been truer—nothing could have had less effect. Walpole was dubbed Cassandra, and the House, accustomed to hear him with devout attention, emptied when he rose to denounce the South Sea affair. The Bill was carried and received the royal assent.

Curiously, no sooner had His Majesty's assent been announced than South Sea stock suddenly fell. The Directors were not prepared for this, but showed themselves more than equal to what was but a momentary crisis. It was quickly put about that the South Sea Company was to be within a year or two " the richest the world ever saw." Spain, by treaty with England, was to grant a free trade to all her colonies, and silver, thus fetched from Potosi, was to be " almost as plentiful as iron." In less than a week the bait began to take. " On the 12th of April, five days after the Bill had become law, the Directors opened their books for a subscription of a million at the rate of £300 for every £100 capital. Such was the concourse of persons, of all ranks, that this first subscription was found to amount to above two millions of original stock.

It was to be paid at five payments, of £60 each for every £100. In a few days the stock advanced to three hundred and forty, and the subscriptions were sold for double the price of the first payment. To raise the stock still higher, it was declared, in a general court of Directors, on the 21st of April, that the midsummer dividend should be 10 per cent., and that all subscriptions should be entitled to the same. These resolutions answering the desired end, the Directors, to improve the infatuation of the moneyed men, opened their books for a second subscription of a million, at four hundred per cent. Such was the frantic eagerness of people of every class to speculate in these funds, that in the course of a few hours no less than a million and a half was subscribed at that rate."

For a while it seemed to be literally the case that every one who was not selling stock was buying it. It is scarcely a figure of speech to say that the whole of London felt the rage, for the stream of speculators that daily flowed to the City was composed of representatives of every class that had a shilling to invest. In 'Change Alley itself the crowd was probably a more typical one than ever swept over Epsom downs on Derby Day, for here were many parsons as clamorous as any of the laity. Peers and peeresses drove in their equipages ; Cornhill " was impassable for the number of carriages." Country squires swarmed as at a meet of hounds. Literary characters like Pope and Gay, and the ecclesiastical historian Bingham, were mixed up with tradesmen, doctors, farmers, " widows with small annuities," actors and actresses, women of fashion and women of the town, and even the penniless of many kinds who hoped that a penny might be turned there if anywhere. It was a hunt for the philosopher's stone, prosecuted by the people with much who wanted more, by the people with little who wanted enough, by the people with nothing who wanted something.

In songs and ballads of the day the scene was imaged. Swift wrote :

> There is a gulf where thousands fell,
> There all the bold adventurers came ;
> A narrow sound, though deep as hell,
> 'Change Alley is the dreadful name.

A popular ballad went :

> Then stars and garters did appear
> Among the meaner rabble,
> To buy and sell, to see and hear
> The Jews and Gentiles squabble.
> The greatest ladies thither come,
> And plied in chariots daily,
> Or pawned their jewels for a sum
> To venture in the Alley.

And Pope touched it ;

> Statesmen and patriot ply alike the stocks
> Peeress and butler share alike the box,
> And judges jib, and bishops bite the town,
> And mighty dukes pack cards for half a
> crown.

Plays were given (or at any rate advertised) entitled ; " The Stock Jobbers ; or, Humours of 'Change Alley," and " " Exchange Alley ; or, The Stock-Jobber Turned Gentleman ; a Tragi-comical Farce." Wright, in his "Caricature History of the Georges," says ; " All other trade but that of stock-jobbing was now neglected ; Exchange Alley was crowded from morning till night with persons of both sexes, and society seemed for a moment turned upside down. In the course of a few days, a multitude of individuals were raised from indigence to a profusion of wealth, which many of them expended in luxurious living and in reckless profligacy. In the park these upstart gentlemen mixed in their carriages with the aristocracy of the land,

but they were singled out as objects of insult and derision by the rabble, and at first the ' stock-jobbers' carriages ' seldom appeared in the streets without being mobbed. A newspaper of the 9th of July says satirically : ' We are informed that since the late hurly-burly of stock-jobbing, there has appeared in London two hundred new coaches and chariots, besides as many more now on the stocks in the coachmakers' yards ; above four thousand embroidered coats ; about three thousand gold watches at the sides of their wives and daughters ; some few private acts of charity, and about two thousand broken tradesmen."

Now, for the first time, political caricatures began to be rife in England; and Wright notes that the first picture of the kind aimed at the South Sea Company was advertised in the *Post Boy* of June 21st, 1720, under the title of " The Bubblers bubbled ; or, The Devil take the Hindmost." " It related, no doubt," says he, " to the great rush which was made to subscribe to the numerous companies afloat in that month." Others quickly followed. In one of the best of them, " re-engraved with English descriptions and applications in London," Fortune is seen charioteered by Folly, " the car being drawn by the personifications of the principal companies who began the pernicious trade of stock-jobbing, as the Mississippi, represented with a wooden leg ; the South Sea with a sore leg, and the other bound with a ligament ; the Bank, treading under foot a serpent, &c. The agents of some of the larger companies are turning the wheels of the car and are represented with foxes' tails, to show their policy and cunning. The spokes of the wheel are inscribed with the names of different companies, which, as the car moves;

72   **LONDON STORIES**

forward, are alternately up and down ; while books of merchandise, crushed and torn beneath them, represent the destruction of trade and commerce."

For, as may be supposed, the South Sea Company was not allowed to enjoy for long a monopoly of the boom. Like the palace in the " Nights," like the beanstalk in the nursery tale, Bubble companies rose as exhalations of the dawn or evening—and for the most part fell as rapidly. As Mr. Benians remarks, the South Sea Company was the giant bubble in an ocean of bubbles. " During the preceding two or three years many projects of various kinds—industrial, commercial and financial—had been advertised, and in the fever of excitement which attended the great operations of the South Sea Company, their number multiplied with astonishing rapidity. Every day saw new schemes put forward by enterprising stockbrokers who took small deposits. The majority at least bore rational titles, and related to fisheries, insurance, colonisation, land improvement, or the establishment of some manufacture, though a few were purely fantastic, and one audacious thief sounded the depth of public credulity with ' a certain . . . design, which will hereafter be promulgated,' and found it bottomless."

A CARICATURE "BUBBLE" CARD

To one at least of these concerns, The Welsh Copper Company, the Prince of Wales lent his support, clearing, it is said, some £40,000 " before a remonstrance from the judges induced him to resign his lucrative position." When the fever had reached its height above a hundred and fifty companies had been launched. There were companies "for building and re-building houses throughout all England"; "for effectually settling the island of Blanco and Sal Tartagus"; " for trading in hair"; "for furnishing funerals to any part of Great Britain"; "for insuring horses"; " for a grand dispensary"; "for extracting oil from sunflower seed"; " for importing a large number of jackasses from Spain"; "for a wheel for perpetual motion"; "for transmuting quicksilver into a fine malleable metal"; " for making deal boards of sawdust"; "for improving gardens"; "for insuring and increasing children's fortunes"; " for importing walnut trees from Virginia"; " for paying pensions to widows and others"; " for furnishing merchants and others with watches"; "for erecting hospitals for illegitimate children"; "for extracting silver from lead"; "for taking up ballast," and " for making salt water fresh." Swift may have borrowed from the amazing prospectuses of the period a hint or two for the Laputa scenes in "Gulliver." Some of these enterprises were kept going for a week or a fortnight, and some for less then four-and-twenty hours. A rogue might open an office in the morning for the sale of share in a concern that hardly owned a name; take money at his leisure during business hours and decamp with it after nightfall. "It was computed," says Mackay, "that near one million and a half sterling was won and lost by these unwarrantable practices, to the impoverishment of many a fool and the enriching of many a rogue."

All too soon for the herd of fools the great crash began. Some lucky fortunes had doubtless been

This evil Solomon espid
Among the Rabble rout
That beggers did on Horse back
Whilst Princes walke on foot [ride]
South-Sea has verify dy Same
Tor Mighty Men of late
Are brough to Poverty & Shame
Whilst Scoundrels ride in state

A CARICATURE "BUBBLE" CARD

achieved, but there was to be a ghastly tale of ruin. There are several stories as to the immediate causes of the panic that issued in such immense disaster, but the following are perhaps the essential facts. Few among the multitude of Bubble Companies had any definite legal status; few, that is to say, were partnerships, few were chartered bodies. But all in some degree meant harm to the South Sea Company, inasmuch as all in some degree appealed to the limitless cupidity of the public. The Directors therefore " procured a writ

against some of them by name and against the others in general. The writ struck consternation on the crowd of operators in 'Change Alley. The proprietors disappeared, and the orgy of speculation suddenly ceased."

In July eighty-six companies were suddenly, and with very scant ceremony, put out of existence. Less than this on the part of Government would have served to terrorise the speculators, few of whom, it may be conjectured, had ever understood what they were embarked in. The alarm was sounded, the panic set in. How did the public know what concerns had been sound and legal, and what had been merely rotten? If eighty-six could be suppressed out of hand, was the dazzling South Sea Company itself a solid and durable affair?

So once again the market was thronged to bursting, but the throng was not now of buyers but of sellers. In such a crisis one knows the course of events. Down plunged the stock—down and down. The Directors sought, says Mr. Benians, " to sustain it by lavish promises of dividends, but a more calculating spirit had succeeded to the frenzy of expectation, and men no longer believed that dividends of thirty and fifty per cent. were possible. By September 20 the stock had fallen to 410." But a few weeks earlier each £100 share had been fetching its £1000 in the market.

A rumour arose that the Bank of England was coming to the Company's assistance and for a moment the stock rose to 675. For a brief space indeed the Bank of England seemed willing to lend its aid, but the governors quickly learned how the Company stood and that hope vanished. The stock sank to 175, to 150, to 135. A run forthwith began upon certain leading goldsmiths and bankers ; some of these—large lenders on South Sea stock—fled the country. A run began next on the Bank itself. That storm was weathered, but ere the Bank was safe, the Bubble had burst.

The great delusion was at an end, but the morrow of it was a frightful one for thousands. The destruction spread far. Scores upon scores of families found themselves reduced at a blow to mere penury, " some of whom," says a writer who was a witness of the wreck, " after so long living in splendour, were not able to stand the shock of poverty and contempt, and died of broken hearts ; others withdrew to remote parts of the world and never returned."

" Cassandra " Walpole—he who had emptied the House when he uttered his warnings—was the man to whom the nation turned. The Minister, convinced that, for all the evils it had wrought, the South Sea scheme had done one fine thing, " by transforming the irredeemable annuities into a redeemable debt," proposed " that eighteen millions of South Sea stock should be engrafted into the stocks of the Bank and the East India Company ; that unsold South Sea Stock, of which there remained some fourteen millions, should be distributed among the existing proprietors as a dividend, and that money subscribers should be released from further payments. In addition, part (afterwards increased to the whole) of the sum promised by the Company to the nation was to be remitted." These proposals were accepted by Parliament, but the other two Companies concerned were opposed to them, and the engraftment of the eighteen millions of stock was never accomplished.

The House of Commons, spurred by a furious public, was in the mood for vengeance, and what are elegantly described as " punitive measures " were proceeded with. The report of the committee appointed to overhaul the affairs of the South Sea Company discovered " a scene of iniquity and corruption." The Company's books would as little stand investigation as many that have more recently been discussed at the Old Bailey. Knight, the Company's cashier had absconded with a register, sorely wanted, called the " Green Book." The Directors, as was but too clearly proved, " had laid themselves open to charges of illegality, corruption and favouritism, and some members of the Government seemed to have been accomplices." " Aislabie, the Craggs, father and son, Charles Stanhope, and Sunderland were all accused of having used their position to make profit from the scheme." Walpole's courageous defence of Stanhope, who was acquitted by a majority of three, " put the town in a flame." Aislabie was expelled the House and committed to the Tower. The Craggs, both father and son, saved themselves from condemnation by the most opportune of deaths, and Walpole, by a final effort of heroism, rescued his ancient rival, Sunderland. Thus ended the madness of the marvellous Bubble.

THOMAS CARLYLE IN LONDON

THOMAS CARLYLE wrote of London as a "wild wondrous chaotic den of discord." "This foggy Babylon," he calls it, "this huge roaring Niagara of things." Here we have the key of Carlyle's attitude, not only towards London, but towards life. London, like life, was a dragon-monster, that required to be grappled with, wrestled with, and during the forty-seven years that Carlyle lived at 5 Cheyne Row, Chelsea, he wrestled with poverty, he wrestled with contempt, even indifference; he wrestled with bodily suffering and intellectual difficulties. It is always as a fighter that we vision Carlyle, battling against shams, struggling through a welter of hypocrisies, fierce often, violent often, urged on by a noble and tireless thirst after uprightness and sincerity. "Creation cannot be easy," he says; "your Jove has severe pains and fire flames in the head, out of which an armed Pallas is struggling."

In his "sound-proof" room at the top of his Chelsea house a stern solitary wrestle went on for thirteen years while Carlyle grappled with his stupendous subject of Frederick the Great. This house has now been bought in trust for the nation, and it is impressive to stand in that attic upstairs and to recall the great intellectual conflict conducted within its walls. It was in this light that Carlyle himself regarded his work—as an immensity to be attacked and conquered. He himself tells us that he had a desperate dead-lift pull all the time, "day and night wrestling with it as with the ugliest dragon which blotted out the daylight and the rest of the world to me till I should get it slain." Carlyle

deified work as he deified strength—he is, indeed, the most thorough worker on record—"he found nothing easy that was great, and he would do nothing little." By sheer force of will he won his way over almost insuperable obstacles. We might imagine him as a Titan, making recklessly for his goal—destroying as he goes, sacrificing himself, sacrificing others, startling the indifferent out of their lethargy, the smug out of their self-satisfaction; he is like a roaring wind uprooting all that would bar its passage, and purifying the air.

His appearance bears out this conception of him. Hallam describes Carlyle in 1837, three years after he had come to London, on the occasion of Carlyle's first lecture on German literature. There he stood, a spare figure, lacking one inch of six feet; long but compact head, which seemed smaller than it really was; rugged of feature; brow abrupt like a low cliff, craggy over eyes deep-set, large, piercing, between blue and dark grey, full of rolling fire; firm but flexible lips, no way ungenial . . . dark short thick hair. . . ."

The "sound-proof" room, constructed after so much consultation and at so much expense, having double walls, and lighted principally from the top, turned out anything but sound-proof. The noises of London were maddening to Carlyle. Born and educated in the Lowlands of Scotland, he chose Chelsea when he came to London in 1834 because this district was then almost in the country. But as the houses crept up the noises increased—pianos, barrel-organs, parrots, "demon-fowls"; and in the sound-proof room, if the noises of the immediate neighbourhood were excluded, more distant sounds became distressingly audible — railways, whistles, bells, and the like—evils that he knew not of in the lower rooms of the house. A man of strong nerves is able to ignore such distractions, is able to despise the smaller discomforts of life that gave Carlyle such acute misery ; but Carlyle was a martyr to dyspepsia, finding only a measure of relief in long rides on horseback ; and chronic indigestion produced a state of insomnia, a state often of physical depression and " chaotic wretchedness " cruel to bear and hard to live with.

Trifles weighed heavily upon Carlyle, and upon his wife too, Jane Welsh Carlyle, whose vivacity and brilliant intellect impressed all with whom she came in contact. Half in joke, perhaps, she stigmatises the ordinary necessary duties of life in terms of blackest exaggeration. She talks of spring-cleaning as a " sack of Troy " ; when painters are in the house, she feels as if death had been dissolved into a liquid, and she had drunk it until she was full. " That wet paint should have the power of poisoning one's soul as well as one's body ! " she writes.

But if small annoyances were a grievous burden to them both, the Carlyles were able to face a serious crisis with heroic courage and magnanimity. John Stuart Mill was a friend of Carlyle's, and was deeply interested in the French Revolution ; he had, indeed, handed over to Carlyle the material he had himself accumulated on this subject. We will tell the tragic story with which he is connected in Froude's words : " Mill borrowed the manuscript as it was thrown off,

that he might make notes and suggestions, either for Carlyle's use, or as material for an early review. The completed first volume was in his hands for this purpose, when one evening, March 6, 1835, as Carlyle was sitting with his wife, ' after working all day like a nigger ' at the Feast of Pikes, a rap was heard at the door, a hurried step came up the stairs, and Mill entered, deadly pale, and at first unable to speak. ' Why, Mill,' said Carlyle, ' what ails ye, man ? What is it ? ' Staggering and supported by Carlyle's arm, Mill gasped out to Mrs. Carlyle to go down and speak to some one who was in a carriage in the street. Both Carlyle and she thought that a thing which they had long feared must have actually happened, and that Mill had come to announce it and take leave of them. So genuine was the alarm that the truth, when it came out, was a relief. Carlyle then learned, in broken sentences, that his manuscript, ' left out in too careless a manner after it had been read,' was, ' except four or five bits of leaves, irrevocably annihilated.' That was all, nothing worse ; but it was ugly news enough, and the uglier the more the meaning of it was realised."

What had happened was this. Mill had lent the manuscript to the lady who afterwards became his wife. By some accident it fell upon the floor ; and a stupid maid-servant had used it to light the fire. Years of anxious preparation and months of painful work were thus lost for ever, and that at a time of cruel penury. Yet after Mill had left the house Carlyle's first thought was for the suffering of his friend. " Well, Mill, poor fellow, is terribly cut up," he said to his wife. " We must endeavour to hide from him how very serious this business is to us." After months of agony the first volume was written again, and the whole book finished January 12, 1837, as the clock was striking ten, and the supper of oatmeal porridge coming up ; and Carlyle exclaimed to his wife: "You have not had for a hundred years a book that came more direct and flamingly from the heart of a living man."

It has been well said that Carlyle's life was a convulsion, as it were, of spiritual forces, gathering to a climax in each of his wonderful books, and after an interval of dissatisfied torpor—not *rest*, for he knew not rest—gathering again to gigantic effort and result.

But though Carlyle desired absolute solitude, and absolute quiet for his work, he was by no means a solitary. On the contrary, he seems to have had a strong capacity for friendship, and with Edward Irving, with Alfred Tennyson, with Professor Masson, and other of his friends, he often took long night-rambles through the streets of London. We have a vivid account of one of these walks from the pen of Professor Masson. "One summer night, about eleven o'clock, we had passed our usual parting-point at Hyde Park Corner and had strolled into the Park itself, lured by the beauty of a specially soft and star-brilliant sky overhead. The soft-

ness and stillness around and the starry brilliance above had touched his soul to its finest and gentlest depths. All roughness, all querulousness, were gone ; he was in a mood of

CARLYLE IN HIS CHELSEA BACK GARDEN

the simplest and most sage-like serenity. As we sauntered to and fro on the grass, the sole human beings peripatetic, where but a few hours before there had been the roar of the carriages in stream and the parallel gallop of the pedestrians, it was the stars and the silence that seemed to work upon him and suggest his theme. From the mystery and the splendour of physical infinitude he passed to what ought to be the rule of human behaviour, the conduct of one's own spirit in a world framed so majestically and so divinely. There was too much jesting in it, he said; too much of mere irony and laughter at the absurd; too little of calm religiousness and serious walk with God. In speaking of the over-prevalence of the habit of irony, sarcasm, and jesting, he used a sudden phrase of self-humiliation which I have never forgotten. ' Ah! and I have given far too much into that myself—*sniggering at things*'; these are the exact words."

With Carlyle, however, friendship did not always manifest itself in such intimate self-revelation; he knew that deeper form of friendship which is not afraid of silence. Down in the dark kitchen at Cheyne Row Emerson and Carlyle sat by the old-fashioned English grate and smoked together one long evening. "The burning weed scented the room, the smoke curled in sympathy with the silent fancies drifting through their brains, and neither man spoke. As they broke the silence, in farewell, Carlyle summed up the splendour of silence in a single phrase: " Mon, we've had a fine time." Tennyson was a frequent caller, and Mrs. Carlyle used to tell what happened on the occasion of his visits. The door would open and Tennyson would enter. " Good evening, Alfred," " Good evening, Tom," were the greetings. The door of the smoke-room would close, there would be the sound of chairs pulled along the floor to the fire, and then a full two hours' silence, broken only by the clay pipes tapping the dead ashes on to the bars of the iron gate. Then, an opening of doors again, " Good night, Tom," " Good night, Alfred," as farewells,

and Tennyson had paid another satisfactory visit.

After Carlyle had smoked his church-warden two or three times he would leave it, filled with tobacco, on the steps of his house, for any passing workman to take. His favourite tobacco was " York River," and one afternoon, we read, when Carlyle's stock had come to an end, on a walk with a friend, " he stopped at a small tobacco shop in Chelsea, facing the Thames, and went in to procure some temporary supply. The friend went in with him, and heard his dialogue with the shopkeeper. York River having been asked for, was duly produced; but as it was not of the right sort, Carlyle, while making a small purchase, informed the shopkeeper most particularly what the right sort was, what was its name, and at what wholesale place in the city it might be ordered. ' Oh! we find that this suits our customers very well," said the man. ' That may be, sir,' said Carlyle, ' but you will find it best in the long run always to deal in the veracities. The man's impression," adds the writer of this account, " must have been that ' the veracities ' were some peculiar curly species of tobacco, hitherto unknown to him."

" The veracities " were what Carlyle demanded, in friendship as in every other relationship of life. He was able to discover something substantial even under the dandified exterior of such a beau as Count D'Orsay. In a letter to his brother John, Carlyle gives an amusing account of the visit of this " complete Adonis " to Cheyne Row. " About a fortnight ago this Phœbus Apollo of dandyism, escorted by poor little Chorley, came whirling hither on a chariot that struck all Chelsea into mute amazement with splendour. Chorley's under jaw went like the hopper or under riddle of a pair of fanners, such was his terror on bringing such a splendour into actual contact with such a grimness. Nevertheless, we did amazingly well, the Count and I. He is a tall fellow of six feet three, built like a tower, with floods of dark auburn hair, with a beauty, with an adornment, unsurpassable on this planet; withal a rather substantial fellow at bottom, by no means without insight, without fun, and a sort of rough sarcasm, rather striking out of such a porcelain figure. He said, looking at Shelley's bust, in his French accent : " Ah, it is one of those faces who weesh to swallow their chin.' He admired the fine epic, &c. &c., hoped I would call soon and see Lady Blessington withal. Finally he went his way, and Chorley with reassumed jaw. Jane laughed for two days at the contrast of my plaid dressing-gown, bilious, iron countenance, and this Paphian apparition. I did not call till the other day, and left my card merely."

In Ruskin Carlyle recognised a spirit as fearless as his own—" one who had plunged his rapier to the hilt in the entrails of the Blatant Beast "— namely, public opinion. To Emerson Carlyle clung in spite of abysmal differences of view. " Has not the Man Emerson from old time been a

CARLYLE'S HOUSE, No. 5 CHEYNE ROW, CHELSEA

Human Friend to me ? " Carlyle writes to him. " Can I ever think otherwise than lovingly of the Man Emerson ? "

And it was " the veracities " at bottom of the nature of his " Heroic Helper" that awoke in Carlyle that lasting devotion he had always felt for his " poor little Jeannie," but which only attained full consciousness after she was dead. " My poor, ever-true life-partner," he writes to her in

1858, "hold up thy heart! We have had a sore life-pilgrimage together . . . much bad road, little like what I could have wished or dreamed for thee!" And in spite of the tragic suffering that the house in Cheyne Row has witnessed, the misunderstandings, the misconceptions, the disappointments, the remorse, we feel braced and stimulated when we visit it by the near consciousness of high aim and pure thought, heroic effort and endurance, strenuous purpose and unconquerable will.

"POODLE" BYNG

A CLUB DANDY OF THE REGENCY

LORD BYRON in "Beppo" speaks glowingly of the Dandies, and about the same time that his poem was written he said, "I like the Dandies; they were always very civil to me; though in general they disliked literary people. They persecuted and mystified Madame de Stael, Lewis (this was 'Monk' Lewis), Horace Twiss, and the like. The truth is that, although I gave up the business early, I had a tinge of dandyism in my minority, and probably retained enough of it to conciliate the great ones at four and twenty."

It would be impossible to recount here all the odd tricks and pranks that these magnificent dandies prepared themselves to perform; sometimes the fun was not on the surface; at other times it was very boisterous and certainly not of an agreeable nature. Beau Brummel was responsible for giving the sobriquet of "Poodle" to the well known Mr. Byng, who had what George Meredith would have said "a way with him and a leg."

From all accounts we learn that the Honourable Frederick Byng in his youth had very attractive and curly hair, and it was one of his little peculiarities to have with him in his curricle a French Poodle dog. One day Beau Brummel, who was on horseback, happened to meet the turn-out with the Honourable Mr. Byng and his dog driving together in the Park; he pleasantly hailed his friend with, "Ah, Byng, how do you do?—a family vehicle I see." As this was said purposely to attract to the other fop, the attention of the many fashionable riders who were moving close by, the name of "Poodle" attached itself to Mr. Byng, and ever after "Poodle" became part of his cognomen. He was a hero of the seas many years before the days of Nelson, was a well-recognised member of Brooks's Club, where he was in the habit of occasionally saying clever things, especially to the disadvantage of some of the old fogies who would persist in monopolising the best seats. In 1816 Byng had the privilege of being elected, through the influence of the Prince Regent, as one of the additional hundred members selected, when it was an honour to be known as belonging to "Brooks's," the most select and austere club in the metropolis.

Thenceforth Mr. Byng became a prominent figure in London society, and made the best of his opportunities. Ralph Nevill says in his work "London Clubs," "As a very small boy Byng had acted as page of honour to Prince George of Wales at his ill-starred marriage with the Princess Caroline in 1795, and used to relate the curious incident of his being taken to Carlton House to be looked at by the Prince before appointment." He was in Paris in December 1815, and was present at the execution of Marshal Ney, of which he gives an interesting account.

They had curious ways these autocrats of the long past manners and days, and the great " Poodle," when he was nearing his end, was particularly domineering in his attitude in regard to etiquette towards most people, whether young or old. At Brooks's Club, on one occasion he severely reprimanded a youthful member for lighting his cigar beneath the balcony outside the Club—the balcony that has long been dispensed with. One odd anecdote is worth relating. The Honourable Mr. Byng was once tremendously disturbed by finding a gentleman seated before the fire in the Club's best room, who had taken off his boots and had rung the bell for the waiter and asked for his slippers. It turned out that the perpetrator of this outrage was a new member—an M.P. for some manufacturing constituency, who, of strangely unconventional habits quite unknown to the Committee, had been elected, without any one troubling or caring much about him. Evidently the gentleman in question would have been far happier at home in the bosom of his family than in the armchair of a fashionable club. However, the Club's wounded susceptibilities were assuaged by the incidental ejection of the offending provincial.

In Captain Gronow's " Reminiscences," we have a good representation of many notable dandies described as " Bond Street Loungers of 1820," including the Earl of Sefton, the Duke of Devonshire, Lord Manners, the Duke of Beaufort, and "Poodle" Byng, who is the only character represented as wearing Wellington boots and the necessary breeches. One notes the pointed toes of all the boots, their high heels and the trouser straps, the use of which lasted well on to the end of the 'forties of the nineteenth century.

Apropos of " Poodle " Byng's fancy in costume the principal variation in men's attire at this period was the way in which they clothed their legs, when breeches and shoes were eschewed by fashionable men and their place was taken by the pantaloon, generally made of some stockinette material fitting tightly to the leg, and to this arrangement " Poodle " Byng clung almost to the last for evening wear, following the example of Lord Petersham, when the Cossack trousers came into vogue. But the most distinguished of all the dandies, including the Prince, even after he became George the Fourth, clung to the knee breeches.

"Poodle" Byng spent the whole of his time, having affluent means, in clubland, recounting the wonderful exploits of his youth—most of which had never happened.

BARON D'AGUILAR AND HIS "STARVATION FARM"

BARON D'AGUILAR, who died in Shaftesbury Place, London, on March 16, 1802, was one of the most extraordinary misers that London has known. "The elements were so mixed up in him" as to form a weird combination of vice and virtue : of misanthropy and benevolence ; of meanness and integrity ; of avarice and liberality ; of pride and humility ; of cruelty and kindness. Prosperous and fashionable during the early part of his life, he was despised towards the conclusion of it by his meanness and degeneracy.

He was the son of Ephraim Lopes Pereira d'Aguilar, who, after rising to wealth and distinction, died in 1759, very rich, leaving his title to his eldest son.

In 1758 Baron D'Aguilar, the subject of this story, was naturalised, and married the daughter of Moses Mendes da Costa, Esq., whose fortune, stated by report to be one hundred and fifty thousand pounds, was settled on her previous to marriage. By this lady he had two daughters, both of whom were living at his death, and inherited his large property.

Having been left a widower in 1763, the Baron, a few years afterwards, married the widow of Benjamin da Costa, a merchant, who brought him a considerable fortune. During his first, and for some time after his second marriage, the Baron lived profusely in Broad Street Buildings, where he kept horses and carriages, and a retinue of servants. Suddenly, and for no intelligible reason, he altered his whole plan of living. On the expiration of his lease he removed from Broad Street Buildings, renounced the character of a gentleman, became rude, slovenly, careless of his person and conduct, totally withdrawing himself from his family connections and society. It may be that, as William Howitt ("The Northern Heights of London") suggests, he was dissatisfied with his second wife. He grew rapidly mean, penurious, and highly eccentric in his manners. He treated his wife with brutality, starved and abused her. For this he was prosecuted and fined in the King's Bench. Here he impudently pleaded poverty, whereas he was extremely wealthy. Although he had quitted his elegant mansion, he had still abundant choice of residences. He had a field and two houses at Bethnal Green, which he kept shut up, though they were filled with rich furniture.

A large house at Twickenham, formerly his country retreat, was also kept shut up, and so was another of his country seats at Sydenham. In addition to these, he purchased a town house in Shaftesbury Place, Aldersgate Street, where he generally slept, and the lease of another in Camden Street, Islington, together with some ground close to the New River, which he converted into a farmyard.

Having relinquished the pursuits of a gentleman, the Baron took it into his head to turn farmer ; but he farmed in a manner altogether his own. His farmyard at Islington was a scandal. From the state in which the cattle were kept, it received the appellation of "Starvation Farm." His wretched animals might be seen amidst heaps of rubbish, some ready to expire and some preying upon others. His hogs would often make free with his ducks and poultry ; for, though brought up a Jew, the Baron had always plenty of pork and bacon for his own consumption. The miserable condition of these animals, doomed to this state of living death, frequently excited the indignation of the Islington people, who would often assemble in crowds to hoot and pelt the Baron. He generally appeared in a very mean and dirty dress, and never replied or took any notice of these unpleasant salutations, but availed himself of the first opportunity to make good his retreat. It is unknown for what purpose he kept the cattle, unless it were for amusement, as he derived from them little or no profit. The only reason he ever assigned for stinting them to such a scanty allowance of food was that they might know their master. Such was the state of his animals that they unnaturally attacked and devoured each other.

a servant that distance to milk them. Here his cattle in the winter time were absolutely perishing, and rather than sell any he would allow them to die, one after another, of want. In all

BARON D'AGUILAR AT HIS ISLINGTON FARM

After his removal to Islington, he would either feed the hogs, cows, and fowls himself, or stand by while they were fed, holding that nothing could be properly done unless he were present. His cows he used sometimes to send from the Starvation Yard to his field at Bethnal Green to grass, sending

cases of this kind, the man whom he employed to look after them was ordered to bury the carcase. Once, however, he disobeyed, and sold the flesh of a starved calf to a dealer in dog's meat. This coming to the knowledge of the Baron, he summoned the fellow and charged him with selling his property. The man confessed that he had sold the calf for one shilling and tenpence, which the Baron deducted from his wages and then discharged him from his service.

This extraordinary man had his generous moods. He was not uncharitable, for his contributions to the poor are stated to have been " manifold and secret." He was also a liberal patron of public institutions, and though his cattle showed that he did not always feed the hungry, yet he was seldom backward at clothing the naked, frequently inviting home ragged and distressed women, for whom he provided clothing. He had also been known to take into his houses fatherless children.

Having, says Nelson (in his " History of Islington "), totally forsaken all genteel society, and given himself up to the most wretched and abandoned pursuits, he never cared to see any of his family or his former respectable connections. " He would sarcastically tell his sons-in-law that they were *gentlemen*, and not fit associates for him, and his daughters that they were too *fine* to sit in his company. The large estate which he lost in America he never attempted to recover, nor would he allow any person to interfere in the business, though with a probability of success. He is said to have been an excellent scholar."

In his last illness, notwithstanding the severity of the weather, and the dangerous nature of his complaint, he would not allow a fire in his house, nor admit a doctor into his presence ; but he followed the prescriptions of a medical man, to whom he sent every day a fee of one guinea, with a statement of his symptoms. He died at his house in Shaftesbury Place, on March 16, 1802, at the age of sixty-two. His body was removed to Islington, and thence carried to the Jews' Burial-ground at Mile End.

The Baron's effects at Islington were sold by auction, which lasted two days ; his stock of lean cattle sold for £128, and his favourite coach, which was almost dropping to pieces, was bought for £7, for the sake of the springs. He had a valuable library in Shaftesbury Place, consisting of Hebrew, English, and foreign literature, which was also sold. His diamonds, jewels, &c., were reported to be worth £30,000 ; and his plate consisted of seven hundred weight, in articles of various descriptions. He had, moreover, a stock of about forty bags of cochineal, and twelve bags of fine indigo, probably worth near £10,000. These articles he had purchased many years before his death on speculation, resolving never to part with them until he had a desirable profit. The total bulk of his property is supposed to have been upwards of £200,000.

THE SUBLIME SOCIETY OF BEEFSTEAKS.

OF Beefsteak Clubs there have been many and various, but the first and most important was undoubtedly that originated by Richard Estcourt, the comedian, who was made Providore about 1700. This fact is mentioned on several occasions by Sir Richard Steele in the *Spectator;* Estcourt was highly praised for his wit, and the dignity with which he invested his office.

He that of honour, wit and mirth partakes,
May be a fit companion o'er Beefsteaks :
His name may be to future times enrolled
In Escourt's book, whose gridiron's framed
    with gold.

As a mark of distinction Estcourt wore the badge of the club, which was a small gridiron of gold, hung about his neck with a green silk ribbon. This club may be counted as the forerunner of the Sublime Society of Beefsteaks.

In Pyne's "Wine and Walnuts" it is stated that George Lambert, the scene-painter of Covent Garden Theatre, when preparing his designs for a pantomime or new spectacle, would often take his chop or steak cooked on an improvised gas stove rather than quit his occupation for the superior accommodation of a neighbouring tavern. "Certain of his visitors, men of taste, struck with the novelty of the thing, perhaps, or tempted by the savoury dish, took a knife and fork withLambert and enjoyed the unexpected treat."

Hence the origin of the Beefsteak Club.

Now let us read another tale of the origin and history of the Sublime Society of the Steaks, which has its pedigree, its ancestry, and its title-deeds. The Gridiron of 1735 is the heirloom gridiron on which its first steak was broiled. Henry Rich, who was known as Lunn, the first English Harlequin, of whom as a comedian Garrick spoke most enthusiastically, is credited with being the founder. There is still a letter in existence written by Nixon the treasurer of the theatre, probably to some artist, granting permission by the Beefsteak Society " to copy the original gridiron, and I have wrote on the other side of this sheet a note to Mr. White at the Bedford to introduce you to our room for the purpose of making your drawing. The first spare moment I can take from my business shall be employed in making a short statement of the rise and establishment of the Beefsteak Society."

Rich having made a fortune through the success of Gay's *Beggars' Opera* which made " Gay Rich and Rich Gay," became manager of Covent Garden Theatre about 1735, and firmly established the club. He was accustomed to arrange the comic business and construct the models of tricks for his pantomimes in his private room at Covent Garden. Here resorted men of rank and wit, for Rich's colloquial oddities were greatly appreciated. Thither came Mordaunt, Earl of Peterborough, the friend of Pope. He was then in advanced years and one afternoon stayed talking with Rich about incense that my Lord could not resist Rich's invitation to share the meal. His servitor was despatched for more meat, and a bottle or two of good wine from a neighbouring tavern prolonged their enjoyment till a late hour. And so delighted was the old

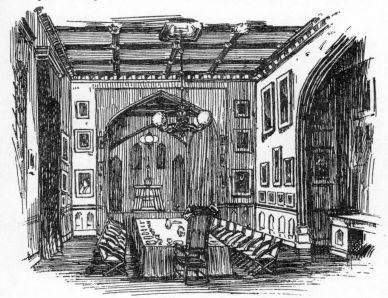

THE DINING-ROOM OF THE SUBLIME SOCIETY OF BEEFSTEAKS

his tricks and transformations, listening to his agreeable badinage, until the pangs of hunger warned Rich that his dinner-hour had arrived. Upon this occasion, accident having detained the Earl's coach later than usual, he found Rich's chat so pleasant that he was quite unconscious that it was two o'clock in the afternoon. Then he observed Rich spreading a cloth and coaxing his fire into a clear cooking flame and proceeding with great gravity to cook his own beefsteak on his own gridiron.

The steak sent up such an inviting peer with the entertainment that on going away he proposed renewing it at the same place and hour on the following Saturday afternoon. He was punctual to his engagement and incidentally brought with him three or four friends, men of wit and pleasure about town, and so truly festive was the meeting that it was at once proposed that a Saturday Club should be held there whilst the town remained full. A sumptuary law, even at this early period, restricted the bill of fare to beefsteaks ; and the accompanying beverages were port wine and punch. However, as we have already said, Lambert was supposed to have been the virtual originator, and Rich simply a worthy follower in very good footsteps.

The members were afterwards accommodated in a room in the playhouse itself, and when the theatre was rebuilt the place of meeting was changed to the Shakespeare Tavern, where for many years hung the portrait of Lambert painted by Hudson, the master of Sir Joshua Reynolds. In the *Connoisseur*, June 6, 1754, we read of the society " composed of the most ingenious artists in the kingdom," meeting " every Saturday in a noble room at the top of Covent Garden Theatre and never suffering any diet except beefsteaks to appear." Another solemn rule ran that every member had the " power of inviting a friend, but pickles are not allowed till after a third helping."

The apartments in the theatre appropriated to the society, varied. Thus we are told of a painting room level with the stage over the kitchen, which was under the stage nearest Bow Street. At one period the society dined in a small room over the passage of the theatre. The steaks were cooked in the same room and when the visitors found it too hot, a curtain was drawn between the company and the fire. Let us now glance at the celebrities who were to be found in the painting room in the Lincoln's Inn Fields Theatre, and the later locations of the club in Covent Garden. To the former came Hogarth and his father-in-law, Sir James Thornhill, stimulated by their love of the painter's art and the equally potent charm of conviviality. Amongst the early members of the society were Richard Brinsley Sheridan, the Earl of Peterborough already

referred to, Lord Sandwich, David Garrick, the Colmans (father and son), John Wilkes, John Churchill (the satirist, whose pen brought him into a great deal of trouble), the Duke of Sussex, the Duke of Leinster, Lord Brougham, the Prince of Wales (afterwards George IV.), John Kemble, the Duke of Norfolk, and his friend Captain Charles Morris, the laureate of the society, many of whose verses are remembered to this day. He died at the good old age of ninety-three, July 11, 1838, the year after Queen Victoria ascended the throne.

Charles Rice and Churchill were considered two of the wittiest members of the society, and it is related that he and Churchill kept the table in a roar. Formerly the members wore a blue coat with red cape and cuffs ; buttons with the initials " B.S " and behind the president's chair was placed the society's halberd which, with the gridiron, was found among the rubbish after the Covent Garden fire of 1808. The officials of the club consisted of a President of the Day, Vice-President, Bishop, Recorder and Boots. The President took his seat after dinner throughout the season, according to the order in which his name appeared on the rota. He was invested with the badge of the society by the Boots. His duty was to give the charted toasts in strict accordance with the list before him, to propose all resolutions that had been duly made and seconded ; to observe all the ancient forms and customs of the society and to enforce them on others. His position was not altogether a joy, for if he made one slip all the members were ready to pounce upon him. In fact he was a target for all to shoot at. The Bishop sang the grace and the anthem. The most important official, however, of all was the Recorder. He had to rebuke everybody for offences, real or imaginary, and with him lay the duty of delivering the charge to each newly elected member, which, of course, was a burlesque performance. The Boots was the last elected of the members and there was a grave responsibility attached to his office. He was the fag of the brotherhood and had to arrive before the dinner-hour not only to decant the wine but to fetch it from the cellar. No one was exempted from this ordeal, and woe to him who shirked or neglected it. The greatest enjoyment seemed to be afforded both to members and guests by summoning Boots to decant a fresh bottle of port at the moment when a hot plate and a fresh steak were placed before him. The Duke of Sussex was Boots from the date of his election, April 1808, to April 1809, when Arnold the composer filled the office, and although the Duke was a most abstemious man he flinched from fulfilling his duties. When any Boots showed signs of temper, or any member was unruly or infringed the rules of the society, a punishment was in store for him. It was moved and seconded that such delinquent should be put in a white sheet and reprimanded by the Recorder; and if the Ayes had it, and they always did have it, the sentence was carried out. The offending party was taken from the room by two members bearing halberds, preceded by a third carrying the sword, and was brought back again in a garb of penitence which consisted of the tablecloth, then, after a lecture from the Recorder, severe or humorous according to the nature of his offence, he was allowed to resume his place at the table.

Some of the most celebrated wits, song-writers, painters and dramatists were members of the club, but to give a list of them all would be like making a catalogue. The author of the "Clubs of London," speaking of the saving of the gridiron when the theatre was destroyed, says; "In that fire, alas, perished the original archives of the society. Lovers of wit and pleasantry have much to deplore in that loss, inasmuch as not only the names of many of the early members are irretrievably gone, but what is more to be regretted some of their happiest effusions; for it was then customary to register in the weekly records anything of striking excellence that had been hit off in the course of the evening. This, however, is certain that the Beefsteaks from its foundation to the present hour has been 'native to famous wits or hospitable.' That as guests or members persons distinguished for rank, and social and convivial powers have through successive generations been seated at its festive board."

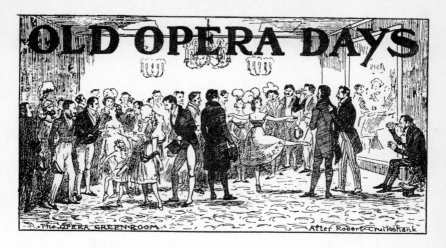

OLD OPERA DAYS

The OPERA GREEN ROOM   After Robert Cruikshank

IT was about the commencement of the eighteenth century that, as Colley Cibber tells us, " The Italian Opera began first to steal into England, but in as rude a disguise as possible in lame hobbling translations, with metre out of measure to its original notes, sung by our own unskilful voices with graces misapplied to almost every sentiment and action." The first special theatre for the purpose of playing Opera was built by Sir John Vanbrugh in 1704 in Lincoln's Inn Fields, where the *Triumph of Love*, as the first piece was called, ran exactly three nights. The first Italian singer who made his mark on these boards was Valentini, who on this occasion sang through his part in his own language, the rest of the company singing in English. The effect was grotesque in the extreme, and may partially account for the fact that for quite twenty-five years of its existence the Opera House was so poorly attended that it scarcely paid its expenses.

In 1729 the Grand Jury of Middlesex prosecuted the management for carrying on the fashionable and wicked diversion called Masquerade, " and par- ticularly the contriver and carrier on of Masquerades at the Kings Theatre in the Hay Market—the second and most famous house of all, on the site of which now stands His Majesty's Theatre— in order to be punished according to law." Horace Walpole, speaking of the various Operas produced here, runs on in his piquant style, in a smart criticism of Vaneschi's Opera of *Fetonte*. " It is," he writes, " in what they call the French manner, but about as like it as My Lady Pomfret's hash of plural persons and singular verbs was to the Italian. They sing to jigs and dance to Church Music. ' Phaeton ' is run away with by horses that go a foot's pace, like the ' Electress's ' coach, with such long traces, that the postillion was in one street and the coachman in another. Then comes ' Jupiter ' with a farthing candle, to light a squib and a half ; and that they call fireworks. ' Reginello,' the first man, is so old and so tall, that he seems to have been growing ever since the invention of Operas. The first woman has had her mouth let out to show a fine set of teeth, but it lets out too much bad voice at the same time. Lord Middlesex, for his great prudence in having provided such very tractable steeds to ' Prince Phæton's ' car, is going to be Master of the Horse to the Prince of Wales ; and, for his excellent economy in never paying the performers, is likely to

events—the introduction of Mozart's music and the first appearance of Madame Catalani. This extraordinarily gifted singer was equally admirable in tragic and comic parts, and for the season of 1809 she received the sum of fifteen thousand pounds, while her

A BOX AT THE OPERA.   *By Thomas Rowlandson*

continue in the Treasury." It may be noted that the *Beggars' Opera* was purposely written by Dean Swift and John Gay to burlesque the Italian Opera and the Italian singers. When Her Majesty's Theatre, as the old King's was re-named after its destruction by fire, commenced its new career, half a dozen managers were landed in the insolvent court owing to the hopeless load of debt and the heavy expenses which swallowed up all the receipts. Then the great English tenor, John Braham, made his début here in 1796, and at once by his marvellous singing secured the favour of the public.

In the year 1806 the history of the theatre was marked by two great

benefit, and the various concerts at which she appeared, produced her eleven thousand pounds more. Captain Gronow, in his " Reminiscences and Recollections," speaks of Madame Catalani, whom he knew, as being, in her youth, the finest singer in Europe, and as much sought after by all the great people during her stay in London. " She was extremely handsome and was considered a model as wife and mother. Catalani was very fond of money, and would never sing unless paid beforehand. She was invited, with her husband, to pass some time at Stowe, where a numerous but select party had been invited ; and Madame Catalani being asked to sing soon after dinner willingly complied. When the day of her departure came her husband placed in the hands of the Marquis of Buckingham the following little billet : ' For seventeen songs, seventeen hundred pounds ' ; this large sum was paid at once without hesitation ; proving of Marlborough, Devonshire, and Bedford, Lady Carlisle, and some others. In their day, after the singing and the ballet were over, the company used to retire into the concert room, where a ball took place, accompanied by refreshments and a supper. There all

A BOX AT THE OPERA. *By Thomas Rowlandson*

that Lord Buckingham was a refined gentleman in every sense of the word." It must be said of Catalani's husband, M. de Valabreque, that he fought more than one duel to protect his wife's honour from those who on several occasions insulted the prima donna. Gronow adds in his agreeable way, " When George the Fourth was Regent, Her Majesty's Theatre, as the Italian Opera in the Haymarket is still called, was conducted on a very different system from that which now prevails. Some years previous to the period to which I refer, no one could obtain a box or a ticket for the pit without a voucher from one of the lady patronesses, who, in 1805, were the Duchesses the rank and fashion of England were assembled on a sort of neutral ground."

Stalls were not invented until the time of the O.P. Riots at Covent Garden, and the pit reached from the back of the house to the orchestra. There is a fine old-world touch about the etiquette that had to be strictly observed in regard to the costume of the gentlemen, who were not admitted in these early days unless they wore knee buckles and ruffles. When there was a Drawing Room the ladies would arrive in their Court dresses and the gentlemen would appear *de rigueur ;* and on all occasions the audience of Her Majesty's Theatre presented a wonderful sight of aristocratic elegance, quite as elegant in its way as Covent Garden of the twentieth century.

George Augustus Sala, who was a lover of the Opera, has much to say about Covent Garden and Her

GREAT LADIES AT THE OPERA HOUSE. *By James Gillray*, 1795

Majesty's Theatres. He recounts the fact of his knowing Sir Michael Costa, who during his conductorship at Her Majesty's used when the curtain fell to seat himself in a large fauteuil in the centre of the stage, close to the curtain ; where for ten minutes or so he would hold a kind of levée, bestowing judicious praise on all the singers for their exertions during the performance. And Sala goes on, " The praise was

valuable. It is not only before but behind the curtain that true dramatic and lyric artists require applause. It is as the air they breathe ; if they have it not they die."

Sala's mother was the great singer and actress, Madame Sala, and consequently he was frequently behind the scenes as a youth and afterwards. He says, with a kind of sorrow of departing things, and still speaking of Her Majesty's Theatre, " The Beefeaters in the Tower have been deprived of those scarlet and embroidered tunics that contrasted so quaintly with the pantaloons and highlows of everyday life, and have been thrust into buttoned-up coats and brass buttons. I have fears for the Opera ; I tremble for the days when there will be bonnets in the upper tiers and paletots in the pit. When I mind the Opera first it was a Subaltern's and not a Serjeant's Guard that kept watch and ward under the portico. The officer on duty had a right of entrance *ex officio* into the pit, and it was splendid to see him swinging his Bearskin and flashing his epaulettes in Fop's Alley."

Fop's Alley, which gave its name later to a sort of arcade at the back of the Opera House where dandies used to congregate, was really the passage between the tiers of benches right and left, in Her Majesty's, and the promenade of the exquisites and descendants of the Macaroni's. Fop's Alley was the centre of attraction for all the aristocracy, where they used to meet their friends and acquaintances, and on Drawing Room nights, the men would attend in their half-mooned cocked hats and the ladies bearing ostrich plumes which were set off by their wonderful diamond necklaces.

The late Queen Victoria in her "Letters" published in 1909, and giving her "Recollections of the Opera," says: Tuesday, July 14, 1835. "At eight we went to the Opera with Lady Theresa and Lehzen. It was the *dear 'Puritani.'* Grisi was in perfect voice, and sang and acted *beautifully;* but I must say, that she shows her many fatigues in her face, and she is certainly much thinner than when she arrived. It is a great pity, too, that she now wears her front hair so much lower than she did. It is no improvement to her appearance, though (do what she may) spoil her face she never can, it is too lovely for that. And besides, she forgot to change her dress when she came on to sing the Polacca. In general she comes on to sing that, as a bride, attired in a white satin dress with a wreath of white roses round her head, instead of which, she remained in her first dress (likewise very pretty) of blue satin with a little sort of hand-kerchief at the back of her head. Lablache, Tamburini, and Rubini were also all three in high good voice. The exquisite quartet 'A te o Cara,' and the lovely Polacca 'Son Vergin Vezzosa,' were both encored, as was also the splendid duet, 'Il .Rival.' After the Opera was over, Grisi, Rubini, Lablache, and Tamburini came out and were loudly applauded. The last two always make a separate bow to our box, which is very amusing to see. We came away immediately after the Opera was over, for the ballet is not worth seeing since La Déesse de la Danse has flown back to Paris again. She appeared for the last time on Saturday, the 4th of this month. We came home at ten minutes to twelve. I was highly amused and pleased. We came in while Tamburini was singing his song, which is just before the lovely duet between Grisi and Lablache."

" After the Opera was over." Queen Victoria inadvertently or perhaps purposely, making use of this phrase, she uses it twice at least, suggested a song to one of the easy writers of a later day, and " After the Opera is over" became one of the most popular ditties that was sung everywhere at the newly arisen music halls in the early sixties and seventies. Her Majesty was a constant visitor to the Opera and the theatres until the death of the Prince Consort.

JOHN CAVANAGH, THE FIVES PLAYER

ONE of the best games ever devised by man is the old-fashioned game of Fives, and the best Fives player who ever lived was John Cavanagh, who exhibited his skill at Copenhagen House, that one-time delightful pleasure-garden in Islington.* The wall against which the combatants played (says Hone) was the kitchen wall, and when the wall resounded more than usual the cook inside would say: " Those are the *Irishman's* balls."

Nevertheless, we should probably have known little about Cavanagh's prowess as a fives player if his skill had not attracted the admiring attention of William Hazlitt, who contributed a brilliant description of Cavanagh at work to the *Examiner* of February 17, 1819. No sportsman can read this appreciation without a sympathetic thrill. Cavanagh died at his house in Burbage Street, St. Giles's, in 1819, when Hazlitt wrote of him as follows :

When a person dies who does any one thing better than any one else in the world, which so many others are trying to do well, it leaves a gap in society. It is not likely that any one will now see the game of fives played in its perfection for many years to come—for Cavanagh is dead, and has not left his peer behind him.

It may be said that there are things of more importance than striking a ball against a wall—there are things indeed that make more noise and do as little good, such as making war and peace, making speeches and answering

them, making verses and blotting them, making money and throwing it away. But the game of fives is what no one despises who has ever played at it. It is the finest exercise for the body, and the best relaxation for the mind.

The Roman poet said that ' Care mounted behind the horseman, and stuck to his skirts.' But this remark would not have applied to the fives player. He who takes to playing at fives is twice young. He feels neither the past nor future ' in the instant.' Debts, taxes, ' domestic treason, foreign levy, nothing can touch him further.' He has no other wish, no other thought, from the moment the game begins, but that of striking the ball, of placing it, of *making* it ! This Cavanagh was sure to do. Whenever he touched the ball there was an end of the chase. His eye was certain, his hand fatal, his presence of mind complete. He could do what he pleased, and he always knew exactly what to do. He saw the whole game, and played it ; took instant advantage of his adversary's weakness, and recovered balls, as if by a miracle and from sudden thought, that every one gave for lost. He had equal power and skill, quickness and judgment. He could either outwit his antagonist by finesse, or beat him by main strength. Sometimes, when he seemed preparing to send the ball with the full swing of his arm, he would, by a slight turn of his wrist, drop it within an inch of the line. In general, the ball came from his hand, as if from a racket, in a straight horizontal line ; so that it was in vain to attempt to overtake or stop it. As it was said of a great orator, that he never was at

* Its name and site are perpetuated in the name of Copenhagen Street.

94

a loss for a word, and for the properest word, so Cavanagh always could tell the degree of force necessary to be given to a ball, and the precise direction in which it should be sent. He did his work with the greatest ease ; never took more pains than was necessary, and while others were fagging themselves to death, was as cool and collected as if he had just entered the court.

His style of play was as remarkable as his power of execution. He had no affectation, no trifling. He did not throw away the game to show off an attitude, or try an experiment. He was a fine, sensible, manly player, who did what he could, but that was more than any one else could even affect to do. He was the best *up-hill* player in the world ; even when his adversary was fourteen, he would play on the same or better, and as he never flung away the game through carelessness and conceit, he never gave it up through laziness or want of heart. The only peculiarity of his play was that he never *volleyed*, but let the balls hop ; but if they rose an inch from the ground he never missed having them. There was not only nobody equal, but nobody second to him. It is supposed that he could give any other player half the game, or beat them with his left hand. His service was tremendous. He once played Woodward and Meredith together (two of the best players in England) in the Fives-court, St. Martin's Street, and made seven and

twenty aces following by services alone —a thing unheard of. He another time played Peru, who was considered a first-rate fives player, a match of the best out of five games, and in the three first games, which of course decided the match, Peru got only one ace.

COPENHAGEN HOUSE AT ISLINGTON

Cavanagh was an Irishman by birth, and a house-painter by profession. He had once laid aside his working dress, and walked up, in his smartest clothes, to the Rosemary Branch to have an afternoon's pleasure. A person accosted him, and asked him if he would have a game. So they agreed to play for half a crown a game, and a bottle of cider. The first game began —it was seven, eight, ten, thirteen, fourteen, all. Cavanagh won it. The next was the same. They played on and each game was hardly contested. ' There,' said the unconscious fives-player, ' there was a stroke that Cavanagh could not take ; I never played better in my life, and yet I can't win a game ! I don't know how it is." However, they played on, Cavanagh winning every game, and the bystanders drinking cider and laughing all the time. In the twelfth game, when Cavanagh was only four, and the stranger thirteen, a person came in, and said, ' What ! are you here, Cavanagh ! ' The words were no sooner pronounced than the astonished player let the ball drop from his hand, and saying, ' What ! have I been breaking my heart all this time to beat Cavanagh ? ' refused to make another effort. ' And yet, I give you my word,' said Cavanagh, telling the story with some triumph, ' I played all the while with my clenched fist.'

He used frequently to play matches at Copenhagen House for wagers and dinners. The wall against which they play is the same that supports the kitchen chimney, and when the wall resounded louder than usual, the cooks exclaimed, ' Those are the Irishman's balls,' and the joints trembled on the spit !

Goldsmith consoled himself that there were places where he too was admired ; and Cavanagh was the admiration of all the fives-courts where he ever played. Mr. Powell, when he played matches in the court in St. Martin's Street, used to fill his gallery at half a crown a head, with amateurs and admirers of talent in whatever department it is shown. He could not have shown himself in any ground in England but he would have been immediately surrounded with inquisitive gazers, trying to find out in what part of his frame his unrivalled skill lay.

He was a young fellow of sense, humour, and courage. He once had

a quarrel with a waterman at Hungerford Stairs, and they say, ' served him out ' in great style. In a word, there are hundreds at this day, who cannot mention his name without admiration, as the best fives player that perhaps ever lived (the greatest excellence of which they have any notion)—and the noisy shout of the ring happily stood him instead of the unheard voice of posterity.

The only person who seems to have excelled as much in another way as Cavanagh did in his was the late John Davies, the racket-player. It was remarked of him that he did not seem to follow the ball, but the ball seemed to follow him. Give him a foot of wall, and he was sure to make the ball. The four best racket-players of that day were Jack Spines, Jem Harding, Armitage, and Church. Davies could give any one of these two hands a time, that is, half the game, and each of these at their best could give the best player now in London the same odds. Such are the gradations in all exertions of human skill and art.

Cavanagh died from the bursting of a blood-vessel, which prevented him from playing for the last two or three years. This, he was often heard to say, he thought hard upon him. He was fast recovering, however, when he was suddenly carried off to the regret of all who knew him.

Jack Cavanagh was a zealous Catholic, and could not be persuaded to eat meat on a Friday, the day on which he died. We have paid this willing tribute to his memory.

> Let no rude hand deface it,
> And his forlorn ' *Hic jacet.*'

FROM A
CONTEMPORARY PRINT

THE LONDON OMNIBUS

ON the morning of July 4, 1829, William IV. on the throne, a great crowd assembled to see the first two omnibuses—one of which is represented above—run from the Yorkshire Stingo at Paddington, along the New Road (by which name Marylebone, Euston and Pentonville Roads were then known) to the Bank.

These pioneer vehicles were the enterprise of Mr. George Shillibeer, who had found his inspiration in Paris. Paris had made an attempt at the bus as far back as 1662, in the reign of Louis XIV., and it is of interest to note that the " carrosse à cing sous," or " twopenny-halfpenny coach," was suggested by the great Blaise Pascal. The twopenny-halfpenny concern came presently to grief, and, says Mr. H. C. Moore ("Omnibuses and Cabs: their Origin and History "), " a century and a half elapsed before vehicles of the omnibus class were again tried in Paris." In 1819, during the reign of Louis XVIII., the banker-politician, Jacques Lafitte, re-introduced the omnibus into Paris. It had now an

immediate popular success, and rival buses were soon running against those of Jacques Lafitte. He, not to be outdone, gave an order to George Shillibeer, for two of the best that could be built. Shillibeer, at this date a leading coach-builder in Paris, had been a midshipman in the British Navy ; but quitted the service and went to Hatchett's, in Long Acre, to learn coach-building. Later he started business for himself in Paris, where English carriages had become the fashion.

While carrying out Lafitte's order, it occurred to Shillibeer that there was as yet no such thing as an omnibus in London. To London thereupon he came, took premises in Bury Street, Bloomsbury, and gave out that he intended to place " a new vehicle called the omnibus " on the streets of the town. " Why omnibus ? " it was asked. " If one vehicle is to be called an omnibus, what are two or more to be called ? " " Omnibuses," said Shillibeer ; " but his questioners were horrified, and to their dying day

preferred to call them 'Shillibeers.'"
But the buses were started on the
New Road, and this was the principal
matter.

Now, though they have not been
commonly remarked upon, there were
at least two sufficing reasons for setting
up popular vehicles in London eight
years before the accession of Queen

upper ten with their carriages—had no
means of locomotion other than the
short-stage-coaches, "which took three
hours to get from Paddington to the
City, and charged two shillings for
outside seats and three shillings for
inside ones.

In the next place, until the very
year that George Shillibeer startled

A Scene in Wellington Street, 1832 (*From a Contemporary Print*)

Victoria. To begin with, the London
of 1829 (provincial as it looks in
so many prints of the period) was
really a great city. At the census
taken two years later, in 1831, London
was found to have an area of
twenty-two square miles. This area,
Sir Walter Besant tells us, was divided
into 153 parishes, embracing 10,000
streets and courts and 250,000 houses.
The population was nearly 1,650,000.
Every day 90,000 passengers crossed
London Bridge. The visitors every
year were estimated at 12,000. Consider that, in a metropolis of this size,
with this population, and this number
of visitors, the general public—the
whole of London, in short, save the

and delighted the West End with
his two fine and commodious buses,
each drawn by three handsome
bays, London had no regular police
force. By day and by night the streets
were unsafe for pedestrians, and even
in the first decade of the nineteenth
century a hackney coach was held up
by robbers in Oxford Street. In July
1829, as was said, the first omnibus
appeared. It was in April of the
same year that Sir Robert Peel introduced his Police Bill, which in two
months became the "Act for improving the Police in and near the Metropolis." Almost at once, ineptitude in
the management of the streets began
to be transformed into efficiency,

London was delivered from that miserable jumble of wards, parishes, hundreds and boroughs, each with its private (and most inadequate) establishment of watchmen and constables. But while all this was being rapidly swept into limbo, the new police had to learn the very A B C of this was at the very season when these thoroughfares began to come under the authority of an organised police force, an important part of whose duty was the regulation of traffic. Briefly, while more people were able to ride, the streets grew less perilous for those who continued to walk.

HANCOCK'S STEAM CARRIAGE "AUTOMATON," 1833

their business; and we are not to suppose that the traffic of the streets—already immense, and every year increasing—was controlled with that perfection of methods which is to-day the admiration of visitors from every quarter of the world. At every point at which vehicular traffic was liable to congestion—such a spot, for instance, as the corner of Chancery Lane—foot-passengers were in danger. Now the new and cheap buses made riding possible for persons who had hitherto been reduced to walking everywhere; and although, of course, in a short time the carriage-ways of the town were more than ever crowded,

The Shillibeer buses — labelled "Omnibus"—were at once in favour with the public. They looked smart, and the bays were cattle to take the eye of the horse-lover. The buses carried twenty-two passengers, all "insides"; the fare from the starting-place to the Bank was a shilling; half way, sixpence. The liberal Shillibeer provided newspapers and magazines free of charge. For conductors he had secured two of his friends, "both the sons of British naval officers," who were attired in "blue-cloth uniforms, cut like a midshipman's." These sparks had resided in Paris, where they had acquired both French and manners;

accomplishments not claimed for the short-stage-coach guards.

Shillibeer was by-and-by taking in £100 a week, and still his conveyances rose in the town's esteem. Sentimental young ladies in poke bonnets strolled down pleasant Paddington to see them start, or journeyed to King's Cross and back for a little French

HANCOCK'S STEAM CARRIAGE "ERA"

conversation with the modish conductors. Alas! the sons of naval officers resigned their posts, which were filled by less attractive characters, who began to filch the takings.

But Shillibeer prospered, "and in less than nine months had twelve omnibuses at work," adventuring now upon Oxford Street and Holborn. Naturally he was not allowed to hold the road unopposed. The Post Office authorities were the first to copy his vehicles, for purposes of their own; competitors arose in one district and another, sundry short-stage-coach proprietors among them, "who had the impudence to paint on the panels of their vehicles the word 'Shillibeer'." Shillibeer retorted by re-naming his own "Shillibeer's Original Omnibuses." This was about 1837.

1837 was the year that saw the graceful young Victoria upon her throne, and a story bearing on our subject is related of her Majesty. A certain John Clark, owning the "Eagle" buses that ran to Pimlico, was driving one of them by Hyde Park Corner, "when suddenly Her Majesty approached on horseback. He endeavoured to pull out of the way, but, as the road was partially blocked, it was not easy to do so. However, being an excellent whip he succeeded, and the Queen, who had witnessed his efforts, most graciously bowed to him as she passed by."

John Clark was gallant, but he was also a man of business, and here was an occasion of advertisement not to be foregone. In commemoration of the incident, he "had the omnibus painted blue, and substituted for the word 'Eagle' on the panels, the words 'Royal Blue.' Moreover, he had a picture of her Majesty on horseback painted on the panel of the door. After a time he called all his omnibuses on that line 'Royal Blues,' but the original 'Royal Blue' was the only one that bore a picture of the Queen. . . . For many years the picture of the Queen painted on the Royal Blue omnibus was one of the sights pointed out to visitors to London. Eventually, wishing to preserve the picture, Clark had it cut out of the omnibus door and framed, and it is now* in the possession of his daughter." When London has a museum such as the Carnavalet in Paris, it will be a fit shelter for this relic of the bus days of old. We are now but eight years from

* 1902.

the bold inception of George Shillibeer at the Yorkshire Stingo, but, says Mr. Moore :

" In 1837 there were fourteen omnibuses running from Blackheath to Charing Cross; twenty-seven from Chelsea to Mile End Gate; forty-one from Piccadilly to Blackwall; nineteen from Hampstead to Holborn, Charing Cross and the Bank; seventeen from the Angel, Islington, to the Elephant and Castle; and twenty-five from Edgware Road (the spot where Sutherland Avenue now joins Maida Vale) to the Bank. There were also many omnibuses running into the City from Putney, Kew, Richmond, Deptford, Greenwich, Lewisham, Holloway, Highbury, Hornsey, Highgate, Hackney, Homerton, Clapton, Enfield, Edmonton, Peckham, Brixton, Norwood, Kennington, Dulwich, Streatham, and elsewhere."

Five years earlier, than this, in 1832, such success had attended the great innovation of the bus that it was necessary to make a new Stage-Coach Act, " specially to permit omnibuses and short-stage-coaches to take up and set down passengers in the streets." The hostility of an old-fashioned class of shopkeepers was partly responsible for the measure. They had raised an outcry that customers of fashion, " driving up to their doors in their carriages," were impeded by the vulgar bus, and it needed an Act of Parliament to convince them that the coaches of the wealthy were not the only equipages permitted to take the air of the public highways.

But we are now at the era of the steam-engine and the railway, and the resolute Shillibeer was confronted with a new problem. The big, brisk, energetic man, " with a florid complexion," believed himself equal to it.

Relinquishing his London business, he opened up a line of omnibuses from London to Greenwich and Woolwich, at the very moment that " a railway from London to Greenwich had been decided upon." So far as the commerce of the bus was concerned, this was Shillibeer's undoing. The railway was laid in 1835, and the earnings of the omnibuses showed forthwith an ominous decrease. Next, Shillibeer was in trouble, on the score of payment, with the Stamp and Taxes Office, and cavalierly handled by this bureau. Faced with ruin, he stepped from the bus into the hearse. He became an undertaker, and—made money anew. In so doing he missed the chance of perpetuating his name (minus its capital letter) in the dictionary. The " Shillibeer," with a large S. as the favourite public vehicle, would gradually have sunk—or been elevated—into shillibeer, with a small one. But the " Shillibeer Funeral Coaches " soon settled the matter, in respect of nomenclature, and Shillibeer's name is forgotten. He died at Brighton in 1866, at the age of sixty-nine.

Steam was now about to be the breath of British nostrils, and nothing was more certain than that attempts would be made to use the new power in the streets of London. Even before Shillibeer's omnibuses were seen, experienced engineers had tried experiments with steam carriages, and Goldsworthy Gurney produced one that ran indifferent well. This, however, could scarcely be described as a true steam omnibus. The first machines to which we may fairly give the name were the invention of Walter Hancock, of Stratford. These, the " Era " and " Autopsy," were placed by Hancock on the London roads in 1833. The " Era," considered to be the better of the two, ran from Paddington to the Bank, carrying fourteen passengers at sixpence apiece. "It travelled at the rate of ten miles an hour, and consumed from eight to twelve lbs. of coke and a hundred lbs. of water per mile." Unfortunately the "Era" had a habit of stopping where nobody wanted to alight, and staying an hour or so when it stopped. Hancock, a sanguine man said the public would get used to this; an hour in the day was no great matter. But he went on trying; and in 1835 started a new steam omnibus ("his last and best") the "Automaton," a nice-looking thing in a print. On the Bow Road on one occasion the "Automaton" covered a mile at the rate of twenty-one miles an hour, to the considerable alarm of the twenty passengers.

Hancock complained to the public of "parties who do not desire that this branch of improvement should prosper," meaning thereby the proprietors of horse-drawn buses, who were suspected of strewing the roads with loose stones to bring the "steamers" to grief. London roads were not then maintained as they are now, but even in the reign of William IV. they were safe from the felonious tricks of the busmen.

The "Automaton," albeit "the best steam omnibus ever built," was "unmistakably a failure." The public stuck to the "osses." "And so came to an end the first attempt to run horseless omnibuses in London."

CATNACH'S COMMENT.

Steam carriages by land are now the order of the day, sir,
But why they haven't started yet, 'tis not for me to say, sir;
Some people hint 'tis *uphill* work—that loose they find a screw, sir,
Such novelties, as Pat would say, of *old* they never *knew*, sir,
    Bow, wow, &c.

From a Catnach Ballad.

DR. JOHNSON IN FLEET STREET

DR. JOHNSON IN FLEET STREET

DR. JOHNSON did not say, "Sir, let us take a walk down Fleet Street," as Mr. Kipling has it in "Many Inventions," and as nine out of ten Londoners who love Johnson devoutly believe. Nor is the other story quite true: George Augustus Sala did not invent these precise words as the motto of the "Temple Bar" magazine. Sala's famous tag ran: "And now, sir, we will take a walk down Fleet Street." Sala confessed that he "imagined" this quotation, and he added (in his "Life and Adventures"): "To the best of my knowledge and belief, Dr. Johnson never said a word about taking a walk down Fleet Street; but my innocent supercherie was, I fancy, implicitly believed in for at least a generation by the majority of magazine readers." It was.

One thing is certain: Johnson was continually walking down Fleet Street, or up Fleet Street, and it is improbable that he ever did so without being seen of men. To meet Dr. Johnson squarely in Fleet Street was interest and adventure for the day, as twenty years ago it was to meet Mr. Gladstone. But we are sure the two sensations were different. To be a young man in London twenty-five years ago, and to meet Gladstone was a sensation, like

Vassalage at unawares encountering
The eye of majesty.

An encounter with Dr. Johnson in Fleet Street was a cruder event. The eighteenth-century street was narrow and cobbled, and until the year 1765, or thereabouts, it had no sidewalks. Johnson was as rough as the cobbles, and his walking manners were imperfect. Kearsly, the bookseller, had often studied the phenomenon, and he describes the doctor's progress as heavily headlong. His gigantic head rolled forward above the heads of the Fleet Street crowd, followed by his huge body in concomitant and proportionate rhythm, while his feet appeared to have very little to do with his motion. One day Bennet Langton saw him fairly drive the load off a porter's back and surge onwards, quite unconscious of what he had done. The porter picked himself up, stared after the giant in speechless wrath, meditating reprisals, but soon thought better of it.

Although, then, the words " Sir, let us take a walk down Fleet Street " are apocryphal, they represent a daily habit of Johnson's life. Johnson's Sunday morning walks to and from St. Clement Danes Church, which he attended, can be traced easily in Boswell's pages. It was in one of them that he met his old college friend Edwards, from whom he had been separated for forty years. " In my return from church I was accosted by Edwards, an old fellow collegian, who had not seen me since —29. He knew me, and asked me if I remembered one Edwards. I did not at first recollect the name, but gradually as we walked along recovered it, and told him a conversation that had passed at an alehouse between us. My purpose is to continue the acquaintance."

The three walked on to Bolt Court, Johnson and Edwards still making plunges into the past. When they reached Bolt Court Edwards was saying : " Sir, I remember you would not let us say *prodigious* at college " ; and it was on this occasion that Edwards made that speech which Burke and Reynolds thought so exquisite : " You are a philosopher, Dr. Johnson. I have tried, too, in my time to be a philosopher ; but, I don't know how, *cheerfulness was always breaking in.*" Altogether, this was one of the doctor's pleasantest walks in Fleet Street.

Dr. Johnson's pew may be seen in the gallery at St. Clement Danes : it is marked with a brass tablet. How frequently he worshipped here is known to every reader of his " Prayer and Meditation," that amazing and touching diary of his spiritual life. He was not often punctual at church. Again and again he confesses a late arrival. April 22, 1764 : " I went to church, came in at the first of the Psalms." ... April 7, 1765 : " I came in at the Psalms." ... September 23, 1771 : " I went to church in the morning, but came in to the Litany." ... April 17, 1778 : " Boswell came in to go to ·hurch ; we had tea, but I did not eat. Talk lost our time, and we came to church late, at the second lesson." Once he explains his non-attendance. March 29, 1777 : " I neither read nor went to church, yet can scarcely tell how I have been hindered. I treated with booksellers on a bargain, but the time was not long."

In his later years Johnson became somewhat deaf, and he would often leave his pew in the high gallery and come to its edge to be nearer the altar during the Communion service. To-day, any one standing in Johnson's pew can see exactly why and how he would approach the altar. The pew is situated just where the gallery widens, by a curve, to a width which brings its eastern end flush with the apse in which the Communion table stands. When Johnson moved to this part of the gallery he must have been prominently visible to almost the entire congregation as he looked down from his perpendicular height into the sanctuary. The pulpit, too, it is believed, formerly stood on the side of the church remote from his pew, instead of, as now, immediately under it.

No street in London is so linked to a single personality as Fleet Street is linked to the name of Dr. Johnson. Even to-day the Fleet Street he knew keeps its old curves and general character. The absence of Temple Bar would stagger Johnson, but the gateway of the Middle Temple, the " Wolsey palace," many old houses, and nearly all the old courts and alleys, and the vista of roofs lifting the eye to the Dome and Cross : these he knew and loved.

On the day in which London mourned the death of King Edward VII., the small statue of Johnson which now stands behind the old Strand church, looking towards Fleet Street, was to have been unveiled by the Princess Louise. The ceremony was postponed, and was carried out quietly at a later date. This memorial was erected on the initiative of the Rev. J. J. H. S. Pennington, the widely known and loved rector of the church, who has since passed away. The statue itself we owe to the pious skill of Mr. Percy Fitzgerald, whose singular privilege it has been to pay his tribute to Dr. Johnson both as editor and sculptor.

VERLAINE IN LONDON

"WHEN I arrived the weather was superb ; *i.e.* imagine a sunset seen through a grey veil." So wrote Paul Verlaine to his friend and biographer Edmund Lepelletier after his arrival in London in the autumn of 1872. It was a characteristic London welcome to this strange man of genius, this poet of modern decadence.

He took lodgings at 34–35 Howland Street, a not inappropriate place if he had happened to know anything of " The Newcomes," which he did not. Howland Street was not cheerful even in the days of Clive Newcome, it was worse in 1872, and it is worse still now. But Verlaine, who knew the garrets of the Quartier Latin, does not seem to have been oppressed by the gloom. It is certain that he fell under the spell of London almost at once, in spite of the unexhilarating fact that he had to give French lessons to its inhabitants at the rate of about a franc an hour. Soon after his arrival he wrote : " As a whole, however, it is very unexpected, and a hundred times more amusing than Italy, and Paris, and the banks of the Rhine."

He coupled the " wax-works " and the " more than royal enthronement of the Lord Mayor " in a letter, and was greatly struck by the " abominable multiplications of little red shoe blacks." It is curious that this acute observer has nothing to say about the great London sights. There is not a word of Westminster, or St. Paul's, or the Houses of Parliament, though he must have seen them all. He insists upon the smallness of everything with the exception of the city and some of the squares. The docks, however, stirred his imagination : " The docks," he said, " are wonderful—Carthage, Tyre, all rolled into one." Perhaps it was his passion for the bizarre that lead him to the Tower Subway—of which he wrote, "There is a unique curiosity, I believe, here ; it is the Tower's Subway, *i.e.* a tube submerged about a hundred and fifty feet in the Thames. One descends a hundred steps. It is literally a cast-iron tube with gas jets at about a man's height, with flooring half a yard wide. It is warm, it smells, and it trembles like a suspension bridge under the immense weight of the water. In short, one is very content with having seen it."

It was natural for Verlaine to haunt Soho and Leicester Square. Here, indeed, he complains of the gloom, the lack of comfort, the tobacco, which is " filthy," and everything else. The Soho of innumerable cheap dining places did not exist then. Again and again he returns to the subject of London taverns and his beloved cafés of the Boul' Mich', though he could no more keep out of one than he could out of the other ; indeed, he formed a taste for whisky almost as deadly as his taste for absinthe. The following passage covers much : " London is

less melancholy than its reputation ; it is true that one must be a searcher like me in order to discover its distractions ; I have found many. But clean cafés, *nix, nix*. One must resign oneself to dirty drinking-shops called ' French Coffee-houses,' or to the commercial travellers' boxes of Leicester Square. No matter, this incredible town is very well, black as a crow and noisy as a duck. . . . Everlastingly glutted in spite of ridiculous tracts about drunkenness immense, although at bottom nothing but a confused collection of clamouring, rival, ugly, and flat little towns ; without any monuments except its interminable docks (which are sufficient for me and my more and more modern style of poetry). It is well enough, in spite of its monstrous absurdities which I have given up enumerating."

Verlaine spent a Christmas in London alone, and found it worse than Sunday : but he had one consolation—" the goose is exquisite." " *Beefsteack*," he asserted, did not exist. But this poet of the heights and depths was just to what he conceived to be the best in the English character, which to him meant London character : " I believe I have found it ; it is something very sweet, almost childlike, very innocent, with an amusing and charming roughness and gaiety."

THE GARROTTERS OF THE 'SIXTIES
A GRIM STORY OF CRIME AND PUNISHMENT

IN London in 1862 there was a sudden outbreak of a rather peculiar form of robbery with violence. The victims before being rifled were garrotted. The attack could hardly be described as a mode of thuggee, for it is improbable that the garrotter had heard of the thug, nor did he seek to strangle his prey outright. He did, however, seize him by the neck and render him, or try to render him, in some degree insensible. The garrotte robberies quickly became epidemic, and London was filled with alarm. It seemed like a return upon the eighteenth century.

Then one night a Member of Parliament was laid hold of, garrotted, and plundered. This was a little more than legislators could stand. How many private persons at this date had suffered from the garrotte we have no means of knowing, but Parliament forthwith applied itself to the question with the double zest of outraged dignity and fright, and in 1863 Lord Norton carried a measure under which garrotters could be flogged.

For years from this date the frequent punishment of the garrotter with the " cat " lent a new relish to the study of the newspaper. The best descriptive hands were punctually told off to Newgate to detail the sufferings of the wretch in the whipping-press, and no one seemed to realise that the law had once again fallen back upon torture. Flogging, variously inflicted, is one of the oldest tortures in almost every country in the world. Scattered up and down the daily papers of the period will be found reports of the exhibitions at Newgate, which must have been looked for by readers, for they were manifestly written with the care that is nowadays given to accounts of first-rate matches on the cricket and football fields. There is a gusto in these ugly records, and sometimes a conscious artistry : the curious may consult the files. Evidence is abundant that the whipping of garrotters became a very popular item of news. It was no longer possible, as in the previous century, to pursue through the streets a criminal tied to the tail of a cart, with the hangman and his scourge behind ; but for easy-going citizens it was perhaps more agreeable to follow at breakfast-time the course of the lash as recorded in the morning paper. Privileged persons friendly with a sheriff were passed into the prison on his order when a garrotter was to be flogged, and there was a run upon tickets as at a bruited trial for murder or divorce.

A well-known Irish journalist, war correspondent, and special correspondent under several skies, the late John Augustus O'Shea, has described " A Morning with Calcraft " in the early days of the flogging of garrotters at Newgate :

" We entered a long, low room, ignorant of furniture, except a sort of press, waist-high against one wall, and a long deal table by the other. What I liken unto the press was the whipping apparatus, with stocks for the prisoner's feet and holdfasts for his hands.* He stepped into this apparatus, and his feet were forthwith

* This whipping-press, of an antique pattern, was a particular property of Newgate, where the triangles were never, we believe, in use. On the demolition of Newgate, the instrument passed into the keeping of the Corporation of London.

imprisoned. Extending his arms, he placed them in the crescent hollow of a plank before him ; another plank was let down, and his wrists were pinioned in rings."

Calcraft, now getting on in years, stood against the table, where the whip lay, and O'Shea continues : " I walked behind the table, and stood beside an elderly man. A short-handled whip, not unlike a hunting-crop, with nine lashes of closely plaited thongs, and nine knots on each, lay on it. I took it up. ' Is this the cat-o'-nine tails of which we hear so much ? ' I asked. ' That's it,' said the elderly man in a choky voice. ' It does not seem to me so formidable a weapon as I expected.' ' Heh ! It tickles 'em all the same, as you'll see.' "

The first prisoner was brought into the flogging-room ; " a sullen, lumpish, thick-skinned brute, with an evil forehead." He was stripped to the waist ; and the " elderly man," Calcraft, took his position, and measured his distance with a glance. At a word from the Governor, Mr. Jonas, the first stroke fell. " The ruffian bore it well. He closed his teeth at first, but he had to groan and draw deep respiration ; eventually, and to evade the descending blow, he curved in his back like a patient in an epileptic spasm. . . . The legal butcher did his work adroitly. He did not stun the criminal by consecutive heavy lashes on one spot, but plied the scourge airily, as a fly-fisher would his line, distributing its favours discriminatingly over the whole expanse of hide."

Another man was tied up who " began to yell before he got a single blow " ; and it may be observed that, among the criminal classes (although their sensibility is often comparatively small), it is very exceptional for a prisoner to take a flogging without a sound. A prison governor once told the writer of a sturdy fellow who, on being cast loose from the triangles, turned to the executioner and said : " Reckon you've done a good mornin's work, sonny, eh ? Go an' git yer 'air cut ! " and Griffiths, in " Fifty Years of Public Service," gives the case of a prisoner whipped at Wormwood Scrubs, who, after the infliction, remarked to the warders in attendance, " Now, I'll fight the best chap among you ! " But these examples of endurance are so rare that the most is always made of them in prison.

The sufferer under the " cat " usually screams, and may well do so, for the chastisement at the hands of a strong and skilful flagellator is a grievous one. Cooper, in his " History of the Rod," says the cries of two convicts who had been flogged " continued after they had been conveyed to their cells, and seemed to indicate that they experienced but little relief from the surgical applications which the doctor put to their wounded backs." O'Shea, who was witnessing his first castigation, bids us note that blood was not drawn. But a practised flogger could draw blood at a stroke or two, both skin and flesh were often torn from the back ; and a cruel performer could make terrible play upon the fine flesh of the ribs. Griffiths mentions a warder who had been a boatswain's mate in the Navy, where he had learned to flog in the savage manner of that service in days gone by. " B. was a short, squat, thick-set man, with the rolling gait of a sailor, and immense physical strength, which, added to his skill, made a very loathsome exhibition of the wretched culprits who were tied

LONDON GARROTTERS AT WORK

up." It may be added that a man flogged in prison is invariably marked for life.

At the present day, however, this degrading punishment (for it has been well said that the very worst of men suffers in his humanity by being triced up and lashed on the naked back, and the stern Justice Hawkins declared: " You make a perfect devil of the man you flog ") is carried out with a greater regard for decency. It is strictly private. Although, of course, no garrotter was ever flogged in public, the hideous affair was made something of a show within the prison walls. Morbid persons, who had no possible right there, were admitted to look on ; a certain number of refractory prisoners were also (or frequently) present with a guard of warders ; and perhaps, too, there were prisoners sentenced to the " cat " awaiting their turn in terror, while observing the writhings and hearing the yells of the felon under punishment. Then, when it was over, the reporters hurried from the scene, and wrote up a flaming story for the public that had not been so fortunate as to see the spectacle at first hand. All this is changed.

The newspapers have ceased to print sensational recitals of the triangles, for their representatives have ceased to be the guests of the prison on flogging mornings. It may be questioned whether any journalist of this generation has ever assisted at a case of corporal punishment in an English gaol ; and the punishment itself, let us add, is now of somewhat rare occurrence. It is witnessed only by the governor or deputy governor of the prison, the medical officer, the chief warder, and the warders who fetch the delinquent to his ordeal. All other prisoners are kept as far as possible from the whipping chamber, which is usually isolated from cell-halls and workshops. Not more than thirty-six lashes may be given at a time, and the number oftenest ordered is from fifteen to eighteen or twenty. The governor has power to remit one-third of the punishment, and the doctor may stop it at any moment he thinks proper. It is a fiery and a debasing discipline, for certain ; yet distinctly less brutal than of old, inasmuch as during the past twenty years the " cat " has carried no knots.

There remains to be said a word in attempted correction of an ancient and quite erroneous opinion as to the efficacy of flogging. As often as this matter comes up for discussion, it is insisted in certain quarters that " After all, flogging put down garrotting ! " It did nothing of the kind. The garrotting epidemic of the sixties was suppressed at least nine months before Lord Norton's Act made flogging a penalty for the offence. In 1900 an argument on the subject was heard in the House of Commons, and an ex-Home Secretary of the Liberals and the Home Secretary of the Conservatives were among the speakers. They made these statements :

Mr. Asquith (Home Secretary 1892–95) : " As to garrotting, that crime had been brought to an end as a serious danger *before* the House, in a fit of panic, due to one of its own members having been garrotted, resorted to legislation. Garrotting was put down without resort to the lash, by a fearless administration of the existing criminal law."

The late Lord Ridley (Home Secretary 1895–1900) : " Reference has been made to the Garrotting Act. He agreed with the history of that Act, at all events as far as London was concerned, given by the right hon. gentleman opposite (Mr. Asquith), and that the rapid and severe action which put down garrotting took place *before* the passing of the Act of 1863."

Corroborative testimony of an official kind has also been given by Lord Aberdare and other Home Secretaries. Flogging is and always has been a complete failure as a deterrent. It failed in Botany Bay, as it has failed in our own country, and at the present day its value as a punishment is scarcely more than legendary.

THE BLUE-STOCKINGS

WE have to chronicle a very interesting phase in the life of London in the eighteenth century — an experiment, largely successful, made by women, to combine the Intellectual with the Social, and to give parties at which Conversation should be the sole form of entertainment.

Though the word *Blue-Stocking* always now denotes a woman, the first Blue-stocking was a man. In the eighteenth century silken hose were worn by men with evening dress, and blue worsted stockings belonged to morning dress. Benjamin Stillingfleet, a botanist of note and an excellent conversationalist, used to come to evening assemblies in morning clothes. " His dress was remarkably grave," says Boswell, " and in particular it was observed that he wore blue stockings." His presence was so much esteemed that it was said, " We can do nothing without the Blue Stockings." Blue Stocking parties were parties of a somewhat unconventional type, where intellectual conversation superseded the entertainment, up to that time universal, of cards.

Mrs. Montagu, " The Queen of the Blue-stockings," held her Blue-stocking receptions, first in Hill Street, and then at the great house she built for herself, Montagu House, still standing, and now 22 Portman Square, the residence of Viscount Portman. She was the acknowledged Queen of her circle because of her wit—her letters, though prolix, are sprightly and entertaining to this day ; because of her beauty—she had brown hair and blue eyes of peculiar animation, dark high-arched eyebrows and a brilliant complexion : and because of her wealth, which enabled her to give entertainments of a vast and luxurious character. Hannah More calls her " not only the finest lady but the finest genius I ever saw," and Dr. Johnson said of her : " She diffuses more knowledge in her conversation than any woman I know, or indeed almost any man." Certain qualities that appealed to the general public established her position as Queen—her tireless vivacity which kept her always flashing before men's eyes, and her love of magnificence, which provided a stately background for her personality. Indeed, the rooms in which she gave her entertainments were famous over London. The " barbarous gaudy goût " of Chinese furniture was then fashionable, and her " Chinese Room " in Hill Street was lined with painted paper of Pekin and furnished with Chinese vases. The curtains were Chinese pictures in gauze, and the chairs, Indian fan-sticks, with cushions of Japan satin painted. Montagu House in Portman Square contained many superb rooms—the Great Room, with pillars of verd antique, and ceilings painted by Angelica Kaufmann ; the " Feather " Room, which contained the feather hangings made by Mrs. Montagu herself, and immortalised in a poem of Cowper's. It is easy to imagine Mrs. Montagu's slight figure " delicate even to fragility," moving restlessly about the great spaces —dressed, perhaps, in that " new pink silver negligée, trimmed too, with silver, *fort galamont* " in which she was told she looked *à merveille*. It is easy to imagine her filling her great rooms with crowded and brilliant assemblies ; and helping to establish the truth, so necessary to be learned in the eighteenth

century, that Wit and Learning may accompany Beauty and Charm, and that Knowledge does not necessarily imply Pedantry.

" To frequent her parties," said Lady Louisa Stuart, " was to drink at the fountain-head : " and all the famous Blue-Stockings, both men and women, were to be found at her house. " Now that I am invited to Mrs. Montagu's, I think the measure of my glory full ! " wrote little Fanny Burney, when she was in the full tide of her happiness over the success of her novel " Evelina." We fancy her at the assemblies, short in stature, brown in complexion, very slenderly made, thrilling with rapture and modesty at the praise lavished upon her work. And the most learned of the Blue-stockings comes here too, the only one who can lay claim to profound knowledge, Elizabeth Carter, the translator of Epictetus. We fancy her in a sober-coloured gown, her hair unfashionably dressed, a bag of knitting on her arm, for it is rather as a listener than as a speaker that she excels : nobility and goodness shine out of her face, and in spite of her Greek, she is perhaps the best loved of the Blue-stockings. We may meet Hannah More at these parties in the days when she was Garrick's friend and loved splendid dress : and we may meet also Dr. Johnson and Horace Walpole and Edmund Burke— to name only a few of the distinguished guests who frequented Mrs. Montagu's receptions.

We can only estimate how remarkable was the change in social intercourse brought about by the Blue-Stockings when we reflect that during the early part of the eighteenth century women had been wholly excluded from the intellectual life of London. In the reign of Queen Anne men assembled in coffee houses—there were over three thousand in London at that time—to discuss the affairs of the day, the political situation, the last poem or satire ; later on, the men's club took its rise ; but mixed assemblies were wholly devoted to cards. How absorbing was this entertainment, how destructive of every other form of social intercourse, may be gathered from Hannah More's poem, the " Bas-Bleu," which gives us an excellent history of the movement.

> Long was Society o'errun
> By Whist, that devastating Hun,

she writes, and she tells how Quadrille, another card-game, conquered colloquial wit and eclipsed conversation. Cards were the great enemy that the Blue-stockings had to overcome, and cards were strictly forbidden at the Blue-stocking assemblies. Conversation was to reign supreme, and even the refreshments provided were to be of the most simple and undistracting kind. " Fragrant tea," Hannah More tells us, and " the milk-white stream " of " thirst-assuaging, cool orgeat," lemonade and biscuits, piled on silver vases—these were the unpretentious ingredients of the entertainment. Dr. Johnson advises his friend Mrs. Thrale, another Blue-stocking hostess, " to give sweetmeats and such good things . . . and she would find company enough come to her " ! but she had little opportunity of profiting by the Doctor's advice, for Mr. Thrale was so anxious for his wife's intellectual development that he forbade her to enter the kitchen! In the later days of the Blue-stockings, Mrs. Montagu indulged in receptions of a much more ambitious nature. Breakfast parties were her favourite form of entertainment, and a French lady gives the following account of a breakfast in

the Chinese Room ; " A long table, covered with the finest linen, presented to the view a thousand glittering cups and dishes, which contained coffee, chocolate, biscuits, cream, butter, toasts and exquisite tea. You must understand that there is no good tea to be had anywhere but in London. The mistress of the house . . . poured it out herself. This is the custom, and in order to conform to it the English ladies wear a white apron and a pretty straw hat, which suits their height admirably, and becomes them well, not only in their own apartments, but at noon, in St. James's Park, where they walk with the stately and majestic gait of nymphs." In the breakfast parties that Mrs. Montagu gave forty-one years later she feasted sometimes as many as seven hundred persons. Naturally conversation, which was the aim and object of the Blue-stocking parties, had little chance under such conditions. But it was carefully cultivated in the earlier and less crowded assemblies. In those days, Conversation was a high art, demanding the most brilliant talents in its service : the Blue-stocking hostesses concerned themselves with anxious thought to ensure the best results by a judicious seating of their guests. What arrangement is most likely to promote conversation ? the circle, the square, or a mere jumble of chairs ? The Blue-stocking hostesses gave different answers to this problem.

During the time when Mrs. Montagu's parties were famous rather for their wit than for their size, she placed the chairs for her guests in a great semi-circle, unbroken during the evening. Conversation at these parties was largely an affair of quip and epigram and repartee, carried on between a few persons, while most of the guests were reduced to the position of audience.

" Every flash being visible, every joke distinctly heard from one end to the other," writes a guest, " the consequent applause may act like a dram on bodily combatants, invigorating wit and provoking fresh sallies." She goes on to add that you might chance to be greatly amused if the conversationalists were brilliant ; on the other hand oue might come in for the dullest long stories, the flattest jokes anywhere to be found." Mrs. Vesey, another Bluestocking hostess, to whom Hannah More dedicated her poem " Bas-Bleu," had a hatred of this formal arrangement of the circle : she desired to make every guest participate in the talk, and set her chairs in most admired disorder, so that sometimes her guests had to sit back to back. General conversation was thus rendered impossible, and though people might form into congenial groups and knots, the hostess was unable to exercise entire direction over the current of talk. This mattered less at Mrs. Vesey's parties, for she possessed the magic gift of sympathy, and the power of kneading the mass well together.

It may come as a surprise to some to learn that the original Blue-stockings were abundantly possessed of all the social graces. To-day the term has come to imply a woman somewhat indifferent to the amenities of life, whose learning savours of pedantry, and who is inclined to regard herself as superior to her fellows. But the women who inaugurated the Blue-stocking movement during the latter half of the eighteenth century answered in no way to this type. The word indeed signified then an intellectual woman, but a woman of society, a woman of brilliant wit and lively conversation, having intense enjoyment in the company of her kind. Plump Mrs. Thrale, with her splendid house at Streatham and her house in London, had extraordinary vivacity and fascination ; Mrs. Vesey had a delicate charm and originality all her own ; while Mrs. Montagu had those qualities of presence and picturesqueness calculated to impress the public gaze. Even her charities were arranged on a scale and in a manner likely to capture the imagination. Every May Day she gave to the little chimney-sweepers of London— those unhappy and ill-treated boys whose lot it was to climb the choking and crooked chimneys—a feast of roast beef and plum pudding outside her house in Portman Square. There is an interesting picture in the British Museum that shows the chimneysweepers dancing before Montagu House.

One wonders if the word *Bluestocking* will ever recover its original significance : if a time will ever come when intellectual conversation will again take rank in London among the highest forms of art ; if we shall see again among us a second Mrs. Montagu " brilliant in diamonds, solid in judgment, critical in talk."

After Gillray.

The Prince at Carlton House.

OF the palace that was known as Carlton House, Thackeray, in "The Four Georges," says: "What palace? The palace exists no more than the palace of Nebuchadnezzar. It is but a name now."

This palace of Frederick, Prince of Wales, father of George III., and afterwards for many years the residence of George IV. when Prince of Wales, stood where now stands Carlton House Terrace, on the north side of the Mall, in St. James's Park. Its splendid grounds and gardens, where the nightingale was heard and rooks built their nests, stretched westward to Marlborough House. All vanished in 1828, "to make room for the central opening of Waterloo Place."

The first Carlton House was erected in 1729 for Lord Carlton. Bequeathed by him to his nephew, the Earl of Burlington, it was bought from this nobleman in 1732 by Frederick, Prince of Wales: a rather plain mansion of red brick, differing not greatly from the houses of noblemen and gentlemen surrounding it. It was immensely altered and embellished for the Prince, and, in its new condition, "was distinguished by a row of pillars in front. . . . The façade of the palace consisted of a centre and two wings, rusticated, without pilasters; and an entablature and balustrade which concealed the roof. The portico, by Holland, was of the Corinthian order, consisting of six columns, with details taken from the Temple of Jupiter Stator, in the Forum at Rome. Above this was an enriched frieze, and a tympanum, adorned with the Prince's arms."

In 1788 and again in 1815 the palace was still further modernised. In the year of Waterloo one of its most ornamental features was the great staircase, which was not seen until closely approached, "when," says a writer of the period, "the most brilliant effect is produced by the magical management of the light." Noteworthy among the magnificent apartments of the palace were the crimson drawing-room in which in 1816 the Princess Charlotte was married to Prince Leopold of Saxe-Coburg; the throne-room; the great ante-chamber; the circular cupola room; and the rose-satin drawing-room. These were chiefly apartments of state. For more domestic uses were the golden drawing-room, the Gothic dining-room, the Hockey-in-the-Hole. The nation lost little by the Prince's premature death ! At Carlton House Pope was one of his guests, and we have the poet's reply to Frederick's question : "How is it that you, so severe upon kings, pass so many

THE HALL AT CARLTON HOUSE

library, and the rare Gothic conservatory.

How many pictures the mind can form of scenes at Carlton House, one period succeeding to another ! They are not all edifying pictures, not all even interesting, but they have their place in the history of the times. Here Frederick kept a " shadowy and extravagant court," a centre of cabal, where his favourites contended for the privileges they were to enjoy in his " future imaginary reign." And from Carlton House Frederick goes out disguised of an evening to visit a fortune-teller or see a bull-baiting at

compliments on me ? " " Oh, sir, it is because I like the lion before his claws are full grown ! "

When George III. came to the throne Carlton House " proved a focus of political faction." Here, to celebrate the return of Fox for Westminster at the fierce election of 1784, the Prince of Wales gave that famous reception on the lawn of his palace, which was rendered more piquant by the fact that the King his father was that day taking his journey in state to open Parliament. Politics also were the chief motive of his Royal Highness's Saturday and Sunday dinners to the place-hunters of the Whig party. "Wine, promises, and personal attentions were not spared," says Wraxall. "Governments, regiments, offices, preferments, titles, here held out in prospect, retained the wavering and allured the credulous and discontented; private negotiations were likewise set on foot to gain over supporters to the Government." The Carlton House court, in short, was kept up in steady hostility to that of his Majesty at St. James's and Kew.

At Carlton House in February 1811, both Houses of Parliament having received the official report on the condition of George III.'s health, the Regency was conferred with high ceremony upon the Prince.

"THE FIRST GENTLEMAN IN EUROPE"

person of my acquaintance, she was so insulted whilst there that every bit of furniture was taken out of the room she dined in, except two shabby chairs; and the pearl bracelets which had been given her by the Prince were taken from her to decorate the arms of Lady Jersey."

An interesting event was the *début* at Carlton House of Princess Charlotte, "the hope of the empire,"as Thackeray called her, for whom the empire was so soon to be in mourning. All eyes, it is reported, were engrossed by the fair-haired royal girl on this occasion of her first public appearance. Not long afterwards Princess Charlotte was giving his *congé* to the Prince of Orange and betrothing herself to Prince Leopold of Saxe-Coburg. It is said that

How wretched was the *ménage* of the Regent and his wife, Princess Caroline of Brunswick, we have all heard a thousand times. The poor lady was undignified, and not very prudent in speech, but she had much to endure at the hands of an unworthy spouse. "Poor Princess!" exclaims the writer of "Memories of the Times of George IV." "She was an ill-treated woman, but a very wrong-headed one. Had she remained quietly at Carlton House, and conducted herself with silent dignity, how different might have been her lot! It is true, as her Privy Purse, Miss Hamilton, once told a

on the night on which Orange was to waltz in public with the Princess as her *fiancé* he came into the ball-room considerably the worse for champagne —that, in fact, his hostess, wishing to spoil the match, had purposely made him drink to intoxication. The story is not absolutely confirmed, but it is certain that not long afterwards she accepted the man whom she really admired, Prince Leopold. She died in child-birth, having given birth to a still-born infant.

We may all remember how contemptuous Thackeray was of that

legendary Prince Regent who so long held his court at Carlton House, and whose flatterers dubbed him "the first gentleman in Europe." The anecdotal Gronow, who was in the inner track, is not much more complimentary than the great novelist. He says that the Regent was "singularly imbued with a petty and vulgar pride. He would rather be amiable and familiar with his tailor than agreeable and friendly with the most illustrious of the aristocracy of the kingdom, and would rather joke with Beau Brummell than admit to his confidence a Howard or a Somerset. And yet he took care always to show good manners in public." His treatment of Brummell, by the way, when the Beau was living in obscurity and poverty at Calais, proves substantially that, far from being the first gentleman in Europe, he was one of the last persons to whom the title of gentleman could properly be applied !

In 1814 that distinguished soldier, Marshal Blücher, was in England, and to Carlton House, of course, he must come. We read that when he arrived there "all attempts to keep the populace out of the courtyard were in vain : the two sentinels at the gate, with their muskets, were laid on the ground, and the porter was overpowered. To indulge the public, the doors of the great hall were thrown open on the occasion ; and here the first interview of the General with the Prince Regent took place."

Blücher was more fortunate in his visit than that eccentric player, "Romeo" Coates, whom Theodore Hook made the victim of a wanton and unwarrantable joke. Getting possession of one of the tickets for a fête to be given by the Prince, Hook "produced a facsimile commanding the presence of Signor Romeo." Coates, who used to take the air of town in a remarkable "bright-pink cockle-shell" with "life-like chanticleers in gilt traps," had himself driven to the palace in this equipage of pantomine. The private secretary to whom the ticket had to be shown at once perceived the forgery, and the poor bamboozled player was driven off again in his blazoned chariot. The Prince, when he heard of this unmannerly jest, was, to do him justice, exceedingly annoyed. "His Royal Highness," says one of Hook's biographers, "sent his secretary next morning to apologise in person, and to signify that as the arrangements and ornaments were still entire, he hoped Mr. Coates would come and look at them. And Romeo went."

There were memoirs of Carlton House which never had the benefit of print. The readers of scandalous chronicles have thereby, no doubt, missed a treat or two, but the loss to history is probably not important. The *chronique scandaleuse*, when it comes up for test in the light of authentic documents, is usually insignificant ; and if any one should at any time discover the private and unprinted MS. which Cyrus Redding ascribes to General Arabin, it is unlikely that he would persuade a publisher of repute to give it to the world.

As has been stated, Carlton House was demolished in 1828. Certain friezes, columns, and mantelpieces of exceptional value were transferred to the National Gallery. "Upon the site of the gardens have been erected the York column and Carlton House Terrace ; the balustrades of the latter originally extended between the two ranges of houses, but were removed to form the present entrance to St. James's Park.

THE BAD OLD BAILEY

NOVEMBER 7, 1783, witnessed the last of the great saturnalia of Tyburn. Shorn of its procession the abominable festival was, however, straightway revived at Newgate; beheld there in full blast on any hanging Monday. Sixty-six years passed, and the debasing spectacle was still enjoyed, to the ever growing disgust of thoughtful and humane men. In the early years of last century the executions which took place outside Newgate prison were an unspeakable scandal, by reason not only of their publicity but of their frequency. As we are about to tell the story of Charles Dickens' famous letter to the *Times* it is well to recall the fact that as early as 1817 George Cruikshank had deeply moved London by his famous "Bank Restriction Note," which is here reproduced. He was proud of it to the end of h s life. At the time he was living in Dorset Street, Salisbury Square, and one morning he had occasion to go to a house near the Bank of England. On his way back he passed Newgate, where he saw several bodies hanging from the gallows, two of the victims being women. He was told that they were hanged for forging one-pound notes. He tells us what he did.

"My residence was a short distance from Ludgate Hill; and after witnessing this tragic scene I went home and in ten minutes designed and made a sketch of this '*Bank-note not to be imitated.*' About half an hour after this was done, William Hone came into my room, and saw the sketch lying upon my table; he was much struck with it, and said, 'What are you going to do with this, George?'

"'To publish it,' I replied. Then he said, 'Will you let me have it?' To his request I consented, made an etching of it, and it was published. Mr. Hone then resided on Ludgate Hill, not many yards from the spot where I had seen the people hanging on the gibbet; and when it appeared in his shop windows, it created a great sensation, and the people gathered round his house in such numbers that the Lord Mayor had to send the City police (of that day) to disperse the crowd.

"The Bank directors held a meeting immediately upon the subject, and *after that* they issued no more one-pound notes, and so there was no more hanging for passing forged one-pound notes; not only that, but ultimately no hanging even for forgery. *After this* Sir Robert Peel got a Bill passed in Parliament, for the 'Resumption of cash payments.' *After this* he revised the Penal Code, and *after that* there was not any more hanging or punishment of death for minor offences."

As Blanchard Jerrold says, Cruikshank assumed too much, but if he was only the fly on the wheel he was at least a very sturdy fly.

To resume the story. Charles Dickens sent to the *Times* his two memorable letters of protest in November 1849, when Queen Victoria had occupied during twelve years the most benignant throne in Europe. True, executions were now less frequent than they had been. In the year that Victoria was crowned, transportation beyond the seas was substituted for the halter in cases of forgery, burglary, highway-robbery, and arson. The labours of the hangman were thus not a little curtailed ; but Calcraft (the last executioner formally appointed by the City of London*) was by no means an idle person, and his public functions were highly relished of the town. " The Execution," in the " Ingoldsby Legends," will be recalled by many readers.

My Lord Tomnoddy he raised his head,
And thus to Tiger Tim he said,
" Malebian's dead, Duvernay's fled,
Taglioni has not yet arrived in her stead ;
Tiger Tim come, tell me true,
What may a nobleman find to do ? "

Tim looked up, and Tim look'd down,
He paused, and he put on a thoughtful frown,
And he held up his hat, and he peep'd in the crown ;
He bit his lip, and he scratch'd his head,
He let go the handle, and thus he said,
As the door, released, behind him bang'd :
" An't please you, my Lord, there's a man to be hanged."

On the morning of November 13, 1849, Dickens saw the execution of the Mannings, husband and wife, in front of Horsemonger Lane Gaol ; and, returning home, wrote a powerful letter to the *Times*.† Often enough of course, the brutal and brutalising

* Marwood, his successor, had no official status. Calcraft, a shoemaker by trade, received a salary of a guinea a week, with an additional guinea for every hanging. He served the Corporation until 1874, when he was pensioned at the rate of twenty-five shillings per week. A simple-minded, not unkindly man, he never remembered what executions he had performed.

† In a year of sensational murders, 1848–9, the crime for which Manning and his wife were hanged was of signal atrocity. The victim, a moneylender named O'Connor, had been a suitor of Mrs. Manning's in the days when she was Marie de Roux, lady's maid to Lady Blantyre. Mrs. Manning had made many ineffectual attempts to get money out of him. At the Mannings' house in Bermondsey one night, the woman enticed O'Connor down to the kitchen ; and as he stood washing his hands at a sink, close to the open grave that she herself had dug for him, she shot him through the back of the head. Manning gave the *coup-de-grâce* with a crowbar, and the pair bestowed the body beneath the kitchen floor.

scene had been described, but the grave indignation of Dickens lent it a new horror. He said :

I believe that a sight so inconceivably awful as the wickedness and levity of the immense crowd collected at that execution this morning could be imagined by no man, and could be presented in no heathen land under the sun. The horrors of the gibbet and of the crime which brought the wretched murderers to it faded in my mind before the atrocious bearing, looks, and language of the assembled spectators. When I came upon the scene at midnight, the *shrillness* of the cries and howls that were raised from time to time, denoting that they came from a concourse of boys and girls already assembled in the best places, made my blood run cold. As the night went on, screeching and laughing, and yelling in strong chorus of parodies on negro melodies, with substitutions of " Mrs. Manning " for " Susannah," and the like, were added to these. When the day dawned, thieves, low prostitutes, ruffians, and vagabonds of every kind, flocked on to the ground, with every variety of offensive and foul behaviour. Fightings, faintings, whistlings, imitations of Punch, brutal jokes, tumultuous demonstrations of indecent delight when swooning women were dragged out of the crowd by the police, with their dresses disordered, gave a new zest to the general entertainment. When the sun rose brightly —as it did—it gilded thousands upon thousands of upturned faces, so inexpressibly odious in their brutal mirth or callousness, that a man had cause to feel ashamed of the shape he wore, and to shrink from himself, as fashioned in the image of the Devil. When the two miserable creatures who attracted all this ghastly sight about them were turned quivering into the air, there was no more emotion, no more pity, no more thought, that two immortal souls had gone to judgment, no more restraint in any of the previous obscenities than if the name of Christ had never been heard in this world, and there were no beliefs among men but that they perished like the beasts.

Four days later Dickens returned the assault, urging, in a long and well-reasoned letter, that from the moment of the murderer's sentence he should be dismissed " to the dread obscurity to which the wisest judge upon the bench consigned the murderer Rush." He showed that public executions had been " the favourite sight of convicts of all descriptions " ; he cited living instances of their hardening

These worthy and humane letters made no small to-do in London and throughout the country, but nearly twenty years were to elapse before a Government of the best and mildest of Queens could be brought wholly

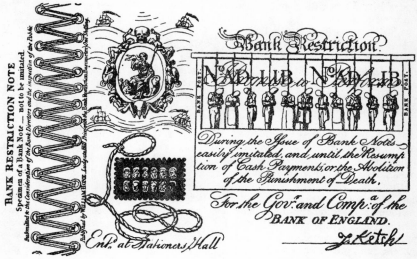

THE CRUSADE AGAINST CAPITAL PUNISHMENT ; GEORGE CRUIKSHANK'S CONTRIBUTION

effect upon the mind ; and strengthened his proposal with some weighty words of the great and wise Fielding, who had expressed his strong conviction that the murderer should die, not—as it were—upon the hustings, but behind the scenes.   Dickens advised the summoning of a " witness jury " within the prison walls, the tolling of church bells, and the closing of shops throughout the town while an execution was taking place, and the posting of minute certificates of death for twenty-one days on the prison-gate and in other public places.*

over to the views of the most splendid of her novelists.   Among the first to argue before Parliament the necessity

did not like it, and after describing his sensations in a tunnel, he goes on : " As long as people think fit to take the lives of criminals, these frightful tunnels would be good places for the operation ; a man might be placed on the top of a carriage (with his back, for mercy's sake, we will say, to the dark) looking at the light growing fainter at the tunnel's end, and the horrible darkness closing round and conquering it ; and—somewhere in the midst of the place . . . just when the light was gone . . . a sort of head-cutting machine might be fixed, calculated just to take the patient at the neck, and . . . against it the rushing engine would come . . . and it might scream and yell all the while in its own horrid, unearthly fashion . . . and when it issued out into the light again the man would be no more, and so no eye could see the murder done upon him.   But this is always said to be mawkish sentimentality ; well, I wish no man hanged, my humble desire goes no farther than that."

* In an early paper by Thackeray, recently published for the first time (*Harper's Magazine*, June 1911), with a prefatory note by Mrs. Ritchie, there is a most curious paragraph. Railway travelling had begun ; Thackeray

of public executions was Mr. Hibbert ; and in January 1864 this question, as part of the larger one of capital punishment, was referred to a Royal Commission. " Full evidence," says Griffiths, " was taken on all points and on that regarding public executions there was a great preponderance of opinion towards their abolition, yet the witnesses were not unanimous. Some of the judges would have retained the public spectacle ; the ordinary of Newgate was not certain that public executions were not the best. Another distinguished witness feared that any secrecy in the treatment of the condemned would invest them with a new and greater interest, which was much to be deprecated. Foreign witnesses, too, were in favour of publicity."

But the weight of evidence was for abolition, and the Commission recommended that capital sentences be carried out within the gaol, " under such regulations as might be considered necessary to prevent abuses, and satisfy the public that the law had been complied with." Among the dissentients, it may be observed, was John Bright, who, with certain other members of the Commission, was " not prepared to agree to the resolution respecting private executions."

In the following session the stalwart Hibbert introduced a Bill " providing for the future carrying out of executions within prisons." Accepted by the Government, it was read for the first time in March 1866, but did not become law till 1868. It was nineteen years since Dickens had first roused the whole social mind upon the subject, and he himself was now within two years of the untimely ending of his high and strenuous career.

At this date there lay under sentence of death in Newgate a Fenian named Michael Barrett. During the late 'sixties, following on the failure of the rising in 1867, Fenians swarmed among the Irish in England ; and here, in this same year, they notified themselves by Clerkenwell explosion and the Manchester rescue. It was the Clerkenwell affair (December 13, 1867) that distinguished and extinguished Michael Barrett.

In December of 1867 a somewhat noted leader of the Fenian party, Richard Burke, was confined in Clerkenwell Prison, and his friends outside were instructed as to the position of the yard in which he exercised. A matter that they were manifestly *not* instructed in was the probable result of an explosion of gunpowder ; for, on the afternoon of December 13, they fired a barrel the contents of which, had Burke been at the spot where they supposed him to be, would have shivered him to atoms. It was intended merely to blow a convenient hole in the boundary wall of the prison, through which Burke was to walk into the street. The actual and tragic happening was vividly summarised in the *Times* (April 29, 1868) :

Six persons were killed " outright " ; six more died from its effects, according to the Coroners' Inquests ; five, in addition, owed their deaths indirectly to this means : one young woman is in a mad house ; forty mothers were prematurely confined, and twenty of their babes died from the effects of the explosion on the women ; others of the children are dwarfed and unhealthy. One mother is now a raving maniac ; one hundred and twenty persons were wounded ; fifty went into St. Bartholomew's, Gray's Inn Lane, and King's College Hospitals ; fifteen are permanently injured, with loss of eyes, legs, arms, &c. ; besides twenty thousand pounds worth of damage to person and property.

There have been few Irish crimes

of mark in which the informer has not played his part, and one Patrick Mullany, of infamous memory in Ireland, named Michael Barrett as the Fawkes of the Clerkenwell explosion. It was, in fact, if the evidence were

And very large lobsters, with very large claws ;
And there is M'Fuze, and Lieutenant Tregooze,
And there is Sir Carnaby Jenks, of the Blues.
All come to see a man " die in his shoes ! "

The last public execution in front

A NEWGATE PUBLIC EXECUTION

good, Barrett who had fired the barrel. In April 1868 he was convicted of murder.

The clock strikes twelve—it is dark midnight—
Yet the " Magpie and Stump " is one blaze of light.
The parties are met ; the tables are set ;
There is " punch," " cold *without*," " hot *with*," heavy wet,
Ale-glasses and jugs, and rummers and mugs,
And sand on the floor, without carpets or rugs,
Cold fowl and cigars, pickled onions in jars,
Welsh rabbits and kidneys—rare work for the jaws !—

of the walls of Newgate (May 26, 1868) was not quite the tremendous affair that, with a due regard for tradition, it should have been ; not quite the tremendous affair anticipated of the police and the Government. Did Barrett, lying in his cell on the lower floor of the prison, within a few hours of death, know that his would be the last face to fascinate a crowd gallows-gazing in the Old Bailey ? Probably he did not—and what would that have mattered to him ? The police were more concerned than he was. " Unusual precautions were taken upon this occasion, as some fresh outrage was apprehended. Both Newgate and its neighbourhood were carefully held by the police, both city and metropolitan. In the houses opposite the prison numbers of detectives mixed with the spectators . . . in the background troops were held in readiness to act if re-quired." But there was no trouble at all. Calcraft, growing old, and primed, as his habit now was, with brandy, shuffled quietly behind a quiet and stolid prisoner ; and a crowd smaller than customary watched with no extravagant display of emotion the brief struggle in the rope of the last murderer who died under the public gaze.

A PORTRAIT IN THE ABBEY

NO object stands out more attractively in the august chaos of Westminster Abbey than the portrait of Richard II., which hangs glowingly in the Sacrarium. It is the oldest contemporary portrait of an English sovereign. Nearly three hundred years ago John Wiener described it as "that beautiful picture of a king sighing." And Richard, who sighed through life, seems in very truth to be drawing his last long sigh of peace in the Abbey which he loved, and in which he is said to sleep with his queen.

Let us leave the picture for a moment and look at the royal tomb in St. Edward's Chapel. Richard completed it for his queen, Anne of Bohemia. She was laid in it with magnificent rites. Richard intended to be laid beside her, and had his effigy sculptured beside hers, his hand clasping his wife's. Does he in fact share her tomb ? This, as Dean Stanley says, is open to grave doubt. We cannot discuss in detail the nature of these doubts, or the long-held superstition that after Richard escaped from Pontefract he lived an imbecile in Scotland, and that the body ultimately deposited in the Abbey with pious pomp by Henry V. was that of his chaplain and "double." We may hope that the beautiful effigies on the Abbey tomb do not form a bitter travesty.

The ornaments of the tomb, crumbled but expressive, include "the ostrich feathers and lions of Bohemia, the eagles of the Empire, the leopards of England, the broomcods of the Platagenets, and the sun rising through the black clouds of Crécy." The royal figures are remarkable for the regal splendour of their habiliments. They are embroidered all over with the royal initials and devices. Among them is the symbol of the white hart, which Richard adopted in the flush of his kingly career only to discover its lurking irony. The legend says that this device was taken from a white stag, caught in Windsor Forest, on whose neck was found a collar inscribed in Latin with the boast, "None may touch me ; I am Cæsar's." This symbol of kingly sanctity was adopted in the decoration of the northern entrance, or "Solomon's Porch," of the Abbey, which Richard rebuilt ; and to this day it is seen painted on a partition between the Nave and the Muniment Room.

Richard, to use a phrase of Stanley, was a peculiarly Westminster king.

In the Abbey the boy of eleven years was crowned with surpassing pomp, and no doubt a sinister omen was recognised in the fact that he fainted at the close of the long ceremonial, and had to be carried out of the church. In the Abbey he was married, and in the Abbey at all times he paid reverence to the shrine of the Confessor, to which he confided a treasured ring. His favourite oath was "By Saint Edward!" He desired to lay his queen as near Edward's shrine as possible, and to allow of this being done the remains of Edward's grandchildren were removed to the chapel of St. John the Baptist.

THE PORTRAIT OF RICHARD II. IN WESTMINSTER ABBEY

A wild scene, suggestive of much in Richard's life, occurred at the funeral. The tombs of the kings were lit up with hundreds of candles brought from Flanders, and the rites were carried out with the fullest pomp. On reaching the Abbey the bereaved king was roused to fury when he found that the discarded Earl of Arundel had come late for the procession, and that he wished to leave before the ceremony was over. Seizing a baton from one of his attendants, the hysterical king struck the earl a blow that brought him to the ground. All those present were horrified to see blood on the pavement. The king had desecrated the Abbey at his queen's funeral. The burial service was suspended in order that the rites of reconsecration might be at once performed, and the night was far gone when the disordered assemblage broke up.

The tomb has been twice reopened, once in the eighteenth century by accident, and again, deliberately, by the Board of Works in 1871. Dean Stanley describes what was seen on the last occasion: "The skulls of the King and Queen were visible; no mark of violence was seen on either. The skeletons were nearly perfect; even some of the teeth were preserved. The two copper-gilt crowns which were described on the first occasion had disappeared; but the staff, the sceptre, part of the ball, the two pairs of Royal gloves, the fragments of peaked shoes, still remained. In this tomb, closing the precinct of the chapel of St. Edward, the direct line of the descendants of its founder, Henry III., was brought to an end; and with it closes a complete period of English history."

Westminster, then, has been kind to the hapless king who, as tradition says, died like a dog in a Yorkshire dungeon. Its historic Hall, to which he gave its magnificent oaken roof, has survived six centuries of change.

To return to the great portrait. In the middle of the eighteenth century the picture, though repainted, preserved much of its pristine character. It was said to have been retouched by Vandyke. It has since been restored again. Thirty years ago it was submitted to Sir W. B. Richmond, who found that the portrait had been greatly altered and coarsened by successive coatings of paint. When these were removed the real old picture, in tempera, came out again—a convincing portrait of the unhappy king on whose failure, deposition, and death Shakespeare has lavished so many splendid lines. "The long thin nose accords with the bronze effigy of the king in Westminster Abbey; whilst the mouth, hitherto smiling and ruddy, has become delicate, but weak, and drooping in a curve, as if drawn down by sorrowful anticipations even in the midst of pageantry." Such was the face that Richard saw in the mirror which Shakespeare makes him consult in Westminster Hall in the hour of his deposition. Shakespeare, following Marlowe's immortal lines on Helen— "Was this the face that launched a thousand ships?"—makes Richard exclaim:

> Was this face the face
> That every day under his household roof
> Did keep ten thousand men? Was this the face
> That, like the sun, did make beholders wink?
> Was this the face that faced so many folks
> And was at last out-faced by Bolingbroke?

To this unique portrait, still hanging in the Abbey, Shakespeare himself may have gone for inspiration.

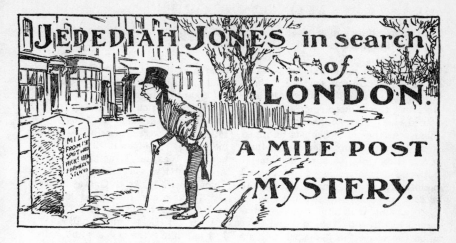

IN days when the journey to and from London was by road, milestones were of great importance to travellers. To-day they moulder, and their place is taken by the smart wooden sign-post to which the goggled eyes of the motorist turn hawk-like as he flies past. The old milestones bear witness to the confused systems under which they were fixed and inscribed, and their number and variety though greatly reduced, will justify to readers of to-day the following delightful skit, which, under the title of "Surburban Milestones" appeared in Charles Knight's "London" more than fifty years ago.

JEDEDIAH JONES (he was called Jedediah in consequence of the admiration his father cherished for the character of Jedediah Buxton, the great calculator) was a schoolmaster at Barnet. His delight in his occupation was hereditary; for the elder Jones had properly impressed his son with a sense of the high responsibilities and privileges of his calling, and had shown him how superior a schoolmaster was to any of the other mighty functionaries of the land—to a judge, or a minister of state, or even to a bishop. Jedediah grew, in time, to be somewhat of an important personage, especially as his love of learning branched out into sundry matters of abstruse inquiry, by his knowledge of which he not only puzzled his wondering pupils, but occasionally perplexed the most sagacious of his neighbours.

He was not a philosopher in the ordinary sense of the word, for he did not busy himself with any of the sciences as they exist in the present day; but he contrived to know something about the theories of these matters as they were received two or three centuries ago, and was always reflecting and experimenting upon propositions that all mankind have agreed to reject as absurd or impracticable. He was acquainted with the past existence of many vulgar errors; but he by no means acknowledged the propriety of that sweeping condemnation of certain opinions which was contained in the title of Sir Thomas Brown's folio. He had considerable faith that he should some day meet the Wandering Jew on the great Holyhead Road; he turned up his nose at the belief that a griffin had not existed, for why should people have them painted on carriages if their ancestors had never seen such things : he was almost certain that he had himself heard a mandrake shriek when he pulled it up—(on purpose to hear it): and he was quite sure that there were only three Queen Anne's farthings coined, and that he had got one of them. As the old alchemists obtained some knowledge of chemistry in their search after gold, so our schoolmaster obtained a smattering of history and philosophy in his search after those crotchety points of learning which history and philosophy have determined to throw overboard ; and thus, upon the whole, he managed to pass with the world as a very wise man, and his school flourished.

There were some matters, however, with all his learning, which puzzled Jedediah Jones exceedingly. One of these dark and important questions was a source of perpetual irritation to him. He took long walks on half-holidays, and generally his face, on these occasions, turned towards London ; for he had a secret conviction that his ultimate vocation was to be in that mighty metropolis, and that he should be summoned thither by a special decree of the Royal Society, or the Society of Antiquaries, and be humbly requested to solve some great enigma, of which all mankind, except himself, had missed the solution. In these long walks he was constantly reminded by the milestones that there was one point of learning as to which he still remained in absolute ignorance. This was grievous. These milestones had proclaimed to him, from the days of his earliest recollections, that it was seven miles, or six miles, or five miles, or four miles, or three miles and a half, " *from the spot where Hicks's Hall formerly stood.*"

Now in all his books he could find not an iota about Hicks, or Hicks's Hall. For ten tedious years had he been labouring at this riddle of Hicks's Hall. It was his thought by day, and his dream by night.

Who was Hicks ? How did Hicks obtain such a fame that even the milestones were inscribed to his memory ? What was his Christian name ? Was he General Hicks, or Admiral Hicks, or Bishop Hicks, or Chief Justice Hicks ? Or was he plain Mr. Hicks ? and if so, was he M.P., or F.R.S., or F.A.S., or M.R.I.A. ?

Why did Hicks build a hall ? Was it a hall like " the colleges and halls " of Oxford and Cambridge, or like the Guildhall in King Street, Cheapside ?

Perhaps it was a hall for public entertainments—perhaps Hicks was a member of one of the City companies, and built a hall which the company, in gratitude, called after his name. How long ago was Hicks's Hall built ? Was it in the Gothic or the Roman style of architecture ? Was it of brick or stone ? Had it a carved roof ? When did Hicks's Hall cease to exist ? Was it burnt down ? Was it pulled down by the mob ? Was it taken down to widen the street ? Was it suffered to go to decay and fall down ? Was anybody killed when it fell down ? Are the ruins still to be seen ? Has anybody written the History of Hicks's Hall ? Has anybody written the Life of Hicks ? Shall I, Jedediah Jones, write this work which the world must be so anxiously looking for ?

Such were a few of the perplexing and yet inspiriting thoughts which had for years passed through Jones's mind, as he walked from Barnet, Highgate-ward. His difficulties at last became insupportable. He took up his resolution, and he was comforted. A week still remained of the Christmas holidays. He would set out for London and not see his house again till he had penetrated the mystery of Hicks's Hall.

With his trusty staff in his right hand, and a small bundle containing his wardrobe in a pocket-handkerchief under his left arm, Mr. Jones sallied forth from Barnet, under the auspices of the New Weather Almanac, on a morning which promised to be "fair and frosty," in January 1838. The morning was misty, with rain, which occasionally became sleet, driving in his face. He courageously marched on through Whetstone, and crossed the dreary regions of Finchley Common—without meeting a highwayman—which was a disappointment, as he had an implicit belief in the continued existence of those obsolete contributors to the public amusement. He at length reached the northern ascent of Highgate Hill, and his spirits, which were somewhat flagging, received a new impulse. The milestone proclaimed that he was only five miles "from the spot where Hicks's Hall formerly stood."

Onward he went, over Highgate Hill, till he arrived at the stone which told him that he was only "four miles" from the shrine to which his pilgrimage was dedicated. But here was a new attraction—an episode in his journey of discovery. He had reached Whittington's Stone, and there he read that this redoubted thrice Lord Mayor of London had passed through these repetitions of glory in the years of our Lord 1397, and 1406, and 1419. Here then Whittington had sat—here he had heard Bow Bells—here he had thought of his faithful cat—here he had returned to cherish his cat once more, and to win all the riches of which his cat was the original purveyor. But then a thought came across him as to

HICKS'S HALL IN CLERKENWELL (*From an Old Print*)

which was the greater man, Whittington or Hicks? If Whittington had one stone raised to his memory, Hicks had twenty; Hicks, therefore, must be the greater man. Who was Hicks? Where was Hicks's Hall? He was only four miles "from the spot where Hicks's Hall formerly stood;" the problem would be soon solved.

He at length reached Islington Green, stopping not to gaze upon the suburban gentility of Holloway, nor going out of his way to admire the architectural grandeur of Highbury. He was now only "one mile from the spot where Hicks's Hall formerly stood." The stone which proclaimed this great truth reared its proud head, unencumbered by houses, at a distinguished distance from the foot-pavement and the high road.

It seemed, as he approached the scene of Hicks's glories, that there was an evident disposition to call attention to the name of the immortal man, whoever he might have been. He was persuaded that he should now learn all about Hicks—the passers-by must be full of Hicks—the dwellers must reverence Hicks. He went into a pastrycook's shop opposite the triumphal stone.

He bought a penny bun, and he thus addressed the maiden at the counter : " Young woman, you have the happiness of living near the spot where Hicks's Hall formerly stood. I have walked ten miles to see that place. Which is the road ? " The young woman replied : " Hicks, the greengrocer, lives over the way; there is no other Hicks about here."

This was satisfactory. Hicks, the greengrocer, must be a descendant of the great Hicks ; so he sought Hicks, the greengrocer, and, bowing profoundly, he asked if he could tell him the way to the spot where Hicks's Hall formerly stood ? Now Hicks, the greengrocer, was a wag, and his waggery was increased by living in the keen atmosphere of the Angel at Islington, and by picking up something of the wit that is conveyed from the West to the East, and from the East to the West, by the omnibuses that arrive every three minutes from the Exchange at one end, and from Paddington at the other. To Jones, therefore, Hicks answered by another question, " Does your mother know you're out ? " This was a difficult question for Jedediah to answer. He had not communicated to his mother— good old lady—the object of his journey ; she might have disapproved of that object. How could Mr. Hicks

know he had a mother ? how could he know that he had not told his mother all his anxieties about Hicks's Hall ? He was unable to give a reply to Hicks, the greengrocer ; so Hicks, the greengrocer, recommended him to get into an omnibus which was standing opposite the door.

Into the omnibus Jedediah Jones accordingly went, and he desired the gentleman called a conductor to put him down at the spot where Hicks's Hall formerly stood. The gentleman grinned ; and something passed between him and another gentleman, called a cad, which had better be trusted to the immortality of their unwritten language than be here inscribed. On went the omnibus, and after a tedious hour Jedediah Jones found the carriage deserted, and the conductor bawled out " Elephant and Castle, Sir."

During his progress our worthy schoolmaster had put sundry questions to his fellow passengers touching Hicks's Hall, but he found them of an ignorant and perverse generation ; they knew nothing of Hicks—nothing of Hicks's Hall—nothing of the spot where Hicks's Hall formerly stood. The ignorance of the people, he thought, was beyond all calculation ; and he determined that not a boy of Barnet should not henceforward be thoroughly informed of matters upon which mankind were called upon, by the very milestones, to be all-knowing.

At the Elephant and Castle our traveller had lost all traces of Hicks's Hall. The milestones had forgotten Hicks and his hall. They were full of another glory—" *the Standard in Cornhill.*"

What was the Standard in Cornhill ? Was it the Royal Standard, or was it the Union Jack ? Perhaps it might be the new standard of weights and measures. He was clearly out of the region of Hicks, so he would make his way to the Standard at Cornhill. Who could tell but he might there find the standard of the English language, which he had long been searching for? At any rate they would there tell him of the place where Hicks's Hall formerly stood.

By the aid of another omnibus our painstaking Jedediah was placed in the busiest throng of the London hive. He was in Cornhill. Jones was somewhat shy, according to the custom of learned men, and he therefore knew not how to address any particular individual of the busy passengers, to inquire about the Standard at Cornhill. He did, however, at last venture upon a very amiable and gentlemanly-looking man—who politely offered to show him the desired spot. The promise was not realised; in a moment his friend slipped from his side, and Jedediah found that his purse containing two pounds seven shillings and sixpence had vanished from his pocket. He forgot the Standard in Cornhill; and in despair he threw himself into a Hampstead stage, resolved not to give up his search after Hicks's Hall although he had only a few shillings in his waistcoat pocket.

In a melancholy reverie Jedediah arrived in the Hampstead stage at Camden Town. He knew that he ought not to go further, unless he was quite prepared to abandon the original object of his inquiry. It was a bitter afternoon. The rain fell in torrents. He had a furious appetite—he had

lost his purse—yet still he would not sleep till he had found the spot where Hicks's Hall formerly stood. He left the Hampstead stage, and there was light enough for him to ascertain whether the milestones were still faithful to Hicks.

A new difficulty presented itself. The milestone in Camden Town in

KNIGHTSBRIDGE: ONE MILE TO HYDE PARK CORNER

formed him that he was *two miles from St. Giles's Pound*. What was St. Giles's Pound? Why did a saint require a pound? If it was a pound sterling, was there not a slight anachronism between the name of the current coin and the era of the saint? If it were a pound for cattle, was it not a very unsaintly office for the saint to preside over the matter of strayed heifers? He was puzzled; so he got into a cab, being disgusted with the ignorance of the people in omnibuses, for the opportunity of a quiet colloquy with the intelligent-looking driver.

" My worthy friend," said Jones, " we are only two miles from St. Giles's Pound—what sort of a pound is St. Giles's Pound?" "For the matter of that," said the cab-driver,

" I have driv here these ten years, and I never yet seed St. Giles's Pound, nor Holborn Bars—no, never—though ve always reckons by them."

" Wonderful ! " replied Mr. Jones ; " then please to drive me to the Standard in Cornhill." " The Standard in Cornhill—that's a good one ! I should like to know who ever seed the Standard in Cornhill. Ve knows the Swan with Two Necks in Lad Lane, and the Golden Cross, and the Vite Horse Cellar in Piccadilly, but I never heerd of anybody that ever seed the Standard in Cornhill." " Then, Sir," said Jones, breathlessly, "perhaps you don't know the place where Hicks's Hall formerly stood ? " " As for Hicks's Hall," said the cabman, " it's hall a hum. There's no such place— no more than the Standard in Cornhill, nor Holborn Bars, nor St. Giles's Pound—and my oppinnun is, there never wor such places, and that they keep their names on the milestones to bilk the poor cabs out of their back carriage."

Jedediah Jones was discomfited. He did not quite understand the cabman's solution ; and he had a vague notion that, if the milestones were placed with reference to the Post-office, or St. Paul's, or some place which *did* exist, the back carriages and other carriages of cabmen and hackney-coachmen would be better regulated. He, however, made the best of his position. He spent one of his remaining shillings upon a *very* frugal dinner ; and, wending his way back to Islington, he bestowed the other upon the coachman of a Holyhead mail to convey him to Barnet without further loss of time or property.

____

[The journey of discovery above narrated was not an impossible one to have been undertaken by a person whose curiosity was greater than his judgment. The suburbs of London long continued to be full of puzzling inscriptions, such as that of Hicks's Hall. The system of measuring the roads out of London by some well-known central object, such as the Standard in Cornhill (a conduit once known to every passenger), was a right system, and ought to have been the uniform one. But the other system was that of measuring the roads from some point where London was *supposed to terminate*. The termination of course depended on the traveller's road. West of London he was given the distances to Tyburn Turnpike or Hyde Park Corner. In South London the milestones usually told him how far he stood from the Standard in Cornhill. On other roads they spoke to him of St. Giles's Pound as a " far off divine event." Doubtless the most absurd inscription, very frequent north of London, was that which measured distances to the spot " where Hicks's Hall formerly stood."

Hicks's Hall had been built in 1612 by Sir Baptist Hicks, of Kensington, as a sessions house for the county of Middlesex. It long remained an important legal centre. In it William Lord Russell was condemned to death, and Count Koningsmarck acquitted— both decisions savouring rather of law than justice. The present Sessions House on Clerkenwell Green, erected in 1782, was the successor of Hicks's Hall.

When Hicks's Hall was pulled down an inscription was placed on a public-house to indicate the *site*, which took the place of the building in the minds of travellers and local authorities. Hence the inscriptions which so sorely puzzled Mr. Jedediah Jones.]

HOW RAILWAYS CAME TO LONDON

THE story of London's railways may be said to commence with the accession of her late Majesty Queen Victoria, for it was in the year 1837 that our first public railway operated by locomotive engines started business. It is true that in 1804 the Surrey Iron Railway had been opened from Wandsworth to Croydon, but this was worked by horses which hauled waggons running on metal rails. Four years later Richard Trevethick's locomotive " Catch-me-who-can " ran on a circular track laid down somewhere near the site of Euston Square, taking passengers, who were sufficiently venturesome to risk their lives behind the " infernal machine," at a charge of one shilling per head. But these hardly count, for in the one case the carriage of goods was the main object, and the other was merely a temporary show railway such as is often associated nowadays with fairs and exhibitions.

Naturally, in view of the developments which had occurred in the north, railway promoters were only too eager to provide the metropolis with railways, and at this period the construction of the London and Birmingham, Great Western, and other lines was already in progress. But in 1837, on December 14, the first railway to be actually completed in London was opened for traffic, and it is interesting to note that this was designed specially to meet the transportation requirements of the metropolis itself, whereas the other lines which were brought into use soon after were intended mainly to provide for transit by machinery between London and other important centres. Moreover, the London and Greenwich, the pioneer line, started at a terminus that was " in the most populous district of the most populous city in the world," instead of commencing away in the comparatively remote north-west, as was the case with Euston, or at the little village of Paddington, about a mile out along the Edgware Road.

In those days a certain section of the Press declaimed very strongly against railways, and it is interesting to note that amongst other dreadful prophecies it was stated that the fumes from the engines would be " more noxious than the pestilential vapours given forth by the fabled dragon of old," and the locality would be " ruined and deserted and become a able, and the Greenwich Railway, while it did not provide an equivalent to the philosopher's stone, was a good paying concern for many years, until it became part of the South-Eastern Railway.

Railway-opening ceremonies in the early years were nearly always made

A "LONDON AND BIRMINGHAM" LOCOMOTIVE

howling wilderness." The promoters of the Greenwich Railway had altogether different ideas, for they claimed that " the traffic will of necessity be so vast and lucrative from both passengers and merchandise that the profits to be derived, if not likely to increase *ad infinitum*, will, nevertheless, cause the position of the happy proprietors to be as much envied as the accredited discoverer of the philosopher's stone."

Such exaggerated language was common in those days, and is not altogether unknown in company prospectuses of later years ; but it is only fair to acknowledge that in the beginning railways were indeed very profit-

occasions for festivities and junketing, but the description of the proceedings on this famous day in December 1837 is too good to be passed over, even at the cost of a somewhat lengthy quotation from a newspaper of the period. On that date the Greenwich Railway was opened from Duke Street, London Bridge, to Deptford. " The directors, with the official staff of management, having arrived at the London terminus, were shown to their allotted seats by ushers in waiting, and the band of music (attired in the garb of the Beefeaters) having taken up its position on the roof of the carriage, the official bugler blew the signal for the start, and the train steamed off amidst the firing of cannon, the ringing of church bells, and the cheers of an excited crowd. Spa Road, the only intermediate station, which was filled to excess with the multitude there assembled, was reached with almost the swiftness of a discharged Congreve rocket, and afterwards Deptford, where

"work of art," a band of musicians "played in" the passengers at both termini for some time.

In such wise was London's pioneer railway brought into use, and on other occasions more or less similar proceedings were indulged in; but, although we are told that the managing director

EUSTON STATION WHEN ENGINES WERE LEFT AT CHALK FARM

a vast concourse, in carriages and on foot, awaited the visitors, with a second band of music, which then took the place of the first on the return journey."

One would have thought that the railway itself constituted a sufficient attraction, but presumably the directors thought it advisable to provide "a special attraction" at Deptford in the shape of a "model of a submarine destroyer, called a naval torpedo, the invention of the Earl of Dundonald," in conjunction with fairs at either end and coloured lamp illuminations along the line, and a pyrotechnic display to liven matters after dark. Moreover, the illuminations were continued into the New Year, and in order that the railway might be further exhibited as a

of the Greenwich Railway, some four miles long be it remembered, was "attended in his movements with a degree of pomp and splendour calculated to excite the admiration of beholders," bigger and more important railways commenced business on much more prosaic lines. Still, it must be acknowledged that London had something to be proud of when its first railway was opened for traffic, and after all, though we may be amused at the details, no one can deny that it was good advertising.

The Greenwich Railway was built on arches, and some of these were fitted up as dwelling-houses. It was also intended to provide a carriageway alongside the rails, on which vehicles and pedestrians were to be allowed on payment of a toll, but the evidence is not very satisfactory that this part of the programme was carried out.

One further reference to this interesting line before we turn to the bigger railways. For third-class passengers open waggons without seats were provided, sometimes described as " standipedes " or " stanups," and it was no easy task to climb into and out of them, while comfort was non-existent. In answer to complaints, however, the directors declared that " there was no justification for the murmur ; if people would insist on travelling at so cheap a rate, it was only reasonable they should pay the penalty in a certain amount of discomfort."

During the following year both the London and Birmingham and the Great Western Railways opened from London. Almost from the beginning Euston was famous by reason of " the fine Doric portico in Euston Square reminding us of the propylæ of the Greek cities." In fact, it would be difficult to find another instance where such a useless erection has justified itself more from the advertising point of view. Euston is far from being the most conveniently located terminus in London, and it is hidden away behind the well-known portico almost as if it were ashamed to own to its existence. Yet no station is better known, not only here but also in other lands, and this is almost entirely due to the famous gateway. The Euston Arch has indeed proved itself a splendid advertisement, though it was erected only in order to provide an imposing entrance to a somewhat obscure station.

It was at first intended to construct the London terminus at Camden Town, as far away from London proper as was Paddington in those days ; but wiser counsels resulted in the extension to Euston Grove. For several years trains were hauled up the incline from Euston to Chalk Farm by means of ropes worked by stationary engines, the two tall and elegant chimneys belonging to the engine-house standing " like monumental columns " on each side of the line.

From 1838 onwards the story of London's railways is far too extensive to be told even with approximate adequacy except at considerable length; but a few remarks must be made in reference to the underground lines. It was mainly in consequence of the comparative remoteness of Euston and Paddington that proposals were made for the construction of what was to be called the " City Railway." Writers of the period seem to have been rather fond of comparing railway trains to a Congreve rocket, for we read in one publication of the City Railway as having been projected " to whirl the impatient traveller like a Congreve rocket over the heads of the astounded citizens of London, and to cause him to alight within a few yards of St. Paul's." This writer was, however, correct in prophesying that " the good people of Gray's Inn need not be very much alarmed by the apprehension of having their midnight slumbers disturbed by the rushing past their garret windows of a train of ' City Railway ' carriages."

The original proposals were for a central terminus somewhere near Farringdon Street, with an extension to the General Post Office, to which all the trunk lines would have connections. Unfortunately that idea was never carried out, and though suggested in another guise in recent years, there is little prospect of its realisation in these days.

As actually constructed, the Metropolitan did not realise this ideal, though how nearly it does so at Farringdon Street will be realised by examination of a railway map of London. But by extending the Great Western to Farringdon Street, and onwards to Moorgate Street and Aldgate, the original line offered enormous possibilities, and although it was fashionable in the later years of steam traction to sneer at its smoky tunnels and its antiquated steam locomotives, there is no question that the Metropolitan, and its associate in the circle traffic, the District, filled a long-felt want.

When first opened trains were run about every fifteen minutes, with expresses between at the busy periods. Each train consisted of three carriages, one for each class. For some time these were provided by the Great Western, and ran on the broad gauge ; but within a few months from the opening from Paddington to Farringdon Street difficulties arose and the Great Western refused to continue. The notice was short, but fortunately the connection with the Great Northern at King's Cross had been made, and that company was already preparing some of its engines for working over the underground, so that they were able to come to the rescue until the engines and carriages on order for the Metropolitan were delivered. These were, of course, for the narrow gauge, but as three rails had been laid down, no difficulty was experienced from this cause.

For some time pleasure trips on the underground were made because of the novelty, but as trains became more frequent and the tunnels more smoky complaints began to arise, and people were not so enamoured of burrowing under houses behind fire machines. Several experimental engines were constructed to overcome the difficulty, among which may be mentioned a hot-water locomotive, and another in which steam was raised by means of hot bricks, and known generally as " Fowler's Ghost." Neither proved satisfactory, and it was not until electric traction provided the remedy that the Metropolitan earned a different character ; but it must not be forgotten that this, the first underground railway in the world, showed what could be done, and has probably rendered better service to London than any other line. Underground travelling was a new field, and, as may be expected, Mr. Punch had his friendly gibe when he pictured the consternation of the maidservant who was suddenly confronted by the grimy visage of a fireman poking his head through the floor of the coal cellar, with the request, " Excuse me; marm, but can you 'blige with a scuttle of coals, as the water in the hengine has gone off the boil ? " But the benefits provided were real, and although now the original Metropolitan is only one part of a comprehensive system of underground and tube railways connecting all parts of the metropolis, the debt of gratitude which we owe to the promoters of the pioneer lines— "London's own" they may be termed in contradistinction to the larger systems which radiate from London—must not be overlooked.

DISRAELI'S GOLDEN YOUTH

THE most astonishing period in the life of Benjamin Disraeli, afterwards to become the Earl of Beaconsfield, was that in which he flitted through the aristocratic Bohemia of London in his early days, as, next to Count D'Orsay, at any rate, the most eminent dandy of his time. It was then that he was drawn by Maclise for *Fraser's Magazine*. He does not appear in the famous group of "Fraserians," in which such men as Coleridge and Carlyle, Thackeray and Lytton, Sir Egerton Bridges and Dr. Maginn, are seated at a round table, enjoying such an ambrosian night as, in fact, so many men of such intellectual prominence in their day never spent in each other's society ; but he had a page portrait to himself, concerning which Maginn wrote, in verse that was concealed as prose : " Oh, reader dear, do pray look here, and you will spy the curly hair, and forehead fair, and nose so high, and gleaming eye of Benjamin D'Is-ra-e-li, the wonderous boy who wrote ' Alroy,' in rhyme and prose, only to show how long ago Victorious Judah's lion banner rose."

Among statesmen Benjamin Disraeli was rather more of a Londoner than any of his contemporaries. He narrowly escaped being born in James St., Adelphi, and actually first saw the light at No. 6 King's Road, Bedford Row, which is now 22 Theobald's Road, a house which overlooks Gray's Inn Garden. At the age of six he was sent to a dame school at Islington, and later on his schoolmaster was John Potticany, at Elliot Place, Blackheath. He used to say that he was despatched to the Islington school so early that he believed he was sent there to learn to speak. A third school was at Epping

Forest, where, he said, " the whole drama of public school life was enacted in a smaller theatre." Sharon Turner, the historian, persuaded his father to allow his children to be baptized, and " little Ben " went through the ceremony of baptism at St. Andrew's, Holborn.

For twelve years Disraeli's home was in Bloomsbury Square, and there he grew up to manhood. When his father desired to make a lawyer of him he was articled to a firm in Frederick's Place, Old Jewry. He was, in fact, a Londoner through and through, and it was in the city of his birth, and at no great distance from his birthplace, that, at a ripe old age, he died.

In Daniel Maclise's portrait Disraeli seems almost too dainty to be human— a thin figure, leaning against a mantelpiece, with legs crossed, hair in carefully arranged curls ; unmentionables immaculate in cut, tight fitting, as was the custom at that period, with straps to keep them from creasing ; a face beautiful as that of a young god, and a background of furniture such as Thackeray describes with appropriate unction in " Codlingsby." It was a pleasant portrait, that of Maclise, without the least spitefulness ; rather, with an artist's appreciation of so much beauty of person and such careful magnificence of attire. It was really graceful portraiture, as was said at the time, the subject " looking for all the world like Apollo masquerading in a suit of Beau Brummel's."

Such a figure as this moved the descriptive pens of the period alike to admiration and to satire. One of them writes of Disraeli's " ringlets of silken black hair," his " flashing eyes," his effeminate and lisping voice," his

BENJAMIN DISRAELI IN HIS YOUTH (*From the Maclise Portrait Gallery*)

" coat of black velvet lined with white satin," his ivory cane with inlaid gold handle, the silken rosettes which adorned his dainty shoes. "Everybody," remarks this almost too-observant contemporary, "laughed at him for being affected; but the women declared that his was an affectation in the best style."

Many of these women affirmed that he would live to be a great man. There were some men who held the same opinion. It needed no ghost from the grave, said one of these, to predict his success in public life. He was silent and reserved, says this authority; but closely observant. The silence obviously depended on the company in which he found himself ; for he is admitted to have had marvellous powers of conversation, only requiring to be stimulated by the attentive hearer and the appropriate subject. When excited he had " a wonderful command of language," with a power of sarcasm phenomenally developed. The most competent of the observers of him in these showy days of his youth took note of his ready wit and of his grasp of mind.

Young Disraeli was to be seen in almost all the great circles of those times. He dined in the company of Lord Melbourne, and told him that he wanted to be Prime Minster. He dined with Lord Lyndhurst, with Lord Durham, and quite frequently at John Murray's, where he met Tom Moore. His friend Bulwer, afterwards Lord Lytton, introduced him in some directions, and that artistic fop, Count D'Orsay, in others, chiefly, of course, to Lady Blessington's, at Gore House, Kensington.

It was in this equivocal household that he was seen by Nathaniel Parker Willis who was in England—making notes for his " Pencillings by the Way," and those other books which excited indignation because they presented too intimate and familiar a view of English society. He saw Disraeli sitting in the deep recess of a window " looking out upon Hyde Park, with the last rays of daylight reflected from the gorgeous gold flowers of a splendidly embroidered waistcoat." The American visitor was constrained to say, " Disraeli has one of the most remarkable faces I ever saw." It was a face lividly pale. " His eye is black as Erebus, and has the most mocking, lying-in-wait expression conceivable." The mouth was alive with a kind of working and impatient nervousness.

" A thick, heavy mass of jet black ringlets falls over his left cheek almost to his collarless stock, while on the right temple it is parted and put away with the smooth carelessness of a girl's, and shines most unctuously ' with thy incomparable oil, Macassar ! ' "

This early portraiture of an always uncommon man is vivid enough, and much alike in all instances. He "carried foppery to an extreme of extravagance," says one. He was " an egregious dandy," says another. He was " singularly handsome." He was " as conscious of his beauty as of his other gifts." One observer describes him as a young man fired by his own eloquence. N. P. or " Namby Pamby " Willis says : " I might as well attempt to gather up the foam of the sea as to convey an idea of the extraordinary language in which he clothed his description " of Beckford, the author of " Vathek," one of the greatly popular books of a day that now seems very far off. Certainly, the young dandy was not despised intellectually, which excepts him from the usual fate of dandyism. There were only some men in the literary circle who were not impressed, like Albany Fonblanque. Disraeli had given, in some conversation, a lively account of how Colonel Sursfield had had some of his blood put in a bottle, as a souvenir for Ireland. Fonblanque said he saw nothing remarkable in the Colonel " decanting his claret," at which sally young Disraeli left the company in high dudgeon.

If the picture were left at this stage it would be dazzling, but incomprehensible. There would be two problems to solve, as there always have been when the life of Disraeli has been viewed only in the light of the earlier biographies. Much has been made of the amazing fact that a lawyer's clerk should have become Prime Minister. If he was only a lawyer's clerk, how did he get into the best society of the day whilst he was still so very young ? If he was a man of real ability as he afterwards proved, how did he come to make such an egregious spectacle of himself ? Let us consider the first question in its due order. One of the early authorities describes him as "the perfumed boy exquisite who forced himself into the salons of peeresses." The truth is that he never had to force his way anywhere. He was cradled in the literary purple. He said of himself, with exact truth, that he was "born in a library, and trained from early childhood by learned men who did not share the pensions and the prejudices of our social and political life." This really meant that from boyhood he was admitted to the most notable society of the time. He was the son of a renowned literary man, who had wealth that was both inherited and earned. He was a lawyer's clerk only as one who enters the office of a solicitor of the first rank with the view of being trained for partnership, and of marrying the solicitor's possibly "ugly and elderly daughter." He never stood in need of money, though he ran to much extravagance in the matter of clothes. When he threw up the practice of the law after three years trial, he was in a position to indulge in expensive European and Eastern travels ; then, too, he was a successful author at twenty. If he chose to make a fool of himself, he had all the necessary means for doing so.

But then comes the next question : Why did he make a fool of himself, if he actually did so ? Neither, we are now able to say, from such exact and cool calculation as that of a celebrated man of our own time, nor from inability to perceive what might be thought of his extraordinary dandyism, nor for the mere uninspired desire for a butterfly existence. Whilst he was figuring as a dandy his mind was in a tumult. His ambitions were tremendous ; his confidence in himself was tremendous ; he knew that he could fly for long distances, but was uncertain as to the desirable route. " At twenty I became pensive and restless," he wrote. " Nothing would satisfy me but travel." When he was pensively resting his elbow on the mantelpiece, as in Maclise's picture, he was a dreamer of dreams. One day, as he wrote, " in reverie he is an Alberoni, a Ripperda, a Richelieu." On the next he had " resolved to be a great historical writer," and " to expound the nature of man and the origin of nations in glowing sentences of oracular majesty." In fact, he felt himself capable of everything, and before he became a dandy he had read twelve hours a day in order to repair what he considered to be the defects of his early education. Then he wanted change.

There was in his strange case a most unusually early experience of life ; there was a correspondingly early experience of literary success ; there was the praise of women, to whose charms he was readily susceptible ; and then there was boredom. " My disposition is now indolent," he wrote to his sister. " I wish to be idle and to enjoy myself, to muse over the stormy past, and to smile over the placid present." " All men of high imagination are indolent," he added. And that explains everything that needs explanation. The dandyism was a diversion, and of course, a passing phase. In the great and historical dandy stage he was still well under his thirtieth year.

THE OLD COGERS

AN OLD FESTIVE FLEET STREET DEBATING SOCIETY

IT is never quite possible to ascertain how or why the meaning of a word gets perverted. The "Cogers Discussion Hall" which was founded as a Debating Society by Daniel Mason in 1775 in Shoe Lane, Fleet Street, has nothing whatever to do with the phrase, "He's an old coger," or "codger," meaning that he is an artful individual who is not altogether to be trusted.

As a matter of fact Coger comes from the Latin word cogito, to cogitate. From this Latin origin we get our word cogent, through *cogens*, a word that was very much in use about the time that the Cogers Hall came into existence, so that the suggestion was, that to be a "Coger" was to be a person of force and power. Burke, in one of his speeches, speaks of "Those principles of cogent expediency to which all just governments owe their birth." From the first, Cogers Hall was a great resort for politicians of all shades, not altogether local, but general. Among its most eminent members, it numbers in its records such names as John Wilkes of notorious memory, Judge Keogh, the great Daniel O'Connell, and that marvellously eloquent Irish barrister, John Philpot Curran, whose wit and good-humour kept the Cogers on the move whenever he spoke, which was tolerably frequently. One writer on the subject of Cogers is very careful to explain that the word Coger does not imply codgers or a drinker of cogs—cogs being small glasses of tipple, but unfortunately through the mispronunciation of the genial London cockney, the word achieved the sound of codger, and only quite recently we heard this institution termed with considerable eloquence and import Codgers Hall !

In the beginning, on the fourteenth

of every June, the Grand, the Vice Grand, and the Secretary were elected, and these gentlemen had very considerable powers of regulating the discussions. The room was always open to strangers, but the members had the right to speak first. Here callow youths rose on their hind legs to set the world straight, and to show how the universe should be governed. Afterwards the majority of them who did not disappear, but made honourable names for themselves, kindly allowed the Universe to flow on as usual.

Mr. J. Parkinson, a well-known gossiper, very carefully, some few years ago, told the story of the Society, at which master tradesmen, mechanics, reporters, budding authors, and sucking young barristers sipped their grog together, what time they sent forth wreathing columns of tobacco smoke from their various pipes and cigars. Mr. Parkinson, with a keen eye for effect, pleasantly related his experiences of the Cogers habitation. He says : " The hall was a long low room like the saloon of a large steamer. Wainscoat dimmed and ornaments tarnished by tobacco smoke and the lingering dews of steaming compounds. A room with large niches at each end like shrines for full-grown saints, one niche containing ' My Grand ' in a framework of shabby gold, the other ' My Grand's Deputy ' in a bordering more substantial. More than one hundred listeners are waiting patiently for My Grand's utterances this Saturday night, and are whiling away the time philosophically with bibulous and nicotian refreshment. The narrow tables of the long room are filled with students and performers, and quite a little crowd is congregated at the

door, and in a room adjacent until places can be found for them in the presence chamber. ' Established 1755 ' is inscribed on the ornamental signboard above us and ' Instituted 1756 ' on another signboard near. Dingy portraits of departed Grands and Deputies decorate the walls. Punctually at nine My Grand opens the proceedings amid profound silence. The deputy buries himself in his newspaper, and maintains as profound a calm as the Speaker ' in another place.' The most perfect order is preserved. The Speaker or Deputy, who seems to know all about it, rolls silently in his chair ; he is a fat dark man, with a small and rather sleepy eye, such as I have seen come to the surface and wink lazily at the fashionable people clustered round a certain tank in the Zoological Gardens. He refolds his newspaper from time to time until deep in the advertisements. The waiters silently remove empty tumblers and tankards and replace them full. But My Grand commands profound attention from the room, and a neighbour, who afterwards proved a perfect Boanerges in debate, whispered to us concerning his vast attainments and high literary position."

To make use of words and to excite discussion were the chief objects of all good Cogers. Numberless briefless barristers used to frequent Cogers Hall in order to give their budding elocution, and hope of future pleadings, a chance of airing, so as to get into the right confidential way of addressing " My Lud " in the Courts of Justice. Actors also were occasionally heard to spout on subjects in which, in after years at any rate, they took not the slightest interest. The curious part about Cogers Hall was that usually the assembled audience were singularly impassive to the most eloquent declarations of the most fervid speaker and generally paid more attention to catching the waiter's eye in order to have their glasses replenshed.

In later years speakers with the wildest notions and disturbing ideas came upon the scene. They promulgated the principles, as they called them, which would cause the downfall of all Kings, Princes, Nations, and Peoples, whose theories did not accord with their own of what Democracy should mean. And Democracy to many of us who try to lead respectable lives — even in this day of great advancement—is a hard thing to understand.

It may be noted that the Cogers were at one time held in some esteem and attracted much attention, and they certainly encouraged the talents of many a rising orator, who later achieved celebrity. It is stated that on more than one occasion both Disraeli and Gladstone were silent guests at the debates, besides which many lesser men of their day were drawn towards the Hall to hear the discussions, which were always of a lively and exhilarating nature. The Cogers still exist, and have their regular members and their outside audiences.

LONDON'S CATCH PHRASES

THE once popular phrase, " I believe you, my boy ! " came from the *Green Bushes*, and was uttered nightly by Paul Bedford for several years ; and there is an old story told of a sailor who every time he came to England paid his annual visit to the Adelphi Theatre, and on each occasion was somewhat astounded to find that the *Green Bushes* was still being played, and was consequently greeted with, " I believe you, my boy." And " I believe you, my boy " gave happy exuberance to everybody in the metropolis. This is easily explained by the fact that whenever Benjamin Webster was at a loss for an attraction he put up the *Green Bushes*, with Madame Celeste in the chief part. " That's the Ticket," is said to have been first used on seeing a benefit ticket etched by Hogarth, for Spiller the actor, because it was exactly the thing he wanted.

" Go it, you cripples ; wooden legs are cheap." This comes from the beggars' scene in *Tom and Jerry*, the play which took all London to the Adelphi Theatre in the early days of the nineteenth century. Now as to " It's all very fine Mr. Fergusson, but you don't lodge here." Captain Fergusson was the companion of the Marquis of Waterford when that young nobleman made himself notorious for his practical jokes in the middle of the nineteenth century. In one of their adventures the two companions got separated and the Marquis found his way home to the house of his uncle the Archbishop of Armagh. The Marquis had gone to bed when a frightful and unseemly knocking came at the front door. The Marquis, suspecting who it was that was making all the disturbance, threw up the window and said : " It's all very fine, Mr. Fergusson, but you don't lodge here " ; and the saying for several years became popular.

THE BIRTH OF THE NATIONAL GALLERY

IN 1799 a significant quarrel occurred within the walls of the Royal Academy, at that time domiciled in the North Front of Somerset House. James Barry, Royal Academician, painter of the interesting cartoons that still adorn the walls of the room belonging to the Society of Arts in John Street, Adelphi, insisted with all the vehemence and earnestness of his excitable nature, that the surplus funds of the Academy should be expended in the purchase of pictures to form a Gallery of Old Masters, for the use of his pupils to aid them in design, composition, and colouring. The Academy did not approve this method of disposing of its funds, and in the end, matters went so far and feeling ran so high, that Barry was expelled from the body. But there is no doubt that he voiced a very wide-felt need : and had his contentions been urged with less violence, our National Gallery might have come into being sooner than it did.

Of course, at this time, and long before, private galleries of pictures existed in large numbers, but these were closed to the ordinary student. Earliest among these was the Royal Gallery of Charles I. This king greatly augmented the collection of pictures which Henry VIII. had begun ; he employed agents commissioned to buy pictures in many European towns; and the purchases made by Charles were marked by rare taste and judgment. He encouraged artists of renown to visit England, among them Vandyk and Rubens, and extended his constant

patronage to English painters. But the Civil Wars put an end to his encouragement of the arts; the King's pictures were sold; the taste for painting began to be regarded as sinful. In the eighteenth century connoisseurship became a mania, and the collection of objects of *vertu* a craze: but a less judicious taste was exercised, and taste was largely a matter of fashion. There existed, however, some very fine collections of pictures, occasionally accessible to art-students; but permission to visit these was, of course, capricious, and James Barry's plea for a Gallery of Old Masters had ample justification.

It was not until the year 1824 that the nucleus of the National Gallery was formed by a Parliamentary grant of £57,000 to purchase the pictures of Mr. Julius Angerstein. This gentleman,

who was of Russian extraction, had risen to wealth as a Lloyds' underwriter, and he had devoted his surplus wealth to philanthropy and the gratification of his cultivated taste for pictures, in the collection of which he had the advice of two presidents of the Royal Academy, Benjamin West and Sir Thomas Laurence.

When Angerstein died in 1823, leaving thirty-eight masterpieces to his heirs, a great crisis was seen to have arisen. The King of Bavaria wished to buy this glorious collection; so did the Prince of Orange, and others. A few influential men, led by Mr. Agar Ellis (afterwards Lord Dover), and Sir George Beaumont, the artist and friend of artists, stepped in with strong speech to the Government. "Buy this collection of pictures for the nation," said Beaumont, "and I will add mine." This, perhaps, turned the scale; Parliament granted £60,000 for the purchase of the pictures and for incidental expenses, and thus the nucleus of the National Gallery was secured.

For some years these pictures and others which were quickly added to them by purchase and bequests, were exhibited in Mr. Angerstein's house in Pall Mall, which stood on the site now covered by the fine building of the Reform Club. In 1826 Sir George Beaumont formally gave his pictures, valued at £7500, to the collection. In redeeming his promise he begged that he might be allowed to keep, till his death, one favourite picture, Claude's *Landscape with the Angel* (now

No. 61) which he loved so well that he had been in the habit of taking it about with him even in his travelling carriage.

As the collection increased, it was felt that it should have worthier times, until they were pulled down to make room for the National Gallery.

W. Wilkins, R.A., was entrusted with the task of designing the National Gallery. Perhaps no building has ever been subjected to more fiery criticism.

THE NATIONAL GALLERY PORTICO IN ITS OLD PLACE IN CARLTON HOUSE

habitation, and finally it was decided to build a special gallery in Trafalgar Square. The site selected was on the North side, where stood the King's Mews. This Mews had as early as the time of Richard II. been appropriated to the keeping of the King's hawks and falcons, when hawking and falconry were the favourite pastimes of king and nobles. The word "Mews" itself, is said to be derived from the "mewing" sound made by the young birds. In 1537 the Mews was burnt down and Henry VIII. had it rebuilt for the reception of his steeds; the King's Stables stood here from Tudor

It has been called the "National Cruet-Stand," a name suggested by the pepper-box-shaped cupolas with which it is crowned. We read that "this unhappy structure may be said to have everything it ought not to have, and nothing which it ought to have. It possesses windows without glass, a cupola without size, a portico without height, pepper-boxes without pepper, and the finest site in Europe without anything to show upon it." It must be admitted, however, that the architect was hampered by many trying conditions; the barracks in the rear were not to be interfered with, nor the view of the portico of St. Martin's Church intercepted. Furthermore, he had to introduce into his design a portico already constructed—the portico, namely, of Carlton House, the Prince Regent's Palace, which had been pulled down. Wilkins was unable to overcome these disadvantages, and the building, which cost the nation some £75,000, admittedly lacks proportion and dignity.

But a more serious charge is brought against the architect. The Royal Academy was to be housed under the same roof as the national collection of paintings, the eastern portion of the building being assigned to it for its school and its exhibition. Wilkins was a Royal Academician, and he is accused of clandestinely contriving the building to suit the purposes of the Academy. The *Times* in a leading article stated that the building had been constructed in a manner to diminish its utility as a receptacle for the national pictures, and even to endanger its safety in case of fire, in order that space and other conveniences might be appropriated to the Royal Academy. Thus from the very first moment that the national collection and the Royal Academy

THE "CLAUDE" (NOW IN THE NATIONAL GALLERY) WHICH SIR GEORGE BEAUMONT MADE HIS TRAVELLING COMPANION

were domiciled under one roof, quarrels began which lasted uninterruptedly for thirty years, increasing in violence as public notice was drawn to them by Press agitation, Parliamentary commissions, and protest of every kind. The public were eager to eject the Royal Academy from a building erected out of the national funds; they denounced the Academy as a royal, aristocratic, privileged, exclusive institution, opposed to social equality. On the other hand, the Academy was anxious to eject the nation's pictures, and secure the whole building to themselves.

Northumberland House in Trafalgar Square, not pulled down till 1874, was suggested as a suitable place for the housing of the national collection; in a letter to the *Builder* in 1846, Buckingham Palace, stated to be quite unsuitable as a royal residence, is said to have special appropriateness as a national gallery. The Academy contended that the National Gallery was unfavourable, on account of its smoky atmosphere, for the preservation of the nation's pictures—"though sufficiently salubrious for their own," adds an indignant writer. "From tenants on sufferance of half," he adds, "they endeavour to instal themselves as masters in fee simple of the whole."

The grounds of complaint against the Royal Academy seem to have been well founded. Want of space was frequently alleged for refusing gifts of pictures offered to the nation ; again, the public paid the Academy for admission to a building built out of the public funds ; and in 1855 the President of the Royal Academy and the Director of the National Gallery came to be united in one person— that of Sir Charles Eastlake—an arbiter against whose judgment there was practically no appeal. The *Times* waxed furious. "Another generation for aught the public is assured to the contrary, will see the daubs of contemporary mediocrity flaring against the walls which should have been graced by the standards of ancient perfection. For a period at present indefinite, Raphael, Sebastiano and Rubens, must give place to Redgrave, Maclise, and Uwins." In 1853 Gladstone had declared that the matter was one in which the public were deeply interested, and ought to be heard: but it was not till fifteen years after that the Academy was finally removed to Burlington House.

Then at last the National Gallery, as we know it to-day, had its birth. Enriched and enlarged by public-spirited benefactors who have left it priceless treasures of the past ; by artists who have bequeathed to the nation their own invaluable works ; by purchases, judicious on the whole : it stands to many Londoners as symbol of golden hours, of memories and joys not to be told in words.

EVANS'S SUPPER ROOMS

"EVANS' late Joy's" was the punning inscription on the lamp when this famous resort first came into existence at the west corner of the Convent Garden Piazza, and became a suitable successor to the old coffee houses, Will's and Button's, where Addison, Steele, Congreve, Pope, Dryden, and other wits used to resort. Evans's was always a resort of men about town. In Thackeray days, the proprietor was Paddy Green, who being a singer himself made music one of the chief attractions of the place for his guests. Amongst these were nearly the whole of the *Punch* staff, including the satirical Douglas Jerrold, Horace Mayhew, Mark Lemon and John Leech. To these should be added the names of the celebrated Serjeant Ballantine, the witty Judge James Hannay, Lionel Lawson of the *Daily Telegraph*, Albert Smith of "Mont Blanc Panorama"

fame, George Augustus Sala, and Charles Dickens. But it was Thackeray who immortalised the place under the name of the Cave of Harmony in "The Newcomes." Therein he gives a full description of Captain Costigan's unseemly conduct on one particular night when he takes Clive, his son, with him, and protested against an unseemly song that Costigan sang, and the dear old Colonel, in his fine British ardour, exclaimed against the disgrace of the wicked old rascal singing ribald songs, and called him a "hoary old sinner," and tells him to go home to his bed.

Lewis Melville, moreover, tells us in his excellent biography of Thackeray that it was outside Evans's that Lowell the American Minister, being on a visit to London, met Thackeray looking quite haggard and worn, and he asked him if he were ill.

"Come inside and I'll tell you all about it," said the novelist. "I have killed the Colonel." At a table in a quiet corner Thackeray took the MS. from his pocket and read the chapter

COLONEL NEWCOME AT EVANS'S
From the drawing by Richard Doyle

that records the death of Colonel Newcombe. When he came to the end, the tears, that had been swelling his lids, trickled down his face and the last word was almost an inarticulate sob."

Evans's Hotel, Supper Rooms, and to some extent Music Hall, was reconstructed from a fine mansion, built in the days of Charles the Second, which was long occupied by Sir Kenelm Digby, the famous physician, and then it passed into the Russell family.

In course of time W. C. Evans of Convent Garden Theatre, having been the manager of the Cider Cellar, in Maiden Lane, took possession of the premises, and using the large dining room as a Concert Hall, made quite a reputation with his musical entertainments. He prospered until 1844, when he retired and disposed of the property to Paddy Green, under whose rule the entertainments became so attractive, that a new Hall was built to which the former singing - room became a sort of vestibule. This vestibule was hung with portraits of celebrated actors and actresses, including Garrick, Mrs. Siddons, and the Kembles. And it is interesting to note that Fanny Kemble was born in a cottage that stood on the site of part of the altered club. On an old programme of Evans's, which was printed "For the Acceptance of Gentlemen visiting this Establishment," is the announcement that "Gentlemen are respectfully requested to encourage the Vocalists by attention; the 'CAFE' part of the Room being intended for Conversational Parties." This was a pretty strong hint for those who will talk while some one is playing or singing. The *Art Journal* in 1855 wrote, with some sense of feeling, about the artistic improvements in "Our places of public resort, which are of so uncommon a kind that we feel bound to devote a few words to a Supper Room recently constructed at the back of Evans's Hotel, Covent Garden, and which may be considered one of the most elegant rooms in London."

"What a jolly old place it was," says Eyre Pascoe. The very atmosphere of the place was old English. . . . Paddy Green's salutation was always "Ah! dear boy! How do you do, dear boy! . . ." He was cordial to everybody and everybody was cordial to him.

In 1867 a genial scribe wrote in *Once a Week*, an entertaining description of the famous Concert Rooms; he gives first of all some particulars of the rather vulgar performances, and the outrageous songs including those that roused the ire of Thackeray, one of which, springing from the Cider Cellar and the Coal Hole, was entitled, "My name it is Sam Hall," and other lyrics of like kidney. He then writes, "The surviving establishment half-supper-room and half-music-hall, and one of the 'lions of London' is situated at the Western extremity of Covent Garden Market. . . . Ladies are not admitted except on giving their names and addresses, and then only enjoy the privilege of watching the proceedings from behind a screen. The whole of the performances are sustained by the male sex, and an efficient choir of men and boys sings glees, and ballads, madrigals, and selections from Operas supplied on the piano and the harmonium."

This famous house, now occupied by a club devoted to sport, had been occupied as a private residence by some of the most eminent persons in literature, politics, and art from about the middle of the seventeenth century, including Nathaniel Crew, the last Lord Crew, and Lord Bishop of Durham from 1681 to 1689. It appears from the books of St. Paul's, Covent Garden, that "almost all the foundlings of the parish" were laid at the door of the house of the Bishop. After having been inhabited by Aubrey de Vere, the twentieth and last Earl of Oxford, it was occupied by the great antiquarian West, and later by Sir John Webb, at whose death the mansion was sold, and was converted in 1773 into a family hotel. A later proprietor advertised the hotel as being equipped "With stabling for one hundred noblemen and horses." At the beginning of the nineteenth century and some years afterwards the great singing-room to which we have already referred, became one of the most popular dining and coffee rooms in the metropolis. It was called the "Star" room from the number of men of rank who frequented it, and it has been stated on undoubted authority that it was no uncommon thing for nine Dukes besides other persons of title to dine there on one day. Of course all this was before the formation of clubs.

One day a gentleman entered the dining-room and ordered the waiter to bring two chops, inquiring at the same time: "John, have you a cucumber?" The waiter said he would step into Covent Garden and see. He returned saying there were a few at half a guinea a-piece. "Then buy two," was the reply. Evidently, Evans's, with its inducements to social intercourse, was the foundation of the many clubs that followed, for example Thackeray formulated the Fielding Club, there and soon after the Garrick was instituted and of course many others. In Thackeray's days Evans's Supper Rooms was capable of dining or supping about eight hundred people.

SALLY IN OUR ALLEY

some annuity." This last assertion made upon what grounds we know not, is certainly not accurate, for all through his days—some prosperous through his own efforts, some miserable through perhaps his own eccentricities—he was fighting with fortune.

It is true that the Saviles, recognising a responsibility that they could not decently ignore, gave him a fairly good musical education, which he turned to all possible advantage. A more or less appreciative writer, Helen Kendrick Johnson, says : " For many years he taught music in schools and families of the middle rank. He was a prolific writer of songs, and in 1729 (? 1720) published two volumes of poems, many of which are good, and one or two of which are widely known. His fame must rest upon the one song, ' Sally in our Alley,' which touched the popular heart." And now let Carey tell us the delightful story in his own quaint words. " A vulgar error having prevailed among many persons, who imagine Sally Salisbury to be the subject of this ballad, the author begs leave to undeceive and assure them it has not the least allusion to her, he being a stranger to the very name at the time the song was composed ; for, as innocence and virtue were ever the boundaries of his muse, so, in this little poem, he had no other view

COMEDY and tragedy are strangely blent in the history of this charming old London ballad. Henry Carey, the author-composer, has a double claim upon our consideration and affections, for he not only wrote and composed " Sally in our Alley," but he was the great-grandfather of Great Britain's most famous tragedian, Edmund Kean. Although Carey was more or less born near the purple, he was nursed in the home of hardship, and very largely bred in despair. If poets learn in sorrow what they teach in song, Carey had his full share of that sadness, which seems ever to be the bedfellow of genius battling with itself. All accounts agree that Carey was the natural son of George Savile, Marquis of Halifax, and was born about 1663, " whose family granted Carey a hand-

than to set forth the beauty of a chaste and disinterested passion in the lowest class of life. The real occasion was this : A shoemaker's 'prentice, making holiday with his sweetheart, treated her with a sight of Bedlam, the puppet-shows, the flying chairs, and all the elegancies of Moor-fields, from whence, proceeding to the farthing pyehouse, he gave her a collation of buns, cheesecakes, gam-mon of bacon, stuffed beef, and bottled ale, through all which scenes the author dodged them. Charmed with the simplicity of their courtship, he drew from what he had witnessed this little sketch of nature ; but, being then young and obscure, he was very much ridiculed by some of his acquaintance for this performance, which nevertheless made its way into the polite world, and amply compensated him by the applause of the *divine Addison*, who was pleased more than once to mention it with approbation.''

This song, with Carey's original music, was at once a success and was seized upon by all the vocalists of the day to sing in the burlettas, and at the afternoon and evening concerts then in vogue. It was first printed in black letter, broadside, somewhere about 1700. His first collected poems, in a small volume, were issued in 1720, '' Sally in our Alley '' being included. In 1739 there came from the press, in two folio volumns, '' The

HENRY CAREY,
THE AUTHOR OF ''SALLY IN OUR ALLEY''

Musical Century, in One Hundred English Ballads on various subjects and occasions, adapted to several characters and incidents in Human Life, and calculated for innocent conversation mirth, and instruction.'' All these were written and com-posed by Carey him-self, with his portrait affixed to the first tome. This caught the taste and fancy of song-lovers to such an extent that a second edition was called for in 1740, and a third in 1743.

An eminent musi-cal authority says, speaking of course of Henry Carey ; '' Of all his com-positions, the most popular, and that which will transmit the name of the com-poser to posterity, is his ballad of ' Sally in our Alley,' one of the most striking and original melodies that ever emanated from the brain of a musician.'' We have quoted this because there is an opinion generally accepted that the melody to which Carey's words are sung is not his. One writer tells us that although he composed a melody to it ('' Sally in our Alley '') '' of some merit '' it has been discarded, and his words fitted to '' The Country Lass,'' which was given in '' Pills to Purge Melancholy '' (1700) and in later editions. Now Carey's own melody was introduced into the '' Beggars' Opera '' as early as 1728, when it was first produced, and it is to be found in all the ballad operas from 1728 to 1760, when all these performances drew their musical values from the popular songs of the day and the English ballads of ancient times. It is true that Carey's tune was to some extent superseded by the other ballad, though both were concurrently in favour. Chappell says; " The two tunes curiously resemble each other . . . and this may have led, first to confusion, and afterwards to the adoption of the one most easy to sing." But as both songs were out together it seems to us that in all probability Carey's original melody may have suggested the second one. Anyhow the likeness between the melodies is very extraordinary.

Here is the first stanza of " The Country Lasse " ;

> Although I am a Countrey Lasse,
>   A loftie mind I beare-a ;
> I thinke myselfe as good as those
>   That gay apparell weare-a.
> My coate is made of honest Gray,
>   Yet is my skin as softe-a,
> As those that with the chiefest Waies
>   Do bathe their bodies oft-a.

Now, let us turn to the simple love song of humble life as Carey sets it forth, one of the prettiest ballads in the language ;

> Of all the girls that are so smart,
>   There's none like pretty Sally ;
> She is the darling of my heart,
>   And lives in our alley.
> There is no lady in the land
>   That's half as sweet as Sally ;
> She is the darling of my heart,
>   And lives in our alley.

and the last stanza ;

> My master and the neighbours all
>   Make game of me and Sally,
> And but for her I'd better be
>   A slave and row a galley :
> And when my sev'n long years are out,
>   Oh, then, I'll marry Sally,
> And then how happily we'll live,
>   But not in our alley.

One very prime and joyous part of lover-like existence, its popularity induced many a parody, burlesque and reply. We can trace six. One is worth a passing glance. It is styled " Sally's Lamentation ; or, the Answer to Sally."

> What pity 'tis, so bright a thought
>   Should e'er become so common ;
> At ev'ry corner brought to naught
>   By ev'ry bawling woman !
> I little thought when you began
>   To write of charming Sally,
> That ev'ry brat would sing so soon,
>   " She lives in our alley ! "

Carey was a man of many good qualities, character, and small benefactions. He was the principal projector of the fund for decayed musicians, their widows and children. In announcing a benefit concert to be given to him, the London *Daily Post* of December 3, 1730, whimsically said ; " At our friend, Harry Carey's benefit to-night, the powers of music, poetry, and painting assemble in his behalf ; he being an admirer of the three arts. The body of musicians meet in the Haymarket, whence they march in grand order, preceded by a magnificent moving organ, in form of a pageant, accompanied by all the kinds of musical instruments ever in use, from Tubal Cain until the present day." They were all supposed to foregather at Temple Bar and proceed to Covent Garden, where, after taking refreshments at the Bedford Arms, they were to march to the theatre. Well, he had a good benefit.

Careless writers declare that he committed suicide in Great Warner Street, Clerkenwell, October 4, 1743, and that " he put a period to a life which had been led without reproach, at the advanced age of eighty." The impulse of this supposed act has been variously assigned to pecuniary embarrassment, domestic unhappiness, and the malevolence of some of his fellow professors. Notwithstanding that this tragic event has been often repeated with many embellishments the manner of his death has never been clearly explained. Moreover, in the *Daily Post* of October 5, 1743, we read : " Yesterday morning Mr. H. Carey, well known to the musical world for his droll compositions, got out of bed from his wife in perfect health, and was soon after found dead. He has left six children behind him." In the same newspaper on November 17, 1743, an advertisement announces a performance on that evening at Covent Garden Theatre " For the Benefit of the Widow and Four Small Children of the late Henry Carey." The widow, who was Carey's second wife, is described as being " left entirely destitute of any provision."

Let us hope that the widow and family of such an excellent man and delightful writer were well provided for, by the public and his professional brethren.

SWISS COTTAGE

THE name of Swiss Cottage—one of the best-known omnibus termini of London—has a pleasant exotic sound, and must often have aroused the curiosity of Londoners as to its origin. That origin is sufficiently explained by the drawing, given on page 156, of the well-known Finchley Road tavern as it appeared about 1840. It was then kept by one Frank Redmond, well known as a connoisseur of the Ring, and as the reputed " best dog-fancier in the Kingdom." The house was considered a delightful " crib " by sporting men, and Frank Redmond's personality was no small part of its attraction. To-day the " Swiss Cottage " is very unlike its original, but it still has a smack of rurality and wayside charm. The associations of the spot cannot be given more truthfully than in the juicy language of a writer of seventy years ago. The Swiss Cottage, he says, is a " delightful summer retreat, and

A merrier, nor a wiser man,
To spend an hour withal,

if it be on sporting subjects, and the moves being made on the fancy board, than the worthy host, it would be hard to name : nor is there a better conducted house within the bills of mortality. It is, in every sense of the word, a snug, complete crib, replete with comfort and convenience ; and to those who are fond of sports of every description, it will be found a very desirable house to obtain information of the best kind, the worthy host generally possessing the earliest intelligence of every event which is on the *tapis.*

" Frank's pugilistic career was not a brilliant one, although at one period he was esteemed so highly as to be matched against the 'Star of the East,' Barney Aaron, with whom he contended on two several occasions ; but the flag of the ' Hebrew race ' (there is another citation for the author of ' Coningsby') floated in the ascendant. Frank, although victory but once smiled on him in his pitched contests within the P.R. ropes, was, and is, far from a smatterer, theoretically or practically, in the ' noble art of self-defence ': although mellowing years have rolled by since he fought ' in his hot blood of youth.' Frank was born on the 26th of Feb., 1803, and therefore now numbers forty-one summers.

"Well versed, then, in all sporting matters is Frank Redmond; and behind a yard of clay, and over a glass of the best Cognac, the proprietor of this hostelrie will discuss with you the merits of a Derby nag, the pluck, game, bravery, and stamina of the aspirant the first water. Thus much for the indoor and creature comforts of the Swiss Cottage; of the outdoor we may say that the grounds and gardens are immensely attractive to visitors, and the neighbourhood the scene of frequent trials of pedestrian rivalry.

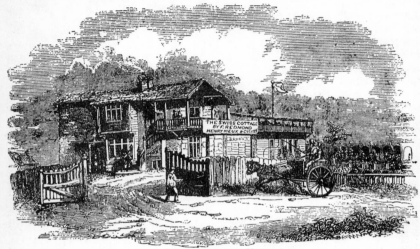

SWISS COTTAGE SEVENTY YEARS AGO

for fistic fame, the construction and merits of a prize-wherry, the skill of a batsman and cricket-bowler, or detail to you the speed and breeding of a crack greyhound.

"On this last theme Frank will become a monopolist: you have touched the chord that will vibrate, for on the subject of the canine species he will become as learned as England's er-mined chief justice on a knotty point of law, or as eloquent as Demosthenes himself. A better judge of the merits, breeding, and qualities of the dog does not exist, and Frank is reputed to be the best dog-fancier in the kingdom, and on that point is generally consulted by the aristocracy and Corinthians of

"Such are a few of the many induce-ments, and we own they are no small ones, which prompt us to notice 'the Cottage.' We say nothing about the accommodation offered to the guests, for it were a libel on Frank's adminis-tration to assert that they are not of the first-rate order; and he must be an epicure, indeed, who could find fault with the *cuisine* of the establishment. Had the Swiss Cottage existed in Shakespeare's days, we should have been inclined to assert that it was from some such a house as this that the 'fat-ribbed knight' first acquired his idea of the comfort a man feels in taking 'mine ease at mine inn.'"

THE GHOST OF BERKELEY SQUARE

AND SOME ATTEMPTS TO LAY IT

THE personality of a London ghost is sometimes quite as persistent as that of the most famous Londoner. One of the most persistent ghosts of all was the famous haunter of No. — Berkeley Square, concerning whom a most minute investigation was held some thirty years ago in the pages of *Notes and Queries*. At that time the man in the street knew very well that a young servant girl had lost her reason, owing to having seen something in one of the bedrooms of the house, and that a young man had soon afterwards died of terror in the same room.

Challenged to supply the facts of the case a correspondent pointed out that No. — Berkeley Square had belonged to an eccentric old miser who had refused to spend money on paint and whitewash. Stories, it seemed, had spread willingly about No. — . But when the old miser's two maid-servants were questioned about odd noises, they replied that they had heard none. Asked if they had seen ghosts, they laughed and answered : " We never see'd none." This was all very tame and the next letter in *Notes and Queries* merely dealt jocosely with the topic of soap, paint and whitewash, after which a correspondent contributes some facts in regard to the mysterious house.

The last name of any occupier of the house, appearing in the London Directory, was that of a certain Honourable Miss ——, who died at the age of ninety in 1859. For the next twenty-one years, it seemed, No. — Berkeley Square had preserved the appearance of an unoccupied house.

This correspondent goes on to quote from a communication by the late Lord Lyttelton to *Notes and Queries* in 1872 : " It is quite true that there is a house in Berkeley Square (No. —) said to be haunted, and long unoccupied on that account. There are strange stories about it, into which this deponent cannot enter. LYTTELTON." Furthermore, in the *Weekly Times* of May 4, 1873, a paragraph appeared stating that a warrant had been issued against a Mr. Myers of No. — Berkeley Square for the prosaic delinquency of having failed to pay his taxes.

All this, however, failed to satisfy the gentleman who had revived the topic in *Notes and Queries* and, after alluding to Miss Rhoda Broughton, the novelist, he once more clamours stoutly for the truth. Then, and not till then, a correspondent comes forward with suitable particulars " extracted from an original letter (lately in my possession) addressed to the late Bishop Thirlwall." This letter, creepy beyond the wildest dreams of the Fat Boy in Dickens, was written on January 22, 1871, and runs as follows :

" Ghosts remind me that I never told you a story Mrs. —— related to us when she was here last, about the haunted house in Berkeley Square ; S—— pointed it out to me last spring.

" The dilapidated, forsaken, dusty look of this house quite suits a reputation for ghosts. Lady M—— declares that the house is watched strictly by police. None of its inhabitants ever cross its doorstep, and false coining is supposed to be carried on there, but has never been detected. Miss H—— (who repeated the tale to Mrs. F——) was told by some R. C. friends of hers that a family they knew hired the haunted house—wherever it is—in Berkeley

for him, and the housemaid was either sleeping there, or else still busy with her preparations, at 12 o'clock the night before his arrival. The hour had

THE GHOST OF BERKELEY SQUARE

Square for a London season, as there were daughters to be brought out, one of whom was already engaged. They spent a short time in the house without finding out anything amiss; then they invited the young lady's lover to join them, and the next bedroom, which they had not occupied, was made ready

no sooner struck than piercing shrieks were heard, loud enough to rouse the whole household; they rushed upstairs, flung open the door of the haunted room, and found the unfortunate housemaid lying at the foot of the bed in strong convulsions. Her eyes were fixed, with a stare of expressive terror upon a remote corner of the chamber, and an agony of fear seemed to possess her, yet the bystanders saw nothing. They took her to St. George's Hospital where she died in the morning, refusing to the last to give any account of what she had seen ; she could not speak of it, she said; it was far too horrible.

"The expected guest arrived that day. He was told the story and that it was arranged that he should not occupy the haunted room. He voted it all nonsense, and insisted upon sleeping there. He however agreed to sit up until past twelve and to ring if anything unusual occurred. 'But,' he added, 'on no account come to me when I ring first because I may be unnecessarily alarmed, and seize the bell on the impulse of the moment ; wait until you hear a second ring.' His betrothed expostulated in vain. He did not believe in apparitions, and he would solve the mystery. She listened in a misery of suspense, when the time of trial drew near. At last the bell rang once, but faintly. Then there was an interval of a few dreadful minutes, and a tremendous peal sounded through the house. Every one hurried breathless to the haunted room. They found the guest exactly in the same place where the dead housemaid had lain, convulsed as she was, his eyes fixed in horror upon the same spot where hers had been fixed the night before, and like her, he never revealed his experiences. 'They were too awful,' he said, 'even to mention.' The family left the house at once. I shall be happy to supply privately the names here left blank."

Naturally enough, one of the clever correspondents to *Notes and Queries* ruthlessly pulls this typical ghost story to pieces, calling it among other things "an intolerable sequence of hearsay," while a Head Porter of Brasenose College, Oxford, adds this first-hand note : "May I be allowed to say that I entered the house, — Berkeley Square, London, on March 20, 1851, in the service of the late Miss ——, who died in May 1859. During the nine years I was in the house, and at all hours alone, I saw no greater ghost than myself." This is distinctly damping, but the next week a correspondent coolly states that he has read the ghost story in the pages of *Temple Bar*. Obviously, there is now a supreme arbiter for the long-drawn wrangle and the ghost story is forwarded to Rhoda Broughton, who writes as follows : "You are mistaken in supposing that my story has anything to do with the so-called Berkeley Square Mystery. Its incidents happened, as I was told by my informant, in the country, and I clothed it in fictitious characters and transposed it to London, which I have since regretted, as so many people have thence assumed that it must refer to the house in Berkeley Square. The slip you enclose is clearly my story mistakenly applied to a wrong house. I am sorry to be unable to assist you in your search, but I can at least divert you from a wrong track."

That closed the correspondence in *Notes and Queries*, but myth-making, even in these later days, is not easily killed. Many a reader must have taken heart at the words "my informant," and if things like that really happened in the country, something odd *must have happened* in No. — Berkeley Square ! At all events, the tale survives as one of the very best ghost stories of modern London.

PAUL'S CROSS
"THE MOST NOTED AND SOLEMN PLACE IN THE NATION"

SO the historian of St. Paul's Cathedral describes the site of Paul's Cross. And yet for over three hundred and fifty years this spot remained without any distinguishing mark or memorial. To-day a high column, surmounted by a figure of St. Paul—on the north side outside the Cathedral—marks the site : but we cannot help regretting that the alternative proposal made by the donor, to erect a facsimile of the Old Cross and Pulpit was not carried out. There are several old prints showing us this " pulpit-cross of timber, mounted upon steps of stone, and covered with lead," picturing for us many of the dramatic scenes in its dramatic history ; and although the varying centuries saw differences in the size and structure of the pulpit, emphasis requires to be laid on the fact that it was as a place of preaching and of penance that Paul's Cross was famous.

The history of Paul's Cross belongs to the history of Old St. Paul's. Old St. Paul's was burned in the Great Fire of London, 1666 ; Paul's Cross was taken down only thirty years earlier by order of the Parliament, which condemned all the crosses about London to be taken away as relics of Popish superstition.

There are, it seems, certain spots consecrated throughout the centuries to the performance of grave and notable functions. Even before the foundations of Old St. Paul's were laid, the site of Paul's Cross was an important gathering-place for the people. Folkmoots, or meetings of the folk, were called here both before and after the Cross was set up ; proclamations were made, both civic and ecclesiastical. We can assign no certain date for the erection of the Cross, but from a document of the reign of Henry III, we gather that it had been then long in existence ; when the spot on which it stood was taken into Paul's Churchyard (*tempo* Edward III.), the Cross came to be used more definitely for ecclesiastical purposes. We read of sermons being regularly preached there from 1361. The Lord Mayor and Aldermen, the City Guilds, high dignitaries of the Church, and sometimes royalty itself, attended the preaching at Paul's Cross.

People of rank were provided with seats—some in an outer gallery of the church, and some on benches ranged before the pulpit. But most of the congregation stood, and Paul's Cross retained to the end its democratic character ; it continued the most important place in London of popular, and sometimes of political, appeal.

We have still the substance of a famous sermon in which the preacher urged the claims of the Duke of Gloucester (afterwards Richard III.) to the throne. It was arranged that Richard should appear at a certain dramatic moment of the discourse, and it was hoped that the people would be moved to cry, King Richard ! King Richard ! But, as the chronicler relates, the people were so far from crying King Richard ! that they stood as they had been turned into stone, for wonder of this shameful sermon. After that, " the preacher got him home . . . and kept himself out of sight like an owl."

And as late as 1553 we read of Ridley, Bishop of Rochester, preaching a sermon in which " he vehemently persuaded the people in the title of Lady Jane, late proclaimed Queen, and inveighed earnestly against the title of Lady Mary."

The political interest of Paul's Cross is however inconsiderable as compared with its religious interest. At its foot were enacted broad, striking episodes which illustrate forcibly the cruder sides of religious feeling and of the religious struggle in England. An open-air meeting always necessitates a somewhat popular exposition of the subject in hand. The wide gesture, the homely instance, were needed to make impression upon the uncultivated populace that formed the bulk of the congregation. When possible, the moral

PAUL'S CROSS
From an Old and Early Print

was pointed by visible and sensational example. Have you failed to keep Lent ? Then you shall stand on a scaffold at Paul's Cross below the pulpit before all the people, holding one pig, ready dressed, in your hand, and having another pig, ready dressed, upon your head. Have you married two wives, when, as a priest, you should not have had even one ? Then you shall do public penance on the same platform, wrapped in a sheet, and having a burning taper in your hand.

To-day the State has taken upon itself the punishment of wrong-doing ; but in mediæval times the Church prescribed penance for many sins, and penance was regarded as a purging process, while punishment only hardens. But though we may admit that penance may sometimes have been used with good effect as a deterrent on an ignorant populace—just as we set a boy in a corner with a fool's-cap on his head—it was too often imposed upon those who differed merely in religious opinion from the ruling powers. By far the greater number of cases of penance at Paul's Cross were performed by recanting Lollards or other "heretics." Their story belongs to the most terrible part of the religious history of England—the bitter persecution practised by the Church upon the Reformers — and afterwards, the cruel retaliations made by the Reformers upon the Romanists. Many acts of penance are recorded in Foxe's " Book of Martyrs." The heretics were paraded in the procession, bearing faggots, or having faggots about their necks (as a symbol of the fate they had escaped, of burning), and then they were made to stand on the platform below the preacher, still holding the faggots. As many as twelve and thirteen Lollards so stood at one time before the pulpit, " shrined with faggots." Sometimes they were compelled to wear ever after the badge of a faggot in flames on their clothes. The preacher no doubt pointed his discourse at the penitents standing below the pulpit, sometimes, we read, actually striking them with a rod. The " Holy Maid of Kent," whose ravings against the divorce of Queen Catherine

PREACHING AT PAUL'S CROSS (*From an Old and Later Print*)

had brought upon her the enmity of Henry VIII., did penance at Paul's Cross ; but her abjuration did not save her life. She was beheaded, and her head stuck on London Bridge.

For now the tide had turned ; the Church was losing its power ; Henry had assumed the title of Defender of the

Faith ; the monasteries were being plundered, and the monks and nuns banished. One striking little scene, one typical episode, illustrates the corruption into which the Church had fallen, and the changed attitude that was coming over the world. There was at Boxley in Kent a wonderful Rood or Crucifix ; the figure of Christ on the Cross used to move its eyes and shake its beard, and sometimes to nod its head and bow with its whole body to those who knelt before it, bringing offerings. In 1538 one Nicholas Partridge, discovered that the figure was worked by wheels manipulated by the priests. The image was taken down, and exhibited at Maidstone and other towns to the scorn and amusement of vast crowds. At last it was brought to Paul's Cross, and elevated on a scaffold, so as to be seen by all the people. There the figure went through its part, with all the machinery exposed; bending its back, nodding, drawing itself up ; till on one Sunday the congregation, mortified that they had been so long deceived, and excited by the warmth of the preacher, threw down the wooden block into the thickest of the throng. " Instantly a confused outcry of many voices arose ; the idol is pulled about, is broken, is pulled one piece from another, is torn into a thousand fragments, and is finally consigned to the flames."

So we come to the era of the Reformation, when the preaching at Paul's Cross reached its highest importance. The age of unquestioning faith had passed, the age of inquiry had come ; the preachers had now to convince their hearers of the truth of their doctrines, to re-establish confidence, to explain new and difficult tenets. The Romanists and the Reformers, as each happened to be in power, seized upon the pulpit at Paul's Cross as the most advantageous point of vantage for popular appeal.

At Paul's Cross was fought out, more fiercely than in any other quarter, the conflict between the old faith and the new. In 1534 " every Sunday at Paul's Cross preached a Bishop, declaring the Pope not to be supreme head of the Church." In Edward VI.'s reign the pulpit was filled by the most eminent preachers of the Reformation. Latimer's sermons, which remain to-day unequalled for shrewd wit and homely illustration, were delivered at Paul's Cross, and among them the famous " Sermon of the Plough." In Mary's reign, behold, another change, and Bishop Gardiner preaching at the Cross ; Cardinal Pole came by water from Lambeth to hear him, and landed at Paul's Wharf, and from thence to Paul's Church, with a cross, two pillars and two pole-axes of silver borne before him ; and about eleven o'clock, King Philip himself arrived by land from Westminster. Another turn of the time-wheel, and we find Elizabeth at Paul's Cross. A special closet was made for the Queen, in the North wall of the Cathedral, that she might hear preached the Thanksgiving Sermon for the destruction of the Spanish Armada.

Charles I., in 1630, was the last sovereign to attend a sermon at Paul's Cross ; and this was almost the last sermon preached there. For the opinions of the Puritans were gaining ground, and all the crosses in London and Westminster fell by Parliamentary decree. But it is a thrilling experience, to stand for a moment or two beneath the modern memorial that marks its site, and to let all the drama and all the passion, and all the tragedy of Paul's Cross crowd into the memory.

SIR WALTER RALEIGH AT ISLINGTON

"MERRY Islington " was scarcely a village in Elizabeth's time. The Islington fields were still the great playing-fields for Londoners, the great archery grounds where citizens came out to shoot with the long-bow—though even in the reign of Henry VIII. the rich had begun to enclose the fields, and it had needed the cry of " Shovels and Spades ! " and a great horde of London apprentices, armed with these implements, to level the hedges and fill the ditches. At this period the village consisted of a few farmhouses ; but it was not till the seventeenth and eighteenth centuries that Londoners flocked to the Islington dairies for the creams, custards, cakes, and gooseberry fools for which the place was famous.

Earlier in the reign of the great Queen the nobles and gentry began to make themselves country-boxes in the neighbourhood of Islington, delighted with its sweet and wholesome air and its pleasant prospect over the valley of Holloway towards Highgate Hill. Fantastic enough were some of these houses, with towers, turrets, and ornamental chimney-pots; others were built in the simple and beautiful Tudor style, decorated within with oak panels and stained-glass windows. One of the greatest of Englishmen—scholar, traveller, soldier, courtier, poet—chose Islington to build himself a residence, returned here after the glitter of courts, rested here after the fierce turmoil of discovery and adventure, studied here, wrote here, smoked here too some of the first tobacco ever smoked in England; for Islington was at one time the home of Sir Walter Raleigh, and his house was actually standing there until the year 1830, when it was pulled down. Prints of it are still to be seen, after it had become the Pied Bull Inn and grown dilapidated, but it retained traces to the end of having been a commodious and comfortable mansion —very different indeed from the narrow prison quarters in which its illustrious owner was afterwards for twelve years to be incarcerated. The site of the Pied Bull Inn is behind the present Frederick Street.

A pleasant story is told of Sir Walter in connection with his most popular discovery, and it is possible that the event actually took place at his Islington residence. "Sitting one day, in a deep meditation, with a pipe in his mouth, he inadvertently called to his man to bring him a tankard of small ale; the fellow, coming into the room, threw all the liquor into his master's face, and running downstairs bawled out, '*Fire! Help! Sir Walter has studied till his head is on fire, and the smoke bursts out of his head and nose!*' It is added that after this affair Sir Walter made it no secret, and took two pipes just before he went to be beheaded." The sign-post of "Sir Walter Raleigh and his Man," depicting this anecdote, used occasionally to be seen over tobacconists' shops. It was in 1583 that Raleigh introduced tobacco into England, and we read that a few years after smoking-houses were as common in London as beer-houses.

In the Pied Bull Inn was a stained-glass window looking from the parlour into the garden. The window had a border of sea-horses, parrots, and leaves representing the tobacco plant, and there can be little doubt that Raleigh himself had this window put in, and chose these emblems as representative of his life. What scenes they must have conjured up before his eyes, in that quiet village, of stormy unknown seas and gorgeous tropical forests, of the delight of battle and the zest of discovery! It is a pitiable thing that Raleigh's house at Islington has not been preserved to the nation, for few Englishmen have had a personality more rich and many-coloured, more vital and daring.

After a print from "Real Life in London"

ALMACK'S ASSEMBLIES

TOWARDS the end of the eighteenth century Almack's Club, established for ladies and gentlemen in King Street, St. James's, took its name from the proprietor, a Scotchman, whose real cognomen was Macall, but by a syllabic transposition he converted it into the title that became more or less famous. According to Major Arthur Griffith's gossipy volumes, Almack's was a club for the two sexes, with this peculiarity that the ladies nominated and voted for the gentlemen and *vice versa*. Some very prominent people, however, were black-balled because the ladies seemed to have the casting vote. Balls took place once a week for three months of the season at a subscription of ten pounds ten shillings, and supper was given ; but to obtain admission was the most difficult trial, for the most vigorous and capricious fancy ruled at the ballot box. Men's tickets were not transferable, and vouchers for them were not easy to obtain. Almack's building, adjacent to the St. James's Theatre, was afterwards known as Willis's Rooms, where many great events took place. Almack, himself, was a tavern keeper, and he opened this establishment in 1765, with a ball at which the Duke of Cumberland, the hero of Culloden, was present. Almack, the most obsequious of men and a great adventurer in clubs, knew which side to work. He was very largely associated with Brooks's Club, and amassed a small fortune out of it. As far back as 1768 an advertisement appeared in the *Morning Advertiser* which ran as follows : " Mr. Almack humbly begs leave to acquaint the nobility and gentry, subscribers to the assembly in King Street, St. James's, that the first meeting will be Thursday, 24th inst. (November).—N.B. Tickets are ready to be delivered at the assembly room." From a satire on the ladies of the age published in 1773 we read

Now lolling at the Coterie and " Whites,"
We drink and game away our days and nights.
    *   *   *   *
No censure reaches them at Almack's ball;
Virtue, religion—they're above them all.

Just previously to this Walpole writes to Montagu : "There is a new Institution that begins to make, and if it proceeds; will make a considerable noise. It is a club of *both* sexes to be erected at Almack's on the model of that of the men of White's. Mrs. Fitzroy, Lady Pembroke, Mrs. Meynell, Lady Molyneux, Miss Pelham and Miss Lloyd are the foundresses. I am ashamed to say I am of so young and fashionable society ; but as they are people I live with, I choose to be idle rather than morose. I can go to a young supper without forgetting how much sand is run out of the hour glass."

Mrs. Boscawen, writing to her friend Mrs. Delany, in Dublin, of this club of lords and ladies, mentions that Ladies Rochford, Harrington, and Holderness were actually black-balled, as also was the Duchess of Bedford, who was subsequently admitted ; but Lady Pembroke, who first started this particular club at an ordinary tavern, was so imperious that even the great Lord March and Brook Boothby were black-balled by the ladies much to their astonishment, but ever so much more to the regret of the ladies afterwards. At Almack's the play ran just as high as it did amongst the men at their own particular clubs. Avarice and extravagance led both men and women on to very great extremes. Mrs. Delany exclaims, with very great indignation, that many men benefited by this craze, like Mr. Thynne, "who has won this year so considerably that he has paid off all his debts, bought a house and furnished it, disposed of his horses, hounds, &c.; and struck his name out of all expensive subscriptions. But what a *horrid reflection* it must be to an honest mind to build his fortune on the *ruin* of others." Still the lady rulers en-

couraged gambling, and we can quite imagine that they were well able to take care of themselves.

Lady Clementina Davies writes in her "Recollections of Society": "At Almack's in 1814 the rules were very strict. Scotch reels and country dances were in fashion. The lady patronesses were all powerful. No visitor was to be admitted after twelve o'clock, and once when the Duke of Wellington arrived a few minutes after that hour he was refused admission." To read of the stories of the great men who knocked in vain at Almack's outer door, reminds one of Thomas Moore's Peri at the Gate of Paradise, and her pathetic desire for admission. Princes and princesses had the greatest difficulty in being admitted to the privileges of this very exclusive assembly, and the lesser folk were absolutely ignored. To get an introduction to Almack's required a very considerable amount of diplomacy, because the female government was so paramount, and therefore under the caprices of that delightful inconsequence which was not altogether innocent of a few feminine prejudices and abuses. It seems an odd thing, and yet not odd, to have serious knowledge of the fact that the ladies of the committee had their own absolute specified notions even as to the kind of trousers a gentleman should wear on entering their premises. Every man as a matter of fact was compelled, if he desired to associate with these charming ladies, to wear knee breeches and silk stockings as well as buckled shoes.

In 1815 Lady Jersey, who had been living in Paris for some years, introduced into London the Quadrille, of which a very quaint illustration is in Captain Gronow's work. The first performers of this new dance were the Marquis of Worcester, Lady Jersey, Clanronald Macdonald, and Lady Worcester. Then at the same famous assembly rooms was introduced within a few months the " mazy Waltz." The quadrille succeeded at once, but the waltz did not come into great favour until, strangely enough, Lord Palmerston, the great Prime Minister, was seen describing an infinite number of circles with Madame de Lieven. After this Baron de Neumann set the fashion by constantly dancing with the celebrated Princess Esterhazy, and, as Gronow says in his " Recollections," the waltzing mania having turned the heads of society generally, descended to their feet, and the waltz was practised in the morning in certain noble mansons in London with unparalleled assiduity.

To revert to the gambling, every indulger in the game was expected to keep at least thirty guineas on the table in front of him, and very often there was as much as ten thousand pounds in gold on the baize. To quote Mr. Ralph Nevill : " The players, before sitting down at the gaming table, removed their embroidered clothes and substituted frieze greatcoats, or turned their coats inside out for luck. They also put on short leather sleeves to save their lace ruffles ; and in order to guard their eyes from the light and keep their hair in order, they wore high-crowned straw hats, with broad brims adorned with flowers and ribbons ; whilst to conceal their emotions they also wore shades or masks."

In July 1821 a splendid Ball was given at Almack's, in honour of the Coronation of George IV., by the special ambassador from France, the Duc de Grammont. The King himself wa present, attended by his brothers, the Duke of Wellington, and many courtiers. This entertainment was a very great success, and the quadrille, the cotillion, and the waltz were some of the features of the evening, and very soon after became attractive. Many great singers and actors, including Mrs. Billington (the singer), John Braham, and Signor Naldi gave various performances, and also in 1844 Charles Kemble, who gave his readings from Shakespeare.

CORONATION ROBES AND HUMOURS

NEVER did the sublime and the ridiculous come nearer to each other in a Coronation ceremony, than on the occasion when George IV. received the crown of England. The scale of expense incurred may be judged by the fact that his Majesty's coronation robes cost £25,000, a sum which no British monarch would now spend on a Coronation costume. But the robes are in existence, and were in part worn by George V. at his Coronation in 1911.

George IV. nearly broke down under their weight during the Coronation ceremony. So loyal a writer as Dean Stanley does not disguise the ridiculous side of the affair :

The heat of the day and the fatigue of the ceremony almost exhausted the somewhat portly Prince, who was found cooling himself, stripped of all his robes, in the Confessor's Chapel, and at another part of the service was only relieved by smelling salts accidentally provided by the Archbishop's secretary. During the long ceremony of the homage, which he received with visible expressions of disgust or satisfaction, as the peers of the contending parties came up, he was perpetually wiping his streaming face with innumerable handkerchiefs, which he handed in rapid succession to the Primate, who stood beside him.

The cause of his Majesty's fatigue was undoubtedly, in large part, the weight of the Coronation robes which he had designed for his own adornment with the professional aid of Sir Thomas Lawrence. Mr. Richard Dancy describes them as follows: "To a tight-fitting satin suit in sixteenth-century style, he added a neo-classical mantle of blue velvet, embroidered in gold, and lined with ermine. It was prodigiously long, and so

GEORGE IV. IN HIS CORONATION ROBES

heavy that, although supported by eight eldest sons of the peers, his Majesty, by the time he reached the altar—he had walked from Westminster Hall—very nearly fainted. Every inch a king he looked, and Lawrence, who afterwards painted him several times in his Coronation robes, declared him the 'finest made man' he had ever seen."

The crushing weight of George IV.'s Coronation robes is further attested by a curious conversation at Hatfield House reported by Richard Redgrave,

in his memoirs, as follows: "In the course of an after-dinner conversation on the rather curious subject of the advantages of perspiration, Lord Salisbury remarked that he was one of the train-bearers at the Coronation of George IV., and that the weight of the robes gave each of the bearers a Turkish bath of some hours' duration. I added that the King seemed equally to suffer on that occasion (I was in the Abbey and close to him). 'Ah!' said my lord, 'the King had an hour's rest and freedom from his robes; for after the Coronation he retired for a time before he left the Abbey, and Lord ——, going into the room which had been fitted up as a dressing-room, found the king walking up and down in a state of nudity, but with the crown on his head.'"

Nor did the most gorgeous of Coronations fail to produce other distresses. Its interruption by the arrival of Queen Caroline, who vainly sought to make good her declared resolve to be present, is matter of history. Attended by Lord Hood, the unhappy Queen tried to pass the military, failed, and retired to the street and to the sympathies of the crowd. Not so well known is the story of the embarrassment of the King when, after the Gargantuan banquet in Westminster Hall, it was time for him to return to Carlton House. The indignation of the crowd at the Queen's exclusion had increased hourly, and now, at eleven o'clock at night, the King was warned that if he attempted to return to the palace by the ordinary route he would be in danger of insult and obstruction. Lord Albemarle, in his " Fifty Years of My Life," tells the rest : " To avert this danger it was suggested that Tothill Fields would be the safer way home. But who knew anything of a region of such ill-repute ? Who but my schoolfellow De Ros, then a lieutenant of Life Guards, and forming that day one of his Majesty's escort ? To him was consigned the pilotage of the Royal cortège ; under his guidance it proceeded up Abingdon Street, along Millbank, through the Halfpenny Hatch and the Willow Walk, leaving the ' Seven Chimneys ' on its right. It next arrived at ' Five Fields,' now Eaton Square, passed through Grosvenor Place and by Constitution Hill to the back entrance of Carlton Palace, which they did not reach till early in the morning. The King, as well might be supposed, was horribly nervous, and kept constantly calling to the officers of the escort to keep well up to the carriage windows."

Meanwhile the mob was dangerous to its own units. There were no police, and an eye-witness of the affair draws a comical picture of Townsend, the famous Bow Street " runner "—of whose career an account has already been given in this collection—advancing before the procession, and hallooing with all his might, " Gentlemen and ladies, take care of your pockets, you are surrounded by thieves," to the intense amusement of the crowd. " Amidst the crowd a respectable gentleman from the Principality hallooed out in his provincial tongue, ' Mr. Townsend, Mr. Townsend, I have been robbed of my gold watch and purse, containing all my money. What am I to do ? What am I to do to get home ? I have come two hundred miles to see the sight, and instead of receiving satisfaction or hospitality I am robbed by those cut-throats called the swell mob.' This eloquent speech had a very different effect upon the mob than the poor Welshman had reason to expect ; for all of a sudden the refrain of the song, ' Home, Sweet Home,' was shouted by a thousand voices, and the mob bawled out, ' Go back to your goats, my good fellow.' "

Such were the incidents of a Coronation which, unlike any that has been enacted since, or is ever likely to be, was designed for the monarch's personal display and glory.

BENJAMIN WEBSTER AT THE ADELPHI

DURING his twenty-seven years reign as manager of the Adelphi Theatre, in the Strand, and as actor and dramatist, Benjamin Webster won many triumphs and was quite the most versatile actor of his age. He was born in Bath as far back as 1798, but lived all his life in London, where he died in 1882. In many respects he was a most extraordinary man, and on one occasion when he had quarrelled with Macready he sent him a challenge to fight a duel on Wimbledon Common. The great William Charles Macready replied that he would accept the challenge when his correspondent had taken rank as a tragedian by a successful performance of Hamlet. Webster first took over the management of the Adelphi Theatre in 1844 and he inaugurated his venture by playing the leading part in *Don Cæsar de Bazan*, whom not even Charles Fechter could surpass in his swift changes from comedy to tragedy. From a business point of view one of his finest productions was the *Green Bushes*, by John Baldwin Buckstone. So long a time did the drama remain in the bills in the Strand, and so frequently was it revived, that there is little exaggeration in the story of the sea-captain who for twenty years made a point of visiting the Adelphi on his return from successive voyages and who never saw anything but the *Green Bushes*, the date of his arrival in this country invariably corresponding with the period of its reproduction.

It was in this play that Paul Bedford first uttered his absurd gag, which took the town and especially the man in the street: " I believe you, my boy!" It was a popular catch phrase for years. A curious circumstance occurred during the early run of the *Green Bushes*. When Madame Celeste, who was representing the character of Miami—the Indian girl shoots the English husband, by whom she had been deserted—a woman started up in the pit and exclaimed in a loud voice, " Serve him right; it's just like my monster!" This explosion of insulted womanhood produced by the " cunning of the scene " and Madame Celeste's powerful acting was followed by shouts of laughter from all parts of the house.

Of Webster's acting in the part of Triplet in *Masks and Faces*, Professor Morley wrote : " There is a poor poet who doubles the scanty callings of painter and player, and whom Gold-smith could not have better described, or Leslie painted, as Webster acts him. The delicacy and strength of this performance took us by surprise. The humour and pathos closely neighbouring each other, smiles playing about the tears, and the mirth always trembling into sadness, belonged to most real art. And it was full of minute touches which showed the discrimination of the actor."

Another fine creation of Webster's was that of Reuben Gwynne in *The Round of a Wrong*. In the beginning he is a happy young man engaged to be married to the girl of his heart, but soon at the instigation of her father the maiden rejects her lover, and he immediately becomes metamorphosed into a being of hate whose sole object in life is revenge. Said Dr. Westland Marston : " His longing for vengeance was the wild outcome of his suffering—the mad desire to give torture which makes the wounded creature turn upon the hunter. When at length the tables were turned, and his enemy, the father of his old love, lay at his mercy, nothing could be truer than the manner —most gradual in its rise, but sudden in its end —in which the cherished purpose of revenge gradually yielded before the prayers and influence of his restored darling." In this part Benjamin Webster held the audience in the palm of his hand.

As an expression of power, however, nothing short of tragic must be cited Webster's rendering of Robert Landry in the first act of the *Dead Heart*. Landry is a young sculptor who by the machinations of a certain Count de St. Valerie and a godless priest—Latour—is immured on false pretexts in the Bastille. The object of St. Valerie in the vile proceeding is to bring within his snare a lovely and innocent girl betrothed to Landry. When he is at last released, eighteen years later, he is as one dying and longing to be dead. John Coleman wrote of the resurrection of the poor prisoners: "with what consummate skill the actor built up this scene; not even Macready's marvellous

THE ADELPHI THEATRE FIFTY YEARS AGO

awakening in Lear; or Jefferson's admirable Rip Van Winkle could excel this extraordinary effect. I can answer for one auditor at least, who never saw it without being stirred to the core; a lump rose in his throat and tears came unbidden to his eyes." Then when Webster cast aside his decrepitude he became a man of iron. His voice became metallic, as he recounted the story of his wrongs: "They cast me into the tomb a living man, but with a dead heart. Do you mark me, Catherine ? The body was living—but the Heart was Dead ! Yes—Dead ! " The effect was electrical and spectators moaned in anguish at his sufferings, and were terrified after at the awfulness of his revenge on the lying Abbe Latour whom he eventually kills in a duel.

Webster's range of rôles was very vast and full of contrasts, but perhaps one of his grandest efforts was the murderer, the " softy " Stephen Hargreaves in *Aurora Floyd*. Says Professor Morley : " The weakness of intellect is shown only in the lowness of its degradation. The make-up of the actor with deformed back, crooked limbs, a Caliban forehead under a thief's crop of red hair, a penthouse of shaggy eyebrow over cunning eyes, and a great cruel witless mouth that, we know not how, seems to be all fang, creates a being in whom not even an expert playgoer, without assurance of the play-bill would easily recognise Mr. Webster. . . . In this spirit Mr. Webster acts the part through with terrible energy. His greed, cunning, and malice become diabolical under unwonted excitement and temptation, and we part from him as he is dragged off screaming unmitigated hate "—to be punished for his vile deeds.

As Tartuffe in Molière's famous play Benjamin Webster was able to startle playgoers for many months by his surprising intensity. He made the character his own. " The play is worthy of the house, the players certainly are not unworthy of the play." Webster produced many adaptations of the Christmas stories of Charles Dickens and several of the works of Dion Boucicault including *Janet Pride*, a terrible tale of misery, drunkenness and crime. As Richard Pride, Ben-

jamin Webster again scored. " The drunken aids, and variations in the temper—the half-sober efforts to stare down suspicion and to hide fear when in the presence of one who may detect crime . . . are marked by Mr. Webster . . . with peculiar refinement." In this piece was first sung the great thieves' song called " Botany Bay."

The *Colleen Bawn* and *Arrah-na-Pogue*—a revival—were also in the bills at different times. In the latter was introduced Boucicault's own version of the " Wearing of the Green " which created an immense furore owing to the ever-present Irish Question being very much to the fore in the early seventies. At last the Government intervened and forbade the singing of the song.

It was in 1865 that Webster entered into a contract with Joseph Jefferson, who had been touring America with *Rip Van Winkle*, to appear in his wonderful impersonation. The play, itself, founded on Washington Irving's story was somewhat crude, but the master hand of Boucicault and the stage management of Webster soon set the drama in order, with the result that eventually it conquered not only the whole of the metropolis but the whole of Great Britain as well.

One night before the piece " caught on " Joseph Jefferson—a most fascinating man and actor—at the end of the last act, eyeing the somewhat scanty benches, varied the tag which is as follows : " I trink your goot healt, and your family's goot healt, and may you all lib long and prosber." On this particular evening he said, advancing to the footlights, with his mug uplifted :

" I trink your goot healt and your family's goot healt and—I vish to gootness, you had brought some of them mit you."

THE REV. DR. DODD

"THE UNFORTUNATE DR. DODD"

THE Rev. Dr. William Dodd lay in his cell at Newgate awaiting the sharp conclusion of death. His name filled the air. In newspapers, in the theatres, in club, coffee-house, and drawing-room he was the universal subject. His case was mentioned with commiseration; he was "the unfortunate Doctor Dodd." He had been condemned to the gallows for forgery.

To be candid, the "unfortunate Doctor" was scarcely an ornament of the Church, even in the eighteenth century. A Royal Chaplain he had been, but for a flagrant act of simony his name had disappeared from the list. He had been a preacher to Magdalens in Goodman's Fields, haranguing, says Walpole, "entirely in the French style," with a certain unctuous in-

delicacy much relished by the fashionable. He had been proprietor, or chief proprietor, of two private chapels—Charlotte Chapel, Pimlico, and Charlotte Street Chapel, Bloomsbury—profitably administered on strict commercial lines. He must have been a sight in the pulpit. Foote hits him off well in the savage satire "Dr. Simony": "with a cambric handkerchief in one hand and a diamond ring on the other; and then he waves this way and that way, and he curtsies, and he bows, and he bounces . . . to show his plump cherry cheeks," &c.

He had trifled with literature, published (in his younger days) a dubious novel, and a volume—not badly done—of "Beauties from Shakespeare." He was a haunter of civic feasts, and liked to sup richly in a tavern after preaching,

All things considered, Dodd was a somewhat raffish clerk, not altogether, perhaps, the most discreditable of his order, but certainly what in those days was dubbed a Macaroni parson. There was something of Sterne in him, but nothing of Sterne's best. Cowper's fiercely penned " Macaroni Parson " was undoubtedly meant for Dodd :

> But loose in morals, and in manners vain,
> In conversation frivolous, in dress
> Extreme, at once rapacious and profane,
> Frequent in park with lady at his side,
> Ambling and prattling scandal as he goes.

For the affair of simony (an attempt to get the living of St. George's, Hanover Square) he was dismissed from the Magdalen, struck off the list of Royal Chaplains, and obliged for a time to beat a retreat to the Continent, where he was seen at races " dressed in a mousquetaire uniform—in very doubtful company." Returning to England, he found himself a little strange in the world that had caressed and spoiled him, and began from this date to move downwards. There is a hint of him in the King's Bench Prison.

In 1777, forty-eight years of age, Dodd " was being very hard pressed indeed." He had parted with his Bloomsbury Chapel, was owing rent, and had debts to tradesmen. On February 1 of this year he went into the city with a bond for four thousand two hundred pounds forged by him in the name of the young Earl of Chesterfield (nephew of the famous Earl), who had been his pupil. All seemed in order, but, on the question of a mere blot, Lord Chesterfield himself was presently appealed to ; and in that moment, of course, the fate of Dr. Dodd was sealed. From first to last Chesterfield's part in the case was not the most generous. Dodd could have made good his attempted fraud to

within some four hundred pounds ; and there seems to have been, in fact, though the point is not established, a more or less desperate attempt to compound the felony. It failed, and Dodd was lodged in Wood Street Compter. " That night," says Mr. Percy Fitzgerald, " the story was all over London. The whole town had the details. Doubting friends and scoffing enemies said now that what they had anticipated had come to pass. . . . Outside in the streets the story was told and sung."

On February 2 Dr. Dodd appeared in the dock. His friends had procured the unhappy man the best assistance, but the evidence against him was decisive, and it took the jury but a few minutes to arrive at a verdict of " Guilty." " The court, the jury, the spectators were all in tears. . . . The miserable prisoner was carried away in a crowd of sobbing friends."

To Newgate, of course, he went, the unreformed Newgate of the eighteenth century, which, however, at this time was in the charge of that humane governor Akerman, whose just praises have frequently been sounded. The quondam shepherd of the Magdalens " had a private room, books, fire, and all comforts. His friends found money and supplied him with everything. But nothing could shut out the grim and terrible associations of the place. Through the walls the horrid riot, the awful saturnalia arising from the promiscuous herding together of prisoners of every shade of crime came to his ears. . . . More chilling still was the booming of St. Sepulchre's bell close by, which by long and pious custom was tolled the night before an execution, for the purpose of announcing to criminals that their end was near ; and as Monday was execution day, this lugubrious memento was heard nearly every Sunday night." Then there was the bellman's chant, beginning:

All you that in the condemned cell do lie,
Prepare you, for tomorrow you shall die.

While Dodd lay here, pouring out in vapid, tasteless blank verse his "Prison Thoughts," one great and noble-minded man was strenuously seeking to save him from the gallows. This was Samuel Johnson, now nearly seventy years of age, through whose intervention the pitiful last days of the Macaroni parson gain a semblance of dignity. Dr. Johnson had once been in Dodd's company, and relished him, we are told, as little as he did "the man Sterne," but his compassion was moved by the stories that reached him from the cell in Newgate.

DR. DODD
From a Portrait taken in Newgate

He would not go there, saying, "It would do *me* more harm than good to *him*"; but he put himself in communication with Dodd, and set to work on speeches and petitions for him.

Three months went by. On May 14 the prisoner was carried again to the bar of the Old Bailey, and told to prepare for his sentence. " His piteous groans then filled the court, and when he was taken away he fell senseless on the floor of the dock." On the 26th he was brought up to receive sentence, and read a speech which Johnson had written for him. " I have fallen from reputation which ought to have made me cautious; and from a fortune which ought to have given me content. I am sunk at once into poverty and scorn; my name and my crime fill the ballads —the sport of the thoughtless, and the triumph of the wicked." There could be no mistaking the author of these rolling periods. After sentence had been passed the condemned man wrote Johnson " a letter of fervent gratitude," and Johnson composed a sermon for him.

From the hour of receiving sentence Dr. Dodd's life became, in Walpole's phrase, " a series of protracted horrors." The whole country was in a ferment over his case. Johnson drew up a petition which an admirer declared to be " one of the most energetic compositions ever seen "; a famous penman engrossed it, and among those who went from house to house collecting names for it was the father of Richard Brinsley Sheridan. With the names attached, this document "was thirty-seven yards and a quarter long, and contained twenty-three thousand signatures." For Mrs. Dodd Johnson drew up another petition, to be laid at the feet of the Queen, and a third which the Common Council was to send in. The Methodists (who owed Dodd no great goodwill) indited their own petition.

Meanwhile Dodd in Newgate was not wholly occupied with his "Prison Thoughts." Woodfall of the *Morning Chronicle* received an urgent appeal asking him to call at the gaol. He did so, and the Doctor pulled out a comedy—*Sir Roger de Coverley*—which he begged him to convey to Harris, the Covent Garden manager. Woodfall was taken aback, "but the Doctor turned the matter off repeatedly, saying, ' O, they will never hang me ! ' "

Incredible as it sounds, on one Sunday the reverend convict was allowed to preach to his brother convicts from the pulpit in Newgate Chapel. It was the sermon Johnson had written for him. "A truly sincere penitent," says Fitzgerald, "would have eagerly seized on the opportunity. But it looks as though this hapless Dodd had clutched at it only as another possible plank by which he might get to shore."

On June 15 the Privy Council met and deliberated for the second or third time on the case of this interesting prisoner, who in our day would probably have been punished with three years' penal servitude. A decision was at last arrived at, and in the London papers of that evening it was read that a warrant had been made out for the execution of Dr. Dodd on Friday the 27th. Mr. Percy Fitzgerald states that the king, after long irresolution on the subject, turned to the Chief Justice, Lord Mansfield, and, finding that he declared for execution, "took up the pen without a word and signed the dreadful paper." The king himself is reported to have said : " If I pardon Dodd I shall have murdered the Perreaus "—wealthy traders in Dodd's own station, who also, a year or two earlier, had been hanged for forgery.

Poor Mrs. Dodd had taken a room on Ludgate Hill, and went every day to visit her husband ; he, every nigh after he had been ordered for execution, wrote her a letter. Johnson, who never ceased his efforts for the wretched man, penned for him a few earnest words to the King, suggesting that a clergyman might at least be spared "the horror and ignominy of a public execution." In his own name he wrote a letter to Jenkinson, Secretary for War, urging that it would be "more for the interest of religion to bury such an offender in the obscurity of perpetual exile than to expose him in a cart, and on the gallows, to all who, for any reason, are enemies to the clergy."

Friends tried to bribe Akerman with £1000, and there was even a wild notion of carrying into Newgate a figure in wax to represent Dodd, who was then to be smuggled out of the cell through the crowd of his visitors. But there was no hope.

On the morning of Friday the 27th, to the booming of St. Sepulchre's bell, Dr. Dodd issued bound through the Felon's Gate. With him walked a young highwayman named Harris, who was to suffer for having robbed a stage-coach passenger of two half-guineas and seven shillings. To this youth Dodd, now at the last tranquil and even manly, spoke words of comfort. Harris climbed into a cart hung with black baize. To the Doctor was granted the favour of travelling to Tyburn in a mourning coach with four horses ; he appeared "in deep black, and in a large full-bottomed wig." His "corpse-like face" was noted beneath a great flapping hat. After them came a hearse and four, containing a white open shell. All the three miles from Newgate to Tyburn Tree London was in the streets, eager and straining for the sight. At St. Sepulchre's, as the bellman came forward with his "All good people pray heartily unto God for these poor sinners who are now going to their death," Harris fainted away. The "poor sinners" were two hours on their journey to Tyburn.

The scene there may be viewed in Hogarth's plate of the execution of the idle apprentice. Charles James Fox, we read, looked on from the top of an unfinished house. Noble old John-son, of course, was not among the crowd. The ghastly ceremonial began. Harris was despatched the first. As Dr. Dodd mounted the cart "a heavy shower came down. Under the great hat his eyes were never lifted, and the corpse-like face was turned to the ground." A gust of wind blew off both hat and wig just before the rope was adjusted, and the people shuddered as they beheld in full that deathly countenance. The execution over, some friends of the Doctor's hurried his body to an undertaker's in Goodge Street, where John Hunter, the surgeon, made a vain effort to restore life to the "unfortunate Dr. Dodd."

A MILLBANK MYTH

"SOME women, like some men, live in criminal history less for what they did than for what they are credited with having done. There was Emily Lawrence. Emily was one of the truly distinguished thieves of the third quarter of the nineteenth century. She may or may not have been superior to the device of hanging hooks beneath her skirts, but certainly in her prime she could "touch" for jewellery by arts less mechanical. Jewellery was Emily's peculiar line; a fashionable jeweller's shop the theatre of her choice. In London she despoiled such establishments as Emmanuel's and Hunt and Roskell's; in Brighton she lifted £1000 worth of jewels while chatting vivaciously with the youthful guardian of the stock; in Paris she was wanted for a matter of "loose" diamonds to the tune of £10,000. These were riflings on the high and splendid scale; yet it is not for such despatches (infinitely as they praise her for a mistress in her craft) that Emily is best remembered. She is best remembered for a stratagem to conceal some portion of her plunder which in all likelihood she not only never attempted but never even thought of. Her second episode of prison—a second sentence of seven years—took her to the old Millbank Penitentiary; and it was persistently asserted that into this place she carried, and here in some way bestowed, a fortune in precious stones.

This preposterous legend was implicitly believed. "Women, it was said, came as prisoners almost voluntarily, in order to carry out their search for the treasure, and a thousand devices were tried to secure a lodging in the cell where the valuables were said to be concealed." Time flowed, and in 1895 Millbank was razed, but no stones were secured that Hatton Garden would acknowledge. Yet to this day there are those who maintain that in some spot beneath the foundations of the Tate Gallery the jewels still lie.

DOLLY'S CHOP-HOUSE

THIS famous City chop-house was in Queen's Head Passage, Paternoster Row, and it stood on the site of an ordinary which had been kept by Richard Tarlton, the famous Elizabethan clown and jester. The eighteenth-century Dolly's took its name from its proprietress, a woman of great character, whose portrait, said to have been painted by Gainsborough, was displayed as the sign of the house. A writer in the *Connoisseur* of June 6, 1754, says: "At Dolly's, and Horseman's, you commonly see the hearty lovers of a beef-steak and gillale." Smollett

DOLLY OF DOLLY'S

seems to have known the house well, for he makes his character Melford (in *Humphrey Clinker*) write to Sir Walkin Phillips: "I send you the history of this day, which has been remarkably full of adventures ; and you will own I give you them like a beef-steak at *Dolly's*, hot and hot, without ceremony and parade." Dolly's was ever famous for its beef-steaks.

But no small part of the popularity of Dolly's was founded in the personality of Dolly herself. She realised that the City merchant relished his midday meal all the more when it was put before him by a pretty maid. In " Curiosities of Biography " (1845) we read : " Dolly's assistants were always selected with a view to draw custom. The barmaid was chosen for her beauty

and obliging disposition—the other female servants were of a similar description, and the waiters were peculiarly smart and clever :

'. All well-bred emblems of the chop-house ware,

As broth reviving, and as white bread fair ;
As small beer grateful, and as pepper strong ;
As beef-steaks tender, and as pot-herbs young.

" It is accordingly said that many customers, including wealthy aldermen and City knights, were often content to pay double for their chop or their soup, merely for the pleasure of being waited upon by Dolly's fascinating female servants. The reputation both of mistress and maids, however, remained untarnished ; and when the former retired for life, it was after a most successful career of industry, and with the satisfaction of associating her name in perpetuity with her beloved chop-house."

Dolly's Chop-house disappeared finally in 1883, and no trace of it remains save in literature. There is no doubt that it was well known to Fielding, Richardson, Dryden, Pope, Hogarth, and many other famous men who liked a little romance to " blow among the chops and steaks." Fifty years ago Dolly's Chop-house shared with the Chapter Coffee-house the patronage of the publishers and booksellers of Paternoster Row, as some can still recall.

THE OLD CANTERBURY.

IT was in the year 1848 that the first actual London music-hall had its genesis, at the Canterbury Tavern, in the Westminster Bridge Road. Charles Morton, who was a friend of Pierce Egan's, commenced his career in a tavern in Belgrave Road, Pimlico, which was a convenient house of call for the "fancy," and particularly too of the Royal servants from Buckingham Palace. Mr. Morton frequently referred to the fact, with a twinkle in his eye, that he had many a time dined at Buckingham Palace ; then he used to add that one of the officials was one of his particular friends. Having saved a little money, he took over the lease of the Canterbury, and at once started a Saturday night "free and easy." This was more or less suggested to him by the success of the supper rooms of Evans's in Covent Garden and in imitation of the "Sing-songs," which were just coming into vogue at the different taverns in and around London. At first Mr. Morton had to rely upon the volunteer efforts of a few musical customers, and as these happy entertainments brought grist to the mill the far-seeing proprietor after a time erected a hall at the back of the premises, the first stone of which was laid by two children, one being his own daughter Lily, the other the niece of Henry Russell. Thenceforward prosperity waited on his footsteps, and when he added a picture-gallery to the establishment, which was quickly filled with oil-paintings and odds and ends of statuary given and lent by various friends and artists of the day, the press lauded the enterprise and the public flocked to enjoy the art and the artists. The fame of the Canterbury very quickly spread, because of the superior class of entertainment given. George Augustus Sala christened it "the Royal Academy over the water" when he was writing for *Household Words*, and he it was, evidently, who induced Charles Dickens and Wilkie Collins to become patrons, for both writers speak of their visits. Thackeray, who loved variety, likewise was a well-recognised figure, and he and many more novelists make references to this "house of call." Stars of all kinds and magnitude eventually were engaged and seen at the Canterbury, which was so called in compliment to the Archbishop, who had his occasional residence at Lambeth Palace close by. Many of the "stars" in their courses made their first appearance there.

Emily Soldene in her vivacious records tells us

A CANTERBURY ADVERTISEMENT OF 1852

upstairs; there was lots of sawdust. Soon I found myself in a long picture-gallery, at the other end of which a rehearsal was being held. The pictures delighted me, but the smell of beer and stale tobacco-smoke revolted me." It was soon apparent that Miss Soldene could sing, and within a year she was acknowledged to be one of the greatest comic opera singers that was ever known in London. She attracted everybody to hear her in *Madame Angot* and many other pieces at different theatres. It is an extra-ordinary fact that *Faust* by Charles Gounod, the

that when a girl she had a letter of introduction to the manager, and Herr Jongmanns, the conductor, was to hear her sing. Miss Soldene, says: "I remember the shock I got when I went under the railway arch, down the dirty, dingy, narrow street, the greasy sidewalk, the muddy gutter, full of dirty babies, to the commonplace-looking public-house. I felt I could not go in; but I did. The people were polite, and showed me

French composer, had its initial English performance at the Canterbury Music Hall, after Gounod's own countrymen had practically condemned the opera on the first night. John Hollingshead relates how Mr. Gye, the director of the Italian Opera at Covent Garden, thought so little of this masterpiece, when he saw it in Paris, that he said there was nothing in it but an ordinary "Soldiers' Chorus." Jongmanns and Morton, however, thought differently, saw their chance, and seized upon it. They gave selections from the opera with Emily Soldene and several other capable singers and a large chorus, to the delight of thousands. *Faust* was played so long and became so popular that every small boy in the street was either whistling or trying to sing the melodies. Men could take their wives, youths could convoy their sweethearts, and they could partake of much innocent enjoyment, spend a good evening, and go home happy and contented. The Canterbury became so well known through the capable management and wise catering, together with the cleverness of the various performers

CHARLES MORTON

engaged to render the best music of the best masters, Continental and English, that it grew to be a regular rendezvous of all classes; and the Lower Marsh and the New Cut inhabitants thus rubbed shoulders with the *élite* of the West End, who were always anxious for novelties. During the early days of its prosperity—a prosperity that never seems to slacken—the performers at the little "Hall over the Bridge" were invariably of the highest class. They included Augustus Braham, son of the great tenor and composer of "The Death of Nelson," whose daughter became Countess of Waldegrave and a prominent member of London society;

Miss Turpin, afterwards Mrs. Henry Wallack of New York; Sam Cowell, whose extraordinary and diverting versions of *Robinson Crusoe, Cinderella, St. George and the Dragon,* and *Bluebeard* created every night he appeared the highest merriment. The "Great Mackney" with his everlasting song and his everlasting chorus, "The Whole Hog or None," together with "Sally Come Up," and particularly "In the Strand "—

I wish I was with Nancy,
In a second floor for evermore,
I'd live and die with Nancy,
In the Strand, in the Strand.

—was another great feature at the Canterbury. A very lively description of the Canterbury is given in Ritchie's "The Night Side of London." The chairman, who has vanished now from the music-hall, was a great authority in those days, and with his hammer used to rap the table to call attention to the fact of the appearance of another "turn." By the way, it was quite a privilege to be permitted to sit at the oblong "mahogany" with the chairman, and this privilege conferred upon you the opportunity of purchasing cigars and other refreshments chiefly for the delectation of the gentleman, who every now and then commanded silence, with a very imperious air, when the gallery or the pit became too noisy.

After Mr. Morton retired from the management of the Canterbury, William Holland at once took over the directorship. He had the house entirely redecorated and rearranged. Then he changed the old programme in order to cater for the different tastes of the newer public. He at once secured the services of George Leybourne; who made a big success with "Airy Fairy Lilian," and of course many other songs; the Great Vance, with his "Chickaleary Cove"; Arthur Roberts, the prince of impromptu comedians; James Fawn, an actor of very great versatility; and Nelly Power, nearly always dressed as a boy or young man, who established a reputation by singing "Captain Cuff," Nelly Moon, and Miss Phyllis Broughton, who later became a great favourite at the Gaiety and the other burlesque theatres in the Strand. Quite a sensation was made at the Canterbury by Farini, who was a rival of Blondin as a tight-rope-walker and who introduced his young and attractive son later as an acrobat under the name of Lulu. This boy at first used to sing a song to emphasise his sex called "Wait till I'm a Man." One peculiarity about the old Canterbury was the custom of providing hot suppers, which the patrons of the house partook of during the intervals, and pipes and porter were the usual accompaniments. Although some of these glories have passed away, many of the old customs of the original house are still maintained.

At the Canterbury, it may be mentioned, the first "sliding roof" was introduced. It is still kept in order, though one particular night when the machinery refused to work the audience received a rain bath that was not either expected or appreciated.

THE JESTER WHO BUILT A HOSPITAL

IN the sanctuary of the church of St. Bartholomew the Great, which has been justly described as one of the architectural jewels of the City, "so serious, so genuine, so un-Wrenlike, so unexpected, so modest," may be found the coloured tomb of the founder of this church and the neighbouring hospital. He is lightly spoken of in one place as "the merry and melodious Rahere." Merry he may have been, and melodious he certainly was, in his youth, for he was minstrel to King Henry; but in his later life he must be pictured as a grave, pious, determined severe man, whose days of mirth had become dim memories.

Rahere was doubtless of Norman blood, as his name implies. Why, when he was still young, he abandoned the jester-minstrel's trade, and turned his back on Courts and voluntarily sank into poverty and obscurity, nobody knows. It may have been love disappointed. It was more probably religion, for he made a pilgrimage to Rome, and was, as an old writer says, "penytant of his synnes."

A great minstrel he must have been; for he was of low kindred and had risen high. It may be that when he left the Court he was fleeing from enemies. After the pilgrimage to Rome he hid himself among the most outcast of the poor. One of the monks of the priory of St. Bartholemew the Great says that he feigned himself an idiot, and collected daily a little band of children, lepers, and poor people, inducing these to collect for him stones from the surrounding waste and morass. This was the place, just outside the City walls, which was afterwards known as Smithfield. "Right unclean it was, and as a marsh drear and fenny, with water almost everywhere abounding; and that that was eminent and dry above the water was deputed and ordained to be the gallows of thieves, and for the torment of others that were condemned by judicial authority."

Why did Rahere induce the children, the lepers, and poor people to collect stones for him? Because he had dreamed a great dream. He had seen through the eye of his mind a noble monastery and an hospital designed for the service of the poor and the sick, and for the shelter of motherless children, rising up on the "drear and fenny marsh." All around lay the ruins of Roman London—fair quarried stones, pillars, fragments of arches. One sees the great heap grow day by day and year after year, unnoticed, perhaps, in those days, and, if noticed, not considered of moment or understood.

In the head of Rahere was brooding the genius of a great architect, and burning within his heart was the passion of

a religious and social reformer. Somehow, whilst living with lepers and the very poor, he took orders, and entered into what seems to have been some irregular service of the Church.

THE TOMB OF RAHERE IN THE CHURCH OF ST. BARTHOLOMEW THE GREAT, SMITHFIELD

He threw off the guise of idiocy, and "went about saying the word of God faithfully in divine churches," and appealing to "the multitude of clerks and laity to follow and fulfil those things that were of charity and almsdeed." At length King Henry I., to whom he had been minstrel, heard of him again, and gave him the land at Smithfield to build on. "Then," says the pious monk who wrote the story of his life, "nothing he omitting of care and diligence, two works of piety began to make. . . . The church; of comely stoneworky tablewise, and a hospital-house a little longer off from the church he began to edify."

Rahere had begun to lay the foundations of the Hospital of St. Bartholomew in the year 1102, and 1123 seems to have been the year in which the Priory was finished. More than twenty years he had spent in building, not, as it appears, without much criticism and opposition. "He that buildeth by the wayside has many masters." His monkish biographer says that they of his own household were made his enemies, that wicked men were against him, and that wickedness was imputed to himself. But the great work was done. Here stood the far-spreading new Priory, of which the present church is only a small part ; and there, not far away, was the hospital which had been seen in visions long ago, "founded for the service of the poor, the sick, and pregnant women, with the care of such children, not of seven years old, as lost their mothers at birth."

This notable architect, builder, priest the minstrel and courtier of times past, had a friend named Alfun, "a certain old man, to whom was sad age and experience of old time." Him he made master of the hospital ; and as for himself he became Prior of his monastery, "and began anew to minister and to exhort, alike in his church and the dwellings of the citizens." There were those who plotted against his life ; but he successfully defended himself against them to a green old age, the king, his old friend and patron, adding now and again so long as his own life lasted, to the privileges of his two houses.

What manner of man was this Rahere ? The old monk of St. Bartholomew's answers this question in a language that does not fall short of eloquence. "He was a man not having cunning of liberal sciences, but that that is more eminent than all cunning, for he was rich in purity of conscience ; attached to God by devotion, to his breathren by humility, to his enemies by benevolence. . . . In feasts he was sober, and yet the follower of hospitality. Tribulations of wretches and necessities of the poor he opportunely admitted, patiently supported, completely relieved. In prosperity not proud, in adversity patient ; and whosoever was unfortunate and came unto him he clipped to him with the bowels of his soul."

They built a most beautiful tomb, those men of the Middle Ages, for Rahere, and there it is to be seen to-day, in the church of St. Bartholomew the Great, in Smithfield, which church was formerly the choir of the conventual church that was finished in 1123.

THE FLEET MARRIAGES

"SIR, will you please to walk
in and be married?"
This civil but astonishing
question was frequently put to Pennant,
the historian of London, when he
walked in his youth through the street
which contained the Fleet Prison. "A
dirty fellow invited you in. The
parson was seen walking before his
shop; a squalid profligate figure, clad
in a tattered plaid night-gown, with a
fiery face, and ready to couple you for
a dram of gin or a roll of tobacco."

That was one type of Fleet parson.
Another was that Dr. Gaynam, who
lived in Bride Lane, and was known
as "the Bishop of Hell," from whom
Sir Walter Besant seems to have drawn
his Gregory Shovel, Doctor of Divinity
and "Chaplain of the Fleet." Of
him it was written during his lifetime:

Long has old G——m, with applause
Obey'd his Master's cursed laws,
Readily practis'd every vice,
And equall'd e'en the Devil for device.

Not for Gaynam the poor reward
of a dram of gin or a roll of tobacco.
"It is customary, my lord," said Dr.
Gregory Shovel to one of his victims,
"to present the officiating clergyman,
myself, with a fee, from a guinea
upwards, proportionate to the rank
and station of the happy bridegroom.
From your lordship will I take nothing
for myself; for the witness I will take
a guinea." Such may have been, and
perhaps was, the large style of the
Fleet parson of the more prosperous
claim. Gaynam celebrated Fleet
marriages from 1709 to 1740. He
died, or retired, four years too early
to crown his remarkable career by
marrying Henry Fox, who afterwards

185

became the first Lord Holland, to a daughter of the second Duke of Richmond, and, therefore, to a great-granddaughter of King Charles II.

How much more easy and expeditious was a marriage in the Fleet than a runaway match to Gretna Green! No banns, no licence, a ceremony of a few minutes, and the expenditure of a guinea or two. To be sure, the parson was liable to a heavy fine; but that was his affair. "It is true that I may be fined a hundred pounds for consenting to perform the ceremony," says Gregory Shovel; "but it will be hard to collect that money."

Henry Fox and Lady Caroline Lennox met at a ball and Horace Walpole tells the story: "There were 197 persons at Sir Thomas's, and yet nobody felt a crowd. He had taken off all his doors, and so separated the old and the young that neither were inconvenienced with the other. The ball began at eight. Except Lady Ancrum no married woman danced. The beauties were the Duke of Richmond's two daughters, and their mother still handsomer than they. The Duke sat by his wife all night, kissing her hand." And at this ball Henry Fox, who was far from being a youth, having been born in 1705, and being already a distinguished statesman, fell over head and ears in love with the Duke of Richmond's elder daughter. It was what in those days was called "a mutual flame." But the course of true love in this instance made no exception to the proverb. When Fox made formal application for the lady's hand he was refused, and a hunt was set up for a more eligible suitor.

Then came the surprise of the Fleet wedding. One morning early in May 1744 a party set out from the house of Sir Charles Hanbury Williams to get promptly married in the Fleet. At which of the well-known matrimonial houses of that day did the event take place? Was it the Hand and Pen, or the Red Hand and Mitre, the Bishop Blaise, the Bull and Garter, or one of half a hundred other places living on the same traffic? At any rate the thing was done, and done irrevocably, to the unbounded astonishment of "the town." It was said at the time that at the opera the news ran along the front boxes exactly like fire in a train of gunpowder. Another contemporary remark was that hardly more noise could have been made if the Princess Caroline had run away with her dancing master. Fox's own brother, Lord Ilchester, found it necessary to exculpate himself from knowledge of his brother's designs. Sir Charles Hanbury Williams was in danger of losing the favours of the Court. The Duke of Newcastle so bemoaned the event that an eminent politician of that day said: "I thought that our Fleet was beaten, or that Mons had been betrayed to the French. At last it came out that Harry Fox was married, which I knew before. This man, who is a Secretary of State, cannot be consoled because two people, to neither of whom he is any relation, have got married without their parents' consent!"

Sometimes, as may be discerned from this instance, almost ideally happy marriages were made in the Fleet. In other cases, too, there were marriages between persons of rank and fortune. The Fleet parson married the Lord Abergavenny of the day, and John Bourke, who became Viscount Mayo, and Lord Banff, and Lord Montagu, afterwards Duke of Manchester, and the brother of the Lord

Chancellor, and Viscount Sligo, and the Marquis of Annandale ; so that there are to this day some noble families which have to trace back their pedigree through the mud of the Fleet Ditch, and in those registers that some Fleet parsons kept and some did not, and that were acquired in the long run, and where possible, for the Registry of the Bishop of London.

Not all those who were married within the Fleet or its liberties went there for that purpose. Many of them were simply hustled into marriage. Three years after the marriage of Henry Fox there was published an engraving representing "A Fleet Wedding between a Brisk Young Sailor and his Landlady's Daughter at Rederiff," with these lines printed underneath :

Scarce had the coach discharged its trusty fare
But gaping crowds surround the amorous pair.
The busy Plyers make a mighty stir,
And whisp'ring cry, " D'ye want the parson Sir ?
Pray slip this way—just to the Pen in Hand,
The Doctor's ready there at your command."
" This way," another cries. " Sir, I declare
The true and ancient Register is here."
The alarmed parsons quickly hear the din,
And haste with soothing words to invite 'em in.
In this confusion jostled to and fro
Th' inamoured couple know not where to go,
Till slow advancing from the coach's side
Th' experienced matron came (an artful guide).
She led the way without regarding either,
And the first Parson spliced 'em both together.

The sailor, it may be remarked, was a favourite bridegroom, for he could be induced to marry in the midst of a debauch, taking on his wife's debts in the process, besides endowing her with all his worldly goods, consisting usually of what remained of the profits of the last voyage. Then he sailed joyfully away as if there had been no marriage at all.

The *Weekly Journal* for June 29, 1723, says : " From an inspection into the several registers for marriages, kept at the several alehouses, brandy shops, &c., within the Rules of the Fleet Prison, we find no less than thirty-two couples joined together from Monday to Thursday last without licences, contrary to an express Act of Parliament against clandestine marriages. . . . Several of the above-named brandy men and victuallers keep clergymen in their houses at 20s. per week, hit or miss ; but it is reported that one there will stoop to no such low conditions, but makes at least £500 per annum of divinity jobs after that manner "—Dr. Gaynam, no doubt, otherwise Sir Walter Besant's Dr. Gregory Shovel.

The parsons each had their own " plyers," or touts, and attacked each other through their announcements, as in this manner : " Marriages with a licence, certificate, and Crown stamp at a guinea, at the New Chapel, next door to the China-shop, near Fleet Bridge, London, by a regular bred clergyman, and not by a Fleet parson, as is insinuated in the public papers ; and that the town may be freed mistakes, no clergyman being a prisoner within the Rules of the Fleet dare marry."

And yet marry they did, by the thousand marriages, and for good or for evil. Here are a few samples of the things done. In 1719 Mrs. Anne Leigh, an heiress, was decoyed from her friends in Buckinghamshire, married at the Fleet chapel against her consent, and barbarously ill-used by her abductors. In 1737 one Richard Leaver, being tried for bigamy, declared he was married in the Fleet without his knowledge." A contemporary memorandum is in these words : " The said Harronson swore most bitterly, and was pleased to say that he was determined to kill the minister, &c., that married him. *N.B.*—He came from Gravesend, and was sober." The last of the Fleet weddings took place on March 25, 1854. It was the day before the new Marriage Act came into operation, and there was so great a rush to take advantage of the disappearing state of things that 217 marriages were entered in one register alone. When the Act was still a Bill before Parliament it was opposed, and even with passion, by Henry Fox. He still thought well of the bridge—the Fleet Bridge—that carried him over.

PAINTING AND RESTORING THE DOME OF ST. PAUL'S

AFTER the completion of St. Paul's Cathedral, it was decided, against the wish of Sir Christopher Wren, to decorate the interior of the dome with paintings. Sir James Thornhill received the commission. Thornhill's speciality was the painting of walls and ceilings. Many royal palaces and noblemen's houses owe their beauty to his brush. He painted the ceiling at the great hall at Greenwich Hospital, where it is said he had to lie so long upon his back that he never stood really erect again. For the dome of St. Paul's he selected eight scenes in the life of St. Paul. These may still be studied—with aching neck and straining eyes. They were never considered a success, and the fact that they were repainted fifty years ago deprives them of much of their historical interest.

It was while painting these gigantic figures that Sir James Thornhill nearly lost his life. Absorbed in his work, he stepped back to observe its effect, and his assistant, Bently French, was horrified to see that he had approached the very edge of the platform. French saved his master from a terrible fall into the nave by flinging a pot of paint on the picture, and so causing Thornhill to rush to its rescue. It will scarcely be believed that Sir James Thornhill's work in the dome was paid for literally by the square yard the pay per yard being 40s. However, Thornhill was so industrious and thrifty that he amassed sufficient wealth to be able to repurchase the old seat of his family at Thornhill, in Dorset.

The effect of Thornhill's paintings has never been considered happy. In the judgment of Dean Milman (" Annals of St. Paul's Cathedral ") the scheme was an egregious mistake. " The cupola, instead of having been brought down by dark and heavy figures, ought to have melted upwards into life. In truth to paint a cupola nothing less was required than the free, delicate, accurate touch, the brilliant colour; the air and translucence of Correggio. Instead of lifting the sight and thought heavenwards, Thornhill's work, with its opaque and ponderous masses, oppresses and lies like a weight upon the eye and mind. It was a fatal fashion of the times ; no ceiling allowed its proper elevation : it was brought down by heavy masses of painting—where sprawl the saints of

Verrio or Laguerre. There is another irremediable fault : the architectural framework of Thornhill's figures does not harmonise with the architecture of the building : it crosses and clashes with the lines and curves of the original structure."

In 1853 the peculiar heaviness of Thornhill's work had been increased greatly by the grime of years. It was proposed to clean the paintings, and the work was entrusted to Mr. E. T. Parris, who was an accomplished artist, and had painted the great panorama of London exhibited at the Colosseum. Mr. Parris found, however, that restoration was impossible and that the pictures needed to be repainted. Bearing the same perils and discomforts which Thornhill had faced a century and a half earlier, Mr. Parris devoted three years to his task. The drawing from which our illustration is adapted appeared in the *Illustrated London News* of August 9, 1856, and the artist wrote: "' Slung up in a basket as I have sketched him, I found Mr. Parris painting away with huge housepainters' brushes, his pots of paint at his feet : a coat covered with a thick mass of dry droppings of colour, canvas overalls on his legs, a thick shawl about his throat, and a skullcap made to cover his ears, and tied under his chin, completed the painter's costume necessary to protect the wearer not only from dirt, but from the gusts of wind which play about the huge vaulted space." This was indeed painting under difficulties and discomforts which would have deterred most artists from such an undertaking ; but it must be remem-

bered that Mr. Parris had fortified himself by the construction of the requisite scaffold and platforms for his arduous

MR. E. T. PARRIS REPAINTING THE DOME OF ST. PAUL'S IN 1833

work, and this at no very great cost ; since but for this ingenious and economical contrivance Thornhill's pictures would in all probability have remained to this day obscured ' by the accumulated dirt and grime of years.' Here, in dreary loneliness, for three years was Mr. Parris pent up."

THE BEAUTIFUL GUNNINGS
The Irish girls who took London by storm.

IT is rather curious that one historian refers to the beautiful sisters Gunning as the Misses Gunn ; but he tells us in his chatty way that they had the kindly protection of the Lord-Lieutenant of Ireland before they made their debut in London, and no doubt he helped them to that distinction which made them so very popular.

"They can't walk in the Park," says Walpole in 1751, of the beautiful sisters, "or go to Vauxhall, but such mobs follow them that they are generally driven away." Eight years later curiosity had not abated. "Two ladies of distinction (who had, it seems, been incommoded by the mob as the phrase is, on the Sunday before) walked up and down the walks (in St. James's Park) preceded by soldiers from the Guard—a precaution which," we are told, "gave no small offence to the rest of the company, who were frequently obliged to go out of their path to make way for the procession." So says the *London Chronicle* for June 23–26, 1759. The ladies in question, we learn from Walpole, were Lady Coventry (the elder of the Gunnings)

and Horace's own beautiful niece, Lady Waldegrave, afterwards Duchess of Gloucester. Sometimes the Gunnings as well as other ladies of position, and the *grandes dames* of the day, appear to have invited inspection by their singularities.

The Gunning family originally came from Cornwall, but in the reign of James I., Richard Gunning, a descendant, who first spelled their name Gonning of Tregonning, went to Ireland and settled there after the year 1587, at Castle Coote, Roscommon. Then a later representative of this Gunning, named John, who had the misfortune to be heir to an impoverished estate in 1731, and having no means of his own—he was a law student—decided to share the same with a beautiful, but dowerless girl, the Honourable Bridget Bourke, a daughter of Viscount Bourke. So they got married, and in England where they had taken up their abode was born to them three lovely baby-girls who were destined to turn the hearts of many men. His father dying, John Gunning naturally came into the luckless estate which was more heavily encumbered than ever.

Mrs. Gunning soon resolved for the benefit of her children to get to Dublin or London, a feat that was not easily accomplished, seeing that they were all in a most dire state of impecuniosity.

However, they were acquainted with the Sheridans, Thomas Sheridan, the father of Richard Brinsley, then being the manager of the Theatre Royal, Dublin, with Miss George Anne Bellamy, the extraordinary daughter of an extraordinary father, It was through Miss Bellamy that Sheridan lent the Misses Gunning suitable costumes from the wardrobe of the establishment in order to attend their first vice-regal ball at Dublin Castle, where they began their triumphant career in the social world.

ELIZABETH (GUNNING), DUCHESS OF HAMILTON

George Anne Bellamy tells us that one day on her way home from rehearsal she heard great cries of distress from one of the houses, and on entering, in the goodness of her heart, she discovered " a lady of most elegant figure, with four beautiful girls and a boy, about three years old, around her." The lady proved to be, to her amazement, Mrs. Gunning, who at once explained the cause of her distress. Their expenses had been so heavy during their residence in Dublin and had far exceeded their income, and the bailiffs were in possession ! Miss Bellamy, taking pity on their unhappy plight, at once carried them off to her own apartments, where, for some considerable time she gave them food and lodging.

One writer says : " During the two years of their residence in Dublin the girls were the toast of all the beaux, the divinity of all the poets, and the admiration of all beholders, but it was a mystery at the time, and it remains a mystery to this day how they managed to pay their way for the ordinary necessaries of existence; and how they obtained the means to lead a life of continual gaiety among the rich in the capital of Ireland."

Rumours got about that the Gunnings had come into a fortune and that the girls would have dowries, but this was denied. Meanwhile, glowing accounts of the beauty of the two Misses Gunning had travelled to London, Bath, Paris, and other fashionable resorts. Mrs. Delany, a society gossip, and letter-writer of some note, wrote to her sister in London on the subject on June 8, 1750 :

" I have stole away to finish my letter, with a promise (this being a *jubilee day*) of playing to them (her guests) on the harpsichord, as soon as I have done. All you have heard of the Misses Gunning *is true*, except their having a fortune, but I am afraid they have a greater want than that, which is discretion."

The young people had their detractors of course, but these they ignored. With the assistance of a grant of one hundred and fifty pounds a year to add to her meagre income, from the Irish Government, by having her name added to the Irish Establishment list as a beneficiary for that amount, Mrs. Gunning was enabled to leave Dublin to take up her residence in London, and the sisters Gunning were duly presented at Court in December 1750, and their conquest of the metropolis was complete.

Suitors on all hands sprang up, but Mrs. Gunning was a careful mother and determined that her daughters should not throw themselves away. Up to the present they had had nothing but gallant admirers ; their mother wanted worthy husbands for them.

Walpole, writing to Sir Horace Mann a year after their debut, says ; " You, who knew England in other times, will find it difficult to conceive what indifference reigns with regard to Ministers and their squabbles. The two Misses Gunning are twenty times more the subject of conversation than the two brothers and Lord Granville. These are two Irish girls of no fortune, who are declared the handsomest women alive." But he qualifies this somewhat, a usual trick with him, by adding that he has seen handsomer women than either. Notwithstanding, they were the belles of every ball and rout and entertainment, capturing all with their entrancing beauty, and were the " cynosure of all eyes " when they went to the opera or theatre. The rather profligate young Duke of Hamilton—who was Duke, by the way, in three countries, England, Scotland, and France—fell violently in love with

Elizabeth, the youngest, and Horace Walpole relates how the marriage ceremony came to be performed that made her a duchess, under date February 27, 1752 : " The event that has made the most noise since my last is the extempore marriage of the youngest of the Miss Gunnings, who have made so vehement a noise of late. About a fortnight since, at an immense assembly at my Lord Chesterfield's, made to show the house, which is really most magnificent, the Duke of Hamilton made violent love at one end of the room while he was playing faro at the other ; that is he saw neither the bank nor his own cards, which were of three hundred pounds each ; he soon lost a thousand. . . . Two nights afterwards he found himself so impatient, he sent for a parson. The doctor refused to perform the ceremony without licence or ring, so the duke swore he would send for the Archbishop. At last they were married with a ring off the bed-curtain at half an hour after twelve at night, at the May Fair Chapel." These clandestine marriages at this notorious chapel were a scandal to the age, and were eventually stopped—but that is another story.

The duke and duchess did not lead a very happy life together, and when his Grace died six years afterwards, and Elizabeth found herself a widow, she kept her liberty for just one year, though even then she had many offers, her most persistent wooer being the Duke of Bridgwater, whom she refused, accepting eventually Colonel John Campbell, who became in 1770 fifth Duke of Argyll, Elizabeth beoming a Queen of Society. The Duchess of Hamilton and Argyll died in 1790 at the age of sixty, beloved by all who knew her, for she is declared to have had a very sweet disposition. In regard to Maria, the eldest sister, she espoused the Earl of Coventry in 1752. The Earl was a curious sort of lover for, though he made love to Maria in a way, it was rumoured that he was diffident about taking the fatal step. He could not decide to let her go, and he could not decide to take her. Many unkind remarks were made and Mrs. Gunning was in a fever of doubt and expectancy, but Lord Chesterfield was of opinion that love and courage would win the day, and presently, as already stated they did, and evil rumour was sent flying.

And now commenced Maria's achievements in society, for which she seemed better

MARIA, COUNTESS OF COVENTRY

fitted than her sister, who was of a gentle disposition, though generally considered the more beautiful of the two. Again we find Horace Walpole recording his opinion.

In July 1752 he writes : " Our beauties are returned (from Paris) and have done no execution. The French would not conceive the Lady Caroline Petersham ever had been handsome, nor that my Lady Coventry has much pretence to be so now. Indeed, all the travelled English allow that there is a Madame Brionne, handsomer and a finer figure." It appears that Lord Coventry was a very sedate young man, and objected to powder and patches and all frivolity, and was of an exceptionally jealous nature. Indeed

it is stated that once at Sir John Bland's, before sixteen guests, he chased his wife round the table, suspecting that she had used a little red on her face. He seized hold of her and scrubbed the colour off by force with a napkin. Whereupon he declared that as she had deceived him once he would at once take her away from the gay city and home and he did. So that Maria could not have been particularly happy with her prudish husband. " Yesterday," writes Mrs. Delany, in 1754— and her " Autobiography and correspondence " is a valuable work — " after chapel the Duchess (Portland) brought home Lady Coventry to feast, and *a feast she was*. She is a fine figure and vastly handsome, notwithstanding a silly look sometimes about her mouth ; she has a thousand airs, but with a sort of innocence that diverts one. Her dress was a black silk sack, made for a large hoop, which she wore without any, and it trailed a yard on the ground ; she had on a cobweb-laced handkerchief, a pink satin long cloke, lined with ermine mixed with squirrel skins ; on her head a French cap that just covered the top of her head of blond, and stood in the form of a butterfly with its wings not quite extended, frilled sort of lappets crossed under her chin, and tied with pink and green ribbon—a head-dress that would have charmed a *shepherdess*. She has a thousand dimples and a prettiness in her cheeks, her eyes a little drooping at the corners, but fine for all that." How kind these ladies are to each other!

Lady Coventry was a curious character and strong. She was long the leader of fashion ; she was not so much loved as admired. She was very mean and possessed a bitter or at any rate half cynical tongue, that made people shy of her. She once told George II. when he was worn with age and very feeble, that there was but one sight she cared to see and that was a Coronation ! As predicted when she was a young girl in Dublin, by a gipsy, she died of consumption which had long been troubling her, at the early age of 27 in 1760.

Kitty Gunning who was also very pretty and the youngest sister of the trio, was evidently the Cinderella of the family in the unfortunate days. We only hear of her in an obscure manner, and then we are told that she " got married, but not to a title." She certainly made no name at Court.

THE BEHEADING OF SIR WALTER RALEIGH

THE scene was Old Palace Yard, not as we know it now, but with houses crowding in and narrowing it, so that it looked like an ordinary London Street. Of all the scenes which have been witnessed there, say the authors of the best book on the King's Palace of Westminster, " that which most fascinates is the tragic end of Raleigh."

That great Elizabethan, who had the misfortune to live into the reign of James I., was beheaded in Old Palace Yard on Michaelmas day, 1618, two years after the death of Shakespeare, whom he had no doubt entertained many a time at Durham House, which looked over the Thames from what is now known as the Adelphi. A sad and silent crowd had gathered to witness the astounding event. It was to behold the execution of the most brilliant of the courtiers, soldiers, and adventurers of the previous reign, because on his return from his last voyage to Guiana he had not brought back shiploads of the gold of El Dorado.

Sir Walter Raleigh was now an old man. His health had been broken by long imprisonment, and his heart by the death of his eldest son ; but he had the undaunted heart and the ready wit of the days of his prime. An old and devoted friend darted forward to give him the support of his arm as he walked to the scaffold, and was repulsed by the guards. " Prithee, never fear, Beeston," said Raleigh, "I shall have a place." He had written the night before those famous and touching lines :

Even such is Time, who takes in trust
  Our youth, our joys, and all we have,
And pays us but with earth and dust ;
  Who in the dark and silent grave,
When we have wandered all our ways,
Shuts up the story of our days.
But from that earth, that grave, that dust,
The Lord will raise me up, I trust.

When he was in his fortieth year, which is to say in 1595, Walter

Raleigh sailed to the West Indies to seize El Dorado, which, as he believed, the greedy Spanish explorers had fortunately missed. According to the passionate dream of the men of those days El Dorado was a province which had for its capital Manoa, a city built in the centre of a great lake whose name was Parimo. It was a city in which there was more gold than in all the rest of the round world. Veins of gold cropped up out of the soil, as rocks do in other countries. Plates of gold were used for roofing its houses. Besides — so the story went — it held all the vanished treasures of the Incas of Peru. Walter Raleigh believed the fable as whole-heartedly as the most ignorant seaman of his time, and he determined to combine the fighting of Spaniards and the finding of El Dorado in a single great adventure.

There was brave fighting of Spaniards no doubt. A new Spanish settlement, important enough to be called a city, was captured and burnt. But El Dorado was not reached on that voyage, or any other, and Raleigh had so confirmed himself as an enemy of Spain as to make his fruitless search lead directly, but at a long interval, to his execution in Old Palace Yard.

The instrument in the hands of Spanish hatred was King James I.

SIR WALTER RALEIGH IN THE TOWER

When that monarch came to the throne Raleigh's life became a series of crushing persecutions. It was found possible in the long run to involve him in a charge to depose James and place the Lady Arabella Stuart on the throne. There was no proof of his complicity; but he was sentenced to death, and then, by the King's mercy, as it was called, was sent as a prisoner to the Tower of London, where he remained for the long period of fourteen years;

and wrote, among other books, his " History of the World."

James liberated him in order that he might go on another search for Manoa, the King putting some of his own money into the venture. Nothing came of it but disaster. There was more fighting with Spaniards, in the course of which Raleigh's son Walter was killed. " My brains are broken," he wrote to his wife ; and he was brought back to England a prisoner in his own ship, " to sue for grace of a graceless face," as Johnny Armstrong said.

The great adventurer had tried again and failed, and then, incredible as it may seem, the former sentence of death was revived against him. The explanation of that iniquity is to be found in a despatch sent to the British Ambassador at Madrid. " Let them know," it said, " how able a man Sir Walter Raleigh was to have done his Majesty service, if he should have been pleased to employ him. Yet, to give them content, he hath not spared him when by preserving him he might have given great satisfaction to his subjects, and had at his command as useful a man as ever served any Prince in Christendom." James's explanation at a later date was that Raleigh had promised either to find

and to capture El Dorado, or return to his imprisonment in the Tower.

The supreme grandeur of the man shone forth in his final hour in Old Palace Yard. To the ecclesiastic who attended him in his last moments he said that he gave God thanks that he had never feared death, and that as to the manner of it, though to others it might seem grievous, yet that he had rather die so than of a burning fever. " This is a sharp medicine ; but a safe cure for all diseases," he said, touching the headsman's axe. Trembling with agitation, the executioner shrank from the block. " What dost thou fear ? " asked Raleigh. " Strike, man ! " But he was still so unnerved that he had to strike twice. " The extraordinary effusion of blood," it has been remarked, " evinced an unusual strength and vigour of constitution."

" The head," says his biographer, " after being as usual held up to the view of the people on either side of the scaffold, was put into a red bag, over which his velvet nightgown was thrown, and the whole immediately carried to a mourning coach which was in waiting, and conveyed to Lady Raleigh."

And so perished the last of the Elizabethan heroes.

CHARLOTTE BRONTË IN LONDON

AT eight o'clock on a summer morning in the year 1848, a grey-haired, elderly waiter stood idly at the door of the Chapter Coffee House at the west corner of Paul's Alley, Paternoster Row. This house was pulled down in 1854, but a wine house on the same spot retains the old name. The coffee house was a rambling building, with heavy beams running across the low ceilings, and a broad shallow staircase in the centre. The waiter looked out—a little dolefully perhaps—at the high dull warehouses hemming in the narrow flagged row; there was no briskness in the coffee house at that hour of the morning; indeed, very few people ever stopped there—a bookseller up from the country sometimes, or a clergyman passing through town.

The waiter may have been an antiquarian—waiters often are; he may have sighed for the time, a century since, when this same coffee house was in its glory—a name to conjure by—the resort of the booksellers, publishers and wits; when the young poet Chatterton, full of confidence first, and then full of despair, haunted its rooms, in the hope of making acquaintance and getting employment. "I am familiar at the Chapter Coffee House," he wrote to his mother in Bristol, "and know all the geniuses there." But now—the waiter may have reflected, nothing happened, year in year out; there were only dull meetings of the trade in the long room upstairs; no wits, no geniuses, ever crossed the threshold—and just at that moment an event somewhat out of the usual did occur; two little ladies entered the coffee house, asked to see rooms, and ordered breakfast. The waiter observed that they were pale, tired and excited; too agitated indeed to eat much breakfast; and eager at once to proceed to Cornhill, asking him for directions as to the best way of reaching it. Ladies did not as a rule stop at the Chapter Coffee House, hidden away as it was in the heart of the City, and appropriated to business purposes; but the simplicity and dignity of the ladies touched the waiter, who did all he could to make them comfortable. No doubt he speculated curiously as to who they might be. But it never occurred to him—how could it ?—that at that moment under the roof of the Chapter Coffee House was a genius as great as any that had been there in the past; that this genius had borne through long years sufferings more terrible than poor Chatterton had known in his few London months; that the solution of a secret that had baffled literary London lay in the keeping of these two shy and quiet visitors.

Who were Currer, Ellis and Acton Bell? This was a question that had for some time past agitated the minds of all the critics. A volume of poems had been published, with contributions under each of these names; then, in 1874, three novels had appeared; " Jane Eyre," by Currer Bell; " Wuthering Heights " by Ellis Bell; " Agnes Grey " by Acton Bell, which created an extraordinary sensation. " Jane Eyre " especially was a type of novel new to our literature. It stood alone for intensity, for passionate force; it was the first book to have for heroine a plain little governess—if we may venture to describe Jane Eyre, compact as she is of purity and fierceness, under this colourless designation. The publishers could throw no light upon the question of the authorship of these novels; they were ignorant even of the sex of the writers. An American publisher, however, stated that he had ground for believing that Currer, Ellis, and Acton Bell were one and the same person, and Messrs. Smith Elder and Co.; publishers of " Jane Eyre," wrote to Currer Bell asking if they could contradict this statement.

The letter reached its destination— a stone parsonage on the bleak Yorkshire moors. It awoke consternation in the minds of three sisters, who with their father lived there a life of intense solitude — Charlotte Brontë (Currer Bell), Emily Brontë (Ellis Bell), and Anne Brontë (Acton Bell). The sisters considered that their honour had been impugned by the suggestion that one of them had been masquerading under three pseudonyms, and Charlotte and Anne started that very day, taking the night train to London, in order to reveal to the publishers the secret of their authorship.

Charlotte, when she had passed through London on her way to Brussels with her father and Emily, had stopped at the Chapter Coffee House, and thither she had come on this occasion, knowing of no other place. She and Anne had arranged to take a cab to Cornhill, where Messrs. Smith Elder had their offices; but in the agitation of the moment they forgot their decision, and set out to walk. The noise and the confusion of traffic bewildered them, and again and again they stood still, unable to proceed. Mr. George Smith, the publisher, has left us an interesting account of the interview. " I was in the midst of my correspondence, and my thoughts were far away from ' Currer Bell ' and ' Jane Eyre.' Two rather quaintly dressed little ladies, palefaced and anxious-looking, walked into my room; one of them came forward and presented me with a letter addressed in my own hand-writing to ' Currer Bell, Esq.,' I noticed that the letter had been opened, and said, with some sharpness, ' Where did you get this from? ' ' From the Post Office," was the reply; ' it was addressed to me. We have both come that you might have ocular proof that there are at least two of us.' "

Mr. Smith at once hospitably urged them to come and stay at his house, but this invitation they declined. He proceeded to make plans for their entertainment, and that evening called at the Coffee House with " two elegant ladies in full dress." He found the sisters in the long dingy room upstairs, clinging together on the most remote window-seats, looking out of the high narrow window into the gloomy row. They were tired out by the fatigue of the night journey and the agitation of the day, and though Charlotte had taken a strong dose of sal volatile to prepare herself in case of visitors, they had not understood that Mr. Smith was taking them to the Opera. " I put my headache in my pocket," says Charlotte, " we attired ourselves in the plain, high-made country garments we possessed . . . . They must have thought us queer, quizzical looking beings, especially me with my spectacles. . . . Fine ladies and gentlemen glanced at us with a slight, graceful superciliousness, quite warranted by the circumstances. Still, I felt pleasurably excited, in spite of headache and sickness and conscious clownishness, and I saw Anne was calm and gentle, which she always is."

This momentous visit with its thunderclap of revelation lasted only three days. London was unaware that

MESSRS. SMITH ELDER'S OLD PREMISES IN CORNHILL; THE SCENE OF CHARLOTTE AND ANNE BRONTË'S HISTORIC INTERVIEW WITH GEORGE SMITH

the author of " Jane Eyre " had been in its midst.

Charlotte Brontë visited London on several other occasions, staying generally at the house of Mr. George Smith, whose mother was a very kind hostess. This house was in Westbourne Place, now a street of shops. Charlotte Brontë saw all the sights of London, and visited the Great Exhibition of 1851 —"that vast Vanity Fair," she calls it. But it was always people rather than things that interested her. And among the literary celebrities of the time, there was one whom she admired before all, and whom she desired before all to meet —William Makepeace Thackeray. Her relations with Thackeray bring out forcibly many of the salient traits of her character ; her almost unconquerable shyness, her fiery spirit when roused, her acute critical perceptions. Thackeray, too, stands before us more clearly by reason of her descriptions and judgments. He impressed her, both mentally and physically, as a giant. " He is a very tall man, about six feet high," she writes to her father,

" not handsome—very ugly indeed . . . a most formidable-looking personage." And again, " He is a Titan in mind. . . . All the others are subordinate."

Eighteenth-century London knew another couple, not unlike these in casual outward appearance—another " formidable-looking personage," and another little lady who had published anonymously a highly successful novel. But how different in essentials was the relationship between Dr. Johnson and Fanny Burney, author of " Evelina," and between Thackeray and Charlotte Brontë. No literary contrast can be greater than Fanny Burney's naïve raptures when her identity became known, and Charlotte Brontë's agonised shrinking from publicity. Fanny Burney basked in Dr. Johnson's open praise of her; Thackeray hurt Charlotte Brontë pitifully by addressing her in a loud voice in a public place as " Jane Eyre." Fanny Burney's sensitiveness was mainly a thing of surface convention, but Charlotte Brontë's Irish nature was sensitive to the core of her being, and her capacity for pain had been increased by the slights she had borne as a governess, by her cruel anxieties for those she loved, and by the intense solitude of her life after her sisters had died. Little wonder if at her first meeting with Thackeray she was " painfully stupid,"—little wonder that she fancied herself in a dream, " and was only certain that it was true because I became miserably destitute of self-possession."

" I saw her first," Thackeray writes, " just as I rose out of an illness from which I thought never to recover. I remember the trembling little frame, the little hand, the great honest eyes. An impetuous honesty seemed to characterise the woman." That is

finely said, and gives in a few words a memorable picture. " New to the London world," he goes on, " she entered it with an independent indomitable spirit of her own ; and judged of contemporaries, and especially spied out arrogance and affectation, with extraordinary keenness of vision. She was angry with her favourites if their conduct or conversation fell below her ideal." Thackeray himself was soon to prove in his own person how fierce that anger might be.

We have an admirable account from the pen of Thackeray's daughter of a dinner and reception given at his house in Kensington in Charlotte Brontë's honour. " One of the most notable persons who ever came into our bow-windowed drawing-room in Young Street is a guest never to be forgotten by me . . . whose small hand nevertheless grasped a mighty lever which set all the literary world of that day vibrating. . . . The door opens wide and the two gentlemen come in, leading a tiny delicate, serious little lady, with fair straight hair, and steady eyes. She may be a little over thirty ; she is dressed in a little barège dress, with a pattern of faint green moss. She enters in mittens, in silence, in seriousness ; our hearts are beating with wild excitement. . . ." Miss Thackeray goes on to relate what a gloomily silent evening followed— how every one waited for the brilliant conversation, which never began at all. " Miss Brontë retired to the sofa in the study and murmured a low word now and then to our kind governess. . . . Mrs. Brookfield leaned forward. . . . " Do you like London, Miss Brontë ? " she said ; another silence, a pause, then Miss Brontë answers, " Yes and No," very gravely. Little wonder that all pronounced it the dullest evening !

At last, after Miss Brontë had left, Thackeray could bear it no longer, but with finger on lip, stole out of the house to his club !

Charlotte Brontë was no passive hero-worshipper, like Fanny Burney. She herself relates the following " queer scene." One morning, Thackeray called upon her at Mr. Smith's house. "The giant sat before me ; I was moved to speak to him of some of his shortcomings (literary of course) ; one by one the faults came into my head, and one by one I brought them out, and sought some explanation or defence. He did defend them like a great Turk and heathen—that is to say, the excuses were often worse than the crime itself." This is how the altercation appeared to an outsider. " When I entered the drawing-room," writes Mr. Smith, " Thackeray was standing on the hearthrug, looking anything but happy. Charlotte Brontë stood close to him, with head thrown back, and face white with anger. . . . The spectacle of this little woman, hardly reaching to Thackeray's elbow, but somehow looking stronger and fiercer than himself, and casting her incisive words [at his head, resembled the dropping of shells into a fortress."

In spite of her admiration for the Titan, Charlotte Brontë judged Thackeray with some severity. After one of his famous lectures delivered at Willis's Rooms, he asked her what she thought of it, and she felt this was prompted by " inquisitive restlesness," which is perhaps a kind way of saying vanity. She condemned him a little for being the " pet and darling " of great lords and ladies ; and she considered him in his books unjust to women.

Charlotte Brontë does not belong to London—would never have been acclimatised to its life. In her there was something elemental, akin to wild and desolate places. She craved companionship, she craved affection, but society would never have supplied that want. Yet her visits to London do help us to realise more vividly her strong and eager personality ; and as we think of her hidden in drawing-rooms that would have acclaimed her had she allowed it, we are struck anew by the contrast between this quiet woman and her volcanic work.

MAJOR FOUBERT'S PASSAGE

IT is now Foubert's Place, but its narrow complexity of old shops and houses, suggesting antiquity, makes an agreeable change from the palatial whiteness of Regent Street. Foubert Place is on the east side of Nash's great thoroughfare, and leads indefinitely into Soho. In any map of London earlier than 1814 you will find Regent Street represented by Swallow Street, but Foubert's Passage may be seen in maps a century and a quarter older. Who was Foubert ?

He was no obscure landlord or builder. Major Foubert fulfilled, in the reign of Charles II. the functions of Domenico Angelo in the reign of George III., and Philip Astley at a later period : he was the fashionable riding-master of the day. On the spot which now bears his name he conducted his academy. According to E. W. Brayley ("Londiniana," vol. ii. p. 170) Monsieur, or Major Foubert came over from Paris in 1681 and established himself here on premises, which, prior to that time, had been the residence of the Countess of Bristol.

Evelyn, in his Diary, mentions, that "the Council of the Royal Society had it recommended to them, to be Trustees and Visitors, or Supervisors, of the Academy, which Monsieur Foubert did hope to procure to be built by subscriptions of worthy gentlemen and noblemen, for the education of youth, and to lessen the vast expense the nation is at yearly by sending children into France to be taught military exercises. We thought good to give him all the encouragement our recommendation could procure."

In a word the French equestrian was a welcome guest in London. In another part of his diary, dated December 18, 1684, Evelyn gives the following description of the exercises practised at this Academy : " I went with Lord Cornwallis to see the young gallants do their exercises, Mr. Foubert having newly rail'd-in a manage and fitted it for the Academy. There were the Dukes of Norfolk and Northumberland, Lord Newburgh, and a nephew of (Duras) Earle of Feversham. The exercises were—1. Running at the ring ;—2. Flinging a javelin at a Moor's head ;—3. Discharging a pistol at a mark ;—and lastly, taking up a gauntlet with the point of a sword ; all these perform'd in full speede. The Duke of Northumberland hardly miss'd of succeeding in every one, a dozen times, as I think. The Duke of Norfolk did exceedingly bravely. Lords Newburgh and Duras seem'd nothing so dextrous. Here I saw the difference of what the French call ' *belle homme à cheval*,' and ' *bon homme à cheval* ;' the Duke of Norfolk being the first, that is, rather a fine person on a horse ; the Duke of Northumberland being both in perfection ; namely, a graceful person, and excellent rider. But the Duke of Norfolk told me he had not been at this exercise these twelve years before. There were in the field the Prince of Denmark and the Lord Landsdown, sonn of the Earle of Bath, who had been made a Count of the Empire last summer for his service before Vienna."

From the above extracts it appears, that Foubert's Riding Academy was as fashionable a lounge for the noblemen and gallants of that period as Tattersall's is at the present day. When Swallow Street was pulled down to effect the Regent Street improvements, the greater part of this passage, including the Riding School, which had been converted into livery stables, shared the same fate. Nevertheless, an air of quaintness and antiquity somehow pervades the little alley. Samuel Rogers loved it, and said that in his youth it was called, in full, Major Foubert's Passage, "and so I should like to see it called still."

OLD·TEA·DRINKING·DAYS·IN·LONDON

SIX years ago (in 1906) Mr. Richard Twining died at the age of ninety-nine. Three years later the historic trading house of which he had been long the head kept its bicentenary. Twining's old tea house is familiar to all who haunt the Strand. Its quiet doorway opposite the Law Courts, with the sculptured Chinamen above it, has been as much a matter for mention by topographers as the church of St. Clement's. In his "Town," published in 1848, Leigh Hunt duly notices this tea house, founded about the year 1710 by Mr. Thomas Twining. His grandson, Richard Twining, who died in 1824, was a man of literary taste, and a close correspondent of his half-brother, the Rev. Thomas Twining of Colchester,

who was at Cambridge with the poet Gray. Richard Twining was succeeded by his son, Richard, who died in 1857; and the third Richard Twining passed away almost two hundred years after the foundation of the business.

Thomas Twining, of Painswick, in Gloucestershire, came up to London in the first years of the century before last, and founded his tea business in the Strand at a time when the Maypole stood within a stone's throw of his premises. For the historic Maypole was not removed until 1717. Queen Anne was the first of the firm's many Royal customers. In 1711, a year after Thomas Twining had started his fragrant business, her Majesty appointed him her "purveyor of teas." A few years later the Queen's tea-drinking was so well known that Pope, referring to Hampton Court, was able to sing :

DR. JOHNSON TAKES TEA AT STREATHAM

Here, thou, great Anna! Whom three nations obey,
Dost sometimes counsel talk, and sometimes tea.

Perhaps Pope did not foresee that a consequence of his couplet would be that generations of school-boys would be told with very doubtful correctness

that tea was formerly pronounced " tay."

In 1710 Tom's Coffee House brought men about town and men of letters to Devereux Court, by St. Clement Danes. The Twining establishment still has an entrance in this court, which was named after Robert Devereux, Earl of Essex, the Parliamentary general. "Tom's" in this court was not *the* "Tom's" (that was in Covent Garden), but it was a famous resort ; and at the instance of Thomas Twining it became the original London depôt for the sale of teas. The "Grecian" coffee-house in the same court contributed to the social bustle. Addison, Steele, Goldsmith, and Sir Isaac Newton often bent their steps to Devereux Court.

So early a poet as Edmund Waller sang the praises of tea, and thought he knew how it should be brewed. A Jesuit, who had been to China, had told him that the boiling water should remain on the leaves, " while you can say the Miserere Psalm very leisurely." As a well-deserved result you got " the spiritual part of the tea "—such tea as Colley Cibber apostrophised as . " Tea ! thou soft, thou sober, sage, and venerable liquid ; thou female-tongue-running, smile-smooth-thing, heart-opening, wink-tipping cordial ! " This was the beverage which Dr. Johnson drank at Mrs. Thrale's, at Streatham, singing no Miserere Psalm, but a blither strain :

And now I pray thee,
   Hetty dear,
That thou wilt give to
   me,
With cream and sugar
   softened well,
Another dish of tea.

But hear, alas! this mourn-
   ful truth
Nor hear it with a
   frown—
Thou can'st not make the
   tea so fast
As I can gulp it down.

We are told that on these occasions t h e Doctor drank as many as twenty- five cups of tea in rapid succession. It is better, however, to be accurate than picturesque, and it must not be supposed that the tea which Mrs. Thrale poured out for Johnson, sometimes till the early hours of the morning, bore much resemblance to the Indian teas of to-day. India was not then a tea-garden, and the Doctor drank a mild Bohea. He drank it, moreover, out of cups not to be compared in size to the usual drawing-room ware of to-day. A Dutch tea enthusiast of the seventeenth century declared that ten or twelve cups of tea after dinner would hurt nobody's digestion, and that he himself could take a hundred cups without any after regrets. But his cups were tiny, and he "made" the tea only once, adding water ninety-and-nine times. The Doctor's performances were probably of much the same character.

Meanwhile, in Red Lion Square, old Jonas Hanway—the first man to carry an umbrella in London—was writing his famous indictment of tea, which

LORD PETERSHAM

he said was sapping England's manhood and destroying the beauty of her women! He was not the first writer, by any means, to attack tea on medical, moral, and economic grounds. The association of tea with scandal began much earlier, and a print of 1710 entitled " The Tea Table " bore these lines :

Here see we Scandal (for our sex too base)
Seat its dread Empire in the Female Race,
'Mongst Beaux and Women, Fans and
   Mechlin Lace,
Chief seat of Slander ! Ever there we see
Thick Scandal circulate with right Bohea.

In reviewing Hanway's essay Dr. Johnson good-humouredly remarked that the author must expect little justice from one who " with tea amuses the evening, with tea solaces the midnight, and with tea welcomes the morning." Even Johnson thought that tea was not a beverage for any but the leisured classes, being "commonly an entertainment merely nominal, a pretence for assembling to prattle, for interrupting business or diversifying idleness."

Among old London tea-drinkers high rank must be given to the eccentric Lord Petersham, who gave his name to a greatcoat and to a snuff mixture. But if he kept his teas, as is said, in the same room as

A FAIR TEA-DRINKER IN 1771

his snuffs one must doubt his connoisseurship. His canisters yielded Congou, Pekoe, Souchong, Gunpowder, and other kinds.

Shakespeare missed tea by half a century. John Wesley loved teadrinking, but gave it up under a conviction that its use by the lower classes was extravagant and harmful. It does not appear that he gave up alcohol for the same reason. It is rather startling to remember that John Keats was once on the point of becoming a tea-broker.

LORD ERSKINE AT HAMPSTEAD

AFTER you have climbed Hampstead Hill, and are approaching the Heath, you will see next to the "Spaniards" a plain white house with a long portico opening upon the roadway. The building is shut out from close observation by a high wall, but the tall windows of its large drawing-room on the second floor are observable, which command a splendid view over Ken Wood and Highgate. In this house there lived, between the years 1788 and 1822, Lord Erskine, the great Lord Chancellor, better remembered as the famous advocate in many a historic trial.

This is not the place to touch upon Lord Erskine's power as a pleader, the dignity of his fine person and stately bearing, the charm of his voice, his eloquence, his pathos, that could mould any jury to his will. We aim at surprising him in his more intimate domestic life, marked as it was by the same untiring energy he displayed at the Bar, and lighted by the same flashes of irrepressible wit.

Lord Erskine's great hobby was gardening. His grounds lay on the opposite side of the road facing his house, and were reached by a subway. Here, when the more onerous duties of the day were over, the Lord Chancellor employed himself digging, planting trees and shrubs with such vigour and such judgment, that the whole hill became famous for the number and beauty of its evergreens, and was known as Evergreen Hill, while Erskine's house was called Evergreen Hall. He is said to have planted with his own hand the extraordinary broad holly hedge separating his kitchen-garden from the Heath, opposite to the Fir Tree Avenue. In this kitchen-garden he did not disdain to work: and when discovered with his spade there, he would say, "Here I am enjoying my 'otium cum *diggin* a *taity*.'" His gardener was a Scotchman, not, we hope, unappreciative of his master's wit. Once, when the gardener complained that the drought had burned up all the vegetables and was killing the shrubs, he replied: "Well, John, all I can do for you is to order the hay to be cut down to-morrow morning; if that does not bring rain, nothing will." A friend of his made the remark that "the soil is not the best in that part of Hampstead where your seat is." "No, very bad," Erskine replied, "for although my grandfather was buried there as an earl near a hundred years ago, what has sprouted up from it since but a mere baron?" He was alluding, of course, to his own title.

Besides enjoying the physical delights of gardening, Erskine was well versed

in horticulture; an anxious client who came to consult him at Serjeant's Inn found on the table of his room there thirty or forty small vials, each holding a slip of geranium; and Erskine seemed much more anxious to describe how

ERSKINE HOUSE, HAMPSTEAD

many kinds of geranium there were, than to discuss his client's case!

But if Erskine had a devotion for flowers, his love of animals was even stronger. Of these he had several at Hampstead—Toss, a Newfoundland dog, whom he had taught to personate a Judge, making him sit up with much gravity on a chair with his paws on the table, and placing a full-bottom wig on his head; "faithful Jack" the goose, who followed him wherever he walked about his grounds; a favourite macaw, and other dumb favourites without number. To quote from a description of a dinner-party at Evergreen Hall, written by Sir Samuel Romilly—"He told us now that he had got two favourite leeches. He had been blooded by them last autumn when he had been taken dangerously ill at Portsmouth : they had saved his life and he had brought them with him to town—had ever since kept them in a glass—had himself every day given them fresh water, and had formed a friendship with them. He said he was sure they both knew him and were grateful to him."

Many stories are related that illustrate the practical turn taken by Erskine's love of animals. One day, crossing Hampstead Heath, he saw a ruffianly driver most unmercifully pummelling a miserable bare-boned pack-horse, and remonstrating with him, received this answer : " Why, it's my own ; mayn't I use it as I please ? " As the fellow spoke he dscharged a fresh shower of blows on the bare back of the beast. Erskine, much irritated by this brutality, laid two or three sharp strokes of his walking-stick over the shoulders of the cowardly offender, who, crouching and grumbling, asked him what business he had to touch him with his stick. " Why," replied Erskine, " my stick is my own ; mayn't I use it as I please ? "

For many years it was Erskine's desire to promote legislation for the prevention of cruelty to animals, and a Bill on this subject was introduced by him into the House of Commons, and afterwards carried.

A very interesting story is told of the visit of Edmund Burke to Lord Erskine at Hampstead. The men admired each other's talents, but had latterly been divided by political opinions. Erskine came of a Whig family, and had ever adhered steadily to the Whig party, but Burke's Liberal tendencies had been checked by the excesses of the French Revolution, and he thenceforward mistrusted " reform." Before Burke's death, he came to see the Lord Chancellor, and holding out his hand, said, " Come, Erskine, let us forget all. I shall soon quit this stage, and wish to die in peace with everybody, especially you." Erskine took him into the garden through the tunnel that divided the house from the shrubbery. All the loveliness of the woodlands and the distant prospect over Hampstead Heath broke upon Burke in the soft light of the setting sun. " Oh," said Burke, " this is just the place for a reformer. All the beauties are beyond your reach ; you cannot destroy them."

We close with the picture of these two great men, these two great orators —so different in character and opinion —standing together reconciled on Evergreen Hill, and looking over Hampstead Heath.

OLIVER CROMWELL'S HEAD

OLIVER CROMWELL'S head has long been supposed to be in existence, and to be the embalmed head now in the possession of the Rev. H. R. Wilkinson. This gentleman delivered an address on the subject at the Royal Archæological Institute in March 1911, when he exhibited the head to his audience. A public discussion followed, and strong opinions for and against the authenticity of the relic were delivered. Sir Henry H. Howorth and Dr. Boyd Dawkins, both eminent antiquaries, declared the skull to be indubitably Cromwell's. Describing the effect of Mr. Wilkinson's remarkable lecture, Dr. Dawkins said :

" It is impossible not to accept this as the real head of the great Protector, the man to whom England owes so much. The meeting was distinctly of this opinion, and the whole question was treated with the reverence due to the name and to the remains of one of the greatest benefactors of our country. It is to be hoped that this unique relic will ultimately find its way into the possession of the nation and be kept as a precious heirloom, which cannot fail to be of the deepest historic interest to all the English people."

What, then, if we should live to see the solemn re-burial of Oliver Cromwell's head in Westminster Abbey !

A re-burial it would be. Cromwell's first burial was in the Abbey, where the site of his tomb is marked to this day by a slab on the bays of Henry VII.'s Chapel. Here the great Protector was laid with fitting pomp, but, it is said, with little lamentation. Two vivid descriptions of the scene have come down to us. " It was," says Cowley, " the funeral day of the man who late made himself to be called

Protector. . . . I found there had been much more cost bestowed than either the dead man, or even death itself, could deserve. There was a mighty train of black assistants ; the hearse was magnificent, the idol crowned ; and (not to mention all other ceremonies which are practised at royal interments, and therefore could be by no means omitted here) the vast multitude of spectators made up, as it used to do, no small part of the spectacle itself. But yet, I know not how, the whole was so managed that methought it somewhat represented the life of him for whom it was made : much noise, much tumult, much expense, much magnificence, much vainglory : briefly, a great show, and yet, after all this, but an ill sight."

" It was," says Evelyn, " the joyfullest funeral that ever I saw, for there were none that cried but dogs, which the soldiers hooted away with as barbarous noise, drinking and taking tobacco in the streets as they went."

Even at this point legend and dispute creep in, for it is said that the real interment had taken place two months before in private, and this mystery, says Dean Stanley, " probably fostered the fables which, according to the fancies of the narrators, described the body as thrown into the Thames, or laid in the field of Naseby, or in the coffin of Charles I. at Windsor, or in the vaults of the Claypoles in the parish church of Northampton, or ' carried away in the tempest the night before.' " A hazy eighteenth-century writer quotes the tradition that Cromwell's mutilated remains were obtained by some of his devoted followers and reverently buried in a field on the north side of Holborn. and that the spot was marked by the obelisk which formerly stood in the middle of Red Lion Square. No credence can be given to this story.

The Royalists were never in doubt that Cromwell had been laid in the Abbey, and at the Restoration they carried out a ghastly disinterment and desecration of his remains and those of Ireton and Bradshaw. Let Anthony Wood tell the story :

After the restoration of King Charles II. Ireton's body with that of Oliver Cromwell was taken up [from their tombs in Henry VII.'s Chapel in Westminster Abbey] on Saturday, 26 Jan., 1660, and on Monday night following were drawn in two several carts from Westminster to the Red Lyon in Holbourn, where they continued that evening. The next morning the carcass of Joh. Bradshaw, president of the high court of justice (which had been with great solemnity buried in St. Peter's Church at Westminster, 22 Nov., 1659) was carried in a cart to Holbourn also ; and the next day following that (which was the 30th January, on which day King Charles I. was beheaded in 1648) they were drawn to Tyburn on three several sledges, followed by the universal outcry of the people. Afterwards they being pulled out from their coffins, were hanged at the several angles of that triple tree, where they hung till the sun was set. After which they were taken down, their heads cut off (to be set on Westminster Hall) and their loathsome trunks thrown into a deep hole under the gallows, where they now remain.

This is one of the most accepted stories, but the truth about the disposal of the body of Cromwell after his disinterment remains dark.

It is not to be doubted, however, that the three heads which Londoners became accustomed to see on the roof of Westminster Hall were those of Cromwell, Ireton, and Bradshaw. A Royalist writer described this exposure of the Protector's skull as " the becoming spectacle of his treason."

There these heads remained for a generation. Then a strange thing happened. When the Great Storm of 1703 (of which a separate account is given in this work) was raging over London a ghastly object fell from the roof of Westminster Hall. It was the head of Oliver Cromwell. A sentry picked it up and, carrying it home, concealed it during the rest of his life. He made a statement concerning it on his death-bed, and his friends sold the relic to a family named Russell. It is said that Sir Joshua Reynolds had a great desire to purchase the head, which was ultimately sold to James Cox, an antiquarian dealer. The sale contract, dated 1787, is now in Mr. Wilkinson's possession, and we know that Cox publicly exhibited this head in Bond Street in 1799. In the *Morning Chronicle* of March 18 in that year the following extraordinary advertisement appeared : " The Real Embalmed Head of the powerful and renowned Usurper, Oliver Cromwell ; with the Original Dies for the Medals struck in honour of his Victory at Dunbar, &c., are now exhibited at No. 5 in Mead Court, Old Bond Street (where the Rattle-snake was shown last year) : a genuine Narrative relating to the Acquisition, Concealment, and Preservation of these Articles, to be had at the place of Exhibition."

The head came into the possession of the Wilkinson family in 1812, under circumstances known and attested. It has passed from father to son, and is now preserved by the Rev. H. R. Wilkinson at Shortlands, in Kent.

A peep at the gas-lights

HOW GAS CAME TO LONDON

THERE is a story, not we think told by Boswell, that Dr. Johnson was one evening leaning out of his window in Bolt Court when he saw the parish lamplighter ascend his ladder to light one of the oil lamps which then feebly mitigated the darkness of London at night. The man had scarcely begun to descend when he saw that the flame had gone out. Quickly returning, he lifted the cover of the lamp and thrust the end of his torch beneath it; instantly the flame was communicated to the wick by the vapour which still issued from it. "Ah!" exclaimed the Doctor, "one of these days the streets of London will be lighted by smoke." A correspondent of *Notes and Queries* in 1852 expressed the opinion that this story "bears the mark of authenticity." We are not quite of that opinion, but Dr. Johnson's unconscious prediction may introduce our present subject.

The discoverer of coal gas as an illuminant was Archibald Cochrane, ninth Earl of Dundonald; the inventor, William Murdock, the Cornishman. The distinction must be made, because the scientific Earl made no successful use of his discovery. In manufactured coal-tar he found that the vapour escaping from his retort through an iron pipe was liable to become ignited, and the idea occurred to him that this escaping gas might be controlled and used as an illuminant. But it was reserved for William Murdock to achieve this result. In 1792 he lighted his house at Redruth with coal-gas, and as late as 1872 Mr. Francis Trevethick wrote: "Those still live who saw the gas-pipes conveying gas from the retort in the little yard to near the ceiling of the room, just over the table. A hole for the pipe was made in the window-frame." This house, the first in the world to be lit by gas, is still standing, and its walls bear a commemorative tablet. Murdock was closely associated with Messrs. Boulton and Watt, of Soho, Birmingham, and it was here that the first extensive application of coal gas to lighting was made in 1802. Other factories followed suit, and a few years later gas was in wide use.

The first gas displays in London were regarded as no more than "philosophical fireworks." The first of these displays was given at the Lyceum Theatre in May 1800. Meanwhile, the man who was to be London's first gas-lighter was studying the illuminant in Paris, where Lebon was making rapid independent

THE LIGHT OF OTHER DAYS
From an Old Print

progress. This was Frederick Albert Winsor, a German "company-promoting expert" ("Dictionary of National Biography"). Returning to London this gentleman gave experimental lectures at the Lyceum Theatre on the coming illuminant. In 1806 Winsor was able to light up the front of Carlton House with gas, and to issue a high-falutin prospectus of "The New Patriotic Imperial and National Light and Heat Company," which might well have suggested to

Dickens (if he saw it) the style and objects of the Muffin and Crumpet Company in "Nicholas Nickleby." For Winsor estimated his Company's profit at £229,000,000 a year, out of which he proposed to redeem the National debt and pay the shareholders dividends of something like 1100 per cent.

Meanwhile various experiments were made in London. According to Matthew's "Historical Sketch of Gas Lighting" (1827) Alderman Ward attempted to light with gas the Golden Lane Brewery, and parts of Beech Street and Whitecross Street. In the Peace Jubilee of 1814, when a mimic British Fleet sailed on the Serpentine, an artificial bridge was to be lit by gas, but the bridge it was that burned !

Sir Humphry Davy, who might have known better, declared that it would be as easy to bring down the moon to London as to light the streets with gas, and Sir Walter Scott, who knew nothing at all, scoffed at the idea of lighting London by "smoke." Nevertheless, Pall Mall and Westminster Bridge were well gas-lamped in 1814. The glittering lights abode in Byron's memory ; hence in describing Don Juan's entry into London he remembered "the lamps of Westminster's more regular gleam."

The line of lights, too, up to Charing Cross,
  Pall Mall, and so forth, have a coruscation
Like gold as in comparison to dross,
  Matched with the Continent's illumination.
But London's so well lit that if Diogenes
  Could recommence to hunt his honest man,
And found him not amidst the various progenies
Of the enormous city's spreading spawn,
  'Twere not from want of lamps to aid his dodging his
  Yet undiscover'd treasure.

The spread of the use of gas in London, and the formation of the great gas companies, cannot be traced here, for the story belongs to business rather than romance. It may be mentioned that the conservatism of the West End squares was long manifested in the opposition to gas-lighting of their inhabitants, and that the last to capitulate was Grosvenor Square, in 1842. Theatres began early to adopt gas, but the lessees of the Haymarket Theatre was bound to use oil until 1853. Church clock faces, according to Timbs, began to be lit up by gas in 1827.

The revolution effected by the gas-lighting of London was soon seen to have its moral aspect, and in 1829 a writer in the *Westminster Review* asked, "What has the new light of all the preachers done for the morality and order of London compared to what has been effected by gas-lighting? Old Murdock alone has suppressed more vice than the Suppression Society; and has been a greater police officer into the bargain than old Colquhoun and Richard Birnie united." We may rejoice, therefore, that the electric light now illumines the blameless West End.

WHERE SCOTS FOREGATHERED

DR. Alexander Carlyle, who was the friend and associate of a great many of the literary celebrities of his day, in the middle of the eighteenth century, says that with Smollett and one or two more he used to resort to a small tavern "in the corner of Cockspur Street," called The Golden Ball, "where we had a frugal supper and a little punch, as the finances of none of the company were in very good order. But we had rich enough conversation on literary subjects, which was enlivened by Smollett's agreeable stories told with a peculiar grace. Soon after our acquaintance Smollett showed me his tragedy of 'James I. of Scotland' [afterwards published as *The Regicide* which he never could bring on the stage."

In Cockspur Street itself, which became a regular thoroughfare for the wits and beaux and critics of *bon ton*, was situated the British Coffee House, which was largely frequented by gentlemen from north of the Tweed. And it was here that later Dr. Carlyle, Smollett, and Home the author of "Douglas," were wont to foregather to meet their compatriots and enjoy the flowing bowl and the pawky conversation for which Scottish men have ever been celebrated.

The "British" was long a house of call for Scotchmen, and was very fortunate in its landladies. It dated back as far as 1722 and was kept in

1759 by the sister of Bishop Douglas, of Salisbury, who was so well known for his work against Lauder, the rash doubter of Milton's originality, and who is described by Lord Brougham as "a person of excellent manners and ability." This lady, Mrs. Anderson, was greatly esteemed by the patrons of the house and was evidently a person of superior character and determination. Every Scotchman visiting London felt it his bounden duty to visit the British Coffee House, knowing that he would meet some of his own fellow countrymen there, and Dr. Carlyle, already referred to, of Inveresk, in his "Autobiography," says: "Having found some of my old friends lounging about the British and Forrests's Coffee Houses, in Cockspur Street, Charing Cross—viz., John Blair, afterwards a Prebendary of Westminster, Robert Smith, afterwards distinguished by the appellation of the Duke of Roxburgh's Smith, who introduced me to Dr. Smollett, with whom he was intimate, and Charles Congalton, arriving in a few weeks from Leyden, who was a stranger as well as myself in London—I was at no loss how to pass my time agreeably." John Blair will always live on account of his funeral sermons. William Robertson, the historian, was a great frequenter of the British, and, in a letter sent from the place, April 20, 1759, he writes: "The Argyll [Archibald, third Duke of Argyll] carried all the Scotch against the turnpike; they were willing to be carried, for the Duke of Bedford, in case it should have come into the Lords, had written to the sixteen Peers to solicit their votes; but with so little deference that he enclosed all the letters under one cover, directed to the British Coffee House."

At the British there was a regular club held, which resolved itself into a weekly meeting, and opened at eight o'clock in the evening. The members were chiefly Scottish physicians from the City and the Court end of the town. "Of the first set were Pitcairn, Armstrong, Orme, and Dickson; of the second were William Hunter, Clephan, Mr. Graham, of Pall Mall, etc.—all of them very agreeable men; Clephan especially was one of the most sensible learned and judicious men I ever knew—an admirable classical scholar and a fine historian. He often led the conversation, but it was with an air of modesty and deference to the company which added to the weight of all he said. Hunter was gay and lively and often came into us at nine o'clock fatigued and jaded." Carlyle continues: "He had had no dinner but supped on a couple of eggs, and drank his glass of claret; for though we were a punch club, we allowed him a bottle of what he liked best, and he repaid us with the brilliancy of his conversation; his toast was, 'May no English nobleman venture out of the world without a Scottish physician, as I am sure there are none who venture in.'" This William Hunter was the eminent anatomist, physician, and surgeon. He was the elder brother of the even more famous surgeon John Hunter, who formed the celebrated Museum of Anatomy now at the Royal College of Surgeons.

The following most interesting anecdote connected with the British Coffee House comes from Dr. Carlyle's "Autobiography: "I was in the Coffee House when the news of the Battle of Culloden arrived, and when London all over was in a perfect uproar. About nine o'clock I wished to go home to Lyon's, in New Bond Street, as I had promised to sup with him that night, it being the anniversary of his marriage night or the birthday of one of his children. [Captain Lyon was Dr. Carlyle's cousin.] I asked Smollett if he was ready to go, as he lived at Mayfair; he said he was, and would conduct me. The mob were so riotous, and the squibs so numerous and incessant that we were glad to go into a narrow entry to put our wigs in our pockets and to take our swords from our belts and walk with them in our hands, as everybody then wore swords; and after cautioning me against speaking a word, lest the mob should discover my country and become insolent, 'for John Bull,' says he [Dr. Smollett] is as haughty and valiant to-night as he was abject and cowardly on the Black Wednesday when the Highlanders were at Derby.' After we got to the head of the Haymarket, through incessant fire, the Doctor led me by narrow lanes where we met nobody but a few boys at a pitiful bonfire, who very civilly asked us for sixpence, which I gave them. . . . Smollett though a Tory, was not a Jacobite, but he had the feelings of a Scotch gentleman on the reported cruelties that were said to be exercised after the battle of Culloden. My cousin Lyon was an Englishman born, though

THE OLD BRITISH COFFEE-HOUSE IN COCKSPUR STREET

of Scottish parents, and an officer in the Guards, and perfectly loyal, and yet even he did not seem to rejoice so cordially as I expected. . . . ' God knows,' said he, ' I heartily rejoice that it [the Rebellion] is quelled, but I'm sorry that it had been accomplished by the Duke of C——, for if he was before the most insolent of all commanders, what will he be now ? ' ''

Judging from the many books of reminiscences of those who visited the British Coffee House, there must have been some lively and tragic scenes in Cockspur Street. Cyrus Redding tells a rather sad story, to the effect that on a short visit to town the proprietors of the *Pilot*, a newspaper of some standing at that time, gave a dinner to some of the officers of the Horse Guards at the British. "After a sumptuous repast, in the fashion of the time, we sat down to wine; there was present a bustling little man, a Scotch Colonel, named Macleod, with his son, a fine young man about twenty years old who sat by me; he was an only son with a number of sisters. The bottle was pushed hard. The youth partook too freely for one of his years. He was seized with fever and died, and the estate entailed, went by his death, to distant relatives; and his mother and sisters who would have to depend on him were left penniless on his father's demise."

Captain David Cheap, who was associated with Anson on his distinguished voyages of discovery, and had been wrecked on the coast of Chili, where he was detained for a long period by the Spaniards, when he arrived in London made his way to the old haunt in Cockspur Street with the object of finding somebody to write a full account of Lord Anson's experiences. Captain Cheap, who had a natural feeling for his own countrymen, having heard of Guthrie, the writer of the *Westminster Journal* and other publications, endeavoured to seek him out with the object of getting him to do the work. Cheap had not been long in the house when Guthrie arrived, dressed in fantastically laced clothes, and talking loudly to everybody all the time. Quite soon he commenced quarrelling with a gentleman about Tragedy and Comedy and the unities, and in a wrangling fashion laid down the law in a most peremptory and even insolent manner, and being weak in logic attempted to support his arguments by cursing and swearing. Captain Cheap who was well acquainted with "strange oaths," was astounded at the flow of language that Guthrie had at his command, and, going to the bar asked who the gentleman was, and, finding it was Guthrie whom he had come down purposely to inquire about, he paid for his coffee and went away in silence. Guthrie, through his outrageous mode of living and his quarrelsome nature, though he wrote many clever works, and was indeed a clever man, ended his days in poverty.

The old British as a building began to show signs at last of breaking up, and it was necessary in 1770 to rebuild the premises. It was re-erected from the design of Robert Adam—one of the Adelphi brothers—and the house was considered of high merit, and had a good architectural facade.

Mr. Wheatley tells us that Lord Campbell belonged to a club of Scotchmen called the Beeswing, which was held at the British, and he goes on, "It consisted of about ten men who met once a month at the British Coffee House to dine and drink Port Wine. Spankie, Dr. Haslam, author of several treatises on Insanity, Andrew Grant, a merchant of great literary acquirements, and George Gordon, known about town as 'the man of wit,' were members and the conversation was as good as I ever joined in; but the drinking was tremendous." For over a century and a half the British Coffee House held sway and was the resort of all good Scottish men; but the building fell into the hands of the housebreakers, and upon the old and joyous site modern shops now stand.

HOW THE CHARTISTS SHOOK LONDON

THE year 1848, says Justin McCarthy, in a rememberable phrase, was a year of unfulfilled revolutions. There was to have been a revolution in London in that year, or such a surrender by the Government as would have been unprecedented in our history. The imagination of the Chartists, mostly poor men living on starvation wages, caught fire at the overthrow of Louis Philippe, as had been the case with that of the poorer classes in most countries of Europe. On May 9 a Chartist Convention assembled in London. On May 10 there was to be a vast meeting on Kennington Common to convey to Parliament a petition containing no less than five million signatures. Many of the Chartists were for peaceful persuasion ; but many others had armed themselves, much after the fashion in which the peasants of Monmouth's rebellion were armed. There was widespread terror in London, alleviated by the news that the Duke of Wellington—" the Iron Duke," the victor of Waterloo— was taking measures to prevent riot, or the passage of any great crowd over Westminster Bridge.

It seems strange in these days that any large body of Englishmen should have worked themselves into a dangerous passion about the Six Points of the Charter. These had no relation, even, to the great question of how to get bread. The Charter—the name was given to it casually, by Daniel O'Connell : " There," he said, " is your Charter "—contained only a series of by no means affrighting political demands. Parliament was asked for, and threatened for not conceding, universal suffrage, vote by ballot, annual Parliaments, equal electoral districts, the abolition of all property qualification for members of the House of Commons, and payment for their services.

Those were the famous " Six Points." There is nothing exciting about them in these days ; but during the ten or a dozen years preceding 1848 men had rioted for them, and gone to prison for them, and been transported for them. Thomas Cooper, and Ernest Jones, and Henry Vincent, were among the men who were convicted and imprisoned because they were leading Chartists. The truth is that behind the passionate political movement there was a pathetic belief in the ability of Parliament to work miracles if only it became possible to return members who were acquainted with the lives and with the condition of the poor. " The towns shall win the Charter for England," says Alton Locke, in Charles Kingsley's fine story, " and then for social reform, sanitary reform, ædile reform, cheap food, interchange of free labour, liberty, equality, and brotherhood for ever." Kingsley knew the movement all through, and interpreted it well. What he puts in the mouths of some of the chief characters in " Alton Locke " is history.

At the head of the Chartist movement was Feargus O'Connor, who was returned to Parliament for Nottingham at the general election of 1847. He was a giant of a man, of good Irish family, and was described by his admirers as " the descendant of kings." The description, it has been said, was probably more warranted in his case than in that of Thackeray's Captain Costigan. He seems to have been what Charles Bradlaugh was long afterwards, the greatest out-of-doors orator of his time. But he was no revolutionist. He should never have had anything to do with a party half of whose members talked about the employment of physical force as a means of bringing about political reform. He led Chartism up to its supreme moment, and then abandoned his followers in fear of their desperation.

If the Chartist movement had succeeded, says Kingsley, it must have let loose on those "who had" in London the whole flood of those "who had not." This is to presume that success would have meant the triumph of the physical force men. But the milder sort of Chartists fell away from the movement before the threats and the braggadocio of the more ruffianly men who were rapidly thrusting themselves to the front. These last had plans for outdoing the French revolutionists. London was to be fired in ever so many places at once. Parliament was to be terrorised and its members assaulted, or worse. The Chartists were to be under arms day and night until their petition was granted, all this tremendous threatening being connected with a roll of paper which was chiefly remarkable for its bulk, and for the forged or invented names which it contained. "Shoplifters, an' idiots, an' suckin' bairns. Long Nose, an' Short Nose, an' Pug Nose; an' seventeen Deuks o' Wellington, let alone a baker's dizen o' Queens." Such was Sandy Mackaye's summary of the description given of themselves by some of those who signed the huge petition which was to be carried from Kennington

Common to the floor of the mother of Parliaments.

What is now known as Kennington Park would not at this day be recognised by those who selected it as the scene of the great gathering at which the Chartist movement was to come to a triumphant head. It is in these days a green railed-in public garden and playground. Its flower-beds are among the most pleasant sights of South London. Its trees are so healthy and so umbrageous, and have flourished so amazingly, that some of them seem to be as old as the Chartist agitation itself. Almost ceaseless lines of tram-cars hem in the Park on three of its sides, and yet it is possible to sit down in places which seem to belong to a wooded country far from the roar of towns.

But Kennington Common was a bare, enclosed space when the followers of Feargus O'Connor decided to meet there.

A popular resort of South London cricketers, it was so highly valued in that character that when it was enclosed there would have been strong public protest had not the Duchy of Cornwall, then being administered by the Prince Consort in behalf of his eldest son, the late King Edward VII., set aside the neighbouring Oval as a cricket ground. As a place for such a national meeting as that which the Chartists contemplated its merits were very considerable. It would hold a vast, a probably unexampled concourse of people; it was within easy distance of Westminster where the great petition was to be taken in procession; and it was well surrounded by roads, vastly convenient should there arise any necessity for a sudden dispersal.

However, the significance of the

THE GREAT CHARTIST MEETING ON KENNINGTON COMMON APRIL 1848

National demonstration on Kennington Common was destroyed in advance by the National Convention of Chartists held on the previous day. There were many noisy advocates of a plan for going to the Common armed. This was what the people of London had been apprehending for some days past. What was looked for in some quarters was, indeed, nothing short of civil war. But nothing could induce Feargus O'Connor to give his approval to even the show of violence, and his was the strongest following. Large numbers of delegates went home from the Convention startled and dismayed by the tone of the physical force men, and determined to take no part in the events of the following day. The defections from the other side were probably not fewer in number. Then, too, a terrified whisper as to spies had gone round, and many of those who had seemed to be the most brave and venturesome, slunk off in fear of the law. O'Connor himself contrived to be called away before the critical moment came, and the leadership was left to an honest, rather stupid, uninfluential man who jumped from the speaker's waggon the day after the Convention declaring that they were all humbugged and betrayed.

Nevertheless, on that ninth of April 1848, London went to bed in fear and trembling, knowing nothing of Chartist dissensions, and having heard much more than was true of Chartist threats, but with a certain confidence in its Iron Duke, who planted cannon on Westminster Bridge, and had soldiers hid away in all convenient places. The public offices were garrisoned. Had the Houses of Parliament been threatened, Palace Square would immediately have filled with troops. Great numbers of citizens were enrolled as special constables, and it is one of the little ironies of history that Louis Napoleon, then a faintly interesting exile in London, afterwards French Emperor, was among those who shouldered a baton and wore a badge in the cause of English law and order.

The gathering at Kennington Common was a partly pathetic and partly comic fiasco—a fiasco of the overwhelming kind. It was to have consisted of half a million of men, and there may have been ten thousand present.

Mr. Justin McCarthy says: "The public at large was not aware that the fangs of Chartism had been drawn before it was let loose to play on Kennington Common that memorable tenth of April. London awoke in great alarm that day. The wildest rumours were spread abroad in many parts of the metropolis. Long before the Chartists had got together on Kennington Common at all various remote quarters of London were filled with horrifying reports of encounters between the insurgents and the police or military, in which the Chartists invariably had the better, and as a result of which they were marching in full force to the particular district where the momentary panic prevailed." And what had taken place ? Nothing but the final dispersion of the Chartist movement.

One bystander has left it on record that he saw the Duke of Wellington, in mufti, watching the miserable-looking crowd at Kennington Common, and that he heard him mutter to himself, " Cannon to those fellows ! Cannon to those fellows ! Why, I could puff them down."

THEODORE HOOK AND THE BERNERS STREET HOAX

THEODORE HOOK, the famous humorist and the author of the Berners Street Hoax, was a particularly handsome man, and the grace of his bearing seemed to appeal strongly to nearly every person that he met. He had a way with him. One writer says: "If fine personal qualities, as a handsome figure and agreeable countenance, quick intelligence and brilliant wit with an unfailing flow of animal spirits, were alone able to secure happiness, Theodore Hook ought to have been amongst the happiest and most fortunate of mankind, for he possessed them all." His life, however, was an uninterrupted succession of boisterous buffooneries, and his whole career was an absolute farce even when he edited *John Bull*. On one occasion he and Terry, the actor, who was a friend of Sir Walter Scott, were rowing to Richmond when they saw a placard at the foot of a garden which read "Nobody permitted to Land Here—Offenders prosecuted with the utmost Rigour of the Law." Hook and his friend immediately landed and walked about the lawn as if the place belonged to them. They made their way into the house and mingled themselves with the jovial party that was assembled. The room being full no notice was taken of them, and long before the host was beginning to wonder who he was, his sallies had already drawn around him a whole congress of the guests who were being tickled by his absurdities.

Barham, of "Ingoldsby Legends" fame, relates, in very agreeable terms, the particularities of this little incident as follows: The master of the house at last perceiving a stranger went up and politely begged his name, as he felt rather at a loss. Hook replied with a perfect torrent of volubility, but expressed in the suavest and most fascinating terms, and effectually preventing any interruption to his discourse. . . An explanation at last came out, that he had mistaken both the house and the hour at which he ought to have dined with a friend. The old gentleman's civility then could not allow him to depart, as his friend's dinner hour must now be long past, and a guest with such a flow of spirits must prove a most agreeable acquisition to his own table. Hook professed great reluctance to trespass thus on the hospitality of a stranger, but was induced, seemingly with much difficulty, to remain and partake of dinner. So delightful a companion and so droll a fellow they had never met before, and so much mirth and jollity had never till now enlivened the mansion. At ten o'clock, Mr. Terry was announced, and Hook, who had seated himself at the pianoforte in the performance of one of his famous extemporaneous effusions, brought his song to a close as follows:

I am very much pleased with your fare ;
Your cellar's as prime as your cook ;
My friend's Mr. Terry the player,
And I'm Mr. Theodore Hook !

In Hook's days, practical jokes were in vogue. All the young blades thought it clever to wrench off door knocker and carry away bell pulls. Hook himself engaged himself in many of these pastimes. One of his freaks was the conveying away of the figure of a Highlander, as large as life, from the door of a tobacconist. This he wrapped up in a cloak, put into a coach and told the driver to take the gentleman home, giving of course, a wholly fictitious address.

During the great trial of Lord Melville, Hook went with a friend to Westminster Hall to watch the proceedings. As the peers began to enter a simple-looking lady from the country touched his arm, and said, "I beg your pardon, Sir, but pray who are these gentlemen in red now coming in?"

"Those, madam," he replied, "are the barons of England; in these cases the junior peers always come first."

"Thank you, Sir; much obliged to you. Louisa, my dear (turning to her daughter who accompanied her), tell Jane these are the barons of England, and the juniors, that is the youngest, you know, always go first. Tell her to be sure and remember that when we get home." The game is continued by Hook, who deludes the visitors in the most fantastic fashion.

THEODORE EDWARD HOOK

Later when he had lied to them with perfect *sang froid*, the old lady of the company said to him when the Speaker of the House of Commons entered in his richly embroidered robes, "Pray say who is that—that fine looking person opposite?"

"That, ma'am, is Cardinal Wolsey."

"No, Sir," was the angry rejoinder, "we know a good deal better than that; Cardinal Wolsey has been dead and buried these many years."

"No such thing, my dear madam," replied Hook without moving a muscle, "it has been reported in the country, but without the least foundation in truth; in fact, these rascally newspapers will say anything."

The provincial dame looked thunderstruck. She opened her eyes and mouth in amazement, and, being deprived of further speech, she, not knowing what might happen next, hurried off with a daughter in each hand, leaving the mischievous wag and his friend to enjoy the joke.

"Passing one day," says the anonymous author of "Theodore Hook—a Sketch" published in 1852, "in a gig with a friend by the villa of a retired chronometer maker, he suddenly reined up, and remarked to his friend what a comfortable little box that was, and that they might do worse than dine there. He then alighted, rang the bell, and on being admitted to the presence of the worthy old citizen, said that he had often heard his name, which was celebrated throughout the civilised world, and that being in

"I BEG YOUR PARDON, SIR, BUT MAY I ASK, ARE YOU ANYBODY PARTICULAR?"

the neighbourhood he could not resist the temptation of calling and making the acquaintance of so distinguished a public character." The old gentleman was so taken with the compliment that he invited Hook and his companion to stay to dinner, and, as may be imagined, Hook paid for it with his own peculiar humour of improvisation and eccentric anecdotes, of which he had a full fund.

One absurd thing of Hook's early days

is thus recorded : Walking along the Strand one day he accosted with extreme gravity a very pompous-looking old gentleman. " I beg your pardon, Sir, but may I ask, are you anybody particular ? " and then passed away before the astonished individual could recover sufficient breath to make a reply.

Hook's escapades are without end; but all were eclipsed by the Berners Street episode, which created a sensation in London in 1809. It is recorded that in walking one day down this street with his companion, Sam Beazeley, who wrote many farces that achieved a certain amount of popularity in their day, he called his attention to the particularly neat and modest appearance of a house the residence of a widow lady. " I'll lay you a guinea," said Theodore, " that in one week that nice quiet dwelling shall be the most famous in all London." The bet was taken. In the course of four or five days Hook had written and de-spatched something like a thousand letters conveying orders to tradesmen of every sort within the " bills of mortality," all to be executed on one particular day and as nearly as possible at one fixed hour. Waggons loaded with coals ; carters from Covent Garden laden with potatoes, cabbages, and all kinds of vegetables ; carriers with books, prints, millinery, dresses, and everything conceivable in the way of costumes and eatables, groceries, and whatever was available from the butcher, and every other tradesman that was necessary, or unnecessary, to any human being, was commanded from scores of dealers from every part of London. Vans with pianos, wedding and funeral coaches all rumbled through and filled up the adjoining streets.

In 1809 Oxford Road, as Oxford Street, was then called, was not approachable either from Westminster, or from the City, otherwise than through a complicated series of small turnings. It may be therefore only feebly guessed what the crash and jam and tumult of that day was.

Such a babel was never heard before in London ; and, to complete the business, who should drive up but the Lord Mayor in his State Carriage ; the Governor of the Bank of England ; the Chairman of the East India Company, and even the Duke of Gloucester.

Hook and his confederates had hired an apartment immediately opposite to the house to see the fun. The consternation caused to the poor lady became quite a serious matter in the end, and Hook himself was alarmed. However, although the matter was made a subject of investigation the perpetrators of the hoax were not discovered till long after.

Hook was a great clubman, and at the Athenæum the number of dinners fell off by upwards of three hundred per annum, after Hook disappeared from the corner he had made so popular, near the door of the coffee room. Champagne and punch were Hook's particular fancies in the way of drinks, and one writer remarks, " many grave and dignified personages being frequent guests, it would be hardly seemly to be calling for repeated supplies of a certain description ; but the waiters well understood what the Oracle of the Corner meant by ' Another glass of toast and water ' or ' A little more lemonade.' " And thus Hook, living if one may say by hook and crook, lived his day—the favourite of princes and the enemy of himself. Debt and nervous depression clouded his last years. He died in 1841, and lies buried in Fulham Churchyard.

After W. Havell

OLD SADLER'S WELLS AND ITS THEATRE

SADLER'S WELLS is still the oldest existing theatre in London. It bears the privilege and honour of being the only old theatre that has never been burnt down. It is acknowledged that amongst the relics of a bygone era very few playhouses can show a past of more enthralling interest than the ancient theatre built by a surveyor of highways named Sadler in 1683. One of Sadler's workmen during the excavations discovered a long-forgotten spring of mineral water. This fact Sadler made much stir about. The well had been stopped up during the Reformation, by the State, as was alleged, to "check the impositions of the priests of the Priory of St. John of Jerusalem who extorted money from the people by making them believe that the virtues of the water proceeded from the efficacy of their prayers."

When Sadler came into possession of the place and into the knowledge of the supposed curative powers of the spring, he at once, with the guarantees of many physicians of note, drew all the fine ladies and their escorts from the West End and the City to drink the waters. "Hundreds of persons daily came to drink them, who were recommended to eat carraways whilst drinking the waters, or to drink a glass or two of Rhenish or white wine, and smoke a pipe of tobacco." For these visitors Sadler devised a combination of variety entertainments. Soon the spring became of secondary consideration, and fascinating performers on the tight rope, and dancers and singers of ballads and comic songs, now ingratiated themselves as the chief attractions.

The story of Sadler's Wells is fertile in changes, not only in managements but in the development of one art and one class, to and from another. It is with considerable interest one reads in the *Weekly Journal* of March 15, 1778 : " Sadler's Wells being lately opened, there is likely to be a great resort of strolling damsels, half-pay officers, peripatetic tradesmen, tars, butchers, and others musically inclined." At this time there were four or five exhibitions in one day, the duration of each depending on circumstances. As soon as the persons outside were numerous enough to form another audience, somebody would go to the back of the seats and call out : " *Is Hiram Fisteman here ?* " which was a cue for the showman, who would rapidly dismiss the unwary audience with a song in order to let in the next waiting contingent of pleasure-seekers.

In those days rope-dancers—in particular there was a ladder dancer, supposed to be of Dutch origin, who climbed up a rope arrangement and tumbled about and in and out the treads in an exceedingly marvellous manner—were a novelty, and then came the first trapeze wonders, men and women who flew from swinging bars right over the very large auditorium. All these performances were free, as note :

You only pay for liquors, not the show,
Such as neat brandy, southern cyder fine,
And grape's true juice as e'er was pressed for wine.

Sadler's Wells was evidently the forerunner of the modern music-hall and hippodrome. It makes startling reading to learn that a hundred and twenty years ago visitors to any places of amusement inside and outside London had to be most anxiously on their guard against footpads and highwaymen, even " Islington way," where even then there was an " Angel." Quite a familiar announcement on the playbills was : " A horse patrol will be sent in the New Road for the protection of the Nobility and Gentry who go from the squares and that end of Town." Similar precautions were taken for the protection of City merchants and City dames who had the courage to venture out for an evening's enjoyment.

Sadler's Wells at the end of the eighteenth century became a great dramatic centre and the home of pantomime. Grimaldi made his greatest successes here, and many years after Samuel Phelps tried to make, and eventually with now-forgotten success, the true meaning of Shakespeare's plays plain to the waiting understanding of legitimate students and lovers of the play.

But to return to some of the early incidents, we may quote from Edward Ward in his satire " A Walk to Islington " :

Lady Squab, with her moonified face,
By the side of the organ resumes her place.

He then speaks of a violinist dressed in scarlet :

Who runs up in *alt*, with a hey-diddle-diddle,
To show what a fool he can make of a fiddle.

Then we hear of the fine ladies who disport themselves in their handsome gowns, with their maids, to the discomfort of their lords and masters, who are in the City labouring for their livings.

Many interesting tales are related of the performers at Sadler's Wells. Edmund Kean, for instance, made his first appearance in London here in a speaking part, as " a juvenile wonder," and recited the great speech of Rolla in Sheridan's *Pizarro*. Then there was the African traveller Belzoni, who exhibited feats of Herculean strength as a gymnast. He posed as the Patagonian Samson, and one of his feats was to walk round the stage supporting on his shoulders a pyramidal framework on which rested eleven men, the topmost of whom reached to the flies. Upon one occasion the stage gave way, owing to their weight, and precipitated the giant and his crew into the water of the New River Company, whose stream meandered beneath the stage. The audience were so delighted at the mishap that they cried for an encore.

At Sadler's Wells was first danced, apart from the tight rope, an extraordinary feat by a popular clown called Dubois, who, wearing wooden clogs, gave a hornpipe, gyrating between a number of well-placed eggs.

Early in the nineteenth century an immense tank, according to Blanchard, was constructed underneath the stage and filled up by a communication with the New River Company. In this was given a mimic representation of the siege of Gibraltar, with mechanical water-pipe arrangements and lights from different parts of the house. The most bewildering effects were secured, and the audiences, who crowded in for many seasons, thought it the most astounding achievement of mankind.

Sadler's Wells, operatic, comic, dramatic, and " various," has to its count the names of some of the greatest actors, dancers, and acrobats that ever lived. Kean and Grimaldi have been referred to, and also, of modern years, Samuel Phelps. Mrs. Siddons has to be added to the roll and also King, who created the part of Sir Peter Teazle in Sheridan's *School for Scandal.*

Sadler's Wells, with many ups and downs, and especially the latter, has yet lived through its many decades of uncertainty ; and it is still a landmark of many memories, that will certainly not be forgotten by those who like to linger on the days that pass.

LONDON CATCH PHRASES

A CATCH phrase popular in London many years ago was, " *How's your poor feet ?* " and this very nearly ruined a play at the Adelphi Theatre called the *Dead Heart.* When Mr. Benjamin Webster, playing the hero, exclaimed, " Alas ! alas, my heart is dead ! " instantly came an inquiry from the gallery, " How's your poor feet ? "

A common saying about which history is silent, " Keep your hair on," is quite explainable, though doubtless exasperating, as it implies an act of irritability on the part of the person so addressed.

Then, again, " Does your Mother know you're out ? " This provoking query used to be addressed to young men who assumed more than was necessary, or, as we say in these days; " swank." It was a question of mock concern and solicitude implying that one so young and inexperienced should be allowed to wander about without the guidance of the maternal parent.

" *If you want to know the time ask a policeman.*" That came from a popular song sung by Herbert Campbell. Then there was " *Where did you get that hat ?* " vulgarised into " Where did you get that tile ? " At Coventry some years ago, an actress who was appearing in one of the Gilbert and Sullivan Operas, at the theatre there, wore an abnormally large confection in millinery, and an exuberant youth in the pit, directly she made her entrance, inquired as to where she had obtained her hat. The refrain, " *Where did you get that hat ?* " was taken up uproariously by the gods, and the performance had to be stopped until the rioters were quelled or expelled.

TENNYSON IN LONDON

WHEN we think of Tennyson in London, we think of a voice suing out of the clouds.is Clouds, it must be explained, of tobacco smoke; for Tennyson in London always looms dim out of a smoky halo. Witness Carlyle's words, when he found Tennyson with Mrs. Carlyle, sitting in the garden at his house in Cheyne Row, smoking comfortably—" dusty, smoky, free-and-easy," he describes him, a man " who swims outwardly and inwardly with great composure in an articulate element of tranquil chaos and tobacco smoke. Great now and then when he does emerge—a most restful, brotherly, solid-hearted man."

As to the voice, it has been variously described—by Carlyle, as having the sound of a pine-wood; by Mrs. Browning, as like an organ, rather music than speech; by Bayard Taylor, as " a strange monotonous chant." The voice, it must be explained, is not indulging in mere conversation, but is reading aloud poems of Tennyson's own composition. We have innumerable vivid little sketches of such readings in London. And it is in no trivial spirit that we remind our readers of Tennyson's love of tobacco smoke; rather we recall it, because it symbolises the social intercourse that before all he preferred—long talks into the night with congenial souls, long rambles through London streets with intimate friends.

" Old Fitz," Edward Fitzgerald, who made that wonderful translation of " Omar Khayyam," writes of " much sitting up of nights till twelve or three in the morning, with pipes in our mouths; at which hour we would get Alfred to give us some of his magic music, which he does between growling and smoking."

The figure of Tennyson in the days of his fame has blotted out the figure of Tennyson in the days of his obscurity and poverty. We are apt to think of his life as always lived on the grand scale, a thing somewhat aristocratic and aloof; it is well to remember that as a young man he had rooms in dingy London lodgings and frequented chop-houses in Fleet Street— not only frequented them, but commemorated them in good swinging verse. But even in early manhood his appearance was sufficiently striking to arrest attention. Imagine him at the age of twenty-three, when he had published but two small volumes of poems, walking down the Strand! He was over six feet in height—" one of the finest-looking men in the world," says Carlyle, " a great shock of rough dusky dark hair; bright laughing hazel eyes; massive aquiline face, most massive yet most delicate; of sallow brown complexion, most Indian-looking . . . clothes cynically loose, free-and-easy . . ." To complete this forcible picture we have only to add that the young man already affected the wideawake, which might have cost him his peerage. For when, in later years, honours came upon him, and Gladstone was commissioned to offer him a barony, the only difficulty in Gladstone's mind was that the new peer might insist on wearing his wideawake in the House of Lords!

Tennyson lived practically all his life in the country, but the " dark Queen-city " had strong fascination for him, and he rejoiced in London's " central roar," and especially delighted in the motley Strand and Fleet Street. "Instead of the stuccoed houses in the West End, this is the place where I should like to live," he would say. After 1833 he lodged hung in glittering rows in the bar. It was famous for its chops and its porter, and its "plump head-waiter" was, according to Tennyson, a very superior person, "not like the common

TENNYSON AT THE COCK TAVERN

a good deal in London, generally occupying rooms in Lincoln's Inn Fields. The chop-house "to which I most resort" was the "Cock Tavern," which used to stand opposite Temple Bar. This tavern retained many of the features of the old inns; it was lined with wainscoting, and the silver tankards of special customers breed that with the napkin dally." The "Cock" has now been swept away, and a bank erected on its site; but the original old oak fireplace, the "boxes" and other fittings have been transferred to a tavern of the same name almost opposite the Fleet Street end of Chancery Lane (No. 22, Fleet Street). Carlyle used to dine with Tennyson at the " Cock," and this tavern is celebrated in Tennyson's " Will Waterproof's Lyrical Mono-logue "—a poem that is full of fancy and humour.

The poet bids the waiter " bring him a pint of port," not such as is set before chance comers, but a special vintage " whose father-grape grew fat in Lusitanian Summers." Port was always Tennyson's favourite wine, and was never omitted when his friends gathered round him in his lodgings. " Head-waiter of the chop-house here," Tennyson sings :

> *We* fret, we fume, would shift our skins,
>   Would quarrel with our lot ;
> *Thy* care is, under polish'd tins
>   To serve the hot-and-hot ;
> To come and go and come again
>   Returning like the pewit,
> And watch'd by silent gentlemen
>   That trifle with the cruet.

It is amusing to read that the " plump head-waiter " was a little offended at the allusions to himself, when he heard of the poem : perhaps on the ground of the old Irish woman who objected to being called " a rectangular parallelogram," he re-sented being compared to " Ganymede from some delightful valley."

Tennyson in London is chiefly a record of Tennyson's friendships, which seem to have included almost all the great men of his time ; and the greatest friendship of his life—the friendship untimely cut off, which survives for all time in " In Memoriam "—had many of its episodes in London. Tennyson's close college friend, Arthur Hallam, lived at 67 Wimpole Street —a number easy to remember, for he was always to be found at sixes and at sevens. Hallam had a den at the top of the house ; and the two young men used to ramble about London, and have long smokes in the den, discussing every possible subject under the sun, literary, political, social. They were both much in earnest, both much concerned at the misery of the poor, both anxious to remedy the evils they saw around them. Their friendship promised soon to be cemented by a closer tie ; for Hallam was engaged to Tennyson's sister Emily. Hallam had always been a little delicate in health, and after an attack of influenza his father planned to take him on a tour in Germany and Austria. Before Hallam set out there was a supper-party at Tennyson's lodgings. " Moxon (the publisher) and Leigh Hunt were there," writes Hallam, " and we did not separate till half-past four o'clock ; Alfred repeated glorious fragments of ' The Gardener's Daughter,' which seemed to produce the proper effect upon Leigh Hunt." Every one knows the tragedy that followed. Hallam died in Vienna in 1833 of the bursting of a blood-vessel near the brain. The sister bereaved of her lover, the brother bereaved of his friend, under-went long months, long years, of anguish ; and *his* grief, and the doubts and questions that beset him, and the key that he found to the riddle of life and death, lie open for us all to read in the pages of " In Memoriam," given to the world in 1850, the year that Tennyson became Laureate, seven-teen years after Hallam's death.

When Tennyson first revisits the street where his friend lived, all is terrible to him :

> Dark house by which once more I stand
>   Here in the long unlovely street,
>   Doors, where my heart was used to beat
> So quickly, waiting for a hand. . . .

But later, hope is born anew, and the very street itself is transfigured :

Doors, where my heart was used to beat
  So quickly, not as one that weeps
  I come once more ; the city sleeps ;
I smell the meadow in the street ;

I hear a chirp of birds ; I see
  Betwixt the black fronts long withdrawn
  A light blue lane of early dawn,
And think of early days and thee.

If Hallam stands beside Tennyson in London in early days, Carlyle is the figure that looms most prominently beside Tennyson in later years. The rugged melancholy Scotchman was attracted from the first to Tennyson ; "a true human soul," he calls him, "to whom your own soul can say 'brother.'" And in his forcible way he adds this striking description of Tennyson : "A man solitary and sad, as certain men are, dwelling in an element of gloom, carrying a bit of chaos about him, in short, which he is manufacturing into Cosmos." Both these great men were alike in their veracity, in their single-mindedness, in their melancholy, though in Carlyle's nature the melancholy was more deep-seated, and he had not those visions of "The Gleam" which irradiated Tennyson's way. Carlyle was more bitter, more impatient ; Tennyson's was the serener nature. But the two men understood each other—they reached in fact that perfection of understanding that is satisfied with silence ; and long evenings they sat

THE ENTRANCE TO THE OLD COCK TAVERN, FLEET STREET

in the kitchen of Carlyle's house at Chelsea, smoking quietly, and no word passing between them. On other occasions they took long walks at night, and Carlyle would rail against the "governments of Jackasserie which cared more for commerce than for the greatness of our Empire"; or would rave against the stuccoed houses in London as "acrid putrescence"; or against the suburbs as "a black jumble of black cottages where there used to be pleasant fields"; and they would both agree that it was growing into "a strange chaos of odds and ends, this London."

It was such intercourse as this that Tennyson enjoyed ; he stood outside the amenities of ordinary social life. Mrs. Carlyle, writing to her husband, tells how she found Tennyson at some private theatricals in 1843, got up by Dickens and Foster. "Passing down a long dim passage, I came upon a tall man leant to the wall, with his head touching the ceiling like a caryatid, to all appearances asleep, or resolutely trying it under most unfavourable circumstances." Carlyle took upon himself to interview Richard Milnes (afterwards Lord Houghton) on the subject of a pension for Tennyson. Milnes asked, "What will my constituents say ? " Solemn and emphatic was Carlyle's response, "Richard Milnes, on the Day of

Judgment, when the Lord asks you why you didn't get that pension for Alfred Tennyson, it will not do to lay the blame on your constituents ; it is *you* that will be damned." The argument proved effective, and a pension of £200 was granted.

But Tennyson's son tells us that the *tête-à-tête* conversations between Browning and his father were the best talk he ever heard, so full of repartee, quip, epigram, anecdote, depth, and wisdom. These brother poets, he adds, were two of the most widely read men of their time, absolutely without a touch of jealousy, and revelling, as it were, in each other's power. On one occasion Browning said he thought he could make a rhyme to any word in the English language. The word " rhinosceros " was suggested. Without a moment's hesitation, Browning improvised as follows :

O, if you should see a rhinosceros
  And a tree be in sight,
  Climb quick, for his might
Is a match for the Gods, he can toss Eros.

Mrs. Browning gives a delightful picture of Tennyson in London, and tells how he " dined with us, smoked with us, opened his heart to us (and the second bottle of port), and ended by reading ' Maud ' through from end to end, and going away at half-past two in the morning. If I had had a heart to spare, certainly he would have won mine. He is captivating with his frankness, confidingness, and unexampled naïveté. Think of his stopping in ' Maud ' every now and then -There's a wonderful touch ! That's very tender ! How beautiful that is ! Yes, and it *was* wonderful, tender, beautiful."

Tennyson, as we have said, seems to have known all the great men and women of his day, great in position, as well as great in intellect. The following amusing story is told of his meeting with the Princess of Wales, which took place at Mrs. Greville's, in Chester Square. The Princess asked him to read the " Welcome to Alexandra." When he had read it, the fact of his having read his own complimentary poem to the Princess herself somehow struck them both as being so ludicrous that he dropped the book on the floor, and both went into fits of uncontrollable laughter.

Tennyson is pre-eminently the poet of English country life ; and the loveliness of England lies in his verse as in a pure and clear shrine. Many of his poems were, however, written in London. " The Princess " was born among the fogs and smuts of Lincoln's Inn. At Chapel House, Twickenham, the corner house in Montpelier Row, running between the Thames and Richmond Road, where he brought his wife after their marriage, the " Ode on the Death of the Duke of Wellington " was written. And he has struck out some memorable descriptions of London. At one time he lived in Epping Forest ; and out of the night journeys between London and Epping grew that splendid line, " The lights of London flaring like a dreary dawn." In 1842 he visited St. Paul's Cathedral with " Old Fitz." " Merely as an enclosed space in a huge city, this is very fine," he said. When they got out into the open, in the midst of the " central roar," he added, " This is the mind ; that is a mood of it,"—a thought that he might well have carved into a sonnet. Though indeed the modern lovers of London have generally preferred to sing her praises in lyric strain.

THE TRIAL OF HENRY FAUNTLEROY

"AT ten o'clock Mr. Justice Park and Mr. Baron Garrow took their seats on the bench, accompanied by the Lord Mayor. The Attorney-General entered the court at the same time, and took his seat at the table, next Mr. Freshfield, the Bank solicitor.

"At five minutes past ten o'clock Mr. Henry Fauntleroy was conducted to the bar, between the two city marshals, the head turnkey of Newgate, and accompanied by Mr. Harmer, his solicitor. He was dressed in a full suit of black, and the firmness which he displayed in the morning seemed for the moment to have deserted him, when he was exposed at the bar to the gaze of the court. His step was tremulous; his face paler and much thinner than when he was first examined at Marlborough Street; his grey hair had rather a lighter hue, as if from the mixture of a little powder; he never for a moment raised his head; but, placing his hands upon the front of the dock, stood with dejected mien while the preliminary forms of the trial were arranging."

This was at the Old Bailey, October 30, 1824.

The prisoner at the bar, Henry Fauntleroy, was just thirty-nine years of age. His father had assisted in the founding, in 1782, of the banking-house of Marsh, Sibbald, and Co., of Berners Street. Eighteen years later, in 1800, the younger Fauntleroy entered the house as a clerk; and he was but twenty-two when, on the death of his father in 1807, the elders of the firm took him into partnership. "His knowledge of the business was extensive, and from the first almost the whole management of the bank and its affairs was left in his hands."

Seventeen years passed, and suddenly the City received a shock. On September 14, 1824, Marsh, Sibbald, and Co. published a statement in the papers to the effect that they were compelled to suspend payment owing to "the very unexpected situation in which we find ourselves placed by the extraordinary conduct of our partner, Mr. Fauntleroy." Henry Fauntleroy, in fine, was in the hands of justice. He had been arrested September 11, and, after private examination before a magistrate, committed to Coldbath Fields. Forgery was the charge against him.

Fauntleroy had been taken into custody in his own counting-house. "The warrant was obtained on the depositions of two trustees of £1000 in 3 per cent. annuities who had entrusted the stock to Fauntleroy; the dividends were regularly paid to them, but it was discovered that the stock had been sold in September 1820 under a power of attorney purporting to be signed by the trustees themselves and by Fauntleroy, and the trustees' signatures were forged." One week from the date of his arrest saw Fauntleroy in the police-court. Evidence was then given that he had similarly made away with other stock, representing sums of £17,500, £46,000, and £5300. On October 1 further charges were dealt with; and Fauntleroy, formally committed for trial, was lodged in Newgate.

Even before these preliminaries were over, an indiscriminate attack on him had begun. The Press would seem to have lent itself to the malice of private and hidden foes, for there was almost no limit to the accusations that were printed. Had he brought ruin upon the widow and the orphan in their thousands, the ex-banker could not have been more liberally or outrageously assailed. He had appropriated trust funds to the amount of a quarter of a million ; this legal plunder he had squandered in riotous living ; he kept houses here and horses there ; his every night was an orgy : such were among the prodigal inventions of the enemy. It may be imagined to what a point public opinion was inflamed against the man who stood in the dock on October 30.

Pleading not guilty, he "put himself for trial upon God and his country." Seven separate indictments were preferred against him, but one of these sufficed for the Attorney-General's case. Fauntleroy had forged a deed in the name of Miss Frances Young, his sister-in-law, for the transfer of £5480 (in one report of the case, unless there was a misprint, the amount is £5450). One and all of the indictments could probably have been proved with very little difficulty, but the Attorney-General relied upon the case of Miss Young. He had a bombshell for the court, one of the most remarkable ever exploded by counsel, and it settled the fate of Fauntleroy. This, in the Attorney-General's words, was "a document of a character so extraordinary, so singularly complete in all its parts, as to leave no possible doubt that the prisoner at the bar was the party who had committed the offence." The Attorney-General went on :

"When the prisoner was taken into custody . . . he, in the presence of the officer, locked his private desk, with a key which was then attached to his watch—that key was afterwards taken from him by the officer ; and when the respectable solicitor for the Bank, who conducts this prosecution, went to search the house in Berners Street for the prisoner's papers . . . he found in one of the rooms of Messrs. Marsh and Co.'s bank . . . one tin box without a name. This led him to examine it. The key was found in the prisoner's private desk . . . and on opening this box was found a number of private papers belonging to the prisoner, and among them the extraordinary document of which I have apprised you."

An extraordinary document it was. It was death-warrant and halter in one. Writing it with his own hand, Fauntleroy had consigned himself to the gallows. It ran :

"Consols, £11,151 standing in the name of my trusteeship ; £3000, E. W. Young ; £6000 Consols, General Young ; £5000, long annuities, Frances Young ; another £6000 ; Lady Nelson, £11,595 ; Mrs. Ferrer, £20,000 4 per cents ; Earl of Ossory, £7000 ; T. Owen, £9400 ; J. W. Parkins, £4000 ; Lord Aboyne, £6000 ; P. Moore and John Marsh, £21,000."

The paper contained a total of sums exceeding £100,000. It was all in Fauntleroy's hand, and he went on to establish his guilt in these following words : " In order to keep up the credit of our house, I have forged powers of attorney, and have thereupon sold out all these sums, without the knowledge of any of my partners. I have given credit in the accounts for the interest when it became due." In his infatuation Fauntleroy had added a damning postscript : "The Bank began first to refuse our acceptances, and thereby to destroy the credit of our house ; they shall therefore smart for it."

What a confession was this, at a date when the convicted forger was practically assured of the most ignominious of deaths! Commenting upon it, the Attorney-General suggested that Fauntleroy in drawing up the paper had contemplated flight—partly perhaps with a design to "protect his partners from any suspicion of participation in his acts." Not having fled, what madness of negligence had stayed him from destroying this incontrovertible proof of his guilt?

The Bank of England, with this information as a guide, had examined the private accounts kept by Fauntleroy with his firm, and found that the accounts of those clients whose moneys he had fraudulently transferred were regularly kept up, and the interest upon the dividends as regularly carried to them every half-year as if the original stock had remained in being.

The case having been formally proved, Fauntleroy (since at that era his counsel could not speak for him) addressed the court in his defence. Admitting his guilt, as he could not but do, he protested that his course of action had been forced upon him by his firm's necessities. At the time he succeeded his father he "found the concern deeply involved in advances to builders and others, which had rendered a system of discounting necessary, and which we were obliged to continue in consequence of the scarcity of money at that time, and the necessity of making further advances to those persons to secure the sums in which they stood indebted." From bad to worse the affairs of the house

FAUNTLEROY IN THE DOCK

had gone. Having exposed the situation pretty fully, Fauntleroy went on: "I declare that all the moneys temporarily raised by me were applied, not in one instance for my own separate purposes or expenses, but in every case they were immediately placed to the credit of the house in Berners Street, and applied to the payment of the pressing demands upon it. . . . I have been accused of crimes I never even contemplated, and of acts of profligacy I never committed; and I appear at this bar with every prejudice against me, and almost prejudged. . . . I maintained but two establishments, one at Brighton, where my mother and my sister reside in the season, the expenses of which to me, exclusive of my wine, were within £400 per annum; one at Lambeth, where my two children lived, from its very nature private and inexpensive, to which I resorted for retirement, after many a day passed in devising means to avert the embarrassments of the banking-house."

Justice Park having delivered his charge, the jury retired, and after a deliberation of twenty minutes returned with a verdict of "Guilty of uttering the forged instrument, knowing it to be forged." Three days later, November 2, at the termination of the sessions, the Recorder passed sentence of death.

Griffiths tells us in his "Chronicles of Newgate" that Fauntleroy, "on account of his birth and antecedents, was allowed to occupy a turnkey's room, and kept altogether separate from the other prisoners until the day of his death." The chaplain of Newgate treated him less feelingly. At this period strangers were admitted to the Sunday service in the prison chapel when the "condemned sermon" was to be preached, the sheriffs attended in state, and there was as much parade as possible. "In the centre of the chapel was the condemned pew, a large, dock-like erection painted black. Those who sat in it were visible to the whole congregation, and still more to the ordinary, whose desk and pulpit were just in front of the pew, and within a couple of yards of it. The occupants of this terrible pew were the last always to enter."

The ordinary of that day, a certain Rev. Cotton, in one of his sermons to the condemned seems to have pointed directly at Fauntleroy and made a kind of exhibition of him. For this he was summoned before the gaol committee of aldermen, who informed him that "the public would not in future be admitted to hear the condemned sermon."

As was often, of course, the case when a person of some distinction lay under sentence of death, every kind of influence was employed to obtain a commutation of the death penalty. Twice the affair was argued before judges on points of law, and to the Home Secretary there were sundry appeals from very influential quarters. One curious and grimly amusing circumstance is recorded. An Italian named Edmondo Angelini begged to be allowed to take Fauntleroy's place on the scaffold. He wrote to the Lord Mayor urging that "his life is useful, mine a burthen to the State." It was not unnaturally thought that the generous Italian was insane.

All efforts to save the banker were unavailing, and on November 30, 1824, he was executed in the presence of a crowd estimated to number 100,000 persons. "Every window and roof which could command a view of the horrible performance was occupied. All the avenues and approaches, places even whence nothing whatever could be seen of the scaffold, were blocked by persons who had overflowed from the area in front of the gaol."

A strange but quite groundless rumour was long believed that Fauntleroy "had escaped death by the insertion in his throat of a silver tube . . . and that on being restored to consciousness he went abroad and lived for many years." Griffiths says the body after execution was handed over to friends and privately buried.

THE BURNING OF THE HOUSES OF PARLIAMENT

O N October 16, 1834, the old Houses of Parliament were destroyed, as all the world knows, by fire. The greater part of the adjoining official residence of the Speaker was burnt down, and though many of the archives of both house were preserved they were considerably damaged by the flames. The much admired tapestry in the House of Lords, representing the defeat of the Spanish Armada, was destroyed, but, curiously enough, the table of the old House of Commons was preserved to find a place in the office of the Board of Works, Whitehall Place.

The fire was not extinguished for several days, and it is certainly remarkable that the libraries and State papers were saved. Six years before, in 1828, Sir John Soane had noticed the large quantity of timber contained in the House of Lords and had asked this ominous question : " Should a fire happen, what would become of the Painted Chamber, the House of Commons, and Westminster Hall. Where would the progress of the fire be arrested ? " As a matter of fact, Westminster Hall was preserved only by the favourable direction of the wind which prevented the flames from the two Houses from being wafted towards its enormous timber roof. Many contradictory stories were circulated at the time in support of the theory that the fire was the work of political conspirators. A Mr. Cooper, for example, an ironmonger of Drury Lane, maintained that he had heard a report of the fire at Dudley, a hundred and nineteen miles from London, only three hours after its commencement.

The fire began at half-past six in the

evening at which time flames were seen to issue forth from near the entrances of both Houses. The whole interior was in flames in less than half an hour, and the fireman and soldiers who had been summoned to the spot, concentrated all their efforts on saving Westminster Hall. Their efforts were crowned by success but the rest of the building was devastated by the flames. In the House of Lords the damage consisted of the destruction of the Robing-Rooms and the Committee-Rooms in the west front. The rooms of the resident officers at the south end of the structure as far as the octagon tower were burnt down. The fire also swept the north end of the Royal Gallery abutting on the Painted Chamber, from the door which led into that apartment as far as the first compartment of columns. In the House of Commons the destruction included the loss of the house, libraries, committee rooms, housekeeper's apartments, the official residence of the Clerk of the House, together with all the rooms of the Speaker's house from oriel window right down to the south side of the House of Commons. " The loss of records by the fire," Sir Walter Besant assures us in " London in the Nineteenth Century," " was not important, nearly everything of value being printed, but among those of the House of Commons destroyed were the test and qualification rolls signed by the members after taking the oaths. The King and Queen came to town the following day on purpose to see the ruins. An investigation was conducted by the Privy Council, whose report in November 8 stated that the fire was accidental, and wholly attributable to carelessness and negligence."

The damage, it seems, had originated in the House of Lords, where the flues had been overheated through the burning of certain old wooden exchequer tallies. This operation had been entrusted to Joshua Cross, a labourer whose services had not been adequately supervised by the Clerk of Works.

No less a person than Charles Dickens has told—with fine satirical humour the story of the fire. The occasion was a speech delivered by him in Drury Lane Theatre at a time when, owing to the mismanagement of the English army in the East, the establishment of an Administrative Reform Association had been publicly demanded. The author of " David Copperfield " said : " Ages ago, a savage mode of keeping accounts on notched sticks was introduced into the Court of Exchequer and the accounts were kept much as Robinson Crusoe kept his calendar on the desert island. In the course of considerable revolutions of time the celebrated Cocker was born and died. Walkinghame, of the ' Tutor's Assistant,' and well versed in figures, was also born and died ; and a multitude of accountants, book-keepers, and actuaries were born and died.

" Still official routine inclined to these notched sticks, as if they were the pillars of the Constitution, and still the exchequer accounts continued to be kept on certain splints of elm wood called *tallies*. In the reign of George III. an inquiry was made by some revolutionary spirit whether pens, ink and paper, slates and pencils being in existence—this obstinate adherence to an obsolete custom ought to be continued, and whether a change ought not to be effected. All the red tape in the country grew redder at the bare mention of this bold and original conception and it took till 1826 to get these sticks abolished. In 1834 it was found that there was a considerable accumulation of them ; and the question then arose—what was to be done with such worn-out, worm-eaten, rotten bits of wood ? The sticks were housed at Westminster, and it would naturally occur to any intelligent person that nothing could be easier than to allow them to be carried away by the miser-

1320 and 1352 the chapel was rebuilt and until its destruction in 1834, it was always regarded as one of the finest examples of architecture in London. This became the House of Commons in the reign of Edward VI., and remained so until the building was destroyed by the fire of 1834. Among its many other memorable dramas it

THE BODY OF A FIFTEENTH-CENTURY BISHOP FOUND IN THE CRYPT OF
OLD ST. STEPHEN'S CHAPEL

able people who live in that neighbourhood. However, they never had been useful, and official routine required that they never should be, and so order went forth that they were to be privately and confidentially burnt in a stove in the House of Lords. The stove overgorged with these preposterous sticks set fire to the panelling ; the panelling set fire to the House of Lords ; the House of Lords set fire to the House of Commons ; the two Houses were reduced to ashes ; architects were called in to build others ; and we are now in the second million of the cost thereof ; the national pig is not nearly over the stile yet ; and the little old woman Britannia hasn't got home to-night.''

Stephen, King of England, founded, according to tradition, St. Stephen's Chapel for a dean and canons. Between

was the scene of the dismissal of Parliament by Oliver Cromwell. The House of Lords, also destroyed by the fire, was the old Court of Requests. The late E. M. Barry, R.A., restored the crypt of St. Stephen's Chapel and fitted it up as a chapel for the use of Members of Parliament. It is also used as a private chapel for the Speaker, and privileged babies are baptized at its font. As late as 1852 the remains of a buried churchman, probably William Lyndwoode, Bishop of St. David's, was ound in the masonry of the wall near the altar, where it had lain for four centuries.

Seventy-seven years ago it is since those walls of St. Stephen's, impregnated with so many memories, crumbled away in flame.

" Who," asks Townsend, in his " History of the House of Commons," "that has sat in the gallery of the House—that venerable building which the calamitous fire of October 16, 1834, reduced to ashes—can fail to recollect his first feeling of disappointment as what intelligent stranger was ever ushered for the first time without a throbbing heart and heightened pulse."

Here since Edward VI. the great men of the nation had one and all

THE RUINS OF ST. STEPHEN'S CHAPEL

he gazed with a sense of wounded pride around the dark and narrow room and looked in astonishment at the honourable members grouped in various attitudes of carelessness and indifference ? Yet such as it was, decked only with a new coating of paint and whitewash, destitute of all architectural pomp by a single monument of sculpture or art—into that building contributed their genius to the memory of the place. Here Raleigh, Charles and Cromwell, Chatham and Canning, had, each after his fashion, poured out their inspirations to the generations to come. The place had been the very heart of England and one understands the spirit in which Townsend continues: "Magnificent as the new building may be, adorned with paintings, and embellished with trophies of our progress in the arts, far more convenient than the old chamber, in splendour not to be compared, can it ever rival in the mind's eye that humbler room empanelled with living memories, and blazoned with illustrations of the past ? "

Turner painted the burning of the Houses of Lords and Commons. It was witnessed from a high altitude by Dean Ireland and Sir Francis Palgrave, as Dr. Arthur Penrhyn Stanley tells us in his " Historical Memorials of Westminster Abbey." For his account the Dean relied partially upon Lord Hatherley, an eye-witness of the fire and partially upon Sir Francis Palgrave himself. " On the night of the fire," writes the Dean, " which consumed the Houses of Parliament in 1834, when thousands were gathered below, watching the progress of the flames, when the waning affection for our ancient natural monuments seemed to be revived in that crisis of their fate, when as the conflagration was driven by the wind towards Westminster Hall the innumerable faces of the vast multitude, lighted up in the broad glare with more than the light of day, were visibly swayed by the agitation of the devouring breeze, and one voice, and one prayer seemed to go up from every upturned countenance : ' O, save the Hall ! ' on that night two small figures might have been seen standing on the roof of the Chapter House overlooking the terrific blaze, parted from them only by the narrow space of Old Palace Yard. One was the Keeper of the Records, the other was Dean Ireland. They had climbed up through the hole in the roof to witness the awful scene.

Suddenly a gust of wind swept the flames in that direction. Palgrave, with all the enthusiasm of the antiquarian and of his own eager temperament turned to the Dean and suggested that they should descend into the Chapter House and carry off its most valued treasured into the Abbey for safety. Dean Ireland with the caution belonging at once to his office and his character, answered that he could not think of doing so without applying to Lord Melbourne, the First Lord of the Treasury.

" It was a true, though grotesque; expression of the actual facts. The Government were the masters of the Chapter House."

Curiously enough, during the last session Mr. Hume had proposed, without success, a vote to erect a larger and more dignified House of Commons. And as the flames played round the venerable building, a wag in the watching multitude cried out : " There is Mr. Hume's motion, being carried without a division ! " But the people of England profoundly regretted their old House of Commons. " Great," writes Dr. C. Mackay, " was the sorrow of every lover of his country, when the ancient seats of the British Legislature were destroyed ; for, though they were but stones and bricks and mortar and wood, they were hallowed in the hearts of Englishmen. Who could help regretting that the very boards on which Chatham, and Pitt, and Fox, and Burke, and Canning trod would never more be trodden by the admirers of their worth ; and that the walls that re-echoed to their words, and to the approving cheers of their delighted auditory had crumbled in the flames ? "

After Robert Cruikshank

THE FISHMONGER WHO CAPTURED THE WEST END

THIS celebrated gambling establishment was started on the west side of St. James's Street, opposite White's, in 1827, by William Crockford. Crockford first started as a fishmonger in the Strand close to Temple Bar. Abandoning this profitable business, and having saved a few hundred pounds, Crockford started as a gaming-house proprietor in Piccadilly, and then in King Street, before he got into the more fashionable thoroughfare of St. James's Street itself —the very centre of all these clubs. His operations with his partners were far from being above suspicion, and on more than one occasion Crockford was sued by his victims when it was discovered that they had been involuntarily playing with false dice, and also that they had been cheated by the operators of the tables. But Crockford, who soon became to be known by the significant title of " Crockey," was cautious enough to compromise every action before it gained absolute publicity in the press. In the games that were played it was always the bank then, as now, who came out the winner, and in a very few months the bank at Crockford's cleared over two hundred thousand pounds. Crockford, of course, was a man of very doubtful principles ; but he was undoubtedly encouraged in his nefarious practices by the gambling spirit of the age.

However, Crockford was a caterer *par excellence*, and provided every sort of culinary luxury that the tastes of the folk of fashion demanded, consequently the very best men about town flocked into Crockford's from the different clubs, including White's and Brooks's, the Theatres and the Opera, to spend the late hours ; and then they were wont to try their luck at the hazard table afterwards. A number of these young bloods, who by degrees felt the impulse of play, having just risked small sums and won, ventured on larger stakes and, of course, eventually lost. But there is a story of a certain young officer who one night secured the price of his " troop " in the Life Guards at Crockford's, and never touched a dice box again.

It was the excellence of the cuisine that attracted so many of the *roués* vagant. It is a well-founded fact that Crockford, in a very few years, though never risking a halfpenny himself at the hazard table, amassed the enormous fortune of one million two hundred thousand pounds.

We cannot resist quoting from Captain Gronow a piquant note about this notorious club: " No one can describe the splendour and excitement

PRINCE TALLEYRAND : A MEMBER OF CROCKFORD'S
From the Maclise Portrait Gallery

and gamblers, who were nearly all men of rank and breeding, and as Mr. Crockford possessed much philosophical acumen he knew exactly how to propitiate the wealthy and the extra- of the early days of ' Crockey.' A supper of the most exquisite kind, prepared by the famous Ude, and accompanied by the best wines in the world, together with every luxury of the season, was furnished gratis. The members of the club included all the celebrities of England, from the Duke of Wellington to the youngest Ensign of the Guards; and at the gay and festive board, which was constantly replenished from midnight to early dawn, the most brilliant sallies of wit, the most agreeable conversation, the most interesting anecdotes, interspersed with grave political discussions and acute logical reasoning on every conceivable subject, proceeded from the soldiers, scholars, statesmen, poets, and men of pleasure, who, when the 'house was up,' and balls and parties at an end, delighted to finish their evening with a little supper and a good deal of hazard at old Crockey's.

"BALL" HUGHES ("THE GOLDEN BALL"): A HEAVY LOSER AT CROCKFORD'S

The tone of the club was excellent. A most gentlemanlike feeling prevailed, and none of the rudeness, familiarity, and ill-breeding which disgrace some of the minor clubs of the present day would have been tolerated for a moment."

It was not only the nobleman who resorted to this " fishy " establishment, but the greatest Foreign Diplomatists, whose power was felt throughout Europe, were constant visitors and belonged to Crockford's as a matter of course. Prince Talleyrand, General Alava, Prince Esterhazy, Count Pozzo di Borgo, the Duke of Palmella, representing their various countries, and nearly all the persons of distinction who arrived in England at this special period. Alas, there were many who regretted the day when they became involved in this fascinating pastime of win or lose.

Scarcely a wit or dandy of the day was not a member of Crockford's. That brilliant statesman to be, Benjamin Disraeli, and Bulwer Lytton, who fell so much under the lash of Thackeray, who was also a visitor though not a member, cast their shafts of wit across the gorgeous supper-tables; the one with his sable curls and satiric wit, the other with his auburn locks and his lisping way of delivering excellent things.

As quite an amusing contrast we have happy references to Horace Twiss, whose appetite for the good things of the table was, apparently, only equalled by Edward Montagu's thirst, " which astonished all beholders." Some of the members of this club, whose memories are only shadows, made bitter jests and said unkind things which have all passed away into the Ewigkeit, while the agreeable and pleasant sayings of Alvanley, Sheridan and even Theodore Hook, now and then Sam Foote, survive still as treasures.

Crockford's Club House, nearly at the head of St. James's Street, on its west side, is now the well-ordered Devonshire Club.

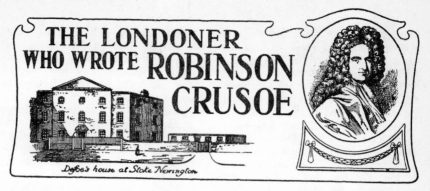

THE LONDONER WHO WROTE ROBINSON CRUSOE

Defoe's house at Stoke Newington

I N Oldfield Road, formerly Hussey's Lane, at Stoke Newington, may be seen a long stretch (about 120 yards) of venerable brick wall, pierced to-day with back-doors. This is part of the boundary wall of Daniel Defoe's little estate at Stoke Newington. Here he lived from 1709 to 1729, and here he wrote "Robinson Crusoe." Defoe Road covers the site of the house, which has utterly disappeared. But in Church Street several very fine old brick houses are standing which must have belonged to Defoe's neighbours, and round the old church many of those neighbours must be sleeping.

The appearance of the house has been preserved in an engraving which is reproduced, with a plan of the garden, in Mr. Thomas Wright's biography of Defoe. It was a very plain brick mansion with twelve windows looking on Church Street. Tradition says that it was full of strange cupboards, and that the locks and bars in various parts of the house were formidable. There is something in this that consorts with Defoe's secretive and rather uncanny nature. There were stables for Defoe's horses and "chariot." In the garden, which was four acres in extent, Defoe walked and talked. Indeed, behind this brick wall in Hussey's Lane his golden years were spent. A frequent visitor to the house, Henry Baker, the naturalist and founder of the Bakerian lectureship, speaks of his "very genteel ways of living," and declares that his "three lovely daughters were admired for their beauty, their education, and their prudent conduct." Indeed, Sophia was so pleasing to Mr. Baker that he married her.

Undoubtedly the claim of Stoke Newington to have been the birthplace of "Robinson Crusoe" has been freely challenged. But the applicants cancel each other. Gateshead-on-Tyne has been mentioned as the place where Defoe, in one of his numerous concealments, wrote his immortal story. The "Rose and Crown," in the Back Lane, Halifax, is also indicated. Harrow Alley in Whitechapel, and "a small room over the wash-house of a cottage in Hartley in Kent" have been pointed out to Defoe's biographers as the real places. But Lee, in his exhaustive "Life," replies to these stories that Defoe was living in London when his book was published, being then in the pay of the Government, and that 'Robinson Crusoe' could only have been written in his own house at Stoke Newington." The fact that Charles Gildon's well-known burlesque dialogue on "Robinson Crusoe," published less than half a year after Defoe's work appeared, laid the scene of that dialogue in a field at Stoke Newington is fairly conclusive evidence.

Not only was the story written at Stoke Newington, but very probably its title originated there. In his youth Defoe entered a Dissenting academy there, kept by the Rev. Charles Morton, and here he had a fellow student in one Timothy Crusoe, who afterwards rose to the ministry, but who is famous, not because he could pray for two hours at a stretch in Scriptural language, but because he lent his surname to the best boys' book in the world.

It was Charles Gildon who annoyed Defoe by asking how Robinson Crusoe could have stuffed his pockets with biscuits when swimming naked to the wreck. To him, nevertheless, we owe a racy phrase descriptive of the extraordinary success of " Robinson Crusoe." In his satire he admits that it was " fam'd from Tuttle Street " (that is to say, Tothill Street, Westminster) " to Limehouse Hole," and that there was " not an old woman who can go the price of it, but buys thy ' Life and Adventures, and leaves it as a legacy with the ' Pilgrim's Progress,' the ' Practice of Poetry,' and ' God's Revenge Against Murther' to her posterity." The publishing office of " Robinson Crusoe " is known beyond a doubt. It was William Taylor's, known as the " Ship," in Paternoster Row The book was published on April 25, 1719.

One would like to think that Defoe had died in peace in the house in which he wrote his one work of genius. This was not the case. He became a discredited politician, and a brokenhearted wanderer. A few months before his death he was a fugitive in Kent, and wrote to Mr. Baker (then married to Sophia) these pathetic lines : " I am so near my Journey's end, and am hastening to the Place where ye Weary are at Rest, and where ye Wicked cease from trouble ; be it that the Passage is rough, and the Day stormy, by what Way soever He please to bring me to the End of it, I desire to finish Life with this temper of Soul in all Cases : *Te Deum Laudamus*. . . . Kiss my dear Sophie once more for me ; and if I must see her no more, tell her that this is from a Father that loved her above all his Comforts, to his last Breath."

The weary old pamphleteer and novelist crept back into London a few months later, and died in Ropemaker's Alley, in Moorfields. It is now Ropemaker Street. Close by is Fore Street, where the butcher's boy had been born. From obscurity he had risen into fame, but from fame he had fallen back into obscurity. They registered his death, thus : " 1731, April 26. Mr. Dubowl, Cripplegate." He was laid in Bunhill Fields, where, over his grave, there now stands an obelisk subscribed for in 1870 by the boys and girls of England under the lead of the " Christian World " newspaper. Bunyan lies near him, Isaac Watts's grave is there, and many a grave divine and good man who fought the battles of dissent and political liberty.

SAMUEL ROGERS AT STOKE NEWINGTON

IT is a quiet, uneventful story, the life of him who came to be called the "Banker Poet" at Stoke Newington during the first thirty years of his life, 1763 to 1793. Its interest lies in the fact that it may be regarded as the typical life of a boy brought up in a prosperous Nonconformist family of the middle class, where discipline is not too rigid and doctrine is not too severe ; the typical life of a man successful in his career and his ambitions going into the City every day and returning to a happy home with his father and sisters and younger brother, and enjoying the society of congenial friends.

Stoke Newington has for generations been the home of earnest religious thinkers, and during the eighteenth century many men of Liberal tendencies lived in the substantial old-world houses which bordered the pretty Green of Newington with its ancient elms and its Presbyterian meeting-house. Well-ordered households they were, characterised by solid comfort and careful administration : the Rogers' house stood on the west side of the Square, and is no doubt "the old mansion frowning through the trees " described in Samuel Rogers' best-known poem, "The Pleasures of Memory." Thomas Rogers, the father, was a highly respected banker of Cornhill ; he manifested a deep interest in the foundation of Hackney College, the great Nonconformist seat of learning, and became its first Chairman. His wife is described by all who knew her as a woman firm and yet tender, a gentle and capable ruler of the household, and of keen intelligence. The five children led a healthful and enjoyable life. Both the active exercise of riding on horseback and the passive delights of reading and study were at their disposal under the pleasantest conditions. The Newington fields had not yet passed into the hands of the devouring builder, and there was much open country to explore : when Samuel Rogers entered the Bank, the office was an easy ride from home—indeed, he often walked the distance. In the library of the house silence was strictly imposed, and any communication between those sitting there had to be made by writing. There " where the shaded lamp's mild lustre streams " Samuel read "ancient books " and dreamt " inspired dreams "—dreams which received pleasant fulfilment in the extraordinary success which attended the publication of " The Pleasures of Memory " (1792).

At Newington Green Rogers met not only many of the leading literary lights of the day but Liberal politicians and Liberal Divines of many shades of opinion. His boyhood's friend, the Presbyterian minister, Dr. Price, was a man of profound learning and widespread fame, who endeared himself to young and old alike by his modesty and high spirits. Rogers related that Price leaped the New River, and tells how, in his attempt to jump over a honeysuckle bush in the Rogers' garden, " he entangled the tree between his legs, and away went the doctor and the honeysuckle together."

Samuel Rogers very nearly made the acquaintance of a more famous doctor, the great lexicographer. Johnson was living in Bolt Court off Fleet Street,

SAMUEL ROGERS THE "BANKER POET"
From the Maclise Portrait Gallery

and the young bank clerk conceived the bold idea of paying him a visit in order to submit his early poetical efforts to the master. He stole with a friend through the quiet court, and knocked at the door : but before the doctor's old negro servant could answer it, the courage of the lads failed them and they retreated in haste !

Samuel Rogers had a curious experience once when he was returning from business. As he was passing by a house in the City Road, " I saw a number of respectable persons of both sexes assembled here, all well dressed in mourning, and with very serious look and behaviour. The door of the house was open, and they entered in pairs. I thought that, without impropriety, I might join them, so we all walked upstairs, and came to a drawing-room in the midst of which was a table; on this table lay the body of a person dressed in a clergyman's robes, with bands, and his grey hair shading his face on either side. He was of small stature, and his countenance looked like wax. . . . After we had gone round the table in our lingering procession we descended as we came. The person that lay before us was the celebrated John Wesley, and at the earnest request of his congregation, they were permitted to take this pathetic and affectionate farewell of their beloved pastor."

THE PORTER AND THE DWARF

ON a house in Newgate Street, too high to be well seen, is a small stone portraying, in low relief, William Evans, the gigantic porter of Charles I., and Jeffrey Hudson, his diminutive fellow servant. On the stone are cut these words, "The King's Porter and the Dwarf," with the date 1680. Evans is described as having been full six feet and a half in height, though knock-kneed, splay-footed, and halting; yet he danced in an anti-mask at Court, where he drew little Jeffrey, the dwarf, out of his pocket, much to the wonder and laughter of the company. Among the curiosities of the Ashmolean, at Oxford, are preserved the waistcoat, breeches, and stockings (the two latter in one piece) of Jeffrey; they are of blue satin, the waistcoat being slashed with figured white

silk. And in the Towneley collection was a rare tract, or "New Yere's Gift," 1636, containing a portrait of Hudson; the binding of the book is a piece of Charles I.'s waistcoat.

At the commencement of the Civil Wars, Hudson became a Captain of Horse in the Royal Army, and in that capacity he accompanied the Queen to France, where he killed his antagonist in a duel, and was, in consequence, imprisoned. After his release he returned to England, and lived for some time on small pensions allowed him by the Duke of Buckingham and other persons of rank. During the excitement of the Titus Oates Plots, Hudson was arrested as a Papist, and committed to the Gatehouse, where he lay a considerable time. He died in 1682, shortly after his release, in the sixty-third year of his age.

THE LEVERIAN MUSEUM

THE creator of the once famous Leverian Museum, Sir Ashton Lever, was the eldest son of Sir Darcey Lever, of Alkrington, near Manchester. After leaving Oxford he lived a country life at Alkrington, indulging his passion for sport and natural history, and the great museum which afterwards drew Londoners to Leicester Square sprang from small beginnings in this village. His hobby consumed him, and we are told that he frequently rode from London to Alkrington, with cages full of birds, which he brought safely home by holding them with a full-stretched arm, and galloping till the arm was tired, and then stopping to change hands. He had, at the same time, the best trained pack of beagles in his neighbourhood, and pointers in such perfection, that he is known to have had fifteen in the field all making a point at the same instant. He had frequently five or six hunters at the same time, all lying down and rising at the word of command, fetching, carrying, opening and shutting doors, and many other tricks. He was equally successful with live birds. He taught a bullfinch to fly from its cage and light upon his hand, sing one of its tunes at the word of command, and fly back to its cage as he directed ; and a goose—we are gravely told—to wait behind his chair at table, with a napkin under its wing. He allowed his grooms to teach his method of managing his horses to any one who desired to see and learn it.

About 1760, Sir Ashton, being at Margate, was in the habit of picking up shells, and he was then told of a quantity of curious foreign shells to be sold at Dunkirk. He hired a boat, sailed to France, and purchased a whole cargo, consisting of several hogsheads, which he sent down into the country. With these he commenced his collections. Fossils, native and foreign, together with shells, for some time took up his attention. Many of his rare birds he gave to his friends, and made a kind of gaol delivery of the rest. He went on to the collection and stuffing of birds. His museum attracted wide local attention, and in 1774 he brought it to London and opened it under the name of " The Holophusikon " in old Leicester House (once the "pouting-place of princes ") in Leicester Square. He charged the curious and forbidding sum of 5s. 3d. for admission, reducing his charge later to half a crown. But the public did not come in " paying " numbers. Among those who did come (she had but to cross the square) was Fanny Burney, who describes Lever's grotesque appearance. " I went this morning (December 31, 1782) with my dear father to Sir John Ashton Lever's, where we could not but be entertained. Sir Ashton came and talked to us a good while. He may be an admirable natural*ist*, but I think if in other matters you leave the *ist* out, you will not much wrong him. He looks full sixty years old, yet he had dressed not only two young men, but himself, in a green jacket, a round hat, with green feathers, a bundle of arrows under one arm, and a bow in the other, and thus, accoutred as a forester, he pranced about ; while the younger fools, who were in the same garb, kept running to and fro in the garden, carefully contriving to shoot at some mark, just as any of the company appeared at any of the windows. After such a specimen of his actions, you will excuse me if I give you none of his conversation."

Lever found himself in serious difficulties, and he was saved from ruin by his undoubtedly high reputation, which secured him sympathy. Dr. Johnson backed a proposal to purchase the museum for the nation, but this scheme came to nothing. In 1788, however, he was authorised by Parliament to dispose of his collection by a lottery of thirty-six thousand tickets at a guinea each. Only 8000 were sold, and the prize fell to a Mr. Parkinson, who thus obtained for a guinea an immense and valuable collection, which included many curiosities collected in the South Seas by Captain Cook. Mr. Parkinson built the Rotunda in Albion Place, Blackfriars, for the display of the Museum Leverianum. But the enterprise failed. Sir Ashton Lever

The Leverian Museum was at once a triumph and a tragedy. Sir William Hamilton told the House of Commons

THE LEVERIAN MUSEUM
From a Drawing in Hone's Everyday Book

died soon after he had parted with his treasures, and in 1806 their new owner brought this unfortunate museum to auction. The sale was conducted by King and Lochee, of King Street, Covent Garden.

that he had seen every public and private museum in Holland, France, Germany, Italy, and Sicily, and he thought Sir Ashton Lever's collection was in every respect the finest he had visited.

THE WILD LORD CAMELFORD

MOST Londoners know—by its boundary wall at least—the retired, almost hidden house which stands at the corner of Park Lane and Oxford Street. To this house, which at a later period was the home of Princess Charlotte in her soon-ended married life, was brought the body of Thomas Pitt, Lord Camelford, on a March day in 1804. He had been killed in a duel with his old naval comrade, Mr. Best, which was fought in a field behind Little Holland House. It was a sorry affair, and it terminated the career of a brilliant but ungovernable man.

Lord Camelford's naval career had been marred by an unseemly and tragic quarrel as to superiority of command between himself and Charles Peterson, when the two men commanded respectively the *Perdrix* and *Favourite*, in an Antiguan harbour. Camelford shot his brother officer. Tried by court-martial he escaped punishment on the court's decision that he was the superior officer, Peterson being therefore judged to be the mutineer. As the result of a later and less serious affair he was deprived of his command of the *Charon*, whereupon he resigned from the Navy and threw himself into London life.

In London this hot-headed man was continually in quarrels and disturbances. On the night of April 2, 1799, he assaulted a gentleman at Drury Lane Theatre, and had to pay damages of £500. Returning home one morning, with his friend Captain Barrie, he indulged himself in the then popular sport of assaulting the watch. After an hour's fight the two aristocrats were escorted by twenty watchmen and lodged in the watch-house, where, according to one account, they gave their captors a guinea apiece and went free. Lord Camelford knew the insides of most of the watch-houses in the west of London. It is even said that, when a prisoner in one or other of them, he would prevail " either by force, or more persuasive methods," on the constable of the night to allow him to take his place. " He would then, with the utmost gravity, examine all delinquents that were brought in by the watch, and rejoiced in the opportunity of exercising the lenity of his disposition by directing the offenders to be discharged."

On the night of October 7, 1801, when London was illuminated for the Peace, he kept his lodgings at No. 148 New Bond Street in darkness. The mob clamoured for it to be lit up. Camelford refused, and the mob threw stones, whereupon his lordship sallied out with a thick cudgel and attacked the crowd right and left. All his windows were broken, and he himself returned to his bed covered with bruises and dirt. We owe a glimpse of these same lodgings in New Bond Street to James and Horace Smith. The witty brothers had witnessed another of Lord Camelford's outbursts —this time at the Royal Circus. " God Save the King " had been called for, accompanied by a general cry of " Stand up ! " and " Hats off ! " A tipsy naval lieutenant, seeing a gentleman slow to obey the call, struck off his hat with his stick, exclaiming, " Take off your hat, sir ! " The person thus assaulted proved to be, unluckily for the lieutenant, Lord Camelford. A set-to in the lobby was the consequence, where his lordship quickly proved victorious. " The devil is not so black as he is painted," said Mr. James Smith to his brother; "let us call upon Lord Camelford, and tell him that we were witnesses of his being assaulted." The visit was paid on the ensuing morning. "Over the fireplace of the drawing-room were ornaments strongly expressive of the pugnacity of the peer. A long thick bludgeon lay horizontally supported on two brass hooks. Above this was placed one of lesser dimensions, until a pyramid of weapons gradually arose, tapering to a horsewhip:

Thus, all below was strength, and all above was grace."

Lord Camelford received his visitors with great civility,

THE ECCENTRIC THOMAS PITT, LORD CAMELFORD, KILLED IN A DUEL NEAR HOLLAND HOUSE, MARCH 7, 1804

and thanked them warmly for the call; adding that their evidence would be material, it being his intention to indict the lieutenant for an assault. "All I can say in return is this," exclaimed the peer, with great cordiality: "if ever I see you engaged in a row, upon my soul I'll stand by you." The brothers expressed themselves thankful for so potent an ally.

The affair which led to Lord Camelford's death was as foolish as any that have been related. It came to his ears that his friend Captain Best had spoken disparagingly of him in a certain quarter. He went in a passion to the Prince of Wales's Coffee House, and seeing Best, said in a loud voice: "I find, sir, that you have spoken of me in the most unwarrantable terms." Mr. Best replied that he was unconscious of having deserved such a charge. Lord Camelford retorted angrily, and called his friend "a scoundrel, a liar, and a ruffian." A meeting was immediately proposed for the following morning; each having appointed his second, it was left to them to fix the time and place.

In the course of the evening Mr. Best sent to Lord Camelford the strongest assurances that the information he had received was unfounded, and that as he had acted under a false impression, he would be satisfied if he would retract the expressions he had employed; but this Lord Camelford absolutely refused to do.

The landlord in Bond Street suspected that a duel was in the air, and lodged an information. But the officers acted too slowly. Lord Camelford avoided them by sleeping at a tavern. He seems to have understood his position. Captain Best was reported one of the best shots in England, and this circumstance, which increased his danger, fixed also his determination to go through with the foolish business.

By appointment the duellists and their seconds met early on the morning of March 7 in a coffee-house in Oxford Street, where Best said : " Camelford, we have been friends, and I know the unsuspecting generosity of your nature. Upon my honour you have been imposed upon. Do not insist on expressions under which one of us must fall." Lord Camelford replied : " Best, this is child's play ; the thing must go on." The mad folly of the duelling system was never more clearly exemplified, for when Lord Camelford spurned this generous offer of reconciliation he knew himself to be in the wrong, and had even put the fact on record. Before going to meet his reluctant antagonist he had inserted these words in his will : " In the present contest I am fully and entirely the aggressor, as well in the spirit as in the letter of the word ; should I therefore lose my life in a contest of my own seeking, I must solemnly forbid any of my friends from instituting any vexatious proceedings against my antagonist ; and should, notwithstanding the above declaration on my part, the laws of the land be put in force against him, I desire that this part of my will may be made known to the King, in order that his royal heart may be moved to extend his mercy towards him."

The party started for the appointed spot on horseback and in a post-chaise. The seconds performed their duties. Lord Camelford fired first, and missed. Then he fell to Best's bullet. The seconds, together with Mr. Best, ran to help him, when he seized his friend by the hand, saying, " Best, I am a dead man : you have killed me, but I fully forgive you." The dying man was carried into Little Holland House, where he lingered till Saturday evening.

An inquest was held, at which the jury permitted themselves to return a verdict of wilful murder against " some person or persons unknown." Captain Best was indicted, but the bill was thrown out by the grand jury.

Lord Camelford was something better than the roystering young man about town. Although not yet thirty, he was widely read, and had a strong taste for science and mathematics. A curious light is thrown on his character by the wish he expressed for his burial. In his travels he had once seen a beautiful spot in Switzerland, in the canton of Berne. Here he desired to be laid. " I wish my body," he said, " to be removed as soon as may be convenient to a country far distant— to a spot not near the haunts of men, but where the surrounding country may smile upon my remains." The spot he had in mind was on the borders of Lake St. Lampierre, and was marked by three trees. The centre tree was to be taken up and there he would rest.

From Little Holland House the body was taken to Camelford House, and thence to a vault in the Church of St. Ann's, Soho, where it was to await removal to Switzerland. But it has never left that vault. It is said that the war prevented the journey to Switzerland, and that eventually the vault was bricked up.

THE APOTHEOSIS OF THE DUCHESS OF DEVONSHIRE (*From a Print of* 1784)

GEORGIANA, DUCHESS OF DEVONSHIRE

IN the popular fancy, Georgiana, Duchess of Westminster, was a beautiful hoyden who kissed a butcher to win a vote for Fox. Whether she did or did not kiss a butcher, we cannot say ; no one can say : wiles less decorous by half have a thousand times been used to cozen voters. What we can say is, that the wife of the indolent but honourable fifth Duke of Devonshire was one of the few exquisite graces of a society none too fastidious, a siren with a heart and a mind, a universal charmer in whom the woman outshone and overtopped the brilliant, energetic queen of the Whigs.

An aristocrat by birth, eldest daughter of the first Earl Spencer, she was married (in June 1774) as a schoolgirl of seventeen to the Devonshire who was then the "first match" in England. Of whatever stock she had come, this alliance must at once have given her absolute place in the very exclusive society of the last quarter of the eighteenth century (when it was more or less unusual for a lord to be seen hand in glove with a commoner) ; but the notion that the young Duchess was a mere female fribble is dispelled by a single stroke of the precise pen of Wraxall. Wraxall, in his " Memoirs," shows her to us, " in the first bloom of youth, hanging on the sentences that fell from Johnson's lips, and contending for the nearest place to his chair." Fanny d'Arblay tells us that, though she perceived in the youthful Duchess not so much beauty as she expected, she found " far more of manner, politeness, and gentle quiet."

There was a touch of the reformer in her, even in the matter of raiment, and when she had been permitted so far to assert herself as to set the fashion in this department, she "introduced a simple and graceful style to supersede the ridiculous hoop." But the Duchess was elegant by instinct, as she was instinctively a

seen at Ranelagh, which was to the gay world of that era an Arabian Night's Entertainment. "Ah!" exclaims the old gentleman in Hone ("Table-Book"): "Ranelagh was a noble place! Such taste! such elegance! and such beauty! There was

WIT'S LAST STAKE, OR THE COBBLING VOTER AND ABJECT CANVASSERS (*After Rowlandson*)

leader. She could sit enamoured at the feet of the grand old Johnson, but she could also attract, and hold her place, among the wits, and be something of a light to them; not solely because she was the radiant young Duchess of Devonshire, but because the air of Parnassus was never foreign in her nostrils. Fox and Sheridan and Selwyn were friends with whom she could hold her intellectual own.

Pray let us remember, too, that she figured splendidly in social junketings, and, as became a Duchess in the vaward of her social order, went wherever there was fun. She was

the Duchess of A——, the finest woman in England, sir; and Mrs. B——, a mighty fine creature; and Lady Susan what's-her-name, who had that unfortunate affair with Sir Charles. Yes, indeed, sir, they came swimming by you like swans. Ranelagh for me!" When the Duchess of Devonshire married, Ranelagh was in its glory. "As no place was ever better calculated for the display of female elegance and beauty," writes Faulkner ("History of Chelsea"), "it followed, of course, that the greatest belles of the day frequented Ranelagh, at the head of whom was the celebrated and beautiful Duchess of Devonshire, a lady eminent for every grace that could adorn the female, and not a few candidates for admiration were in her train."

At Devonshire House, the palatial residence in Piccadilly (which for two years "played the part of a pouting-place for princes"), the Duchess at the summit of her beauty and renown must have been a peerless hostess. Devonshire House was perhaps the chief rendezvous of the Whig party, and hither came to the court of the "belle châtelaine" Fox, Burke, Windham, Sheridan, Fitzpatrick, Selwyn, and others of that brilliant crew. Wraxall has left us a fascinating picture of Georgiana as the mistress of the Devonshire House of this period. "Her personal charms constituted her smallest pretension to universal admiration; nor did her beauty consist, like that of the Gunnings, in regularity of features and faultless formation of limbs and shape: it lay rather in the graces of her deportment, in her irresistible manners, and the seduction of her society. Her hair was not without a tinge of red, and her face, though pleasing, had it not been illumined by her mind, might have been considered an ordinary counte-

II

nance. Descended, in the fourth degree, lineally from Sarah Jennings, the wife of John Churchill, Duke of Marl-

AN HISTORICAL KISS

borough, she resembled the portraits of that celebrated woman. In addition to the external advantages which she received from nature and fortune, she possessed an ardent temperament, susceptible of deep as well as strong impressions, a cultivated understanding, illumined by a taste for poetry and the fine arts, and much sensibility, not exempt, perhaps, from vanity and coquetry."

Strange that so rare a creature should be chiefly remembered as the aristocrat who kissed a butcher at election time ! As if her matchless Grace of Devonshire were on a par with a Comtesse Dubarry ! But the Middlesex election of 1784 (occurring in that General Election which, it has been said, " determined for more than forty years the question of the government of England ") was assuredly a famous affair, and assuredly also the Duchess played a famous part in it. Charles James Fox was her candidate. The Duchess was twenty-seven, and one of the forces of society. Fox was thirty-five, and—as an orator, at least—probably the greatest force in Parliament. Pitt, his eloquent, intrepid rival, styled him a magician who laid a spell upon his hearers so long as words issued from his lips.

The cries were : " Pitt and the Constitution ! " and " Fox and Free Government ! " The Tories compassed earth and heaven to exclude Fox, the champion of the Whigs, from the representation of Westminster. The poll continued open from April 1 to May 17, and during all these days the air was electric. " At the hustings at Covent Garden, hour after hour, the orators strove to out-argue and the mobs to out-bawl each other. All day long the open space in front resounded with alternate clamours, while the walls were white with placards, and the newspapers teeming with lampoons. Taverns and public-houses were thrown open at vast expense. Troops of infuriated partisans, decked with party ribbons and flushed with gin and wine, were wont to have fierce conflicts in the streets, often with severe injuries inflicted."

As the day drew near, and the numbers were almost even, the Duchess set out in her coach to beat up the voters in the outlying suburbs. The ballad-makers went before her.

Arrayed in matchless beauty, Devon's fair
In Fox's favour takes a zealous part ;
But oh ! where'er the pilferer comes—beware !
She supplicates a vote, and steals a heart.

In the course of her canvass, says the " Cornwallis Correspondence," she entered " some of the most blackguard houses in the Long Acre," where she was now and then " coarsely received by some worse than tars." Nothing daunted, the young Duchess went forward for Fox and free government, and it is reported that to a butcher halting in his allegiance she offered her lips for a promise of his vote. Suppose it true, and the butcher in his apron among his carcases, the action was less a hoyden's than a heroine's. Rowlandson, in one of his caricatures, represents the Duchess seated on Fox's knee and presenting her dainty shoe to be sewn by a voting cobbler while to his wife she hands money. The scene is laid in Peter Street, Westminster, and the cobbler's stall has a board lettered, " Shoes made and mended by Bob Stichett, cobbler to her Grace the tramping Duchess." To the same campaign belongs another story, that of the Irish labourer who " asked to light his pipe by the fire of her beautiful eyes." It is on record that the Duchess herself treasured this among the compliments of her life. Free government carried the day in Westminster ; Fox was returned by a majority of 236.

On another occasion, to serve her

friend Sheridan, the Duchess turned her wit to account in a practical joke. Sheridan had just got into Parliament, and Fox and other cronies wanted him for Brooks's Club, membership of which, says Walford, "was a sort of crucial test by which the Whig party of the time were distinguished." But Sheridan was personally unpopular with two of the wire-pullers of the coterie, Selwyn and Lord Bessborough, and one black ball disposed of a candidate for Brooks's. The merry Duchess put the Foxites up to a trick of comedy, and "when the time for the ballot came on, they sent false messages, conveying alarming news of the illness of near relatives, to both of the dissentients. The bait took in both cases, each no doubt supposing that the other would be in his place to give the black ball"—and Sheridan was duly elected. It may have been about this time that Horace Walpole, summing up the gifts and qualities of the Duchess, pronounced her "a phenomenon." Certainly she was little familiar with defeat.

How many canvases have preserved for us some semblance of this divinity we cannot with certainty declare, but she is known to have sat to Reynolds, Gainsborough (each of whom painted her both in childhood and in her radiance), Cosway, Downham, and Nixon. Thirty-five years ago a very sensational robbery gave a new celebrity to the most admired of the Gainsborough pictures. Early in 1876

this fine and seductive portrait became the property of the Messrs. Agnew, art dealers, who had purchased it at Christie's for 10,100 guineas, "the highest price ever paid at an auction for a portrait." The Gainsborough was on exhibition in a Bond Street gallery, and on a night of May in 1876 it vanished. "The picture had been very neatly cut from the stretcher." says Major Arthur Griffiths ("Mysteries of Police and Crime"), "after it had been removed from the gilt frame in which it hung upon the wall. The stretcher was left, and it showed that no unpractised hand had operated upon the canvas, for the picture itself had been completely removed, leaving nothing but the clean cut canvas at the edges on which it had been mounted."

All trace of the work was instantly lost, and, so far as the public were concerned, the mystery was unbroken for five and twenty years. In 1901 the Duchess was returned, and the story of the theft was gradually revealed. The thief was Harry Raymond, *alias* Wirth or Worth, a master of crime in several departments, sometime known, we believe, as "the American porch-climber." The "stolen Duchess" was re-sold by Messrs. Agnew for £30,000.

On March 30, 1806, in her forty-ninth year, the Duchess died at Devonshire House, her Piccadilly home. The Prince of Wales, on hearing of her death, exclaimed: "Then we have lost the most amiable and best-bred woman in England!"

STATESMEN AT PLAY
QUESTIONS AND ANSWERS

IN Queen Anne Street, Cavendish Square, lived, eighty and more years ago, the Right Honourable Joseph Planta, M.P., who had risen to distinction through the Foreign Office and had, in turn, acted as private secretary to Canning and to Lord Castlereagh. At his dinner-table he entertained a number of distinguished persons, including Mr. Canning, Count Lienen (the Russian Ambassador), Mr. Robinson (then Chancellor of the Exchequer and afterwards first Earl of Ripon), Mr. Huskisson, Lord George Bentinck, and Mr. Richard Rush (the American Minister). From the last-named gentleman's book of memoirs, "A Residence at the Court of London," we take this entertaining account of the intellectual exercise indulged in, one night, by the company :

It would not have been easy to assemble a company better fitted to make a dinner-party agreeable, or to have brought them together at a better moment. Parliament having just risen, Mr. Canning and his two colleagues of the Cabinet—Mr. Huskisson and Mr. Robinson—seemed like birds let out of a cage. There was much small talk, some of it very sprightly. Ten o'clock arriving, with little disposition to rise from table, Mr. Canning proposed that we should play "Twenty Questions." This was new to me and the other members of the diplomatic corps present, though we had all been a good while in England. The game consisted in endeavours to find out your thoughts by asking twenty questions.

The questions were to be put plainly, though in the alternative if desired ; the answers to be also plain and direct. The object of your thoughts not to be an abstract idea, or anything so occult, or scientific, or technical, as not to be supposed to enter into the knowledge of the company ; but something well known to the present day or to general history. It might be any name of renown, ancient or modern, man or woman ; or any work or memorial of art well known, but not a mere event —as a battle, for instance. These were mentioned as among the general rules of the game, serving to denote its character. It was agreed that Mr. Canning, assisted by the Chancellor of the Exchequer, who sat next to him, should put the questions ; and that I, assisted by Lord Granville, who sat next to me, should give the answers.

Lord Granville and myself were, consequently, to have the thought or secret in common, and it was well understood that the discovery of it, if made, was to be the fair result of mental inference from the questions and answers, not of signs passing or hocus-pocus of any description. With these as the preliminaries, and the parties sitting face to face on opposite sides of the table, we began the battle.

FIRST QUESTION (by Mr. Canning) : Does what you have thought of belong to the animal or vegetable kingdom ?

Answer : To the vegetable.

SECOND : Is it manufactured or unmanufactured ?

Manufactured.

THIRD : Is it a solid or a liquid ?

A solid.

(How could it be a liquid, said one of the company, slyly, unless vegetable soup ?)

FOURTH : Is it a thing entire in itself or in parts ?

Entire.

FIFTH : Is it for private use or public ?

Public.

SIXTH : Does it exist in England or out of it ?

In England.

SEVENTH : Is it single or are there others of the same kind ?

Single.

EIGHTH : Is it historical and is it existent at present ?

Both.

NINTH : For ornament or use ?

Both.

TENTH : Has it any connection with the person of the King ?

No.

ELEVENTH : Is it carried, or does it support itself ?

The former.

TWELFTH : Does it pass by succession ?

(Neither Lord Granville nor myself being quite certain on this point, the question was not answered ; but, as it was thought that the very hesitation to answer might serve to shed light upon the secret, it was agreed that the question should be counted as one, in the progress of the game.)

THIRTEENTH : Was it used at the Coronation ?

Yes.

FOURTEENTH : In the Hall or Abbey ?

Probably in both ; certainly in the Hall.

FIFTEENTH : Does it belong specially to the ceremony of the Coronation, or is it used at other times ?

It is used at other times.

SIXTEENTH : Is it exclusively of a vegetable nature, or is it not, in some parts, a compound of a vegetable and a mineral ?

Exclusively of a vegetable nature.

SEVENTEENTH : What is its shape ?

(This question was objected to as too particular, and the company inclining to think so, it was withdrawn ; but Mr. Canning saying it would be hard upon him to count it, as it was withdrawn ; the decision was in his favour on that point, and it was not counted.)

SEVENTEENTH (repeated) : Is it decorated, or simple ?

(We made a stand against this question also, as too particular ; but the company not inclining to sustain us this time, I had to answer it, and said that it was simple.)

EIGHTEENTH : Is it used in the ordinary ceremonial of the House of Commons, or House of Lords ?

No.

NINETEENTH : Is it ever used by either House ?

No.

TWENTIETH : Is it generally stationary or movable ?

Movable.

The whole number of questions being exhausted, there was a dead pause. The interest had gone on increasing as the game advanced, until, coming to the last question, it grew to be like neck-and-neck at the close of a race. Mr. Canning was evidently under concern lest he should be foiled, as by the law of the game he would have been if he had not now solved the enigma. He sat silent for a minute or two, then, rolling his rich eye about, and with a countenance a little anxious, and in an accent by no means over-confident, he exclaimed, " I think it must be the wand of the Lord High Steward ! " And it was—EVEN SO.

This wand is a long, plain, white staff, not much thicker than your middle finger, and, as such, justified all the answers given.

After John Doyle

LOUIS NAPOLEON IN LONDON

LOUIS NAPOLEON, afterwards Napoleon III., and husband of the Empress Eugénie who is still among us, visited London for the first time in May 1831. His mother, Queen Hortense of Holland, accompanied him and he seems to have formed the most agreeable impressions of the English capital which was to be a second home to him in years to come. Cut off from the throne of the great Emperor, his uncle, the future victim of Sedan had only too early commenced to look longingly towards the throne of Louis Philippe. The Revolution of 1830 had changed one dynasty for another; the turn of the Napoleons would surely come.

In October 1838, Louis Napoleon, already surrounded by a certain halo of prestige, returned to the English capital and remained in this country until August 1840. For some time, after leaving Fenton's Hotel, he lived in Carlton Terrace, and it was from here that he issued his famous work, " Les Idées Napoléoniennes," in which he extolled his uncle's policy, and urged that it should be adopted in France. The book seemed to the English the work of a mere dreamer, but it appealed to the imagination of the French. The future Napoleon III. became a frequent visitor at Gore House, and was a constant companion of the expelled Duke Charles Frederick

of Brunswick. Attracted by all feats of chivalry, Louis took part in the famous Eglinton Tournament, which was held in the summer of 1839. In the winter of the same year he moved to Lord Ripon's house in Carlton Terrace. His life at this time has been minutely described by a contemporary writer in the *Lettres de Londres*. " The Prince is an active working man, severe towards himself, indulgent towards others. At six A.M. he is in his study, where he works till noon—his hour of *déjeuner*. After this repast, which never lasts longer than ten minutes, he reads the newspapers and has taken notes of the more important events and opinions of the day. At two he receives visits; at four he goes out on his private business; he rides at five and dines at seven; then generally, he finds time to work again for some hours in the course of the evening." Enemies of the Prince maintain that he was a gambler and a spendthrift, but it is more fair to say that he lived at this period the fashicnable life of the set in which he found himself.

But under the surface he was still a dreamer, and he believed more devoutly than ever in his star. Undoubtedly, while apparently devoting himself to riding in the Park and field sports, he was planning that political coup, which was to be ridiculed all over the world as the blunder of

Boulogne. The steamship *Edinburgh Castle* had been chartered for this hazy attempt to win back the throne of the great Emperor, and on the night of August 3, 1840, the vessel put in at the Custom House Wharf, near London Bridge. Early the next morning, under the supervision of Count Orsi, nine horses, two ponderous vehicles, numerous packages of uniform, and a large quantity of spirits and wine were brought on board. It was said afterwards by Captain Crowe, the skipper of the *Edinburgh Castle*, that most of the followers of Prince Louis Napoleon were drunk, but Archibald Forbes in his "Life of Napoleon III." maintains that the "wild orgy" story was of a piece with that of the "live eagle" which the Prince was said to have carried on his shoulder on arrival at Boulogne. "The story," writes Archibald Forbes, "of this historic fowl, was very simple. Colonel Parquin, during a delay while the *Edinburgh Castle* was anchored off Gravesend, was obstinately determined to go ashore for the purpose of purchasing some decent cigars, those on the ship being detestable. He had his way in spite of all remonstrance; and on the way to the cigar-shop accompanied by Orsi and Thélin, he noticed a boy on the wayside feeding an eagle with shreds of raw meat. The eagle had a chain fastened to one of its claws, with which it was secured. Returning towards the landing-place Parquin, whose obstinacy was sustained, approached the boy and looking at the eagle asked 'Est-il à vendre?' The boy turned to Orsi and said, 'I do not understand the gentleman.' Orsi entreated, 'My dear Colonel, I do hope you don't intend to buy that eagle? For my sake don't think of such a thing!' The stubborn Parquin insisted. 'Why not? I will have it. Combien veux-tu?' The boy shrugged his shoulders; and at last Parquin asked him in broken English, 'How mooch?' 'One pound,' answered the boy. The eagle was put into the boat, Parquin insisting vehemently."

The eagle was fastened to the mainmast by the boy and no notice was taken of it until it was captured by the authorities at Boulogne. The episode, as all the world knows, ended in disaster, and the English eagle may be taken as its symbol. But very soon afterwards, Prince Louis Napoleon proved that he knew how to play a dignified and even generous rôle before the Chamber of Peers. "I represent before you," he exclaimed—and this was the very substance of his famous London book—"a principle, a cause, a defeat. The principle is the sovereignty of the people; the cause is that of the Empire; the defeat is Waterloo. . . ."

Of England, the Prince retained the kindliest memories. He was fond of the English ways, and he was particularly fond of hunting. On one occasion, when hunting with Baron Rothschild's stag hounds in the Vale of Aylesbury, he had fallen no less than seven times from the same horse. Long afterwards as Emperor he would talk to his intimates of this period of his exile. "There is nothing," he used to say, "comparable to the position of an English nobleman or squire. All our French imitations of your hunting and your shooting parties are like salt that has lost its savour."

A sentence of perpetual imprisonment followed the blunder of Boulogne, and when the Prince next visited London it was as the world-famed escaped prisoner from Ham. From

May 1846 until February 1848, he lived unostentatiously in this country. Early in 1847 he occupied a newly built house in King Street, St. James's, where he busied himself in collecting family portraits, books, and portfolios. His losses on the Turf at this period were heavy, and he was certainly " almost moneyless " when, on hearing of the flight of Louis Philippe after the Revolution of February 1848, he started for France on the 28th of the month. He was back again, however, very soon afterwards, and wielded the truncheon of a special constable in Park Lane on April 30 of the same year.

The Coup d'État followed in a few months, and when Louis Napoleon returned to London on April 16, 1855, it was as absolute master of France and a powerful ally of England in the Crimean War. Of Napoleon III. Queen Victoria noted in her Diary : " Nothing can be more amiable or more well-bred than the Emperor's manner—so full of tact," while of the Empress she wrote : " Her manner is the most perfect thing I have ever seen—so gentle and graceful and kind ; and the courtesy so charming and so modest and retiring withal."

When next Napoleon landed in this country another period of imprisonment had ended. He was old and worn, but the English crowd greeted him at Dover on March 20, 1871, with all their old warmth and kindness. Wherever he appeared in public, as, for example, at a Review of the Woolwich Garrison, and also during the Thanksgiving Progress of the Prince of Wales to St. Paul's Cathedral, of which ceremony he was a spectator, there were demonstrations of sympathy. But for the most part he remained with the Empress and his son at Camden Place in Chislehurst. The sad routine of these last days has been sketched by an intimate : " The Emperor would walk up and down the long corridor of Camden Place with his arm on the young Prince's shoulder, while he talked to the lad of men and things. After the midday breakfast, at which the little Court met for the first time in the day, he would sit in the morning-room in his arm-chair by the wood fire and talk cheerfully with the Empress or with any visitors who had come. It was but a small circle in which the Imperial couple moved, but it was one of steadfast friends. The Emperor talked willingly and freely of the remote past, but he was only a listener when contemporary politics were under discussion. If he interfered it was to counsel moderation of speech or to protest against reprisals."

The end was very near, and the series of operations by which the Emperor's last days were harassed began on January 2, 1873. Two were comparatively successful, but it was decided that a consultation should be held on the 9th at 11 A.M. as a third and final one would probably be necessary. Sir Henry Thompson, however, discovered at 10.25 that morning that the Emperor had only a few minutes to live, and twenty minutes later he was dead.

Londoners came in crowds to view the dead body of the Emperor. The English at least were still faithful to that unfortunate Prince who had whispered to Dr. Conneau with his dying breath, " Étiez-vous à Sedan ? "

ROUND ABOUT NORTHUMBERLAND HOUSE

NORTHUMBERLAND HOUSE lasted on into modern times; witnessed the clearing-away of its lowlier neighbours which took place for the making of Trafalgar Square in 1830; formed a prominent feature in the view from the portico of the National Gallery; was shaken by railroad traffic and saw the coming of electric light before it was finally sacrificed to the Metropolitan Board of Works in 1874.

Many still living can remember Northumberland House, "the most conspicuous feature in London," as it has been called, "the most notable house in the most characteristic of streets." Its destruction was accounted by many "barbarous and ridiculous" —a needless piece of vandalism. It is true that the house itself had been

so continually altered and rebuilt that little of the original structure remained; but the beautiful gateway was almost as Inigo Jones had designed it, and the plain front was not without a certain dignity. "Commenced by a Howard, continued by a Percy, completed by a Seymour," it stood symbol of some of the greatest names in England. Here, too, history was made, for the restoration of Charles II. was first proposed in direct terms within its walls.

Almost all the stories we have in connection with Northumberland House are coloured with a solemn and almost oppressive magnificence. The house was built in 1605, of brick, by the Earl of Northampton, and was considered a very fine specimen of Jacobean architecture. It passed through marriage to the Northumberland family in 1642, who continued the reconstruction carried on through several centuries. All these alterations aimed at making the house a more cheerful place of abode. The famous architect, Inigo Jones, transferred the principal apartments from the Strand side to the river side, and planned a new garden-front; but we feel that more drastic measures than this were necessary to dispel the almost Spanish rigidity of etiquette that prevailed within the walls. In 1670 Lady Elizabeth Percy, who was twice a widow and three times a wife before she was seventeen, married the " proud " Duke of Somerset. (Her father was the last of the old male line of the Percies, and the title of Earl, and afterwards Duke, of Northumberland passed in the middle of the eighteenth century to Sir Hugh Smithson, who had married Lady Elizabeth Seymour.) The " proud " Duke of Somerset never allowed his daughters to sit down in his presence, even when they were nursing him for days and nights together in his eighty-seventh year, and he omitted one of his daughters from his will because he caught her involuntarily napping by his bedside!

Eighty years later, in 1750, we still find the owners of Northumberland House trying to make the front look " less like a prison," as the then Duchess of Somerset writes to a friend in a letter in which she gives minute details about the alterations. " My lord's bed on the ground floor is crimson damask with tapestry hangings; the next room is furnished with green damask on purpose to set off the pictures. . . . The great waiting-room with Saxon green cloth chairs with gilt nails, and green lute-string (glacé silk) window curtains, marble table and large glass between the windows. . . ." It was perhaps into this waiting-room that Oliver Goldsmith was ushered when he came with a letter of introduction to the Earl of Northumberland. The Earl was Lord-Lieutenant of Ireland, and willing, on representation, to extend his patronage to an Irishman of talent. We can imagine Goldsmith, dressed in those gay colours of which he was so fond, adventuring into the gloom and formality of that great mansion. According to Washington Irving, Goldsmith used to give this account of his visit: " I dressed myself in the best manner I could, and after studying some compliments I thought necessary on such an occasion, proceeded to Northumberland House, and acquainted the servants that I had particular business with the Duke. They showed me into an antechamber, where, after waiting some time, a gentleman very elegantly dressed made his appearance. Taking him for the Duke, I delivered all the fine things I had composed, in order to compliment him on the honour he had done me, when, to my great astonishment, he told me I had mistaken him for his master, who would see me immediately. At that instant the Duke came into the apartment, and I was so confounded on the occasion that I wanted words barely sufficient to express the sense I entertained of the Duke's politeness, and went away exceedingly chagrined at the blunder I had committed." We read, however, that when the Earl expressed a desire to do Goldsmith some kindness, the poet recovered sufficient presence of mind to ask that some help might be given, not to himself, but to his brother, a clergyman in Ireland.

If the inside of the house, with its 150 rooms, was somewhat gloomy and awe-inspiring, the populace managed to extract some amusement from its exterior features. The crest of the Percies, a lion, adorned the top of Northumberland House. (This lion, which was cast in lead, and was about twelve feet in height, has since been removed to a similar position at Sion House, Isleworth, the suburban residence of the Dukes of Northumberland.) It is related by Mr. Macmichael how some nameless wag undertook, for some trifling wager, to collect a crowd in the streets of London upon any pretence, however absurd. "He accordingly took his stand opposite Northumberland House and gazed very earnestly up at the lion. Joined by one or two passers-by, he took out a spy-glass, and looked still more intently. A hundred people quickly assembled, and it went round that at a certain hour the lion would wag its tail! The crowd increased until the Strand was rendered impassable. The greatest curiosity was manifested; several swore positively that they saw the tail wagging, and long arguments ensued *pro* and *con*. The story adds that the crowds were not dispersed till a smart shower came on, and even then some of the most pertinacious believers ensconced themselves in covered alleys and under doorways to watch the phenomenon."

In 1874 the Metropolitan Board of Works purchased the house for £500,000, and the material of which it was built was sold under the auctioneer's hammer. The famous marble staircase, which fetched £360, was removed to 49 Prince's Gate. Northumberland Avenue, with its three monster hotels—the Grand, the Victoria, and the Métropole—rose on the site of Northumberland House and its gardens. So perished one of the most impressive links with an older London—so fell the last of London's riverside palaces.

THE LION, NORTHUMBERLAND HOUSE

Northumberland House long had for its companion the equestrian statue of Charles I. now at the head of Whitehall. As we look at the figure of the King, full of grace and dignity, we are dazed with memories of the Stuart time, so thick and fast they crowd upon us. This beautiful statue had been modelled by Hubert Le Sœur, a Frenchman who came to England about 1630. It was commissioned by the Earl of Arundel, and cast in bronze in the narrow purlieus of Bartholomew Close. It was erected just before the beginning of the serious quarrel between Charles and his Parliament. By order of the Revolutionary Government it was taken down and sold to one Rivett, a brazier, who lived at the Dial near Holborn Conduit. Rivett was given strict orders to break up the statue. Whether he was an ardent Royalist or a cunning rogue we cannot tell; in any case he gave out that he had obeyed these injunctions, and that he had for sale a number of knives and forks with bronze handles made from the statue.

Royalists bought these as mementoes of the martyred King; Parliamentarians bought them as symbols of their triumph; and Rivett drove a thriving trade. Meanwhile he had carefully hidden away the statue in the vaults of St. Paul's Church, Covent Garden.

The statue was brought from its place of concealment and set up in 1674 upon its present pedestal. The pedestal, which is sculptured with the Royal arms of England, trophies, cupids, palm-branches, &c., is reputed to be from the design of Grinling Gibbons.

NORTHUMBERLAND HOUSE AS DRAWN BY CANALETTI

The Commonwealth wore to a close: Charles II. became King. On the very spot where had stood the Eleanor Cross, where Charles I.'s statue was afterwards to stand, the few remaining regicides were executed with every accompaniment of ignominy. "I went to Charing Cross," says Pepys, "to see Major-General Harrison hanged, drawn, and quartered, which was done there, he looking as cheerful as any man could in that condition. Thus it was my chance to see the King beheaded at Whitehall and to see the first blood shed in revenge for the King at Charing Cross."

Charles I. was not, we believe, much given to practical joking during his lifetime, and he would no doubt have viewed with disapproval the participation of his bronze counterpart in a large number of practical jokes. Young men up from the country used to be given letters of introduction to Charles Stuart at Charing Cross, and their gradual perception of the hoax that had been played upon them was a source of infinite amusement to the onlookers. Young men up from the country may not be so green to-day; but indifference is a less laughable matter than ignorance.

A DRURY LANE ROMANCE

THE "QUEEN OF HEARTS" AND LORD CRAVEN OF CRAVEN HOUSE

PICTURESQUE for a while, in the social history of London, and of old Drury Lane in particular, is Elizabeth of Bohemia. Within a small orbit she was one of the women created for the conquest of hearts, yet her victories were less those of the girl than of the woman, well set in years, for she was full thirty-six when her beauty and high bearing fascinated and subdued Lord Craven. The brief passage that follows may be cited as an introduction : " William Lord Craven, the hero of Creutznach, by his romantic attachment to Elizabeth, the titular Queen of Bohemia, has inseparably associated their names in history. According to the old Yorkshire tradition, Craven's father, Lord Mayor in 1611, was born of such poor parents that they sent him, when a boy, by a common carrier to London, where he became a mercer in Leadenhall Street, and grew rich. His son, the soldier of fortune, distinguished

himself under Gustavus Adolphus ; and at the storming of Creutznach in 1632 his determined bravery led to the fortress being taken after two hours' conflict, in which all the English officers were wounded. Craven then attached himself to the King and Queen of Bohemia."

Elizabeth was of royal origin, and had in her veins both Scottish and Danish blood. The eldest daughter of our James I. and Anne, daughter of Frederic II. of Denmark, she was born in 1596. The fates were but indifferent kind to her in marriage, for she became, in 1613, the wife of Frederic V., Elector Palatine of the Rhine, who was possibly as deficient in all stirring and stimulating qualities as a prince may contrive to be. It is said that the consent of the princess's parents to the union was reluctant enough, and that her mother " used to twit her with the title of Goody Palsgrave."

In November 1632 King Frederic

died of the plague ; and the Queen of Hearts (as she was so happily called) was left to face the world alone, in circumstances not the happiest. She gradually withdrew into private life, being indeed sorely pressed for money.

Brighter days at length dawned on the long-exiled Stuarts, and in 1660 Elizabeth saw her nephew, Charles II., set out for England. Money (no great sum at first) was presently voted to her Majesty by Parliament, her steadfast champion, Craven, exerting himself to the uttermost in her behalf. Elizabeth's biographer, Mrs. Everett Green, says : " The devoted generosity with which Lord Craven had for years past thrown his heart and fortunes into the cause of the Palatine family has led to the supposition that some warmer and closer tie than that of a loyal and platonic friendship united him to the Queen of Bohemia ; in fact, that a private marriage had taken place between them. This opinion, however, is incorrect : the whole character of Lord Craven shows him to have been a man of a large heart and noble-spirited benevolence ; one of the few chivalrous spirits of an age in which selfishness and party feeling were rampant ; and he needed no secondary motives to spur him on to generous and high-souled action." Elizabeth; it may be added, was sixty-four at the date of the Restoration. It is possible —and this report was current at Court—that Lord Craven wished to marry Princess Elizabeth; eldest daughter of the Queen of Bohemia, who was not more than seven years his junior. Mrs. Everett Green assures us that the warmest sentence in the extant correspondence between Craven and the Queen occurs in reference to the news which he forwarded to his royal friends of an infectious disorder

which had attacked one of her nieces : " For God's sake ! have a care of yourself ; for if your majesty should miscarry, that loss were never to be repaired. God in his infinite mercy protect you ! "

Elizabeth's residence at The Hague, where she had long been established, grew more and more distasteful, and now again she indulged hopes of returning to England. Her nephew on the throne, who had scant affection to bestow upon an aged relative, delayed to send for her ; and it was under the advice of Sir Henry Howard that she finally resolved to come. She would not force herself as a guest on Charles, but it was a very different matter to accept the hospitality of Lord Craven, who placed at her disposal his own house in Drury Lane.

Three ships of war had been provided by the States for Elizabeth and her little retinue. The French Ambassador at The Hague, De Thou, in a letter to Louis XIV., said : " Although here she is in debt, more than 200,000 crowns, to a number of poor creditors and tradespeople, who have furnished her subsistence during the disgraces of her house, nevertheless, from the friendship they have for her person, they let her go without a murmur, and without any other assurance of their payment than the high opinion they have of her goodness and generosity."

Charles, one thinks, might have given her apartments in one of the royal palaces, but the Queen went straight; as Lord Craven's guest; to his mansion in Drury Lane. " Craven House was originally built by Sir William Drury, from whom it was purchased by the Craven family. Lord Craven built large additions to it, so as to make it rather resemble several houses placed together. The entrance was through

THE MURAL PORTRAIT OF THE EARL OF CRAVEN WHICH FORMERLY DECORATED
A WALL NEAR CRAVEN STREET

a pair of gates leading into a large coach-yard, and behind was a beautiful and extensive garden. Drury Lane and the Strand were at this period the fashionable parts of London, and chief places of residence of the gentry. Craven House was taken down in 1809."

Early in 1662, unwilling to trespass too far on the generosity of the devoted Craven, Elizabeth hired from the Earl of Leicester his mansion in Leicester Fields. Her high character made itself felt in some degree even at the Court of Charles II., and she was seen frequently with him in public (Craven usually in attendance on her), "always welcomed by the people, who regarded her with reverential affection."

But her residence at Leicester House was very brief. A severe illness seized her almost in the hour of her arrival, and on the morning of February $\frac{13}{23}$, 1662, she died, sitting in her chair. Her papers and portraits were bequeathed by Elizabeth to Lord Craven, by whom they were deposited at his country seat, Combe Abbey. "There they still remain ; so that the home of Elizabeth's happy girlhood "—she had resided there with her tutor, Lord Harrington, and Lady Harrington— "has become the fitting shrine for these valuable relics of her brilliant and eventful after-life." She died at the age of sixty-five years, forty of which had been spent in exile. Mrs. Carteret says : "Her own proudest title, of 'Queen of Hearts,' has been super-added to that of 'Queen of Nations,' in the person of the descendant of her youngest child—her Majesty Queen Victoria."

Chroniclers have preserved for us another memory of the chivalrous Lord Craven. He had an interest in fires such as George Selwyn had in executions ; but it was the interest, not of a morbid sightseer, but of a zealous citizen. Wherever a fire blazed (and fires were frequent in those days) he was on the spot to render help. His very horse, it was said, could smell flames from a distance, "and galloped off with his master unguided to the scene of action." Lord Craven died in 1697, aged nearly eighty-nine years. This romance of Drury Lane still lives in Lord Dorset's ballad :

The people's hearts leap, whenever she comes;
And beat day and night, like my Lord
   Craven's drums ;

but more especially in Sir Henry Wotton's beautiful verses beginning :

Ye meaner beauties of the night,
   Which poorly satisfy our eyes
More by your number than your light,
   You common people of the skies,
What are you, when the Moon shall rise ?

" Th' eclipse and glory of her kind " he calls her. A romantic pair in old Drury Lane ! Of Lord Craven a writer in Chambers's " Book of Days" says : "His city birth, warlike fame, and romantic connexion with a Queen—for Elizabeth was always styled in England by her fatal title of Queen of Bohemia— rendered him the most popular man in London, and his quiet remonstrances would disperse a riotous mob more effectually than a regiment of soldiers."

We easily remember the tall blank wall which closed the end of Craven Buildings—named after Craven House —in the Kingsway-Aldwych area, from which so many storied lanes and sites disappeared seven years ago. From that wall there had long disappeared a large fresco painting representing Lord Craven on his white charger. It must have been a unique outdoor decoration, and indeed it had been one of the regular sights of London. " Rainy Day " Smith, that diligent recorder of such things, who died in 1833, made a careful etching of this picture, which we have here reproduced.

Craven House disappeared in 1803, and on its site Philip Astley, who is the subject of a separate sketch, built his Olympic Pavilion. Long after its disappearance Lord Craven's mansion was represented by the Craven Head public-house, and the memory of the woman he loved was oddly perpetuated in the sign of a tavern —the " Queen of Bohemia " in Drury Lane.

THE LION COMIQUE

THE first "Lion Comique" was George Leybourne, upon whom the title had been conferred by J. J. Poole, of the South London Music Hall, who had an original aptitude for drawing up attractive bills and inventing fine sounding sobriquets for his artistes.

George Leybourne, who started life as a mechanic, had a magnificent voice and a manner of delivering his songs that caught the audience by his exaggerated imitation of the supposed manner of the West End "swell." Notwithstanding this he had a hard struggle to reach the top of the tree. His success began when he met Alfred Lee, a composer. One day, having only a penny between them to pay for the toll over Waterloo Bridge, they trudged to Sheard's offices, and there, in a little top room in Holborn, Lee sat down at the piano with the MS. of "Champagne Charlie" in front of him ; Leybourne sang it, and Sheard the publisher said to Lee, "What do you want for it ? " Lee, very nervous, and seeing a chance at last, went on improvising at the piano and suggested that he should talk to George about it. And after a parley Sheard said he would give five pounds down. Leybourne sang the song first of all under his proper name of Joe Saunders in the East End of London. It was so popular that he was almost immediately engaged for the West End.

"Champagne Charlie" was the rage of London, and George Leybourne suddenly found himself, as another song put it, "par excellence, the idol of the day." In "Champagne Charlie" he always came on the stage wearing a long Newmarket coat, underneath which he had on an immaculate evening dress suit. His wig was fair, his whiskers were straw-coloured, and he invariably wore white gloves with which he made great play. Once at the Princess's Theatre, where he was specially engaged to play in the music-hall scene of *After Dark* he was just on the point of singing when he suddenly discovered that he had forgotten something, and cried out, to the amusement of the audience, "Hang it all, I've forgotten my gloves." A pair being promptly handed to him from the wings, he was able to commence his song and bring down the house as usual.

George Leybourne eclipsed every singer of his time, not with one song alone but with many. His well-known turnout of four horses and an elaborate carriage became one of the talks of the Town. From a few sovereigns a week George Leybourne was able to command almost any sum he pleased, and at one time, by singing at various places of entertainment, he earned one thousand pounds a week.

Another great "lion comique" was Alfred G. Vance, whose style of dress was entirely different from that of Leybourne. He particularly delighted in red plush coats and chess-board trousers, and a blue waistcoat. Occasionally he varied his attire by donning impeccable white "ducks." He had a vast store of pocket handkerchiefs, which he distributed about the stage during the singing of his various songs. One of Vance's biggest successes was "Walking in the Zoo," with which he alternated "Clicquot, Clicquot, that's the wine to make you jolly," and "Slap ! Bang ! Here we again."

Next comes Arthur Lloyd, first of all

an actor, then an entertainer, and then he came out at the Oxford Music Hall as a "lion comique" and set the town ringing with "I like to be a Swell,"

THE LION COMIQUE

"Not for Joseph," "I Fancy I can see her now," and his "German Band."

Then there was "Jolly John Nash," with his irresistible laughing songs and "Sister Mary walks like this," and J. W. Rowley, of "Going to the Derby" fame.

George Hastings Macdermott became the most famous "lion comique." He caught the fancy of the public directly he made his appearance at the Pavilion, in Piccadilly, after a long training as an actor at the Grecian Theatre in the City Road. He came

to the front with the singing of "Where was Moses when the light went out?" then he sang "When the Pigs begin to Fly," which had a very strong political suggestion. But the greatest achievement of George Macdermott came when, during the great crisis, which occurred a little over thirty years ago between England and Russia, he burst upon the town with a song written by G. W. Hunt, called, "We don't want to Fight," the chorus of which ran:

We don't want to fight,
But by Jingo if we do
We've got the ships, we've got the men,
We've got the money too;
We've fought the Bear before
And while we're Britons true
The Russians shall not have Constantinople.

When the "Great" Macdermott, as he was afterwards styled in the bills, walked upon the boards attired in faultless evening dress, and sang the first verse of this now historic song, the applause that greeted him was tremendous, but when he came to the refrain, quoted above, the enthusiasm of the audience knew no bounds. It is said that members of both Houses of Parliament not only went to hear Macdermott, but several Cabinet Ministers wrote letters to him to congratulate him on his patriotism. The song was translated into French and sung heartily in all the café's concerts. Macdermott made a considerable fortune—and kept it.

THE BIRTH OF THE BRITISH MUSEUM

WHEN we look at the vast mass of the British Museum, built of stones of such magnitude as have not been employed in structure since the days of ancient Rome, when we consider the various collections it contains, drawn from all countries and all ages, we are driven to ask ourselves : In what brain did this stupendous idea of a national museum first take shape ?

It was at Cotton House, which stood on the site of the present House of Lords, that Sir Robert Cotton housed his world-famous collection of manuscripts and printed books. Sir Robert Cotton (1570–1631) had as a young man travelled over the northern counties with Camden, the famous antiquarian. Cotton was largely instrumental in the foundation of the first Society of Antiquaries ; before the close of the sixteenth century the renown of his library was wide-spread on the Continent. He was consulted on recondite points by kings ; he had a voluminous correspondence with the eminent men of his day ; Ben Jonson put difficult questions to him concerning ancient Roman geography ; and Sir Walter Raleigh wrote to him from the Bloody Tower, beseeching him to supply a desolate prisoner with historical material.

But the point on which we would lay special emphasis is the extraordinary devotion that Cotton had for his books. He was of liberal disposition, and the lavish hospitality that he dispensed at Cotton House to the wits and wiseacres of his day was extended also to students in the use of his library. This library was his passion ; separation from his beloved books killed him. It is fitting that the virtual founder of the British Museum should have been possessed of this great love ; but tragic that it should have been put to so cruel a test. The story is a dramatic one ; and well worth telling briefly.

Cotton had incurred the anger of Charles I. by reason of his alliance with the Parliamentary leaders; and this anger was manifested at Charles's coronation in the following petty way : the water-stairs by which the King usually entered Whitehall were at that time under repair, and it was expected that he would land from the royal barge at the water-gate of Cotton House and cross the garden to the palace. Cotton decorated his house, and invited many guests for the occasion. The ladies, in fair attire, were standing from the water-gate to the house-door, to do respectful obeisance, when; by a sudden order of the king's, prompted by Buckingham, the barge passed to the ordinary stairs belonging to the backyard of the palace (where the landing was dirty), ran on the ground and stuck fast before it reached the causeway. The king and Buckingham had to leap across the mud—certainly an unusual incident in a coronation show !

Not satisfied with this insult; the king later on found a flimsy pretext for throwing Cotton into prison. Afterwards, when he was released, in a spirit of almost incredible meanness, the king had his library sealed up (1629). In vain Cotton petitioned Charles to give him access to his books; telling how his manuscripts were perishing from neglect ; his prayers were disregarded; and, troubled beyond measure by the deprivation, his ruddy appearance fell away, and he became sallow and haggard. As he lay on his death-bed he said : " Tell the Lord Privy Seal and the rest of the Council that their so long detaining my books from me has been the cause of this mortal malady." One of his contemporaries remarked : " If you could look at Sir Robert Cotton's heart ' My Library '

would be found inscribed there, just as Queen Mary said ' Calais ' was printed deeply on hers."

In 1700 Cotton's great-grandson bequeathed this great library to the nation. Sir Robert Cotton had himself strenuously advocated the foundation of a public library, and one is glad to think that the books and manuscripts he loved so well are now a national possession, the nucleus of the great collections which have since accumulated. Later, two royal libraries were presented to the nation, the Old Royal Library, given by George II. in 1757, and the King's Library, collected by George III.; and given by George IV. in 1821. The stories of these two collections possess features of special interest.

The virtual founder of the Royal Library was Henry, eldest son of James I., a prince of great liberality and promise, who died in 1612 at the age of eighteen. One cannot help speculating how, had he lived, and succeeded to the throne instead of his brother Charles, the whole course of English history might have been changed. It is certainly remarkable in so short a life to have acquired so high a name for wisdom and learning ; remarkable in so brief a time to have accumulated so considerable a library with such skill and judgment.

We find a very different royal collector in George III. It is a somewhat striking paradox that this king; narrow as he was in culture and limited in range, should have been able to form a library—the King's Library— which is perhaps larger and finer than any like collection ever made by any one man even under the advantageous conditions of royalty. It is true that George III. was possessed of infinite patience; and was willing to forego even personal enjoyments that he might have more money to spend on books. But probably the library owes most of its excellence to the fact that the librarian applied to Dr. Johnson for advice, and followed the advice given. Nothing shows more on an expedition to the West Indies. He continued them under favourable auspices, becoming President of the College of Physicians, and succeeding Newton as President of the Royal Society. His life has special associations with Chelsea ; he gave the

THE BRITISH MUSEUM REPLACING MONTAGU HOUSE, 1845–49

clearly the sound and wide practicality of Johnson's judgment than the counsel he gave on this occasion. For this library Parliament erected a special building in 1828.

The reader may object that the British Museum is by no means a storehouse for books only, and in Sir Hans Sloane we have a collector of all kinds of miscellaneous objects —minerals, precious stones, corals, crystals, insects, shells, antiquities from Egypt, Greece, China, Rome, and even America. Hans Sloane began his collections when acting as physician

Company of Apothecaries the entire freehold of their Botanical Garden there : and removed his collections from his house at Bloomsbury to the Manor House at Chelsea, once the residence of Sir Thomas More. On his death in 1752 he bequeathed his collections to the nation, on condition that £20,000 should be paid to his family— a sum that in no way represented the exceeding value of his gift.

But how raise the money ? " I don't think there are twenty thousand pounds in the Treasury," said George II. And so the Government resorted to a most extraordinary expedient. They decided to raise the sum by public lottery. There were to be 100,000 shares at £3 a share. £200,000 was to be allotted as prizes; the remaining £100,000 was to be applied to the purchase of the Sloane and the Harleian collection; the providing of a repository, and the creation of an annual income for future maintenance. The management of the lottery became a great public scandal; there was a disgraceful traffic in lottery tickets, the price of which was artificially inflated, and cruel loss was inflicted on many unsuspecting persons. Private individuals had done their part nobly in making these collections; but the Government was grudging, supine, and indifferent; and the British Museum was born amid fraud and recrimination, gambling and misery.

However, a sum of money was raised, and Montagu House, in Great Russell Street, was bought in 1754 to be the repository of the national collection— a noble house, built of brick and stone, having a charming garden in the rear.

Montagu House was opened to the public on January 15, 1759. The southern range of the present museum occupies the exact site of Montagu House. The walls of Montagu House were removed piecemeal as the building of the present museum progressed between 1845 and 1849.

It is the birth of the British Museum we have set ourselves to chronicle : we have no space here to tell of the vast accretions by gift and purchase which have enriched the galleries. The building of the great Reading-room—which has the largest dome in the world, except the Pantheon at Rome—belongs rather to the maturity of the museum than to its infancy. But when we gaze upon this great completed whole, when we avail ourselves of the advantages of liberal and delightful education in the collections and in the library, it is pleasant to look back on the men who stand behind, whose zeal, whose public spirit, whose initiation, have made all this possible, who first nourished the idea which has since taken outward and visible shape.

DANIEL LAMBERT

INASMUCH as a writer no less distinguished than George Meredith describes London as " the Daniel Lambert of cities " it is impossible to refuse a place in this collection to the man whose corpulence could suggest such a phrase. The " Dictionary of National Biography " admits Lambert to its pages as " the most corpulent man of whom authentic record exists." On Ludgate Hill, close to St. Paul's, stands a tavern which bears his name.

Daniel Lambert was born in Leicester in 1770, his father being the

Keeper of the gaol. He was apprenticed to a button-engraver in Birmingham, and as a youth was active in sports. It was when he was nineteen that his future greatness began to be foreseen by himself or his friends. On his father's resignation of his post at the prison Lambert succeeded him, and his bulk forthwith increased rapidly. He is said to have been a very humane gaoler, and on his discharge in 1805, under a scheme of reorganisation, he was awarded a pension of £50. Meanwhile Lambert had become exceedingly corpulent. In 1793 his weight had been thirty-two stone, but it was now a little over fifty stone.

Lambert's reluctance to exhibit himself was gradually overcome, and in 1806 he resolved to visit London. To accomplish the journey, he had a carriage specially constructed, and in this vehicle he arrived at his lodgings at No. 53 Piccadilly. From the first he seems to have been well liked and respected by his visitors, though he had sometimes to repel impertinences. After exhibiting himself here for five months, Lambert returned to Leicester. He came to London again in 1807, and gave receptions in Leicester Square. He died at the Waggon and Horses Inn, at Stamford, on July 21, 1809. He was buried in St. Martin's burial-ground, Stamford. "His coffin was six feet four inches long, four feet four inches wide, and two feet four inches deep. This coffin, which consisted of 112 superficial feet of elm; was built on two axle-trees, and four cog wheels. Upon these his remains were rolled into his grave, which was in the new burial-ground at the back of St. Martin's Church. A regular descent was made by sloping it for some distance. It was found necessary to take down the window and wall of the room in which he lay to allow of his being taken away."

A tomb-stone; with the following epitaph, was erected in St. Martin's burying-ground, Stamford.

DANIEL LAMBERT

In remembrance of that prodigy in nature,

DANIEL LAMBERT,

a native of Leicester.

who was possessed of an excellent and convivial mind, and in personal greatness had no competitor.

He measured three feet one inch round the leg, nine feet four inches round the body. and weighed 52 stone 11 lbs. (14 lbs. to the stone).

He departed this life on the 21st of June, 1809, aged 39 years.

As a testimony of respect, this stone was erected by his friends in Leicester.

E. A. SOTHERN AS LORD DUNDREARY

THE LORD DUNDREARY MANIA

LORD DUNDREARY, the theatrical rage of London in the sixties, was the creation of an accidental moment. On May 12 1858, Laura Keene, at her own theatre in New York, produced a play called *Our American Cousin*, written by Tom Taylor, at that time a barrister friend of Thackeray, and contributor to the pages of *Punch*. *Our American Cousin*, having failed to find a home in England, was sent across the seas and, after having been rejected by one or two managers, Miss Laura Keene, who was a very imperious lady, decided to produce the piece because the character of Mary Meredith appealed to her. Edward Askew Sothern was at the time playing what is generally known as " walking on " parts, and much to his disgust, Miss Keene, who had not much opinion of Sothern, cast him for the subordinate character of Lord Dundreary, who was intended to be an old man, and who had only forty-seven lines to speak.

In his interesting biography of Sothern, the late Mr. T. Edgar Pemberton says : " At first he declined to play the part, but subsequently, on the condition that he should be permitted to rewrite it on lines of his own, he undertook it. Then he commenced putting into it everything he had seen that had struck him as wildly absurd. There was not, he afterwards used to declare, a single look, word, or act in Lord Dundreary that had not been suggested to him by people whom he had known since his early boyhood." It should be stated that Sothern was an Englishman who had played all round the English provinces before he sought for success in America, which will account for the fact that in this character that was to make his reputation he was reproducing an exaggerated version of the London dandy and swell. Strange to say, in the beginning Sothern aspired to play heroes, and was highly commended for his pathetic power by Charles Kean, but this small part in Tom Taylor's piece revolutionised the whole project of his career.

Everything about the part—the extraordinary make-up, the wig, and the elaborate side whiskers, not exactly " Piccadilly Weepers," but very like them, and especially the eyeglass and then the eccentric, yet faultless, costume, the lisp and the stutter, and the ingenious distortion of old aphorisms—made the character so new and original to the American public that it caught on at once. One thing connected with the impersonation— the quaint little hop which became a sort of impediment in the gait, as well as the carefully developed impediment in his speech—was the result of accident. According to all the records—and Joseph Jefferson, who was the original Asa Trenchard, repeats the story in his " Reminiscences "— one cold day, Sothern who was naturally of a restless disposition, was endeavouring to keep himself warm by hopping about at the back of the stage, when Miss Laura Keene sarcastically inquired if he was going to introduce that into the part of Lord Dundreary. The actors and actresses who were rehearsing laughed at this remark as being quite a brilliant sally, emanating from the manageress, and Sothern, who at the time was out of tune with his character and nettled, replied, in a rapid and grave manner, " Yes, Miss Keane, that's my view of the character." Having thus committed himself, he, of course, was bound to go on, and finding, as the

rehearsal progressed, that the whole company, including the scene-shifters, were convulsed with laughter, he, on the first night increased the extravagance of his hop and skip, and the very absurdity " brought down the house."

After playing Lord Dundreary in America for over three years, he was engaged by John Baldwin Buckstone for the Haymarket Theatre, when it was modestly announced that on November 11, 1861, Mr. Sothern " formerly of the Theatre Royal, Birmingham, and from the principal American Theatres," would make his first appearance in London in a character which he had already acted for upwards of eight hundred times. It was cheerfully predicted that as Lord Dundreary was supposed to be a gross caricature of an English nobleman that Sothern and the play would be condemned out of hand. Sothern himself had many misgivings, and felt that although he was going to be supported by all the clever members of the well-known Haymarket company that he had to face a tremendous ordeal. Buckstone himself became frightened, and was on the point of withdrawing the play after a few nights, but Charles Mathews, who had seen and appreciated Sothern's excellent impersonation, advised him to keep it in the bill, and to wait and see. Mathews was right in his judgment, as the sequel quickly proved. " The fame of his lordship spread far and near ; the success of the performance became as great as it was then unprecedented, and for four hundred consecutive nights the Haymarket was crowded with eager, delighted and uproariously mirthful audiences."

Thus Sothern came into his own after the struggles and perseverance of many arduous years. The impersonation took London by storm. Its humour was at once understood. Dundreary, with his absurd affectations of speech, his lisp and his general manner, was talked about by everybody. Dundreary whiskers were affected as well as his coats, which were absurdly long in the tail, also his neckties, and his waistcoats, in fact everything was " Dundreary " and became the rage. His dressing room, says Pemberton, at the Haymarket, was crowded with sufficient parcels of clothes to last him for a lifetime, and after a while energetic haberdashers simply flooded him with neckties of peculiar patterns with the hope that he would wear one or the other of them. Hatters, bootmakers, and tailors were equally anxious for his patronage, and " Dundrearyisms," as they came to be called, were the fashionable *bon mots* of the day. Even little books dealing with the imaginary doings of Dundreary, under every conceivable and inconceivable condition, were sold in their thousands in the shops and at the street corners.

Sothern's greatest feature in the play was the reading of the celebrated letter from his brother Sam, and the joke about the dog wagging his tail in order to prevent the tail from

THE REIGN OF DUNDREARYISM
GEORGE LEYBOURNE IN HIS SONG " I'M AWFULLY CLEVAH "

wagging the dog. The letter from Sam (the immortal Sam who never had a " uel ") which used to be the great success of the evening and which delivered as it was, we give with the full stage directions.

The history of this letter is worth recording. It supplies an instance of Sothern's ability to rise to an occasion. Sothern had promised to play for the benefit of John J. Raymond, an American of considerable repute, at a town called Mobile. On his arrival there from New Orleans, the first object that greeted his astonished eyes was an announcement to the effect that, in the course of his performance of Lord Dundreary " Mr. Sothern would read a letter from Brother Sam." Now, in the play as Sothern had presented it, although Brother Sam was incidentally mentioned, there was no suggestion of any correspondence or anything else. Sothern for the moment did not know what to do. But he determined to be equal to the occasion, and so on the back of a playbill he scribbled the remarkable epistle which we here reprint and delivered it to the amazement of John J. Raymond, who thought he had put Sothern in a corner.

To proceed. (Before opening letter

read N.B. outside it.) "N.B. If you don't get this letter, write and let me know." "That fella's an ass whoever he is." (Opens letter, taking care he holds it upside down.) "I don't know any fella in America except Sam ; of course, I know Sam, because Sam's my brother. Every fella knows his own brother. Sam and I used to be boys when we were lads together, both of us. We were always together. People used to say, 'Birds of a feather' —what is it birds of a feather do?—oh, 'Birds of a feather gather no moss.' That's ridiculous, that is. The idea of a lot of birds picking up moss. Oh, no ; it's the early bird that knows its own father. That's worse than the other. No bird can know its own father. If he told the truth, he'd say he was even in a fog about his own mother. I've got it—it's the wise child that gets the worms. Oh, that's worse than any of them. No parent would allow his child to get a lot of worms like that. Besides the whole proverb's nonsense from beginning to end. Birds of a feather flock together ; yes, that's it. As if a whole flock of birds would have only one feather. They'd all catch cold. Besides there's only one of those birds could have that feather, and that fella would fly all on one side. That's one of those things no fella can find out. Besides, fancy any bird being such a d—d fool as to go into a corner and flock all by himself. Ah, that's one of those things no fella can find out. (Looks at letter.) Whoever it's from; he's written it upside down. Oh; no; I've got it upside down. (Laughs.) Yes, this is from Sam ; I always know Sam's handwriting when I see his name on the other side. 'America.' Well, I'm glad he's sent me his address. 'My dear brother.' Sam always calls

me brother; because neither of us have got any sisters.

"'I am afraid that my last letter miscarried, as I was in such a hurry for the post that I forgot to put any direction on the envelope.' Then I suppose that's the reason I never got it ; but who could have got it ? The only fella that could have got that letter is some fella without a name. And how on earth could he get it ? The postman couldn't go about asking every fella he met if he'd got no name. "Sam's an ass. 'I find out now' (I wonder what he's found out now ?) 'that I was changed at my birth.' Now, what d—d nonsense that is. Why didn't he find it out before ? 'My old nurse turns out to be my mother !' 'What rubbish.'"

Then Sothern, in the character, began counting his fingers to find out what relation Sam is to him, and what relation Sam's mother was to him, and he gets so confused that he discovers all the fingers on his hand leaving his thumb out, are all mothers which, as he says, no "fella can find out." In one of the postscripts Sam tells him that he has bought an estate on the banks of the Mississippi and sends him a pill box containing a sample of the soil, he also requests him to forward him the purchase-money.

All through this speech, and in fact all through the play, Sothern's stutter was one of the most comical individual points, so that it is rather amusing to learn that one indignant playgoer went out of the theatre saying that Lord Dundreary was the worst played part in the piece, because the actor had such an "unfortunate impediment in his speech."

In the comedy Dundreary tells an extraordinary story to Georgina which is absolutely incoherent from end to end, but; as delivered by Sothern, was vastly amusing. Here is a part of it and, of course, it is about the irrepressible Sam, whom nobody ever sees. " There was another fella—an old chum of Sam's—and he was born with a bald head . . . well, that fella died and made himself very comfortable in that sort of way—and his cousin by another fella's godmother married a girl that I was going to marry—only I didn't get up, or something like that—my man didn't call me—or something of that sort—so she married this other fella—a very nice fella he was, and I wanted to do him a good turn—and there it was."

The absurd counting of the fingers was a transcript of an incident that Sothern had seen. " You remember," said the actor, " that in one act I have a by-play on my fingers in which I count from one to ten, and then reversing begin with the right thumb and count ten, nine, eight, seven, six, and five are eleven, holding up the other hand. This has frequently been denounced by critics as utterly out of place in the character, but I took the incident from actual life, having seen a notoriously clever man on the English Turf as quick as lightning in calculating odds completely puzzled by this ridiculous problem."

Sothern in private life, or shall we still say professional, was always playing practical jokes, Once when he was invited to see the Lord Mayor's Show from the roof of the offices of *Punch* in Fleet Street, he found himself on the wrong side of the road, and as pedestrians were not allowed to cross Sothern induced a well-known inspector, whom he knew, to handcuff him and so lead him across to *Punch* and *Punch's* lively associates. Lord Dundreary was never intended to be an absolute fool. He was simply a man without ballast, who tried to grasp at original ideas and always missed them. There was no power of concentration. John Oxenford very carefully analysed the character of Lord Dundreary.

When London could not get away from him or have half enough of him, then he was " a person who must be seen." Oxenford, the *Times* critic, said, " After all, what is this queer lord, who is always varying, is still ever the same ? In what consists his identity ? Let us hazard an answer to the interrogatory by saying that his sense of the ludicrous is most keen; his susceptive faculties are even over-developed."

Lord Dundreary was, like many others, an incomplete man—though his morals were quite irreproachable— but he was born askew, and curiously enough his great creator was born Askew—Edward Askew Sothern—on the first of April, too, 1826. He died in 1881.

THE EXECUTION OF LORD DERWENTWATER

THE Earl of Derwentwater paid the penalty on Tower Hill for his share in the Jacobite Rebellion of 1715 on Friday, February 24, of the following year. The youth of this gallant peer, his great popularity at his seat at Dilston, Northumberland, and, above all, the resolute devotion of his wife, who again and again appealed to the King to spare him, and rushed down from the North to London on a last desperate effort on his behalf—all these things enhanced the tragedy and pathos of this historic punishment. He was, indeed, a noble and dignified figure to whom a touching tribute has been paid in the poem entitled, "Lord Derwentwater's Farewell":

Farewell to pleasant Dilston Hall,
My father's antient seat,
A stranger now must call thee his;
Which makes my heart, to greet.
Farewell each kindly, well-known face,
My heart has held so dear;
My tenants now must leave their lands,
Or hold their lives in fear.

No more along the banks of Tyne
I'll rove in autumn gray;
No more I'll hear at early dawn
The lav'rocks wake the day.
And who shall deck the hawthorn bower,
Where my fond childhood strayed?
And who, when spring shall bid it flower,
Shall sit beneath the shade?

*　　*　　*

And although here, in London Tower
It is my fate to die;
O carry me to Northumberland,
In my father's grave to lie.
And chant my solemn requiem
In Hexham's holy towers;
And let six maids of fair Tynedale
Scatter my grave with flowers!

In that profoundly sympathetic volume, "Dilston Hall," William Sydney Gibson quotes Father Pippard's letter to Lady Derwentwater, in which he describes minutely the last days of the gallant Earl. Father Pippard was his confessor, and he was on his knees in the very act of making his last confession, when Major Sole entered the apartment to tell him that the coach, that was to take him to London, was waiting for him. "He asked," writes Father Pippard, "with much sedateness if he might be allowed a few minutes more, to which he was civilly answered he might. Then he finished what he had begun, with all the moving sentiments imaginable. This being over, he walked down to the coach. One of the keepers and I went in with him, and going along, the buffetiers, and guards, and most of the company were weeping, whilst his lordship, with a composed countenance, was devoutly praying." The sad procession left the Tower at about ten in the morning, Lord Derwentwater and Lord Kenmure, his no less gallant fellow sufferer, being conveyed from the Tower Gate in two hackney coaches. At the City Bar, they were received by the Sheriffs of London. They were now in sight of the scaffold, which was guarded on all sides by three detachments of the Life Guards, Horse Grenadiers, and Foot Guards. Alighting at some little distance from the scaffold, the two noblemen were conducted to the Transport Office on Tower Hill, from which a passage leading directly to the scaffold was formed.

Lord Derwentwater was now informed by the Sheriffs that a room had been prepared for him in which he might retire, in case he so desired, for a little while. The Earl accepted the concession gratefully, and spent about half an hour there in prayer. He then, according to Father Pippard, who witnessed the final scene, "walked majestically to the place of execution," while Lord Kenmure remained below. A crowd of many thousands watched the Earl as he ascended the steps of the scaffold. He was seen to grow pale at first, but he very quickly recovered, and "his behaviour was resolute and sedate." He was dressed in black velvet, and a gold crucifix hung suspended from his neck. His broad-brimmed beaver hat was ornamented with a black plume, beneath which the curls of his flaxen wig fell upon his shoulders. His hose also was black, as were his leather shoes with their high heels and silver buckles. In his hand he carried two books of devotion.

The father of Dr. Gibson, the Roman Catholic Bishop, accompanied him as well as Father Pippard and some others on the scaffold, where he was offered once more both his life and his fortune if he would conform to the Established Church and pledge his honour to the House of Hanover. The Earl of Derwentwater replied that these terms "would be too dear a purchase," whereupon Sir John Fryer offered him all the time that he might wish for his last preparation. The Earl said that he would only read a few prayers, and asked leave to read aloud a paper. Permission having been given, he knelt down and prayed, after which he rose from his knees and approached the rails of the scaffold. Then, in a clear, calm voice, the Earl of Derwentwater pronounced his last manifesto, in the course of which he said : "Some means have been proposed to me for saving my life, which I looked upon as inconsistent with honour and conscience, and therefore I rejected them ; for, with God's assistance, I shall prefer any death to the doing of a base unworthy action." The paper concluded with this significant postscript : "If that Prince who now governs had given me my life, I should have thought myself obliged never more to have taken up arms against him."

Sir John Fryer then asked for this paper, which is said to be written in the Earl's own hand. Lord Derwentwater handed it to him, saying "I have sent a copy of it to my friends." After this he repeated several penitential Psalms and a short prayer. "He prayed a second time," continues Father Pippard, "so movingly, that everybody there, and there were about thirty-five persons, seemed more concerned than himself. The very executioner knelt down and prayed and wept like a child, and so did many more—many at the same time praising and extolling his courage. For I heard some say, 'No Cæsar could die greater,' others commended his piety and truly Christian behaviour ; and though I have assisted many dying, I never was with any who gave such visible signs of a predestinate happy soul."

The Earl then took off his wig and coat, after which an unseemly interruption took place. "A strife arose," says his confessor, "about his wig between the keeper from the Tower who came with him and the executioner ; the like contest arose about his velvet clothes, during which he gave me a whisper to beg your ladyship to be in no concern about his burial, for he did not care what they did with his corpse. This he said, because he saw the Sheriff did not interpose when the executioner took his clothes, though the keeper made his complaint to him that they had been given to himself by his lordship, and he thought that what he desired about his burial might be likewise contradicted. This sort of scuffle was no sooner over, which grated others more than his lordship, when he prepared to kneel down."

Lord Derwentwater examined the block, and finding a rough place on it, asked the executioner, with a coolness that amazed the spectators, to make it smooth, so that it might not hurt his neck. "I forgive all," he then exclaimed, "that are concerned in my execution, and I forgive all the world !" At this point the executioner interposed with, "I ask your lordship's forgiveness," to which Lord Derwentwater replied immediately, "With all my heart ; I forgive all my enemies ; I forgive the most malicious of them ; and I do forgive you." He then gave the executioner "two half broad pieces," and told him that he would receive an additional present from the gentleman who was holding his hat and wig. "He bade the executioner," says Father Pippard, "not to strike till he had made a short prayer and pronounced the name of Jesus three times loudly. He then knelt down and placed his head on the block, and I stooped to him and gave him the last absolution, after which he made a short low prayer : then, with a loud voice, he said, 'Dear Jesus, be merciful to me,' after which he made a short pause, then repeated the same words still louder, and, stopping a little moment, he repeated them a third time, louder, and his head was in the instant severed from his body. It is impossible to describe the consternation that appeared in the faces of all that were there, that vast multitude really seemed to give a groan not unlike the hollow noise of the sea at a distance."

Thus, in his twenty-seventh year, James, the third Earl of Derwentwater, paid the penalty of death for his religion, and for him whom he regarded as his lawful king.

His last request had been that his body might be buried with his ancestors at Dilston, but from fear of a rising in the North, it was refused. The headless corpse was wrapped in black cloth and conveyed from the scaffold to the Tower in a hired coach. It was to have been interred in the Tower if the dead Earl's friends had not contrived to obtain possession of it. First of all, a faithful attendant brought the head wrapped in red velvet to the Earl's friends, and on the Tuesday following his decapitation the body itself was conveyed in a hearse from the Tower to the surgery of a Mr. Metcalf in Brownlow Street. Here both head and body were embalmed, after which they were taken to the house of an undertaker in Great Wilde Street named King. The coffin, covered with crimson velvet, was then conveyed to Dagenham Park, a place near Romford, which the Countess of Derwentwater had rented during the Earl's imprisonment. In this house was a Roman Catholic chapel in which the coffin rested until the Earl's friends were able to gratify his last wish and bring his remains to the quiet home of his ancestors.

The Northumbrian peasants believed firmly that marvellous appearances marked the day on which the young Earl was beheaded in London. They said that the Divelswater stream had acquired the hue of crimson as though the domains of Lord Derwentwater had been sprinkled by his blood. They maintained, too, that on the very night of his death the aurora borealis was seen for the first time, and they read in these "red streamers of the North" the vengeance of Heaven. They have been called ever since "Lord Derwentwater's lights."

A SHAKESPEAREAN CHARACTER

SIR TOBY BELCH'S mention in *Twelfth Night* of "Mistress Moll's picture" is said to refer to Moll Cutpurse; who is named in many Elizabethan plays and is the heroine of Middleton and Dekker's *The Roaring Girl*. Her real name was Mary Leith, and she was a noted pickpocket and associate of thieves. Her most signal exploit was robbing General Fairfax upon Hounslow Heath, for which she was sent to Newgate; but from here she is said

to have bought her liberty. Her biographers notice, as a remarkable feature, her passion for smoking tobacco; in the frequent use of which she long indulged herself. It was, at that time, almost as rare a sight to see a woman with a pipe, as to see one of the sex in man's apparel. On her thieving expeditions she often wore male dress and was accompanied by a dog which she had trained to assist her. She died in 1659 in Fleet Street.

THE LITERARY DUSTMAN AT HOME

THE OLD LONDON DUSTMAN

ALL the old cries and sounds of London are dying fast away. The sweep with his " Sweep O!" is never likely to pass, but the dustman, who of course will ever be present, now simply calls out "Dust O!" Even far up in the nineteenth century he used to come round ringing his bell with a clang that woke the children and roused the maids from their slumbers. And it used to be a saying with mothers that, when the dustman's bell was heard, " If you are not a good child, I'll give you to the dustman," and " Dust-hoy-e !" was the great cry all through the streets. The dustman's attire was one gorgeously decorated smock, and a curly brimmed hat which was adorned with a magnificent band, usually of red or blue and often

the two colours blended. He was generally a good-natured sort of fellow, not averse to a good strong glass of beer, especially Burton, with now and then a little drop of gin to mingle in between his arduous duties. Curiously enough, although the dustman was and still is hated of dogs, children took a great interest in him when they had grown out of the age of being frightened by his appearance. The dustman, notwithstanding his popularity, was always a favourite subject with the humorist, and *Punch* in particular made him the topic of many of his jokes, and many an old piece of verse was written about him.

There is no doubt that the dustman gave Dickens his idea for the chief character, Harmon, in " Our Mutual

Friend," because the huge dust-hills which at one time were to be seen in various open spaces round about

THE LONDON DUSTMAN OF FIFTY YEARS AGO

London, were known to contain much incidental wealth. Harmon of course made a large fortune, which he left to Nicodemus Boffin. An old gentleman recorded, not long since, a reminiscence of his early days. Quite enthusiastically he tells of a dustman's wedding procession on a Whit Monday, in the neighbourhood of Old Street, St. Luke's.

There was a loud clangour of hand-bells and the beating of a drum, then suddenly appeared upon the scene " four sturdy Dustmen in full regalia of velveteens, white slops, new flip-flaps, short pipes, and each adorned with a large bunch of flowers on his breast, and each one ringing his bell for all it was worth. These were followed by four more carrying on their shoulders the bridegroom in a large washing tub— probably the property of the bride. He too was smoking a short clay; and had on his breast a bouquet of flowers of the dimensions of an ordinary cabbage." The gallant bridegroom was also attired in velveteens, and the bashful bride, and her bridesmaids all on foot, were gorgeously attired in all the colours of the rainbow, with high flowing hats decorated with flowers and brilliant ribbons. Evidently the bride was connected with the laundry business, and as the husband was what one might say the delight-ful dustman, no doubt the combination eventually proved of extreme value.

At Vauxhall Gardens and other popular resorts, songs about the dust-men were quite a feature. The famous and excellent song of "The Literary Dustman," was written and sung by Robert Glindon, who was a very well-known and popular performer.

THE LITERARY DUSTMAN

Some folks may boast of sense, egad,
    Vot holds a lofty station,
But tho' a dustman, I have had
    A lib'ral hedication ;
And tho' I never went to school,
    Like many of my betters,
A turnpike man what warn't no fool,
    He larnt me all my letters.
They calls me Adam Bell 'tis clear,
    As Adam was the fust man,
And by a co-in-ci-dence queer,
    Vy, I'm the first of Dustman.

At sartin schools they make boys write
    Their alphabet on sand, sirs ;
So I thought dust vould do as vell,
    And larnt it out of hand, sirs ;
Took in the " Penny Magazine,"
    And " Johnson's Dictionary,"
And all the Pe-ri-o-di-cals,
    To make me literary.
            They calls, &c.

My dawning genius fust did peep,
    Near Battle-Bridge, 'tis plain, sirs,
You recollect the cinder-heap
    Vot stood in Gray's Inn Lane, sirs ?
'Twas there I studied picturesque,
    Vhile I my bread was yearnin ;
And there, inhaling the fresh breeze,
    I sifted out my larnin.
            They calls, &c.

Then, Mrs. Bell, 'twixt you and I,
    Vould melt a heart of stone, sirs,
To hear her pussey's wittals cry,
    In such a barrow tone, sirs.
My darters all take arter her,
    In grace and figure easy,
They larns to sing, and as they're fat,
    I has 'em taught by Grisi !
            They calls, &c.

Ve dines at four, and arter that,
    I smok a mild Awanna,
Or gives a lesson to the lad
    Upon the grand piana.
Or vith the gals valk a quadrille,
    Or takes a cup of coffee ;
Or if I feels fatigu'd or ill,
    I lounges on the sophy.
            They calls, &c.

Or arter dinner read a page
    Of Valter Scott or Byron—
Or Mr. Shikspur on the stage,
    Subjects none can tire on.

At night we toddles to the play,
    But not to the gallery attic,
Drury Lane's the time of day,
    And quite aristocratic.
            They calls, &c.

I means to buy my eldest son
    A commission in the Lancers,
And make my darters every one,
    Accomplished hopra dancers.
Great sculptors all conwarse wi' me,
    And call my taste diwine, sirs ;
King George's staty at King's Cross
    Was built for my design, sirs.
            They calls, &c.

And ven I'm made a member on,
    For that I means to try, sirs ;
Mr. Gully fought his way,
    And vherefore shouldn't I, sirs ?
Yet vhen I sits in Parli'ment,
    In old Sin Stephen's College,
I mean to take, 'tis my intent,
    The " taxes off o' knowledge."
        They call me Adam Bell, 'tis true,
        'Cause Adam was the fust man—
        I'm sure it's wery plain to you
        I'm a literary dustman.

The success of this remarkable composition was so great that Glindon followed it up by writing and singing " The Dustman's Brother," and as it was evident that more of the family should come in he added " The Dustman's Sister," in which the lady is extolled in a manner that is graceful to her merits and qualities :

My brother Adam, you're aware, is quite a
    nat'rul genus,
Possessing talents very rare, and such as
    seldom seen is ;
The turnpikes taught him how to read
    without the aid of Walker,
A running hand he larnt with speed of Ben
    the pavement chalker.

    In elegance I won't give place,
        To Madam, Miss, or Mister ;
    You'll recognise the Dustman's face
        In Dora Bell, his sister.

Although somewhat rugged in his appearance the dustman always had a kind of familiarity that was not unpleasant.

There is a well-authenticated story of the beautiful Duchess of Devonshire, who was one day stepping out of her carriage, when a dustman accidentally standing by was about to regale himself with his accustomed whiff of tobacco when he caught a glance of her countenance, and instantly exclaimed, " Love and bless you my lady, let me light my pipe in your eyes."

The Duchess was so delighted with this unexpected compliment that she rewarded him with a guinea, and when she frequently afterwards received the adoration of her admirers she used to say to her friends, " Oh, after the dustman's compliment all others are insipid."

The dustman is still with us and is likely to remain. He is such an absolute institution in London that neither the metropolis nor the suburbs could do without him.

AN ECCENTRIC LADY

JOHN THOMAS SMITH tells us in his " Book for a Rainy Day," that Miss Sophia Banks, the sister of Sir Joseph

SOPHIA BANKS

Banks, President of the Royal Society, " was looked after by the eye of astonishment wherever she went, and in

whatever situation she appeared." Her dress contained two immense pockets stuffed with books, and she was usually followed by a footman carrying parcels. She was a great collector of ballads, tradesmen's cards and tokens, and other curiosities. With all her eccentricities she was a woman of lofty character, and was devoted to her brother, for whom she kept house at 32 Soho Square, helping him to receive his distinguished guests at his Sunday evening conversaziones. Sophia Banks's collections are now in the British Museum, and have considerable value, especially her collection of Visiting and Invitation Cards. She died in 1818.

The old house in the south-west corner of Soho Square, a picturesque example of its period, is now a small hospital

SOME EARLY LONDON HIGHWAYMEN

O N the night of January 21, 1670, in a room of the Tangier Tavern, St. Giles's, there was a lying in state. Wax tapers to the number of eight burned in the chamber, which was hung all with black. The bier, whereon scutcheons were displayed, was guarded by eight "tall gentlemen in long black cloaks." Among the visitors admitted to this temporary chapel in a tavern were women who had come in coaches or sedans from the rich quarters of the town. By-and-by flambeaux streamed from the Tangier to Covent Garden Church, and in the long train of mourners women were most numerous. Thus was laid in state, and thus to earth the highwayman, Claude Duval.

But a few hours earlier his body had been carried in a mourning coach from Tyburn Tree to the Tangier. He was twenty-seven years of age.

When I was mounted on my Steed,
I thought myself a Man indeed ;
With Pistol cock'd and glittering Sword,
Stand and Deliver, was the word
Which makes me now lament to say,
Pity the fall of great *Devol*.
Well a day, Well a day.

Not "with age and dust," but with the running blood of early manhood was the highwayman liable to pay scot to the gallows. Claude Duval at twenty-seven, Jack Sheppard swung at twenty-three. To retire betimes with the swag, or to fall to the bullet of a better man upon the road ; these were almost the sole alternatives of the halter.

Claude Duval was born in the fit place. He was a native of Domfront, in Normandy. The curé of this village was puzzled to know how it chanced that he, who had baptized a hundred children, was never in request for a burying. Pushing the inquiry beyond his own borders he was at last informed that persons born at Domfront were commonly hanged at Rouen. He may have died in the conviction that Claude Duval was the one white sheep in a spotted flock.

By his parents, humble folk in a hungry France, Duval was destined to domestic service, but at thirteen, orphaned or cast loose, he set his face for Paris. There he was befriended by some aristocratic English royalists, with one of whom, at the Restoration, he came as footman to England. During a great part of the seventeenth century, and the whole of the eighteenth, footmen in families of mark or wealth were fatally attracted to the "road." They handled (and no doubt often wore) the fine clothing of their masters ; horses and weapons were familiar creatures to them ; they saw gambling, and learned to gamble ; they were tacked to the skirts of intrigue and adventure, above the ruck of base and sweaty people. Claude Duval in England went early on the road.

He seems to have had for it figure, nerve, and general aptness, since his reputation was not long in making. His name, when he was still new to the business, " stood first in a proclamation issued for the arrest of certain dangerous highwaymen." Spoliation of travellers on the king's highway was at this date a branch of crime to which ingress had grown easy. It was popular and somewhat crowded ; reputation in it was therefore not too readily achieved. Duval, amid the little host of those who go in masks, is clearly a notable practitioner. French by blood and birth, he has his stage in two countries. Proclaimed in England, he returns for a space to Paris, and does a little trade there and thereabouts. A Frenchman of the seventeenth century, he would naturally, on his proper soil, have a fling at black magic ; and his game with the Jesuit miser, to whom, while robbing him, he imparted the secret of the philosopher's stone, is one of the original strokes that give him a place slightly apart among contemporary knights of the path. Tyburn, calling him at twenty-seven, extinguished a fair talent in Claude Duval.

The close of the Civil War threw upon the country many honest, distracted friends of the vanquished side, probably

JOHN COTTINGTON (" MULLED SACK ")
From a Contemporary Print

a greater number of adventurers of the quality of Pistol. As far as the records can be trusted there is reasonable evidence that certain highwaymen assumed the mask as a desperate last protest in the cause of the King who had already perished at Whitehall ; though how many were out for vengeance, and how many for victuals or adventure, it is not possible to say. There was Captain James Hind, for instance, a hero of chap books. Hind was a King's man, un-

doubtedly, and had carried a sword for Charles at Worcester, but it seems equally sure that before this he had carried a pistol for himself, on his Majesty's highway, and one anecdote shows him as ready as the boldest of his class to plunder unprotected women. It runs that, somewhere between Petersfield and Portsmouth ; he overtook a coach " full of ladies," whose courage in travelling alone might have moved a highwayman to be shield and buckler to them. It moved Hind to lay hands on the bag of £1000 that formed part of the dowry of one of the ladies.

It was not; however, as robber, but as Royalist, that Captain Hind, in 1651, was had to Newgate. He stood " indicted upon high treason by the Counsel of State," escaped on this count, and was despatched to Reading there to be tried for murder or manslaughter. But it was a hard task to attach this man to the gallows. Released from Reading, he was forwarded to Worcester, where he stood a new trial for high treason. Worcester, mindful perhaps of the rout of the Parliamentary Horse, was more easily satisfied, and in September 1652, Hind was both hanged and quartered.

Captain Philip Stafford is another Royalist outlaw who, in the old phrase, began highwayman after the sequestration of his small estate. Having, by several lucky touches, put together a cosy fortune, Captain Stafford retired to a village in the north, where he so edified his neighbours that they " chose him to fill the place of minister of their congregation." In this position, from the blackmailing of women of quality, the regenerate " bounce " turned to pulpit homilies, until, wearying of his own good works, he fled with the church plate. On the Reading road he did a stroke of business in the old line, was pursued, headed for London, fell a prize to the watch, and was very quickly adorned with a Tyburn tippet.

JOHN COTTINGTON AT WORK

the name he thereafter went by. A skilled thief and " magsman " even in his novitiate, he was not long in mounting into the hierarchy of the mask. Hounslow Heath was a dreaded region when Mulled Sack frequented there. From a government waggon he took £4000 that was travelling to the army; he seized a jeweller's whole stock at a spot between London and Reading, and at Reading " robbed the Receiver's office of £6000 in hard cash, which he carried off on horseback." One of the first highwayman who organised a system of spies, Cottington was almost as well served from this source as Jonathan Wild in the succeeding century. Apprehended for the

Jack Cottington may also have leaned to Royalism, since at Westminster once he was caught with a hand in the pocket of Oliver Cromwell, and had before this taken (in church) a watch set with diamonds from Lady Fairfax, wife of the Parliament's great general. But Cottington, a liberal sportsman, sought his game in all coverts. He had graduated from chimney-sweep, and in this walk, admittedly a thirsty one, gave such exhibitions of his skill as a drinker of mulled sack, that " Mulled Sack " was

Reading robbery, he contrived to be acquitted, and made away to the Continent. At Cologne he depleted Charles II.'s chest of £1500 in plate, and with this booty set foot again in England, dressed from top to toe, praised in the rhymes of the gutter, and holding the gallows as cheap as a man of his fortune might do. But the life of every highwayman was a daily challenge to its end. In any pleading in a court of criminal justice Cottington was wanted upon many counts. There was the murder of Sir John Bridges, with whose wife Cottington had had some intrigue; there were robberies of which the proceeds had swelled to a sum that the seventeenth century would regard as fabulous. An attempt on Cottington's part to make his peace with Cromwell by the offer of secret correspondence obtained from Charles II. came to nothing, and once in Newgate he was easily levelled on one accusation or another. He took his wages of the hangman the year before the Restoration.

This was a great criminal for the age he practised in, and his genius returns in William Nevison, who furthers the credit of the craft in Charles II.'s reign. Nevison (whose real name is said to have been Brace or Bracy) has his birth assigned by some chroniclers to Pontefract, by others to Burton Agnes in the East Riding. Tradition favours him as "a man

JONATHAN WILD

of pleasing address, gentlemanly demeanour, of large stature and unparalleled courage." Charles II., to whose court his celebrity had penetrated, dubbed him "Swift Nick," and more than once indeed, he seems to have been, if not like Mrs. Malaprop's Cerberus, "three gentlemen at once," at several places simultaneously. He worked with a gang and one of his followers may now and again have been credited with an exploits of the chief's. He is himself to be credited with the most widely bruited feat in the annals of the road, that ride to York of which Turpin is the putative hero. Nevison is another of whom it is told that he would never level pistol at a Royalist, though how, in the casual rencounters of the road, Royalist and Roundhead were distinguished, one does not readily surmise.

Nevison, after bolting with his father's spoons, started "on the crook" in London, and was either hunted from the capital or quitted it to take service with the Duke of York's English Volunteers in Flanders. He is next heard of as a highwayman at home, and then, like Stafford, as a reformed character, on the morrow of a grand coup, living decorously with his father, whom he doubtless presented with a new set of spoons. The father dies and the son again sets foot in the stirrup. Arrested during the season of the plague (this episode, however, lacks proof), Nevison received a potion from a friendly doctor, under the influence of which he was carried out of prison, a supposititious corpse, in a coffin. There is a second version to the effect that he was condemned and reprieved, "when he was drafted into Kirke's Lambs and served for a time at Tangier. From this he soon deserted to resume his old calling in England." The undisputed fact concerning his end is, that he met it in the noose at York. It seems past question that Nevison took the great jaunt from London to York, of which (among the nomads of the circus tent especially) Turpin, to this day, enjoys the fame. The date can be fixed with no precision. As Griffiths says, "it must have been in summer when the daylight hours were long." Did Nevison at dawn or daybreak of a summer's morning commit a robbery in London, and, fancying himself recognised, spring to the saddle and gallop apace for the north? This is like enough, if he had beneath him a horse of the fabled mettle of Black Bess. But we have another account, and the second is just as plausible as the first. It is that " the robbery was committed at Gadshill, that he rode thence to Gravesend, crossed the Thames, reached Chelmsford, and baiting there, rode on through Cambridge and Godmanchester to Huntingdon, where he again baited and rested an hour, then remounting, rode on at an even pace until sunset, when he entered York, having ridden the distance, two hundred miles, in fifteen hours." An average of thirteen miles an hour for fifteen hours on end is tremendous going (and remorseless riding) for one horse,* but the long-distance military test rides abroad have proved it compassable. The object in chief of the flight was the establishment of the alibi that the elder Mr. Weller considered of cardinal importance, and this point Nevison made good with a jury. On the bowling green at York, whither he repaired after a change of clothes, he got recognition from the Lord Mayor, and was noticeable to other persons. This was between seven and eight on the evening of the day of the robbery in London or at Gadshill,

and it was deemed incredible that, in the span of fifteen hours, a man should show himself in places so remote.

Through all the later years of the seventeenth century the highwayman

JONATHAN WILD IN THE HANGMAN'S CART

rides prospering. " The roads were infested with banditti. Innkeepers harboured and assisted the highwaymen, sympathising with them, and frequently sharing in the plunder. None of the great roads were safe ; the mails, high officials, foreigners of distinction, noblemen, merchants, all

* Archibald Forbes's brilliant rides in war would, of course, not compare with this, and Frederick Burnaby's historic ride to Khiva was a very different affair.

alike were stopped and laid under contribution." Now it is a captain on his way to Portsmouth, robbed of the £5000 of his men's wages ; now the mails from Holland, robbed of £5000 on the road near Ilford ; now the Worcester waggon, robbed of "£4000 of the King's money " near Uxbridge ; now the Manchester carrier, robbed of "£15,000 King's money " ; now the purser of a ship landed at Portsmouth, robbed of "£6000 worth of rough diamonds belonging to some London merchants, which had been saved out of a shipwreck." " All manner of men took to the road. Some of the Royal Guards were apprehended for robbing on the highway. Life-guardsmen followed the same gentlemanly occupation when off duty. . . . One, Smith, a parson and lecturer at Chelsea . . . was found to be confederate with two highwaymen, with whom he had shared a gold watch, and planned to rob Chelsea Church of its plate. . . . Disguised highwaymen were often found in reputable citizens and quiet tradesmen, who, upon the surface, seemed honest folk. A mercer of Lombard Street was taken out of his bed and charged by a cheesemonger as being the man that had robbed him two years previously."

Curious it is to reflect that, at a period when, in Smollett's words, " thieves and robbers are now become more desperate and savage than they had ever appeared since mankind was civilised," when " no thoroughfare was free from the tyranny of the fraternity of highwaymen," the plain remedy " of maintaining a properly paid and equipped police was never tried." The best expedient that suggested itself to the wisdom of the age was, in truth, about the worst that could have been adopted. It was " the

offering of rewards to all and sundry to encourage the apprehending of highwaymen." By Captain Melville Lee, in his " History of Police in England," this policy (begun in 1692, 4 William and Mary, c. viii.) is rightly described as disastrous. The provisions of the Act were afterwards extended to London, " and first and last were responsible for an appalling sum of wickedness. The bait of bloodmoney, and the lack of a salaried or professional class of detectives, were answerable for the appearance of amateur thief-takers ; these men were mostly ex-thieves who had given up their old vocation for the safer, more lucrative, but infinitely baser rôle of fattening on the conviction of the innocent, and on the execution of those whom they had themselves corrupted." It was largely, if not mainly, to his traffic in blood-money that " Jonathan Wild the Great " (Fielding's title, of course, and it is to Fielding's masterpiece in satirical biography that the reader should betake him) owed both his power and his wealth.*

* Captain Melville Lee arraigns Wild effectively in a few incisive sentences : " This arch-ruffian had a most complete knowledge of all the thieves in England, and at one time practically monopolised in his own person the trades of receiver of stolen property and trafficker in blood money. He established warehouses all over the country, and even bought himself a ship to export what he could not dispose of at home. To those thieves who submitted to his authority, and who brought him the proceeds of their robberies, he extended a protection that must have been dependent to a certain degree on the connivance of some person or persons in authority. Grand master of espionage, and holding in his talons the threads of all villainy, Wild could manufacture whatever evidence he chose, could ruthlessly destroy any who opposed him, and deliver up to justice those thieves who were bold enough to take their spoils elsewhere for disposal. When this supply of victims ran short, or when it suited his purpose to shield the real culprit, he was content to take the reward offered for the conviction of the innocent. It is comforting to know that his carcass, the foulest fruit the fatal tree ever bore, eventually swung at Tyburn, at the same spot where so many of his victims had preceded him."

AN OLD DUELLING RESORT

THE name of Chalk Farm is said to be a corruption of Chalcot. It was from Chalk Farm, near Primrose Hill, that the trains of the old London and Birmingham Railway were hauled to and

Montgomery and Capt. Macnamara on April 6, 1803, in consequence of a quarrel between them in Hyde Park, when a meeting was arranged for at Chalk Farm that same evening. Capt. Macnamara's bullet entered the right

Chalk Farm
— when a duelling ground. —

from Euston by a cable, and to-day it is a great railway appanage of Euston. But of old it was a rural resort where Londoners were amused with theatrical entertainments, dances, prize-fighting, and other sports. It was also for a long period one of London's duelling grounds. Here, in 1816, Tom Moore and Jeffrey fought the serio-comic duel of which the story has already been given in this work. Three years earlier the place was the scene of a fatal duel, which is thus described by Mr. E. G. Newton, the industrious historian of Hampstead. "One of the earliest recorded as having taken place at Chalk Farm was that between Lieut.-Col.

side of Col. Montgomery's chest, and passed through the heart ; he instantly fell without uttering a word, but rolled over two or three times, as if in great agony, and groaned. Being carried into Chalk Farm he expired in about five minutes. . . . Macnamara was tried at the Old Bailey on April 22, when he received an excellent character from Lords Hood, Nelson, Hotham, and Minto, and the jury returned a verdict of not guilty."

A later duel was that between Mr. Christie and Mr. John Scott, the editor of the *London Magazine*, which took place in March 1821. Scott was killed, and Christie was acquitted.

CHATEAUBRIAND IN LONDON

FRANÇOIS RENÉ, Vicomte de Chateaubriand, came to London for the first time in 1793. Many of his relatives were already among the victims of the Terror and his brother and sister-in-law had gone to the guillotine in the same tumbril as that aged M. de Malesherbes, who, in Carlyle's phrase, "defended Louis and could not speak, like a grey old rock dissolving into sudden waters." Chateaubriand's mother was a prisoner in Paris and his wife and his sister, Lucille, were prisoners at Rennes. He himself had joined the army of the *émigrés* and, during the retreat of the Prussians, had been left for dead near Namur, from which town he escaped a little later to England.

In these early days of his exile he rented a lodging in Holborn at a guinea a month from Bayliss, the printer, who, four years later, printed his "Essai sur les Révolutions." He was desperately poor and kept aloof from most of his brother *émigrés* with the exception of Hingant, who had been a councillor of the parliament of Brittany but was now as poor as himself. Hingant lived at that time quite near Bayliss "at the bottom of a street running into Holborn," and Chateaubriand used to breakfast with him every morning at ten. In the evening the friends would meet again and dine together in an eating-house at the cost of a shilling a head, a sum which had soon to be reduced to sixpence. Sometimes they were on the verge of starvation and every now and then they were reduced literally to bread and water. The future author of the "Génie du Christianisme" busied himself with hack translations from Latin and French. His health had broken down and he suffered from hæmorrhages. It is no wonder, then, that in recalling, nearly thirty years afterwards, these literary struggles he spoke of having " his tombstone for a desk."

Years afterwards, while Chateaubriand was engaged in writing these recollections, he had become French Ambassador at St. James's, and one night he attended the annual dinner of the Royal Literary Fund. The French Ambassador was seated next to Canning, and his health was proposed in very gracious terms. After this, the usual collection was made and naturally enough the memory of his own bitter youth in London revived, and he was moved to tears as, in the words of his secretary, M. de Marcellus, " He emptied both his purse and mine." On the way back to the Embassy Chateaubriand is said to have leaned back in his coupé and to have quoted with deep feeling the " Sunt lachrimæ rerum " of Virgil, as he reflected how much in need of the benevolence of such a fund he himself had been in 1793. As a matter of fact the Society was in existence in that year, though it was only three years old. Undoubtedly, too, its beneficence was open to foreigners, and at that very dinner which the French Ambassador had attended, the Secretary of the Society reported the discovery of a " venerable bard of Iceland where he patiently reclined beneath a shed of poverty."

There is a story to the effect that Chateaubriand had been assisted by the Society, but in his " Memoirs " he writes : " Had the Literary Fund existed when I arrived in London from Southampton, on the 21st of May, 1793, it would, perhaps, have paid the visits of my physician to the attic in Holborn ; where my cousin, La Boriètardais, the son of my Uncle de Bedée, had hired a lodging for me." Chateau-

briand had disdained to avail himself of the shilling a day allotted by the British Government to all destitute French *émigrés*. Nearly starving as he was, he would wander aimlessly through the London streets or recline under the trees of Kensington Gardens. In his " Lectures on Modern History and Biography," Professor Robertson tells how Chateaubriand, in later and happier days " would stroll under these beautiful trees, where in the days of his exile he used to meet his fellow sufferers, the French priests, reciting their breviary—those trees under which he had breathed many a sigh for his home in La Belle France, under which he had finished ' Atala ' and had composed ' Rene.' "

Chateaubriand was very fond of Westminster Abbey and on one occasion he passed the night there, having been locked in by accident. " After some hesitation," he tells us, " in the choice of my lair, I stopped near the monument of Lord Chatham, at the bottom of the gallery of the Chapel of the Knights and that of Henry VII. At the entrance to the steps leading to the aisles, shut in by folding gates, a tomb fixed in the wall, and opposite a marble figure of death with a scythe, furnished me a shelter. A fold in the marble winding-sheet served me as a niche ; after the example of Charles V., I habituated myself to my interment."

The young exile was fond of musing in the precincts of the Poet's Corner. " The bust of an unknown, like me," he would say to himself sadly, " will never find its place among those famous effigies." But as he looked back, something of his youth certainly stirred the heart of the French Ambassador when he wrote : " I wonder if any of the beautiful women there divined the invisible presence of René."

So far, no English woman had entered his life, but he was about to meet Charlotte Ives, the clergyman's daughter, whose memory remained always one of the few gleams in his dreary exile. Chateaubriand speaks of an advertisement in a Yarmouth paper having been brought to his notice by his old friend Pelletier, the journalist. A Frenchman was wanted it seems, to help in deciphering some old French manuscripts belonging to the Camden Collection. Two hundred guineas were offered for his services, and Chateaubriand was obviously the very man for the post. At all events he maintains that he applied for it successfully, and that he and Pelletier celebrated the occasion with a typical English dinner of roast beef, plum pudding and port at the London Tavern.

After his secretarial episode in Beccles, Chateaubriand returned to London still haunted by the glamour of Miss Charlotte Ives, whom he was to meet again in 1822 in the zenith of his fame. And now, pursued by her memory, Chateaubriand became a wanderer throughout the environs of London : " Within a circuit of thirty miles round London, there was not a heath, a road, a church, which I did not visit. The most deserted spots— a meadow bristling with nettles, a ditch planted with thistles, all that was neglected of man, became to me objects of preference, and in such places Byron already breathed."

According to Chateaubriand, Shakespeare was the only author who maintained his influence in England, a fact which he considers easily accounted for by this little incident : " I was one night at Covent Garden

Theatre, which takes it name, as is generally known, from an ancient convent, on the site of which it is built. A well-dressed man seated himself near me and asked soon afterwards where he was. I looked at him with astonishment, and answered, ' In Covent Garden.' ' A pretty garden indeed !' exclaimed he, bursting into a fit of laughter, and presenting to me a bottle of rum. It was a sailor who had accidentally passed this way as he came from the City, just at the time the performance was commencing ; and having observed the pressure of the crowd at the entrance of the theatre, had paid his money and entered the house without knowing what he was to see." And, shocked at this state of things, René asks : " How should the English have a theatre to be termed supportable, when the pit is composed of judges recently arrived from Bengal, and the coast of Guinea, who do not even know where they are ? Shakespeare may reign eternally in such a nation."

Chateaubriand considered St. Paul's the most beautiful modern, and Westminster Abbey the most beautiful Gothic building in England. He loved to wander about the precincts of Whitehall. " I have sometimes stopped," he tells us, " and listened to the wind moaning round the statue of James the Second, which points to the spot where his father perished. I never found any person in this place but workmen cutting stone, whistling as they pursued their labours. Having asked one day what this statue meant, some of them could hardly give me any answer, and others were entirely ignorant of the subject. Nothing ever afforded a more just idea of human events and our littleness."

The publication of the "Essai sur les Révolutions," which was published in England, 1797, attracted considerable attention among the members of the French Colony. Chateaubriand left his lodgings in Tottenham Court Road, took much better lodgings in the Hampstead Road, and began to mix once more in good society. Among his new friends, he mentions the Comte de Montlosier, the Chevalier de Panat, Abbé Delille, and that Abbé Carron, who was afterwards to write the life of his sister Julie. Chateaubriand was, at this period, welcomed in the salon of Mrs. Lindsay, an Irish lady, "the last of the Ninons" as he calls her, who was in later years to become the *chère amie* of Benjamin Constant. Already it was perceived among the *émigrés* that Chateaubriand would shed lustre upon the Colony, and one of them observed prophetically: "He will go further than any of us." It was in London, too, that he became a friend of the poet, Fontanes, whom he had known slightly before the Revolution.

Often, while strolling through Hyde Park, Chateaubriand would catch a glance of Pitt, who, "cast a disdainful glance" at him, and the rest of the *émigrés* and then "walked on with his nose in the air." Sometimes he would ramble through Harrow where Byron was then at school. The future author of the "Childe Harold" wrote him a letter, which he left unanswered, an act of discourtesy, which, in his opinion, prevented Byron from ever acknowledging his indebtedness to the inspiration of René. At Strawberry Hill Chateaubriand's old friend, Pelletier, picked him up and took him for a driving tour through the Thames Valley. He saw Herschel and his famous telescope at Slough, and at Windsor he bribed a servant to hide him so that he might catch a glimpse of the King. In August 1798, he was at Blenheim and learned there the news of Nelson's victory in Aboukir Bay. He was meditative as ever and after musing for a long time in a country church-yard he made a translation of Gray's "Elegy."

He spent a part of the summer of 1799 in Richmond, and was among the crowd who went to see the newly arrived kangaroos in Kew Gardens. He was already busy with the "Genius of Christianity," and after working at his book he would bathe in the Thames from a boat and stroll at random through Richmond Park. In the following May he left for France and when he returned to England in 1822 it was as ambassador extraordinary at the British Court.

AN OLD LONDON BOAT

During the sinking of the foundations of the County Council Hall, on the south side of Westminster Bridge, there was recently laid bare the keel and some of the timber of a large boat of apparently Roman fashion. It was probably used in the days of the Roman occupation, as a ferry-boat between the south and the north side of the Thames at Westminster, when the river was of much greater width than now. The boat measures about 50 ft. in length. It is now a principal treasure in the new London Museum in Kensington Palace. What follows will be read as reasonable fantasy,, not historic fact.

I T was in those days when Agricola, in the disparaging phrase of the Roman poet, "trudged about that weary Britain." Caedwellyn, who plied a large boat for hire between the shores that are now united by Westminster Bridge, lay in the shadow of the wide tongue of land which the men of later days called Thorney Isle, crouching forward, with every nerve intent, listening for the splash of bare feet among the not far distant sedges.

All night there had been fierce cries and the clash of arms, and within the Druids' temple on the nearest hill there had been leaping flames, so that the great circle of trilithons stood out against the glare like the remains of some giant forest of a time long gone by ; for the Roman con-querors—who were only conquerors at intervals, so stubbornly, and often so victoriously, did the Britons return to the fight—had destroyed the central altar, proposing to build a new temple of wood with altars to gods of their own. Wherefore the chieftains of those days had called the Trinobantian tribes together, and those whom the Romans called the Attrebatii and the Cantii, and had made great slaughter alike of Romans and of Romanised Britons, themselves placing lighted torches beneath the piles of dried wood which were to shelter the statues of new deities.

But when the flames were at their highest they flared up only to announce a sudden need to the Roman fleets which were scattered on the broad waters that have since been hemmed in to make the Thames, and to become a pharos to the generals who had won so many of Agricola's victories, so that wild triumph was almost at once turned into crushing defeat, and there was flight where there had been exultation, and over marshes, and by half-submerged forests, and by many devious ways, parties of defeated Britons came to where they could hail Caedwellyn's boat, and thus escape to where no Roman galleys could pursue them.

Caedwellyn was a man not only of great strength, but of ingenious mind. From the new conquerors he had learned the great art of building a boat of the Roman size and pattern. He had acquired the Roman speech. It seemed indifferent to him whether he carried Romans or Britons to and fro ; for which reason he was suspected by his countrymen, for none of them knew of the savage but smouldering fire of patriotism within his heart.

Yet it was to the place where Caedwellyn plied his trade that so many of the defeated men made their difficult way after the battle on the hill. Of what use was a coracle to them—a mere basket enclosed in hide ? Caedwellyn's boat could hold more fugitives than a score of coracles, and could be impelled swiftly over the shadow waters by sail as well as oar. So, from the first dawn of the morning, the boatman, silent and sullen through heaviness of heart and declining all proffer of reward, carried his dejected countrymen over to where they could disperse themselves southwards, or, mayhap, divesting themselves of all arms and signs of the warrior's trade, take service with those who, under Roman direction and for Roman pay, were then carrying on that work of embanking the Thames which was begun in what even then were remote ages, and which was carried on until long after Norman kings had come to the English throne.

And Caedwellyn, almost worn out with long and heavy toil, leant forward in his boat, wearily listening for the approach of more fugitives. This time, however, there was such a plash in the waters as is made by men who keep their feet covered, and a jingle as of armed skirts, and those who came into sight on the further bank were plainly Roman soldiers, two of them, as it seemed to Caedwellyn, of high degree.

There was a quick, peremptory summons, to which the tired boatman made only a slow response ; but the two chief Romans, to whom the others seemed to act as guard,

were too busily talking to each other to take note of the ferryman's manners.

" You will have good enough reason to be pleased with this night's work,

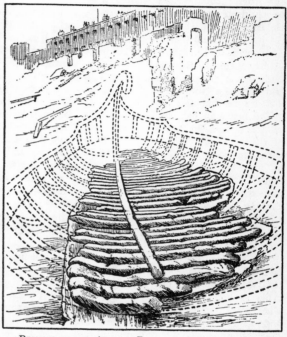

REMAINS OF THE ANCIENT BOAT DISCOVERED IN 1911 IN THE THAMES MUD NEAR WESTMINSTER BRIDGE

Carusius," said one to the other, as they took their places in the boat.

" What, I ? With the wound of a dart in my arm ? "

" Aye, for I doubt not that what has now taken place will despatch thee straight to Rome. Camelodunum; and a feast of those glorious shell-fish, and then a swift passage over sea and land with the news of the last great fight in the south of Britain ! "

" The last great fight, think you, Lucillus ? "

" Aye, the Britons of the south are conquered once and for all, Carusius. They are our slaves. They shall hew their trilithons into stones for our temples ; they shall become our beasts of burden ; their women shall bear to us children that we will not own ; on the site of their hideous orgies the joyous Apollo shall be worshipped. The spirit of this part of Britain is utterly broken, Carusius. Ah," he said, pausing to look round him, and addressing a soldier of the guard, " Smite me that man ! "

The boatman had ceased to use his oars and had sat down in the stern of the boat, which was now drifting with the tide. As the soldier struck at him he fell forward, less, as it seemed, to avoid the blow than as a man in a doze, but at once he arose, shaking himself, and using his oars with such effect that on the instant the boat was again heading for the further shore.

" A brief space and we must say farewell, Carusius," said the elder of the two officers, seeming to forget the order he had given. " Forget not me when you offer up your prayers to the gods at home ; nor fail to remember me in your revels when I am toiling under inclement skies for the glory of Rome."

" And whither do you now depart, Lucillus ? " asked his companion.

" I ? Oh, I go northwards, into the Hyperborean regions where Agricola is, there to fight against a race that, as I hear, is fierce as the lions of Numidia, and as strong."

As he spoke, his companion suddenly drew his short sword and lunged at the boatman with savage fury ; but Caedwellyn had seen the light of anger and fear leap into his eyes, and plunged overboard before any mischief befell him, speedily swimming to a distance to which no dart could be flung.

" The rascal Briton has drawn the plug from the boat. We are sinking, Lucillus, and in these arms and accoutrements we cannot swim."

But Lucillus had seized the oars which Caedwellyn had cast down in the boat as he leaped into the wide and swift waters, and was using them with the skill of one with experience of such things.

" Before the boat sinks we may reach the shore, Carusius," he said, recovering his balance with nimbleness after a long, fast-propelling stroke ; but the gods had ruled otherwise, for the soldiers of the guard leapt to their feet as the water rushed in, and the boat swayed over through their ill-balancing of themselves, and there was a cry of horror and despair as they found themselves struggling with each other in the effort to keep themselves afloat.

Carusius was not seen again at Rome, where no messenger told of the fight which gave London to the Empire ; nor did Lucillus ever join Agricola in the inhospitable North ; but many a Roman galley was thereafter sunk in the night by some mysterious enemy as it lay anchored under the hill where the trilithons had stood, and where there was now a stone temple dedicated to Apollo ; and, when almost twenty centuries have passed away, when the forests and marshes of those old days had become a tradition, and when the greatest of the world's cities hemmed in the river to a channel not much more than a bow-shot wide, men digging for the foundations of a municipal palace larger and more splendid than any building of ancient Rome found Caedwellyn's old boat.

After Hogarth

JOHN WILKES

JOHN WILKES is an unforgettable Londoner. His fame, which was never truly the most honest, is no doubt considerably dimmed, but extinguished it cannot be. Though the mere pawn of Fate, he was the central figure in that tremendous Middlesex election of 1768 which was fruitful of much for the democracy of this country. It was the struggle of a powerful and intelligent section of the people against their own House of Commons—more exactly, perhaps, of this section against a royal and most stubborn opponent of all popular aspirations, George II. Were the people to be free to choose their own representatives or not? This was the meaning that underlay the rallying cry of "Wilkes and Liberty!" The Middlesex election was the first great platform campaign in England. It resulted in the first great platform victory. On a memorial tablet in South Audley Street Chapel are inscribed the words from Wilkes's own pen, "The Remains of John Wilkes, a Friend to Liberty," and all Londoners are familiar with the obelisk to his memory at Ludgate Circus, erected in 1775.

Jack Wilkes! Fame alights where she will, and sometimes seems to set her seal in pure irony. She chose a graceless, good-humoured, witty, and brilliant rogue in Wilkes; an adventurer albeit of the most intrepid sort, and a first-class fighting man. He is eminently of his century in England, as Casanova—with whom it is often possible to compare him—in France. Pity is it for the personal vanity of the incompressible demagogue and "rake on principle" that posterity knows him best by the malicious portrait of Hogarth (with whom he had rashly quarrelled)—that leering, impudent, squint-eyed face, and the cap of Liberty poised upon a bludgeon. Yet the ugly British Wilkes was as irresistible with the sex as the ugly French Mirabeau. To Lord Townshend he said: "Your lordship is one of the handsomest men in the kingdom, and I am one of the ugliest. Yet, give but half an hour's start, and I will enter the lists against you with any woman you choose to name, because you will omit attentions on account of your fine exterior, which I shall double on account of my plain one." Wilkes sometimes said that it took him just half an hour to talk away his face.

Gallant among women, Wilkes was witty and companionable among men. He was a popular sinner. Dr. Johnson could be brought to meet him only by a stratagem on the part of Boswell, but he ended by saying, "I would do Jack a kindness rather than not." Gibbon called him "a thorough profligate in principle as in practice, his life stained with every vice," yet this did not prevent him enjoying Jack's company for the sake of his "inexhaustible spirits, infinite wit and humour, and a great deal of knowledge." The central incident of Wilkes's

tortuous and noisy political career was the issue of the famous No. 45 of his journal the *North Briton*. But for this single number, which has probably been the cause of more writing than any other sheet ever printed in this country, the *North Briton* would scarcely have found mention in history, and an imposing obelisk would not be keeping the name of John Wilkes before Londoners. No. 45 appeared on April 23, 1763, and the offence lay in a mordant criticism of the King's Speech, in which, however, the whole blame was cast upon his Ministers. These gentlemen chose to construe the article as an attack upon his Majesty himself, and in no long time Wilkes was lodged in the Tower. But the Tory Cabinet had blundered. A week later Wilkes was released by the Court of Common Pleas; he was a member of the House of Commons, and the privilege of Parliament had been violated in his person. Thus he had been persecuted and imprisoned and had triumphed within a few days; and already there had gone up for him those shouts of the populace which were the prelude to the battle-call of "Wilkes and Liberty!"

Jack Wilkes was a lucky man nearly all his life, but error occasionally overtook him. In the flush of victory he reprinted No. 45; the Commons took the earliest opportunity of voting it a "false, scandalous, and seditious libel"; and, in accordance with a foolish and feeble custom of the age, the precious piece was publicly burned by the common hangman. The House of Lords was taking note of Wilkes for another cause. Among the papers seized at his house was an obscene thing called "An Essay on Woman," a parody on Pope's "Essay on Man," the composition possibly of Potter, but attributed to "our hero." It had undoubtedly been set up at his private press. The "Essay" was in no sense of the word published, and had doubtless been penned solely for the delectation of Wilkes's companions at Medmenham Abbey; but in certain notes attached to it a wittily offensive use had been made of the name of Bishop War-burton, and their Lordships ordered Wilkes to be prosecuted in the Court of King's Bench. He thereupon decided for a change of air, and found it in Paris. He was expelled from the House of Commons January 19, 1764.

WILKES ASSURING GEORGE III. THAT HE HAD NEVER BEEN A WILKITE   *After Gillray*

to sue the King in vain for a pardon. Then it was that he resolved to appeal from the King to King Mob, and the protracted and dramatic struggle began. Undaunted by his failure in the City of London, he offered himself to the electors of Middlesex, who placed him at the head of the poll. He appeared before the King's Bench, and was sentenced to twenty-two months' imprisonment. The Commons once again expelled him. It was no matter. His prison cell, thronged every day with conspicuous Whigs, served him as a splendid platform. Four times the men of Middlesex carried him to the top of the poll. His head was adopted as a tavern sign; and Franklin, travelling down to Winchester, tells us that for fifteen miles out of town almost every door or window-shutter bore the magic legend: "Wilkes and No. 45 for ever!"

The Paris of Louis XV. was no bad retreat for an outlaw with the social gifts of Wilkes, and the wit that he was never shy of using was his passport into all gay circles. To Madame de Pompadour's question, "How far he considered that an Englishman could safely go in attacking the Royal family?" he replied: "That, Madame, is precisely what I am trying to find out." In Paris and elsewhere abroad he remained until 1768, "receiving £1000 a year from the leading Whigs."

But London was Jack Wilkes's proper habitation, and thither he returned

Yet to such a height did the "Wilkes and Liberty!" fever rise that Benjamin Franklin wrote in amazement:

"'Tis really an extraordinary event, to see an outlaw and exile of bad personal character, not worth a farthing, come over from France, set himself up as a candidate for the capital of the kingdom, miss his election only by being too late in his application, and immediately carrying it for the principal county. The mob, spirited up by numbers of different ballads, sung or roared in every street, requiring gentlemen and ladies of all ranks, as they passed in their carriages, to shout for 'Wilkes and Liberty!' marking the same words on all their coaches with chalk, and No. 45 on every door, which extends a vast way along the roads into the country. I went last week to Winchester, and observed that for fifteen miles out of town there was scarce a door or window-shutter next the road unmarked; and this continued, here and there, quite to Winchester, which is sixty-four miles."

Meanwhile Sheridan was writing his epigram:

Johnny Wilkes, Johnny Wilkes,
Thou greatest of bilks,
How changed are the notes you now sing;
Your famed forty-five
Is Prerogative,
And your blasphemy, "God save the King."

To all this there could ultimately be but one issue, and at the end of his unparalleled contest Wilkes sat in Parliament for Middlesex from 1774 until 1790.

One incident in that election will suffice to reveal the inner mind of the demagogue. It is related that Colonel Luttrell and Wilkes were standing on the Brentford hustings, when Wilkes asked his adversary, privately, whether he thought there were more fools or rogues among the multitude of Wilkites around the platform. "I'll tell them what you say, and put an end to you," said the Colonel. Seeing that Wilkes was unperturbed, he added, "Surely you don't mean to say you could stand here an hour if I did so?" Wilkes answered with a gesture of contempt,

"Why, you would be dead one instant after." "How so?" "I should merely say it was a fabrication, and they would destroy you in the twinkling of an eye."

Many are the stories of Wilkes's wit, effrontery, and resource, and the best of these have been collected by Timbs in his "Century of Anecdote."

What is called a "City career" fell to this irrepressible demagogue, diner-out, and wit. He was by turns Alderman, Chamberlain, Sheriff, and Lord Mayor. Rogers, when a lad, was proud to shake his hand in his father's bank, and thus he recalls his figure: "I think I see him at this moment walking through the crowded streets of the city, as Chamberlain, on his way to Guildhall, in a scarlet coat, military boots, and a bag-wig—the hackney-coachmen in vain calling out to him, 'A coach, your honour?'" As Franklin surveyed Jack's political success with astonishment, so Dr. Johnson exclaimed: "It is wonderful to think that all the force of government was required to prevent Wilkes from being chosen chief magistrate of London [he was elected after two defeats], though the liverymen knew he would rob their shops—knew he would debauch their daughters." This was going too far, yet Wilkes heard it from Boswell with perfect good humour. Wilkes was one of those men who may steal a horse with impunity where a better man may not look over the hedge. It was said that wagers were sometimes laid that from the time he left his house in the West End till he reached Guildhall no one would speak to him without going away with a smile or a hearty laugh. And George III. must have laughed when, after dubbing him "that devil Wilkes," the impudent dog assured his Majesty that he had never "really been a Wilkite." There was no defeating him.

Wilkes's duels with Lord Talbot (Lord Steward at the Court) and Samuel Martin (Secretary to the Treasury under Bute) showed his mettle in the field. Having ridiculed Talbot's horsemanship at the coronation of George III., he bantered him for weeks through the post, and finally exchanged shots with him at Bagshot Heath. Martin the fought in Hyde Park, receiving a bullet wound in the stomach which sent him to bed, where, says Walpole, "he was all spirits and riot." Of his humorous effrontery with the pen we have an inimitable example in his letter (after discharge from commitment to the Tower) to Lords Halifax and Egremont, Secretaries of State. Touching on the seizure of his papers under Halifax's warrant, "I find," he says, "that my house has been robbed, and am informed that the stolen goods are in possession of one or both of your lordships." Next morning he repaired to Bow Street, and demanded a warrant "to search the houses of Lords Egremont and Halifax for goods stolen out of his house." He did, in fact, in the end get "thumping damages."

"PARIS IS BUT A DOG-HOLE TO IT"

BONNEL THORNTON, in his "Connoisseur," No. 79, describes a conversation with a London tradesman whom he met in an inn about forty miles from London.

"Our meal being ended, my companion took his pipe ; and we laid our heads together for the good of the nation, when we wanted the French terribly both by land and sea. At last, among other talk, he happened to ask me if I lived in the City. As I was desirous of hearing his remarks, I answered that I had never seen London. 'Never seen it?' says he. 'Then you have never seen one of the finest sights in the whole world. Paris is but a dog-hole to it.' There luckily hung a large map of London over the chimney-piece, which he immediately made me get from my chair to look at. 'There,' says he, 'there's London for you ; you see, it is bigger than the map of all England.'

"He then led me about, with the end of his pipe, through all the principal streets from Hyde Park to Whitechapel. 'That,' says he, 'is the river Thames ; there's London Bridge ; there my Lord Mayor lives ; that's Poule's ; there the Monument stands ; and now, if you was but on the top of it, you might see all the houses and churches in London.' I expressed my astonishment at every particular ; but I could hardly refrain from laughing when, pointing out to me Lincoln's Inn Fields, 'There,' said he, 'there all the noblemen live.' At last, after having transported me all over the town, he set me down in Cheapside, which he said was the biggest street in the city. 'And now,' says he, 'I'll show you where I live. That's Bow Church, and thereabouts, where my pipe is, there, just there my shop stands.' He concluded with a kind invitation to me to come and see him ; and pulling out a book of patterns from his coat pocket, assured me that if I wanted anything in his way he could afford to let me have a bargain."

THE WRITING ON THE WALL
Memorials of Prisoners in the Beauchamp Tower

THERE are few records more tragic than the inscriptions left on the wall of the Beauchamp Tower in the Tower of London. These ingenious devices, these pious maxims, these curious riddles, these quaint verses, were cut by prisoners—by men undergoing the most terrible stress of mind. Many of them had experienced the most terrible stress of body as well, in the torture of the rack; many of them were wasting after long incarceration; many of them lay under sentence of death.

The Beauchamp Tower is one of the oldest parts of the Tower of London, having been built probably in the reign of King John; and though its exterior has been somewhat recklessly restored, so that it looks quite modern, its interior still retains many

of the features of a Norman keep. It has three floors, each of which consists practically of one large room, and these are connected by a winding staircase. All these rooms were used for the confinement of prisoners of state; the men of highest rank were incarcerated in the prison chamber on the middle floor. This tower owes its very name to one of its earliest prisoners—to Thomas Beauchamp, Earl of Warwick, who occupied the peculiarly difficult post of Governor to King Richard II. Richard resented the actions of his Governor, and when he felt himself strong enough imprisoned Beauchamp in this room (1397), whence he passed to execution. The Earl left no inscription on the walls. The earliest inscription is dated 1462; but the most interesting records, the most illustrious prisoners, the most poignant tragedies, the most exciting dramas connected with the Beauchamp Tower belong to a later period—to Tudor times, and to the sixteenth century.

Our readers have no doubt stood in this prison-chamber, and reconstructed it as it was in ancient times. In each of its four large recesses was a slit of a window;

these have of late been stopped up, and two other casements made towards the east. The cells adjoining the room were probably used for the better securing of prisoners at night. It is difficult to say which most stir the imagination —the inscriptions

cut by prisoners whose names and whose fates are unknown—an initial, a date— and then no more; or the inscriptions of those whose lives are large in history. In the first case we are moved to all manner of curious speculation, and may dream over the devices and weave romances, as Sir Walter Scott did over the inscription PEVEREL. This is an elaborate device : in one compartment is a cross, on which hangs a bleeding heart ; in another is the figure of a skeleton ; in another, a shield with heraldic arms. Sir Walter Scott made both his own Peveril (of the Peak) and his Nigel prisoners in the Beauchamp Tower. But even the fiction invented

by the Wizard of the North is not more strange than the true history of many a prisoner within these walls.

The stories of comparatively unimportant prisoners are often full of thrilling incident. Take, for instance, the name THOMAS FITZGERALD cut by himself, and the verses by Thomas Miagh.

There ran an ancient prophecy in Ireland that five sons of an earl should come to England in the belly of a cow and should never return. Now Thomas Fitzgerald, Earl of Kildare, who had been in open rebellion against Henry VIII., was taken prisoner, and with his five uncles conveyed to England. When his uncles discovered that the name of the ship was *The Cow*, they remembered the ancient prophecy, and lost all hope of pardon. They were imprisoned with their nephew, a young man only twenty years of age, in the Beauchamp Tower ; and the prophecy was fulfilled, for all six of them were hanged and quartered at Tyburn in the year 1538.

Thomas Miagh (who was also an Irishman) has left more than one inscription on the walls. His verses have a special interest, as they bear witness to the torture commonly employed upon prisoners.

Thomas Miagh whiche lieth here alon,
That fayne would from hens be gon ;
By tortyre straynge mi troyth was tryed,
Yet of my libertie denied. 1581 Thomas Myagh.

The Tower records contain extraordinary evidence of the steadfastness of this man, who refused to betray his comrades. He withstood the torture of Skevington's Irons, applied "with so much sharpness as was for the man and his cause convenient," and the Lieutenant of the Tower gave authority to put him to the rack. This inscription was cut after he had undergone so unflinchingly unspeakable anguish, and when we remember the circumstances under which it was carved it becomes invested with a new pathos, with a new nobility. Of his subsequent fate no tale is told.

One of the most piteous stories of English history is the story of Lady Jane Grey. Jane herself, and her husband, Lord Guildford Dudley, and his four brothers, John, Ambrose, Robert, and Henry, were all imprisoned in different parts of the Tower of London. John Dudley, Robert Dudley, and Guildford Dudley were incarcerated in the Beauchamp Tower, and have left their marks upon its walls. There is perhaps no inscription in this room that attracts more pathetic interest than the carved name of JANE. (It was cut twice; but one of the inscriptions has

been removed in the making of the new window.) Who carved the name of Jane ? Was it her husband, young Guildford Dudley, still in his teens, like his girl-wife a victim to his father's ambition, and, like her, to make expiation on the scaffold ? Was it some other unfortunate adherent to her cause? There the name stands, tragic in its simplicity, shaped by what love, by what anguish we shall never know.

John Dudley, Guildford's eldest brother, has left an elaborate device. Within a frame formed by a garland of roses, geraniums, honeysuckle, and oak-sprigs are a bear and a lion supporting a ragged staff, the Dudley crest, with these lines beneath :

Yow that these beasts do wel behold and se,
May deme with ease wherefore here made they be,
With borders eke wherein (there may be found)
Brothers' names who list to serche the ground.

It is conjectured that the A in Acorns (on the oak-sprig) represents the initial letter of Ambrose ; the R in Rose, Robert ; the G in Geranium, Guildford ; the H in Honeysuckle, Henry ; but whether this is indeed the right reading of the riddle no man may say.

John Dudley died in prison ; another fate was reserved for Robert Dudley. You will find on the walls his device of an oak-tree bearing acorns; beneath, the initials R.D. No death's head and crossbones, no skeletons, of which so many carvings appear on these walls, testify to the melancholy of his thoughts; he may have had some faint foresight of the triumphs and the glories that were in reserve for him. For he was to emerge from prison into the dazzling court of Queen Elizabeth, to be created Earl of Leicester, and even to aspire to the hands of two Queens— Elizabeth herself and Mary Queen of Scots—he, the brother-in-law of Lady Jane Grey, he whose brother and whose father met their deaths on the scaffold. Truly time has its whirligigs! Robert Dudley was only twenty when he was imprisoned in the Beauchamp Tower; but he was already the husband of Amy Robsart.

One of the most amazing stories of this prison chamber is connected with Philip Howard, Earl of Arundel, several of whose inscriptions appear on the walls. Over the fireplace he has cut a Latin inscription which may be translated as follows:

The more suffering with Christ in this world, the more glory with Christ in the next. Thou hast crowned Him with honour and glory, O Lord! In memory everlasting He will be just. Arundell, June 22nd, 1587.

Arundel's father, grandfather, and great-grandfather had all been be-headed on trifling pretexts. He himself was a devout Roman Catholic, and his hopes were centred in Spain. In prison he was, of course, forbidden all the consolations of his religion, and his wife conceived the daring plan of contriving to have mass said in his very cell, under the Queen's very nose! By a bribe of thirty pounds she managed that a priest imprisoned in the Belfry Tower should gain access to his room; she smuggled in a chalice and vestments; a rough altar was raised; and there, in the heart of the Tower, Father Bennett said a mass for the success of the Spanish Armada! Truly an almost unbelievable incident in the history of this room! Arundel was tried for high treason when this fact became known, and was sentenced to death (1589), but was reprieved from time to time. He died in gaol 1595, and his last years were spent in austerities and devotions.

Edmund and Arthur Pole, imprisoned for conspiracy to put Mary Queen of Scots on the English throne, were of royal blood, being grandchildren to George Duke of Clarence, brother of Edward IV. Both these brothers have left interesting inscriptions on the walls. "A passage perillus maketh a port pleasant," Arthur Pole cuts with date 1568.

How pathetic is the device with the motto "I am waiting for my liberty"!

Another prisoner, T. Salmon, counts the wearisome months, weeks, days and hours of his confinement : " Close prisoner 8 monethes, 32 wekes, 224 dayes, 5376 houres." From bitter experience some are moved to give sage advice, as Charles Bailly, who writes :

> Wise men ought circumspectly to see what they do—to examine before they speake—to prove before they take in hand— to beware whose company they use, and above all things, to whom they trusts.

Indeed, all types of mind, from those who looked for consolation to religion and to high philosophy, to those who sought solace in riddles and ingenuities, are represented on these walls. Heroism, martyrdom, and treachery have all left here their record ; and we may fittingly close our brief sketch with the words of Sir Walter Scott, who said of the Beauchamp Tower : " It was like the roll of the prophet, a record of lamentation and mourning, and yet not unmixed with brief interjections of resignation, and sentences expressive of the firmest resolution."

A QUEEN'S FUNERAL TRIUMPH

THE unhappy Queen Caroline died at Brandenburgh House, Hammersmith, on August 27, 1821, having left instructions in her will that she should be buried in Brunswick beside her father and brother. George IV.'s Government appointed Tuesday the 14th inst. as the day on which Her Majesty's remains should be removed from Brandenburgh House to Harwich for embarkation to the Continent.

During the preceding week a correspondence took place between the ladies of Queen Caroline's Household and the Earl of Liverpool, and the Under Secretary of State, Mr. Hobhouse, in regard to the day appointed for the funeral. Both Lady Anne Hamilton and Lady Hood wrote to Mr. Hobhouse on Saturday, the 11th, to say that they had only heard that afternoon of the preparations for the funeral, and that their mourning dresses could not possibly be ready before Tuesday night. Unless the day was changed to Wednesday they maintained it would be impossible for them to attend the funeral. Mr. Hobhouse replied the next day expressing surprise that they should have been in ignorance of the arrangements, and the matter was then referred to Lord Liverpool who decided that the order for the funeral on Tuesday was irrevocable.

At half-past four o'clock on Tuesday morning, Mr. Bailey of Mount Street, Grosvenor Square, who had been appointed conductor of the Queen's funeral procession, left his house to attend to his duties. Between five and six thirteen mourning coaches and six, a hearse and eight horses with all the usual paraphernalia of mourning, drew up in front of the Royal residence in Hammersmith. Sir George Nayler, Clarencieux - King - at - Arms, accompanied by Mr. Wood, Pursuivant-at-Arms, arrived at six o'clock, when they were ushered into the State apartment of Brandenburgh House. A little later, Dr. Lushington, one of Queen Caroline's executors, made his appearance to be joined shortly afterwards by the other executor, Mr. Wilde. Several other gentlemen followed, including Mr. Thomas who was acting for Mr. Mash, of the Lord Chamberlain's office.

A squadron of the Oxford Blues had formed into line in front of Brandenburgh House at six o'clock. The church bells had commenced to toll to minute time, and minute guns were fired from the bank of the river immediately opposite to the dead Queen's residence. The London Escort Committee were headed by Mr. Hume and Mr. Hobhouse, while the Hammersmith Committee was under the control of the Churchwarden and Mr. Bowling.

Everything seemed to be in readiness, but when Mr. Bailey entered the State Room to order the Lord Chamberlain's officers to deliver up the Queen's body to those in waiting, Dr. Lushington at once intervened. An unpleasant altercation ensued after which Mr. Wilde handed Mr. Bailey a written protest against the removal of Queen Caroline's corpse. He maintained that it was being taken by force and against the will of the executors, after which he demanded information from Mr. Bailey as to the route and destination of the funeral procession. After protesting that those whose duty it was to attend the removal were being impeded in every way, Mr. Bailey took a paper from his pocket and read aloud in the presence of the Queen's executors the route of the procession. "The funeral cavalcade to pass from the gate of Brandenburgh House, through Hammersmith, to turn round by Kensington Gravel Pits near the Church, into the Uxbridge Road to Bayswater; from thence to Tyburn turnpike, down the Edgware Road, along the New Road to Islington, down the City Road, along Old Street, Mile End, to Romford &c. A squadron of Oxford Blues from Brandenburgh House to Romford, to attend the procession; a squadron of the 4th Light Dragoons from Romford to Chelmsford, another squad of the same regiment from Chelmsford to Colchester; another escort from Colchester to Harwich, where a guard of honour is in waiting."

At last, shortly after seven o'clock, the Procession started. Twelve of the Oxford Blues headed it, and it was closed by the escort Committees of Hammersmith and London. Each side of the hearse bore the Royal Arms, and each of the horses was decorated with an escutcheon. Postillions dressed in black were mounted upon the two leading horses. The letters C.R. attached to an Imperial Crown decorated the end of hearse.

The rain was pouring in torrents, but the procession moved slowly along without obstacles of any kind until it arrived at Kensington Church. Here, a large body of men formed up nearly twenty deep across the streets, and a severe fight took place between them and the police, many being injured on both sides. Several attacks were made in the vicinity of the Gravel Pits, where the mob tore up the pavements and threw trunks of trees across the road to bar the passage of Queen Caroline's funeral procession. The populace was determined that the funeral should pass to the City through Hyde Park

Corner gates, and after a stout resistance the Procession passed through Hyde Park to Cumberland Gate where another serious fracas took place. "Stones and mud," says a contemporary writer in the *Gentleman's Magazine*, "flew about in all directions, and the Horse Guards fired upon the mob. The Guards kept galloping about in all directions. Richard Honey, a carpenter, was shot at the corner of Great Cumberland Street and the body was carried to the General Townshend, in Oxford Street. Others were carried to St. George's Hospital."

The Procession, amidst loud outcries from all quarters, passed down Edgware Road towards Paddington, but it was compelled to halt on arriving at Tottenham Court Road, for at this point all the streets that led to the City Road were blockaded by waggons and carts and various other obstacles. Forced out of its route, the procession was forced to move in a straight line towards St. Giles's, all the streets leading out of Tottenham Court Road in the direction of the New Road being effectually blockaded by a determined mob. It proceeded then down Drury Lane and entered the City through Temple Bar. Here it was joined by the Lord Mayor and the City authorities. The shops were closed and on all sides nothing but mourning was to be seen, while the church bells tolled for Caroline of Brunswick who was leaving England for the last time.

There were no further scenes of discord and the procession proceeded quietly to Whitechapel and from there to Romford, arriving at Chelmsford at two o'clock on Wednesday morning. At twelve o'clock the same day it proceeded to Colchester and arrived at Harwich for embarkation, at five o'clock on Thursday afternoon.

GEORGE CRUIKSHANK IN THE HAMPSTEAD ROAD

ABOUT half a mile up the Hampstead Road from the Euston Road, just before you reach the pleasant foliage and enlarged sky which Mornington Crescent and Harrington Square enclose, stands, on the left, a tall, stuccoed house marked by a circular tablet. Here the good old George Cruikshank lived for twenty-eight years, and here he died on February 1, 1878, at the age of eighty-six.

The great span of Cruikshank's life can be judged by the way in which it enclosed Dickens's career. At the south end of the same terrace in the Hampstead Road stood, until quite recently, the corner house in which Dickens was going to school in 1824. Jones's Academy, as it was called, is the original of " Salem House " in " David Copperfield," where the Welsh schoolmaster, William Jones, figures as Mr. Creakle. But in 1812, when Dickens was acting as ringleader to his schoolfellows in the fields above Drummond Street, George Cruikshank had fully established himself as a public idol by the humour and fecundity of his art.

Thackeray, who deeply admired Cruikshank's genius, and devoted an admirable essay to it, thought that he reached his apogee in 1822—when Dickens was still a small boy in the Hungerford blacking factory. Recalling these years in his essay of 1840, he says : " Knight's, in Sweeting's Alley ; Fairburn's, in a court off Ludgate Hill ; Hone's, in Fleet Street— bright, enchanted palaces, which George Cruikshank used to people with grinning, fantastical imps, and merry, harmless sprites—where are they ?

Fairburn's shop knows him no more ; not only has Knight's disappeared from Sweeting's Alley, but, as we are given to understand, Sweeting's Alley has disappeared from the face of the globe. Stop ! The atrocious Castlereagh, the sainted Caroline (in a tight pelisse, with feathers in her hand), the Dandy of Sixty, who used to glance at us from Hone's friendly windows—where are they ? Cruikshank may have drawn a thousand better things since the days when these were ; but they are to us a thousand times more pleasing than anything else he has done."

What Thackeray loved in Cruikshank's art was its humorous portraiture of common life near the bone : the life in which Cruikshank was born and bred, and in which he took his careless pleasures long before he mounted the teetotal rostrum. He loved George's Tom and Jerry scenes, his gallery of dustmen, his " Mornings at Bow Street," his Irish rows, his Jews and tipplers and post-boys. All these had been vitally true to the age.

Still, some of Cruikshank's best work was done in his house in the Hampstead Road. Here, in 1853, he illustrated " Uncle Tom's Cabin " for John Cassell ; here he did his twenty etchings for Robert Brough's " Life " of Sir John Falstaff, including the wonderful Death of the Knight ; the delightful " Epping Hunt " for Thomas Hood's " Whimsicalities " ; and the eight illustrations for " Peter Schlemihl," from which Thackeray selected for special praise the picture of the little old gentleman, who has just struck his bargain, in the act of lifting Peter' shadow from the ground, and folding it

GEORGE CRUIKSHANK
From the Maclise Portrait Gallery

Cruikshank arrived a teetotaler in the Hampstead Road. For many years he had been flirting with temperance, and he had long made the evils of drink a subject of his art. To this many influences inclined him. His father, Isaac Cruikshank, had been a confirmed toper, and had actually died as the result of winning a whisky-drinking contest. At the grave of Gillray Cruikshank had realised how drink could destroy talent. From time to time he had conveyed startling lessons to the public in such drawings as his "Sunday in London," "Introduction to the Gout," "Deadly Lively," and "A Gin Jugganaut." But his personal reform dated from 1847, when he brought out his set of eight plates called "The Bottle." Anxious that his first elaborate temperance sermon should reach the masses, Cruikshank took these plates to Mr. William Cash, chairman of the National Temperance Society. This shrewd Quaker, after carefully looking through the series, turned to the artist and asked how he could himself have anything to do with the bottle, which by his own showing led to every evil. Cruikshank declared afterwards that he was completely staggered by this question.

From that day till the end of his life he shunned and denounced drink, and he carried into his temperance advocacy the impetuous and ludicrous zest which he had always shown as a

up neatly to put in his pocket. And these are but a drop in the ocean of work in which Cruikshank was immersed in his later years. His last plate of all was the frontispiece to Mrs. Blewitt's "The Rose and the Lily," which he signed : "Designed and etched by George Cruikshank, age 83, 1875."

viveur. Not one man in a million could have comported himself as Cruikshank did now. He did not abandon his social circles. The club and the banquet knew him as of old. His bright, head-strong personality had not changed. He simply refrained from drink, and

This was the man who now thundered against gin at Exeter Hall. Any other man would have estranged his friends, but "dear old George's" sincerity and fundamental goodness kept them loyal. Once at a ball given in Fitzroy Square by Mr. Joshua Mayhew,

GEORGE CRUIKSHANK'S TOTAL ABSTAINERS' MEETING AT SADLER'S WELLS

denounced it with unblushing freedom and courage. It did not matter that he had been the ruling spirit of many a tavern and club room, or that Maclise had portrayed him sitting on a beer barrel. It did not matter that Dickens had seen him walk into his library at Devonshire Place smelling of tobacco, beer, and sawdust, and afraid after a night's revelry to go home ; or that W. H. Wills remembered, after a long bout, how Cruikshank's boisterous spirits had broken out in the street until his companions, unable to lead him home, had left him in the act of climbing a lamp-post.

Cruikshank danced vigorously with the young folks, but when the wine began to go round he crept round to the head of the supper-table, and, laying his hand on his host's shoulder, said in a deep tone of remonstrance, " Sir, you are a dangerous man." At the Mansion House, when the loving cup was passed round, Cruikshank would shake his hand angrily at the Lord Mayor, and go through a pantomime of grimace and gesture to express his horror of strong drink. On the platform he put no restraint on his tongue, and once he told a Bristol audience : " My mother first lifted the poisoned chalice to my lips." That venerable lady was then sharing his house in the Hampstead Road! Her indignation was boundless. "What!" she cried. "Am I to be told publicly at eighty years of age that I, who always begged and prayed him to be sober, taught him to drink?" The old lady nursed her wrath till her son came home, and then he heard some plain speaking. But Cruikshank had meant no evil. He had merely been carried away by his enthusiasm.

All this temperance gospelling withdrew Cruikshank from the favour of his old public. His laborious work, "The Triumph of Bacchus," for the execution of which he received financial aid, was a complete failure when it was exhibited at a little gallery next to the Lyceum Theatre in Wellington Street. Many years before this, in his two drawings "Born a Genius" and "Born a Dwarf," Cruikshank had satirised the very different receptions accorded to B. R. Haydon and "Tom Thumb." He knew now, as Haydon did then, the bitterness of desertion. It was in the illustration of fairy tales that Cruikshank found his happiest self-expression in these last years. In 1875 the house in Hampstead Road was crowded with his friends and admirers, who came to drink tea with him on the celebration of his silver wedding. A guard of honour from his old volunteer corps was in attendance. When his friend, S. C. Hall, spoke a few appropriate words to the company, Mrs. Cruikshank was so affected that she sobbed on her husband's neck. Cruikshank was then eighty-five, but in bidding good-bye to Blanchard Jerrold he laughingly said, "You are down on our list of visitors for the golden wedding." On Cruikshank's grave these lines are inscribed:

In memory of his Genius and his Art,
His matchless Industry and worthy Work
For all his fellow men; this monument
Is humbly placed within this sacred Fane
By her who loved him best, his widowed wife.
ELIZA CRUIKSHANK.

The "sacred fane" is St. Paul's Cathedral.

THE MARBLE ARCH

THE Marble Arch was copied by its architect, John Nash, with modifications, from the Arch of Constantine at Rome. It stood for some years in front of the chief entrance to Buckingham Palace. The archway, as first designed, was found to be too small to admit the Royal coach, but the mistake was remedied in time. A colossal bronze group emblematic of Victory was to have been the crowning ornament, but the intention was altered in favour of an equestrian statue of George IV., executed by Chantrey at a cost of 9000 guineas. The statue, in turn, never reached the Marble Arch, and it is now in Trafalgar Square. In removing the Marble Arch to Cumberland Gate of Hyde Park, at the end in Oxford Street, an important and beautiful frieze was irreparably damaged, and has not been replaced. The sculptured decorations are by Flaxman, Westmacott, and Rossi, all men of genius. The big central gates are said to be the largest in Europe, and among the finest. The entire cost of the Arch was about £80,000. Paris paid £416,666 for her Arc de Triomphe.

THE EMPIRE AT HOME
THE STORY OF NUMBER 10 DOWNING STREET

ALL the world knows of Downing Street, and particularly of that famous residence of Prime Ministers which links Mr. Asquith to Sir Robert Walpole, but many are quite ignorant of that George Downing, who appeared " a perfidious rogue " to Samuel Pepys, no mean judge of rogues. The man who gave his name to Downing Street was the son of Emanuel Downing, a Puritan gentleman who had emigrated with his family to Salem in New England. His son George, born in 1623, was second on the list of first-class graduates of Harvard in 1642 and shortly afterwards returned to his native England.

Filled with ambition the young Puritan had procured introductions to the leading Roundheads, including Oliver Cromwell himself. At first, however, George Downing had to content himself with the modest position of chaplain in the regiment of a certain Colonel Okey, one of the three regicides whom he was afterwards mercilessly to hunt down. Downing was not long a chaplain but managed to have himself appointed Scouts-Master-General of the Parliamentary Army. Eventually he became Cromwell's ambassador to the Netherlands but when the Restoration came George Downing was by no means out in the cold.

In 1660 he was Pepys' superior officer and looked up to by the little man of Axe Yard, who always tried to look to the right people. Downing had asked him to join his suite when he returned to Holland in order to assist in the designs of General Monk. Moreover, he told Pepys that he had a kindness for him, by which he meant a clerkship of the Council. But the suspicious Pepys distrusted this kindness, " fearing that his doing of it was only to ease himself of the salary which he gives me." All the same, nine days later appears this contented note : " To Mr. Downing's lodgings. Then came he in and took a very civil leave of me, beyond my expectations. So I went down and sent a porter to my house for my best fur cap ; but he coming too late, I did not present it to him." Pepys knew his George Downing. Possibly he had at least heard of him in the early days when he was preaching against the Monarchy in Okey's regiment. Pepys had known him as a member of both Cromwell's Parliaments, and had watched him while " he was doing the lacqueying to Cromwell's coach." Afterwards Pepys learned of his correspondence with Cromwell's Secretary, Thurloe, about the Royalist doings in Holland. And Pepys knew every step that Downing took in that hunt after the three regicides with which his name is as closely associated as Downing Street itself. Okey, in particular, his old Colonel, would have escaped but for the direct interference of his former chaplain, an act upon which Pepys makes this characteristic comment on March 12, 1662 : " This morning we had news that Sir George Downing (like a perfidious rogue ; though the action is good and of service to the King ; yet he cannot with a good conscience do it) hath taken Okey . . . in Holland."

In private life his reputation was equally unenviable. He refused to support his aged mother after his father's death and allowed her, in spite of his great wealth, to lack the necessaries of life. In Salem the phrase "an arrant George Downing" survived as a reproach for trickiness, and his munificence is attested by the donation, in 1667, of £5 to Harvard University. At all events he got what he wanted

10 DOWNING STREET

as Mr. Charles Eyre Pascoe shows in his valuable record, "No. 10 Downing Street, Whitehall," in the course of which he sums up this unusual career : "Election to the House of Commons in Cromwell's time, Tellership of the Exchequer, Secretaryship of the Treasury, Commissionership of Customs, Diplomatic rank, Knighthood, Baronetcy; all that parcel of land now named Downing Street—a London memorial of his name, enterprise and ability—and all the houses thereon erected by himself (1663-74) ; and last, not least, £80,000 (so we are told) in bonds and good sterling English."

It was only three years, indeed, after the Restoration that directions were given to prepare a lease of these famous premises to Sir George Downing, " with power to build thereon, but not to build any further westward towards his Majesty's Park of St. James's than the westermost part of (where) his Majesty's house called the Cockpit is now built ; whereof the Surveyor-General of his Majesty's Works for the time being is to take care." The Surveyor-General referred to was Sir Christopher Wren.

When Charles II. granted this tract of land to Sir George it was stipulated that " the house to be built upon the premises, so near to the Royal Palace, shall be handsome and graceful." Sir George built not one but several houses, none of them handsome and graceful, upon the site and in one of these he lived happily before retiring to Haltey in Cambridgeshire. In which house did he live ? " That is difficult to say," answers Mr. Pascoe ; " but we incline for various reasons, to think it was one of the three larger than the others, originally standing at the top of the street, fronting on what was known as Downing Square; and of these three the one which stood at the northwest corner—later to become the old Colonial Office." If this interesting surmise is correct it is quite probable that the dining-room of George Downing of Salem, the " perfidious rogue " of Pepys became the world-famed Cabinet Room of No. 10.

THE MACARONIS

IN 1770 appeared the Macaronis, those ultra-dandified young men. It was about then that they began to irradiate the town; possibly a year or two later. Mrs. Stirling says: "The reign of the Macaronis commenced about 1770, and was at its height between the years 1772 and 1775." According to Wright: "The grand phenomena of the years 1772 and 1773 were the Macaronis." They were certainly phenomenal for some while after 1773, but a year or so is not of moment in their entertaining history.

So greatly did the Macaronis take the town by surprise that there were sundry speculations to explain them. In the earlier part of the reign of George II. the gentlemen of fashion were commonly styled Beaux. Towards 1750 they began to be dubbed Fribbles, and this name they carried through the first stage of the long era of George III. But who were these youthful Macaronis, so fantastically clothed? "One will naturally inquire," observes a writer in the *Universal Magazine* (April 1772), "whence originated the prolific family of the Macaronis? who is their sire? To which I answer that they may be derived from the *Homunculus* of Sterne; or it may be said the Macaronis are indeed the offspring of a *body*, but not of an individual. This same body was a many-headed monster in Pall Mall, produced by the demoniac committee of depraved taste and exaggerated fancy, conceived in the courts of France and Italy, and brought forth in England." Horace Walpole, whose finger was in every pie, had his venture on the subject. Throwing a glance at the vast wealth created for us by our successes in India, he goes on: "Lord Chatham begot the East India Company; the East India Company begot Lord Clive; Lord Clive begot the Macaronis; and they begot poverty; and all the race are still living."

Evidence of poverty among the Macaronis would not have been easily produced. If most of them were not young men of affluence, their tailors must have been of a generous kidney; and whence came the moneys that they poured upon the gaming-tables, and their frequent subscriptions to the arts? The "courts of France and Italy," as the writer in the *Universal* hints, had certainly shed their influence.

In brief, the Macaronis were chiefly young men of some birth and some intelligence (with a sprinkling of genius), who, having made the grand tour of Europe, had returned to England imbued with new ideas about food and clothes and dress, and social deportment in general. They formed themselves into a social order called the Macaroni Club, partly no doubt because the name was likely to take, and partly "from a dish then little seen in England, and which in accordance with their adoption of foreign customs, was always placed on the table at their dinners." But macaroni, eaten as we may suppose in the Italian style, was of very indifferent importance in the hierarchy of the Macaronis.

Supereminently they were young men of clothes; a body sartorial. If caricatures of the period may be trusted, the human creature was never before attired in this manner, and never again could be. Pantomime nowadays would be a setting too sober for the Macaroni, he would be a monster on the stage of the music-hall. His most important baggage was his hair. Of this he wore at the back a prodigious artificial knot, which in some of the prints of the day has the

THE MACARONIS
"WELL-A-DAY, IS THIS MY SON TOM?"
From a Contemporary Print

form and likeness of a vegetable marrow grown for the show tent. At a later date the Macaroni wig soars into the air rather in the style of a modern military balloon, ballasted with two enormous bags of hair upon the shoulders. But the Macaroni was redundant only in his hair. The coat or jacket was extremely attenuated,

short and clipping the figure. Breeches were of similar dimensions. The hat was a tiny, cocked affair, like a child's. The "buttonhole" alone rivalled the wig in size; a kind of nosegay attached to the lapel of the coat. In his hand the Macaroni sported a cane such as Mr. Whistler among the moderns used sometimes to display on private-view days at the picture galleries; and the cane was decorated with great emblematic tassels.

We may speak of the Macaronis as veritable pets of London. Those who laughed made haste also to imitate. It was Macaroni this and Macaroni that in all polite seats of London. "The Macaronis soon made an extraordinary noise; everything that was fashionable was *à la* Macaroni. Even the clergy had their wigs combed, their clothes cut, 'their delivery refined' *à la* Macaroni. The shop windows were filled with caricatures and other prints . . . there were portraits of 'turf Macaronis,' and 'Parade Macaronis,' and 'Macaroni divines,' and 'Macaroni scholars,' and a variety of other species of this extensive genus. Ladies, who carried their head-dress to the extreme of the mode"—even then, however, it was less terrific than that of many Parisiennes a few years later—"set up for female Macaronis.

Macaronis were the most attractive objects at the ball or in the theatre. Macaroni articles abounded everywhere. There was Macaroni music, and there were Macaroni songs set to it." A successful five-act drama of the day was called "The Macaroni."

Now had the Macaronis been the simple nincompoops of the caricaturist and the satirist, had they been drunken and criminal bullies as the Mohocks were, they could scarcely have carried it so far and so long in the most refined and exclusive coteries of London society. There was a great deal of licence in fashionable sets, a great deal of grossness, a great deal of profligacy; but there was also (and this somewhat widespread) an increasing interest in ideas, an admiration of good talk, a deference accorded to charm in alliance with originality or cleverness. People with titles, it is true, held themselves in the main somewhat apart from people who had none (we have Godfrey Bosville writing that, "The Nobility hold themselves uncontaminated with the Commons, you seldom see a Lord and a private Gentleman together"); but accomplishments and the renown of travel were beginning to overthrow the barriers of caste. Sheer attainments—for instance, the intellectual eminence of a Johnson—furnished as yet no

A MACARONI

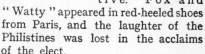

passport to the drawing-rooms of the great; but young men of an acknowledged origin, who had visited a few continental capitals, and could discuss their journeys, and had purses deep enough for the nightly calls of the card table, were important enough (noble or not noble) to set things going to quite a new tune in the very bosom of patrician London. And this, in fact, in a small way, is what the Macaronis did.

On the whole, we need not wonder too much that the Macaronis, having first surprised the town, carried it by storm. George III., our royal "good-man Dull," banned them and all their antics and their frolics, but this was no great matter. Walpole's sneer at the "travelled young men who wear long curls and spying glasses," was not more effective. Fox and "Watty" appeared in red-heeled shoes from Paris, and the laughter of the Philistines was lost in the acclaims of the elect.

But the Macaroni was not an essential fop. In an age of downright swilling he sipped tea and capillaire, a syrup prepared with maidenhair fern. In an age of dicers' oaths, such as moved to expostulation even the genial and free-living Harry Fielding, he recommended as a suitable expletive, "May I be deaf at the Opera!" He gambled, of course, or he could scarcely have exercised his apostleship in society ; but the delirious excesses of Fox at the table fall in his post-Macaronic days.

At Almack's the Macaronis were supreme. They had also their *Sçavoir Vivre* (which, had they stooped to English, they would have called "The Gentleman's "), the club at which " good eating and drinking went hand in hand with connoisseurship." Thus, they " decided to award every March a gold medal and a banknote of £100 for the best poem, the best picture and the best work of sculpture produced during the year, and smaller awards for the best musical composition and the best engraving on copper."

Altogether, there are worse things recorded of the eighteenth century than the pranks of the Macaronis.

A MACARONI

THE COLOSSEUM

A LONDONER'S memory must go back to 1875 if he is to boast of any personal knowledge of the once famous Colosseum, whose architectural splendour was declared by Samuel Rogers to be " finer than anything among the remains of architectural art in Italy." The Colosseum overlooked Regent's Park, and was devoted to the exhibition of artistic and mechanical marvels, and notably Hornor's famous panorama of London. Mr. Hornor painted his scenes from a perch specially constructed for him on the top of St. Paul's Cathedral in 1821, when the ball and cross were being renewed. The old ball and cross were exhibited at the Colosseum.

The Panorama of London was a wonder of the age. " It covers," says a contemporary writer, " upwards of 46,000 square feet, or more than an acre of canvas ; the dome on which the sky is painted is 30 feet more in diameter than the cupola of St. Paul's ; and the circumference of the horizon from the point of view is nearly 130 miles. Excepting the dome of St. Paul's Cathedral, there is no painted surface in Great Britain to compare with this in magnitude or shape, and

even that offers but a small extent in comparison." Describing Hornor's artistic feat this writer says : " After his sketches were completed upon 2000 sheets of paper, and the building finished, no individual could be found to paint the picture in a sufficiently short period, and many artists were of necessity employed : thus, by the use of platforms slung by ropes, with baskets for conveying the colours, temporary bridges, and other ingenious contrivances, the painting was executed, but in the peculiar style, taste, and notion of each artist ; to reconcile which, or bring them to form one vast whole, was a novel, intricate, and hazardous task, which many persons tried, but ineffectually. At length, Mr. E. T. Parris, possessing an accurate knowledge of mechanics and perspective, and practical execution in painting combined with great enthusiasm and perseverance, accomplished the labour principally with his own hands ; standing in a cradle or box, suspended from cross poles or shears, and lifted as required by ropes. The panorama is viewed from a balustraded gallery, with a projecting frame beneath it, in exact imitation of the outer dome of St.

Paul's Cathedral, the perspective and light and shade of the campanile towers in the western front being admirably managed ; whilst art cannot exceed the contrast of the bold and broad buildings in the foreground with the receding mid-distance, and the minuteness of the horizon. The spectator is recommended to take four distinct stations in the gallery, and then inspect in succession the views towards the north, east, south, and west ; altogether representing the Metropolis of 1821."

The Panorama of London was opened in the Colosseum in 1829, and it kept its popularity for twenty years, when a second edition of the same idea was carried out and called "London by Night." This scene was illuminated in such a way as to secure the illusion of moonlight ; the lamps from the streets and the shops and the bridges, as they sent forth their rays, fell with pleasing effect on the rippling river.

In 1848 a panorama of Paris by Night was exhibited, and was the more popular because it showed the localities of the recent revolution. This seems to have been a very fine effect, and a description of it by a writer in Charles Knight's " London " is agreeable reading even to-day. We read of the fall of night over the gay city. "The bell rings again, a curtain rises, and we are looking on the time-worn towers, transepts, and buttresses of Notre Dame, its rose window on the left, and the water around its base reflecting back the last beams of the setting sun. Gradually these reflections disappear, the warm tints fade from the sky, and are succeeded by the cool grey hue of twilight, and that again by night—deepening by insensible degrees till the quay and the surrounding buildings and the water are no longer distinguishable, and Notre Dame itself scarcely reveals to us its outlines against the sky. Before we have long gazed on this scene the moon begins to emerge slowly—very slowly—from the opposite quarter of the heavens, its first faint rays tempering apparently rather than dispersing the gloom ; presently a slight radiance touches the top of one of the pinnacles of the cathedral, and glances as it were athwart the dark breast of the stream ; now growing more powerful, the projections of Notre Dame throw their light and fantastic shadows over the left side of the building, until at last, bursting forth in serene unclouded majesty, the whole scene is lit up, except where the vast cathedral interrupts its beams, on the quay here to the left, and where through the darkness the lamps are now seen, each illumining its allotted space."

Already the Colosseum had changed hands several times, and its fortunes continued to vary. In 1857 Dr. Bachhoffner opened it as a science lecture hall. The doors were again closed in 1863, and the building was demolished in 1875 to make way for a terrace of houses.

THEODORE, KING OF CORSICA

KING AND BANKRUPT
THE STRANGE STORY OF THEODORE, KING OF CORSICA

IN the burial-ground of the quaint Dutch-looking Church of St. Anne's, Soho—so visible from Piccadilly Circus—may be seen a tablet bearing the following inscription:

Near this place is interred Theodore, King of Corsica, who died in this parish, December 11th, 1756, immediately after leaving the King's Bench Prison by the benefit of the Act of Insolvency; in consequence of which he registered his kingdom of Corsica for the benefit of his creditors.

The grave, great teacher, to a level brings
Heroes and beggars, galley-slaves and kings;
But Theodore this moral learn'd ere dead;
Fate pour'd its lesson on his living head—
Bestow'd a kingdom and denied him bread.

The story of the monarch whose melancholy record is thus summed up in a London churchyard is as follows.

Born in Metz in 1696, Theodore von Neuhoff, afterwards King of Corsica, and finally an exile in London, served in the French Army, and by a freak of fate was thrown among the leaders of the Corsican revolt from the yoke of Genoa. In return for his military and other services, he was elected king by the General Assembly. But he was never actually crowned, and when popularity and money failed him, he came, as is the habit of Continental adventurers, to London. Here, on somewhat slender grounds, he was welcomed as an exiled monarch, and he was fortunate in winning the sympathy and friendship of one of the most brilliant leaders of society, Horace Walpole.

Walpole, who is our best authority

for King Theodore's sorry career in London, describes him as " a comely, middle-sized man, very reserved, and affecting much dignity." This was in 1749, March 23, when Walpole writes : " King Theodore [of Corsica] is here : I am to drink coffee with him to-morrow at Lady Schaub's. I have curiosity to see him, though I am not commonly fond of sights, but content myself with the oil-cloth picture of them that is hung out, and to which they seldom come up." (Horace Walpole was cynical even when he was kind.) The smiles of London society were not long for the Corsican King, who had neither money nor the sense of its value. From the drawing-rooms of the West End he descended, as a debtor, to the King's Bench Prison, and of his life there a picture may be found in Smollett's novel, " Ferdinand, Count Fathom." Walpole continued, however, to befriend the exile, and wrote a paper in the *World* to promote a subscription in his aid, but the results were not encouraging.

" His Majesty's character," says Walpole, " is so bad, that it only raised fifty pounds ; and though that was so much above his desert, it was so much below his expectation, that he sent a solicitor to threaten the printer with a prosecution for having taken so much liberty with his name —take notice, too, that he had accepted the money ! Dodsley (the publisher) laughed at the lawyer ; but that did not lessen the dirty knavery. It would, indeed (continues Walpole), have made an excellent suit !—a printer prosecuted, suppose, for having solicited and obtained charity for a man in prison, and that man not mentioned by his right name, but by a mock title, and the man himself not a native of

the country !—but I have done with countenancing kings ! "

However, the money proved of service, and enabled Theodore to obtain his release from prison. Theodore did not long survive his liberation ; he died on December 11, 1756.

" Your old royal guest, King Theodore (writes Walpole to Sir Horace Mann), is gone to the place which, it is said, levels kings and beggars ; an unnecessary journey for him, who had already fallen from one to the other : I think he died somewhere in the liberties of the Fleet." In another letter of January 17, Walpole continues : " In my last I told you the death of a monarch, for whom, in our time, you and I have interested ourselves— King Theodore ! He had just taken the benefit of the Act of Insolvency, and went to the Old Bailey for that purpose : in order to it, the person applying gives up all his effects to his creditors : his Majesty was asked what effects he had ? He replied nothing but the Kingdom of Corsica— and it is actually registered for the benefit of the creditors. You may get it intimated to the Pretender, that if he has a mind to heap titles upon the two or three medals that he coins, he has nothing to do but pay King Theodore's debts, and he may have very good pretensions to Corsica."

Walpole then describes how the ex-king died. " As soon as Theodore was at liberty, he took a chair and went to the Portuguese Minister, but did not find him at home : not having sixpence to pay, he prevailed on the chairmen to carry him to a tailor he knew in Soho, whom he prevailed upon to harbour him ; but he fell sick the next day, and died in three more." The friendly tailor was himself so poor as to be unable to defray the cost of his funeral. His remains were, therefore, about to be interred as a parish pauper, when one John Wright, an oilman in Compton Street, declared that *he for once would pay the funeral expenses of a king*, which he did, in the churchyard of St. Anne's, Soho.

Walpole, although he had been dis gusted with the ex-king's conduct, paid the last honours. He writes to Sir Horace Mann, September 29, 1757 : " I am putting up a stone, in St. Anne's Churchyard, for your old friend, King Theodore : in short, his history is too remarkable to let perish. You will laugh to hear that when I sent the inscription to the vestry for the approbation of the minister and church-wardens, they demurred, and took some days to consider whether they would suffer him to be called King of Corsica. Happily, they have acknow-ledged his title ! " The inscription has already been quoted. Walpole adds : " I think that at least it cannot be said of me as it was of the Duke of Buckingham entombing Dryden :

> And help'd to bury whom he help'd to
> starve.

I would have served him, if a king, even in a gaol, could he have been an honest man."

Timbs mentions (" Romance of Lon-don ") that Theodore left a son, Colonel Frederick, who came to a sad end. The old man walked from the coffee-house at Storey's Gate to the porch at Westminster Abbey, and there shot himself. He had long been familiar to the inhabitants of London, and was distinguished by his eccen-tricities and gentlemanlike bearing. He had fulfilled many employments, and witnessed many strange incidents. One strange passage in his life was his dining at Dolly's, with Count Ponia-towski, when neither the son of the late King of Corsica, nor he who was afterwards King of Poland, had where-with to settle the bill. Distress drove the Colonel to commit suicide, and his remains rest by those of his father, in St. Anne's Churchyard, Soho. The Colonel's daughter married a Mr. Clarke, of the Dartmouth custom-house. Four children were the issue of this marriage. One of them, a daughter, was established in London at the beginning of the present century, earning a modest livelihood as an authoress and artist. The following is a copy of the card of this industrious lady :

MISS CLARK,

Granddaughter of the late Colonel Frederick, Son of Theodore, King of Corsica, PAINTS LIKENESSES IN MINIATURE, FROM TWO TO THREE GUINEAS, No. 116 NEW BOND STREET.

Hours of Attendance from Twelve in the Morning until Four.

WHITE'S

ORIGINALLY it was known as White's Chocolate House. Attached to the building was a garden with alcoves, from which, in the summertime, many a highwayman, having regaled himself, would take himself off to Knightsbridge, there to waylay any unfortunate passenger, whether protected or not.

The first " White's " was burnt down in April 1733, and it is handed down to us in the various chronicles that the King and Prince of Wales were present for above an hour during the conflagration to encourage the workmen and firemen engaged in subduing the flames. His Majesty ordered that twenty guineas should be distributed amongst the most energetic of the helpers, while the Prince personally gave five guineas to the firemen. " The incident of the fire " (at White's, says Cunningham) " was made use of by Hogarth in Plate VI. of the ' Rake's Progress,' representing a room at White's. The total abstraction of the gamblers is well expressed by their utter inattention to the alarm of fire given by watchmen, who are bursting open the doors."

Everybody of any importance in the early days of its establishment seemed to go to White's to gamble. Swift says that Robert Harley cursed it as "the bane of half the English nobility." The chief members were the Duke of Devonshire, the Earls of Cholmondeley, Chesterfield, and Rockingham ; Sir John Cope, Major General Churchill, Bubb Doddington, and Colley Cibber.

The Honourable Algernon Bourkes' " Chronicle of White's " is very interesting, and full of information. He goes into details that give the history of this famous house from its very inception.

Mr. Algernon Bourke, who was a brother to Lord Mayo, a few years ago related, for the benefit of everybody interested in clubland, the internal history of this most extraordinarily fascinating association of gentlemen, who were, to use Dr. Johnson's word, " clubable," and a clubable man has been generally known to be one of wit.

White's ranks amongst the most venerable and valuable institutions of this country. It is just one year older than the Bank of England. Moreover, if White's was a club given over to good living, high spirits and high play, it was also a club of high politics, the politics always on the side of the reigning monarch. There were one or two singular wagers made at White's, and many of these eccentricities make very extraordinary reading at this period. For instance, " Mr. Primrose bet Sir George Talbot fifteen guineas to five that a certain person understood between them does not marry a certain lady within six months from this day, April 24, 1815.

" GEORGE TALBOT.

F. W. PRIMROSE (Paid by the letter)."

During the Napoleonic era everybody seemed to be seized with the desire to bet either against or for his fortunes. And as it was rumoured that Buonaparte, after his many adventures on the continent, resolved to conquer England, in many parts of the country the people were in a tremendous state of terror, and at White's Club the famous Bow Window was constantly filled with members who were anxious to know whether Buonaparte could possibly secure a landing on the coast, and so the stakes rose high on each side. "Boney" was a perpetual bugbear, and everybody seemed to be in a condition of confusion as to what would happen next. One critic says that there was a continual matter of doubt at White's Club as to whether Buonaparte, the Corsican ogre, was really alive at the time when all these mental disturbances in England occurred. "For instance, on September 7, 1812, the very day on which the battle of Borodino, the most bloody general engagement of the century was fought, Colonel Stanhope bets Colonel Osborne ten guineas to one that Buonaparte is alive." After the fatal termination of the attempted French invasion of Russia was known and understood in England, we find Beau Brummell betting Mr. Methuen "two hundred guineas to twenty guineas that Buonaparte returns alive to Paris." The belief in "Boney's" elasticity of resource and vitality seems to have been held by many members of White's to an almost extraordinary degree.

In the course of years the club had its many managers and there were many curious alterations; and as Ralph Nevill carefully relates, in his "London Clubs, their History and Treasuries," about 1780, there was a regular club dinner at White's when Parliament was sitting at twelve shillings a head; then the charges varied and, in 1797, one of the rules decreed "that every member who plays at Chess, Draughts, or Backgammon do pay one shilling each time of playing by daylight, and half a crown each by candle light."

It was in 1811 that various alterations occurred in regard to the commonplace odd sashes in the Bow Window, which through its historical associations has made itself one of the prominent features of the West End of London. When it was resolved to remove the entrance by converting the second window from the bottom of the house into a door and to enlarge the morning room by utilising the old entrance hall, it gave room for an additional window. And this additional window being

Going to WHITE'S.

LORD ALVANLEY
After a drawing by Dighton

built over the entrance steps and significantly rounded, secured the name by which it is so well recoguised—that is the Bow Window of White's. When Beau Brummell was at the height of his fame, he and a few of his choice spirits made it a shrine of fashion, and only those who were initiated, chiefly through Brummell's patronage, were permitted to sit in the Window. An ordinary member of the club would not dare to take his seat there except on the approbation of the Beau. There were so many questions of etiquette in regard to this Bow Window that quite solemn conclaves were held as to who and who should not be admitted. So exclusive become that these ridiculous dandies become that after much discussion it was decided amongst them that they would not even doff their hats to any one in the street, including the ladies of their acquaintance, who passed by the club, or rather the " Bow Window."

The cachet of White's Window was carried by the members so far that Beau Brummell on one occasion, being pressed by one of his creditors for the sum of five hundred pounds, said : " I paid you." " Paid me, when pray ? " " Why, when I was standing at the Window at White's, and as you passed I said, ' How d'ye do ? ' "

Brummell was an inveterate gambler at White's, and on one occasion after a long run of ill-luck his friend, Pemberton Mills, heard him moan out that he had lost every farthing he possessed, and he wished that some one would bind him down never to play again.

Mills said, " Very well, Brummell, I will take you at your word," and taking a ten pound note out of his pocket offered it to Brummell on the condition that if he broke his vow he would pay Mills a thousand guineas.

For a few days, having taken the ten pound note, the Beau absented himself from the club, but soon after this Mills caught Brummell gambling at White's again. Of course the thousand guineas were forfeited ; but, according to Ralph Nevill, his friend, instead of claiming the thousand guineas, said : " Well, Brummell, you might at least give me back the ten pounds you had the other night." Lord Alvanley, who seemed to spend his life in getting into debt, and ordering extravagant dinners, was another frequenter of the Bow Window. Once Lord Alvanley arranged for a dinner at White's, at which it was settled that whoever could produce the most expensive dish should dine for nothing. The winner was the organiser, whose dish was a fricassee, composed entirely of the *noix*, or small pieces at each side of the back, taken from thirteen kinds of birds, among them being one hundred snipe, forty woodcocks, and twenty pheasants, with other " game." The cost of this mad dish amounted to £108 5s.

Lord Allen, whose income was very limited, was a very frequent visitor at the Window, and to show his mode of life only one anecdote is necessary. He eked out his living by dining out whenever he could get an invitation. An unpleasant remark to an elderly lady one night at dinner caused her to answer : " My lord, your title must be as good as board wages to you ! "

Many distinguished people were to be seen at White's Bow Window, including Sheridan, of course, whose wit carried him everywhere ; but though Louis Napoleon, during his exile in London, tried to be admitted as a member of this most exclusive club, he never succeeded, nor did Count D'Orsay meet with any better luck.

White's was the notorious gambling

WHITE'S CLUB IN 1811

centre in the metropolis, and the great "Betting Book" is still in existence. Some of the wagers were of the most extraordinary nature. Chess was one of the chief attractions for "sportsmen," and it is set down that Lord Howe entered into an arrangement " to play twelve games at Chess with Lord Egmont, and bets Lord Egmont twelve guineas to six guineas on each game."

Then the odd Lord Montfort; whose wastefulness was the talk of London; and who eventually committed suicide;

made a very peculiar bet "as to his powers as a horseman."

July ye 17th, 1732.
Lord Montfort to ride six days running.
1st Ld. Montfort gives Ld. Downe one guinea to receive 10 gs. when he rides 35 miles within the first day.
2nd Ld. Montfort gives Ld. Ashburnham 1 guinea to receive 10 gs. when he rides 25 miles within the second day. Pd.

There are numbers of these foolish debts entered in White's Betting Book. There is another wager that is worth printing. It runs this way :

Ld. Montfort wagers Ld. Ravensworth One Hundred Guineas, Duke of Devonshire Fifty Guineas, and Ld. Hartington Fifty Guineas that Mr. Arthur is not married in three years from ye date hereof, March 11, 1754.
N.B.—Bob goes Twenty Guineas with Ld. Montfort in this bet.

It is well known that this "Bob," the waiter, married, the daughter of Mr. Arthur, who was the proprietor of White's, grew prosperous, and was eventually knighted and became Sir Robert Mackrith, and then sat as a member for Castle Rising in the House of Commons.

Some of the bets were so ridiculous that one can scarcely credit the fact that sane men could make them. One more wild example will suffice.

Mr. F. Cavendish bets Mr. H. Brownrigg 2-1 that he does not kill the bluebottle fly before he goes to bed.
W. FREDERICK CAVENDISH.
HENRY M. BROWNRIGG. Recd. H.B.
July 17, 1856.

Lord Rivers, on one occasion at White's, is known to have lost £3400 at Whist, simply through forgetting the cards that had been played ; but he is also credited with having won over £100,000 ; and, of course, it all went at Crockford's and other places. Certain "fashionable" highwaymen, who managed to get into the club without their real characters being suspected, would note the winners and waylay and rob them at the point of the pistol of all their gains. A mad world !

A MEMORABLE PARTY

AT No. 58 Lincoln's Inn Fields, lived Charles Dickens's friend and biographer, John Forster. Dickens made this house the home of Mr. Tulkinghorn ("Bleak House").

Here, on December 2, 1844, Dickens read "The Chimes" to a little company of his friends that included Thomas Carlyle. Referring to Maclise's sketch of that memorable scene, Forster says : "All are now dead who were present at it excepting only Mr. Carlyle and myself. Among those, however, who have thus passed away was one, our excellent Maclise, who, anticipating the advice of Captain Cuttle, had 'made a note of ' it in pencil. It will tell the reader all he can wish to know. He will see of whom the party consisted ; and may be assured (with allowance for a touch of caricature to which I may claim to be considered myself as the chief victim), that in the grave attention of Carlyle, the eager interest of Stanfield and Maclise, the keen look of poor Laman Blanchard, Fox's rapt solemnity, Jerrold's skyward gaze, and the tears of Harness and Dyce, the characteristic points of the scene are sufficiently rendered." The original drawing by Maclise is now in the Forster Collection at South Kensington.

CHARLES II.'S RETURN TO LONDON

IT was on Tuesday, May 29, 1660, on his birthday, that Charles II. left Rochester in his coach on the final stage of his triumphant journey to London. Past the Plain of Blackheath, he took horse and found many famous troops of cavalry waiting for him. But the reception was not only military, for young country lads danced to tabor and pipe a merry Morris dance which was typical from first to last of the English people's attitude towards the Restoration.

Only four days before Samuel Pepys, who had accompanied Sir Edward Montague on his mission of bringing back the King, had witnessed the landing at Dover: " I went and Mr. Mansell, and one of the King's footmen and a dog that the King loved, in a boat by ourselves, and so got on shore when the King did, who was received by General Monk with all imaginable love and respect at his entrance upon the land at Dover. Infinite the crowd of people and the gallantry of the horsemen, citizens and noblemen of all sorts. The Mayor of the town came and give him his white staff, the badge of his place; which the King did give him again. The Mayor also presented him from the town a very rich Bible, which he took and said ' *it was the thing that he loved above all things in the world.*' A canopy was provided for him to stand under, which he did, and talked awhile with General Monk and others, and so into a stately coach there set for him, and so away through the town towards Canterbury, without making any stay at Dover. The shouting and joy expressed by all is past imagination."

We learn that the following troops marched in front of the restored King of England : " Major General Brown, The Merchant Adventurers, Alderman Robinson, the Lord Maynard, the Earls of Norwich, Peterborough, Cleveland, Derby, Duke of Richmond, and His Majesty's Own Life Guards."

At Deptford a hundred young girls all in white and with scarves about their shoulders waited for Charles II. " These," in the words of a chronicler, " having prepared many flaskets, covered with fine linen, and adorned with rich scarves and ribbons ; which flaskets were full of flowers, and sweet herbs, strewed the way before him as he rode." The Lord Mayor and Aldermen of London in their scarlet robes were waiting for him in St. George's Fields in Southwark. Here, too, were the Recorder and other members of the City Council in a large tent hung about with tapestry. In the tent was placed the Chair of State, covered by a rich canopy ; and when the King had arrived, the Lord Mayor presented to him the City sword and the Recorder greeted him with a speech. These proceedings being finished, the King made his way into the tent and partook of the rich banquet which had been prepared for him.

The progress from the tent is thus outlined by the chronicler already quoted : " First the City Marshal, to follow in the rear of His Majesty's Life Guards, next the Sheriffs' trumpets; then the Sheriffs' men in scarlet cloaks, laced with silver on the capes, carrying javelins in their hands. Then divers eminent citizens well mounted, all in black velvet coats, and chains of gold about their necks, and every one his footman, with suit, cassock and ribbons of the colour of his Company ; all which were made choice of out of the several companies in this famous City and so distinguished : and at the head of each distinction the ensign of that Company."

The City Council followed two by two, close after the Aldermen, and after these, well-known noblemen and their sons. The King's trumpets followed, after which there came in order, the Heralds at Arms, the Duke of Buckingham, the Earl of Lindsey, Lord High Chamberlain of England, and, most important of them all, the Lord General Monk. After these came Garter, Principal King of Arms, with the Lord Mayor on his right bearing the City Sword, and on his left was a Gentleman Usher. On each side of them were the Serjeants at Arms with their Maces.

Then came the King himself with his equerries and footmen on each side and at a few paces distance his brothers, the Duke of York and the Duke of Gloucester. Behind these came many of the King's servants who had served him abroad, while last of all came these troops : the Duke of Buckingham, Earls of Oxford, Northampton, Winchelsea, Lichfield, and Lord Mordaunt's, together with five regiments of horse belonging to the army. The King entered the Borough of Southwark at about half-past three in the afternoon and arrived at London Bridge an hour later. On all sides the streets were thronged and every window was crowded with people eager to catch a glimpse of their King. Tapestry and other costly hangings lent richness to the scene, and at many points of the route the King was hailed by loud music, while as he passed the conduits ran with claret. The different companies attended in their liveries, bearing with them their ensigns, while the trained bands of the

City stood along the line of route and joined in the universal acclamation of the King. " And within the rails," continues the Chronicler, " where Charing Cross formerly was a stand of six hundred pikes, consisting of knights and gentlemen, as had been officers in the armies of his late Majesty of blessed memory ; the truly noble and valiant Sir John Stowell, Knight of the Honourable Order of the Bath (a person famous for eminent actings and sufferings) being in the head of them. From which place the citizens in velvet coats and gold chains being drawn up on each hand, and divers companies of foot soldiers ; his Majesty passed betwixt them, and entered Whitehall at 7 o'clock ; the people making loud shouts and the horse and foot several volleys of shots, at this, his happy arrival. Where the House of Lords and Commons of Parliament received him, and kissed his royal hand."

Never before had such pomp attended a procession. Charles had been conveyed from Holland to Kent by a strong fleet and conducted to London by gallant troops. But his welcome lay primarily in the hearts of his subjects and of the many thousands that flocked to greet him at Dover—

few hailed him with dry eyes. And now at about seven o'clock in the evening, while the House of Lords and the House of Commons were saluting their King, a different scene was being enacted in the Royal Chapel of King Henry VII. of Westminster. Here, the Reverend Bishops of Ely, Salisbury, Rochester and Chichester met in their episcopal habits in honour of the occasion. With them were many of the orthodox clergy who had been so long oppressed, and together they sang a Te Deum and gave thanks to the Deity for having delivered the King from so many dangers and restored him to the Kingdom of Great Britain which was his by right of birth and by the choice of his people. Little wonder that the old magic of kingship seemed to have been permanently restored, and with it even the old belief in the King's touch. Charles II, indeed, is said to have " touched " nearly twenty-four thousand persons during the first four years of his reign, a fact which in itself proves how sure a hold his picturesque personality had upon the English people. On the Tuesday, May 29, 1660, so far as the people were concerned, there was but a single sentiment—" The King has come into his own again, Long Live the King."

"THE SPECIOUS ORATOR": JAMES CHRISTIE THE FIRST

THE STORY OF CHRISTIE'S

THE era of the first expansion of the picture market was that which witnessed the steady rise of James Christie. A Perth man, born in 1730, he served some years in the Navy, and settled afterwards in London and learned the business of auctioneering as assistant to one Annesley, of Covent Garden. He was Annesley's partner for a while, and in 1763 or 1766 " he started on his own account at the rooms in Pall Mall, formerly occupied by Richard Dalton, print-seller," where he had his first sale in December. In 1768, says Mr. Roberts in his interesting Memorials of Christie's, ‹‹ the Royal Academy took possession of a part of the house in which Mr. Christie had been established. In 1770 Mr. Christie removed westward to No. 125, adjoining Schomberg House, where Gainsborough, on his arrival in London from Bath in 1774, set up.

"Christie's ‘ Great Rooms ’ were to be found next to Schomberg House until the autumn of 1823, when the next move was to 8 King Street, St. James's Square, the present position, which covers what was formerly Wilson's

European Emporium, or Museum, prior to which the place had an unenviable notoriety as a gambling-hell."

This first Christie was a man of some blood and excellent natural parts, "of tall and dignified appearance, remarkable for eloquence and professional enthusiasm." He was not, it is reported, exactly a connoisseur, but gathered gradually, in professional and friendly commerce with artists and collectors, the precise degree of knowledge that he needed for the rostrum. There was a coterie— "Christie's Fraternity of Godfathers" —drawn to his table by his own intrinsic qualities as much as by the qualities of his venison and claret, who paid him a little learning in return for much admirable feeding. We get a relish of the best of the period in some of the tales of his intimacy with Gainsborough, Reynolds, Garrick, Richard Wilson, and others; and there must have been some flashes when a company of this sort, dining with Christie, "gave loose to their crazy fancies in their travesties of every remarkable picture that had passed the ordeal of the ivory hammer."

According to one of his biographers, Christie, before opening in Pall Mall, was established for a while in Spring Gardens, Charing Cross; and a story of this period reveals both the auctioneer and his friend the great actor in a very amiable light. At Spring Gardens, it seems, Christie "experienced his first great loss, the precursor of those misfortunes to which his generous nature too frequently exposed him throughout life. He became, under particular circumstances of friendship, security for a minor of great expectations, to the amount of £20,000. The young gentleman died just before the expiration of his minority, and Christie lost the whole sum. Happily he had many friends, among others the illustrious Garrick," who, by the way, often in his lifetime was unjustly charged with meanness. "No sooner was this great player acquainted with Christie's loss than he generously advanced him the loan of £10,000, which the borrower within a given period repaid; and such was his grateful recollection of the circumstance that when deputed by Garrick's widow to sell part of her honoured husband's effects, Christie very feelingly related the whole affair from the rostrum." Another and perhaps more probable version places the amount of Christie's loss at five thousand.

Less agreeable to modern taste is the story of the upright and gifted auctioneer under the patronage of that imperial snob, the Earl of Chesterfield. Christie had for disposal a valuable collection of pictures, of high reputation abroad, many of which Lord Chesterfield had seen during his travels. Christie, as John Taylor relates, "told his lordship how anxious he was that these pictures should excite the attention they deserved, and he requested that his lordship would condescend to look at them. His lordship promised to attend the public view, and gave Mr. Christie leave to announce his intention among his friends, or wherever he thought proper, and in order to give éclat to the occasion he promised to come in state. On the day appointed, therefore, the room was crowded in the expectation of seeing this venerable and celebrated nobleman, who arrived in a coach-and-six, with numerous attendants. The company gave way and afforded a convenient space for his lordship. He was attended by Mr. Christie, who took the liberty of directing his lordship's attention to some pictures, and requested to be favoured with his opinion of the chief productions in the room. . . . The auditors pressed as near as respect for his lordship would permit them, in order to hear and circulate his opinions." It is a typical vignette of a period when the lordly patron was still a power in the land. How the great Dr. Johnson dealt with and disposed of the great Earl of Chesterfield every one should remember.

We are inclined to think that the institution of the Private View arose in Christie's "Great Rooms" in Pall Mall. A familiar print by Gillray, "A Peep at Christie's: Tally-ho and his Nimeney Pimeney, Taking their morning Lounge," bears upon the subject. Tally-ho is the Earl of Derby, and Nimeney Pimeney (the part she played in Burgoyne's *Heiress*) is the accomplished actress, Miss Farren, who became his second wife. Lord Derby is admiring a sporting picture in the gallery, and Miss Farren (both nobleman and actress shockingly caricatured) a classical piece. The Rooms at this date were, in fact, on private view days, a promenade of the world of fashion; and during the season, says Mr. Roberts, " when any remarkable collections were on view, occasional evening receptions took place. The great room was then lighted up, and persons of quality attended in such large numbers that an official of the Opera was stationed at the entrance to prevent the intrusion of those not belonging to the upper world." It was much like a *soirée* at the R.A. in our own day; and there were few more distinguished-looking persons in the room than the host himself, whom Gainsborough painted.

James Christie died at his house in Pall Mall, November 8, 1803, aged 73, and was buried at St. James's burial-ground in the Hampstead Road. The *Gentleman's Magazine*, in a vein of well-intentioned snobbery, remarked that, " with an easy and gentleman-like flow of eloquence, he possessed in a great degree the power of persuasion and even tempered his public addresses by a gentle refinement of manners."

James I. was succeeded by his eldest son, James Christie the Second, educated at Eton, and intended for the Church. James II. had a taste for authorship, and published, among other works, an essay with this tremendous title:—"An Enquiry into the Antient Game, supposed to have been invented by Palamedes, antecedent to the Siege of Troy; with reasons for believing the same to have been known from remote antiquity in China, and progressively improved into the Chinese, Indian, Persian, and European Chess; also two dissertations on the Athenian Shiophoria, and on the mystical meaning of the bough and umbrella in the Skiran rites." 4to. London, 1801.

During all the latter part of the nineteenth century the spacious and handsome rooms in King Street were a noted and peculiar resort. Hither ofttimes came to the hammer (James I.'s original ivory mallet and fine old Chippendale rostrum are still in service) the artistic rarities of the world: pictures, books sumptuously bound, great sets or pieces of wondrous furniture, weapons, tall vases, strange and beautiful inlaid things, jewels, intaglios, cameos — treasures that countries and continents had been ransacked for. And at this or that famous sale were to be seen faces and figures familiar in society, in the Church, literature, the drama, science, the Army, politics, and art. It might be a scholarly collector of books like Lord Acton, of European fame as a student ; or a statesman of the renown of Mr. Gladstone ; or a poet like Mr. Browning or Mr. Swinburne ; or an admired divine like Dean Stanley ; or a painter like Leighton or Millais; or a courted player like Irving or Bancroft ; or a connoisseur of such celebrity in the trade as Agnew ; or a great private buyer of the standing of a Rothschild; or some beautiful woman whose features appealed in the windows of West End studios. Sometimes the sale was romantic in a curious way, as when, soon after his death in 1872, the pictures gathered by Joseph Gillott in his Edgbaston residence fetched £164,530 ; and the purchasers perchance remembered that the steel-pen maker began his career as an " operative grinder " in Sheffield, and rose to be paymaster to hundreds of workmen. Sometimes the interest was in a measure pathetic, as when, just a month after the untimely ending of Dickens, such pictures from Gad's Hill were put up as Frith's

A CONNOISSEUR AT CHRISTIE'S
From a Print published in 1771

Dolly Varden and *Kate Nickleby at Madame Mantalini's*, and Leslie's *Pickwick and Mrs. Bardell ;* and again, as when, but recently, certain " lots " came up from a flat in 17, Stratton Street, and men and women of many degrees (remembering the almost tragic death in Bradford), crowded to secure some token of that most admired and beloved genius of the modern stage, Henry Irving.

Undoubtedly, however, the most extraordinary art sale ever held, not merely at Christie, Manson, and Woods', but in England, was that of the Hamilton Palace Collection, in June and July 1882. Alexander, tenth Duke of Hamilton, who began the amassing of this splendid heap—the mere inventory of which sends the fancy back to another Cave of Aladdin— was born in 1767. Travelling during many years, he bought on this hand and on that gem-like things of every sort, from great cabinets to miniatures, rings, and candlesticks, as a banker's clerk, on a fortnight's inexpensive holiday in Brittany or Belgium, gathers picture post-cards to remind him in the winter of his little summer's progress. Member of the House of Commons (as Marquis of Douglas), British Ambassador to the Court of St. Petersburgh, Member of the House of Peers in 1806, Lord High Steward at the Coronation of William IV. and of Victoria, holder of two dukedoms, two marquisates, three earldoms, and eight baronies, this golden star of the peerage married "the beautiful heiress, Susan Euphemia Beckford, second daughter of William Beckford of Fonthill, the author of ' Vathek,' " and died at his Portman Square mansion in 1852. It was the twelfth Duke of Hamilton (1845–95), son of the eleventh Duke by Princess Marie of Baden, at whose order the fabulous collection was dispersed.

During seventeen days a select and animated fraction of the society of London filled the rooms of Christie's, and gazed astonied as the auctioneer put forward, now a bust of the Emperor Augustus, of antique Egyptian porphyry (500 gs.) ; now a great jug, carved out of a solid mass of avanturine jasper, and mounted in gold (2350 gs.) ; now a Louis XVI. commode of parqueterie (2200 gs.) ; now a great silver-gilt standing cup and cover, some German goldsmith's work (3090 gs.) ; now a Louis XIV. armoire by Buhl, with frame of ebony and panels of tortoise-shell, once in the Louvre (11,500 gs.); now a ewer of ancient Oriental glass, enamelled and gilt (2600 gs.) ; now a writing-table and cartonnière of the Duc de Choiseul (5300 gs.) ; now a hexagonal Henri II. salt-cellar (800 gs.) ; now a secretaire made for Marie Antoinette by Riesener, with her cypher (4400 gs.) ; and now Thorwaldsen's bust of Napoleon I., crowned with bay (610 gs.). When the final bid had accounted for the final thrill, Christie had on his books £397,562 0s. 6d. The Hamilton sale, completed elsewhere, realised in all £554,005.

A FAMOUS PLAYER AT DRAUGHTS

WHEN passing Hanway Street, close to the foot of the Tottenham Court Road, one may notice that the tavern at the corner bears the name of the Blue Posts.

This house (now rebuilt) was once kept by a man named Joshua Sturges. He was the author of a well-known "Guide to the Game of Draughts," published in 1800, and dedicated by permission to the Prince of Wales. Sturges's epitaph in St. Pancras churchyard has long been obliterated, but it bore curious testimony to his skill as a draughts-player and his qualities as a man. Here it is, as preserved in an old volume of *Notes and Queries ;*

"Sacred to the memory of Mr. Joshua Sturges. Many years a Respectable Licensed Victualler in this Parish ; who departed this Life the 12th of August, 1813. Aged 55 years. He was esteemed for the many excellent Qualities he possessed, and his desire to improve the Minds, as also to benefit the Trade of his Brother Victuallers.

"His Genius was also eminently displayed to create innocent and rational amusement to Mankind, in the Production of his Treatise on the difficult game of Draughts, which Treatise received the Approbation of his Prince, and many other Distinguished Characters. . . .

"May his Virtues be rewarded in the next. Peace to his Soul, and respected be his Memory."

GLORIOUS SIDDONS

IT is a significant fact that to Sarah Siddons was raised the first statue in London to any stage-player, in June 1898, when Sir Henry Irving unveiled the monument that bravely stands on Paddington Green. Sarah Siddons was a great woman in many ways. Hazlitt declared that "she was not less than a goddess or a prophetess inspired by the gods. Power was seated on her brow, passion radiated from her breast as from a shrine ; she was tragedy personified." Indeed, Mrs. Siddons, by the contemporaries of her own day and by her fellow actors, was hailed as the incarnation of the sublime in the expression of dramatic passion. On this particular occasion just referred to Sir Henry Irving said : "This is not only the image of a great actress ; it is the image of indomitable energy and perseverance. When she came to London first she was a conspicuous failure. She went back to the hard life of the provincial theatre and matured her powers by unflagging industry. This is no memorial of casual and irresponsible genius, but a triumphant witness to the merits of those comrades-in-arms of all true endeavour—application and a stout heart." It turned out rather prophetically that Irving himself should be accorded the honour of a statue, which stands at the back of the National Gallery.

Sarah Siddons was born in the theatre and nurtured on rose-pink, in the green-room—she was the daughter of players and married a player. She captured the ever-captious Horace Walpole in his old age, when she played Jane Shore at Drury Lane Theatre, with such effect that "not only were sobs and shrieks heard from the ladies; but men wept like children." Henderson, the handsome tragic actor, and the Duchess of Devonshire were her most influential friends and pushed her forward when her heart seemed to fail her in her enterprises. John Scott, who was destined to become Chancellor, Lord Eldon, wrote of her : "She is beyond all idea capital. I never saw an actress before, in my notion, of just affecting, action, and elocution. She beats our deceased Roscius (meaning Garrick) all to nothing."

There must have been something unusually imposing and grand about this famous impersonator of Lady Macbeth—authorities declare that no woman ever could supersede her—for we learn that she was run after everywhere by everybody, from the King and Queen downwards. Anecdotes galore are told of her and her characteristics, and yet withal she was a prudent woman and a model mother to her many offspring. One invalid Scotch lady, whose doctor had forbidden her to go to the theatre, went unintroduced to Mrs. Siddons's residence in Gower Street, and calmly sat down, gazed at her for some minutes, and then walked silently away. Sir Joshua Reynolds painted his name on the hem of her garment in his portrait of her as the Tragic Muse, and Dr. Johnson kissed her hand and called her "my dear madam" on his own staircase. Statesmen were glad, when she played, to sit among the fiddlers ; and the fine gentlemen of the day, including the Prince of Wales, visited her in her dressing-room "to make their bows." Said Dr. Johnson to Dr. Glover, who wrote many plays in his time : "She is a prodigiously fine

347

woman ! " Dr. Glover agreed, but suggested that she was much finer upon the stage when adorned by art—in other words, " made up." " Sir," answered Johnson, " when she is on the stage art does *not adorn* her ; *nature* adorns her there, and *art* glorifies her." One night when Mrs. Siddons was playing Isabella in *The Fatal Marriage*, and uttered the words (on discovering her first husband, in whose absence she had married again), " Oh ! my Biron; my Biron," a young heiress, Miss Gordon, sent forth a scream as wild as that of Isabella, and, taking up the words in a hysterical frenzy, was carried out, still uttering them. Next year this impressionable young lady was wooed and won by John Byron, by whom she became the mother of the famous poet, Lord Byron.

David Garrick, having heard good reports of Mrs. Siddons, at first engaged her for Drury Lane at the sum of five pounds per week, but she had so many enemies in the regularly engaged actresses at the theatre that on the retirement of Garrick she was compelled to go into the country again. She was very soon to return, and with such triumphant emphasis that she became the topic of conversation in polite society and the idol of the hour amongst all classes.

On the eventful night of her reappearance as Isabella she herself says : " I never heard such peals of applause in all my life. I never thought they would have suffered us to end the play." With the echoes of the shouting audience ringing in her ears she wended her way home, she and her father and husband sat down to a frugal supper, only interrupted by the glad exclamations of her proud partner, a not very versatile comedian, but always " reliable " and a trustworthy man. Her

immediate success brought her suitable recognition from the theatrical treasury, and from five pounds a week she jumped to ten, twenty, fifty, and a hundred. In every way, on and off the stage, her manner was ever intentionally or unintentionally dramatic. Her conversation, like that of her brother, John Kemble, frequently flowed into blank verse. Sir Walter Scott, who was a capital mimic, often repeated her tragical exclamation to a foot-boy during a dinner at Ashestiel : " ' You've brought me water, boy— I asked for beer ! ' " Serjeant Talfourd, who was a popular dramatist, speaks thus of Mrs. Siddons : " We think of Mrs. Siddons now not only as the greatest tragic actress of whom there is any trace in living memory, but as a splendid exception to the rules of nature—an artist above her art ; one who not only surpassed all others in degree, but excelled them in kind."

After playing innumerable parts in the old plays, in some of which she seems to have been not well suited, she astounded the whole of critical London, including the gossiping Walpole and all the fine ladies and gentlemen of his circle, by her impersonation of Lady Macbeth in 1785. The originality of her conception of the part and the terror which she was able to convey to the audience at once stamped her as the most striking representative of this character in Shakespeare's tragedy. She made " points " all through the play. Richard Brinsley Sheridan, who was the manager of the Theatre Royal, Drury Lane, had some doubts as to her success, because Mrs. Siddons in the great sleep-walking scene absolutely refused to carry the candlestick about with her—a piece of business that was supposed to be traditionally correct. Evidently she made all her effects with the by-play of her hands,

down his opinion in this wise : "Her countenance, aided by a studious and

MRS. SIDDONS (*After Sir Joshua Reynolds*)

and on the first night so roused the audience that many ladies in the pit fainted dead away.

Lord Harcourt, who was a playgoer all his life, and had seen all the greatest actresses of several generations, set

judicious choice of head-dress, was a true picture of a mind diseased, in the sleep-walking scene, and made one shudder ; and the effect as a picture was better in that than it had ever been with the taper, because it allows of variety in the actress of washing her hands."

In private life Mrs. Siddons was extremely modest and lived only for the benefit of her family. She refused many invitations to great houses and great dinners, but, notwithstanding, she did not escape the malice of many who envied her for the position she attained. To Dr. Whalley she wrote and said amongst other things : " I have been charged with almost everything bad, except incontinence ; and it is attributed to me as thinking a woman may be guilty of every crime, provided she retain her chastity. God help them and forgive them ; they know but little of me."

After startling the town with her Lady Macbeth, Mrs. Siddons played Desdemona in *Othello* with such beauty and charm that old playgoers were hard to persuade that it was the same actress who was appearing before them. Once when Mrs. Siddons was playing Agnes in Lillo's *Fatal Curiosity* she made the flesh of the audience creep at her suggestion of murdering the stranger in the play, who happened to be her own son, and several people were carried out suffering from hysteria. From all accounts, apart from her majestic beauty, her graceful walk, and eloquent gesture, she had a charm of manner that at once marked her supremacy on the stage.

As Charles Mayne Young, equally celebrated as Romeo and Hamlet, tells us, Mrs. Siddons had " a mute eloquence of gait and movement that were irresistible." For instance, in *Coriolanus* an ovation in honour of the victor was introduced in which some two hundred and forty persons marched across the stage. Mrs. Siddons, who had to walk in this procession, remembering that the was Volumnia, the proud mother of a proud son and conquering hero, gave such distinction to her conception of the character that the pit and gallery sprang to their feet electrified by the transcendent execution of her embodiment of the part.

Inevitably there is bound to be the comic side of most things tragic. Mrs. Siddons when playing Lady Macbeth one night was parched with thirst, and the manager sent for a pot of porter —her favourite stimulant. She was in the midst of the great sleep-walking scene when the messenger returned. He asked where Mrs. Siddons was, and in reply a scene-shifter pointed to her on the stage. The boy, with the foaming pot in his hand, coolly walked on and presented it to her. In vain she haughtily waved him away, while the people at the side, in the wings, frantically waved to him and beckoned him to retire, and at last, amid roars and shrieks of laughter, he was got off the stage. But Mrs. Siddons never lost her presence of mind even in this trying ordeal and carried on her impersonation to the end of the act with marvellous force, gaining the usual applause.

Her farewell performance was given on June 29, 1812. The play was *Macbeth*. The crowd was immense. In the sleep-walking act the excitement was so great that the audience stood on the benches and demanded that the performance should end with that scene. The curtain was then dropped for twenty minutes. When it rose Mrs. Siddons was discovered at a table dressed in white. She came forward, amidst a perfect thunderstorm of applause which endured for many moments. When silence was at last secured she recited her farewell address with very considerable emotion.

THE OLD NIGHT HAUNTS

I. THE CIDER CELLARS

IN that curious turning from Southampton Street, Strand, which wends its way towards Bedford Street, at No. 20 Maiden Lane was at one time a tavern called the Cider Cellars, which gained some popularity in its day. It was frequented by very many of the cleverest men of the period. The celebrated Professor Porson was one of its regular patrons, and so was J. M. W. Turner, who lived opposite. The place was opened about 1730, and was then described as a midnight concert-room in a work called " Adventures Underground." Professor Porson had a very great affection for cider, and cider from Devonshire was a highly popular beverage, and the Cellars became his nightly haunt, for, wherever he spent the evening, he finished it up in Maiden Lane. But everything eatable and drinkable could be obtained there. One night as the Professor sat smoking

his pipe, in 1795, he turned to his friend George Gordon, and abruptly said : " Friend George, do you think the Widow Lunan an agreeable sort of personage as times go ? " Gordon agreed that she was. " In that case," replied Porson, " you must meet me to-morrow morning at St. Martin's-in-the-Fields at eight o'clock." Without more ado Porson paid his reckoning and went home. Gordon, being naturally curious as to what was going to happen, repaired to the church the next day, and there found Porson with Mrs. Lunan and a lady friend, and the parson ready to begin the ceremony. John Timbs then tells us that, " the service being ended, the bride and her friend retired by one door of the church and Porson and Gordon by another. The Bride and Bridegroom dined together with friends, but after dinner Porson contrived to slip away, and passed the rest of the day with a learned friend, and did not leave till the family were about to retire for the night, when Porson adjourned to the Cider Cellar and stayed there till eight o'clock the next morning."

The Cider Cellar really was a cellar, for it was deep underground. Its festive glooms enticed many of the nobility, men about town, and all the young sprigs who aspired to fashionable life. The notorious Dr. William Maginn and nearly all the writers connected with *Fraser's Magazine* were more or less regular visitors. Napoleon III. before he became President of the French Republic was to be seen there constantly, as also was Dr. Maguire, and young Benjamin Disraeli made it one of his haunts. Charles Dickens, Douglas Jerrold, Mark Lemon, John Leech, and most of the *Punch* contributors made a joyous company at the Cellars on many occasions. But most famous of all, perhaps, was Thackeray, who here heard Sloman— the "Nadab" of "The Newcomes"— sing his improvisations, and to him he referred in one of his ballads :

Sloman repeats the strains his father sang,

appending to this line a note : "It is needless to speak of this eminent vocalist and improvisatore. He nightly delights a numerous and respectable audience at the Cyder Cellars."

Although it has been a question of some controversy as to whether the Cider Cellars, or the Coal Hole in the Strand, or Evans's Supper Rooms in Covent Garden, was the scene of "The Cave of Harmony" described by Thackeray in "The Newcomes," it is very certain that the great novelist had in his mind, when writing, all three places. But the one great song, "Sam Hall," which has become historic as given by Ross the comedian, was originally sung at the Cider Cellars, and in October 1848, according to Lewis Melville, Thackeray went at least twice "to hear the man sing about going to be hanged." For long this famous, or infamous, song drew the town, as Albert Smith tells us in "The Adventures of Mr. Ledbury," to the Cider Cellars.

It is curious to read how this extraordinary place took the public fancy, and how it was written about in the most respectable journals. Percival Leigh, who wrote a kind of parody of "Pepys' Diary" in *Punch* under the signature of "The Professor," which he called "Mr. Pipps' Diary," said: "To supper at the Cider Cellars in Maiden Lane, wherein was much company, great and small, and did call for kidneys and stout, and then a small glass of aqua vitæ and water, and thereto a cigar. While we supped the singers did entertain us with glees and comical ditties, but alack to hear with what little wit the young sparks about town are tickled, but the thing that did most take me was to see and hear one Ross sing the song of 'Sam Hall' the chimney-sweep going to be hanged. For he had begrimed his muzzle to look unshaven, and in rusty black clothes, with a battered old hat on his crown and a short pipe in his mouth, did sit upon the platform leaning over the back of a chair, so making believe that he was on his way to Tyburn. And then he did sing to a dismal Psalm tune how that his name was Sam Hall, and that he had been a great thief and was now about to pay for all with his life ; and thereupon he swore an oath which did make me somewhat shiver, though divers laughed."

The after-history of the Cider Cellars, when the premises were resorted to by many of the scamps and irresponsible hangers on of the metropolis, need not be detailed. The place fell into frank disrepute and was closed.

II. THE COAL HOLE

NOBODY seems to have properly ascertained why the tavern in Fountain Court, Strand, should have been called the Coal Hole, and yet the origin of the name is quite simple. Fountain Court is situated nearly opposite Exeter Hall, and quite adjacent to the Hotel Cecil, close to Simpson's and the Savoy Theatre. On the site of the old Coal Hole now stands the theatre built by Charles Wilmot, who introduced Jennie Lee to London in her husband's (J. P. Burnett) version of Charles Dickens's "Bleak House" called, *Jo*, and now owned by Edward Terry, who was associated with Wilmot in its erection. Wilmot about 1872 arriving from Australia re-christened the ancient hostelry the Occidental Tavern, as will be gathered from this advertisement, which appeared in the "Era Almanack" for 1873.

"The Occidental Tavern, later Coal Hole, Fountain Court, Strand. The extensive alterations being completed the Profession and the Public will find every accommodation and comfort combined with moderate prices, at the above celebrated tavern. . . . The Sustentation Department is under the management of Her Majesty's Royal Artillery Messman,
WILLIAM KERRIDON
who will provide good dinners after Rehearsal, and Recherche Suppers after Performance, for ONE SHILLING. At five o'clock a Table d'Hote including Soup, Fish, Joints, Poultry, Sweets, Cheese, Salad, &c., Two Shillings. . . . Proprietor Charles Wilmot formerly of America, Australia and New Zealand."

Charles Wilmot carried on the traditions of the house as a theatrical resort, for here assembled in the times of its early resuscitation some of the greatest actors of their various careers.

First, however, the Coal Hole was run by John Rhodes, at the beginning of the eighteenth century, who obtained a licence to supply the coal-heavers and coal-whippers from the Thames wharves that lined the river bank, and that added a picturesque appearance to the ancient "old time stream that flowed by from Parliament House to the Tower, and, so on, the sea." It became a meeting house also for members of the theatrical profession in the better parts of the premises because the rooms were large and the viands supplied were inexpensive. Also because it gave the comforts of a club and was close to the theatres. It was Edmund Kean who made it a tavern of Thespis, just after his marvellous success at Drury Lane as Richard the Third, in which part he seemed to have captured his audiences by lightning flashes of brilliant inspiration, as he progressed in the portrayal of the insidiousness of Richard's character. In Kean's days the Coal Hole was quite respectable, but it degenerated about the year 1859, when it sank under the sway of Renton Nicholson.

Of this man and his "Judge and his Jury" entertainments it is unnecessary to write in detail. Next upon the scene came Charles Wilmot, as already stated, and the house again attracted the theatrical brotherhood of the old school, such as Charles Dillon and Barry Sullivan, Charles Sullivan and Shiel Barry. The old Bohemian haunt where many joyous days and nights were spent had to give place to Terry's Theatre, which was opened in October 17, 1887.

GEORGE MORLAND IN LONDON

THAT unhappy genius, George Morland, to whom London life meant temptation and wreckage, was born in the Haymarket, London, on June 26, 1763. He was an artist almost from the cradle, being both the son and grandson of a painter. He is said to have turned out drawings at five years of age equal to those produced by brilliant art students in their early manhood. His father seems to have utilised him as an infant prodigy in a very harsh manner, and then to have changed his tactics and indulged his son with luxuries. Once, when Nathaniel Hone was visiting the elder Morland, the proud father, pointing to his lad, said, " Is not my son a hopeful boy ? " While he was gone from the room to fetch some specimens of the youngster's work Hone looked reflectively at the boy, who, though only thirteen, was dressed like a man of twenty, in buckskins and boots, and was standing with his coat-tails on his arms and his back to the fire. " Well, Master George, and how do you employ yourself now ? " he asked. George at once rapped out an oath, and answered, " In kissing the maids." When the father re-entered the room Hone remarked, " I have been talking with George in your absence, Mr. Morland, and certainly he is—a hopeful boy ! "

Morland is said to have first tasted gin in a dram-shop near Exeter Change when, as a boy, he was attending the Academy School at Somerset House. It is certain that when he obtained release from his seven years' apprentice-ship to his father he broke out into forms of dissipation which he had already liked and understood. From the day on which he left his home he never possessed a book. Margate was the scene of his first open follies. There he acted as an amateur jockey in the local races, and was mobbed by sporting mariners for his pains. His later career is an old and wretched story, and it does not belong to the Haymarket.

When he left his father's roof Morland —" in the very extreme of foppish puppyism " as to dress and behaviour— went to Margate to enjoy himself and paint portraits. Already his fame was considerable, and he did not want for wealthy sitters, but he put them off and disgusted them, returning to London with poor results. His com-panions were jockeys, postboys, and prize-fighters, and swearing and swilling were his delights. Under these cir-cumstances he married the beautiful sister of his friend and brother painter, William Ward, who, in his turn, married Morland's sister Maria. The two artists essayed to set up house-keeping together in a good house in High Street, Marylebone, but the inevitable friction between the young wives caused their separation, and Morland moved to Great Portland Street. In a very short time his old propensities returned. Utterly neg-lecting his wife, he began that amazing life of industry and dissipation which was to end his career. He worked that he might waste. He gathered in order to scatter, and the two processes soon became mixed. He gave his beautiful pictures in exchange for horses and in exchange for drink. At one time he owned eight saddle-horses, which he kept at the White Lion Inn at Padding-ton, and his splendid painting, *Inside of a Stable*, now in the National Gallery, depicts a scene at that inn. Always a crowd of vampire dealers

CONNOISSEURS EXAMINING A COLLECTION OF GEORGE MORLAND'S
From a Caricature by Gillray

surrounded him, extracting pictures from him by every kind of wheedling or threat, and often taking a picture in settlement of a guinea that would sell for ten. His paintings were copied and sold as genuine with shameless system. A biographer says: " I once saw twelve copies from a small picture of Morland's at one time in a dealer's shop, with the original in the centre, the proprietor of which, with great gravity and unblushing assurance, inquired if I could distinguish the difference." This was nothing to Morland, who could create beauty faster than other men could copy it, and whose one desire was an unhampered week of drink and ribaldry.

The extraordinary life led by Morland in his years of debt and disaster may be judged by the statement that he was once found at work in a lodging in Somers Town under the following circumstances, as set down by Pilkington : "His infant child, that had been dead nearly three weeks, lay in its coffin ; in one corner of the room an ass and foal stood munching barley straw out of the cradle ; a sow and pigs were solacing themselves in the recess of an old cupboard, and himself whistling over a beautiful picture that he was finishing at his easel, with a bottle of gin hung upon one side, and a live mouse sitting for its portrait on this scene." This story may not be true in detail, for according to Cunningham Morland never had a child ; but the picture does not really misrepresent this great painter in the years when, after sowing the wind, he reaped the whirlwind.

GEORGE MORLAND

Yet Morland's career is a contradiction in terms, for this feckless, good-natured, and prodigiously gifted painter did not accept the privilege of idleness so often accorded to genius. In quantity and quality of achievement he stands almost alone. It has been computed that he painted no fewer than four thousand pictures, and these have never been a drug on the market.

The end came in October 1804, when, palsied in himself and shunned by his friends, Morland was taken for a publican's debt to a sponging-house in Eyre Street, Coldbath Fields. Here he sought to drown his miseries by drinking spirits and succeeded. He suggested that his epitaph should be, "Here lies a drunken dog." After being "eight days delirious and convulsed, and in a state of utter mental and bodily debility," this man of genius died at the age of forty-two. His wife's grief, when she heard of it, rose above all her wrongs, and the poor woman died of distress four days after her husband. In life they had been divided, but in death they were lowered together into one grave in St. James's Chapel, in the Hampstead Road.

A DEBUT AT DRURY LANE

THE father of Edmund Kean was the posthumous son of the author of "Sally in our Alley." The mother was Nance Carey, whose intimacy with Aaron Kean, or Moses Kean—at any rate, one of the two—resulted in the advent of Edmund, whom she neglected from almost the day of his birth. Kicks and cuffs and little halfpence were this mite's portion, and love was never known to him except through Miss Tidswell, who was a friend of the unnatural parent. And they both made money out of him and his cleverness, for even as a child he was so beautiful that he was chosen for all the "pretty parts" in the pieces these two women tramped with from fair to fair.

On one occasion he impersonated Cupid at the Opera House in Covent Garden, and when John Kemble was supreme at Drury Lane he was employed to play one of the imps, attendant on the witches, in *Macbeth*, and Mrs. Siddons was the Lady Macbeth.

Little Edmund was born in London. The pavement was his only heritage. What happened to the poor waif during several years it is only possible to conjecture. "A little outcast, with his weak legs in 'irons,' day and night, he sleeps between a poor married couple, whose sides are hurt by his fetters." Then Miss Tidswell, an actress of some emotion, comes to the rescue, and taking a fancy to the child, and admiring, maybe, his beauty, teaches him to speak properly, and coaches him and corrects him, sometimes with that kindness that blends harshness with it. And then he goes out into the world.

At Windsor we learn he made such a reputation as an elocutionist that King George sent for him and so enjoyed a taste of his quality that the young Thespian carried away with him a couple of guineas, which his manager doubtless annexed. But this speaking in higher circles gave the observant youth a new impulse to his desires—and his desires were always London. "A better time will come by and by," that was always the promise he made to himself, through all the awful, miserable wanderings; when sometimes, crushed by his misfortunes, he now and then fell by the way. Once he played with the great Sarah Siddons, who thought that he acted very well; but "there was too little of him wherewith to make a great actor." The passion-stirred Kean overheard, and resolved. He resolved that if perseverance could win him to the highest pinnacle he would be there. Another time a generous colleague said, when Kean had a colourless character to enact : " Look at the little man ; he is trying to make a part of it."

"Who is that shabby man ?" said Mary Chambers, a young Waterford girl, who had been a governess, and who was going through her probationary time as an actress at Gloucester.

"Who the deuce is *she* ?" asked Kean; who had been rated by her for spoiling, as she thought, one of her scenes. "She was what Kean," as Dr. Doran records; "never thoroughly knew her to be—his good genius—worth more than all the kinsfolk he had ever possessed, including Miss Tidswell, who once gave him a home and the stick. The imprudent young couple, however, fell in love ; they married ; and the manager paid his compliments to them by turning them out of his company. . . . Beverley (the manager) dismissed them on the ground that the lady was of no use to him whatever, and that the attraction of Kean would wane, now he was no longer a young *unmarried* tragedian."

the kind of part for which he had engaged Kean. He was engaged, that was all, and he was in London dancing attendance upon those who were in power. It was at the end of 1813 that Kean reached London with his wife and his son Charles. Howard, the other boy, was dead. Drury Lane

EDMUND KEAN AS RICHARD THE THIRD
From a Contemporary Print

But they loved, these two ardent souls, and starved, and notwithstanding the unparalleled misery of their lives they clung to each other for the brighter days that Kean kept on saying would dawn. His industry was so intense that to a large extent he lived the life of the characters he had to portray. And London still. " If I could only get there," he cried in his anguish, " and succeed! If I should succeed I shall go mad ! "

Then at last he got to London. And he was shabby and felt ashamed of his shabbiness. Not so much, perhaps, because he was reminded of it, as because he knew it. We shall see. Arnold, the stage manager of Drury Lane theatre, had not stipulated

was in a terrible state of stagnation at this period. Nobody and nothing drew the public.

There in the cold hall of Drury Lane stood the genius—cold himself, a little dark-eyed restless man in the coat of many cakes and patches, ignored of all. Listen to the chronicle of his trusting, and his despair : " In Cecil Street, his family was living on little more than air ; and he was daily growing sick as he stood, waiting in that hall for an audience with the manager, and subject to the sneers of passing actors. . . . Even Arnold treated him superciliously, as a *young man*, as he condescended to speak, and put him off." Several actors got their chances and were heard of no more. Stephen Kemble was tried in *The Merchant of Venice*, but his Shylock was voted old-fashioned and no good. Others also came and went in Shylock and other parts. Why not try a new actor? And the little man stood within, and yet without the gates. "Let me but have my foot before the floats and I'll show them——!"

So at last the permission came. But he must play Richard. He refused. "Shylock or nothing," was his determined reply. He dreaded Richard on account of the smallness of his stature. So, after some argument, he had his way. For him it was the Jew or nothing. And bankruptcy stared the theatre in the face.

EDMUND KEAN.
DIED. MAY 1833.
AGED 46.

A MEMORIAL ERECTED BY HIS SON,
CHARLES JOHN KEAN.
1839.

THE MEMORIAL TO EDMUND KEAN IN KEW CHURCH

At the one morning rehearsal he fluttered his fellow actors, and scared the manager by his originality and independence. "Sir, this will never do," cried Raymond, the acting manager. "It is quite an innovation; it cannot be permitted." "Sir," said the poor, proud man, "I wish it be so"; and the actors smiled. Edmund Kean went home—to the humble lodgings in Cecil Street—through the cold, foggy weather, with hunger and hope battling in his breast. It was January 26, 1814, and Kean said: "To-day, I must dine." Then, kissing his wife, as the tears streamed down their cheeks, he gathered the few necessary personal properties for Shylock together and went off to the theatre.

Pale, quiet and pondering, he dressed himself in a room shared by several others, and went down to the stage and waited at the wings. Up to that moment no one had spoken to him except genial Jack Bannister, the chief comedian of the company, who gave him a hearty word of cheer; and Oxberry, who tendered him a glass of wine and wished him good luck.

At length he made his entrance with Rae as Bassanio, and numerous members of the company stood at the side of the stage to note the business of the newcomer. Dr. Drury, the headmaster of Harrow, who took a great interest in Kean, looked fixedly at him from his box as he came forward. Shylock bent over his crutched stick with both hands; and looking askance at Bassanio, said: "Three thousand ducats?" paused and then added—"Well?"

"He is safe," said Dr. Drury. And Kean's success was assured. He was safe.

His brightest dreams were realised; and staggering home to Cecil Street he caught his faithful wife in his arms and cried: "Mary, you shall ride in your carriage yet!" And then, taking his son Charles in his arms, he added, "and you shall go to Eton."

LOUIS PHILIPPE

LOUIS PHILIPPE IN LONDON

LOUIS PHILIPPE, Duke of Orleans, eldest son of the notorious Egalite, who shocked the world by voting for the death of Louis XVI., after many wanderings in the north of Europe and in the United States of America, determined to come to England with his two younger brothers, the Duke de Montpensier and the Comte de Beaujolais. The royal French exiles arrived in Falmouth Harbour from New York early in February 1800, and requested George III.'s permission to land on British soil and proceed to London. The permission being graciously granted, the exiled princes arrived in London on the fifth of the same month. The Thames and the scenery about Richmond particularly delighted them, and they took up their residence at Twickenham, while Louis XVIII. was holding his forsaken Court at Mittau.

The two younger brothers paid a visit to Clifton, and on their return, all three brothers dined with " Monsieur," the French King's brother, at whose house they met for the first time the famous Mr. Pitt. Other important introductions to powerful families in England followed. On March 1 Lord Grenville entertained them and other distinguished French exiles at his house in Cleveland Row. The following Sunday the same nobleman, by George III.'s permission, introduced the French princes to the King of England at a levée held for that purpose at the Queen's house This kindness on the part of the English King to the exiled Bourbons caused them to be welcomed all over England. Count Woronzow, the Russian Ambassador, entertained them a few days later at his house in Harley Street, and shortly afterwards they were invited to Carlton House by the Prince of Wales, afterwards George IV.

" The Duke of Orleans," says the Reverend Mr. Wright in his interesting Biography of Louis Philippe, " was now initiated into fashionable life in London, and no grand soirée or sumptuous banquet was complete if it wanted the presence of the three princes. Reminiscences of the Orleans family were eagerly sought after, and recollections revived of a somewhat painful nature to the young men themselves. Amongst these was a exhibition, advertised in the public journals of a beautiful portrait of Madame Buffon, which had been painted for the gallery of the late Duke of Orleans, the luckless Egalité. This untimely exhibition was got up at the European museum in St. James's Square, and although sufficiently distressing to the princes, who were devoutely fond of their wretched father, such an Orleans mania pervaded society at the West end that the announcement proved attractive and lucrative to the proprietor of the portrait." The Marchioness of Salisbury entertained the young princes, and Lady Harvey Combe, the lady mayoress, threw open the Egyptian Hall in a splendid civic entertainment in their honour. The Duke of Clarence, afterwards William IV., entertained them at a most sumptuous State dinner at his residence in the Stable-Yard. Louis XVIII.'s brother had of course been invited, but he was unable to attend, owing to an accident. While playing at the tennis court in the Haymarket, it seems, monsieur had been struck on the head by a tennis ball.

In the end the hospitality to the exiled princes became so lavish that the royalist journals in Paris remarked, not without chagrin, "that the dethroned royal family had been entertained by the aristocracy of England with a splendour equal to the most brilliant periods of French history." Louis Philippe was now living in a house at Twickenham belonging to a Mr. Gosling, but afterwards he occupied Orleans House which had been formerly the country seat of General Pocock. Before leaving Twickenham for good Louis Philippe, among many acts of benevolence, granted twenty annuities of £20 each to poor people in the neighbourhood.

But now, in 1800, the first year of a long exile in Twickenham, Louis Philippe and his brothers grew restless and obtained a free passage from the British Government in a vessel of war to Minorca. Owing, however, to the hatred of the Spaniards for the very name of Orleans they did not go on to Spain as they had intended but returned to this country. They settled down again at Twickenham to bear their exile in patience, but in the May of 1807 fate struck them yet another blow in the death of the Duke de Montpensier, who died on the eighteenth of that month and was buried in the aisle of that part of Westminster Abbey which is near the great entrance of Henry VII.'s chapel. The next year Louis Philippe took his surviving brother to Malta, and he died the same year from the same malady—consumption—that had killed his brother. The Comte de Beaujolais was a very gallant young prince. One night, as he was sitting in a box at Covent Garden, he was informed that a frigate was on the point of starting for Boulogne. Louis Philippe's youngest brother immediately begged to be allowed to take part in the reconnoitring expedition. He was told that the French would do their uttermost to sink the frigate, "No matter," he replied, "no matter, if I should perish, I shall at least have the consolation of once more beholding the shores of that adored country to which I am destined never to return." The prophecy was only too true, but the reconnoitring expedition which the young prince accompanied was a success.

In the autumn of 1808 Louis Philippe, now alone in the world, returned to London on a mission on behalf of the Queen of the Two Sicilies whose daughter, Marie Amelie, he was to marry the following year, after having been granted a passage in an English frigate to the Mediterranean. Time passed and on March 24, 1815, Louis Philippe abandoned by the royalists, was compelled to leave France and return to his second home, Twickenham. But the "July revolution" of 1830 made him King of France at last, and it was as a King that he paid his next visit to England, when he was entertained at Windsor by the late Queen Victoria in the October of 1844. On this occasion he visited his favourite Twickenham and another English spot that he was to know in the future only too well—Claremont.

For yet once again the luckless Louis Philippe was to seek refuge in England. He came as a dethroned King in March 1848. He travelled as " Mr. Smith " and his first words on reaching Newhaven were : " Thank God, I am on British ground ! " After passing the night at Newhaven the King and Queen left the next morning for Croydon, where they were to meet members of their family who had made their escape a little earlier. This meeting at Croydon has been described by an eye-witness : " Upon the arrival of the royal carriages, Captain Hotham put his head out, and gave a signal to the directors. When the door of the royal carriage was opened, his Majesty stepped out, and upon seeing him, his daughter, the Duchess of Coburg, gave a stifled scream. He was immediately locked in the arms of his son, the Duke de Nemours, whom he embraced with great warmth, and instantly after he pressed his daughter to his bosom in the most affectionate manner. His Majesty was overpowered, and shed tears, as did his daughter also. The scene was a most moving one, and one not easily forgotten. The Queen upon stepping from the carriage also affectionately embraced her children, and was greatly agitated."

The royal party remained together for a few minutes in the waiting-room to which they had been ushered by the directors They then took their places in the three carriages that were to convey them to Claremont. Here Louis Philippe died on August 26, 1850.

THE SPECTATOR'S LONDON.

Sir Roger de Coverley at the Temple Stairs.

IN No. 1 of the *Spectator*, issued on Thursday, March 1, 1711, Addison emphasised a side of the *Spectator's* character which was to remain prominent throughout the matchless series of essays. It was as an observant Londoner that he came before his readers. "I have passed my latter Years in this City, where I am frequently seen in most publick Places . . . there is no place of Resort wherein I do not make my appearance," and in this essay alone we have descriptive mention of many of the social centres of Queen Anne's London, including Will's Coffee House, Child's Coffee House, the St. James's Coffee Houses, the "Grecian," the "Cocoa Tree," Drury Lane Theatre, Change Alley, and many more.

Of all flavours in the *Spectator*, that of London is the most pervading. The mere name of a street lends charm to many a page, as when Dick Steele begins a discourse on the duties of wives: "I was the other day driving in a Hack through Gerard Street." As often it is some curious detail that quickens the attention, as when Addison, in an essay on Tragedy, remarks that the tremendous stage battles at the Haymarket Theatre could be heard sometimes, at Charing Cross. Our interest in Robin Bridegroom's complaint, that he and his newly-made bride were awakened on the morning after their wedding by "the Thunder of a set of Drums," is all enhanced by the punctilious dating of his letter from "Birchan Lane." And Jack Toper's scrupulous testimony to the character of his servant—whose steadiness was more than such a master desired—gains in the same kind when he writes :

We were coming down Essex Street one night a little flustrated, and I was giving him the word to alarm the Watch ; he had the impudence to tell me it was against the Law.

Again, when Dick Steele pursues in a hackney coach the young lady, similarly conveyed, whose glances he encountered in Covent Garden, you may follow the chase through Long Acre, King Street, Newport Street, and St. Martin's Lane with all a Londoner's recognition of the route.

Hardly a characteristic of London in Addison's day is unmentioned in these intricately interesting essays. The extent of London for instance, is indicated when the "Widow Gentlewoman," who advertises her willingness to instruct parrots and starlings in human speech, tries to recommend her house by stating that it stands in Bloomsbury Square, "commodiously situated next the Fields in a good Air." At once we have the limits of London in that quarter. When Addison tells us that Sir Roger de Coverley's town lodgings were in Soho Square, we know little about the matter until we see that Soho Square was on the very edge of London. Oxford Street (then the Tyburn Road) had only a south side, and this extended only as far as Bond Street. North of the road the fields stretched away to Paddington. The Tottenham Court Road ran northwards through open fields, and was called the road to Hampstead. Bloomsbury scarcely existed; nevertheless, Red Lion Street ran up to Great Ormond Street. Bedford Row was being built when the *Spectator* was flourishing.

But the "Spectator's" pictures of London, as often as not, are deliberate. "I have sometimes employed myself," says Addison, "from Charing Cross to the Royal Exchange in drawing the characters of those who have passed by me." To Steele we owe the most complete picture of a London day in the whole *Spectator*. In No. 454 he undertook to give an account of the twenty-four metropolitan hours. He had been sleeping at Richmond, rose at four, and took boat down to London. At once we have this river piece:

When we first put off from Shore we soon fell in with a Fleet of Gardeners bound for the several Market-Ports of London ; and it was the most pleasing Scene imaginable to see the Chearfulness with which those industrious People ply'd their Way to a certain Sale of their Goods. The Banks on each Side are as well peopled and beautiful with as agreeable Plantations as any Spot on Earth ; but the Thames itself, loaded with the Product of each Shore, added very much to the Landskip. It was very easie to observe by their Sailing, and the Countenances of the ruddy Virgins, who were Super-cargoes, the Parts of the Town to which they were bound. There was an Air in the Purveyors for Covent-Garden, who frequently converse with Morning Rakes, very unlike the seemly Sobriety of those bound for Stocks Market.

Presently our early risen essayist lands "with Ten Sail of Apricock Boats at Strand Bridge, after having put in at Nine Elms and taken in Melons consigned by Mr. Cuffe of that Place to Sarah Sewell and Company, at their stall in Convent Garden."

The finest London scenes in the *Spectator*, as the first in portrayal of human character, are those in which Sir Roger De Coverley figures. Who can forget his visit to Westminster Abbey in a coach, which he stopped on the way at a tobacconist, to "take in a Roll of their best Virginia" for the coachman's solace ? It would be a delightful thing—why have we never done it ?—to go to the Abbey and walk there in Sir Roger's footsteps, to see what he saw, and to linger where he lingered. Is not the ugly pomposity of Sir Cloudsley Shovel's monument more than half redeemed by Sir Roger's tribute ? Passing by it, " he flung his Hand that way, and cry'd Sir Cloudsley Shord ! a very gallant Man ! " The Coronation Chair itself is enhanced by Sir Roger's attention to it. For Sir Roger

after having heard that the Stone underneath, which was brought from *Scotland*, was called *Jacob's Pillar*, sat himself down in the Chair ; and looking like the Figure of an old *Gothic* King, asked our Interpreter,

What authority they had to say that *Jacob* had ever been in *Scotland*? The Fellow, instead of returning him an Answer, told him, that he hoped his Honour would pay his Forfeit. I could observe Sir ROGER a little ruffled upon being thus trepanned; but our Guide not insisting upon his Demand the Knight soon recovered his good Humour, and whispered in my Ear that if WILL WIMBLE were with us, and saw those two Chairs, it would go hard but he would get a Tobacco-Stopper out of one or t'other of them.

It is easy to follow Sir Roger round his London. Behold him at Squire's Coffee House in Fuller's Rents—that purlieu of Holborn which disappeared when the "Tube" railway was making. There his venerable figure drew the eyes of the whole room upon him, and the servants ran to supply him with a clean pipe, a paper of tobacco, a dish of coffee, and the "Supplement" with such devotion that "no Body else could come at a Dish of Tea till the Knight had got all his Conveniencies about him." See him, finally, at the Temple Stairs, stepping down to the boat that was to take him with the *Spectator* to Vauxhall, and picking out from the crowd of watermen a poor fellow with a wooden leg. For, as he explained, "I never make use of anybody to row me that has not lost either a Leg or an Arm. I would rather *bate* him a few strokes of his oar than not employ an honest man that has been wounded in the Queen's service. *If I was a Lord or a Bishop, and kept a barge, I would not put a fellow in my Living that had not a Wooden Leg.*"

THREE POETS IN ONE COURT SUIT

WHEN Sir Robert Peel wrote to Wordsworth urging him to accept the Poet Laureateship the poet pleaded his age (he was seventy-four) as a bar to his acceptance of this post; but on his being assured that little or nothing would be expected from him, he resigned hi self to the honour. A few weeks later Wordsworth was invited to London to attend a State Ball in his new character, and he obeyed the summons. Grasmere's lake was exchanged for London streets. "And will you put on a Court dress?" said Haydon, the painter.

To Wordsworth this was an unforeseen problem. He possessed no Court dress, and probably had little liking for the expense of obtaining one. Who should come to the rescue but Samuel Rogers? Rogers was always coming to the rescue. He fitted up Wordsworth with a shabby Court suit of his own. True, Wordsworth was twice Rogers's size, and was only got into the clothes by much pulling and hauling.

Thus attired, and with Sir Humphry Davy's sword whipping his shins, the venerable poet presented himself before his Queen. But the awkwardness of Poet Laureates is not so easily exhausted. Five years later Wordsworth died, and on November 5, 1850, Tennyson received a letter offering him the Laureateship in succession to Wordsworth. And to him came an invitation to Court, and with it the same problem of a suitable dress. Rogers's greatness of mind asserted itself again. He had himself been offered the Laureateship, but had refused it on the score of old age. He had seen one poet forced into his shabby old Court suit. Why not another? Hearing of Tennyson's difficulty, he promptly offered him those versatile garments. And Tennyson wore them. The coat did well enough, but his friends were consumed with anxiety about the nether garments, which he did not try on until the fateful morning.

THE GOLD HEADED CANE AND ITS OWNERS.

A REMARKABLE relic is preserved in the clubroom of the Royal College of Physicians in Trafalgar Square. It is a gold-headed cane. The physician's gold-headed cane was once the symbol of his profession as definitely as the striped pole is the symbol still of the barber's; and between the cane and the pole there is even an actual connection into which space forbids us to enter in this narrative.

The cane now so religiously preserved by the Royal College of Physicians was used, or worn, by five successive members of the medical profession, each of whom left a great name; and perhaps no single object is regarded by British physicians with more veneration. Oddly enough, it is not the typical physician's cane of bygone days. It is not, that is to say, a knobbed cane, whose knob is fitted with a lid and whose interior was used as a vinaigrette or receptacle for disinfectants. It is a cross-handled cane. Its gold handle bears the engraved arms of each of its successive owners. Originally possessed by Dr. John Radcliffe, it was bequeathed by him to Dr. Richard Mead. But let us set forth the dynasty in form. This unique gold-headed cane descended as follows:

Dr. Radcliffe (1650–1714).
|
Dr. Richard Mead (1673–1754).
|
Dr. Anthony Askew (1722–1774).
|
Dr. David Pitcairn (1749–1809).
|
Dr. Matthew Baillie (1761–1823).

Dr. John Radcliffe, racily described by Jeaffreson (in his "Book About Doctors") as "the physician without learning, and the luxurious *bon vivant*, who grudged the odd sixpences of his tavern scores," was born at Wakefield in the year 1650. Whether he had learning or not, he uttered the very bold confession, all the more significant after a career of the highest distinction, that when he was a young practitioner he possessed twenty remedies for every disease, and finally found that there were twenty diseases for which he had not one remedy. He fought his way upwards in the reign of William and Mary against astute and bitter rivals. In 1686 he was appointed physician to Princess Anne of Denmark, and this is how he looked after her Royal Highness: "Shortly after the death of Queen Mary, the

Princess Anne, having incurred a fit of what is by the vulgar termed 'blue devils' from not paying proper attention to her diet, sent in all haste to her physician. Radcliffe, when he received the imperative summons to hurry to St. James's, was sitting over his bottle in a tavern. The allurements of Bacchus were too strong for him, and he delayed his visit to the distinguished sufferer. A second messenger arrived, but by that time the physician was so gloriously ennobled with claret that he discarded all petty considerations of personal advantage, and flatly refused to stir an inch from the room where he was experiencing the happiness humanity is capable of. 'Tell her Royal Highness,' he exclaimed, banging his fist on the table, 'that her distemper is nothing but the vapours. She's in as good a state of health as any woman breathing, only she can't make up her mind to believe it.'" But the *cure by insult* had not then become popular, still less was it acceptable at Court, and Radcliffe—who weakly repented and hurried to his Royal client next morning—was thrown out of favour, and had to fall back on ordinary wealthy clients, out of whose ailments he piled up a fortune. According to some of his critics, Radcliffe killed Queen Mary by his treatment and Queen Anne by his not treating her. He deeply offended King William III. by telling him that he would not have his Majesty's legs for his three kingdoms. Radcliffe died in his house in Bloomsbury Square in 1714, leaving magnificent bequests to Oxford University.

Immediately on his death, and indeed before the funeral, Dr. Richard Mead moved into Radcliffe's house, and took over his practice and the Gold-headed Cane. He had long paid court to Radcliffe, a circumstance which did not escape his enemies and satirists. It is said that one day Radcliffe had found him reading Hippocrates in the original Greek, and said, "Why, I never read Hippocrates at all." "You have no occasion to do so," replied Mead, "for you are Hippocrates himself." This audacious reply is stated to have procured him the friendship of Radcliffe, to whose patronage the foundation of Mead's practice has been generally attributed. According, however, to one author, Mead "had his rise in life from being called to see the Duchess of —— at midnight. She unfortunately drank to excess. The doctor also was very often much in liquor, and was so that night. In the act of feeling her pulse, slipping his foot, he cried, 'Drunk! by God!' meaning himself. She, imagining he had found out her complaint, which she wished to conceal, told the doctor if he kept her secret she would recommend him. She did so, and made his fortune." When engaged at home Mead generally spent his evenings at Batson's coffee-house in Cornhill, and apothecaries used to come to him at Tom's, near Covent Garden, with written or verbal reports of cases, on which he prescribed, without seeing the patients, for half-guinea fees. Alexander Pope was one of his many distinguished patients :

I'll do what Mead and Gheselden advise.

From Bloomsbury Square Mead soon moved to a palatial house in Great Ormond Street. Here his library was adorned with busts of the Greek philosophers and Roman emperors, with bronzes and gems and vases and coins, besides ten thousand volumes. Hospitable, cultured, and magnificent, Mead was unfortunate only in living too long and descending into second childhood.

Mead died in 1754, and the wand of success, whose history is entertainingly told in Munk's *Gold Headed Cane,* passed to Dr. Anthony Askew, who is remembered now chiefly for his attainments as a classical scholar. A great traveller and a great linguist, he collected rare manuscripts abroad, and at home filled his house in Queen Square, Bloomsbury, with books until it could hold no more. Here, to friends like Sir William Jones and Dr. Parr, he produced his rare editions and large-paper copies. He valued some of his treasures so much that he would not allow visitors to touch them, but only to survey them in glass cases, or he would mount a ladder and himself read aloud passages from his first edition of Boccaccio. Of his medical work the records are slight.

Askew died in 1774, and the Gold-headed Cane passed to Dr. David Pitcairn, a Scotch physician, who began to practise in London in 1779, rose to the top of his profession, and arrived at the conviction " the last thing a physician learns is to know when to do nothing but quietly to wait and allow Nature and time to have fair play."

By this time the Gold-headed Cane of Radcliffe, Mead, Askew, and Pitcairn had become a treasure too precious for ordinary use. Indeed, the custom of carrying a gold-headed cane had declined in the profession. Dr. Matthew Baillie, the great morbid anatomist, kept the sacred symbol in a corner of his consulting-room in Grosvenor Square, though he would occasionally take it with him when he was joining some circle of professional friends. He uttered precepts which might be used as annotations to Mr. Bernard Shaw's " Doctor's Dilemma." He would say : " I know better perhaps than any other man, from my knowledge of anatomy, how to discover a disease, but when I have done so I do not know better how to cure it." It was Baillie who told a fine lady with an imaginary ailment that she might eat oysters, shells and all. He died in 1823, and his bust is in Westminster Abbey. He was the last private owner of the Gold-headed Cane.

THE COCKNEY OF OLD TIME

HE was such a man as Washington Irving's cheesemonger, of Little Britain.

" He passed the greater part of his life in the purlieus of Little Britain, until of late years, when, having become rich, and grown into the dignity of a Sunday cane, he begins to take his pleasure and see the world. He has therefore made several excursions to Hampstead, Highgate, and other neighbouring towns, where he has passed whole afternoons in looking back upon the Metropolis through a telescope, and endeavouring to descry the steeple of St. Bartholomew's. Not a stage coachman of Bull-and-Mouth Street but touches his hat as he passes ; and he is considered quite a patron at the coach-office of the Goose and Gridiron, St. Paul's Churchyard. His family have been very urgent for him to make an expedition to Margate, but he has great doubts of those new gimcracks, the steamboats."

This centripetal devotion to London, which was the root of the Cockney character, is not only weakened, but is now replaced by a centrifugal tendency that grows stronger every year.

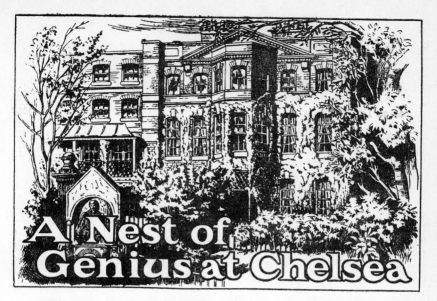

A Nest of Genius at Chelsea

POETS AND PAINTERS UNDER A CHELSEA ROOF

AT Tudor House, 16 Cheyne Walk, Chelsea, between the years 1862 and 1882, lived Dante Gabriel Rossetti. He lived in retirement from the world ; but hither came young poets, young painters, many of them unknown, untried ; unfledged, without the proper knowledge or use of their wings. And by the example of Dante Gabriel Rossetti, pre-eminent in the two arts of painting and poetry, because of the unfailing sympathy and generous praise he was always ready to bestow on work that was worthy, the young aspirants learned under his roof to turn promise into performance, to trust themselves to wider and stronger flights, and finally to build reputations for themselves in lasting material. And so we have called Rossetti's house at Chelsea "a nest of genius," for here, under the guidance and inspiration of the master, the young birds tested their wings.

The sway that Rossetti exercised over his circle—over all with whom he came in contact—was absolutely magical. In early years he was associated with men of intense individuality and rugged character, yet even these he dominated and dazzled by a charm of personality which William Sharp calls "bodily genius." He pressed Millais and Holman Hunt into the Pre-Raphaelite Brotherhood — that wonderful little group of artists he amalgamated in 1848 to resist convention, and return to nature ; and of these three men, only one of whom was of age, his was the ruling personality. His magnetism seemed almost hypnotic. Ruskin himself fell for a time under his sway ; William Morris, stubborn and independent as he was, yielded to the spell of his influence ; he determined the career of Burne-Jones, and among men of the younger generation he awakened a loyalty and devotion almost unparalleled in literary history. "What a supreme man he is!" exclaimed Philip Bourke Marston, the young blind poet whom Rossetti considered the most brilliant in promise of his contemporaries; "Why is he not some great exiled king, that we might give our lives in trying to restore him to his kingdom?"

Rossetti was rather over middle height; his face, we read, was strong and passionate in expression, and full of melancholy. His eyes were dark grey, wide open, deeply set, his eyebrows dark, thick, well arched, the forehead large and well rounded, and the strongly marked brows produced a remarkable fulness at the ridge of the nose, which was well cut and had large breathing nostrils. A natural kingliness was indeed native to him, and all who knew him are agreed that the man was greater than his work. It has been well said that his work was only the faint expression of an inner force, and streamed from him like light from the sun. Those burning canvases of his, which glow with a richness and depth of colour we cannot match, except by going back to the early Italian painters, were but a pale reflection of the smouldering fire of colour within. His lyrics, dewy-fresh: his sonnets exquisite in wrought workmanship, were but a frail and partial representation of the passion for beauty that possessed his soul. When we add to these dazzling qualities of character, a buoyant delight in the work of others, a magnificent generosity in bestowing help and praise, a matchless eloquence, we may arrive at some slight understanding of the astonishing power he exercised over his age and over his generation.

Rossetti established himself at Cheyne Walk after the death of his wife in 1862, because he could not bear to continue in the rooms where his married life had been spent—Chatham Terrace, Blackfriars Bridge—a Terrace which has since been swept away. Ten years he had known and loved Elizabeth Siddall before their marriage, and seven years they had been engaged. She was a girl of extraordinary beauty with brilliant complexion, pale blue eyes, and a mass of coppery-gold hair. In May 1860 they were married, and in 1862 she died. On the day of the funeral the distracted lover and husband came into the room where her body lay. He had in his hand a little manuscript book of poems, and speaking to her as though she heard, he said that the poems were written to her and were hers, and that she must take them with her. Then he put the volume on her hair, and it was buried with her in Highgate Cemetery. Seven years afterwards, through the pressure of friends, Rossetti gave his consent to have the book exhumed, and it was published with additions in 1870 under the title of "Poems."

The face of Rossetti's wife looks out from many of his canvases, but the best portrait of her is the *Beata Beatrix*, in the Tate Gallery, though it was painted after she was dead—painted with what anguish of longing, what bitterness of regret, we may not guess. She sits in a trance symbolic of death—Dante's Blessed Beatrice—on a balcony overlooking the city; a bird drops between her hands the poppy of Sleep. This picture was painted in the studio at Cheyne Walk.

At first the house had three sub-tenants—George Meredith, Swinburne, and William Michael Rossetti, the poet's brother—the idea being that they should live a kind of collegiate life together; but the arrangement did not last long. It is hard to measure Rossetti's influence over Meredith ; his influence over Swinburne was, however, profound. To the end of his life Rossetti was deeply attached to the poet. We know no instance of poetic frenzy so striking as that described by Henry Dunn, a painter and friend of Rossetti. The scene took place in Rossetti's studio, and Dunn alone was present. " It had been a sultry day," he writes, " and with the advancing twilight, heavy thunder-clouds were rolling up. The door opened, and Swinburne entered. . . . Like the storm that had just broken, so he began in low tones to utter lines of poetry. As the storm increased, he got more and more excited and carried away by the impulse of his thoughts, bursting into a torrent of splendid verse that seemed like some grand air with the distant peals of thunder as an intermittent accompaniment. And still the storm waxed more violent, and the vivid flashes of lightning became more frequent. But Swinburne seemed unconscious of it all, and whilst he paced up and down the room, pouring out bursts of passionate declamation, faint electric sparks played round the wavy masses of his luxuriant hair. . . ." In Rossetti's presence the geniuses did not as a rule indulge in such raptures ; indeed, in spite of his enthusiasm and encourage-

DANTE GABRIEL ROSSETTI

ment, they stood in considerable awe of him. But before we touch upon the somewhat timid twitterings of his nestlings, it behoves us to say something about the nest itself.

Anguished with grief at the loss of his wife, Rossetti sought distraction in the collector's pursuit. He is said to have inaugurated the present mania for old furniture, china and bric-à-brac. He haunted the old shops of Hammersmith and Leicester Square, and every nook and cranny of his great " barn of a house," as he called it, was filled with objects beautiful and curious. Even the spare bedroom—Watts's Bedroom, it was called, for Theodore Watts-Dunton used to be a constant visitor at Cheyne Walk—was so full of " old carved heads and gargoyles of the most grinning and ghastly expression," and " Chinese Buddhas of every degree of placid ugliness," that Hall Caine, when he stayed with Rossetti, very much doubted if sleep could be induced to visit him amid such terrifying surroundings.

The garden was filled with an even more curious assemblage—this time of animate objects—strange animals, armadillos, a wombat, woodchucks, a peahen " with two little whining queernesses at her heels, no bigger than ordinary chicks," a raccoon, a kangaroo, a deer, a chameleon, a salamander, and even a zebu, a fierce little animal not much bigger than a Shetland pony, which cost him £20. It was a delicate business to carry the zebu, even securely bound, through the museum of a house, into the garden, where it was tied to a tree ; and the tale is told how the animal finally tore up the tree by the roots, and chased Rossetti round the garden.

Undoubtedly the most interesting room in the house was the studio, where Rossetti painted, where he wrote, where he often dined when alone, and where, after his dinner-parties, his guests assembled, to talk in the dim light before the blazing fire, till the early hours of the morning. The studio was on the ground floor, large and roomy, and opened into the garden, which was almost an acre in extent. The eastern window was darkened by a sycamore tree, " whose large delicate leaves," William Sharp writes, " with the innumerable lights and shadows, made in summer a ceaseless shimmer of loveliness, and in autumn waved to and fro like gold and amber flakes." This tree appears in many of Rossetti's canvases. A number of fine drawings in chalk hung on the walls of the studio, and easels of various sizes stood about the floor. The room was filled not only with " properties " useful to the painter, but with curios of the most miscellaneous description, heaped in confusion, which overflowed the room. For Rossetti bought Japanese furniture and old oak ; his shelves groaned under his fine collection of blue china ; Oriental stuffs glimmered from the shadows, and in the dimness was the glint of sacramental cups and jewelled ware.

What talk the studio must have heard ! Rossetti's conversation had wonderful ease, precision, felicity, and incisiveness. Sometimes he would be persuaded to read aloud passages from the poems he admired ; this he did with a voice of rare power and clearness. But more frequently some young poet would recite his latest poem, and Rossetti, who had " an ungrudging, outspoken loyal and unselfish delight " in the work of others, would give, in full measure and running over, sympathy and praise.

Hither came personalities as diverse as that butterfly of wit as of art, J. M. Whistler, and William Morris, hiding under the exterior of a solid British farmer, unfathomable sweetnesses of dream. Hither came, later on, that young Viking, William Sharp, whose work under the name of Fiona Macleod was to form one of the most puzzling literary problems of time— a problem that neither he himself nor his wife were able to read and which perhaps must remain a riddle until we have developed faculties of greater subtlety. Walter Pater came, too, he whose style is limpid as a crystal stream, and Lewis Carroll of " Alice in Wonderland " fame ; Arthur O'Shaughnessy, the young Irish poet, and Philip Bourke Marston ; Rossetti's old friend, Ford Madox Brown, Burne-Jones, and Swinburne.

Towards the close of Rossetti's life, Hall Caine became acquainted with him, and the novelist has left us a vivid picture of his visits to Cheyne Walk. " Rossetti's house to me the appearance of a plain Queen Anne erection," he writes, " much mutilated by the introduction of unsightly bay-windows ; the brickwork seemed to be falling into decay ; the paint to be in serious need of renewal ; the windows to be dull with the accumulation of the dust of years . . . and round the walls and up the reveals of doors and windows were creeping the tangled branches of the wildest ivy that ever grew untouched by shears. . . . The hall had a puzzling look of equal nobility and shabbiness. . . . Very soon Rossetti came to me through the doorway in front. . . . Holding forth both hands and crying ' Hulloa,' he gave me that cheery, hearty greeting which I came to recognise as his alone, perhaps, in warmth and unfailing geniality among all the men of our circle. It was Italian in its spontaneity, and yet it was English in its manly reserve." When he next passed through London, Caine was asked to spend the night at Cheyne Walk ; and as they were going up to bed Rossetti invited him to look into his bedroom. It was an inner room, dark with heavy hangings on the walls and round the antiquated four-post bed, and thick with velvet curtains before the windows, so that the candles hardly seemed able to light it. " ' My curse,' said Rossetti, ' is insomnia. Two or three hours hence I shall get up and lie on the couch, and, to pass away a weary hour, read this book '—a volume of Boswell's ' Johnson,' which I noticed he took out of the bookcase as we left the studio. It did not escape me that on the table stood two small bottles sealed and labelled, together with a

little measuring-glass. Without looking further at it, but with a terrible suspicion growing over me, I asked if that were his medicine. ' They say there is a skeleton in every cupboard,' he said in a low voice, ' and that is mine; it is chloral.' "

This drug induced in Rossetti periods of terrible gloom, and at such times he was dependent on the tender ministry of his friends for comfort and support. Loyally did his little band of devoted followers rally to his need. There is no work written on Rossetti that does not pay the highest tribute to Theodore Watts-Dunton for his " brotherly devotion and beneficial influence, almost without parallel in the beautiful history of literary friendships." " He is a hero of friendship," Rossetti himself said. Hall Caine, too, was much with him during the last months of his life. Rossetti died at Birchington-on-Sea, at the age of fifty-three, and is buried there.

His house at Cheyne Walk still stands (cleared of its rank growth of ivy), though even in Rossetti's time the greater part of the garden was taken away for building purposes. In the Embankment Gardens, sitting on the seat opposite, one may easily meditate on Dante Gabriel Rossetti and his nest of geniuses.

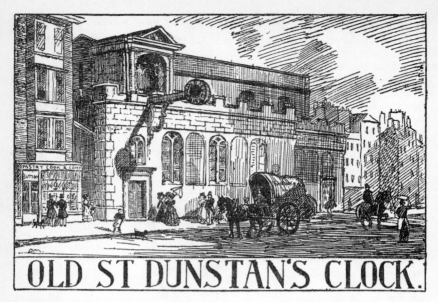

OLD ST DUNSTAN'S CLOCK.

FROM the year 1671, when it was set up by a Water Lane clock-maker named Thomas Harris, down to 1830, the clock of old St. Dunstan's Church was one of the free sights of London. The dials were projected well over the pavement, and behind them, in a large alcove, stood the famous figures which struck the hours and quarters. Many generations of Londoners, and many hundreds of famous men, stopped in Fleet Street to see the performance. This clock is referred to frequently in literature, for example in Goldsmith's " Vicar of Wakefield " and (though with anachronism) in Scott's " The Fortunes of Nigel." Cowper, too, in his " Table Talk " has the oft-quoted lines

When labour and when dulness, hand in
    hand,
Like the two figures at St. Dunstan's stand,
Beating alternately, in measur'd time,
The clock-work, tintinnabulum of rhyme,
Exact and regular the sounds will be,
But such mere quarter-strokes are not for me.

Strype describes the figures as " two savages, or Hercules." Ned Ward in his " London Spy " (1698) refers to " the two wooden horologists at St. Dunstan's."

The popularity of St. Dunstan's two "bell-thumpers," as the author of " Real Life in London " calls them, is thus attested by " Aleph " in " London Scenes and London People." " The giants stood in front of the building, about 30 feet from the road, on a covered platform, each wielding a club—the bell being hung between them—which at the quarters, as well as whole hours, they struck, but so indolently, that spectators often complained that they were not well up to their work. The mechanism, too, was rough and clumsy. You could not help noticing the metal cord inserted in the club to which its motion was due, the tall fellows who appeared to hold it being evidently a mere sham. Gog and Magog are giants in full dress. The pair at St. Dunstan's were nude almost to impropriety ; their aprons were exceedingly narrow and a rough, straggling uncombed " fell of hair " formed the sole covering for the rest of their bodies. . . . They were universally admired. Punch was hardly so popular, and scarce a single unit—man, woman, or child—of the living stream flowing by failed to pause and pay them a look of recognition. Country folks and strangers to London were not content with a transient glance ; they must not only gaze but wait till the clubs were slowly upheaved and the dumb bell made vocal. Many persons made special visits to St. Dunstan's during the forenoon from nine to twelve o'clock as most favourable for the display of automaton power."

The most *striking* wonders in the metropolis, as they were facetiously called, were taken down in 1830 when the old church itself was doomed. We have the word of Edward Moxon that Charles Lamb wept to see them go. Yet they found a new home in London. The Marquis of Hertford, who had often been brought as a boy to see the figures perform, purchased the clock, bells, and figures for two hundred guineas and set them up in his villa in Regent's Park, where they still remain in working order. One cannot but cherish the dream that they may some day strike the hours above the portico of that Museum of Old London, which has long been talked of and is, at last, in the way to be realised.

The older church of St. Dunstan's rose out of a nest of bookseller's shops, and many books, famous or notorious, were published here. John Smeth-wicke, one of Shakespeare's publishers (he issued *Hamlet* and *Romeo and Juliet*) had his shop " under the diall " of St. Dunstan's, and one of the three publishers of Milton's " Paradise Lost," who between them undertook to pay the poet a conditional sum of £20, was Matthias Walker, a St. Dunstan's bookseller. Here also were issued by Richard Marriot two most famous and divine books, Butler's " Hudibras " and Walton's " Compleat Angler." Old Isaak ranks as St. Dunstan's most interesting parishioner. He lived on the north side of Fleet Street, in a house two doors west of the end Chancery Lane, next to a house which bore the sign of the Harrow. " Now the old timber-house," continues his biographer (writing in 1760), " at the south-west corner of Chancery Lane, till within these few years, was known by that sign : it is, therefore, beyond doubt, that Walton lived at the very next door ; and in this House he is, in the deed above referred to, which bears date 1642, said to have followed the trade of a *Linen-draper*. It further appears by that deed, that the house was in the joint occupation of Isaac Walton and John Mason, hosier ; from whence we may conclude, that half a shop was sufficient for the business of Walton." Walton subsequently removed into Chancery Lane, a few doors higher up, on the left hand, where in 1632, he carried on the business of a *Sempster*, or *Milliner*. He was then married : his wife was Anne, daughter of Thomas Ken, of Furnival's Inn, and sister of the Rev. Thomas Ken, afterwards Bishop of Bath and Wells.

GEORGE AUGUSTUS SALA

GEORGE AUGUSTUS SALA

GEORGE AUGUSTUS SALA, although of mixed foreign parentage, was a Londoner born, and a born Londoner. He was a great traveller and visited nearly every city in the world, either as war correspondent or special commissioner, especially for the *Daily Telegraph*, with which paper he was connected the greater part of his journalistic career, and his heart was ever true to Fleet Street. Madame Sala, the great journalist's mother, was a very distinguished actress, singer, and dancer, chiefly associated with the St. James's Theatre when John Braham was producing the operettas and burlettas of Charles Dickens and others, and thus, one way and another, George Augustus became affiliated to the Stage, Music, the Drama, and the painting of scenery at the Princess's, the Standard, and other theatres.

There is a great deal of pathos associated with Sala's early struggling days. At the Princess's Theatre, for the ridiculous sum of fifteen shillings a week, he not only worked in the painting room, but he also translated and adapted comedies and farces from the French for Mr. John Maddox, the lessee, besides which he had to copy out the parts, draw up the advertisements, take stock of the wardrobe, and occasionally hold the prompt book at the wing, and, if the treasurer wanted assistance in making out his accounts, the worthy Jew proprietor was ever ready to call upon Sala's services.

Once even the eccentric Maddox was moved to generosity ; when the manager was about to produce in London *L'Ambassadrice* George Augustus Sala told him that he had seen the piece when it was originally produced in Paris when he was a child, and could remember how the opera was staged. And so, for attending all the rehearsals and giving his advice, he received the lordly sum of one golden guinea.

After adventuring as an etcher and artist, Sala at last found his *métier* and became by degrees one of the most brilliant journalists of his day. One of his first and most agreeable works was "Twice Round the Clock," which is full of the life, the gaiety, the tragedy, and the aspect of the daily life of London some sixty years ago. Another of his Town vignettes was "The Key of the Street," which appeared in *Household Words*. He had become personally associated with Charles Dickens. Sala himself wrote in his "Life and Adventures" the following interesting self-portrait, which gives an idea of the manner of costume donned about the middle of the nineteenth century. Says Sala: "Sir Edward Lawson, coming to me the other day at Brighton, gave me in the course of conversation a most humorous description of my personal appearance on the occasion of my first visit to the offices of the *Daily Telegraph*. He said that I had got myself up for the interview, and that I was attired in a chocolate-coloured frock-coat, a double-breasted plaid velvet waistcoat, trousers of uncertain hue and much too short for me, and Blucher boots. I plead guilty to the chocolate frock-coat and the too brief pantaloons; I acknowledge the Blucher boots; but I join issue with my old friend on the subject of the waistcoat . . . it was a black camlet vest, profusely embroidered with beads and bugles of jet."

Sala, besides being a very deeply read man, had many whimsical turns of mind. When he was appointed the first editor of *Temple Bar* he put as a motto on the title-page : " 'And now, Sir,' said Dr. Johnson, ' we will take a walk down Fleet Street.' " This sham quotation Sala originally coined in one of his " Gas-light and Daylight " papers. This " quotation " has ever since been attributed to the great lexicographer, but nobody has ever been able to discover it in his works ! Sala, indeed, admitted that it was an invention of his own.

It was tolerably well known that George Augustus Sala was often chaffed about his broken nose. How this misfortune occurred he himself relates in speaking of a certain establishment kept by a Jew with his wife in Panton Street, Haymarket. It appears that "G. A. S." had a little dispute with Mrs. " Jehosaphat " in regard to the charge of fifteen shillings for a bottle of champagne. "Mr. Jehosaphat interfered ; there was a fight, I took the floor, Mr. Jehosaphat kneeling on my chest ; and then by a cleverly directed blow with his left hand, the fingers of which were plentifully garnished with diamond rings, he split my nose throughout its entire length. Then he dexterously rolled me into the street." Sala continues that he was rescued by a certain Jack Coney, who lived next door. " I was bleeding like a pig. He picked me up, tied a table napkin tightly round my face, put me in a cab, and took me to Charing Cross Hospital, where the house surgeon swiftly sewed up my damaged nasal organ." Years afterwards, when Sala was in Melbourne staying at Menzies Hotel, he was waited upon by an oily youth of the Hebrew persuasion. He confided to Sala that his name was Jehosaphat. " ' Eh, what ? ' I exclaimed ; ' I think I knew somebody of that name some years ago.' ' Yes, sir, you did,' replied the many-ringleted youth, with a courteous bow; ' which I am the nevvy of the gentleman which had the honour to split your conk open at his saloon in Panton Street.' "

When Sala began to make his first hit he thought that he would like to enter the bonds of matrimony, and married a lady with whom he had been acquainted ever since she was a little child. Sala says: " And this is a reminder of the peculiar formalities in vogue in the early part of the nineteenth century—that when I asked her to name the wedding day she called me ' Sir,' and expressed her opinion that the following Monday would be quite a nice time for the wedding." It must have been a quiet affair because the beadle gave the bride away and the pew-opener was bridesmaid. Having his work to do at the *Daily Telegraph*, Sala put his young bride into a hansom cab and bade her engage some apartments at Brompton. This was the beginning of a long and very happy married life. It was at this period that Sala, as a writer about London contributing to *Household Words* and the new-founded *Temple Bar* magazine, was pestered to death by literary aspirants and poets who would call upon him with their lucubrations, although all and every were warned not to; so he devised a scheme to thwart his enemies. During business hours he sported his oak at his chambers in Clement's Inn to keep all intruders away. Those who were privileged to enter his sanctum had to throw a penny through the large aperture in his letter-box, and then when the coins rang upon the floor " G. A. S." would arise and the callers were admitted, including, of course, Edmund Yates, the sub-editor.

History does not record the fate of the pennies. While editing *Temple Bar* and doing much outside work as well, " G. A. S." was referred to by the rather cynical Matthew Arnold as " one of the young lions of the *Daily Telegraph*," and the phrase is still in a flourishing condition.

On December 12, 1867, Sala was sent for hurriedly by a messenger from the *Telegraph*, who told him that an explosion had taken place at the Clerkenwell House of Detention and requested him to repair thither at once. " The swiftest of hansoms conveyed me to the prison. It was nightfall when I arrived at the House of Detention. There was a strong cordon of police round the scene of the explosion to keep off the mob; but the inspectors on duty knew who I was, and allowed me to pass. My eye lighted on the strangest of spectacles. All the cells in the prison were lighted up; the wall in front was one great black mass, in the middle of which, low down, there was a huge cavity, through which you could descry the gas lamps in the prison yard. The *débris* of that yawning chasm in the wall had formed a high mound in Corporation Lane; and on the top of the hillock of broken bricks stood Captain Eyre Massey Shaw, directing, with his usual coolness and decision, the operations of the firemen." This was one of the most terrible explosions caused by the Fenians that ever took place in London, and the present writer as a child remembers feeling the shock as far as the Brixton Road close to the White Horse Tavern.

George Augustus Sala was the thirteenth child of his parents, and was born in New Street, Manchester Square, in 1828, and passed away at Brighton in 1895.

The Trial of Lord W. Russell.

THE EXECUTION
OF LORD WILLIAM RUSSELL.

NO more affecting historical drama has had London for its scene than the trial and execution of Lord William Russell, who, on very corrupt evidence, was condemned to death at the Old Bailey in July 1683 for participation in the Rye House Plot. He had undoubtedly led, with uncompromising zeal, the movement to debar the Duke of York (afterwards James II.) as a Roman Catholic, from succession to the throne, and he had allowed himself to mingle with associates whose desperate designs to murder both King Charles II. and the Duke he neither shared nor understood. The verdict of history is well and briefly stated by Dr. A. W. Ward (" Dictionary of National Biography ") in these words : " He cannot be said to have found his way through the intrigues which beset his path with notable insight or discretion, but he brought his personal honour out of them unstained."

An exquisite note is brought into the tragic story by the devotion of Lady Russell to her husband in his last dark hours. Rachel Wriothesley was the second daughter of Thomas Wriothesley, fourth Earl of Southampton, and had been the widow of Francis Lord Vaughan, when Russell wooed and won her. To great beauty she joined the virtues of a perfect wife. Her letter to her husband breathes of a great love. " I know of nothing new since you went," she ends one letter to him : " but I know as certain as I live, that I have been for twelve years as passionate a lover as ever woman was, and hope to be so twelve years more ; happy still and entirely yours——"

Over the happiness of these two lovers the shadow of death was brooding in 1683. Lord Russell had warning that he would be accused of conspiracy ; but considering, and also being advised, that flight would appear as a confession of guilt, he remained at home, and allowed himself to be taken and brought before the king in council. To all the charges preferred against him of being concerned in treasonable matters, he gave but one reply : that he knew nothing of the nature of a treasonable plot.

On July 13, 1683, Lord Russell stood within the bar of the Old Bailey, to take his trial upon a charge of high treason. The character of the trial is well summed up by a modern writer. The evidence was contradictory and insufficient. At the most it proved that Russell had attended a meeting where a rising was discussed. It was not shown that he consented to any such schemes, which, certainly, were never carried into effect. An illegal construction

LORD WILLIAM RUSSELL

was put on the 25th of Edward III., the statute under which he was indicted. But, in the nomination of the panel, the sheriffs, who were the creatures of the court, had fully secured his conviction. He was found guilty of high treason, and the atrocious sentence provided in such cases was pronounced thus : " That you be carried back again to the place from whence you came, and from thence be drawn upon a hurdle to the place of execution, where you shall be hanged up by the neck, but cut down alive, your entrails cut off from your body, and burned in your sight, your head to be then severed from your body, and your body divided into four parts, and disposed at the king's pleasure. And the Lord have mercy upon your soul."

Russell had thought of himself as of a dead man from the moment of his arrest. But for the entreaties of his wife, and for his love that could refuse her nothing that could make for her peace, he had been content to die without a word of appeal. But he gave her leave to do as she would, and his friends worked night and day to save him.

Lady Russell threw herself at the King's feet to implore her husband's pardon. " If I do not kill him, he will soon kill me," Charles had said in another place ; surely a cowardly apprehension ; but perhaps to be understood in the son of a murdered king.

Neither gratitude for old services, nor pity for the high estate of the condemned, nor even the charm of the loving and lovely woman at his feet could move Charles from his resolution. One last hope remained. Louise de Kerouaille, the fair and covetous Duchess of Portsmouth, spurred by a promise of £100,000, forsook her plays and masquings to plead for a man's life ; but not all her wiles and supplications could coax even a few weeks respite from the implacable king. Hope was gone ; but despair was not yet come.

Russell jested to the last ; although the careless, impulsive, imaginative Essex, unable to face the horrors of a trial for treason, with its foredoomed end, had died by his own hand in prison on the day Lord Russell was brought into court.

The last days of Lord Russell's life dragged on. He read the scriptures, prayed with his chaplain, conned over and over the little love-notes his lady contrived to smuggle to him with his food. He wrote his last statement, a justification rather than an apology.

" A violent death is a very desirable way of ending one's life," he said to his chaplain. " It is only the being exposed to be a little gazed at, and to suffer the pain of one minute, which, I am confident, is not equal to the pain of drawing a tooth." And on the night before his death, when the rain beat against his barred window, he exclaimed : " Such a rain to-morrow will spoil a great show, which is but a dull thing in a rainy day."

The last morning dawned ; the crowd gathered in Lincoln's Inn Fields. The playhouse stood deserted ; no one walked under the mulberry trees ; but round the great scaffold, hung with black, the orange-girl jostled the citizen's wife and the crippled beggar the fine cavalier, for a sight of the headsman waiting there and the sheriff shading his eyes from the sun as he watched for the prisoner's coach.

LORD WILLIAM RUSSELL PARTING FROM HIS FAMILY
After the picture by Robert Smirke, R.A.

Lord Russell, who had slept soundly all night, rose early and drank a little tea and sherry. He wound his watch : " Now I am done with time," said he, " and am ready for eternity."

Then he asked what he must give the executioner. They told him ten guineas. " A pretty thing," said he smiling, " to give a fee to have one's head cut off."

The scene of the execution, which

happily was more merciful than the sentence, was the centre of Lincoln's Inn Fields. A tablet now marks the spot in the children's play-ground. Crowds lined the streets, and many wept. Russell, looking at them, said, "I hope I shall soon see a better assembly." He sang in a low voice the first words of the 147th Psalm. As he turned with the Dean of Canterbury into Little Queen Street he said, "I have often turned to the other hand with great comfort." He was referring to Southampton House, the noble mansion of the Wriothesleys in Bedford Square, the home of his wife.

Both had left their hearts in the little cell at Newgate. So they came to the green pleasaunce of Lincoln's Inn and the sheriff waiting in the sun on the sable-hung platform.

Then Lord Russell, fronting the yelling crowd, delivered this speech:

Mr. Sheriff,—I expected the noise would be such that I should not be very well heard. I was never fond of much speaking, much less now ; therefore I have set down in this paper all that I think fit to leave behind me. God knows how far I was always from designs against the King's person or of altering the Government. But I have now done with this world and am going to a better! I forgive all the world heartily, and I thank God I die in charity with all men ; and I wish all sincere Protestants may love one another and not make way for popery by their animosities. I pray God forgive them and continue the Protestant Religion amongst them, that it may flourish so long as the Sun and Moon endure. I am now more satisfied to die than ever I have been.

His last word to man spoken, Lord Russell addressed himself to God. Then, pulling off his peruke, his cravat, and his coat, he put some money into the executioner's hand, bidding him do his office without a sign. And thus died Lord William Russell, surnamed the "Patriot."

MISER AND LANDLORD

A GREAT deal of Marylebone, Portman Place and Portman Square district, was built by John Elwes, who had, in consequence, many houses on his hands. To save expense he would live in any one of his houses which happened to be empty, and the moment he had let it he moved into another. Two beds, two chairs, a table, and a poor old woman, were all the movables this great London landlord had to consider. To-day they were in the Haymarket, to-morrow in a Marylebone attic ; and their wanderings were too rapid and fitful to be followed.

In his last years Elwes lived in Welbeck Street, with two maidservants. One of these girls all but succeeded in marrying him. He was then reaching his dotage. But every morning, long

before it was necessary, he would trot off to Marylebone to superintend the workmen on his new houses, becoming known to the wondering neighbours as "the Old Carpenter" His sight and memory failing him, he sometimes lost himself in the streets, and was brought home by an errand boy, whom he rewarded with a polite bow. He became an automaton with one idea, that of keeping the wealth which he could not even estimate. He would cry out in the night, "I will keep my money, I will ; nobody shall rob me of my property." He refused to undress himself, and would be found in bed fully clad, even to his boots, hat, and stick. He died at last without a sigh in his son's house at Marcham, leaving £800,000.

VOLTAIRE IN LONDON

ON Whit Monday of 1726 Voltaire, then in his thirty-third year, landed at Greenwich. It was a brilliant day. The sun shone, the river rippled under a westerly breeze, and to the great exile who, for the second time, had escaped from the rigours of the Bastille, England, in this smiling aspect, seemed something more than a pleasant haven. Moreover, it was the day of Greenwich Fair. In his correspondence Voltaire tells us that the river was covered by two rows of merchant ships, which occupied a space of six miles. Their sails were all set to do honour to the king and queen, who made a royal progress in a gilded barge, preceded by boats carrying musicians. The brilliant exile was intoxicated by the lovely climate and by the air of liberty which he breathed. He wrote afterwards :

I fancied that I was transported to the Olympian games ; but the beauty of the Thames, the crowd of vessels, and the vast size of the City of London soon made me blush for having dared to liken Elis to England. I was told that at the same time a fight of gladiators [a prize-fight, no doubt]

was in progress in London, and I immediately believed myself to be among the ancient Romans. A courier from Denmark, who had arrived that morning, and who was fortunately returning to Denmark the same evening, was beside me during the races. He seemed overpowered with joy and astonishment ; he believed that the entire nation was always gay, that all the women were sprightly and beautiful, and that the sky of England was always pure and serene.

There is a vein of banter here, and Voltaire goes on to tell how next day he found every one morose, and murder abroad ; the wind was in the east. Greatly astonished by this change in the manners of the people he inquired of a Court doctor, who told him that he had nothing to be astonished at, and that in November and March, if he stayed, he would see people hang themselves by the dozen—the wind being then in the east. In those months, the doctor told the astonished Frenchman : " Every one looks stern and cross, and is disposed to form desperate resolutions. It was precisely in an east wind that Charles I. was beheaded and that James II. was dethroned. If you have any favour to ask at Court, never go to ask it unless the wind is in the west or south."

Voltaire was particularly struck by the beauty and clear complexions of the English women whom he saw at Greenwich ; they appeared, like the wherrymen, to indicate a nation entirely happy and well-fed. On a pole at the head of a race-course he saw a silver pitcher, which he was told was the prize for the winner of the horse-race. On another pole were a hat and a chemise ; these, he was surprised and delighted to hear, were for the women winners. A man, marching up and down another course, exhibited a full purse, which was to go to the winner of the foot races. These things reminded him of the Olympic games, but everything here was on so big a scale that " he blushed to have compared Greece with England." On the course he was fortunate enough to meet certain merchants to whom he had letters of introduction. They, apparently, did him the honours of the fair.

It is probable that Voltaire's first evening in London was spent at the house of Lord Bolingbroke, whose writings, both political and philosophical, were so largely to influence his outlook and even his style. With the evening came somewhat of disillusion to the exile. When he spoke to the fashionable ladies present of the glories of Greenwich Fair, they turned up their noses ; evidently there was something wrong. Then he discovered that the fine men and noble women whom he had so much admired were only servants, villagers, scholars, and apprentices. One can imagine his sardonic shrug as he glanced round at Bolingbroke's aristocratic guests. On the following morning Voltaire found the city magnates in a dirty coffee house. It pleased them to say that they had never seen him before, and Greenwich Fair—what was Greenwich Fair ? The wind, they said, was in the east. That accounted for their gloom and their forgetfulness.

A good deal of obscurity still surrounds Voltaire's doings in England, though Professor Churton Collins, in his " Voltaire in England," did something to lift the veil, as also did Mr. J. Parton in his valuable " Life " of the great satirist. We know that he had his home with Everard Falkner, a silk and cloth merchant who was also something of a virtuoso ; and we know that through Bolingbroke and the Walpoles he knew everybody, from Pope to Berkeley, from Congreve to Byng, from Swift to John Gay.

Landor might have done a notable Imaginary Conversation between Congreve and Voltaire. The author of *Love for Love*—the most sparkling prose comedy in the language—was then old in body, if not in years, and he lived in Surrey Street, Strand. He had ceased writing almost thirty years before, and desired to forget, in the affluence of pensions and sinecures, that he had ever belonged to the great band of scribblers. Voltaire wrote : " He was infirm and almost dying when I knew him. He had one fault, that of not sufficiently esteeming his first trade of author, which had made his fame and fortune. He spoke to me of his works as trifles beneath him, and told me, at our first conversation, to visit him only on the footing of a gentleman who lived very simply. I replied that if he had had the misfortune to be only a gentleman like another, I should never have come to see him ; and I was shocked at a vanity so ill-placed." It is an extraordinary picture—the English dramatist who had finished his work at thirty, now nearly blind and prostrated by gout, talking thus slightingly of his work to the great Frenchman, then in the flush of his powers. Voltaire was essentially a man of letters ; he stood, indeed, for that great republic of letters whose freedom he upheld, though he did not always respect that freedom. And here was the pet of courts wishing to forget that he had ever descended into that great arena.

Voltaire modified his first enthusiasm for London as seen through the glamour of Greenwich Fair. Later he declared that London was not the equal of Paris in material things. There was, he said, " five hundred times more silver plate in the houses of Paris *bourgeois* than in those of London." In Paris a notary, or a solicitor, or a draper, was better lodged than a magistrate in London. In the affairs of the mind, however, he respected the freedom and sincerity of England, in spite of the brilliant insincerity of his friend Bolingbroke. It is possible that he may have heard at Bolingbroke's table Robert Hooke's reasons for preferring England before all other countries : " The first was liberty, the second was liberty, and the third was liberty."

Voltaire was enormously struck by what he regarded as the English liberality of appreciation and outlook in the funeral of Sir Isaac Newton. He saw the procession to Westminster Abbey ; he saw as pall-bearers two scientific dukes, three learned earls, and the Lord Chancellor ; he saw a great concourse of people showing respect to the greatest of physicists and one of the most simple-hearted of men. " In extreme old age," writes Mr. Parton, " his eye would kindle and his countenance light up when he spoke of

his having once lived in a land where a professor of mathematics, only because he was great in his vocation, could be buried in a temple where the ashes of kings reposed, and the highest subjects in the kingdom felt it an honour to assist in bearing thither his body." It is to Voltaire that we owe the familiar version of the story of Newton and the apple, that accident that crystallised the law of gravitation in Newton's mind.

Voltaire, being an excellent business man as well as a great writer, did not neglect his opportunities in England. To the London edition of his " La Henriade " he prefixed a dedication in English to Queen Caroline, which brought from George II. a gift of 2000 crowns. Nor was he above getting his friend to solicit for subscribers, and over the table of a coffee house he would himself sell his own work. He learnt English because, as he put it, it was a " learned language," and his knowledge of it stood him in good stead in an emergency. Once he was mobbed in Maiden Lane because he was a Frenchman. He saved the situation by crying, " Brave Englishmen ! Am I not sufficiently unhappy in not having been born among you ? "

When Pope was dying Bolingbroke tearfully spoke of how much he had " loved that man," and Pope paid Voltaire one of the most terrific compliments which even that fulsome flatterer ever achieved. " I really think," he said, " that there is something in that great man which looks as if he were placed here by mistake. When the comet appeared to us, a month or two ago, I had sometimes an imagination that it might possibly have come to our world to carry him away, as a coach comes to one's door for other visitors."[1]

THE GIBBET.
After Hogarth.

THE THAMES PIRATES

A T the end of the eighteenth century, as related by Major Arthur Griffith in his "Mysteries of Police and Crime," the plunder of "merchandise and naval stores in the river Thames had reached gigantic proportions. Previous to the establishment of the Thames river police in 1798, the commerce of the country, all the operations of merchants and shipowners, were grievously injured by these wholesale depredations, which amounted at a moderate computation to quite half a million [sterling] per annum. There were, first of all, the river-pirates, who boarded unprotected ships in the stream."

One gang actually weighed a ship's anchor, hoisted it into their boat with a complete new cable and rowed away with their spoil. These villainous rascals hung about the newly arrived vessels and cut away everything within reach. They were invariably armed with cutlasses and pistols, and were so desperate that they would fight to the death for whatever they determined to seize. They were severally known as the "heavy horsemen" and the "light horsemen," the "game watermen," the "game lightermen," the "mud larks," who still exist on the Thames and at the seaside resorts, and the "scuffle-hunters"—the latter being generally the last to get aboard while the attention of the crew would be concentrated on the more dangerous thieves.

Some of these, with the connivance of watchmen or without, would cut lighters adrift, and lead them to remote places where they could be pillaged and their contents carried away. Cargoes of coal, Russian tallow, hemp, and ashes were often secured in this way.

The "light horsemen" did a large business in the spillings, drainings, and sweepings of sugar, cargoes of coffee or rum, all of which were greatly increased by fraudulent devices and carried off with the connivance of the mates, who shared in the profit. The "heavy horsemen" were smuggled on board to steal whatever they could find. The "game watermen" worked by quickly receiving what was handed to them when cargoes were being discharged, which they conveyed at once to some secret place; the "game lightermen" were of the same class, who used their lighters to conceal stolen parcels of goods which they could afterwards dispose of. A clever trick, says Major Griffiths, was told of one of these thieves, who long did a large business in purloining oil. A merchant who imported great quantities was astonished at the constant deficiency in the amounts landed, far more than could be explained by ordinary leakage. He determined to attend at the wharf when the lighters arrived, and saw that in one of them all the casks had been stowed with their bungs downwards. He waited until the lighter was unloaded, and then visiting her, found the hold full of oil. This the lightermen impudently claimed as their perquisite; but the merchant refused to entertain the idea, and, having sent for casks, filled nine of them with the leakage. Still dissatisfied, he ordered the deck to be taken up, and found between the timbers of the lighter enough to fill five casks more.

There was nothing sacred to these rapscallions, and of course they were assisted by the "receivers" or "fences," like Fagin in "Oliver Twist," most of whom carried on in a sort of ostensible manner some respectable trade. It has been computed that there were several thousands of these men in London alone, who would buy goods without asking any questions. Many were publicans or dealers in second-hand clothes, and styled themselves "marine store" merchants. When it came to a question of gold and

silver to be melted down, there were many quite opulent people engaged in the trade who never made any inquiries as to where the materials came from. They had a command of capital and their supposed respectable positions raised them above suspicion. "These high-class operators had extensive connections" with all classes of people beyond the seas and on the continent, who would take any jewels as they were sent, having been removed from their settings so as to avoid any possible chance of recognition.

We owe the first great institution of the police force to Jeremy Bentham and Dr. Colquhoun. The latter in 1798 turned his attention to the question of the long-wanted river police. The rich cargoes of West India merchantmen lying in the Thames had long afforded opportunities to the water predatories, and the absence of any proper guard gave the chances to the persons always on the look-out to take advantage of honest men's property. Robberies were therefore of daily occurrence, and the value of the property annually stolen from incoming ships and from the wharves has been calculated, as we have said, at over half a million sterling. In these circumstances, the principal shipowners, despairing of receiving adequate protection from the Government in return for the heavy taxes they were called upon to pay, applied to Dr. Patrick Colquhoun, who was a London police magistrate with many great and good ideas of reform. He agreed to their request, and wrote a work called "A Treatise on the Commerce and Police of the River Thames," and very soon after the Government saw the wisdom of establishing an efficient water-police with headquarters at Wapping; and composed for the most part of regular sailors who were experts in all their ways.

Dr. Colquhoun was very straight-forward in his remarks about river piracy. " This species of depredations was carried on by the most desperate and depraved class of the Fraternity of nautical vagabonds aided by Receivers (equally noxious and hostile to the interests of society), who kept

PIRATE-LAND; THE OLD RIVERSIDE

old iron and junk shops in places adjacent to the river ever ready to deposit and conceal the nocturnal plunders of these marauders." It is astonishing to read of the daring of these gangs who, knowing that there was no river guard, defied the law at every point. To show the culpable impertinence of these culprits it is known that they actually established a club amongst themselves to which they subscribed so much per week in order to defray " all expenses arising from detections, penalties, and for-feitures."

Outward-bound vessels were equally liable to be plundered. Sometimes a man would enrol himself as a mariner solely for the purpose of making an arrangement to plunder the cargo

in the course of its stowage. The stories of these robberies are too trivial, though sometimes tragic, to go into detail, because they were of such frequent occurrence. Nearly all the piracies were committed through a conspirator on board the vessel, and were done through the obtaining of the original keys of the trunks and boxes, of which the receiver immediately had duplicates made so that he was able to send his accessories on board to achieve the object that they all had in view. The " night plun-derers," as Colquhoun calls them; were the most pernicious by far, as their pillage, accom-plished by a great variety of secret and artful practices; was carried out to an extent that is almost incredible to believe nowadays. They acted upon a pre-concerted plan with the cognisance of the mates and the Revenue Officers; " oiling their palm " with certain sums of money for the privilege of removing from accessible casks of rum and brandy, as much liquor as they thought fit and convenient, and from the packages just as much sugar, coffee, tea, and other useful luxuries, as could be conveyed away in the dead of the night.

There was a class of depredators who were designated Lumpers, and they were principally employed in the lading and discharging of ships and vessels in the Thames. These labourers, or " heavy horsemen," through long practice made themselves well acquainted with all the receivers of goods stolen or otherwise, and they never failed to wear such garments as would allow them to hide whatever property they chose to lay their hands upon in such a way as to defy detection. Many of them had an under-dress, which was professionally known as a " Jemmy" with pockets before and behind, and they also managed to manipulate certain pouches which were secured to the legs and upper part of their very wide trousers. Some of the ship owners and masters, being foolishly parsimonious, would not feed the Lumpers on board, while they were at work, consequently these individuals had very good excuse for going ashore several times a day ; and each time they went they were careful to carry some concealed and valuable spoil. Another class, who were great assistants to the Lumpers and other plunderers, and who got away with plenty of things of nefarious exploits, were the rat-catchers, who were necessary auxiliaries when our ships were known as the " Wooden Walls of old England."

According to the clever Colquhoun there were very few of the lightermen who could be trusted, and they had a habit of abstracting something from all the cargoes under their charge, and he adds, " they resorted to those various devices in which the minds of men in a course of Criminal Turpitude are but too fertile." And so we may be now grateful for the institution of the Thames River Police, as well as our everyday constables.

A DANDY "WHIP"

LORD BARRYMORE, one of the most famous dandies of the Regency, and intimate friend (for a time) of the Prince Regent, was celebrated for his skill as a coach-man. He was one of the founders of the Whip Club. " The first time I ever saw Lord Barrymore," says Captain Gronow, " was one fine evening while taking a stroll in Hyde Park. The weather was charming, and a great number of the *bon ton* had assembled to witness the departure of the Four-in-Hand Club. Conspicuous among all the ' turns-out ' was that of his Lordship, who drove four splendid greys unmatched in symmetry, action, and power. Lord Barrymore was, like Byron and Sir Walter Scott, club-footed." Gronow gives an unedifying account of Barrymore's choice of language when, irritated by something wrong in the harness, he addressed his servants. In addition to his " drag " Lord Barrymore " sported a very pretty Stanhope, in which he used to drive about town, accompanied by a little boy, whom the world denomin-ated his tiger. The " tiger " was Lord Barrymore's invention, and the first tiger was Alexander Lee, who in after life was well known as a musician and composer. Many not very creditable records of Lord Barrymore's amuse-ments and eccentricities are given by Henry Angelo, whereof one of the most innocent is this : " Lord Barrymore's phaeton was a very high one ; and after our midnight revels in town, I have often travelled in it with him to Wargrave. One dark night, going through Colnbrook; he kept whipping right and left, breaking the windows; delighted with the noise as he heard them crack—this he called ' fanning the day-lights.' " This story, however, may refer to Barrymore's elder brother, known as " Hellgate." The subject of this sketch was, from his lameness, called, " Cripple-gate." A third brother owned the sobri-quet of " Newgate," while the sister was, justifiably, dubbed " Billingsgate."

NELSON IN LONDON

LONDON has many memories of her great sea captain, who was living in the autumn of 1787 at No. 5 Cavendish Square with Mrs. Horatio Nelson as she was then. Exactly ten years later, 1797, he was at 141 New Bond Street, where he was suffering great pain after the Battle of Cape St. Vincent and the Expedition against Teneriffe, where he had lost his arm. "He had scarcely any intermission," writes Southey, "day or night, for three months after his return to England. Lady Nelson, at his earnest request, attended the dressing of his arm, till she had acquired sufficient resolution and skill to dress it herself. One night, during his state of suffering, after a day of constant pain, Nelson retired early to bed in hope of enjoying some respite by means of laudanum. He was at that time lodging in Bond Street, and the family was soon disturbed by a mob knocking loudly and violently at the door. The news of Duncan's victory had been made public, and the house was not illuminated. But when the mob was told that Admiral Nelson lay there in bed, badly wounded, the foremost of them made answer : ' You shall hear no more from us to-night.' "

Four years later Lord and Lady Nelson were living in Arlington Street. Mr. Haslewood, Lord Nelson's executor, visited them there, and on one occasion was present at a very important interview. " I was breakfasting," he writes, to Sir Harris Nicolas, " with Lord and Lady Nelson at their lodgings in Arlington Street, and a cheerful conversation was passing on indifferent subjects when Lord Nelson spoke of something which had been done or said by ' dear Lady Hamilton,' upon which Lady Nelson rose from her chair, and exclaimed with much vehemence, ' I am sick of hearing of dear Lady Hamilton, and am resolved that you shall give up either her or me.' Lord Nelson with perfect calmness said, ' Take care, Fanny, what you say ; I love you sincerely ; but I cannot forget my obligations to Lady Hamilton, or speak of her otherwise than with affection and admiration.' Without one soothing word or gesture, but muttering something about her mind being made up, Lady Nelson left the room, and shortly after drove from the house. They never lived together afterwards."

The Hamiltons were living with William Beckford at No. 22 Grosvenor Square when Lord Nelson returned to London after the Battle of the Nile. He was constantly in the house at this time, when there happened to be a general scarcity of bread. So scarce indeed was that commodity, that people of every rank in life denied themselves the use of it at dinner. One night, Lord Nelson was dining at Mr. Beckford's and found no bread on the dinner-table, whereupon he immediately asked for it in spite of the fact that such a request was contrary to etiquette. One of the servants told him that bread was not served at Mr. Beckford's dinner-table. Irritated by the refusal, Nelson took a shilling from his pocket, and ordered the servant to procure him a loaf then and there, remarking at the same time that it was hard that he who had fought so strenuously for bread, should be denied it by Englishmen.

Another favourite resort of Nelson was the house of his old friend and agent, Alexander Davidson, whose residence was on the south side of St. James' Square, and whose office was at the other side of the house in Pall Mall. It was in Pall Mall that Charles Lamb first made Nelson his hero. " Wasn't you sorry," wrote Elia to Hazlitt on November 10, 1805, " for Lord Nelson ? I have followed him in fancy ever since I saw him walking in Pall Mall (I was prejudiced against him before) looking just as a hero should look ; and I have been very much cut about it indeed. He was the only pretence of a great man we had, nobody is left of any name at all. His secretary died by his side. I imagined him a Mr. Scott, to be the man you met at Hume's, but I learn from Mrs. Hume that it is not the same." The conqueror of Trafalgar was the subject of one of Charles Lamb's epigrams :

Off with Briareus, and his hundred hands,
Our Nelson with one arm, unconquer'd stands !

The only time that Nelson met the Duke of Wellington was in Downing Street, and the interview took place in the small waiting-room in the old Colonial Office. The story of their interesting encounter has already been given in this collection.

Nelson's famous Aboukir coffin was kept in readiness for him by Peddiesin's, the undertaker in Brewer Street, and before embarking for the last time he went there in person to give instructions about it. He had given orders for a large quantity of cabin furniture to be sent on board

the ship, and the upholsterer called with his account in the middle of a farewell party. Nelson, however, saw him in the dining-room and was informed that everything was packed and would be taken in a waggon from a certain inn at six o'clock. " And you," said Lord Nelson, " go to the inn, Mr. A—, and see them off." " I shall, my lord ; I

LORD NELSON'S VILLA AT MERTON

shall be there punctually at six." " A quarter before six, Mr. A—," insisted the admiral, " be there a quarter before ; to that quarter of an hour I owe everything in life."

Mr. W. Clarke Russell has pointed out in his " Life of Nelson " how thoroughly Nelson had mastered on shore the manœuvres by which he was so soon to conquer the combined French and Spanish fleets. In his last letter to his old friend, Lord Sidmouth, the Admiral wrote : " On Tuesday forenoon, if Superior Powers do not prevent me, I will be in Richmond Park, and shall be happy in taking you by the hand and to wish you a most perfect restoration to health." Years afterwards, Lord Sidmouth would tell how Nelson, at this last meeting with him, explained the coming battle by

After J. P. Knight A.R.A.

THE ONLY MEETING OF NELSON AND WELLINGTON IN THE OLD COLONIAL OFFICE
From the Picture by J. P. Knight

diagrams on his little study-table. "Rodney," he said, "broke the line in one point; I will break it in two." Lord Sidmouth had inscribed upon his study-table a brief record of this remarkable scene: "On the 10th day of September, 1805, Vice-Admiral Lord Viscount Nelson described to Lord Sidmouth, upon this table, the manner in which he intended to engage the combined fleets of France and Spain, which he expected shortly to meet. He stated that he should attack in two lines, led by himself and Admiral Collingwood, and felt confident that he should capture either their van and centre, on the 21st of October following, in the glorious battle of Trafalgar."

On January 5, 1806, on Sunday morning, the public were admitted to the Great Hall of Greenwich Hospital to view the corpse of Nelson. The crowd had been waiting for a long time in a state of great eagerness and tension, and it was estimated that more than ten thousand people had to be refused admission at the doors. The same scene took place on the second and third days, but owing to the arrival of some troops of horse guards who co-operated with the volunteers, the crowd was controlled more effectually, though many people sustained injuries.

High above the corpse in the funeral saloon there was suspended a canopy of black velvet festooned with gold. The festoons were decorated with the plume of triumph known as the *chelenk*. This was ornamented with Nelson's coronet and with the stern of the Spanish Admiral's ship which had already been quartered to his arms. Surmounting the whole on a gold field encircled by a wreath of gold, the one word "Trafalgar" was written in characters of mourning.

On Wednesday the 8th the aquatic side of the procession took place, and Nelson's remains, brought on a state barge to Whitehall, were removed to the Admiralty amidst a double line of troops, minute guns were fired the whole time of the procession by water, and the flags of all vessels in the river were lowered in the masts." Captain Hardy carried the banner of emblems during this procession of barges, which was nearly a mile long.

Before dawn on the next day vast

NELSON'S TOMB IN THE CRYPT OF ST. PAUL'S CATHEDRAL

military preparations were in progress throughout London. By ten o'clock more than a hundred and sixty carriages, sixty of which were mourning coaches; had assembled in Hyde Park. All the cavalry and infantry regiments quartered within a radius of a hundred miles, who had taken part in the campaigns in Egypt after the victory at the Nile, were drawn up in St. James's Park. There was also a detachment of flying artillery together with twelve field pieces, and their ammunition, tumbrils, &c. The procession from the Admiralty to St. Paul's was headed by the Duke of York and his Staff. It started at about eleven in the morning.

The City Officers were waiting at

Temple Bar to take their places in the Procession. "Upon arriving at the Cathedral," writes J. Timbs, the well-known London chronicler, "they entered by the west gate and the great west door (fronting Ludgate Street), ranging themselves according to their ranks. The seats were placed under the dome, in each archway in front of the piers and in the gallery over the choir. The seats beneath the dome took the shape of the dome and held 3056 persons : from the dome to the great west door, behind an iron railing, persons were allowed to stand. The body was placed on a bier, erected on a raised platform, opposite the eagle lectern." At the end of the service a procession was formed to the grave of Nelson.

NELSON'S MONUMENT IN ST. PAUL'S CATHEDRAL

Over the coffin a great funeral canopy of state was borne by six admirals. It was of black velvet, and before the body was lowered it was removed so that the spectators might see more easily the splendidly decorated coffin of the national hero. "There was," says the writer in the *Gentleman's Magazine*, "an excellent contrivance for letting down the body into the grave. A bier rose from the oblong aperture under the dome, for the purpose of supporting the coffin. This bier was raised by invisible machinery, the apparatus being totally concealed below the pavement of the church. The procession departed in nearly the same order in which it arrived. When the Duke of Clarence ascended the steps of St. Paul's, he suddenly stopped and took hold of the colours that were borne by the *Victory's* men, and after conferring with one of the gallant tars, he burst into tears. On the entrance of the tattered flags, within the Communion rails the Prince of Wales, after conferring with the Duke of Clarence, sent and requested they might be brought as near the grave as possible, and on observing them although at some distance, the tears fell from his Royal Highness."

The coffin began slowly to descend into the grave, and just as his flag which covered it was on the point of being withdrawn, the sailors who held it with one accord rent it in pieces, each one of which would be treasured from father to son as a record of the great national hero who meant even more to the seamen of England. The interment being completed, Garter proclaimed the style of the last ceremony of all, after which the Comptroller, Treasurer, and Steward of the dead Admiral broke their staves and handed the pieces to Garter who threw them into the grave.

Every Prince of the Royal Family

had taken part in this final ceremony of homage, but there was that in the hearts of the common people which no ceremony in the world could express. For them, as for the gunner of the Victory, Nelson had passed beyond the confines of ordinary manhood, and for them even the victory of Trafalgar was dwarfed by the death of him to whom it was owed. "The people of England," writes Southey, "grieved that funeral ceremonies and public monuments and posthumous rewards were all which they could bestow upon him, whom the King, the legislature and the nation would have alike delighted to honour; whom every tongue would have blessed; whose presence in every village through which he might have passed would have wakened the church bells, have given schoolboys a holiday, have drawn children from their sports to gaze upon him, and 'old men from the chimney corner,' to look upon Nelson ere they died."

A FAMOUS DWARF

THE Chevalier Desseasau attracted much notice in London in the early years of the reign of George III. Circumstances had compelled him to leave his native Prussia for England, where he soon became acquainted in London with Dr. Johnson, Goldsmith, and other well-known men, while his favourite resort was Old Anderton's coffee house in Fleet Street. Debt brought him to the Fleet Prison, but his sense of honour was so well recognised that he was allowed to walk about London freely during the daytime. His quaint little figure, gold-headed cane and sword, became a familiar sight; and his habit of writing and "spouting" poetry a good joke. Desseasau died in Fleet Market; aged more than 70, in 1775, and was buried in St. Bride's churchyard.

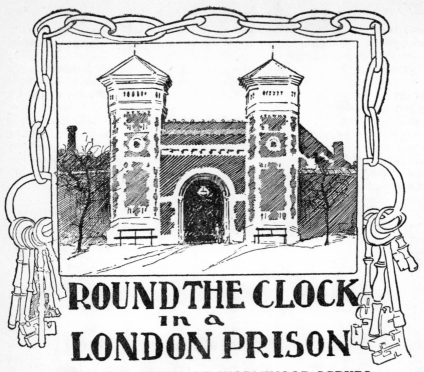

ROUND THE CLOCK in a LONDON PRISON

THE DAY'S WORK AT WORMWOOD SCRUBS

WHEN judge and magistrate have meted out their sentences, and bench and dock are silent, a quiet bustle begins in the precincts of the courts. Black Maria is gathering her fares for the prisons. The door of the van is backed up close to where the prisoners issue one by one, but outside may generally be seen a cluster of friends shouting a send-off to some of them. "By-bye, Billy! See you in a moon an' a 'alf [six weeks]! Do it on yer 'ead, ole man!"

A few old stagers in the van seek to hearten up the rest. One has a packet of cigarettes, and hands round a last whiff apiece. Some one else starts a chorus. The warder in charge is lenient.

Black Maria shall be driven to Wormwood Scrubs, known to felonry as "The Scrubs," that collection of great pentagonal buildings, west of Paddington, on the outskirts of London. Jabez Balfour, entering the portals to begin a sentence of fourteen years' penal servitude, tells us that though he had often noticed the pile "when travelling on the Great Western Railway, to and from my house in Oxfordshire," he had never "troubled to think what it was." He adds (in the fifth chapter of that impressive work, "My Prison Life"): "As 'Calais' was written on the heart of Queen Mary, so I am sure is ' Wormwood Scrubs ' stamped on the brain of every English convict who passes its portals for the first time."

Through solid wooden gates the van is driven into the outer court of the prison, and through iron gates into the second. A big bell has clanged, and everywhere there is a flourishing and jangling of keys. The door of the van is thrown open, and as the prisoners descend and are marshalled in a row the officer who has conducted them calls out the number, which is answered with an " All correct " by the principal warder in waiting. The contrasts presented by the prisoners are sometimes very curious—the silk hat and morning coat beside the tatters of the tramp and so forth ; and some men show a face of utter woe and some are unconcerned and jaunty. This is the first stage of the reception.

Then they are marched into what is called the Reception Hall. It is evening ere the new-comers reach the prison, and with the exception of a few who are acting as orderlies they would see no other prisoners. Everything is chill and silent. The " halls " of a modern prison are, as Jabez Balfour says, " great brick barns filled with iron staircases, landings and cells."

The prisoners are passed on to the bathroom, and after the first bath in prison comes the supreme transformation : the felon must don his felon's livery. For convicts it is a knickerbocker suit, with red-striped black stockings ; the short-term men (those up to two years) wear trousers ; and every article of attire is besprinkled with the broad arrow.

Hard upon the toilet follows an interview with the doctor, whose word so profoundly influences the destinies of prisoners. It is the doctor who decides what kind of labour a prisoner is fit for —first-class hard labour, industrial labour, light labour—what diet he shall be placed on, &c. In general the doctor sees the new-comers in one of the halls or wards, but he may order a prisoner to be brought to him in his private office for a special word of advice or even of consolation. Some convicts, hurled on a sudden from eminence in a social or official sphere, enter prison half demented and wholly dazed under a staggering sentence of penal servitude. Such unhappy creatures a wise and humane doctor takes in hand forthwith, reasons with them out of his experience, lets in a little kindly light upon the first hour of darkness, and bids them play the man. Such prisoners also he is careful to keep a watch upon. Let it be added that the returned convict often hails the doctor as an old friend, asks after his health, hopes the governor and the staff in general and their families are keeping fit, and the " hotel " is running as well as ever.

It is now a question of supper—a very late hour for supper in prison. In a recent volume, curiously entitled " A Holiday in Gaol," by Frederick Martyn, the writer speaks humorously of his first supper at "The Scrubs": "We were ushered into a room where there was a bright fire burning, and told to sit in a row on a form facing a table at which a warder sat with a book in front of him. Presently a khaki-clad prisoner in his shirt sleeves appeared with a large can of oatmeal porridge and some eight-ounce loaves of brown bread. ' Who sez a late dinner ? ' he asked in a subdued tone, as if he didn't want to disturb the warder sitting at the desk. ' This is the way we live here, me boys ; ain't you glad as you've come ? ' "

Supper over, it is probably close on

ten o'clock, an unheard-of hour for prisoners to be up. Night warders in shoes of felt are on duty in the quiet halls as the new-comers are guarded to their cells. A prison cell, beheld for the first time, is another shock. Spotlessly clean it is (or should be) and excellently ventilated, but about as comely an abode as a scullery. Bare walls (the stark rules of the place suspended upon one), bare floor, a small deal table and stool, a few primitive utensils in tin, a narrow window on high, a diminutive shelf, a door with a spy-hole for the warder. But the ugliest piece of furniture in the cell is the naked plank—no morsel of mattress or shred of coverlet on which the prisoner is to sleep. This Spartan bed forms, as it were, the introduction to life in prison, but is a form of penance which the doctor remits at his discretion, and many delinquents have never known the plank.

There are two nights during a sentence of penal servitude or imprisonment on which it may be conjectured that few prisoners ever sleep : the first and the last. Old stagers, or recidivists, no doubt experience but little discomfort ; but to the unhappy creature who has never before felt the taint of prison, and who, when the door of the bleak cell closes on him, realises his awful break with the world, the first night is often one of incommunicable horror. Indeed, during a crisis of this sort the prisoner is sometimes lodged in a special cell connected with the infirmary.

At six in the morning the din of the bell wakens the prison to the daily round. The warders, whose day is long and arduous, are already about. Prisoners must turn out, and scour and dress themselves and put their cells in order. Presently another bell goes,

and now the prison is well astir. From hour to hour the huge machine moves with a terrible precision, a terrible monotony, and very little noise. The convict " cleaners " come round collecting slops and replenishing water-cans. Breakfast is served. Jabez Balfour writes : " It was my first of nearly 4000 identical breakfasts, and consisted of a pint of impossible tea and an eight-ounce brown loaf—but this eight-ounce loaf is not so ample as it may seem, for a substantial portion of every loaf consists of crust. The wise prisoner soaks his loaf in his tea."

After this, the silent world is paraded for chapel. At Wormwood Scrubs, which is not a convict establishment, but what is called a " local " prison (a prison, that is to say, for short-term men), there is always, among the ten or twelve hundred inmates, a certain crowd of convicts beginning a sentence that may be for three years or for life. The convicts, who are kept apart from the locals, enter chapel first, and take the front seats. " Then," as Martyn correctly says, " come the hard-labour men of the general class, who can see the convicts, but cannot see any class superior to themselves. Next in order are the 'Star' men [first offenders] ; behind them again come the 'Second Division,' and right at the back are the 'Debtors,' who can see all classes in the prison, but cannot be seen themselves."

The warders occupy raised seats, the better to observe their flock, but a good deal of surreptitious talking goes on in chapel. Silence is the rule throughout the prison, but a dumb prison would soon become a mad-house, and this prescription is easily and habitually evaded. During hymns and responses new-comers are questioned about their sentences, and old chums recognise each other and pass round the news of prison and of the world they have temporarily quitted. No newspaper is ever admitted into prison, but what is happening is known there. As a warder once said to the writer : " If you want to know what's doing outside, come into prison ! "

Conversation is renewed, as far as twenty-three hours of whitewashed cell, but was largely made up of the little tit-bits of news from outside that went round the circle at such times. The silent system is more or less a dead letter, for it is not and cannot be so strictly enforced as to prevent communication, and, notwithstanding the watching warders, conversation is

THE BLACKSMITH'S SHOP AT WORMWOOD SCRUBS

chance allows, at exercise. In fit weather every prisoner gets an hour's exercise, and this is usually taken after chapel. The exercise ground at Wormwood is a fair wide space with a grass plot and elliptical asphalted paths, where about eighty prisoners take the air together, walking in Indian file. This, says an ex-convict, " was the brightest hour of the whole twenty-four for me. This brightness did not come altogether from the open air and the restful green of the grass, which were pleasant enough in all conscience after

pretty brisk at exercise time, and at many other times too for that matter."

To this brief interlude of ease succeed the serious tasks of the day. A new prisoner may find himself idle a while before the right sort of employment is found for him ; but for all the rest the day's labour is ready prepared ; and in cell, workshop, and hall the effort is made to carry on a variety of industries. Prison labour constitutes a very difficult problem. It is impossible to teach a useful trade to men serving short sentences, and there are always old and decrepit prisoners fit only for the infirmary, and half-witted creatures who ought to be anywhere but in prison, and tramps and other wastrels who have no use for work of any kind. For prisoners whom it is more or less profitable to instruct, Wormwood Scrubs has roomy and airy workshops, in which tailors, carpenters, shoemakers, tinsmiths, and others are engaged, not altogether unsuccessfully, in earning their eight marks per diem. If there is a really lucrative industry in prison, as mat-making once was, the trade unions raise an outcry (though the interference with free labour could never be serious), and at present the principal work is done for Government. Jabez Balfour at the outset of his term was put on mail-bags. " I do not suppose I had ever done any sewing in my life. After breakfast some heavy canvas was tossed into the cell ; a ball of thread, a lump of wax, and two large needles were handed to me, and I was told to begin to sew it as strongly and neatly as I could. . . . My output for the first day was exactly half a bag, and very badly done at that. I feared that I should be severely reprimanded, and perhaps lose some marks ; the fear spurred me on to renewed efforts, but I suppose that through the spy-hole the warder had seen that I was doing my best, and far from being reprimanded, I was rather encouraged."

The first interruption of work is dinner. Meals are early in prison, and prisoners as a rule are sharp-set. At 11.30 the orderlies, under the supervision of their warders, are carrying round the dinner-baskets ; and, according to the day, it is boiled fresh beef with bread and potatoes, or suet pudding with bread and potatoes, or haricot beans and a cube of fat bacon with bread and potatoes, or, on Sundays,

preserved meat, known to the lags as " Harriet Lane." Lord William Nevill, in his reminiscences of penal servitude, states that prisoners badly need a larger supply of fresh vegetables.

A convict is more liberally fed than a short-term man, and a three-months man than a one-month man, and prisoners can be punished with change or diminution of diet. The thoughts of many prisoners run a good deal upon food, and Frederick Martyn tells how he suffered from a little practical joke over the Christmas Day menu. A fellow prisoner had told him : " They gives you roast beef, plum duff, an' a pint o' beer for dinner, an' 'addicks for tea." Martyn's warder was privy to the jest. At the regular hour a dinner-tin was handed in to him. " So far there was nothing out of the ordinary course, but the warder made a remark as he put the tin in that was a great departure from rule. ' Roast beef course,' he said jocosely ; ' beer and duff to follow.' Then he banged the door, and left me to my long-anticipated enjoyment. . . . I took the top tin out of the other . . . the tin only contained the usual dinner set down in the dietary for that day of the week. . . . Truth compels me to say that my chagrin was so bitter as to cause me actually to sink down on my stool, hide my head on my arms, and blubber."

Prisoners being served, the warders go off to their own dinner, so that the whole interval is of the duration of about an hour and a half. Many men spend the major part of it in reading ; and as the library of an establishment like Wormwood Scrubs is nowadays very well furnished (from fiction and *belles lettres* to history, science, and philosophy), this interlude is greatly prized by book-lovers. It is at the dinner-hour that the chaplain and his assistant generally make their rounds.

The return of the warders is the signal for the resumption of work, which is continued until supper-time at about 4.30—tea or cocoa with bread, or a pint of stirabout (" skilly "), according to the prisoner's sentence or his class in gaol. For the staff of the prison, from the governor and his deputy down to the clerks in their office, there is never less than a full day's work to be got through. The governor has his rounds and holds his court. The chief warder has his rounds and holds his court. The chaplain has his visiting to do, the library to supervise, reports to prepare, representatives of aid societies to interview, letters to write to prisoners' friends. The doctor and his assistant have a score of multifarious duties : sick prisoners in cells or the infirmary, complaints about malingering to be investigated, petitions of prisoners regarding work or food or health, and the new arrivals to be attended to every evening. The schoolmaster is fully occupied in his own department. The warders, from principals to juniors, have their especial tasks. There are warders who attend solely to the discipline of the prison, and warders who attend solely to its industries. In the great kitchen, the master cook and his convict orderlies are baking or boiling or stewing during most of the day. The prison barbers in one department are cropping heads, the photographers in another are taking realistic (and most unflattering) portraits, and in a third the officials of the finger-print system are engaged upon those simple yet marvellous impressions—no two alike !—which in recent years have led to the undoing of so many old offenders. The inspector of prisons, the visiting justices, the visiting chaplain, the comptroller of industries, and other important persons must be received on their respective days of call. There are days on which prisoners write letters home, and days on which they are privileged to receive a visit from relative or friend. Almost every evening there are prisoners to take in, almost every morning prisoners to send out.

Towards half-past six in the evening the vast criminal hive begins to sink into repose. The day's work is put out from the cells ; scissors and other tools are collected ; and the cells are then locked for the night. There is still another period for reading, or the mild pastime of slate and pencil. At eight o'clock lights are extinguished in the cells. The felon's day of fourteen hours is ended.

ST. PETER'S-AD-VINCULA CHAPEL IN THE TOWER OF LONDON

THE LAST HOURS OF MONMOUTH

SHORTLY after the Battle of Sedgemoor, Monmouth was conveyed from Ringwood to London in a coach together with his fellow prisoner, Grey. The Duke was under the escort of an officer whose orders were to kill him in the event of a rescue being attempted. The party arrived at Vauxhall at the end of three days. A State barge was in waiting for them, and they were immediately conducted to Whitehall Stairs where the rebels were, in turn, to meet the King of England face to face. Monmouth was scarcely equal to such an ordeal, though he himself had pleaded for it. Unlike his fellow prisoner, Grey, who had chatted agreeably on field sports and dogs and horses all through that grim journey, the Duke had shown himself already overwhelmed by his desperate position. In this mood, with his hands tied behind him by a silken cord, he was ushered into his Royal uncle's presence.

Monmouth wept on his knees at the King's feet, protesting that he had neither written nor read that rebellious Declaration which had spoken so openly and so flagrantly of James. "Do you expect me to believe," asked the King, "that you set your hand to a paper of such moment without knowing what it contained?" Monmouth, who had nothing to say to this, hinted eagerly that he might yet be reconciled to his uncle's faith. James offered immediate spiritual help, but made no mention of reprieve. "Is there then no hope?" asked the prisoner as the King turned away from him in silence. Monmouth then rose to his feet and retired with a show at least of his old manhood. Grey, who followed immediately afterwards, seems to have astonished James by his disdainful fortitude. But his courage availed him as little as Monmouth's weakness and both prisoners were conducted by water to the Tower. On the way the

402

Duke begged Dartmouth to intercede for him. " I know, my lord," he said, " that you loved my father. For his sake, for God's sake, try if there be any room for mercy." Dartmouth answered that the King had spoken truth when he had said that for such treason as Monmouth's there was no pardon in this world.

But in the Tower, where so many of his race had lingered during their last hours, Monmouth thought always of pardon. His wife visited him and with her came the keeper of the Privy Seal, the Earl of Clarendon. Monmouth received her distantly and spoke earnestly to Clarendon of pardon. The same evening Turner, Bishop of Ely, and Ken, Bishop of Bath and Wells, visited the prisoner with a message from the King. It was Monday night already, and on Wednesday morning Monmouth must assuredly pay the penalty of death. He wrote numerous letters of appeal to the King, but all were useless. He rejected, however, the absolution of the Roman Catholic Church. At the same time he shocked, by the view of his liaison with Lady Wentworth, the Anglican Bishops, Ken and Turner, who refused to administer the Sacrament to him.

On the morning of his death the Duke requested that Dr. Thomas Tenison should visit him. He hoped for more leniency from that divine but he was mistaken, for Dr. Tenison, too, refused to administer the Eucharist to Monmouth.

And now that the final scene was very near, terror of death and longing for life passed out of the Duke's heart. He became utterly apathetic and received his wife and his children without the slightest emotion, though the bystanders wept at the misery of this deserted wife.

At precisely ten o'clock the coach of the Lieutenant of the Tower was ready to convey Monmouth to his death. Urged by the Duke to accompany him, his spiritual advisers reminded him that it would be their duty to continue their exhortations to the very last. Monmouth was firm and tranquil now and, passing through the ranks of the guards, he saluted them with a smile and ascended the scaffold with quiet dignity. All over Tower Hill the people waited in absolute silence to hear the last words of the man who was still the idol of their hearts. " I shall say little," he began. " I come here not to speak, but to die. I die a Protestant of the Church of England." Here he was interrupted by the Bishops, who reminded him that he was not a member of the Anglican Church unless he accepted the orthodox view of non-resistance. Monmouth went on to speak of Lady Wentworth, maintaining that he could not die without publicly expressing his unalterable love and devotion to her. At this point the Bishops again interrupted, protesting against the expression on the scaffold of sentiments which had already deprived the Duke of the last Sacrament of the Church. They pressed again the orthodox views of non-resistance upon Charles II.'s son, but their abstract arguments left him unconvinced. But when they passed from abstractions to remind him of all those gallant followers whose corpses had remained on Sedgemoor, Monmouth was touched and said, " I do own that. I am sorry that it ever happened." The Bishops then prayed with him fervently and Monmouth took part in all their petitions until a blessing was invoked on James II. The Duke listened to this in silence. " Sir," exclaimed one of the Bishops, " do you not pray for the King with us?"

After some struggle with his innermost feelings, he responded, "Amen." But when he was urged to speak to the soldiers and the people on the subject of obedience to the King's Government, he refused absolutely. "I will make no speeches," he said. "Only ten words, my lord," urged the Bishop. Monmouth turned away and called his servant, into whose hand he put a tooth-pick case, which was considered to be a symbol of unhappy love. "Give it to that person," he said and passed on to the executioner, John Ketch. "Here are six guineas for you," he said. "Do not hack me as you did my Lord Russell. I have heard that you actually struck him three or four times. My servant will give you some more gold if you do the work well." Monmouth then felt the edge of the axe and expressed doubt as to its being sharp enough. After this, being already undressed, he laid his head on the block while the Divines repeated more and more earnestly: "God accept your repentance! God accept your imperfect repentance!"

John Ketch then proceeded to his business. He struck an agitated blow which inflicted a slight wound. Monmouth staggered to his feet from the block, and looked at the excutioner in silent reproach. The Duke resumed his place, and again and yet again that agitated stroke was repeated. But still the neck of the Duke of Monmouth remained upon the block while his whole body writhed in agony. As the horrified fury of the crowd increased,

Ketch flung down the axe, exclaiming with a curse, "I cannot do it, my heart fails me." "Take up the axe, man," said the Sheriff, to which the mob responded with, "Fling him over the rails." Ketch at last obeyed the Sheriff, and succeeded in killing Monmouth with two more blows. A knife however, was necessary to complete the act of decapitation. Ketch was conveyed away under a strong guard and so saved from the crowd who would undoubtedly have torn him in pieces had they been able to get at him. Handkerchiefs meanwhile were dipped in Monmouth's blood, for he was regarded by the vast majority not as a rebel but as a martyr of the Protestant faith.

Monmouth's head and body were placed in a coffin covered with black velvet, and were deposited beneath the communion table of Saint Peter's Chapel in the Tower, where rested so many other famous and restless rebels. "Thither," in Macaulay's words, "have been carried, through successive ages, by the rude hands of gaolers, without one mourner following, the bleeding relics of men who had been the captains of armies, the leaders of parties, the oracles of senates, and the ornaments of courts." Here were interred, after execution, Queen Catherine Howard, Anne Boleyn, Lady Jane Grey, and also the Protector Somerset, Sir Thomas More, and Robert Devereux, Earl of Essex— all beheaded. Within four years the remains of Jeffreys were placed close to those of the Duke of Monmouth.

AETER H. ALKEN

TATTERSALL'S

NEAR the corner of the Brompton Road, just where it turns away from Knightsbridge, there is a triangular space of greensward, with three plane trees, enclosed within a modestly ornamental iron railing. This, until London spread out like the billows of the sea, was an actual village green and had its maypole, like the Strand. Now it is flanked by the farge front of Tattersall's, and otherwise neighboured by some of the most famous of the London shops.

Tattersall's is renowned all over the world as what may be called the chief temple of English sport. There the great horse sales are held ; the betting which takes place there regulates that of the country at large ; among those who gather in the vast sale-room which was rather clumsily pictured by Gustave Dore may be seen at one time or another all the most eminent sportsmen of their day and generation. Tattersall's is a national institution. If it suddenly ceased to exist there would follow an alarming dislocation of society here and elsewhere.

And yet it is only a family affair; carried on at present by two brothers Tattersall. A family affair it has continued to be through several generations. The first Tattersall was born in 1724, and died in 1795. His Christian name was Richard, and he became stud or training groom to the second Duke of Kingston. But no ordinary stud groom was he. Educated at Burnley Grammar School, he imbibed the political leanings of a large part of Lancashire, and left home because his father would not let him join the Jacobites. This shows gentlemanly tastes, which were always recognised in him, after his unimpeachable integrity, as his leading characteristics. The Duke of Kingston, by whom he was employed, was the brother of Lady Mary Wortley Montagu, sometimes the friend of Pope and sometimes not quite so much his friend. The Duchess, who, when he undertook to sell the stud of his former patron, became his active and determined opponent, was that Elizabeth Chudleigh who shocked a somewhat lax generation by attending

405

a ball in a costume rather too readily suggesting that of mother Eve.

The position which Richard Tattersall held was one in which it was possible for an honest man to do very well. In 1779 he was able to buy from Lord Bolingbroke a horse named Highflyer, at the then unprecedented price of £2500. He was at that time officially described as " Richard Tattersall, in the Parish of St. George's in the East, Liberty of Westminster and County of Middlesex, gentleman." Up to that day there had been no such horse as Highflyer. A picture of it was painted by Stubbs, who was an Associate of the Royal Academy, and whose fame as a painter of horses has endured to our own time. To be the owner of Highflyer was at once to become eminent. When Richard Tattersall's own portrait was painted, to be hung in the famous " rooms," and to be preserved by his family, there was included, at his own request, the proud statement that " Highflyer is not to be sold."

It was probably this fortunate investment that suggested the establishment of a horse mart on a then unprecedented scale. At any rate, the " regulations " of Tattersall's, something too sacred to alter, bear date a year after the purchase. The site decided upon was not the village green at Knightsbridge. That was too far away from the world

RICHARD TATTERSALL

of fashion. Just the space that was needed was to be found at Grosvenor Place, next to St. George's Hospital. A narrow lane led down to it, and it was said to be celebrated for nightingales and footpads. Here Richard Tattersall, already a wealthy man, the possessor, not only of Highflyer, but also of a residence named Highflyer Hall, established what soon became known as " The Corner." There at once clustered all who were interested in horses or sport. These included the Prince of Wales, afterwards George the Fourth, the Marquis of Queensbury, disparagingly known as " old Q.," and a general ruck of peers, bishops, soldiers, admirals, and country squires. Tattersall's, in fact, at once took rank as easily the first of the institutions of its kind.

Richard Tattersall, " one of nature's noblemen," became the personal friend of many of the most eminent of his customers. It is recorded of him that at his place, New Barns, near Ely, he regaled such choice spirits as the Prince of Wales, Charles James Fox, and William Windham. His port was the best in England his guests assured him, and they were none of them inexperienced judges. But " Old Tatt," as he came to be called, was not a frivolous, or showy, or hard-drinking man. He had personal qualities of the highest class. A fine, substantially built, gentleman-farmer-looking man one pictures him, with a calm air and a commanding head. A man, too, with an easy and assured style. His popularity was so great that he was said to be " free of the road," as no highwayman would molest him, and even a pickpocket returned him his handkerchief " with compliments." " From his indefatigable industry, and the justice of his dealings," it was said of him at his death, which, as we have said, took place in 1795, " he acquired a degree of affluence which was exercised for the general good without ostentation."

Such was the founder of Tattersall's. The place itself was something much more than a horse mart from the beginning. The proprietor fitted up two rooms for the convenience of the members of the Jockey Club. They were called " subscription rooms," and they soon became the favourite resort of the sporting world. There the odds were arranged ; and the betting at Tattersall's regulated sporting prices at all places to which they could be conveyed in the days before telegraphs. They regulate the betting in all places between Knightsbridge and the ends of the earth in our own.

One Tattersall has followed another down to the present day. There was an " Edmund I." and an " Edmund II.," with " more to follow," as the newspaper reporters say. Some of the Tattersall's had literary and artistic interests. It was " Old Tatt " who began it, by becoming proprietor of the *Morning Post*. There was a George Tattersall who wrote a book on " The Lakes of England," and was editor of the *Era*. He was an architect also, and designed " The Palladium," which stands in the centre of the present selling mart, something half fountain and half memorial to George the Fourth, a classical work, with a dome on four pillars, surmounted by what is not nowadays easily recognised as a bust of the first gentleman in Europe.

Tattersall's removed to its present situation, near the Brompton Road, in 1865. One enters the building through a hugh arched gateway and almost immediately is standing in the world-renowned mart, with " The Palladium " in the centre, and in the far corner to the right is the dignified and spacious rostrum from which so many of the best horses that ever come under the hammer are stated to be " going, going, gone." There is an arcaded gallery round this splendidly lighted hall, and beyond the walls of the quadrangle, on both sides, there are great lengths of stables, generally full.

And here, on Mondays and Thursdays, the great sales take place, and here, also, in the rooms that stand on either side of the entrance, the " tone " is given to the sporting world.

THE BELLMAN OF HOLBORN

IN London, and probably other English cities, in the seventeenth century, the Bellman was the recognised term for what we would now call a night watchman, being derived from the hand-bell which the man carried in order to give alarm in case of fire. In the Luttrell Collection of Broadsides (British Museum) is one dated 1683-4, entitled "A Copy of Verses presented by Isaac Ragg, Bellman, to his Masters and Mistresses of Holbourn Division, in the parish of St Giles's-in-the-Fields." It is headed by a wood-cut representing Isaac in professional accoutrements, a pointed pole in the left hand, and in the right a bell, while his lantern hangs from his jacket in front. Below is a series of verses, on St. Andrew's Day, King Charles the First's Birthday, St. Thomas's Day, Christmas Day, St. John's Day, Childermas Day, New Year's Day, on the thirtieth of January, &c., all of them very proper and very insufferable ; the "prologue" is, indeed, the only specimen worth giving here, being the expression of Mr. Ragg's official duty ; it is as follows :

Time, Master, calls your bellman to his task,
To see your doors and windows are all fast,
And that no villany or foul crime be done
To you or yours in absence of the sun.
If any base lurker I do meet,
In private alley or in open street,

THE BELLMAN OF HOLBORN

You shall have warning by my timely call,
And so God bless you and give rest to all.

In a similar, but unadorned broadside, dated 1666, Thomas Law, bellman, greets his masters of "St. Giles, Cripplegate, within the Freedom," in twenty-three dull stanzas, of which the last may be subjoined :

No sooner hath St. Andrew crowned November,
But Boreas from the North brings cold December,
And I have often heard a many say,
He brings the winter month Newcastle way ;
For comfort here of poor distressed souls,
Would he had with him brought a fleet of coals !

It seems to have been customary for the bellman to go about at a certain season of the year, probably Christmas, amongst the householders of his district, giving each a copy of his broadside—firing a broadside at each, as it were—and expecting from each in return some small gratuity, as an addition to his ordinary salary. The execrable character of his poetry is indicated by the contempt with which the wits speak of "bellman's verses."

Robert Herrick has a little poem giving his friends a blessing in the form of the nightly addresses of the Bellman :

From noise of scare fires rest ye free,
From murders benedicitie ;
From all mischances that may fright
Your pleasing slumbers in the night.
From Chambers' "Book of Days."

THE GREAT STORM OF 1703

HOW IT WRECKED LONDON AND MADE A WRITER'S FORTUNE

LITTLE WILD STREET in the Old Clare Market region of London is no more. It has been swept away in the great Kingsway improvement. But the few Londoners who really wander about London remember it, and they remember, too, a dingy old chapel which stood there, This chapel had for nearly two hundred years been famous for its connection with the GREAT STORM which devastated England in November 1703. The effects of this storm on land and sea were so dreadful that a public fast was observed throughout the country, and an annual service of thanksgiving, and of allusion to the dire event, was kept up year by year in Little Wild Street Chapel. An annual sermon had been instituted by a Mr. Joseph Taylor, a member of the Baptist Church meeting in Little Wild Street, who sought in this way to commemorate his own merciful preservation during the tempest.

For many years these sermons were regularly printed, but this practice was discontinued in 1821. The bills announcing them commonly took the following form :

GREAT STORM.

On Sunday Evening, November 27th, 1825, The

𝕬nnual 𝕾ermon

In commemoration of the Great Storm in 1703, will be preached

In Little Wild Street Chapel,

Lincoln's Inn Fields,

By the Rev. Thomas Griffin,

of Prescott Street.

Service commences at half-past six o'clock

The storm spread death and havoc everywhere, and some of its worst effects were felt in London. It killed the Bishop of Bath and Wells and his wife ; it killed Lady Penelope Nicholas, sister to the Bishop of London—in both cases by the fall of buildings. One hundred and twenty-three persons of less note were killed in the same manner, and the number of people drowned by the flooding of the Severn and Thames is said to have run into thousands.

Two thousand stacks of chimneys were blown down in London. The damage in the city alone was computed at nearly two millions. Many people believed that the war of the elements was accompanied by an earthquake. In the Thames any number of ships were driven down stream, and over five hundred wherries were lost.

One great tragedy was the utter destruction of the Eddystone Lighthouse, together with its architect, Mr. Winstanley.

In the sermons preached at Little Wild Street these happenings were frequently recalled, possibly with embellishments. Preaching there, on the anniversary in 1734, Dr. Andrew Gifford related that in a country town a large stable was swept off its foundations and carried across the highway, clean over the heads of five horses and the man who was feeding them, neither man nor horses being hurt in any way, whilst the rack and manger remained untouched, and were for " a considerable time the admiration of every beholder."

Of " special providences " there were

hundreds. A house in the Strand, containing fourteen persons, collapsed, and no one was hurt. In Poultry two boys were lying in a garret. A huge stack of chimneys falling in made their way through their floor, and all the other floors down to the cellar, followed by the bed with the boys in it, who awoke in the nether regions quite unhurt. Narratives like this go far to explain the popularity of the Little Wild Street sermons.

It is an interesting fact that this storm made the fortune of no less a literary genius than Joseph Addison, whose *Spectator* essays are immortal. In the year following the storm, Sidney Godolphin, whose position as Queen Anne's Tory Minister was none too firm, bethought him that what the Tories needed was a stronger representation in literature. In an age when every Government kept its little corps of hack writers this was a serious defect in the Tory position, and it was the more patent because the Whigs were just then well served by writers. Macaulay tells us that Godolphin was not a reading man; but it did not take a very keen critic to perceive that the poems just then appearing in honour of Marlborough's great victory at Blenheim were exceedingly bad. Macaulay illustrates this by three exquisitely absurd lines taken from one of them:

Think of two thousand gentlemen at least,
And each man mounted on his capering beast:
Into the Danube they were pushed by shoals.

So one fine morning Godolphin went out to find a poet. " He understood how to negotiate a loan, or to remit a subsidy; he was also well versed in the history of running horses and fighting cocks; but his acquaintance among the poets was very small." He questioned Halifax, and Halifax, after some uncertainty, mentioned Addison. Addison was then occupying a garret up three pairs of stairs over a small shop in the Haymarket. Here the needy author was surprised by a visit from no less a person than the Right Honourable Henry Boyle, Chancellor of the Exchequer. Persuaded by him, Addison readily undertook to write a poem on Marlborough's great victory. The result was " The Campaign," and, what was more important to Addison's reputation, the famous simile of the Angel riding the whirlwind. Wishing to glorify Marlborough's generalship, it occurred to him to recall that awful storm which, after nine months, still haunted the public imagination. He did so in the following lines, which not only won him the warmest favour of Godolphin, but captured the admiration of the whole country:

So when an angel, by divine command,
With rising tempests shakes a guilty land
Such as of late o'er pale Britannia past,
Calm and serene he drives the furious blasts
And, pleased the Almighty's orders to perform
Rides in the whirlwind, and directs the storm.

Before the poem had been out many days Addison was appointed to a commissionership worth £200 a year, and from that date his rise to much higher emoluments was assured. He took his rightful place in the world of rank and fashion; and in the Haymarket, where he had been a lodger up three pairs of stairs, he now filled his tortoise-shell snuff-box at Fribourg and Treyer's, whose quaint bow-windowed shop stands unaltered to this day.

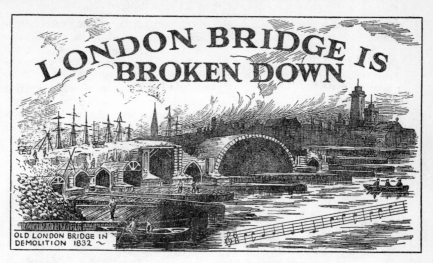

LONDON BRIDGE IS BROKEN DOWN

OLD LONDON BRIDGE IN DEMOLITION 1832

IT is almost impossible to be sure of the origin of many of the ancient songs and legends about London and London Bridge. Who, for instance, was the writer of the children's folk-song of " London Bridge is Broken Down ? " Every child knows it, every child—meaning a girl—sings it. When the first London Bridge was erected about 994 trouble and tragedy began to take possession of its very limited space.

In the year 1008, in the reign of Ethelred II., the Unready, there was a bridge already for, according to Snorro Sturleson, " Olaf the Norwegian, an ally of Ethelred, attacking the Danes, who had fortified themselves in Southwark, fastened his vessels to the piles of London Bridge, which the Danes held, and dragged down the whole structure." That was the first time the bridge was " broken down." Then in the reign of Stephen another wooden London Bridge was burnt down, and on several subsequent occasions London Bridge was broken down in sections. Indeed, it was always meeting with misfortunes, and, truth to tell, it is the history of the catastrophes which befell the many structures that is told in the nursery song. The stone bridge was built between the years 1176 and 1209 by Peter of Colechurch, and survived in some shape until 1851. But its vicissitudes were many and its need of repair a proverb. Edward Walpole very aptly says : " If old London Bridge had a fault, it was, perhaps, its habit of occasionally partly falling down. This it did as early as 1437, when the great stone gate and tower on the Southwark end, with two arches, subsided into the Thames."

It will thus be understood why London Bridge soon became the subject of the satirists and the ballad-mongers.

London Bridge is broken down,
　Dance o'er my Lady Lee ;
London Bridge is broken down,
　With a gay ladye.

How shall we build it up again ?
　Dance o'er my Lady Lee ;
How shall we build it up again ?
　With a gay ladye.

Silver and gold will be stole away,
   Dance o'er my Lady Lee ;
Silver and gold will be stole away,
   With a gay ladye.

Build it up again with iron and steel,
   Dance o'er my Lady Lee ;
Build it up with iron and steel,
   With a gay ladye.

Iron and steel will bend and bow,
   Dance o'er my Lady Lee ;
Iron and steel will bend and bow,
   With a gay ladye.

have been Leeds. At any rate, here is another account of the supposed origin of the ballad which, at least, is worth some consideration. It is presented with only a few abbreviations. " In the year of grace 1536, when London Bridge was covered with houses, over-hanging the pent-up turbulent stream . . . Sir William Howitt, citizen of London, inhabited one of these temptations of Providence. His only child,

WILLIAM IV. AND QUEEN ADELAIDE OPENING NEW LONDON BRIDGE ON AUGUST 1, 1831

Build it up with wood and clay,
   Dance o'er my Lady Lee ;
Build it up with wood and clay,
   With a gay ladye.

Wood and clay will wash away,
   Dance o'er my Lady Lee ;
Wood and clay will wash away,
   With a gay ladye.

Build it up with stone so strong,
   Dance o'er my Lady Lee ;
Huzza ! 't will last for ages long,
   With a gay ladye.

The " Lady Lee " mentioned is supposed to have been the one referred to by Sir Walter Scott in " Woodstock," the scene of which is, of course, laid in the times of Elizabeth. However instead of Lee the name might

a pretty little girl, was playing with a servant over the water and fell into the dangerous rapids. " Many a one beheld the fearful sight in the help-lessness of terror, without dreaming of venturing into the stream. But there was one to whom the life of the perishing child was dearer than his own, and that was the apprentice of Sir William Howitt. He leaped into the perilous water after his youthful mistress, and by the aid of a bold heart and strong arm bore her in safety to the shore ; and he had his reward."

The reward was, of course, the heart and the hand of the maiden when she grew up. She was, however, on account of her wondrous beauty, wooed by many gallant noblemen, " but fairer in her eyes was the 'prentice cap of the daring youth, who had snatched her from the whirling waters than the coronet of the Peer, and with the single-minded disinterestedness of a true woman she gave to her untitled pre-server, Edward Osborne, the hand and the heart which the Earl of Shrewsbury, the heir of the lofty house of Talbot, had sighed for in vain."

Eventually by industry and merit, George William Frederick Osborne rose to be the Duke of Leeds, and it has been suggested more than once that his duchess was the lady—Lady Lee, or Leeds—named in the ballad.

This story, interesting for its own sake, has probably no connection what-ever with the old song, the origin of which is wrapt in obscurity, and was perhaps never made the subject of inquiry during many centuries. In 1823, a contributor to the *Gentleman's Magazine* wrote as follows : " The projected demolition of London Bridge recalls to my mind the introductory lines of an old ballad, which more than seventy years ago I heard plaintively warbled by a lady who was born in the Reign of Charles II., and who lived till nearly the end of that of George II." That gives us a pleasant flavour of the song's antiquity. It is known that in the reign of Edward II., the Master of London Bridge had some property and liabilities in certain mills on the River Lea. Stow found the record and says : " The Keeper of the Bridge House had, in ancient times, an in-terest in certain mills upon the River Lea, near Stratford. It has been

conjectured that the song was com-posed on one of the occasions that the Bridge was in ruin." Dr. Rimbault, however, writing in *Notes and Queries*, in 1850, probably comes nearest to reasonable truth when he says : " If I might hazard another conjecture I would refer it to the period when London Bridge was the scene of a terrible contest between the Danes and Olave of Norway. There is an ani-mated description of this ' Battle of London Bridge,' which gave ample theme to the Scandinavian scalds, in Snorro Sturleson ; and singularly enough, the first line is the same as that of our ditty :

> London Bridge is broken down
> Gold is won and bright renown ;
> Shields resounding
> Warhorns sounding,
> Hildur shouting in the din ;
> Arrows singing,
> Mail-coats ringing,
> Odin makes our Olaf win.

There is no doubt that the song has had many adventures, and that it has been re-written and added to by many hands. It has even entered into a Christmas carol beginning

> Dame, get up and bake your pies,
> On Christmas Day in the morning.

The dame objects that

> London Bridge is broken down
> On Christmas Day in the morning,

the sense being that until London Bridge is built up again she cannot proceed with her pies. But unless the battle referred to above was fought at Christ-mas it is difficult to see why the falling of London Bridge should furnish ma-terial for a carol of that season.

SYDNEY SMITH IN LONDON

"THE house is in Amen Corner—an awkward name on a card and an awkward annunciation to the coachman on leaving any fashionable mansion." So wrote Sydney Smith in taking up his residence in 1831 as a Canon of St. Paul's Cathedral.

St. Paul's Cathedral is a grave and serious structure : it is associated in our minds with religious aspiration, with beauty, with history, with the glory of England's great men ; but because of Sydney Smith's connection with it, we associate it also with his lambent wit, his gay flights of fancy, and his extraordinary command of imagery. Who does not remember his remark when he saw a child stroking a tortoise " to please it " ? He told the child he might as well stroke the dome of St. Paul's to please the Dean and Chapter ! Wit is a rare possession among Englishmen, and Sydney Smith's bon-mots remain a national heritage, while we have forgotten all about his early poverty, his hard struggles, and the drudgery so cheerfully undertaken in lonely country parishes. Yet these bon-mots are many of them kept fresh by some salt of common sense, some preservative of wisdom ; and so they often contain the very essence of the man himself.

Sydney Smith was sixty-three when he became a canon : our illustration gives us in slight caricature the strong, intellectual face, speaking energy and determination in every feature, the short and burly figure " of the family of Falstaff." Sydney Smith was of dark complexion, and at this time his hair was iron-grey ; his fine eyes were quick and penetrating, and his countenance was illumined by an expression of benevolence. Yet sometimes his sense of fun carried him away. As canon he was deeply interested in the restoration of St. Paul's and its preservation from fire. The subject of placing wood pavement round the cathedral came up one time for discussion in the chapter-room of St. Paul's. Sydney Smith is reported to have said in his most matter-of-fact tones, and with his usual innocent look : " If my reverend brethren here will but lay their heads together, the thing will be done in a trice ! " It is not every canon that would take such humour in good part ; and little wonder that Sydney Smith exclaimed : " The whole of my life has passed like a razor—in hot water or a scrape."

His gravity of demeanour added very considerably to the zest of the joke. A lady, for instance, who mistook the term " vergers " for " virgins " asked Mr. Smith if it was true that he walked down St. Paul's with three virgins holding silver pokers before him. He shook his head and looked very grave and bade her come and see. " Some enemy of the Church," he said, " some Dissenter, had clearly been misleading her." His power of ludicrous exaggeration is well illustrated in the following anecdote. St. Paul's Cathedral used in his time to be excessively cold, and the Canon despaired of ever heating it. " You might as well try and warm the county of Middlesex," he said. " The thermometer is several degrees below zero," he wrote to a friend; " my sentences are frozen as they come out of my mouth, and are thawed in the course of the summer, making strange noises and unexpected assertions in various parts of the church."

The famous *Edinburgh Review* was started at Sydney Smith's suggestion, and he contributed a large number of articles to it. He was acquainted with most of the distinguished men of his day, and Thomas Moore the poet says that as a conversational wit he surpassed them all. Of Macaulay—another great conversationalist—Sydney Smith wrote: "Oh yes! we both talked a great deal, but I don't believe Macaulay ever did hear my voice. Sometimes, when I have told a good story, I have thought to myself, 'Poor Macaulay! he will be very sorry some day to have missed hearing that.'" Samuel Rogers, the banker-poet, was also one of Smith's friends, and from Rogers we get the following story. Smith's medical man said to the Canon on one occasion: "You must take a walk on an empty stomach." The patient looked up with a glance of inquiry, and naïvely uttered but one word— "Whose?"

Sydney Smith was wholly devoid of snobbery, and when a heraldic compiler called upon him to ask permission to include his armorial bearings in a coming work, the Canon replied: "The Smiths never had any arms, and have invariably sealed their letters with their thumbs." When he was informed that his daughter's marriage was announced in the London papers under the heading of "Fashionable Intelligence," he exclaimed, with a merry twinkle in his eye, "How absurd! Why, we pay our bills!" Gout, he said on one occasion, was the only enemy he did not wish to have at his feet.

People have often wondered why Sydney Smith did not receive a bishopric when the Whigs were in power, for throughout his life he had been a consistent and active supporter of their policy. His "Peter Plymley's Letters," written in support of Catholic Emancipation, made an extraordinary sensation, and undoubtedly his speech

SYDNEY SMITH
From the Maclise Portrait Gallery

at Taunton, delivered in 1831 when the House of Lords rejected the Reform Bill, had a notable effect on public opinion. In this speech he compares the efforts of the House of Lords to restrain the rising tide of democracy to the ludicrous efforts of Mrs. Partington to sweep back the waves of the Atlantic Ocean from her door. " Dame Partington, who lived upon the beach, was seen at the door of her house with mop and pattens, trundling her mop, squeezing out the sea-water, and vigorously pushing away the Atlantic Ocean. The Atlantic was roused ; Mrs. Partington's spirit was up ; but I need not tell you the contest was unequal."

Even to-day allusions are not infrequent to Mrs. Partington and the Atlantic Ocean, and at the time the phrase was in everybody's mouth.

It is a little surprising that another of Smith's political phrases, the " Foolometer," has not received the same wide acceptance. By this " common precaution " he meant the acquaintance and society of three or four British fools as a test of public opinion. " Every Cabinet Minister should judge of all his measures by his foolometer, as a navigator crowds or shortens sail by the barometer in his cabin."

It is clear that Sydney Smith himself expected ecclesiastical preferment, but " whether I get preferment or not,"

was his quiet remark to a friend, " I shall always be the same, and, like the patent flannel at seven shillings a yard, will never shrink in heat or cold ! "

But though his great personal gifts and his unusual talents never advanced him beyond a prebendary stall at St. Paul's, he was able to enjoy in old age the satisfaction of a well-spent life.

In so short a space we have been able to indicate by a few examples only the range of Sydney Smith's wit. His conversation has been compared to a stream of fireworks, brilliant, incessant, and perfectly harmless ; and we have shown that he was able to touch at will the notes of irony, of sarcasm, and of fun pure and simple. We have given a few instances of his droll powers of expression, and his command over ludicrous imagery ; but had we been able to multiply our examples a hundred-fold, they would still have lacked the zest of the living personality, of the occasion that gave their readiness so much point. One of the most charming features of Sydney Smith's character is indicated by Macaulay, who visited him in his lonely Yorkshire parish. " It seems to be his greatest luxury," wrote Macaulay, " to keep his wife and daughters laughing for two or three hours every day." On this delightful picture we must close our brief record.

LONDON'S FIRST BALLOON AND PARACHUTE

ON September 15, 1784, nearly two hundred thousand people were assembled in and around the Honourable Artillery Company's grounds in Moorfields. They had come to see the first balloon ascent in England.

The circumstances under which this ascent was made by Vincent Lunardi, an Italian, are of singular interest to-day. England looked to France for her first balloons; and in late years she has looked to France for aeroplanes. Montgolfier's balloon had soared above the Champs de Mars in August of the previous year, and the feat had produced a profound impression in England. History, indeed, has no more startling coincidence to offer than that of the apprehensions which were felt lest the new invention should be turned to military account against this country. A caricature appeared in London in 1784 entitled " Montgolfier in the Clouds, constructing Air Balloons for the Grande Monarque." The French aeronaut was represented blowing soap-bubbles and saying, " O by Gar, dis be de grand invention. Dis will immortalise my King, my country, and myself. We will declare the war against our enimie ; we will make des English quake, by Gar. We will inspect their camp, we will intercept their fleet, and we will set fire to their dock-yards, and, by Gar, we will take Gibraltar in de air-balloon ; and when we have conquer de English, den we conquer de other countrie, and make them all colonie to de Grande Monarque."

Vincent Lunardi was a young attaché at the Neapolitan Embassy in London when he was seized with the balloon frenzy. It was his intention to have ascended from the gardens of Chelsea Hospital, but the royal permission to do so was afterwards withdrawn, and he found a new scene for his attempt in the Honourable Artillery Company's parade-ground.

His balloon, which was spherical in form, and $32\frac{1}{2}$ feet in diameter, was composed of oiled silk, arranged in alternate stripes of blue and red. This immense globe, inflated with common air, was for some time exhibited at the Lyceum ; but the rough treatment it received there compelled Lunardi to obtain assistance from the magistrates, to remove, by force, his machine and apparatus to the Artillery Ground.

On Wednesday, September 15, 1784, the day appointed for the ascent, every avenue leading to the spot was crowded to excess, and Moorfields, then entirely open, was covered by a dense multitude. Charles James Fox and Edmund Burke were two of the many distinguished spectators. The Prince of Wales was present, and expressed his wishes for the safety of Lunardi, and of Mr. Biggin, who was to be his companion in the ascent. The balloon was inflated by hydrogen under the direction of Dr. George Fordyce. Through the impatience of the multitude (the hour fixed for the ascent having long elapsed), the machine could not be completely filled, and when the daring aeronauts entered the gallery, which was attached to the net work, its buoyancy was found to be inadequate to carry up both individuals. Lunardi, therefore, determined to ascend without his com-

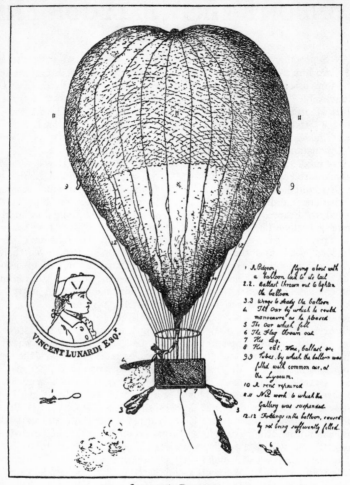

LUNARDI'S BALLOON
From a Contemporary Print

panion, and at five minutes after two o'clock the ropes were cut, and the balloon rose majestically into the air, amidst the acclamations of one of the greatest crowds London had ever seen. "The effect," to use the words of Lunardi himself, "was that of a miracle on the multitudes which surrounded the place, and they passed from incredulity and menace, into the most extravagant expressions of approbation and joy."

As Lunardi sailed over London he was intently observed by the King through a telescope, from St. James's.

He descended at Ware to find himself famous. He was presented at Court, and his name was given to wigs, coats, and bonnets. He exhibited his balloon at the Pantheon, and it was seen there by Dr. Johnson, who, although much impressed by the event, said characteristically, "The vehicles can serve no one till we can guide them." Horace Walpole said, and his words have a singular application to aeronautics to-day: "Balloons occupy senators, philosophers, ladies, everybody. France gave us the *ton ;* and, as yet, we have not come up to our model."

Lunardi printed an account of his voyage which, according to Chambers' "Book of Days," exhibits him as a vain and excitable young man. "He tells us how a woman dropped down dead through fright, caused by beholding the wondrous apparition in the air but, on the other hand, he saved a man's life, for a jury brought in a verdict of 'Not guilty' on a notorious highwayman, that they might rush out of court to witness the balloon. When Lunardi rose, a cabinet council was engaged on most important State deliberations; but the King said : 'My lords, we shall have an opportunity of discussing this question at another time, but we may never again see poor Lunardi ; so let us adjourn the council, and observe the balloon ! '"

Yet Lunardi seems, like other heroes,

to have been quickly forgotten in London, for a year after his ascent Rowlandson depicts him as "Aerostation out at Elbows." The aeronaut is seen carrying his deflated balloon on his back, and the caricature is explained in the following lines :

"AEROSTATION OUT AT ELBOWS"
After Rowlandson

Behold a hero, comely, tall and fair !
His only food is philogistic air . . .
Now drooping, roams about from town to town,
Collecting pence to inflate his poor Balloon.
Pity the wight and something to him give,
To purchase gas to keep his frame alive.

In January 1785, while Lunardi was in the dumps, the world was amazed by the great feat of J. P. Blanchard and the American Dr. Jeffries, who crossed the Channel from Dover to Calais in a balloon.

Lunardi died in 1806, and in the meanwhile a French aeronaut, M.

Garnerin, had become the hero of the air. His first ascent was made from Ranelagh on July 28, 1802, accompanied by Captain Snowden. The day was a wild one, and the travellers were glad to descend at Colchester. After further ascents from Lord's old cricket ground and from Vauxhall, the daring aeronaut made his great experiment of ascending in his balloon in order to descend from it in a parachute. In his Vauxhall ascent he had safely sent a cat to earth in a parachute ; he was now to use one himself. From St. George's Parade, in North Audley Street, Garnerin ascended in a basket attached below his parachute, which was hung to the balloon.

He rose above the town to a great height, and then, as he said, " with a conscience void of approach," he cut the cord and saw the balloon rise as his parachute fell. His own account of his sensations proceeds : " I saw that all my calculations were just, and my mind remained calm and serene. I endeavoured to modulate my gravitation, and the oscillation which I experienced, increased in proportion as I approached the breeze that blows in the middle regions : nearly ten minutes had elapsed, and I felt that the more time I took in descending, the safer I

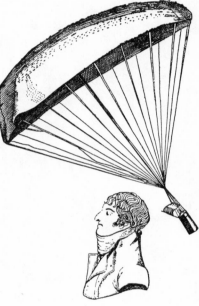

M. GARNERIN

should reach the ground. At length I perceived thousands of persons, some on horseback, and others on foot, following me ; all of whom encouraged me by their wishes, while they opened their arms to receive me. I came near the earth, and, after one bound, I landed, and quitted the parachute without any shock or accident. The first person that came to me pressed me in his arms ; but, without losing any time, I employed myself in detaching the principal circle of the parachute, anxious to save the instrument that so well guaranteed me ; but a crowd soon surrounded me— laid hold of me, and carried me in triumph, till an indisposition, the consequence and effect of the oscillation I had experienced, obliged the procession to stop. I was then seized with a painful vomiting, which I usually experience for several hours, after a descent in a parachute. The interval of a moment, however, permitted me to get on horseback ; a numerous cavalcade approached to keep off the crowd, whose enthusiasm and transports incommoded me not a little. The spot at which Garnerin landed was near St. Pancras churchyard. The exploits of later London balloonists, Graham, Green, Glaisher, and others belong to later history.

HENRY FIELDING (*b.* 1707, *d.* 1754)

HENRY FIELDING AT BOW STREET

IN 1749 Henry Fielding, less known as a magistrate than as the father of the English novel, sat in his squalid Bow Street Court room, administering justice with all his might. If was the way of Fielding to do things with all his might. The office of Justice of the Peace was assuredly not a splendid one for the man who had created the English novel, shaken the theatre with laughter, and dealt swashing blows as a political pamphleteer ; but it was all that the Government of George II. did for Fielding. He had even to be indebted for certain benefactions to the Duke of Bedford before he could declare—as was necessary for a county magistrate—that he was the holder of landed estate worth £100 per annum. The sole estate of Henry Fielding had been his valiant and ever-active pen.

But he set about his new duties with all his might. At the beginning of the last five years of his crowded life

(1707–1754) he flung himself into a conflict with the multiform and epidemic crime of the London of the eighteenth century.

Fielding was just forty-three, and already his great constitution was failing him. Both as professional literary man and as boon companion he had lived hard. He had known sore domestic trials, he had been all his days battling for bread, he had been bitterly assailed by public and private foes ; but his courage of mind and native gaiety of heart were no jot abated. "It is a pity he was not immortal," exclaimed his kinswoman Lady Mary Wortley Montague ; "he was so formed for happiness." "His genius," said the greatest of his disciples, Thackeray, "had been nursed on sack posset, and not on dishes of tea." His pedigree, observed the critic Ninto, will always be remembered by one of the eloquent passages of Gibbon : "Our immortal Fielding was of the younger branch of the earls of Denbigh who drew their origin from the counts of Hapsburg, the lineal descendants of Eltrico, in the seventh century Duke of Alsace. Far different have been the fortunes of the English and German divisions of the family of Hapsburg ; the former, the knights and sheriffs of Leicestershire, have slowly risen to the dignity of a peerage ; the latter, the Emperors of Germany and Kings of Spain, have threatened the liberties of the old and invaded the treasures of the New World. The successors of Charles V may disdain their brethren in England ; but the romance of *Tom Jones*—that exquisite picture of humour and manners—will outlive the Palace of the Escurial and the Imperial Eagle of Austria."

No sooner was he appointed magistrate than he seemed as if he had all his life been holding court at Bow Street. Arthur Murphy, in the essay prefixed to the first collected edition of Fielding's works, tells us that " whatever he desired he desired ardently " ; and of his resolve to purge London " of some of the crying evils of his time," we have evidence in his first charge to a grand jury, which, Mr. Austin Dobson informs us, is " still regarded by lawyers as a model exposition." Henry Fielding had to deal with a London which was " a kind of nightmare of lawlessness " ; and in which, though punishments were often atrociously cruel, the odds were mainly in favour of the criminal classes. Fielding himself has told us that, at an era when peaceful and decent citizens needed the best of protection, their interests were entrusted mainly to a body of old men, the Watch, who were barely capable of carrying the " pole " they were armed with, and who owed their offices not to their fitness but to

their sheer infirmities. In these poor old hands was the guardianship of the peace at a period when the peace was flouted by the readiest, most energetic and most uncivilised rogues that modern justice has had to cope with. The pistol, the bludgeon, and the cutlass were among their habitual weapons ; and not less habitual were outrages—often committed in daylight—of which the " apache " in suburban Paris has still to learn the secret.

The geography of the London of that day was of no small assistance to the law-breaker. Innumerable lanes, alleys, courts, rookeries, and byplaces afforded both means of escape and sanctuary to thieves, robbers, and murderers. There were whole districts of which Fielding said that " had they been intended for the very purpose of concealment, they could scarce have been better contrived. Upon such a view the whole appears as a vast Wood or Forest, in which a Thief may harbour with as great Security as Wild Beasts do in the Deserts of Africa or Arabia." Crime, moreover, was well organised : " there are at this time a great Gang of Rogues whose Number falls little short of a Hundred, who are incorporated in one Body, have Officers and a Treasury ; and have reduced Theft and Robbery into a regular System." Prosecutors were bribed or terrorised ; and " rotten Members of the Law " were ready to forge a defence which any number of false witnesses would support.

Fielding's house in Bow Street became the centre of a strenuous campaign against all manner of depredators, from the highwayman to the professional gambler. The Justice's method of procedure was twofold. " He dealt vigorously with the individual criminal," says his latest biographer, Miss Godden ; "and he sought to remove some of the causes by which these criminals were engendered." This second part of Fielding's policy was, in the eighteenth century, almost a new thing ; but this profound considerer of human life perceived at once that while the root of crime in the metropolis was left untouched the tree would continue to yield fruit. In the address to the Jury to which reference has been made, he glances at the open profligacy of the town, the gaming houses and masquerade rooms, "temples of inquity." "Gentlemen," he cries, "Our News-Papers, from the Top of the Page to the Bottom, the Corners of our Streets up to the very Eves of our Houses, present us with nothing but a View of Masquerades, Balls, and Assemblies of various kinds, Fairs, Wells, Gardens, &c., tending to promote Idleness, Extravagance, and Immorality among all sorts of People " ; and he adds that many of the public make diversion "no longer the Recreation or Amusement, but the whole Business of their Lives."

Almost immediately after this charge was delivered, a riot, lasting three days, broke out in the streets, which it fell to the Bow Street magistrate to suppress ; and we see him haranguing the rioters from his window, and sitting up all night with the officer in command of the soldiery. The riot quelled, he returned to his desk and roughed out a "Bill for the better preventing street Robberies." Miss Godden says : "This eventful year, the year which had seen the publication of *Tom Jones*, the shackling of Fielding's genius within the duties of a London magistrate, the issue of two pamphlets on criminal reform and administration, the drafting of a proposed Criminal Bill, and the suppression of a riot, closed sadly with the death of Fielding's little daughter, Mary Amelia, when barely twelve months old."

But we are hardly permitted to speak of his magisterial work as "the shackling of Fielding's genius." It was altogether too important, and, its importance apart, it left his creative power so far untrammelled that he was able to finish and present to the public the novel that set the seal upon his literary fame. Had he lived to a ripe age, instead of dying prematurely exhausted at 47–48, his experiences at Bow Street would have given him an immense fund of new material for the enrichment of other stories. What a diverse crowd flows through his justice's chambers ! By advertisement in the press he invited all "Persons who have been robbed," with their servants, to wait on him "at his House in Bow Street," and this in itself might well have drawn half the town to the magistrate's official doors ! There also; when no weighter affair was toward; he sat to hear and compose the quarrels of porters from the markets and beggars from the thoroughfares. The reward of these manifold endeavours is somewhere alluded to by Fielding as "about £500 a year of the dirtiest money upon earth." By this harsh qualification he means us to know that his justice's income dribbled in as fees ; and since we have it upon record that he steadfastly refused to "take a shilling from a man who most undoubtedly would not have had another left," we readily understand how the nominal stipend of £500 was "reduced to little more than £300, a considerable portion of which remained with his clerk." A poor man all his days, he was more than ever open-handed when a slender certainty was assured to him.

He never rested from his labours. The pen so often engaged upon trenchant or witty dialogue, or scenes of fiction that could hold Johnson enthralled (though, to be sure, the doctor damned " Tom Jones " !) was now preparing " An Enquiry into the Causes of the late Increase of Robbers, &c., with some Proposals for remedying this growing Evil." In this pamphlet is depicted, with the skill of an artist and the passion of a true moralist, all the darker side of the London Fielding knew. He assigned for the increasing demoralisation of " the most useful Part " of the people, three causes in chief : (1) The " immense number of places of amusement " ; what would Fielding have said to our hundred and twenty theatres ? (2) The epidemic of gin drinking, " a new Kind of Drunkenness unknown to our Ancestors . . . lately sprung up among us." (3) Gambling among the " lower Classes of Life "—a school wherein " most Highwaymen of great eminence have been bred." He added, as a fourth great cause, the general condition of the London poor.

The " Enquiry " was published at the beginning of 1751. In six months from this date the Tippling Act received the royal assent. In March 1752, were passed an Act " for the better preventing Thefts and Robberies " and an Act " for better preventing the horrid Crime of Murder." With these measures in view, may we not justly infer that the noble spirit of Henry Fielding is reflected in the Statute Book itself.

THE GOLDEN BALL

THE house numbered 40 in Upper Brook Street, W. was taken about the year 1822 by that brilliant young worldling Hughes Ball Hughes, who gave Wyatt the architect *carte blanche* to furnish it with buhl furniture, costly hangings, statues, bronzes, and pictures. Hughes inherited £40,000 a year from his uncle, Admiral Hughes. He fell in love with Lady Jane Paget but was refused at the eleventh hour. He then made love to Miss Floyd whom fate had reserved to be the wife of Sir Robert Peel. Finally, he ran away with Mercandotti, the Spanish dancer.

BALL HUGHES

All London stared, and Ainsworth produced his epigram :

> The fair damsel is gone,
> And no wonder at all
> That, bred to the dance
> She is gone to the ball.

Hughes was a born gambler ; he and Lord Petersham once played battledore and shuttlecock all night for money. When his career seemed likely to point a moral it began to adorn a tale of London's growth. He bought Oatlands palace, a speculation that proved fortunate, and Hughes was again a Golden Ball. He died in obscure luxury at St. Germain in 1863.

CLAPHAM IN 1800

THE CLAPHAM SECT

I T is curious that a body of men similar in their religious opinions, and united in the methods they advocated for attaining social reform, should have been grouped round Clapham Common. Chance, perhaps, brought Henry Thornton and William Wilberforce to the spot; Zachary Macaulay (father of Lord Macaulay) followed because his friends had settled there. His house, on the south side of the Common, formerly stood back from the road, but has since thrown out a shop-front, and lost all traces of being a private gentleman's residence. Lord Teignmouth's house, "the cradle of the Bible Society," stood at the corner of Clapham Common, and is now—curious turn of fortune—turned into a college and monastery of Redemptorist monks. Thornton's house was on the north side

of the Common, at Battersea Rise, and while they were both unmarried Wilberforce shared this charming villa with him. The house, wreathed with wistaria and honeysuckle, looked across the beautiful lawn to distant vistas of spreading fields and forest-trees. The oval library had been planned for Thornton's residence by the great statesman, William Pitt; and here the Clapham sect met in friendly intercourse or in serious deliberation. "It arose at his (Pitt's) bidding," writes Sir James Stephen in his "Essays," "and yet remains, perhaps a solitary monument of the architectural skill of that imperial mind. Lofty and symmetrical, it was curiously wainscoted with books on every side, except where it opened on a far extended lawn, reposing beneath the giant arms of aged elms and massive tulip-trees."

Wilberforce was "the sun of the Claphamic system," and these others we have named were some of its leading members. It behoves us now briefly to summarise the religious views of the sect and their social aims.

In the eighteenth century the life of the Church of England had fallen to its lowest ebb. Its revival of active energy was very largely due to the Clapham sect, which was composed chiefly of members of the Low Church party of the Established Church. The Clapham sect was essentially evangelical ; its members were men and women of deep devotional feeling, but they were by no means narrow. Nonconformists were included in the sect, and Wilberforce occasionally attended places of Nonconformist worship. The Claphamites took up with intense earnestness the work of evangelisation ; and to their efforts we may attribute the establishment of those two far-reaching organisations, the Bible Society and the Church Missionary Society. Lord Macaulay writes, with perhaps some slight exaggeration : " The truth is that from that little knot of men emanated all the Bible Societies and almost all the Missionary Societies in the world." " Bibles, schools, missionaries," says another writer, "the circulation of evangelical books, and the training of evangelical clergymen . . . war through the Press and war in Parliament against every form of injustice which either law or custom sanctioned—such were the forces by which they hoped to extend the kingdom of light, and to resist the tyranny with which the earth was threatened."

But the work by which the Clapham sect will be remembered by those of all nations and of all creeds is the part they took in the Abolition of the Slave Trade—" that monster iniquity which fairly outstripped all abhorrence, and baffled all exaggeration "—and in the emancipation of the slaves. Zachary Macaulay had himself been a slave-overseer in Jamaica ; he had made a voyage in a slaver to investigate the condition of the slaves ; he had been Governor of Sierra Leone, the colony established for freed slaves : and when he settled down in Clapham in 1803 he sacrificed, without a single thought of self, time and health and fortune to the crushing of this monstrous evil. He was possessed by this one idea, animated by this one master-passion ; night and day it haunted him, and spurred him to unceasing effort. He established a paper, the *Christian Observer*, to awaken public opinion, and never relaxed his labours till the end was accomplished.

William Wilberforce worked unremittingly in Parliament, and in 1789 proposed the Abolition of the Slave Trade in the House of Commons. But it was not till 1807 that the Bill for the Abolition of the Slave Trade was passed, and not till 1833 that the Bill for the Total Abolition of Slavery throughout the British Dominions received the Royal Assent. But the emancipation of the slaves was only one among Wilberforce's myriad benevolent schemes. Sir James Stephen draws for us a most illuminating picture of the variety of causes that claimed his aid : " Eloquent deputies from Hibernian schools would be awaiting audience in the drawing-room ; in the ante-chamber, the advocates of an improved prison-discipline ; in the spacious library, ladies anxious to explain their plans for visiting the sick Quakers under a concern for transported convicts, the founders of savings-banks, missionaries from Seramfore and the Red River. . . . And then would emerge from his closet Mr. Wilberforce, the prime minster of that disjointed state, passing from one group to another, not without a smile, which revealed to the initiated his involuntary perception of the comic aspect of the scene, but still more clearly disclosing by his voice, his gestures, and his kindling eye the generous resentment, the glowing admiration, or the tender sympathy with which he listened to one and another tale of injustice, of self-denial, or of woe. . . ." Henry Thornton, both by his pen and in Parliament, ably seconded the efforts of Wilberforce, and had we space, there is many another name that should be added to Clapham's glorious roll; not forgetting the name of Granville Sharpe, a clerk in the Ordnance Office, who, to establish the right to freedom of a negro he had rescued, spent two whole years studying the laws of England, and caused some of the greatest justices of England to reverse former decisions.

There is an account of the Clapham sect, written wholly from the outside, in the opening chapters of Thackeray's " Newcomes." It gives in satiric vein an admirable picture of the variety of interests that occupied a member of that sect. " To attend to the interests of the enslaved negro ; to awaken the benighted Hottentot to a sense of the truth ; to convert Jews, Turks, Infidels and Papists ; to arouse the indifferent and often blasphemous mariner ; to guide the washerwoman in the right way ; to head all the public charities of her sect, and to do a thousand secret kindnesses that none knew of ; to answer myriads of letters, pension endless ministers ; . . . to hear preachers daily bawling for hours, and listen untired on her knees after a long day's labour, while florid rhapsodists belaboured cushions above her head with wearisome benedictions ; all these things had this woman to do, and for near fourscore years she fought her fight womanfully."

In this picture Thackeray has left out of account the factor that helped this woman to fight her fight—the strong spiritual force, the uplifting joy and hope by which members of the Clapham sect felt themselves sustained ; which enabled them to carry gigantic reforms against the ranked opposition of indifference and commercial cupidity ; which transfigured trivialities and illumined errors ; and which makes of Clapham a place of pilgrimage for all who are interested in the history of religious thought and of social reform.

SIR ROBERT PEEL

THE DEATH OF SIR ROBERT PEEL

ON Saturday, June 29, 1850, Sir Robert Peel was thrown from his horse on Constitution Hill, and on July 2 he died from his injuries in his house in Whitehall Gardens. On the 6th Charles C. F. Greville wrote in his political diary : " The death of Sir Robert Peel, which took place on Tuesday night, has absorbed every other subject of interest. The suddenness of such an accident took the world by surprise, and in consequence of the mystery in which great people's illnesses are always shrouded, the majority of the public were not aware of his danger till they heard of his death. The sympathy, the feeling, and the regret which have been displayed on every side and in all quarters are to the last degree striking. . . . When we remember that Peel was an object of bitter hatred to one great party, that he was never liked by the other

party, and that he had no popular and ingratiating qualities, and very few intimate friends, it is surprising to see the warm and universal feeling which his death has elicited."

The circumstances of the accident which deprived England of Sir Robert Peel's great abilities were as follows. Peel was riding shortly after five in the afternoon at a slow pace from Buckingham Palace, where he had just entered his name in her Majesty's visiting-book. He had arrived nearly opposite the wicket-gate leading into the Green Park, when he met Miss Ellis, one of Lady Dover's daughters, on horseback, attended by a groom. Sir Robert had scarcely exchanged salutes with this young lady when his horse became slightly restive. He was observed for a moment to sit very unsteadily, rolling from side to side, and the next instant the horse turned sharply round and threw Sir Robert over its head upon his face. Two gentlemen (Mr. Fowle, of Chesham Place, and Mr. Barker, connected with the firm of Savory and Moore, Bond Street) who were close to the spot ran forward and raised Sir Robert,

Dr. Foucart's question as to whether he was much hurt, he replied, " Yes—very much."

Mrs. Lucas, a lady resident in Bryanston Square happened to be passing shortly after the accident, and at once made an offer (which was

SIR ROBERT PEEL'S HOUSE IN WHITEHALL GARDENS AFTER HIS FATAL ACCIDENT

holding him in a sitting posture. Mr. Barker then ran with all speed to St. George's Hospital for surgical aid. Dr. Foucart, a medical gentleman residing in Glasgow who happened to be passing at the moment, was the third gentleman to render assistance. He saw the accident from a distance of one hundred and fifty yards, and hastening forwards reached the spot just as Sir Robert had been raised by the other two gentlemen. Sir James Clarke also came up in a few moments afterwards. Sir Robert on being raised groaned very heavily, and, in reply to

immediately accepted) to give up her carriage, in order to convey the injured statesman to his residence. During the few moments which elapsed before a carriage was procured Sir Robert became unconscious, in which state he remained until after he had been assisted into the carriage. He then slightly revived, and, again in reply to Dr. Foucart, said, " I feel better." The carriage was then ordered to drive slowly through the park to Whitehall Gardens, Sir Robert being supported by Dr. Foucart and the two gentlemen who had first raised him from the ground. Sir James Clarke also accompanied him in the carriage to Whitehall.

In a few minutes after he had entered the carriage Sir Robert became much excited, and endeavoured to raise himself up, which it was thought necessary to prevent. He then again sank into a state of half - unconsciousness, in which he remained until his arrival in Whitehall Gardens. On being lifted out of the carriage he revived, and walked, with assistance, into the house. On entering the mansion, Sir Robert was met by Lady Peel and the members of his family, who had been awaiting his arrival in acute anxiety after having received news of the accident. Lady Peel was overwhelmed, and the effect of the meeting upon Sir Robert was painful. He swooned in the arms of Dr. Foucart, and was placed upon a sofa in the nearest apartment (the dining-room). From this room, whose windows are seen in the drawing here reproduced, Sir Robert was never removed, and so sensitive to pain did he become that it was only after difficulty that he could be removed from the sofa to a patent hydraulic bed which had been procured for his use. An examination was immediately made and the following bulletin was issued :

" Whitehall Gardens, June 29, seven P.M.—Sir Robert Peel has met with a severe accident by falling from his horse. There is severe injury of one shoulder, with a fracture of the left collarbone. There is great reason to hope that there is no internal injury.
" (Signed) Cæsar Hawkins."

The fracture was a comminuted one, and the symptoms were of the most serious character, though, at times, up to Tuesday, Sir Robert's recovery did not appear quite hopeless. From two o'clock to six o'clock on the afternoon of that day the change for the worse in his symptoms was progressive. He died at nine minutes after eleven o'clock on Tuesday night, his last words being, " God bless you."

It appeared that Sir Robert for many years past had ridden a favourite bay mare. This animal having become very old, Sir Robert was advised to obtain a more sure-footed horse ; and the animal from which he was thrown had been bought at Tattersall's a few months earlier by Mr. Beckett Denison, who intended to offer it to Sir Robert Peel. Mr. Denison rode him daily for a week. He met the troops with their bands playing, as well as omnibuses and carriages in Piccadilly— all which the horse passed without showing the smallest disposition to shy. Mr. Denison insisted upon Sir Robert riding him for a week before he decided on keeping him. He did so and then requested he might have him.

Sir Robert Peel was buried in the church of Drayton-Bassett. It is not unfitting to quote the words in which he had said farewell to office five years earlier : " I shall leave a name execrated by every monopolist, who, from less honourable motives, clamours for protection because it conduces to his own individual benefit ; but it may be that I shall leave a name sometimes remembered with expressions of goodwill in the abodes of those whose lot it is to labour, and to earn their daily bread by the sweat of their brow, when they shall recruit their exhausted strength with abundant and untaxed food, the sweeter because it is no longer leavened with the sense of injustice."

HAZARD AT BROOKS'S

THE MECCA OF REGENCY GAMBLERS

IT is very difficult to decide the origin of some clubs; but it is almost certain that the establishment of Brooks's was occasioned by the blackballing of Mr. Brook Boothby and Mr. James, two well-known men about club and town, at White's Club, which was first started at Almack's, in opposition to White's, and was farmed by Almack himself until a wine merchant named Brooks took over Almack's and removed the club to St. James's Street.

Brooks, it appears, was in the money-lending line, as were nearly all the club proprietors of that date. He is described by Robert Tickell—who is not to be confounded with Thomas Tickell, the friend of Pope—in a set of verses addressed to Richard Brinsley Sheridan, when Charles James Fox had arranged to give a supper at his own lodgings, which were situated quite near the Club:

Derby shall send, if not his plate, his cooks,
And know I've bought the best champagne from Brookes—
From liberal Brookes, whose speculative skill
Is hasty credit and a distant bill;
Who, nursed in clubs, disdains a vulgar trade,
Exalts in trust and blushes to be paid.

This first Brooks's had its home in Pall Mall, and Lord Crewe, who was one of its founders, died in 1829, after sixty-five years membership. Among the early members of the club were Burke and Sir Joshua Reynolds, David Garrick, Hume the historian, Horace Walpole, Gibbon, the author of the "Rise and Fall of the Roman Empire," Wilberforce and Sheridan, and everybody who was of any real importance. When the club was moved to the west side of St. James's Street, where a magnificent dwelling-place was erected at the expense of Brooks himself, from the designs of Henry Holland, the architect, in October 1778, the new establishment did not prosper, and James Hare, in one of his letters to George Selwyn, writes six months later : " We are all beggars at Brooks's, and he threatens to leave the house as it leaves him no profit." Yet Brooks's became a very popular club and its members were certainly full of gaiety and bonhomie.

R. Tickell is again responsible for this lively description :

Soon as to Brookes's thence thy footsteps bend,
What gratulations thy approach attend !
See Gibbon tap his box ; auspicious sign,
That classic compliment and evil combine.
See Beauclerc's cheek a tinge of red surprise,
And friendship gives what cruel health denies.
Important Townshend ! what can thee withstand ?
The lingering blackball lags in Boothby's hand.

Sheridan, who was one of the most prominent members of Brooks's, was ever ready to take up the welcome jest. One day the conversation turned upon Lord Henry Petty's projected tax upon iron. One member said that as there was so much opposition to it, it would be better to raise the proposed sum upon coals. " Hold, my dear fellow," said Sheridan, " that would be out of the frying-pan into the fire."

The history of Brooks's Club is associated with that awful stupidity that catches some men—to their downfall—gambling. Charles James Fox gambled there until he lost all his fortune ; and yet, while he was unwise in this matter, he for a long time was able to conduct affairs of State.

It was in the bosom of this club that Fox may be said to have spent the happiest hours of his life. The one characteristic of Brooks's was that it was absolutely a gambling club, even

more so than was White's. Faro and Macao were played to such an extent that men won and lost fortunes during a few hours abandoned gambling. There is one extraordinary anecdote told of this club in regard to Lord Robert Spencer, who practically lost every shilling in gambling with the large sum of money given to him by his brother, the Duke of Marlborough. General Fitzpatrick, who was also a very great loser, and Lord Spencer agreed between them to raise a sum of money sufficient to keep a Faro bank. This they accomplished, and Lord Robert Spencer carried off as his share of the proceeds one hundred thousand pounds. " He retired, strange to say, with the money in his pocket and never again gambled." To belong to Brooks's Club in the days of Pitt and Fox was a sort of test as to the likelihood of the appreciation of the Whig or opposite party. And to be a member meant a passport to Holland House, Devonshire House, and even to Carlton House, especially when the Prince Regent was at some antagonism with his father. Sheridan, whose intimate acquaintance with the Prince of Wales was well known, was extremely unpopular with two opponent wits and politicians of the day—the sarcastic George Selwyn and Lord Bessborough, and these two resolved to keep him out of the club. But the Foxites; with the assistance of the sparkling Georgiana, Duchess of Devonshire, who was the presiding genius of the Whig party, permitted themselves to send false messages, which conveyed the most urgent news of the illness of near relatives of both the dissentients. The bait took, in both cases, as each imagined that the other representative and friend would be in his place to give the one necessary blackball, and the result was that as no one else was against him Richard Brinsley Sheridan was immediately elected.

Sir Philip Francis, who has generally been supposed to have been the author of the " Letters of Junius "—though he would be a rash man who would attempt to state definitely who was the real progenitor of those stirring epistles—was one of the most successful players of Whist that Brooks's Club ever knew. It has been estimated that his winnings amounted to thirty thousand pounds ; and he made the best use of them.

When George IV., as the Prince of Wales, gave an intimation that he would like to be a member of Brooks's he was elected at once with enthusiasm ; and it is interesting to learn that he was the only member admitted whose name was not put to the ballot of the committee.

The better side of Brooks's is reflected in a picture of the club drawn by Gibbon in 1762. He thus describes it : " This respectable body, of which I have the honour of being a member, affords every evening a sight truly English. Twenty or thirty perhaps of the first men in the kingdom in point of fortune and fashion supping at little tables covered with a napkin in the middle of a coffee-room, upon a bit of cold meat or a sandwich, and drinking a glass of punch. At present we are full of King's Counsellors and lords of the bedchamber, who, having jumped into the ministry, make a very singular medley of their old principles and language with their modern ones."

OLD HARRY

ABOUT the beginning of the eighteenth century, Old Harry was a remarkable character in London, his notoriety being established by the facetious manner in which he described the sights to be seen in his raree-show. According to all accounts, it was a treat, both to old and young, to hear his learned and elaborate description of every subject and article which his attractive little cabinet contained. Pierce Tempest, in his " Cries of London," from drawings by Marcellus

OLD HARRY ; A LONDON FAVOURITE
OF QUEEN ANNE'S DAY

Laroon, has described Old Harry with his cabinet on his back, strolling the streets, and bawling aloud for an audience to his *show*. Sutton Nicholls, the engraver and printseller, published two representations of him, from one of which we have taken our s k e t c h. According to Caulfield, Harry contrived to make a comfortable living by thus amusing the public at a very trifling expense. In the latter period of his life, he had two or three successful rivals.

PETER THE GREAT

PETER THE GREAT IN LONDON

PETER the Great visited Holland in April 1697 in the rôle of an inferior official attached to an Embassy of which Lefort, the famous Genevese who had done so much to initiate him into the mysteries of civilisation in Russia, was the chief. On January 21, the following year, at the express invitation of William III., Peter, who had become a shipwright at Amsterdam and afterwards at Zaandam, came to London to increase yet further his store of Western knowledge. He stayed at a house in Norfolk Street, Strand, where William III. sent a Chamberlain to call upon him at once and placed Admiral Mitchell at his service. Three days later, the English King visited him in person and the Czar received him in his shirt-sleeves. Apart from this informality, the atmosphere of the room was intolerable, as Peter himself, the Prince of Imeritia and several others had slept in it. A window had to be opened for the benefit of the English King, though the weather was very cold. A few days later, Peter, dressed in the Russian costume, returned the visit and talked in Dutch with his brother of England.

Owing to the hard frost a visit to the English Fleet was postponed and Peter had to be contented with the ordinary attractions of London. When he went to the theatre, he would take his place behind his suite in order to avoid notice. He visited in turn the Royal Society, the Tower, the Mint, and the Observatory at Greenwich ; he also attended a Masquerade. He and Lord Carmarthen used to sup together in a tavern near the Tower, which is still known as the "Czar of Muscovy." Sir Godfrey Kneller painted his portrait, and he certainly became very quickly a personality in London life. Of Parliament, the proceedings of which he watched on one occasion through a small aperture in the ceiling, he thought very little, considering its power a menace to the Royal prerogative. And when he saw a number of people in wigs and gowns while he was visiting Westminster Hall, and was informed that they were

lawyers, the Czar of Russia exclaimed :
" What ! all these lawyers ! Why I
have only two in my dominions, and I
intended to hang them when I go
back."

On the other hand, as Mr. Oscar
Browning notes in his " Peter the
Great," the Czar thought well of
English divines and paid a visit to
the Archbishop of Canterbury besides
attending a Quaker Meeting. Bishop
Burnet saw a great deal of him and
has left this note on Peter the Great
in his History of his own Times : " I
waited often on him, and was ordered,
both by the king and the archbishop
and bishops to attend upon him, and
to offer him such information of our
religion and constitution as he was
willing to receive ; I had good in-
terpreters, so I had much free discourse with him ; he is a man of a very
hot temper soon inflamed, and very
brutal in his passion. He raises his
natural heat by drinking much brandy,
which he rectifies himself with great
application : he is subject to convulsive
motions all over his body, and his head
seems to be affected with these : he
wants not capacity and has a larger
measure of knowledge than might be
expected from his education, which
was very indifferent ; a want of
judgment, with an instability of
temper, appear in him too often and
too evidently. He is mechanically
turned and seems designed rather by
nature to be a great ship carpenter
than a great prince."

Peter the Great is said to have made
a stay during this memorable visit at
number 8 Bayswater Hill. As to
the residence in the Strand there has
been some doubt as to its exact
locality, though it has been described
minutely enough as " a large house at
the bottom of York Buildings on the

east side over against Pepys." As a
matter of fact, however, the famous
Samuel Pepys had retired from York
Buildings some eight years before to
spend the greater part of the remainder of his life in Clapham. York
Buildings, it must be remembered, was
a general name for all streets and
houses erected on the site of old York
House, afterwards restricted to a single
street, the name of which was originally
George Street. While at this house
Peter was so annoyed (says Thornbury)
with the vulgar curiosity of intrusive
citizens, that he would sometimes rise
from his dinner, and leave the room in
a rage. Here the Quakers forced
themselves upon him, and presented
him with Barclay's " Apology," after
which the Czar attended their meeting
in Gracechurch Street. He once asked
them of what use they were in any
kingdom, since they would not bear
arms.

When the weather became better
the Czar made numerous excursions
on the river. He moved down
to Deptford where he occupied Sayes
Court, the property of John Evelyn
which was at that time let furnished to the gallant Admiral Ben-
bow. In a letter to his master,
Evelyn's servant says : " There is a
house full of people and right nasty.
The Czar lies next your library, and
dines in the parlour next your study.
He dines at ten o'clock and at six
o'clock at night, is very seldom at
home a whole day, very often in the
King's Yard " (the Dockyard) " or by
water in several dresses. The King is
expected there this day ; the best
parlour is pretty clean for him to be
entertained in. The King pays for all
he has." After the Czar's departure
Evelyn made this note in his famous
diary : " I went to Deptford to see

how miserably the Czar had left my house after three months making it his Court. I got Sir Christopher Wren, the King's surveyor, and Mr. London,

Peter and, according to Dew's "Deptford," there was "in one of the old shipbuilding sheds in the dockyard, now used for housing foreign cattle, a

PETER THE GREAT'S HOUSE IN YORK BUILDINGS; NOW DEMOLISHED

his gardener, to go and estimate the repairs, for which they allowed £350, in their report to the Lord of the Treasury." During his stay at Deptford Peter added to his knowledge of shipbuilding at the Dockyard, he also visited Woolwich and was interested in the different experiments with new cannon. On March 20, he witnessed the naval manœuvres at Portsmouth. Here, he was particularly struck by the iron hammers, the bridges and the docks, and he considered the skill of the English sailors superior to anything that he had seen in Holland.

Deptford certainly remembered

plain wooden tablet, on which is painted the following inscription: 'Here worked as a ship carpenter, Peter, Czar of all the Russias, afterwards Peter the Great, 1698.'" And Dew adds: "A small thoroughfare near the old dockyard gates is called Czar Street."

But undoubtedly it was poor Evelyn who remembered Peter best of all. "Not content," says Mr. Austin Dobson in his Introduction to the Diary, "with wantonly damaging the grass-work and fruit-trees, and beating the bowling-green into holes, one of Czar Peter's morning exercises was to cause himself to be trundled on a wheelbarrow through Evelyn's famous five-foot holly hedge, long the crowning glory of the Deptford grounds." It is no wonder that in " Sylva " Evelyn speaks mournfully of "my now ruined garden, thanks to the Czar of Muscovy."

All this exuberance on the part of the Czar is rather surprising in view of the fact that so far as shipbuilding was concerned, he was accustomed to subject himself to the most severe discipline. Before visiting England he had worked for four months and a half in the East India Docks at Oostenburg in Holland. Here, he would rise early, light his own fire, cook his own food, and live the life of an ordinary carpenter. His master did not encourage visitors, but on one occasion a distinguished Englishman—either Marlborough or Portland—visited the Docks in order to see the Czar at work. Wishing to point out his famous carpenter the " Baas " called out, " Peter, carpenter of Zaandam, help those men to carry that wood." The Czar instantly obeyed.

Peter on his return from Portsmouth paid visits to Southampton, Windsor, and Hampton Court. He also went to Oxford, where he received the Degree of Doctor of Law.

As time passed Peter produced a more favourable impression on both the King of England and the English people. Count Auersperg in reference to the Czar's approaching visit to Vienna writes to the Emperor : " As concerns the person of the Czar, the Court here is well content with him, for he is not now so afraid of the people as he was at first. They accuse him of a certain stinginess only, for he has been in no way lavish. All the time

here he went about in sailor's clothing. We shall see in what dress he presents himself to your Imperial Majesty. He saw the King very rarely, as he did not want to change his manner of life, dining at eleven o'clock in the morning, supping at seven in the evening, going to bed early, and getting up at four o'clock, which very much astonished those Englishmen who kept company with him."

Peter paid his last visit to the King on April 18, and on saying "goodbye" he is said to have taken from his pocket a wisp of brown paper which he presented to William. On opening it the King discovered a magnificent uncut diamond. Three days later Peter the Great sailed for Holland which, owing to stormy weather, he did not reach for many days. Innumerable stories accentuated the eccentricity of this powerful personality and too many of them have been taken on trust. "The story of Peter," writes Dr. Schuyler, "in Holland and in England gave rise to numberless anecdotes. The stories of Dutch carpenters who had assisted him in Russia, the tales told by the English captains of his familiarity at Archangel, of his bathing with them in public, and of his drinking bouts and familiar conversation, had in a measure prepared the public mind, and the spectacle of the ruler of a great country who went about in sailor's clothing, and devoted himself to learning shipbuilding, rendered it possible and easy to invent." Similar anecdotes to this day attach themselves to picturesque and distinguished travellers and even if they have a substratum of truth at first it is soon lost through the process of telling and re-telling.

THE BOAR'S HEAD IN EASTCHEAP

NO inn in all London teems with more mellow memories than does the famous Boar's Head Tavern of Eastcheap, the original of which was destroyed by the Great Fire in 1666. But, forgetful of this destruction of the original inn, Goldsmith, sitting in front of a fire in the old Eastcheap tavern, evoked the hostess of Sir John Falstaff, as he mused upon the joyous days of Prince Hal and Bardolph and Poins : " The watchman had gone twelve. My companions had all stolen off, and none now remained with me but the landlord. From him I could have wished to know the history of the tavern that had such a long succession of customers. I could not help thinking that an account of this kind would be a pleasing contrast of the manners of different ages. He continued to doze and sot and tell a tedious story, as most other landlords usually do, and though he said nothing, yet was never silent. One good joke followed another good joke ; and the best joke of all was generally begun towards the end of a bottle. I found at last, however, his wine and his conversation operate by degrees. He insensibly began to alter his appearance. His cravat seemed quilted into a ruff, and his breeches swelled out into a farthingale. I now fancied him changing sexes ; and as my eyes began to close in slumber I imagined my landlord actually converted into as fat a landlady. How-

ever, sleep made but few changes in my situation. The tavern, the apartment, and the table continued as before. Nothing suffered mutation but my host, who was fairly altered into a gentlewoman, whom I knew to be Dame Quickly, mistress of this tavern in the days of Sir John, and the liquor we were drinking seemed converted into sack and sugar."

And it must have seemed to the Irish poet, dreaming there among the friendly ghosts, that once again the great philosopher of laughter, who had lent his immortality to the Boar's Head Tavern, had just arrived from Gad's Hill, and was even then puffing out to Prince Hal : " If sack and sugar be a fault, God help the wicked ! If to be old and merry be a sin, then many an old host that I know is damned. If to be fat be to be hated, then Pharaoh's lean kine are to be loved. No, my good lord ! Banish Peto, banish Bardolph, banish Poins ; but for sweet Jack Falstaff, kind Jack Falstaff, true Jack Falstaff, valiant Jack Falstaff, and therefore more valiant, being, as he is, old Jack Falstaff—banish not him thy Harry's company ! Banish plump Jack, and banish all the world ! "

Poor Goldsmith died in 1774, but he must have been present in spirit at the Shakespearean dinner which took place some ten years later at the Boar's Head Tavern. Both Wilberforce and Pitt, however, were present in the flesh, besides many another famous guest.

But among all the wits that were assembled at that great dinner, it was agreed by common consent that Pitt was the most amusing and the most gracious. " He was," comments Wilberforce, " the wittiest man I ever knew, and what was quite peculiar to himself, had at all times his wit under entire control. . . . I was one of those who met to spend an evening in memory of Shakespeare at the Boar's Head in Eastcheap. Many professed wits were present, but Pitt was the most amusing of the party, and the readiest and most apt in the general allusions."

Boswell refers to the famous tavern : " I mentioned a club in London at the Boar's Head in Eastcheap, the very tavern where Falstaff and his joyous companions met, the members of which all assume Shakespeare's characters. One is Falstaff, another Prince Henry, another Bardolph, and so on " : to which Dr. Johnson makes the characteristic response : " Don't be of it, Sir ; now that you have a name you must be careful to avoid many things not bad in themselves, but which will lessen your character."

The Boar's Head, situated in Great Eastcheap, between Small Alley and St. Michael's Lane, appears first as a tavern in a lease dated 1537. After the Great Fire it was rebuilt of brick, its door being in the centre with a window immediately above. Next to the window a boar's head was cut into the stone with the landlord's initials (L. T.), and the date, 1668, by the snout. Writing in 1785, Hutton, in his " Journey from Birmingham to London," says that " on each side of the doorway is a vine-branch, carved in wood, rising more than three feet from the ground, loaded with leaves and clusters ; and on the top of each

a little Falstaff, eight inches high, in the dress of his day."

Washington Irving, the urbane American writer, visited Eastcheap in 1818, in search of relics of Sir John Falstaff. At the Mason's Arms, Twelve Miles Lane, he found a tobacco-box and a sacramental cup from the neighbouring St. Michael's Church, which, in his enthusiasm for Sir John, he mistook for a tavern goblet of long ago. The tobacco-box was enormous : " I received it with becoming reverence ; but what was my delight on beholding on its cover the identical painting of which I was in quest ! There was displayed the outside of the ' Boar's Head Tavern ' ; and before the door was to be seen the whole convivial group at table in full revel, pictured with that wonderful fidelity and force with which the portraits of renowned generals and commodores are illustrated on tobacco-boxes, for the benefit of posterity. Lest, however, there should be any mistake, the cunning limner had warily inscribed the names of Prince Hal and Falstaff on the bottom of the chairs."

An inscription, almost obliterated, on the inside of the cover of this remarkable tobacco-box recorded that it was the gift of Sir Richard Gore for the benefit of vestry meetings at the Boar's Head Tavern, and that it had been " prepared and beautified by his successor, Mr. John Packard, 1767." On the second relic the American writes : " The great importance attached to this memento of ancient revelry (the cup) by modern churchwardens at first puzzled me ; but there is nothing sharpens the apprehension so much as antiquarian research ; for I immediately perceived that this could be no other than the identical ' parcel-gilt goblet ' on which Falstaff made his loving but faithless vow to Dame Quickly ; and which would of course be treasured up with care among the regalia of her domains as a testimony of that solemn contract."

One at least of the waiters of the glorious and historic tavern has been preserved from oblivion. His tomb in the burial-ground of St. Michael's Church had this significant and fitting epitaph :

Here lieth the bodye of Robert Preston, late drawer at the "Boar's Head Tavern," Great Eastcheap, who departed this life, March 16, Anno Domini 1730, aged twenty seven years.

Bacchus, to give the toping world surprise, Produced one sober son, and here he lies. Tho' nurs'd among full hogsheads, he defy'd The charm of wine, and every vice beside. O reader, if to justice thou'rt inclined, Keep honest Preston daily in thy mind. He drew good wine, took care to fill his pots, Had sundry virtues that outweighed his fauts [sic]. You that on Bacchus have the like dependence, Pray copy Bob in measure and attendance.

The Boar's Head was eventually split up into two houses and ceased to be a tavern. A gunsmith was occupying it in 1831, when it was demolished to make room for the new London Bridge.

MADAME DE STAËL IN LONDON

AFTER her many wanderings over the Continent, the famous author of " Corinne " arrived in London towards the end of June 1813, and took lodgings at No. 30 Argyll Street, Oxford Street.

In his " Fifty Years' Recollections " Mr. Cyrus Redding speaks of this house being about the middle of the western side of Argyll Street, and "nearly opposite to Lord Aberdeen's." He speaks of calling on her there between one and two o'clock, which was long before her time for receiving visitors, as she spent her mornings in reading and writing in bed. In Redding's opinion the famous Frenchwoman liked to see her drawing-room full in exactly the same sense that an actor welcomes a "full house." He adds : "Madame de Staël's drawing-room in Argyll Street was a daily levée. All the world went to see her, and she went to see all the world. If she had some little vanity, she had a just claim to be excused that fault. It would be difficult to find any female writer

since to approach her in ability. She thus gained a precedence she never used ungracefully. Her critical remarks on Teutonic literature, her extensive acquirements and reading, and the aim she had in her writings of fiction, always elevated, and never downward or mean in tendency, showing the worthiest aspirations, made me, as I still am, one of the admirers of that renowned lady."

The following month Madame de Staël took up her residence at No. 3 George Street, Hanover Square, and it was here that Crabbe Robinson found her with Mr. Murray, the publisher, and assisted in drawing up the agreement which secured her eighteen hundred guineas for her book on Germany. On the 24th of the same month, Miss Berry writes from Twickenham to Sir William Gell : " When we shall see you here, Heaven knows, for you will be one of the great lions of London yourself, and you have just come in time to save Madame de Staël's life, who certainly would have roared herself to death in another week." During this visit to London the illustrious Frenchwoman heard of the death from typhus fever of her first lover, M. de Narbonne. She also heard of the death of her second son, Albert, whose head was severed from his body in a duel with a Cossack officer. But in spite of these private griefs and the harsh facts of her exile, Madame de Staël was pleased at being lionised, and never failed to supply amazed English men and women with draughts of rhetorical eloquence. " She talks folios," said Byron, who came sixty miles to be presented to her. On the whole the English poet was not disappointed, maintaining that " she justified what I had heard ; but ' was still a mortal and made long speeches.' " " She preached," Byron adds, " politics to the politicians, and the sovereign himself was not exempt from this flow of eloquence."

Madame de Staël was the veritable lion of the season, following Maria Edgeworth just as that distinguished Irishwoman had followed Byron. Miss Berry met her at a dinner-party on the very evening of the day on which she had heard the news of de Narbonne's death. " One must acknowledge," she comments in her Journal, " that one could not lose an old lover more gaily, as it was said of Charles the Seventh of his kingdom." Madame de Staël could not live without the animation produced by her own personality. All the memoirs and diaries of the period abound in references to her. She met everybody, and she charmed everybody. Coleridge forced her to listen to him while he has been accused of " monopolising Curran." She met Sheridan and Gratton at Sir Humphry Davy's house, and Sir Samuel Romilly at Lord Lansdowne's country place.

She was the guest of Lord Liverpool and her prestige compelled the Prince Regent to visit her before she consented to wait on him at Court. The Duchess of Devonshire took her in her barouche to pay a call and Madame de Staël " related for nearly an hour, the works that she thought of writing."

But in spite of the enthusiasm with which she was received, the Frenchwoman, who so constantly gave advice, was not for a moment the victim of illusions in regard to the attitude of the English towards her. " What ascendency," she asks, " could a woman have, amiable as she might be, amid popular elections, parliamentary eloquence and the inflexibility of the law ? " " This," says Albert Sorel in his admirable monograph, " was to avow that neither in the monarchy of 1791, nor in the republic of the year III., nor in any other representative government—that is to say on any of her chosen forms of government—was there any more place for her *salon*, her influence, or indeed for her political ideals." Briefly and boldly London wanted a lion on the old tried lines, but not at all a *salonière* on the new. Moreover, though she appreciated " the best circle of clever men that England, and consequently the world can offer," there were many who shrank from her society. Schiller had wished to escape from her in Germany, and Walter Scott experienced the same aversion in England.

But her London visit was wholly successful, so much so, indeed, as to have taken her attention not only from the dead Narbonne, but also from the living Albert-Michel-Jean de Rocca to whom she was secretly married. She was a lion to the end, and it was as a lion that she returned to Paris on the abdication of her old enemy, Napoleon.

NEWCASTLE HOUSE AND ITS DUKE

WRITING of Lincoln's Inn Fields in his " A Wanderer in London " some half a dozen years ago, it was possible for a London writer to say of the west side that " although the wave of reform that flung up Kingsway and Aldwych washes its very roots," it is still standing " much as it was in the great days of the seventeenth century, except that what were then mansions of the great are now rookeries of the law." London changes fast, although it is not, as Carlyle maintained, rebuilt every seventy years ; and this can no longer be said. Some of the more notable features of the west side of Lincoln's Inn Fields remain. There are the two great brick pillars which are a monument to the genius of Inigo Jones ; but the building behind them is not the former town house of the Earl of Lindsay, but something much more recent. Close at hand there are handsome piles of offices, so new that they are as yet unsoiled by London smoke ; and quite half of the houses on this west side of the great square, which now has most of the attractions of a park, are in that state of disrepair which indicates the expiration of leases and forebodes a speedy rebuilding.

But the principal house of the square, No. 67, that with the clumsy-looking arcade covering the public footway, at the corner of Lincoln's Inn Fields and Great Queen Street, remains still much as it was when it was the residence of Thomas Pelham Holles, first Duke of Newcastle of the line. The differences are that the single doorway has been made into two, the interior of the fine old mansion having been divided, and that an additional house has been built where there was an arcade balancing that in Great Queen Street. Nor can the decorative designs, of coronets and coats-of-arms, have belonged to the original building, as, indeed, is proved by old engravings.

No. 67 Lincoln's Inn Fields was built when the English nobility had scarcely, as yet, taken to its westward flight. Henry Fielding wrote in 1752, when the Duke of Newcastle was living here as one of the most influential men of the realm : " Within the memory of many now living, the circle of the people of fascination included the whole parish of Covent Garden and great part of St. Giles's-in-the-Fields ; but here the enemy broke in, and the circle was presently contracted to Leicester Fields and Golden Square. Hence the people of fashion again retreated before the foe to Hanover Square, whence they were once more driven to Grosvenor Square, and even beyond it." The oasis, further east even than St. Giles's, was this west side of Lincoln's Inn Fields, where dwelt persons of so much social consideration that they could disregard the pressure of those whom, says Fielding, " they are pleased to call the vulgar."

Newcastle House, as it is still called by those who know its history, had Powis House for its first name ; for it was built for the Marquis of Powis about 1686, and was purchased from his family by the nobleman often described as " the great Duke of Newcastle," and by Leigh Hunt as " the well-known fantastical Duke of that name, Minister of George II." Newcastle was great only in the respect that he was one of the renowned bigwigs of the day, and that the political influence which he was enabled to acquire in devious ways helped him to drive Sir Robert Walpole from

Stanhope passes a more elaborate judgment on him. He says: "His peculiarities were so glaring and ridiculous that the most careless glance

NEWCASTLE HOUSE, LINCOLN'S INN FIELDS

power. Sir Robert's son, the malicious but always delightful letter-writer, did not forget the obligation. The Duke of Newcastle is never mentioned apart from Walpole's saying that "Mr. Pitt does everything, and the Duke gives everything. So long as they agree in this partition they may do what they please." The Pitt alluded to here was afterwards the undoubtedly great Earl of Chatham. "The miserable incapacity of the Duke of Newcastle" is J. R. Green's phrase. Lord

could not mistake, nor the most bitter enmity exaggerate, them. Extremely timorous, and moved to tears on the slightest occasions, he abounded in childish caresses and empty protestations. Fretful and peevish with his dependents, always distrusting his friends, and always ready to betray them, he lived in a continual turmoil of harassing affairs, vexatious opposition, and burning jealousies. What chiefly maintained him in power was his court-craft, his indefatigable perseverance, his devoting every energy of his mind to discover and attach himself to the winning side."

And thereby hangs a tale. His energy in corruption was so great that he would travel a long way, at great cost, to influence a contested election. Then, too, he would promise anything. At an election in Cornwall " his Grace poured forth acknowledgments and promises without ceasing on the fortunate possessor of the casting vote," the Duke's side having won by one. The Cornish voter asked for a small place for a relative. " My dear friend," said the Duke, " why do you ask for such a trifling employment ? " The relative should certainly have the place the moment it became vacant. As soon as the then ailing incumbent died the man with the casting vote was to post off from Cornwall to Lincoln's Inn Fields, and there, by night or by day, the Duke would see him at once. The emergency arose in a few months' time, and the contemporary narrator of the story goes on to say : " The Duke of Newcastle, on the very night that the decisive vote was at his door, had sat up anxiously expecting despatches from Madrid. Wearied by official business and agitated spirits, he retired to

rest, having previously given particular instructions to his porter not to go to bed, as he expected every minute a messenger with advices of the greatest importance, and desired he might be shown upstairs the moment of his arrival." Anybody can imagine the remainder. It is like a scene from a rollicking eighteenth-century comedy. " Vexed at so untimely a disturbance, and disappointed of news from Spain, he frowned for a few seconds ; but chagrin soon gave way to mirth at so singular and ridiculous a combination of opposite circumstances."

This is one of those stories to which there is no conclusion. Nobody knows —nobody ever will know—whether the relative of the man with a casting vote got his appointment.

Newcastle House just missed a sort of apotheosis. Pennant says that Government had it once in mind to buy it and settle it on the Great Seal, as Walpole settled his Downing Street house on the Treasury. " At that time it was inhabited by the Lord Keeper, Sir Nathan Wright." The project came to nothing, or the Lord Chancellor might now have been living in Lincoln's Inn Fields. But No. 67 had a further great destiny, nevertheless. It was once occupied by the Society for the Diffusion of the Bible.

J. M. W. TURNER AS A YOUNG MAN

TURNER IN MAIDEN LANE

A THOROUGHFARE that has established its name in the history of London is Maiden Lane, which leads from the west side of Southampton Street, and runs right through into Bedford Street. Here at the corner of Hand Court, a small paved place with an arched entrance which stood opposite the Cider Cellars (opened about 1730, but which at the time of the painter's birth was the studio of a society of artists), at the house numbered 26, Joseph Mallord William Turner was born on St. George's Day, April 23, 1775.

His father, William Turner, was a Devonshire man, though he started early in life to live in London, where he set up business in Maiden Lane as a barber. He married a Miss Mallard, or Mallord, of Islington, a lady who seems to have had a peculiar temper and a great obstinacy of nature.

It has been stated that the Turners lived most of their time in the cellar under the hairdresser's shop. This story may have been circulated to get a sort of dramatic effect, and obtain a contrast by lowering the father in order to elevate the son. However, we know the elder Turner was in humble circumstances for many years, and was certainly close in money matters, if not parsimonious. Although his son did not secure a good education, his parent sent him to several schools, until he was fourteen years of age, and then he apprenticed him first to an architectural firm. Eventually young Turner obtained the opening that gave his budding genius full play. He was sent to an art academy in St. Martin's Lane, and through the good offices of some of his father's theatrical customers he obtained an introduction to Sir Joshua

Reynolds, who took a great interest in the lad.

However, the starting-point in the career of the embryo painter was on the occasion of his going with his father to Mr. Tomkinson's when the barber was engaged to friz a wig and to shave the "white hair from the smooth blue flesh." While the father was at work, the boy with observant eye was at work too. He sat gazing with all the might of his bright blue eyes at a silver salver (emblazoned with the Tomkinson arms) which leant against the wainscot. A certain rampant lion especially astonished him.

The little barber continued his work, the wig was frizzed and snowily powdered till it resembled the cauliflower of the garden, and finally Turner senior, having finished his work, took his departure with his little boy.

THE BIRTHPLACE OF TURNER IN MAIDEN LANE

"The boy is silent and thoughtful all that day," says Walter Thornbury; "he sits upstairs all apart, brooding over a sheet of paper. Mother wonders what ails him; Father is consulted at tea-time; and they call for Billy, who with impetuosity produces his paper and exhibits a not unintelligible lion, twin brother to the royal and wilder one on the salver at Mr. Tomkinson's. The gods be praised—the

boy is a genius." From that time the boy's fate is fixed; and while the elder Turner is busy with his razor in the little shop in Maiden Lane to the constant questions of his customers his invariable reply is: "It's all settled, sir; *William is going to be a painter.*" Never was a proud father's prediction more gloriously fulfilled.

An interesting view of Turner's upbringing, as the son of a working barber in the heart of London, is adopted by the late Philip Gilbert Hamerton, who in his thoughtful "Life of Turner" writes:

"He was born exactly in that rank of society where artistic genius had, at that time, the best chance of opening, like a safely-sheltered flower. To perceive the full truth of this we have nothing to do but imagine him born in any other than the humbler middle class. If his father had been a little lower in the world, the boy would have been fixed down to some kind of humble labour from his childhood, and held down to it afterwards by want; this at least is so probable as to be almost a certainty, for Turner's genius discovered itself very gradually, and he had no explosive originality at the beginning. But what is *quite* a certainty is, the stifling of his gift in any English family of that time which had the slightest pretension to aristocracy. If Turner had been what is called a gentleman, he would have been exposed to influences which are as deadly to artistic genius as an unbreathable gas is to the animal organism."

If Maiden Lane in the last quarter of the eighteenth century was favourable to the development of genius, its direct influence on Turner's art was, in Ruskin's eyes, not less apparent. " He attaches himself with the faithfullest child-love to everything that bears an image of the place he was born in. No matter how ugly it is— has it anything about it like Maiden Lane, or like Thames' shore ? If so, it shall be painted for their sake.

Hence, to the very close of life, Turner could endure ugliness which no one else, of the same sensibility, would have borne for an instant. Dead brick walls, blank square windows, old clothes, market-womanly types of humanity—anything fishy and muddy, like Billingsgate or Hungerford Market, had great attraction for him ; black barges, patched sails, and every possible condition of fog."

It is a satisfying circumstance that when Turner became famous and successful he took his thrifty old father out of the Maiden Lane shop to live with him. The old man was happy in stretching canvases and mixing paints for the son whose genius he had nourished.

BENJAMIN FRANKLIN AS A LONDON COMPOSITOR

FRANKLIN lived in London at various periods ; the house in Craven Street, where he lived as the agent of the American colonies, is marked with a tablet. He probably always retained an affection for the Lincoln's Inn Fields district, where he worked at Watts's printing works in Wild Court as a compositor. There his fellow printers dubbed him the " American Aquatic " because he drank water at his meals, their own consumption of beer being, according to Franklin, not less than five pints a day per man. But they recognised young

BENJAMIN FRANKLIN

Franklin's brain-power, and allowed him to revise the laws of their " chapel." They borrowed money from him with such regularity that the table on which the weekly wages were paid was also the table on which they settled with the " Aquatic." Franklin's landlady was the widowed daughter of a Protestant clergyman who had married a Catholic and become one herself. She and Franklin vied in frugality ; " half an anchovy, a small slice of bread and butter each, with half a pint of ale between them, furnished commonly their supper."

THE ADMIRALTY SEMAPHORE

THE Marconi apparatus on the roof of the Admiralty building, in Whitehall, is perhaps the most fascinating object in London. Through that delicate web of wires Britain speaks to her war-captains around her coasts and for many hundreds of miles to sea. But these Marconi masts have but taken the place of telegraph wires which, again, had superseded the old hand-worked semaphore by which, in Nelson's day, messages were sent from roof to roof and hill to hill until at Portsmouth they reached the quarter-decks.

What a sight for a London boy must have been those mysterious rising and falling shutters whose message was understood in the station at St. George's Fields and was at once transmitted to the next point of observation! As late as 1841 such a boy watched them spell-bound; his name was George Augustus Sala. Dickens, one imagines, must often have seen this predecessor of the telegraph during his dreary years in the blacking warehouse hard by.

The rapidity with which messages could be sent down from the Admiralty to Portsmouth or Deal was remarkable. It is even said that, under favourable conditions, the expert signallers could convey a message all the distance in less than a minute.

AN ADMIRALTY SEMAPHORE STATION; EXTERIOR

There were twelve stations between London and Plymouth, eight of which were part of the Portsmouth line, the separation taking place in the New Forest. Another chain of nineteen stations extended from London to Yarmouth. The route between London and Portsmouth was as follows: The Admiralty — Chelsea — Putney — Kingston— Cooper's Hill — Chatelly — Pearly—Bannick — Haste — Holder — Beacon — Compton Down—Portsdown Hill— Southsea Beach—High Street, Portsmouth. The distances between the stations on all the lines averaged about eight miles.

For a graphic picture of the working of these interesting naval signals we turn to Sir Richard Phillips's interesting book " A Morning's Walk from London to Kew " (1820). That worthy bookseller and alderman stayed, in his " Walk," to examine very thoroughly the signalling station at Chelsea, and the particulars he gives of the methods employed are as follow :

" After about twenty years' experience, they calculate on about two hundred days on which signals can be transmitted throughout the day ; about sixty others on which they can pass only part of the day, or at particular stations ; and about one hundred days in which few of the stations can see the others. The powers of the stations are exceedingly various. The station in question is generally rendered useless during easterly winds by the smoke of London, which fills the valley of the Thames between this spot and Chelsea Hospital ; or more commonly between the shorter distance of the Admiralty to Chelsea. Dead flats are found to be universally unfavourable ; and generally stations are useless nearly in proportion to the miles of dead flat looked over. On the contrary, stations between hill and hill, looking across a valley, or series of valleys, are mostly clear ; and water surfaces are found to

AN ADMIRALTY SEMAPHORE STATION; INTERIOR

produce fewer obscure days than land in any situation. The period least favourable of the same day is an hour or two before the sun's passage of the meridian, particularly on dead levels; where the play of the sun's rays on the rising exhalations renders distant vision exceedingly obscure. The tranquillity of the morning and evening are ascertained to be the most favourable hours for observation.

" A message from London to Portsmouth is usually transmitted in about fifteen minutes ; but, by an experiment tried for the purpose, a single signal has been transmitted to Plymouth and back again in three minutes, which by the Telegraph route is at least four hundred miles. In this instance, however, notice had been given to make ready, and every captain was at his post to receive and return the signals. The progress was at the rate of one hundred and seventy miles in a minute, or three miles per second, or three seconds at each station ; a rapidity truly wonderful ! "

Phillips adds that the number of signals provided was sixty-three— " by which they represent the ten digits, the letters of the alphabet, many generic words, and all the numbers which can be expressed by sixty-three variations of the digits." His statements regarding the speed at which messages could be transmitted are very remarkable, but they do not appear to be exaggerated. A note in Cobbett's " Rural Rides " tells us that the hour of one was transmitted daily from Greenwich to Portsmouth and returned to Greenwich in forty-five seconds, the distance being eighty-five miles one way.

There are many people living who have seen these famous mechanical telegraphs at work. Professor Walter W. Skeat communicated in April 1909 to *Notes and Queries* his recollection of seeing the semaphore signal on One Tree Hill, near Peckham, in operation. This was about 1843 or 1844.

GARIBALDI IN LONDON

ON Monday April 11, 1864, Garibaldi, the Italian Liberator, who had become one of the few heroes of the British public, approached Nine Elms railway station, Vauxhall. From cottage doors and quiet lonely woods salutations had come to him as the train flashed by, but now at a quarter past two, at the entrance to the Vauxhall Station, an indescribable scene of tumultuous welcome was in store for him. The station was black with people, and on trucks and locomotives, on piles of timber, on walls, on piled-up luggage and every possible point of vantage, the railway workmen and their wives and daughters were waiting to see Garibaldi.

The sympathies of the English people were undoubtedly on the side of Italy, and not on the side of the French and Austrian holders of Rome and Venice. It was not simply one class but all classes of Englishmen who welcomed the General whose sustained gallantry against heavy odds had captured the imagination of Londoners. His political object was to induce the British Government to help Denmark in her desperate conflict with Austria and Prussia, but of this Londoners knew little and cared less. Their welcome was for Garibaldi, the man, rather than for the politician.

Enthusiasts among the demonstrators at Nine Elms wore sashes with stripes of green on white and red silk, while the Working-men's Committee were conspicuous with a tri-coloured ribbon, stamped with the Cross of Savoy, and having woven into it in silk a portrait of the General.

As the train approached there was a cry of "Hats off!" and the Italian band played "Garibaldi's Hymn." On all sides the shouts and cheering became tumultuous.

As Garibaldi passed on down the platform, the enthusiasm increased, so much so, indeed, that he appeared almost dazed by it, until on reaching the dais, he turned to receive the addresses with all his accustomed calm and dignity. The first address came from the City Committee, which was followed by that of the workmen. Garibaldi replied to both with grateful appreciation, but his voice shook with emotion as he addressed the workmen in these words : "I wish to say to the workmen particularly, that I am very grateful, and shall never in my life forget the welcome of a class to which I consider that I have the honour to belong, I like to call my brothers the workmen of every part of the world."

His reception in London from first to last had been spontaneous, and on every possible occasion during Garibaldi's short visit it was repeated. On the next day, Tuesday, he lunched at Chiswick with the Dowager Duchess of Sutherland, and on his way called at Cambridge House, where he spent a quarter of an hour with Lord Palmerston. On Wednesday evening the Duke and Duchess of Sutherland gave a great entertainment in his honour at Stafford House and among the guests were Mr. and Mrs. Gladstone. He visited the Royal Italian Opera the following evening, and two days afterwards he received a tremendous ovation at the Crystal Palace. On the Wednesday following Garibaldi proceeded to the Guildhall to receive that historic privilege, the freedom of the City, his reception culminating in a magnificent banquet given in his honour by the Lord Mayor and City of London.

The visit to England was, as everybody knows, abruptly and unexpectedly terminated for political reasons and on April 21 the General wrote to his friends : " Thanks from my heart for yo r sympathy and affection. I shall be happy to return among you under more favourable circumstances, and to enjoy at ease the hospitality of your noble country."

Garibaldi, in the words of a French writer in the *Courier du Dimanche*, " came to England to get the surplus of the balance of the Chancellor of the Exchequer for his million muskets with which to establish Italian freedom; half a million people came to look at Guiseppe Garibaldi, who in his own country is but a pardoned rebel, and has no birth or title." And the cynical Frenchman goes on to prophesy that the Italian would get plenty of plumpudding and turtle soup but no money for his muskets ! As a matter of fact the Liberator's life startled the inmates at Stafford House by its simplicity. " He rose," writes Mr. J. T. Bent in his biography of the great Italian, " at five, and breakfasted at six off bread, grapes, cheese, and a glass of wine, and then he smoked a cigar in the garden whilst his ducal host was still in bed. One morning a servant came to announce his frugal breakfast. ' Oh, I have had it,' said Garibaldi, and it turned out that he had drunk a mug of beer and eaten a bit of bread which had been left from his equally frugal supper of the night before." But the Frenchman had been right in his prophecy about the muskets, and Garibaldi was also disappointed in not having secured help for Denmark in her hopeless struggle against Prussia and Austria. He gives no description of the visit in his memoirs, but it is on record that, like so many other distinguished foreigners, he saluted the London policeman.

After a design by Johannot

THE CRYSTAL PALACE

THERE are many stories told of the birth of the Crystal Palace, which had its original glory in Hyde Park. Here it was first erected in 1851 chiefly through the influence and good offices of the Prince Consort, as the dazzling palace of the Great Exhibition.

The original design of the Crystal Palace as submitted by Sir Joseph (then Mr.) Paxton, may be inspected in the Fine Arts Gallery at Sydenham, drawn on a sheet of blotting-paper. Also, the original model of the Crystal Palace may still be seen. It is a small lily-house standing close to the head gardener's villa on the Duke of Devon-

shire's estate at Chatsworth. Sir Joseph Paxton had chanced to visit Chatsworth whilst seeking a design for the Exhibition buildings in Hyde Park, and was struck by the possibilities presented by the structure. " Tell me," he said to the Duke's agent, John Marples, " could you extend that from here to Chatsworth House." " Certainly," replied Marples. " Then it's done," cried Paxton. And so the idea of the " Great Palace of Windows " was born.

Now this statement must be taken with a very large grain of salt, because Joseph Paxton practically began life as a gardener's boy on the Chatsworth Estate, and he became so expert as a gardener (and in after years a horticulturist and architect) that the Duke of Devonshire proved his great friend to the end of his days. As a matter of fact, it was Paxton himself who designed the lily-house referred to, for the cultivation of the Victoria Lily, and it was through the use he had made of iron and glass in the construction of the conservatories on that estate that Paxton got his conception.

The immense house stood in the convenient position between Rotten Row and the Ladies' Mile, running parallel with the Knightsbridge Road, and close by that spot where stands the Albert Memorial.

SIR JOSEPH PAXTON

Thackeray, in his "May Day Ode," published in the *Times*, May 1, 1851, says:

> But yesterday a naked sod,
> The dandies sneered from Rotten Row
> And sauntered o'er it to and fro
> And see 'tis done!
>
> As though 'twere by a wizard's rod
> A blazing arch of lucid glass
> Leaps like a fountain from the grass
> To meet the sun.

The English Government did nothing and has done nothing towards the cost of the erection or the up-keep of what should be a national possession—the beautiful palace of crystal which has for so long been the scene of so many national gatherings, and so many festivals, to celebrate English and Foreign achievements in every depart-

ment of the world's history and the world's advancement, especially in science and art, and above all in music,

The origin of the present Crystal Palace may be stated in a few words. "When in 1852 the Government declined to purchase the building which had been so successfully raised in Hyde Park, by the genius of Sir Joseph Paxton, for the Great Exhibition of 1851, a few enterprising gentlemen stepped forward and rescued it from destruction with the avowed purpose of rebuilding it on some appropriate site." These gentlemen resolved that the building—the first example of a new and striking style of architecture—should rise again in increased grandeur and beauty, to form a "Palace where, at all times, protected from the inclement varieties of our climate, healthful exercise and wholesome recreation should be easily attainable." It was transferred to the chosen site at Sydenham, to a fine estate of three hundred acres, and it is interesting to note that nearly seven thousand men were employed upon the gigantic task.

The Sydenham Palace differs in many essential values from the parent edifice, which was somewhat monotonous in its outline and appearance, and in every respect it is a great improvement.

One authority says: "The design of the Crystal Palace is most simple: one portion corresponds with another; there is no introduction of needless ornament. Nor is this unity confined to the building. It characterises the contents of the glass structure, and prevails in the grounds—the most glorious grounds and gardens of their size, by the way—all the component parts blend, yet all are distinct : and the effect of the admirable and harmonious arrangement is that any confusion in the vast establishment, within and without, is avoided." This is perfectly true. The visitor to the mighty maze can proceed by easy stages from point to point, from one department to another in perfect comfort and ease, gathering information and amusement at every step.

The history of the Palace is full of surprises, and even Herbert Spencer allowed himself to wander into superlatives when speaking of the building when it was newly opened : " I have been once at Sydenham," he wrote. " It surpasses even my expectations, though I have seen it in progress. It is a fairyland and a wonder surpassing all others." Charles Dickens and Ruskin were equally enthusiastic.

Since Queen Victoria opened it on June 10, 1854, when it was computed that some forty thousand people were present, and recorded in her " Diary " that the sight had been magical—so vast, so glorious, so touching," it has been the scene of many notable events. Alexander II. of Russia, the German Emperor, the late Shah of Persia, and many other continental and Asiatic potential personages have been fêted at the Palace. Here some of the greatest singers of the days, past and present, have sung. Amongst these may be mentioned Madame Tietjens, the great opera soprano singer, who exclaimed towards the end of her career, " If I am to die, I will play Lucrezia once more." And she did, and died in 1877. Madame Adelina Patti has sung often at the Palace, and the late Madame Belle Cole, the charming American vocalist, Madame Albani, Melba, Madame Christine Nillsson, Sims Reeves, Sir Charles Santley, Joseph Maas, and Edward Lloyd. It is worth recording that nearly all Sir Arthur Sullivan's serious works were first heard at the Crystal Palace, including the " Martyr of Antioch " and " The Golden Legend."

The Palace, under the late August Manns, created quite a monopoly of oratorio, and presented from time to time all the great masterpieces of this class of music ever written. Then the choirs were the best to be heard and the orchestra one of the most artistic.

The Handel festivals were one of the greatest achievements and successes that the Palace ever had. Here, too, was held the great Festival of Choirs of few years back.

In the Coronation year of King George V. and Queen Mary the Palace was the scene of the gayest and perhaps best organised fête in history, when the King and Queen, with the Prince of Wales went down to see one hundred thousand London children enjoy the Festival of Empire.

"GENTLEMAN" JACKSON THE PUGILIST

IT is not often that men of the Ring are remembered outside sporting circles and those journals which make it their business to record their exploits, but John Jackson was quite an exception to the general rule. He was an athlete of considerable importance in his day and had the great privilege of teaching Lord Byron how to box. It is noteworthy that on the altar tomb, with athlete figures of Jackson, in the Westminster and West London Cemetery, there is a somewhat pompous epitaph in verse which shows that in any case he must have made a great number of friends during his lifetime.

"Stay, Traveller," the Roman record said,
To mark the classic dust beneath it laid ;
"Stay Traveller," this brief memorial cries
And read the moral with attentive eyes ;
Hast thou a lion's heart, a giant's strength,
Exult not, for these gifts must yield at
    length ;
Do health and symmetry adorn thy frame,
The mouldering bones below possessed the
    same ;
Does love, does friendship, every step attend,
This man ne'er made a foe, nor lost a friend.
But death full soon dissolves all human ties,
And, his last combat o'er, here Jackson lies.

John Jackson, who by one enthusiastic admirer, was called the "Nestor of the Ring," was born in London in 1768. His father was a builder who had a taste for sport himself, and encouraged his son Jack to go in for all those manly exercises that are bound to develop, if nothing else, at least the physical part of a boy's character. As a youth he was known as an agile dancer, a very good wrestler and was able to use the single stick with great ability. His father intended him to follow his own calling, but young Jackson being in appearance something like

another Apollo, and as brave as a lion, decided to enter the arena of fisticuffs.

Jackson's pugilistic career need not be here related. He became "Gentleman" Jackson when he opened a Gymnastic Academy at No. 13, Old Bond Street, where the aristocracy flocked to take lessons ; for everybody boxed and everybody used the single stick. Here it was that Lord Byron, who was a very good amateur sparrer, first became acquainted with Jackson, and by him was initiated in the art of "putting up the dukes." When Jackson taught the author of "Don Juan" he was about double the age of his pupil, but Byron, being lame, had very little chance with such a powerful antagonist. In a note to the Eleventh Canto of "Don Juan," Byron speaks of "My friend and corporeal pastor and master, John Jackson, Esquire, professor of pugilism, who I trust still retains the strength and symmetry of his model and form, together with his good-humour and athletic as well as mental accomplishments." Byron refers several times to the fact of dining at "Tom Cribb's Parlour," and Tom Cribb was celebrated for gathering all the "sports" of the day around him. He was another champion who is frequently mentioned by Pierce Egan in "Life in London." Byron adds, "I have been sparring with Jackson for exercise this morning and mean to continue and renew my acquaintance with my muffles. My chest and arms and wind are in very good plight and I'm not in flesh. I used to be a hard hitter and my arms are very long for my height (five feet eight and a quarter inches) ; at any rate exercise is good, and this is the severest of all ; fencing and the broad sword never fatigued me half so much "

Constantly in Byron's Letters and Diary he refers to Jackson and the

"GENTLEMAN" JACKSON
From a Contemporary Portrait

delight he took in sparring, and as Byron was not blessed with the best of health, and lived an extraordinary life in the way of eating and drinking, there is no doubt that this exercise did him a vast amount of good One description of Jackson from a veteran writer is worth repeating : " There were the Lades, the Hangers, the Bullocks, the Vernons, but give me Jack Jackson as he stood alone amid the throng. I can see him now as I saw him in '84 walking down Holborn Hill, towards Moorfields. He had on a scarlet coat worked in gold at the buttonholes, ruffles and frill of fine lace, a small white stock, no collar (they were not then invented), a looped hat with a broad black band, buff knee-breeches and silk strings, striped white silk stockings, pumps, and paste buckles. His waistcoat was pale blue satin, sprigged with white. It was impossible to look on his fine ample chest, his noble shoulders, his waist (if anything too small), his large, but not too large, hips (the fulcrum of the human form, whether male or female), his limbs, his balustrade calf, and beautifully turned but not over delicate ankle, his firm foot, and peculiarly small hand, without thinking that nature had sent him on earth as a model. On he went at a good five miles and a half an hour, the envy of all men, and the admiration of all women."

John Jackson in many ways was a very remarkable man, because although his origin was obscure he was always aiming at higher things and was even a student of Lavater, one of the first exponents of the value of physiognomy and a very rapid reader of character, and through his own self-developed knowledge, he was not only able to judge people, but, by never being obtrusive, he made many friends, and was always on good terms with almost everybody with whom he came in contact. He was a great theatre goer also, and, whenever any gymnastic or equestrian or pedestrian show was forward at Astley's or the Surrey Theatre, he was almost invariably present.

At the Coronation of George the Fourth, Jackson was applied to to

furnish an unarmed force (surely there is a bull here) to be ready for emergencies, and consequently he gathered together all the pugilists and prize fighters of the hour. Dressed as Royal Pages they formed a most extraordinary corps, which was certainly equal to quelling any disturbance that might have occurred during the processions. There is little more to say except that Jackson's life was most exemplary and his kind heart made him loved and respected by all with whom he came in contact from the King downwards. He died on October 7, 1845.

THE "O. P." RIOTS

THERE have been theatrical riots ever since the days of Shakespeare, when Tarleton, the comedian, was saluted on the cheek with an apple from an occupant of the gallery who was offended because the actor had deviated from the text. In other words, he had " gagged." But the " O.P." riots were the most serious of all. These riots, so well known in theatrical circles, really meant the Old Prices fight over the alteration in the charges for the seats made when Covent Garden was re-opened in 1809. The " O.P." riots must not be confused with the half-price riots at the same theatre and Drury Lane in 1763.

Wright, in his " Caricature History of the Georges," gives a very full account of these notorious scenes, an abbreviation of which, and particulars from other sources, will enable us to comprehend the situation. Covent Garden Theatre was burned to the ground on September 19, 1808, involving the loss of many lives, and the destruction of property valued at a quarter of a million. The first stone of the new building was laid by the Prince of

Wales on the last day of the year, 1808, and such progress was made that the new theatre was opened to the public on Monday September 18, 1809, with John Philip Kemble as Macbeth.

A storm was impending. In the new arrangement a row of private boxes formed the third tier under the gallery. The furniture of each box, and of the adjoining room was to be according to the taste of the several occupants— who might almost be called renters. To make these extraordinary accommodations for the great comfort of the wealthy patrons, the comfort of the rest of the audience was considerably diminished. To crown all the theatre opened with an increase of their prices, the pit being raised from three shillings and sixpence to four shillings, and the boxes from six shillings to seven shillings. To make it clear in regard to the pit it is necessary to understand that there were no stalls in those days. The pit occupied absolutely the whole floor of the theatre, from the back wall to the orchestra. The manager said that this was necessary to cover the enormous expense of rebuilding the theatre, but the public declared that the old prices were sufficient and that the new ones were a mere exaction to enable Kemble to pay enormous salaries to foreigners like Catalini—all foreign performers were hated by the the full-headed, sturdy Britons of 1809!—and it was known that Catalini had been engaged at one hundred and fifty pounds per week, to perform two nights only. On the first night of the representation the curtain drew up to a crowded house, and the audience seemed to be lost in admiration at the beauty of the decorations, until Kemble made his appearance on the stage. "A faint attempt at applause got up by his own friends was in an instant drowned by an overpowering noise of groans, hisses and yells which drove him from the stage."

Excited by the accounts given in the newspapers, the public prepared to go to the theatre on the second night in a spirit more warlike than ever, and on the third night Kemble gave more offence to the audience by saying to them: "I want to know what you want." So, for a whole week, these disgraceful proceedings continued. On Friday the 24th, Mr. Kemble, worn out and exhausted by the unkindly opposition, proposed that the decision of the dispute should be put to a committee composed of the Governor of the Bank of England, the Attorney-General and others. On Saturday night this was agreed to and the theatre was shut up until the verdict was obtained, the obnoxious Catalini having, in the meantime, agreed to cancel her agreement.

The theatre, to the loss and detriment of the management, was closed until the following Wednesday week, when, on the re-opening, the uproar became worse, and more turbulent than ever, because the report of the committee, who were all shareholders, by the way, was entirely in favour of the management and their attitude. Again the house was closed and a full report of the committee re-considered was printed on the playbills for October 4, showing that only on the principle of the new prices could the theatre hope to show profits.

Finally, the discontents formed themselves into a party resolved to disturb the performance night after night until their demands were acceded to. Unfortunately, the proprietors sent in hired "bruisers," and the rattles, drums, whistles and catcalls from the audience disgraced the proceedings and drowned the voices of all. This caused more trouble, and a burlesque song was written called "Heigh ho! says Kemble," which was caught up by all the balladmongers, and even sung beneath poor Kemble's house-windows in Great Russell Street, Bloomsbury. Then ensued a series of struggles which lasted during the extraordinary period of ten weeks and which were not ended until the "Treaty of Peace" was formed on December 17, 1809. As it soon proved too expensive to keep on this siege night after night, the rioters began to adopt the plan of coming in at halfprice, the curious effect of which was that three acts of a play were listened to in the usual, orderly manner by peaceful visitors, while of the remaining two acts not a word could be heard.

The management might have conquered in the end, but the introduction of prize fighters and an action at law brought against Mr. Kemble by an assaulted playgoer weakened the whole case, and in the end Kemble had to make apology to those who had treated him so shamefully!

SHOOTING THE BRIDGE

OLD London Bridge with its many small arches, some of which were obstructed by waterworks, offered no easy passage to small boats or barges. The river rushed through the openings like a great mill-race, and when the tide was going out a fall of four to six feet was encountered on the lower side of the bridge. The Thames watermen were skilful, but " Shooting the Bridge " was for centuries a dangerous, if sometimes an exhilarating, experience. Dr. Johnson cared for it so little that, like other prudent Londoners, it was his custom in going down the river to land above the bridge and take another boat below it. This he did in 1763 when taking a sculler at the Temple Stairs for Greenwich. He and Boswell landed at the Old Swan and walked to Billingsgate to re-embark.

The author of " Chronicles of London Bridge " gives some interesting particulars of the conditions under which the passage of old London Bridge could be safely navigated as late as 1823, when to the usual dangers were added those of the New Bridge cofferdams. He says : " The celebrated fall is, of course, most evident at low water, when it is about 4 feet 6 inches, or 6 feet in the winter season ; and the most hazardous time for passing through any of the bridge locks, is probably half an hour previous to, or, for barges, the last two hours before, low water below bridge. The safest time of the tide is at high water, or slack low water : but boats may pass with safety for 2½ hours after flood, and the last half-hour of the drain of the tide at ebb above bridge ; the tide having then flowed nearly 4 feet below. Deeply laden barges also take the drain through at low water. . . . Though the works of the new bridge have at present closed several of the arches of the ancient edifice, yet the fourth and fifth locks from the Southwark end have been thrown into one, with a strong wooden vaulting, parapet, and roadway above, to increase the waterway beneath. Since the commencement of these works, the fall of the river has also become less dangerous for barges, from the returning tide sooner meeting with resistance ; and instead of a direct fall of 6 feet in 50, it is now only about 6½ feet in 250."

Reverting to Dr. Johnson's period we read of strange accidents at London Bridge. Thus it is related in the *Public Advertiser* of Monday, December

29, 1760 : "On Tuesday, a large old French ship, that was coming through the Draw-Lock at London Bridge, to be broken up above Bridge, stuck in the Lock, and still continues there, having done considerable damage to the same ; and it is thought that she cannot now be got out, but must be broken up where she now lies." The same paper for Friday, January 9, 1761, states that "Yesterday the workmen, who have been employed, for this fortnight past, in breaking up the large French ship that stuck in the Draw-Lock at London Bridge, as she was going up the river, endeavoured, on the strong flow of the tide, to get her through the Bridge, but could not effect it. This ship, it appears, was but 18 inches wider than the Lock." At length, however, in the same paper for Friday, January 30, it was announced that "Yesterday the watermen cleared the Draw-Lock at London Bridge of the large French ship that stuck there some weeks ago."

Hundreds of Londoners were drowned in "Shooting the Bridge," and several famous suicide tragedies are associated with these dangerous rapids. Thus, in 1689, Sir William Temple's only son, lately made Secretary at War, leaped into the river from a boat as it darted through an arch : he had filled his pockets with stones, and was drowned, leaving in the boat this note : "My folly in undertaking what I could not perform, whereby some misfortunes have befallen the King's service, is the cause of my putting myself to this sudden end ; I wish him success in all his undertakings, and a better servant." Pennant adds to the anecdote that Sir William Temple's false and profane reflection on the occasion was, that "a wise man might dispose of himself, and make his life as short as he pleased ! " In 1737, Eustace Budgell, a *soi-disant* cousin of Addison, who wrote in the *Spectator* and *Guardian*, when broken down in character and reduced to poverty, took a boat at Somerset Stairs ; and ordering the waterman to row down the river, Budgell threw himself into the stream as they shot London Bridge. He too had filled his pockets with stones, and rose no more : he left in his secretary a slip of paper, on which was written a broken distich : "What Cato did, and Addison approved, cannot be wrong."

A pleasanter story is that of Edward Osborne who, in 1536, leapt into the rushing tide from the window of a house on the bridge and saved his master's infant daughter, who had been dropped into the river by a nursemaid. The father, afterwards Lord Mayor, gave his daughter in marriage to Osborne, and their great-grandson became the first Duke of Leeds.

JEAN JACQUES ROUSSEAU IN ENGLAND

ON Monday, January 13, 1766, the historian and philosopher David Hume escorted Jean Jacques Rousseau to London after a passage from Calais to Dover which had taken twelve hours. There was no little excitement among Londoners about this visit. "All the world," said the *London Magazine* "are eager to see this man, who by his singularity has drawn himself into much trouble."

The trouble had certainly not been mitigated by his visit to Paris in the December of the preceding year, during which he had called attention to the fact that he was defying an *arrêt* of the Parliament by making himself as conspicuous as possible and appearing in the gardens of the Luxembourg in his world-famed Armenian costume. Naturally enough, he very soon received a hint from the French Government, and he was only too grateful to accept the escort of the man with "that broad unmeaning face" to this country.

He had not been in London many days before the king's brother-in-law, the hereditary prince, called on him incognito. The Duke of York, too, visited him, but found him not at home. Garrick not only gave a supper in his honour, but played two characters especially to please him—Lusignan in the "Zaïre" of Aaron Hill, and the triple character in "Lethe" of the Frenchman, poet, and drunken man. The theatre was of course crowded in anticipation. "Rousseau," writes Cradock in his "Literary and Miscellaneous Memoirs," "was highly gratified, but Mrs. Garrick declared that she had never spent a more unpleasant evening in her life, the recluse philosopher being so anxious to display himself, and hanging over the front of the box so much that she was obliged to hold him by the skirts of his coat to prevent him from falling over into the pit. After the performance, however, he paid a very handsome compliment to Garrick by saying, 'I have cried all through your tragedy and laughed all through your comedy, without being at all able to understand your language.' At the end of the play Rousseau was entertained at supper at Garrick's house in the Adelphi, where many of the first literary characters of the time were invited to meet him."

Hume's troubles, as may be imagined, had commenced in earnest. Lady Sarah Bunbury informed Lady Susan O'Brien in a letter dated February 5 of the same year that the Genevese philosopher was going to live at a farm in Wales in the companionship of mountains and wild goats. "That all London," observes the late Professor Churton Collins, "should be running after a philosopher who had lodgings in St. James's and who lived as his friend Hume lived, would have afforded him no gratification but that all London should be running after a recluse who occupied with a dog and a mistress two squalid rooms in a farmer's cottage at Chiswick—that was quite to his taste." As a matter of fact, Thérèse had not yet arrived from Paris, and Hume's first experiences of house-hunting on behalf of his friend were with a market-gardener at Fulham. These negotiations having proved unsatisfactory, lodgings at Chiswick were secured, and here he settled for a time, though without much satisfaction. Thérèse, escorted from Paris by no less a person than Boswell, joined him at Chiswick. Of this lady Hume had a poor opinion, and he had already written about her very plainly to Madame de Boufflers in a letter dated January 19, 1766: "This woman forms the chief encumbrance to his settlement. M. de Luze, our companion, says that she passes for wicked and tattling, and is thought to be the chief cause of his quitting Neuchâtel. He himself owns her to be so dull that she never knows in what year of the Lord she is, nor in what month of the year, nor in what day of the month or week, and that she can never learn the difference of value of the pieces of money in any country. Yet she governs him absolutely as a nurse does a child. In her absence his dog has obtained that ascendant. His affection for that creature is above all expression or conception." Rousseau, indeed, was almost as devoted to his dog as he was to Thérèse, and when General FitzPatrick called on him at Chiswick he found him in the greatest distress at having lost it. Hume, however, had managed to find the dog, and came in with it shortly afterwards, whereupon Rousseau expressed the deepest gratitude and embraced the dog with tears. The little village of Chiswick was amazed at the occupant of this farmer's cottage, which is described in Mr. Edward Walford's "Old and New London" as a small grocer's shop. "He sits in the shop," says a writer in the Caldwell Papers, "and learns English words, which brings many customers to the shop."

Vanity is the characteristic in Rousseau that seems most forcibly to have struck the English. "When Hume and Rousseau," Lord Charlemont is quoted in Hardy's biography as saying, "arrived from France, happening to meet with Hume in the Park, I wished him joy of his pleasing connection, and particularly hinted that I was convinced he must be perfectly happy in his new friend, as their sentiments were, I believed, nearly similar." To this, however, the historian demurred. "Why, no, man," he said, "you are mistaken. Rousseau is not what you think him; he has a hankering after the Bible, and indeed is little better than a Christian in a way of his own." But Lord Charlemont seems to have thought no better of him on that account, for he continues: "Excess of vanity was the madness of Rousseau. When he first arrived in London, he and his Armenian dress were followed by crowds, and as long as this species of admiration lasted, he was contented and happy."

At all events he was not contented and happy at Chiswick, and he and Thérèse went to Wooton, a village in Derbyshire, in the March of the same year. A rupture with Hume followed only too quickly, and the historian's final estimate of Rousseau was that he was "a composition of whim, affectation, wickedness, vanity, and inquietude, with a very small, if any, ingredient of madness." This is even more harsh than the verdict of Burke, who said: "We had the great professor and founder of the *philosophy of vanity* in England. As I had good opportunities of knowing his proceedings from day to day, he left no doubt on my mind that he entertained no principle, either to influence his heart or to guide his understanding, but vanity." On the other hand, a certain Mrs. Cockburn rose gushingly to the occasion. ": Oh, bring him with you," she almost sang in a letter, "the English are not worthy of him. Sweet old man, he shall sit beneath an oak and hear the Druids' songs; bring dear old Rousseau." In the May of the next year, however, Rousseau deserted enemies and flatterers alike and sailed for Calais.

A REMARKABLE EPITAPH

On a Monument for Richard Humble, Alderman of London, and his two wives, in Southwark Cathedral, erected in 1616, is the following *Epitaph*.

LIKE to the damaske rose you see,
Or like the blossom on the tree,
Or like the dainty flower of May,
Or like the morning of the day,
Or like the sun, or like the shade,
Or like the gourd which Jonas had,
 Even so is Man, whose thread is spun,
 Drawn out, and cut, and so is done.
The rose withers ; the blossom blasteth ;
The flower fades ; the morning hasteth ;
The sun sets ; the shadows flies ;
The gourd consumes ; the Man he dies.

DON SALTERO'S MUSEUM AND COFFEE-HOUSE

HALF-WAY along Cheyne Walk, Chelsea, from the year 1690 till 1866, there was a place of entertainment known as Don Saltero's Coffee House, the feature of which was its curious combination of gimcracks and knick-knacks gathered from all sources, and especially from Sir Hans Sloane.

James Salter had been for long a faithful servant to Sir Hans, and when he retired from service his master presented him with all sorts of odds and ends of curiosities, and with these Salter set up his museum, much to the edification of his numerous friends.

One of Salter's early and consistently valuable patrons was Vice-Admiral Munden, who had long been on the coast of Spain, where his knowledge of Spanish titles suggested to this happy salt the waggish thought, as he was a genial visitor to the house, of christening James Salter Don Saltero, and, ever after, until its extinction the house was known by the name conferred upon it by this well-known sailor, Don Saltero's Museum and Coffee House. However, had it not been for an accidental visit by Sir Richard Steele the place would probably have never been known outside the precincts of its parish.

DON SALTERO'S COFFEE-HOUSE

Steele in the *Tatler* of June 28, 1700, immortalised the Don and his establishment by quite an enthusiastic description of the place. He speaks of the necessity of travelling to know the world, and of his journey for fresh air no further than the village of Chelsea, of which he fancied he could give an immediate description from the "Five Fields, where the robbers lie in wait, to the Coffee House where the literati sit in council."

"When I came into the coffee-house," says Steele, "I had not time to salute the company, before my eyes were diverted by ten thousand gimcracks round the room, and on the ceiling. When my first astonishment was over, comes to me a sage of thin and meagre countenance, which aspect made me doubt whether reading or fretting had made it so philosophic; but I very soon perceived him to be of that sort which the ancients call 'gingivistee'; in our language 'tooth-drawers.' I immediately had a respect for the man; for these practical philosophers go upon a very practical hypothesis, not to cure, but to take away the part affected. My love of mankind made me very benevolent to Mr. Salter, for such is the name of this eminent barber and anti-quary."

The Don was celebrated for his skill in making punch, and as a player on the fiddle. One of his favourite pieces was the "Merry Christchurch Bells" which he seems to have played well; but he confessed that he did it to show that he was orthodox rather than that he valued himself upon the music. Salter, though he had little lore of his own, had many attractive qualities that drew all sorts and conditions of men to his coffee-house, whose windows looked across the Thames and over the reaches that extended beyond Wandsworth and Putney.

In the *Weekly Journal* of June 22, 1723, Don Saltero published a rhymed announcement of the treasures, qualities, good fare, and many other things which he provided at his estab-lishment. Saltero's Poetic Address, signed by himself, from the Chelsea Knackatory, was as follows :

SIR,
Fifty years since to Chelsea great,
    From Rodman, on the Irish main,
I strolled, with maggots in my pate,
    Where, much improved, they still
    remain.

Through various employs I've passed—
    A scraper, virtuoso, projector,
Tooth-drawer, trimmer, and at last,
    I'm now a gimcrack whim collector.

Monsters of all sorts here are seen,
    Strange things in nature as they grew so,
Some relics of the Sheba Queen,
    And fragments of the famed Bob Crusoe.

Knicknacks too dangle round the wall,
    Some in glass cases, some on shelf ;
But what's the rarest sight of all,
    Your humble servant shows himself.

On this my chiefest hope depends—
    Now if you will my cause espouse,
In journals pray direct your friends
    To my Museum Coffee-house.

And in requital for the timely favour,
I'll gratis bleed, draw teeth, and be
    your shaver :
Nay, that your pate may with my noddle
    tally,
And you shine bright as I do—marry,
    shall ye
Freely consult your revelation, Molly ;
Nor shall one jealous thought create a
    huff,
For she has taught me manners long
    enough.

Don Saltero, according to Babillard, wore a sort of old grey muff which he elevated close to his nose, and "by this he was distinguishable at the distance of a quarter of a mile." The Don made his museum very attractive and drew crowds to the coffee-house. Smollett and many of his boon com-panions were visitors and donors to the exhibition. To give an idea of the rarities presented for public approba-tion we take the following from a catalogue issued in 1760 : Tiger's tusks ; the Pope's Candle ; the skeleton of a Guinea Pig ; a Fly-Cap Monkey ; a piece of the True Cross ; the Four Evangelists' Heads cut out on a cherry stone ; . . . Queen Elizabeth's prayer book ; Mary Queen of Scots' Pin-cushion ; and a Pair of Nun's stockings. Then we light upon Job's Tears which grew on a Tree, to which may be added a list of five hundred more odd relics.

However trivial and absurd the Don's collections of curiosities at Chelsea might seem to us to-day, they certainly induced a very large number of the aristocracy and men about town to take the "journey from London to Chelsea."

The exit of Don Saltero is shrouded in mystery, and nobody appears to know how he passed away or dis-appeared. Although one of his daughters carried on the business for some few years after his demise, when the whole place was sold up by auction.

GEORGE AUGUSTUS SELWYN

WIT AND ECCENTRIC

UNLIKE the ephemeral Beau Brummell, George Augustus Selywn was an aristocrat born and a wit of the purest water to boot. He was the son of a Gloucestershire country gentleman, Colonel John Selwyn, who had served under Marlborough, and it was from his mother, Mary, daughter of General Farington, that he is said to have inherited his wit. George, their son, was born on August 11, 1719.

Selwyn took Brummell's place when that gentleman had to go abroad for the benefit of his health—and stay there. Whenever he played at White's or Brooks's or Arthur's he always speculated with his own money, which cannot be said of all the gamblers of the Regency—especially of those who frequented White's. It has been said of Selwyn that, in his inconsistent gossipy letters to his many friends, he "made it his profession to collect and catalogue the follies of the town." Trevelyan somewhat spoils his own attempt to whitewash Fox when he says—the Charles is, of course, Fox— " Selwyn was glad to dine at Charles's table, whenever the brokers had left him a piece of furniture that he could call his own ; but, all the while he was listening to the young man's sallies, he watched him like a cat. And then he would sit down at home with Charles's claret and venison in him and pour out on paper his budget of tattle."

This, judging from the generous character of Selwyn, is particularly unfair. He was a dandy and gave much employment to the Bond Street tailors. Dandy as he was, however, Selwyn had a keen eye for business.

He succeeded his father as a member of Parliament for the City of Gloucester, representing it for twenty-six years.

It must be admitted that of Selwyn's wit, of which so much has been written, scarcely any thing remains of any permanent value. It was persiflage, pure and simple. A joke here and there of the time and the moment, but—and here of course the point lay—all that he said was appropriate of the moment. Going into White's one night and seeing James Jeffries playing at piquet with Sir Edward Fawkener, the Postmaster-General, " Look," cried Selwyn to his companion, " there is Jeffries robbing the mail." At Newmarket, one race day, observing Mr. Ponsonby, the Speaker of the Irish House of Commons, throwing about his bank-notes at a hazard table, he observed : " How easily the Speaker passes the money bills."

Walpole in a letter to Lady Ossory wrote in June 1780 : " You ask about Mr. Selwyn. Have you heard his incomparable reply to Lord George Gordon, who asked him if he would choose him again for Ludgershall ? He replied his ' Constituents would not.' ' Oh, yes, if you would recommend me, they would choose me if I came from the Coast of Africa.' ' That is according to what part you came from. They would, certainly, if you came from the Guinea Coast.' "

A namesake of Charles James Fox having been hanged at Tyburn, Fox inquired of Selwyn whether he had been present at the execution. " No," was the rejoinder, " I make a point of never attending rehearsals."

The wit of Selwyn and the extreme primness of his dress went well together. He was always demure. His cleverest things were uttered, so to speak, unconsciously; he never allowed himself to be surprised into recognising the delightful incident that he had said anything out of the common. From all accounts he had an appealing way of projecting his whims. Walpole on several occasions refers to Selwyn's characteristic demureness, both of countenance and the movement of his hands, and particularly to his "habit of turning up the whites of his eyes when giving expression to one of his drolleries."

Selwyn, the beau, was perhaps the most extraordinary mixture of contradictions that ever lived. He did not care for women, yet loved children—other people's children—inordinately. Loving children, he was yet passionately devoted to the exhibition of criminals and their execution! Tyburn Tree was to him a sort of trysting-place! Let us have the indisputable evidence, because several unauthorised writers have tried to varnish this peculiar idiosyncrasy and make believe that the wit had no large taste in this direction. This is rather an odd way of putting things, but Mr. John Fyvie

is nothing if not blunt. This is of Selwyn: "Not only did he attend every execution that he could conveniently get to, but when it was

SELWYN AND THE CHIMNEY-SWEEPS
After a Drawing by H. K. Browne

impossible for him to be present one or more of his friends were commissioned to send him detailed accounts of the whole ghastly performance." We do not think it is beneficial to quote much more on this side of Selwyn's character, but we have to remember the times. As an example there is Lady Harrington, whose porter was to be hanged—hanged, mind you—for a theft of jewelry, who writes in this lively strain : " I presume we shall have your honour's company if your stomach is not too squeamish for a single swing ! " Good heavens !

Much pleasanter is the story of Selwyn walking with Lord Pembroke, and being obstructed by some young chimney-sweeps. " I have often heard of the sovereignty of the people," he said, " I suppose your highnesses are in Court mourning."

George Augustus Selwyn lived his life—perhaps one of the most intricate of lives that a man, who was a cultured wit and dandy at the same time, could live. He held such sway in his long reign that everybody with whom he came in contact had a good word for him, and he passed away on January 25, 1791, in his seventy-second year. Walpole said at the time of his death : " Him I really loved, not only for his infinite wit, but for a thousand good qualities." And most decidedly Horace Walpole was not one to throw chaff to the winds.

DANIEL DEFOE IN THE PILLORY

DURING the seventeenth and eighteenth centuries we descry in the pillory many political offenders of greater or less importance. Every one no doubt remembers that the author of " Robinson Crusoe," Daniel Defoe, himself stood there. It is, indeed, one of the oddest facts of its class in literature that the most concise, realistic pen-portraits known to us of Defoe must be sought in the description issued of him by the police in 1703 ! In this curt account he is called " a middle-sized, spare man, about forty years old, of a brown complexion, and dark brown coloured hair, but wears a wig ; a hooked nose, a sharp chin, grey eyes, and a large mole near his mouth." It was no mean artist in the Force who drew that sketch !

How came Defoe in the pillory ? During a debate in the Lords on a Bill against occasional conformity, he wrote and published his " Shortest Way with the Dissenters," a parody—in scathing terms—of the pamphlets that the High Church party was just then scattering broadcast. He was prosecuted instanter for " a horrible slander upon the Church." Lying low for a time, it came to his knowledge that the printer and publisher of his brochure had been haled to prison and he then at once gave himself up. Tried at the Old Bailey in July 1704, he pleaded guilty, and was condemned to pay a fine of " 200 marks," stand three times in the pillory, be imprisoned during the Queen's pleasure (Queen Anne), and find sureties for seven years for his good behaviour. On the last three days of July the genius of English narrative stood in the pillory—in Cheapside first and then in the Temple. He had a triumph there. The notable " Hymn to the Pillory," which he had composed in prison, was chanted by the crowd. The flower-girls of the disrict wreathed the pillory with chaplets of their own weaving. Money, said to have been subscribed by the High Church faction " for his torment," circulated mysteriously among the audience, who spent it in liquor with which they drank his health. Still we are not to forget that the creator of " Crusoe " stood three times in the pillory, victim of clerical hatred.

AN OLD HOUSE IN PALL MALL

SCHOMBERG HOUSE, in Pall Mall, is to-day the residence of the Princess Christian, and though the east wing has been taken down it still retains many of the features that characterise it in the old prints—the pediment, and caryatid porticoes, for instance. It was built for the Duke of Schomberg, a German favourite of William III., who, at the age of eighty-one, fell in the Battle of the Boyne. But it very soon acquired that association with art which makes it unique among the houses of London. The painter Astley purchased the mansion for £5000, and divided it into three parts, living himself in the centre part, which he fitted up in a whimsical manner. In early years Astley was poor, and the following story is told about him. " On one occasion a party of young students was formed to go out into the country ; they became very hot, and all took off their coats but Astley. The reason for his reluctance to disrobe was apparent when he at last took off his coat, for a foaming waterfall was displayed on his back, to the great surprise and amusement of his companions. He had made his waistcoat out of one of his landscapes ! " Astley married a rich wife, became known as " Beau Astley " or " Lucky Astley," and lived at Schomberg House with some show of magnificence.

Another painter who for some time, dwelt there, one Nathaniel Hone, R.A. is remembered, not for the excellence of his pictures, but for the satire he aimed at Sir Joshua Reynolds. See him walk down Pall Mall, a tall upright, large man with a broad brimmed hat and a lapelled coat buttoned up to his satin stock. He is nursing in his heart a bitter jealousy, a jealousy against the most famous painter of the day, Reynolds, whose fellow student he had been in Rome. This jealousy finally bore very extraordinary fruit. Hone painted a picture which was meant as a direct accusation against Sir Joshua of plagiarism. It is an admitted fact that Reynolds used to borrow suggestions of attitude and composition from the Old Masters for his own sitters. Hone's picture was called " The Conjurer displaying his Whole Art of Optical Deception," and represented Reynolds performing incantations over a cauldron. A number of prints and sketches from which Reynolds had taken hints for his pictures rise into the air. The Academicians rejected this picture with scorn as a malicious attack upon their President. Hone then exhibited " The Conjurer " in a large room in St. Martin's Lane.

But the house takes its glory from succeeding tenants — from Gainsborough who lived in the west wing from 1774 to his death in 1788, and, in a less degree, from Richard Cosway, who was in the centre part from 1781 to 1791. The division of the house into three portions is still distinctly traceable ; the caryatid figures supporting the porch of the front door still remain, though a window now replaces the door. Let us again take our stand opposite the house and try and catch a glimpse of the painters themselves. Gainsborough, though he is in the full tide of his fame, living at a full thousand a year expense, as he himself tells us, has put down his coach, and does not think it fitting to drive up to his front door in anything so mean as a hackney cab ; so he dismisses it in St. James's Square, and walks the rest of the way. He is a handsome man, of a fair complexion, regular features, tall and well-proportioned. His forehead is broad and strongly marked, his nose Roman, his mouth and eye denoting humour and refinement. He is dressed in a rich suit of drab, with laced ruffles and a cocked hat.

And here comes Richard Cosway down the street, a little man, refined and vivacious of expression, full-dressed in his sword and bag; with a small three-cornered hat on the top of his powdered toupee, and a mulberry silk coat profusely embroidered with scarlet strawberries! Indeed, Cosway was so absurdly foppish in his attire that a caricature was exhibited of him in the Strand as "The Macaroni Miniature Painter." But, nevertheless, he was a miniature painter of great skill and refinement, easy and airy in his touch; his miniatures are excellent, and possess a sprightly *naïveté* that is very charming. His success with a portrait of

Mrs. Fitzherbert brought him the patronage of the Prince of Wales, and Cosway is said to have obtained from his Royal Highness in one year no less a sum than ten thousand pounds.

Within Schomberg House there was a gay continuity of labour. Gainsborough's success in London was imme-

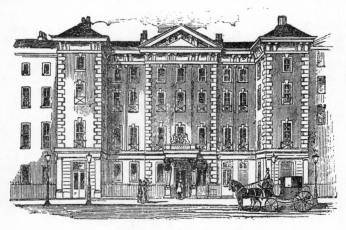

SCHOMBERG HOUSE, PALL MALL

diate, owing partly to the patronage of George III.,who had been struck by the beauty of Gainsborough's works shown at the Academy and other exhibitions. (The Royal Academy was established in 1768.) Gainsborough was the favourite painter of the King and Royal Family, and was frequently at the palace. He painted George no less than eight times. The following account gives us a vivid and delightful picture of a day of his life: "He generally rose early, commenced painting between nine and ten o'clock, wrought for four or five hours, and then gave up the rest of the day to visits, to music, and to domestic enjoyment. He loved to sit by the side of his wife during the evenings, and make sketches of whatever occurred to his fancy, all of which he threw below the table save such as were more than commonly happy, and these were preserved, and either finished as sketches or expanded into paintings." The painter never exercised his genius more lovingly and successfully than in the portrait of his wife, who was very dear to him. There is a charm, a magic touch about it, that none can describe.

Gainsborough was a man generous to a fault, impetuous, sometimes capricious, and quick of temper. "Whenever he spoke crossly to his wife, a remarkably sweet-tempered woman," says his biographer Fulcher, "he would write a note of repentance, sign it with the name of his favourite dog Fox, and address it to Margaret's pet spaniel Tristram. Fox would take the note in his mouth and duly deliver it to Tristram. Margaret (his wife) would then answer, 'My own dear Fox, you are always loving and good and I am a naughty little female ever to worry you, as I too often do, so we will kiss and say no more about it. Your own affectionate, Tris.'"

Though Gainsborough and Reynolds were never very intimate, each had high appreciation of the work of the other, and when Gainsborough was dying he asked that Reynolds would come and see him. The meeting between the two great painters took place in a second-floor room of Schomberg House. "If any little jealousies had subsisted between us," says Reynolds, "they were forgotten in those moments of sincerity." Gainsborough said that he did not fear death, but regretted leaving his art, more especially as he now began to see what his deficiencies were. His words began to fail, and the last he uttered to Reynolds were, "We are all going to heaven, and Vandyck is of the company." He died in 1788, in his sixty-second year, and was buried in Kew churchyard. In 1857 some frescoes painted by Gainsborough were discovered on the walls of Schomberg House.

Not only was the art of painting practised at Schomberg House during Gainsborough's life; not only was the studio filled with beauty and radiant colour; not only did human loveliness and genius shine from the canvases and landscapes instinct with the freshness of nature; but the house vibrated with "concord of sweet sounds," for Gainsborough was an enthusiastic lover of music and moved to the very soul by tender harmonies. Gainsborough played on several instruments; his son-in-law Fischer was a famous hautboy player; his unmarried daughter, an exquisite performer upon the harpsichord. Music also was a favourite recreation of Cosway and his wife. Mrs. Cosway was a miniature painter of great talent, "a golden-haired, languishing Anglo - Italian, graceful to affectation, and highly accomplished, especially in music." Her Sunday evening receptions, her assemblies, were attended by all the fashion of the day, and on these occasions Pall Mall was blocked with carriages, sedan-chairs, link-boys and lacqueys. Mrs. Cosway was generally the chief performer at these receptions, "while her odd little husband, dressed up in the very extreme of fashion, flitted about through his gaily decorated rooms, ogling, flirting and bowing, receiving his patrons with the air of a prince." In later years Cosway became a Swedenborgian. He retained his artistic powers to a very advanced age, and was, as his wife reported, "toujours riant, toujours gai."

THE HUMORIST OF CRAVEN STREET

IN walking down Craven Street from the Strand you may observe a curious shallow bow window on the first floor of a house on the left hand side. Through this window of his own house James Smith, the brother of Horace Smith, and joint author with him of the famous "Rejected Addresses," often looked out upon the quiet street, when he was not bubbling with humour and reminiscence at the Athenæum or the Garrick Club. A bachelor, he was ministered to by a worthy housekeeper, of whom he wrote in his diary under May 1, 1838 : "Mrs. Glover reminded me on Tuesday, that on that day she had just been twenty-four years in my service. What a lapse of time ! How different was I then from that which I am now ! then a rollicking, lively, fresh-coloured man of the town, running from dinner to rout, and from tavern to opera ; and now quiet and contented with all my social eggs in one basket. May the basket never break ! "

The "basket" was the Union Club in Trafalgar Square, whither in his old age, this out-and-out Londoner hobbled daily on crutch-sticks. Somewhat earlier he had contributed much to the gaiety of the Garrick Club, and it is there that he is pictured by Dr. Maguin.

"There sits James Smith with his feet pressing a soft cushion, his elbows dropped by the arms of an easy chair, his hand resting on a crutch, his hair departed from his head, his nose tinged with the colours of the dawn, and his whole man in a state of that repose which indicates that he has had much work in his way while sojourning in this world, and that, like Falstaff, he is taking his ease in his own inn, the Garrick. . . . Let him have his praise. His single talent was a good talent, and there is no reason why he should wrap it up in a napkin. . . ."

Smith's talent was that of being a most agreeable club talker, yet apart from the "Rejected Addresses" his light verse, nearly all of it concerned with London, is still quoted. Two of the best, "St. James's Park" and "London Misnomers" are printed elsewhere in this work. And here we will give ourselves the pleasure of transcribing a third piece, which has literary merit and also London interest.

His book is successful, he's steep'd in renown,
His lyric effusions have tickled the town ;
Dukes, dowagers, dandies, are eager to trace
The fountain of verse in the verse-maker's face ;
While, proud as Apollo, with peers *tête-à-tête*,
From Monday till Saturday dining off plate,
His heart full of hope, and his head full of gain,
The Poet of Fashion dines out in Park Lane.

Now lean-jointured widows who seldom draw corks,
Whose tea-spoons do duty for knives and for forks,
Send forth, vellum-cover'd, a six o'clock card,
And get up a dinner to peep at the bard :
Veal, sweetbread, boil'd chickens, and tongue, crown the cloth,
And soup *à la reine*, little better than broth ;
While, past his meridian, but still with some heat,
The Poet of Fashion dines out in Sloane Street.

Enroll'd in the tribe who subsist by their wits,
Remember'd by starts, and forgotten by fits,
Now artists and actors, the bardling engage,
To squib in the journals, and write for the stage.
Now soup *à la reine* bends the knee to ox-cheek,
And chickens and tongue bow to bubble and squeak—
While, still in translation employ'd by "The Row,"
The Poet of Fashion dines out in Soho.

JAMES SMITH
From the Maclise Portrait Gallery

Push'd down from Parnassus to Phlegethon's
brink,
Toss'd, torn, trunk-lining, but still with some
ink,
Now squab city misses their albums ex-
pand,
And woo the worn rhymer for " something
off-hand " ;
No longer with stilted effrontery fraught,

Bucklersbury now seeks what St. James's
once sought,
And (O what a classical haunt for a bard !)
The Poet of Fashion dines out in Barge
Yard.

It would be hazardous to say that
James Smith's prose writings still find
readers, though students of London

know that there are pickings in his "Kit-Cat Sketches" and "Grimm's Ghost." His epigram on Craven Street is amusing and it recalls the time when this street descended to the river mud, before the construction of the Thames Embankment.

In Craven Street, Strand, ten attorneys find place,
And ten dark coal-barges are moored at its base ;
Fly, Honesty, fly ! seek some safer retreat ;
For there's *craft* in the river and craft in the street.

To this his friend Sir George Rose replied :

Why should Honesty fly to some safer retreat,
From attorneys and barges, 'od rot 'em ?—
For the lawyers are *just* at the top of the street,
And the barges are *just* at the bottom.

James Smith made a quiet exit in Craven Street from the London which he had known and loved through his long life, and was buried in the vaults of St. Martin's Church.

PIERCE EGAN

PIERCE EGAN, the author of "Life in London," that harum-scarum chronicle so admired by Thackeray, was a remarkable man in every way. His knowledge of street phrases and slang are exemplified in the "Slang Dictionary." He was originally a compositor, then a bookseller, and then a reporter of sporting news, events of "the ring," cock fighting, and all the doings of the "fancy." As a contributor to the sporting papers, "He was the greatest man in England. In the event of opposition to his views and opinions, he and those who looked up to him had a mode of enforcing authority which had the efficacy without the tediousness of discussion." Yet we are explicitly told that although he was not physically strong he had very great courage and had a quickness of action that generally served him at opportune moments. Egan was employed by the proprietor of the *Weekly Dispatch* to record the "doings of the ring," in which occupation his extraordinary way of expressing himself, and his knowledge of the prize ring, the low life and the "swagger," particularly that of the "flash" and

demi-monde, gave him a position that was not easily assailed and rendered him for a time an almost impregnable authority. He was present at every pugilistic encounter whether it occurred in Seven Dials or St. James's Street. This quotation is sufficient to explain how universal his talents were : "He was flattered and petted by pugilists and peers : his patronage and countenance were sought for by all who considered the road to a prize-fight the road to reputation and honour." In 1869 it was written of Pierce Egan, "Sixty years ago, his presence was understood to confer respectability on any meeting convened for the furtherance of bull-baiting, cock-fighting, and also wrestling, boxing and all that comes within the category of manly sports."

Pierce Egan spent his last years in some retirement. He died on April 3, 1849, at his house in Pentonville, aged 77. In *Bell's Life* it was written of him : "Pierce was, with all his oddities, a right-minded fellow, and was respected by all to whom he was known." It was added that he left a large family, "most of whom are able to take care of themselves."

WYLDE'S GLOBE, LEICESTER SQUARE

IN 1851 the area of Leiester Square was occupied by a large domed building, in which was exhibited a gigantic Globe, erected in the very centre of the Square—a building sixty feet in diameter, which, and of the Russians correctly laid down each day as the information arrived in England from the seat of war, and especially from the graphic letters of Howard Russell, who was the war correspondent of the *Times*;

WYLDE'S GREAT GLOBE : THE BUILDING IN LEICESTER SQUARE

with four sections for other exhibitions, nearly filled the whole of the enclosure—and the whole world was figured in relief on the inside of the Globe and viewed from galleries at various elevations.

Attendants were always at hand to explain everything from Beersheba to Dan and from China to Japan. The enterprising Mr. Wylde introduced in 1854 a magnificent model of the Crimean War, presenting the positions of the different armies of the Allies

Later Mr. Wylde substituted representations of the war of the Mutiny, panoramas of St. Petersburg and Moscow, and other attractions, with explanatory lectures. The Globe lasted for about ten years, and then the whole erection fell into desuetude and Leicester Square became a disgraceful wreck, until Baron Grant with the permission of Queen Victoria's Government, had it converted into the agreeable pleasaunce known to-day.

A TRAGEDY OF LONDON LITERARY LIFE

THE DEATH OF CHATTERTON

VISITORS to the Tate Gallery always stand a moment or two before a picture by Henry Wallis, which represents a youth lying dead upon his bed. Through the casement window of the attic a summer dawn is just beginning to break, and in the faint green light the roofs of houses and steeples of churches show blue and shadowy. We know that we are in the heart of London, for the dome of St. Paul's is clearly visible ; as a matter of fact, the picture shows an attic in Brooke Street, Holborn. The boy in shirt and breeches lies on the bed under the window : the dawn-light touches his face, which is beautiful in death, and falls upon his tumbled brown-red hair. One arm drops loosely over the side of the bed, and the fingers still grasp a little phial—a phial that held poison. On the floor is a box full of fragments of paper, and torn-up papers strew the floor. It is an arresting picture, and paints for us rather the peace of death than the agony that wrought it.

And this is perhaps just as well ; the subject is so harrowing that we could not bear to have put before us in more detail the cruel evidences of suffering and starvation that led to this suicide. London holds many tragedies in her annals of misery, but none more pitiful than the death of Chatterton.

We must carry our minds back to a time four months before Chatterton's death. On April 25, in the year 1771, at about five o'clock in the evening of a bright frosty day, a well-built youth of middle size got down from the Bristol coach with a few guineas and a bundle of poems in his pocket. Thomas Chatterton had come up to London to make his fortune—London, as the poet says, " the goal of every man's desire." Bristol, his native place that he hated and despised, was left behind—Bristol and the bluecoat school at which he had been educated— Bristol and the attorney's stool on which he had sat. London lay before him with its vast possibilities, a world to conquer. It is not difficult to picture the high spirits, the high hopes that animated this youth as his feet touched London pavement, the exhilaration that he felt in the knowledge that he had thrown himself on his own nerve and pluck and brain power, his sense of superb confidence in himself and his genius.

And indeed he had some cause for this confidence and self-reliance. Though only seventeen and a half years old, he was no raw youth. At the early age of ten he had dropped some verses into the letter-box of a local weekly newspaper of some standing, " Felix Farley's Bristol Journal," and they had duly appeared in print. This was the beginning of his career as a poet. Some of the poems written by Chatterton when he was only twelve years old are among the treasures of English literature. Soon he acquired among some of his fellow citizens the reputation of a lad of extraordinary abilities and large antiquarian knowledge. This local celebrity was won in a very curious way. Chatterton had produced a number of poems and other pieces in an antique style, which he claimed to have transcribed from manuscripts of the fifteenth century written by a priest, one Thomas Rowley. Chatterton's ancestors had from the time of Elizabeth been sextons at the Church of St. Mary Redclyffe at Bristol, which possessed many chests of manuscripts, and it did not seem improbable that old documents regarded as useless should have fallen into the boy's hands. But as a matter of fact Chatterton himself was the author of all these " Thomas Rowley " poems, and they were such clever imitations of the antique that they deceived many learned men.

So, with these poems in his pocket —poems that will carry his name down through all time—he got off the coach, and that very evening—such were his energy and determination—he called upon four of the leading publishers of the town. He was willing to work hard and live frugally ; his mind was teeming with ideas ; he soon caught the popular style of the moment, he was able to turn his pen to anything ; he did articles for the journals, he composed songs, little operettas to be performed at the public gardens, squibs, poems ; and letters are still extant written to his mother and his friends at Bristol telling of his successful appearance in many of the leading papers.

CHATTERTON

The pay, no doubt, was miserable and uncertain, but it enabled him to have a glimpse of eighteenth-century London ; to drop into the coffee houses which were the great social rendezvous for the wits and geniuses of the day ; to visit the pit at Drury Lane ; possibly to spend an evening or two at Ranelagh or Marylebone Gardens. He is full of plans and projects : he writes to his sister, of whom he was very fond, that he will soon be engaged on a voluminous history of London, to appear in numbers, the beginning of next winter. And—the pathos of it !—he sends home a box containing a china tea-service for his sister, and a snuff-box " right French and very curious in my opinion " :" for his mother," and "some British herb-tobacco for my grand-mother with a pipe," besides two fans and other trifles.

The letter describing these gifts is dated July 8, from Mrs. Angell's, sack-maker (which means dressmaker), Brooke Street, Holborn.

Chatterton had enjoyed two months of unparalleled success when the tide began to turn. One of his publishers was imprisoned for debt ; another was thrown into Newgate on account of his political views. Lord Mayor Beckford from whom Chatterton had some hopes of patronage, died unexpectedly, and the months of July and August were then, even more than now, the slackest portion of the London year. Towards the end of July—three weeks after he had sent his mother and sister and grandmother the box of presents—Chatterton was at his last shilling.

The writer of this sketch has stood in one of the garrets of Brooke Street that might have been Chatterton's room (the exact house where he lodged is uncertain). It seemed as if the very walls held the black anguish of those last days of his. Age brings with it philosophy and balance : youth is the time of hopeless despair. Chatterton was a mere boy. His landlady, aware of his extreme want, begged him to keep back part of the rent ; Cross the apothecary invited him again and again, as delicately as he could, to take a meal with himself and his wife : but "he was so proud," as Cross said at the inquest, he would never consent. "He was so proud," that he would not apply to his relatives in London ; "he was so proud " that he would not allow his mother and sister to know of his straits ; "he was so proud " that he would ask charity of no man, though we cannot doubt there were many kind hearts in London who would have helped him in this hour of dire need.

We quote Professor Masson's description of the final scene.

" ' He called on me '—is Mr. Cross's statement—' about half past eleven in the morning.' As usual he talked about various matters, and at last, probably just as he was going away, he said he wanted some arsenic for an experiment. Mr. Cross, Mr. Cross, before you go to your drawer for the arsenic, look at that boy's face ! Look at it steadily ; look till he quails ; and then leap upon him and hold him !

Mr. Cross does not look. He *sells* the arsenic (yes, *sells ;* for somehow in that walk in which he has disposed of the bundle he has procured the necessary pence) ; and lives to repent it. Chatterton, the arsenic in his pocket, does not return to his lodgings immediately, but walks about, God only knows where, through the vast town. ' He returned,' continues Mrs. Angell, ' about seven in the evening, looking very pale and dejected ; and would not eat anything, but sat moping by the fire with his chin on his knees, and muttering rhymes in some old language to her.' After some hours, ' he got up to go to bed,' and ' he then kissed her—a thing he had never done before.' Mrs. Angell, what can that kiss mean ? Detain the boy ; he is mad ; he is not fit to be left alone ; arouse the whole street rather than let him go ! She does let him go, and lives to repent it. ' He then went upstairs,' she says, ' stamping on every stair as he went slowly up, as if he would break it.' She heard him reach his room. He enters and locks the door behind him."

They buried him in the burying ground of Shoe Lane workhouse—at least, so says the parish register—but there is a story that his mother, with the help of a relative in London, obtained the coffin containing his body and had it secretly interred in the churchyard of St. Mary Redclyffe. After he was dead all literary London rang with the controversy about the Rowley poems, some maintaining that they were genuine pieces of antiquity and others that they were forgeries. But of all this Chatterton recked nothing, nor of the high value that posterity would put upon his work, nor of the tears that would be shed over his fate : for him " life's fitful fever " was over.

LONDON-BY-THE-SEA

LONDON - BY - THE - SEA!
London with its shops and its
fashions, its nobility and its
commoners, its court and its assemblies, bordered by the glittering ocean,
and fanned by salt breezes! Such was
Brighton in the hey-day of its triumphs;
such it remains to some extent still,
reproducing, as no other seaside resort
does, many of the features of London
life, and so close to the capital that
it has actually been called a suburb of
London.

Look at the Pavilion! This amazing
structure, which has been described by
every possible ludicrous image, is part
of the history of England. With its
" stone pumpkins and pepper-boxes,"
it stands symbol of the character of
one of England's kings (George IV.) ;
the money of England's people was
squandered upon it in reckless profusion, so that Byron proposed in
" Don Juan " to

Shut up—not the King, but the Pavilion,
Or else 'twill cost us all another million.

It typifies, more completely than any
other building, one aspect of eighteenth-century life, with its dissipation, its
hard drinking, its rough practical jokes.
Every cranny of this palace is filled
with stories, just as the town itself
has associations, literary, historical,
humorous, at practically every street
corner.

As the beginnings of mediæval
London have a fascination for us,
when barbarians lurked in its deserted
Roman ruins, so we look back with
a strange interest to the beginnings of
London-by-the-Sea. In the early
eighteenth century Brighton—Brighthelmstone as it was then called—was
a poor fishing-village, so poor that the
people had no money to spend on
paving or lighting the streets, and
it seemed hardly worth while to try
to keep out the sea from encroaching
on so wretched a place. The fame
of Brighton—as of so many other
popular resorts—was in the first place
due to a doctor. In 1750 Dr. Richard
Russell wrote a pamphlet in which he
stated the importance of sea-bathing
and of drinking sea-water for various
complaints ; he remarked on the purity
of Brighton's air, and analysed its
waters, particularly an uncommon
mineral spring, long discovered. A
few people began to come to Brighton,
lodging-houses were opened, and in
1787 Carey wrote that the town

Few years ago was worse than Wapping
Not fit for human souls to stop in ;
But now, like to a worn-out shoe
By patching well, the place will do. . . .

But much as Brighton owes to its
early doctors in advertising its merits,
it owes much more to Royalty. George
Prince of Wales (afterwards Prince
Regent, and finally George IV.) came
there in 1782 to visit his uncle, the
Duke of Cumberland, and so many
candles were consumed in the illumination on this occasion that it
caused a considerable rise in the
price of tallow ! The Prince was so
enchanted with the place that he bought
a small house belonging to Mr. Kemp,
which was, as Dr. Doran well says, the
seed which grew the Chinese pumpkin.
The Prince began his palace in 1784,
and went on adding wing to centre,
turnip to turnip, bulb to bulb ; thirty-three years after, the building was still
going on ! The Dome, then called the
Rotunda, was used for the royal stables;
and Hazlitt writes : " The King's

horses (if they were horses of taste) would petition against so irrational a lodging."

The ventilation of the Prince's dining-

THE PRINCE REGENT AT BRIGHTON

room in the Marine Pavilion was so very defective that his associates suffered greatly from the heat, to which the Prince himself seemed quite indifferent. On one occasion Sheridan asked George Hanger, "How do you feel yourself?" "Hot, hot, hot as h—l," Hanger answered, and Sheridan, nodding in sympathy, remarked, "We may as well be prepared in this world for what we know will be our lot in the next." And, indeed, the Prince's boon companions were anything but angelic. Richard, the seventh Lord Barrymore, was known familiarly as "Hell-gate"; Henry, the eighth earl, because of his club-foot, as "Cripple-gate"; another brother, Augustus, as "New-gate," because this was said to be the only gaol in which he had not been imprisoned; while a sister, Lady Caroline, was called "Billings-gate," because of her command of bad language. The rowdy set of companions who surrounded the Prince when he first came to Brighton were succeeded in later years by the dandies, who, though quieter, were not less vicious.

"How long do you stay here?" Beau Brummell asked Lord Alvanley, a famous dandy.

"Thirty-five pounds," was the strange reply.

"Thirty-five pounds!" the other repeated, bewildered.

"What I mean by thirty-five pounds is that, after allotting ten pounds for posting from London and back, I have a 'pony' to spend here, and as long as that lasts I shall remain," Lord Alvanley explained. "I think two more dinners, and breakfast at the York Hotel will clear me out." Notorious gourmet as he was, we can yet hardly wonder that a golden shark on Brighton's church should have appeared to strangers "an emblem of its trade."

As an example of the practical jokes

in which the Prince delighted we will tell the story of the treatment of the old Duke of Norfolk—" Jockey of Norfolk," he was called—as related by Thackeray : "The Prince of Wales had concocted with his brothers a notable scheme for making the old man drunk. Every person at table was enjoined to drink wine with the duke —a challenge which the old toper did not refuse. He soon began to see that there was a conspiracy against him; he drank glass for glass ; he overthrew many of the brave. At last the First Gentleman of Europe (the Prince) proposed bumpers of brandy. One of the royal brothers filled a great glass for the duke. He stood up and tossed off the drink. ' Now,' says he, ' I will have my carriage and go home.' The Prince urged upon him his previous promise to sleep under the roof where he had been so generously entertained. ' No,' he said ; he had had enough of such hospitality. A trap had been set for him ; he would leave the place at once and never enter its doors more. The carriage was called and came ; but in the half-hour's interval the liquor had proved too potent for the old man ; his host's generous purpose was answered, and the duke's old grey head lay stupefied on the table. Nevertheless, when his post-chaise was announced, he staggered to it as well as he could, and, stumbling in, bade the

MARTHA GUNN
THE BRIGHTON BATHING WOMAN

postillions drive to Arundel. They drove him for half an hour round and round the Pavilion lawn ; the poor old man fancied he was going home. When he awoke that morning he was in bed at the Prince's hideous house at Brighton. . . . I can fancy the flushed faces of the royal princes as they support themselves at the portico pillars, to look on at old Norfolk's disgrace ; but I can't fancy how the man who perpetrated it continued to be called a gentleman."

It is not to be wondered that the *Morning Post* of 1785 should remark: "The Brighthelmstone intelligence has nothing to recommend it : merely a repetition of the old story : morning rides, champagne, dissipation, noise, and nonsense ; jumble these phrases together, and you have a complete account of all that's passing at Brighthelmstone."

The Prince of Wales did not disdain to play his practical jokes on people of less importance than the Duke of Norfolk, as the following story shows. One of the " institutions " of Brighton was Martha Gunn, the Bathing Woman of whom we give an illustration. " The veteran Priestess of the Bath," the *Morning Herald* calls her, and we read " how many of our lovely belles took ducks for breakfast this morning, purchased of their cateress, Martha Gunn." Martha Gunn was a favourite with the Prince, who enjoyed her racy conversation. He would sometimes send for her to the Pavilion, to amuse him and Mrs. Fitzherbert, the lady to whom he was privately married, and whom Martha Gunn always persisted in addressing as "Mrs. Prince." Martha had also the run of the royal kitchen. One day, when a cook was giving her a pound of butter, the Prince entered unexpectedly. Martha, not knowing if he would approve the gift, hastily put it in her pocket. The Prince pretended that he had not noticed the proceeding, and entered into conversation with her as usual. He contrived, however; maliciously to edge her closer and closer to the great kitchen fire. Martha grew hotter and hotter, partly by the heat, partly from terror that the butter would melt. It did melt ; and when it ran down the old woman's clothes, and formed a stream on the floor, the Prince burst into hearty laughter.

The Royal Bather was also a well-known Brighton character, "Smoaker Miles," of whom the following anecdote is told. On one occasion when the Prince was bathing, he ventured further out than was prudent, and took no heed of Old Smoaker's remonstrances. Whereupon the Bathing Man seized him by the ear, and pulled him, willy-nilly, to the shore. "I ar'n't agoen to let the King hang me for lettin' the Prince of Wales drown hisself ; not I, to please nobody, I can tell 'e," was his outspoken remark. The Prince's sense of humour got the better of his indignation, and he proved a kind friend to the old man and to his widow. There were races at Brighton once a year, and the Prince established the "Smoaker Stakes" in memory of the Royal Bather.

SMOAKER MILES
THE BRIGHTON BATHING MAN

The distance between London and Brighton, even in the eighteenth century, was easily traversed. In 1784 the Prince drove a three-horse tandem from London to Brighton in four and a half hours, and back the same day in five and a half hours. In 1834 the "Criterion" coach performed the journey in three hours forty minutes. In 1822 there were sixty coaches on the Brighton road, thirty coming and thirty going. The longest and most expensive way of travel was by post-chaise. In 1827 this cost for the double journey over twenty pounds, and occupied about twenty-four hours each way.

Till the railway came in 1841 Brighton was still remote enough to attract those who desired quiet, and consequently it had its literary coteries. The season, however, was sufficiently important to necessitate a Master of the Ceremonies at £1000 a year! Horace Smith, part author of the famous parodies, "Rejected Addresses," gathered round him at his two successive houses, the first in Hanover Crescent and the second in Cavendish Place, a group of men that included Samuel Rogers the banker-poet, Sydney

Sunday-afternoon receptions were, we read, the most noted institutions in Brighton after the Chain Pier. For in Horace Smith's time—he was in Brighton 1826–1849—the Chain Pier was still fashionable, though not so brilliant as when all the gay world of the Prince's Court made it their promenade. After a time, however, the tide of fashion set westward, and the pier was left desolate and deserted.

BRIGHTON CHAIN PIER A HUNDRED YEARS AGO

Smith, Charles Kean the actor, Macaulay, Harrison Ainsworth, Dickens, and Thackeray. When Thackeray came to lecture at Brighton on George IV. he told Horace Smith's daughter how relieved he was to find that the lecture was not to be delivered in the Pavilion. Thackeray had described George as "nothing but a coat and wig and a mask smiling under it—nothing but a great simulacrum." "I didn't like," he said, "the idea of abusing a man in his own house." The famous Mrs. Pipchin in "Dombey and Son" lived, it will be remembered, up a steep street in Brighton. Horace Smith's

In its decaying old age it achieved an interesting literary association. During the concluding decades of the last century a solitary man, slight and spare of figure, might have been seen in all weathers pacing for hours up and down the pier. This was William Black the novelist, who found here solitude and inspiration, and who, as he tramped the boards, shaped in imagination those books which were to prove so popular. All his novels written at Kemp Town were thought out on the old Chain Pier. He used to write on alternate days, taking long walks on the days between.

THE MOHOCKS

IN the London in which, after
nightfall, was

> No light, but rather darkness visible,

and in which as yet no policeman
walked, there were terrible men with
terrible names. The seventeenth
century knew them, and better still
perhaps the eighteenth. Macaulay
says: "Thieves and robbers plied
their trade with impunity; yet they
were hardly so terrible to peaceful
citizens as another class of ruffians.
It was a favourite amusement for
dissolute young gentlemen to swagger
by night about the town, breaking
windows, upsetting sedans, beating
quiet men, and offering rude caresses
to pretty women. Several dynasties
of these tyrants had, since the Restoration, domineered over the streets.
The 'Muns' and 'Tityre Tus' had
given place to the 'Hectors,' and the
'Hectors' had been recently succeeded
by the 'Scourers.' At a later period
arose the 'Nicker,' the 'Hawcubite,'
and the yet more dreaded name of
'Mohawk.'"

This is, for Macaulay, a very mild
description of the audacities and
atrocities of the Mohawks, or Mohocks,
and their forerunners, to whom Milton
doubtless makes a reference in the
first book of "Paradise Lost":

> When night
> Darkens the streets, then wander forth
> the sons
> Of Belial, flown with insolence and wine.

Milton, as far as we know, escaped
assault, but Dryden has told us how
he was waylaid and beaten at the
corner of Rose Street and King Street,
Covent Garden. The pedestrian returning home at night, whose ears
were suddenly assailed by the cry, "A
sweat! A sweat!" had two courses
open to him. He might take to his
heels, or, if a citizen of heart, plant his
back against the nearest wall and pluck
out his sword. Taken in the rear, he
could scarcely escape blood-letting.
Steele, in No. 332 of the *Spectator*
(March 21, 1712), gives a lively account
of the rite. "It is, it seems, the
custom for half a dozen or more of
these well-disposed savages, as soon as
they have inclosed the person upon
whom they design the favour of a
sweat, to whip out their swords, and,
holding them parallel to the horizon,
they describe a sort of magic circle
round about him with the points. As
soon as this piece of conjuration is
performed, and the patient without
doubt already beginning to wax warm,
to forward the operation, that member
of the circle towards whom he is so
rude as to turn his back first, runs his
sword directly into that part of the
patient whereon schoolboys are
punished; and as it is very natural
to imagine this will soon make him
tack about to some other point, every
gentleman does himself the same justice
as often as he receives the affront.
After this jig has gone two or three
times round, and the patient is thought
to have sweat sufficiently, he is very
handsomely rubbed down by some
attendants, who carry with them instruments for that purpose, and so
discharged."

It is in his 324th number (March 12,
1712) that Mr. Spectator first applies
his whip to these fine-dressed murderous
bullies of the night, not one of whom
seems ever to have travelled at the
tail of a cart: "a set of men (if you
will allow them a place in that special
of being) who have lately erected

themselves into a nocturnal fraternity, under the title of the Mohock club, a name borrowed it seems from a sort of cannibals in India, who subsist by plundering and devouring all the nations about them." According to Steele, the Mohocks had a president styled " Emperor," whose arms " are a Turkish crescent, which his imperial majesty bears at present in a very extraordinary manner engraven upon his forehead." Having drunk themselves to a pitch, the Mohocks set out from club or tavern and made a general sally. " The particular talents by which these misanthropes are distinguished from one another consist in the various kinds of barbarities which they execute upon their prisoners. Some are celebrated for a happy dexterity in tipping the lion upon them, which is performed by squeezing the nose flat to the face, and boring out the eyes with their fingers. Others are called the dancing masters, and teach their scholars to cut capers, by running swords through their legs, a new invention, whether originally French I cannot tell. A third sort are the tumblers, whose office it is to set women on their heads, and commit certain indecencies, or rather barbarities, on the limbs which they expose."

In an ironical manifesto of " Taw Waw Eben Zan Kaladar, Emperor of the Mohocks," in No. 347 of the *Spectator*, by Budgell, is this passage : " That the sweat be never given but between the hours of one and two ; always provided, that our hunters may begin to hunt a little after the close of the evening, anything to the contrary herein notwithstanding. Provided also, that if ever they are reduced to the necessity of pinking, it shall always be in the most fleshy parts, and such as are least exposed to view.

" It is also our imperial will and pleasure that our good subjects the sweaters do establish their hummums in such close places, alleys, nooks, and corners, that the patient or patients may not be in danger of catching cold."

The attacks of Steele and his brother essayists availed nothing. Presently, in the reign of George II., we have the poet Shenstone complaining that the Mohocks " come in large bodies, armed with couteaus, and attack whole parties " leaving the theatres. Shadwell's comedy, *The Scourers*, presents a picture little less than appalling of the condition of London's thoroughfares at night. Swift informs us that he seeks his lodgings early, "to avoid the Mohocks." Gay writes :

Who has not heard the Scourers' midnight fame ?
Who has not trembled at the Mohocks name ?

Arthur Murphy, that epicurean and versatile Irishman of parts (so maligned by Churchill as " Learned without sense, and venerably dull "), in his letters to Garrick, draws a splendid sketch of " Tiger Roach" the bully of the Bedford Coffee-house in 1769, and " one of the best of the race."

Certain historians have held that vice in England reaches its culmination in the reign of George II. (1727–1760). And are not the manners of the age summed up in the circumstance that society at large thought it a rather humorous thing of the Mohocks to assault women obscenely in the streets of his Majesty's capital ?

THRICE FOUND "NOT GUILTY"

THE GREAT HONE-ELLENBOROUGH STRUGGLE

IT is impossible not to be in sympathy with William Hone. The man himself, ever spited by fortune, never cringing to her, is interesting, pathetic, likeable. Thrice called on to defend himself at law, he made three really great fights of it, giving the eminent Lord Ellenborough the worst peppering of his life. It was as a blasphemous person that Hone was tried, and this should have sufficed to create against him something worse than prejudice in an English court of justice. But the jury stuck by him throughout, and public opinion sided with the jury. It was, in fact, immediately realised in all circles where liberal opinions held sway that Hone was in no true sense a blasphemous person, but a witty political fellow who had given mortal offence in powerful and august quarters. Time had been, no doubt, when Hone would have lost his ears in the pillory. Time had come, however (so at least it was thought by many intelligent people in London), when a present of money, raised by subscription, was a more suitable award for a needy and humorous writer at grips singlehanded with the law of libel. But some of the most signal of Hone's improprieties shall be reproduced, and readers of our own day shall pronounce on them.

To not a few among us Hone must be still in a little way familiar as the compiler of such quaintly interesting works as " Ancient Mysteries Explained," the " Every-day Book," the " Table-Book," and the " Year-Book." He brought George Cruikshank to the front. In the preparation of the books just mentioned he had the warm approval of Southey and the practical help of Charles Lamb. These productions, however, belong to Hone's later period, though he was then, as always, plodding among the children of adversity.

Born in 1780, he was placed by his father, a man of the straitest religious views, in the office of a London attorney. But his tastes were incurably bookish, and in 1800, being then married, he " started a book and print shop and a circulating library in Lambeth Walk." The arts thriving but poorly in Lambeth Walk, the young man " soon after removed to St. Martin's Churchyard, where he brought out his first publication, Shaw's *Gardiner*, and suffered much loss from a fire." Having thus early failed to make money for himself, he conceived a plan whereby the more fortunate might lay out theirs at interest, and, with another amateur financier, sought out the Right Hon. George Rose at the Board of Trade and " proposed the establishment of popular savings banks." But where money was in question fate would not suffer Hone to benefit either himself or anybody else, and the popular savings banks were not then begun.

He declined into bookselling again, and was presently a bankrupt. A mocking fortune continued to play the strangest tricks with Hone, for we find him by-and-by engaged upon " independent investigations into the conduct of lunatic asylums," with the now customary reward of " difficulties and failure." Somewhat later he is lodged, " with his now large family," in the thoroughfare of the Old Bailey, hiring for business purposes a small shop, " or rather box," in Fleet Street. The Fleet Street box is " on two separate nights broken into," and valuable books purloined that had been lent for display.

Meanwhile, Hone, getting forward in his thirties, had discovered a thoroughly efficient talent for parody and squib, such as would nowadays ensure his regular employment on the Press, and such as ought then to have guaranteed a competency to a writer not living in the constant element of ill-luck. From the spring to the late autumn of 1817 he published the *Reformist's Register*, in which his pen was very active in lively and ingenious satire. It was through Hone's gift of satire that the Attorney-General, Sir Samuel Shepherd, was able to land him at Guildhall in December of this year.

" On the morning of the 18th of December, 1817, there was a considerable crowd round the avenues of Guildhall. A bookseller was to be tried in the Court of King's Bench for printing and publishing parodies, at 55 Fleet Street, and 67 Old Bailey, three doors from

WILLIAM HONE

Ludgate Hill. The doorkeepers and officers of the Court scarcely knew what was going to happen, for the table within the bar had not the usual covering of crimson bags ; but ever and anon a dingy boy"—this was Hone's younger brother— " arrived with an armful of books, and the table was strewed with dusty and tattered volumes. . . . Sir Samuel Shepherd took his seat and looked compassionately, as was his nature to do, at the pale man in threadbare black, William Hone. Mr. Justice Abbott arrived in due time ; a special jury was sworn ; the pleadings were opened ; and the Attorney-General stated the case against William Hone for printing and publishing an impious and profane libel upon the Catechism, the Lord's Prayer, and the Ten Commandments, thereby bringing into contempt the Christian religion."

The offending publication, as put forward by the Attorney-General, was : " The late John Wilkes's Catechism of a Ministerial Member, taken from an Original Manuscript in Mr. Wilkes's Handwriting, never before printed, and

adapted to the Present Occasion.—
With Permission." Hone had sold it
at twopence at his places in Fleet
Street and the Old Bailey. The Catechism was, "An Instruction, to be
learned of every person before he be
brought to be confirmed a Placeman
or Pensioner by the Minister."

The Attorney-General proceeded to
recite, and it must be confessed that
the Court was diverted. Here is a
part of the parody of the Creed : " I
believe in George, the Regent Almighty,
Maker of New Streets and Knights of
the Bath, and in the present Ministry.
his only choice, who were conceived of
Toryism, brought forth of William
Pitt, suffered loss of Place under
Charles James Fox, were execrated,
dead, and buried. In a few months
they rose again from their minority ;
they reascended to the Treasury
benches, and sit at the right hand of a
little man with a large wig ; from
whence they laugh at the Petitions of
the People who may pray for Reform,
and that the sweat of their brow may
procure them Bread."

We may call this profane, but in no
sense is it obscene, and the aim of the
piece is manifestly political and nothing
else.

The Lord's Prayer, parodied as the
" Minister's Memorial," ran as follows :
" Our Lord who art in the Treasury,
whatsoever be thy name, thy power
be prolonged, thy will be done throughout the empire, as it is in each session.
Give us our usual sops, and forgive us
our occasional absences on divisions,
as we promise not to forgive them that
divide against thee. Turn us not out
of our places ; but keep us in the
House of Commons, the land of Pensions and Plenty ; and deliver us from
the People. Amen."

Hone, who defended himself, spoke
" near six hours " ; and an extraordinary performance it was for one
who had neither legal training, nor
knowledge of the procedure of courts,
nor any practice in discoursing. It
is unlikely, indeed, that a professional
advocate would have done half so well
for him as he did for himself ; since,
being able to plead ignorance of
technicalities, he was suffered to abuse
the Court and amuse the audience.
Counsel and judge interrupted him,
but Hone was considerably too much
for them. Once he replied to Mr.
Justice Abbott : " My Lord, your
lordship's observation is in the very
spirit of what Pope Leo X. said to
Martin Luther : ' For God's sake don't
say a word about the indulgences and
the monasteries and I'll give you a
living ' ; thus precluding him from
mentioning the very thing in dispute.
I must go on with these parodies or I
cannot go on with my defence." So
he went on hour after hour, reading
page upon page of parodies by the
editor of *Blackwood*, who had parodied
a chapter of Ezekiel ; by Luther, who
had parodied the Psalms ; by Dr. Boys,
Dean of Canterbury, who, in the pulpit
itself, had parodied the Lord's Prayer
(Our Pope, which art in Rome, hellish
be thy name," &c.) ; by Bishop Latimer,
who illustrated a sermon by a game of
cards ; by the reverend translator of
Æsop, Croxal, who had parodied the
Canticles ; by the author of the " Rol-
liad " ; by Canning, the notable Mr.
Canning, who, said Hone dramatically,
ought to be sharing his seat in the
dock. " I have been dragged from
behind my counter—and for what ?
For doing that which a Cabinet Minister
has been suffered to do with impunity.
I say that the Attorney-General will
act wrongly and partially and unfairly
if he does not bring Mr. Canning

forward. **If I** am convicted, he ought to follow me to my cell. If my family is ruined, his family ought to be made to feel a little. If I am injured by this indecent, this unjust prosecution, he ought not to be suffered to escape unpunished."

It will be perceived that " the pale man in threadbare black " was not so badly advised in undertaking his own defence. Vainly did the judge charge the jury. After a deliberation of less than a quarter of an hour they returned with an emphatic " Not guilty."

"The loudest acclamations were instantly heard in all parts of the Court. ' *Long live the honest Jury,*' and ' *An honest Jury for ever.*' were exclaimed by many voices : the waving of hats, handkerchiefs, and applause continued for several minutes. . . . Mr. Justice Abbott interposed, and desired that those who felt inclined to rejoice at the decision would reserve the expression of their satisfaction for a fitter place and opportunity. The people accordingly left the Court, and as they proceeded along the streets the language of joy was most loudly and

LORD ELLENBOROUGH

unequivocally expressed; every one with whom they met, and to whom they communicated the event, being forward to swell the peal."

Next morning, December 19, Hone again entered the Court with his battery of books. He was now to be indicted for the parody entitled " The Political Litany." In his own report, or the one that was prepared for him, he tells us that " the curiosity of the public became so intense this morning, as well on account of the importance of the case as of the triumphant defence of Mr. Hone the former day, that at a very early hour all the avenues of the Court were literally blocked up by a multitude of spectators."

To the general surprise, Lord Ellenborough took his seat on the bench. Ellenborough was not the ideal judge to try a cause of this kind, but he was this day to meet his match. The alleged libel was put in by the Attorney-General, and read by the clerk. The opening clauses will serve as a sample :

O Prince, ruler of the people, have mercy upon us, pension-paying subjects.
O Prince, ruler, &c.

O House of Lords, hereditary legislators, have mercy upon us, pension-paying subjects.

O House of Lords, &c.

The Attorney-General, in the course of his address to the jury, affirmed that " whatever might be the object of the defendant, the publication had the effect of scoffing at the public service of the Church." Hone then took up his parable again, and the Lord Chief Justice, looking ever more threateningly on the lean-visaged student from Grub Street, was given a fair surfeit of parody. Particular play was made by Hone with the skits upon the Litany in which the Cavaliers lashed Roundhead and Puritan. Again and again the judge broke in with an opinion of his own ; " but," cried Hone, " let me say that after all it is but the opinion of *one* man ; it is not *his Lordship's* opinion."

There was " loud huzzaing," and Ellenborough called for a victim, but the distracted Sheriff could produce none. Ellenborough grew furious. " Open your eyes, and see ! " he exclaimed to the Sheriff. " Stretch out your hands, and seize ! " but no one was taken. It was impossible to put down Hone. The jury, as sensible men, said the judge, " should not have their time taken up in this manner " ; and the defendant instantly retorted : " My Lord, I understand your Lordship's notion of sensible men in a jury-box very well. What your Lordship means by calling the jury sensible men is that they will find me guilty ! " In this spirit Hone kept up the attack during seven hours, and towards the end Ellenborough's frame of adamant was visibly oppressed. There was fire enough left in him, nevertheless, for a charge to the jury in which, unhesitatingly adopting the *rôle* of prose-

cuting counsel, he declared that Hone's " Litany " transcended in profanity and impiety everything that had been read by him in Court. The jury's rejoinder to this was a verdict of " Not guilty."

Hone looked weaker than ever when he came into Court on the following morning, December 20, but repelled the suggestion of a postponement of the case. This day it was : " The King against Hone, for the *Sinecurist's Creed.*" It was thought by many that this third action would be dropped. There were two reasons why such a course might have been (and probably should have been) adopted by the Government. In the first place, two verdicts had just been given in Hone's favour by two different juries. In the second, Hone, wearied by two successive combats, representing together thirteen hours of strife, in an unfamiliar arena, might fairly be argued unfit to take the floor a third time without the lapse of a single day. It is likely, however, that the Government made their deliberate reckoning on the assumption that the professional assault of the third day would beat the weakened man to his knees. They were disappointed.

Of the deadly humour of the " Sinecurist's Creed " the opening verses are a just example :

Whosoever will be a Sinecurist, before all things it is necessary that he hold a place of profit.

Which place, except every Sinecurist do receive the salary for, and do no service, without doubt is no Sinecure.

And a Sinecurist's duty is this : that he divide with the Ministry and be with the Ministry in a Majority. Neither confounding the Persons : nor dividing with the Opposition.

For there is One Ministry of Old Bags, another of Derry Down Triangle : and another of the Doctor.

The very first attack of the judge seemed to brace the enfeebled Hone, who had entered the Court "pale and agitated." Ellenborough accused him of misstating a certain statute. "Gentlemen," said Hone, turning to the jury, "it is you who are trying me to-day. His Lordship is no judge of *me*. You are *my* judges, and *you only* are my judges. His Lordship sits there to receive your verdict. He does not even sit there to regulate the trial, for the law has already regulated it."

He made two other effective appeals to a jury who were already with him, and the first of these was another tremendous stroke at Ellenborough. "His friends," he said, "had recommended him to counsel, but some objections were urged against all whom they pointed out to him. Some from motives of etiquette could not attend upon him in prison. Others, though they might have talent, had not courage to undertake his defence. Without courage, it would be useless to attempt it. The question he put was, 'Has he *courage*? Will he be able to stand up against my Lord Ellenborough? Will he withstand the browbeating of my Lord Ellenborough?'"

In his second point Hone stooped a degree, but got well home with it. He was sorry, he said, for the shabbiness of his appearance before the Court; he had resolved "to get a new suit of clothes for these trials, but the money I had provided for that purpose I was obliged to give for copies of the informations against me"; and then he drew a lightning sketch of himself in his battle with the Government. "See the odds against me! It is one farthing against a million of gold!" It was a direct and well-laid appeal to the gallery; but both jury and public were quite aware that it was backed by truth. The verdict for the third time was "Not guilty."

It has been generally supposed, though the supposition may be incorrect, that these defeats in two consecutive cases which he was bent on winning for the Crown hastened the death of Lord Ellenborough.

HONE AND CRUIKSHANK CONSULTING

THE TOURNAMENT ON THE BRIDGE

SINCE early daybreak, from the London side and from the Southwark side, the citizens had crowded on to London Bridge. Wooden houses were built along the top of the bridge, but there were vacant spaces where you could see the river ; and the widest of these was large enough for miniature tournaments and jousting and tilting matches, which were of frequent occurrence on the bridge. To this spot the people flocked with noisy excitement ; they were to witness a show more full of spice and adventure than any mere progress of kings or Lord Mayor's pageant, a sport more full-flavoured than any mere jousting match. The day was St. George's Day, April 23, and the year 1390.

You might see, from the bridge, London lying small and compact within its walls, its forests of steeples and towers glittering in the smokeless air ; along Bankside there were but a few poor houses of watermen and fishermen. The river roared through the nineteen narrow arches of the bridge with a deafening sound. The parapet was hung with cloth of gold ; flags and streamers flapped from the windows of the houses. For to-day the honour of two great rival countries was to be put to the test ; there was to be a solemn trial of valour between two renowned champions, an English and a Scottish knight ; and the king himself, Richard II., was to preside at the tournament. The whole width of the bridge—it was only forty feet wide— was given to the lists ; the spectators thronged at either end of this space. A " summer castle " was put up for the king—an erection of wood and pasteboard, hung with tapestries and painted cloth. Here was assembled a company as brilliant and as gorgeously clothed as any history has to offer ; knights in splendid apparel, carrying the whole wealth of an estate on their backs, and ladies whose stiff dresses glittered with jewels.

The origin of the match was as follows ; at that time between England and Scotland was bitter warfare, and even in times of truce fierce jealousies and bitter feuds prevailed. Now the English Lord Wells was King Richard's ambassador in Scotland, and being at a solemn banquet, a question arose as to the respective valour of the two countries. To settle the controversy, Lord Wells challenged Sir David Lindsay, Earl of Crawford, to a passage of arms. The challenge was accepted, Richard II.'s consent obtained, Lord Wells named the place and Sir David the day.

Sir David had come hundreds of miles through a perilous country to fulfil his pledge. Still to be seen in the Rolls of Scotland is the safe-conduct granted to him by the English king " for coming into our country with twenty-and-nine persons of his company and retinue in armour, and twelve other knights with their esquires, varlets, and pages, and with thirty horses." No doubt, as Sir David passed under the gate of London Bridge, he thought of the time, only some eighty years ago, when the head of that noble patriot Sir William Wallace had been exposed on a pole above it, and no doubt the thought was a spur to his courage. But no bitterness of memory marred the perfect chivalry of his actions, as will appear hereafter.

Trumpets flourished, heralds proclaimed the lineage of the champions, and the combatants rode into the lists, clad in armour from head to foot, each having on shield, banner, and trappings the arms of his house. The signal being given, " tearing their barbed horses with their spurs (as the old chronicle tells us); they rushed hastily together with a mighty force, and with square-ground spears to the conflict. Neither party was moved by the vehement impulse and breaking of the spears ; so that the common people affected to cry out that David was bound to the saddle of his horse, contrary to the law of arms, because he sat unmoved amidst the splintering of the lances on his helmet and visage. When Earl David heard this he presently leaped off his charger, and then as quickly vaulted again on his back without any assistance ; and taking a second hasty course, the spears were a second time shivered by the shock, through their burning desire to conquer. And now a third time were these valorous enemies stretched out and running together ; but the English knight was cast down breathless to the earth, with great sounds of mourning from his countrymen that he was killed. Earl David, when victory appeared, hastened to leap suddenly to the ground ; for he had fought without anger and but for glory, that he might show himself to be the strongest of the champions, and casting himself upon Lord Wells, tenderly embraced him until he revived, and the surgeon came to attend him. Nor, after this, did he omit one day to visit him in the gentlest manner during his sickness, even like the most courteous companion."

Three months Earl David remained in England at the king's desire, and when he returned to Scotland, to commemorate that glorious St. George's Day, the Scotch knight founded a chantry at Dundee, with a gift of £32 yearly, for seven priests and divers virgins to sing anthems to the patron saint of England.

In Sir David's courtesy to his adversary ; in the high honour paid to the Scotchman as victor, even though he was a foreigner and a foeman, we find represented the best traditions of chivalry; and it is pleasant to associate this historic tournament, which illustrates so finely the mediæval ideal of knighthood, with the little lists on London Bridge.

THE STORY OF

THE NELSON COLUMN.

PERHAPS no letter to the *Times*, embodying a popular and practical proposal, has been more successful than the one which appeared in that newspaper on September 9, 1837, signed " J. B." and expressed, in part, as follows :

Allow me to suggest through your columns the favourable opportunity and most appropriate situation now afforded of erecting in the centre of the Square some worthy monument or statue, commemorating the glorious victories of the immortal Nelson.

The idea of honouring Nelson's memory in this manner was so favourably received that in the *Times* of April 27, 1838, the following notice appeared :

NELSON MONUMENT.—The committee for erecting a monument to the memory of Lord Nelson hereby give notice that they are desirous of receiving from architects, artists, and other persons, designs for such a monument, to be erected in Trafalgar Square.

The committee cannot, in the present state of the subscriptions, fix definitely the sum to be expended, but they recommend that the estimated cost of the several designs should be confined within the sum of £20,000 to £30,000. This condition, and that of the intended site, are the only restrictions to which artists are limited.

Committees and meetings were organised, and the site as well as the monument was the subject of much debate. On February 22, 1838, a meeting was held at the Thatched House, in St. James's Street, at which it was resolved "that a subscription be raised for the purpose of creating a national monument in a conspicuous part of the metropolis."

We think it is a forgotten, as it is certainly an interesting, fact that the Trafalgar Square site was agreed upon at a meeting at the London Tavern presided over by the Duke of Wellington.

The project moved slowly, and, indeed, it was destined to be an unconscionably long undertaking.

In April 1839, the *Gentleman's Magazine* was able to report the result of the competition. This it did as follows :

The designs of the competitors for the Nelson Memorial, 124 in number, have been publicly exhibited at Mr. Rainy's gallery in Regent Street, the three prizes having been previously assigned by the Committee. It is generally agreed that the designs, on the whole, betray a lamentable deficiency of invention, and that by far the larger majority are conceived without adequate reference to the intended site (the vast area of Trafalgar Square) or to the surrounding buildings.

The first premium was adjudged by the Committee to the proposition of W. Railton, architect, for a fluted Corinthian column, 174 feet high, on a pedestal ornamented with reliefs, and surmounted by a statue 17 feet high. This design can, of course, make no pretension to originality ; and besides is open to various other objections.

The second prize was awarded to Mr. E. H. Baily, R.A., to whom ultimately fell the commission for the statue.

In 1840 the contract to erect the column within two years was given to Messrs. Ginsell and Peto, for the sum of £17,860. The foundation-stone of the great national monument was laid, strange to say, without ceremony. This was on September 30, 1840. Despite the terms of the contract it was three years before the raising of Baily's statue to the summit was begun.

The figure, which stood 17 feet high and weighed 18 tons, was made of stone from the Duke of Buccleugh's Granton quarry. It was, of course, in segments, but these were put together on the ground so that the public might inspect the complete work. In the two days during which it was on view it was visited by 100,000 persons. The following is a contemporary account of the elevation of the statue, on November 3, 1843, to its present position :

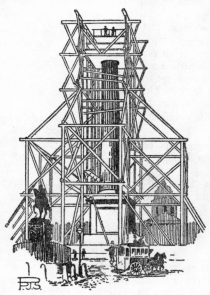

THE COLUMN DURING ITS ERECTION

" The statue of Lord Nelson, by Baily, reached its destination on the top of the column, erected under the management and after the design of Mr. Railton. The lower part was got up on Friday morning, after six hours' labour, and the upper portion followed on Saturday morning, and the arm was also in the course of the day united to the body. A flagstaff was erected which reached above the head of the figure, and from it was displayed the Union Jack, which is the identical flag under which the hero fell at the battle of Trafalgar.

" This figure breathes the very soul and spirit of Nelson ; there we behold the intrepid firmness of his mind—the determination to achieve his purpose, unawed by any terrors which the foes of his country could evoke. The simplicity of the attitude is very striking : here is no extended hand with truncheon or with telescope ; it is Nelson himself on his quarter-deck, cool and collected. Like the Angel introduced in Addison's *Campaign*, as an emblem of Marlborough's imperturbed spirit— calm and serene, he drives the furious blast of battle ; rides in the whirlwind and directs the storm ; and of Nelson it might indeed be truly added, from the same source,

In joys of conquest he resigned his breath,
And, filled with England's glory, smiled in
   death.

" Even when his life-blood was ebbing from his wound, reducing to a few short moments the current of his existence, Nelson's spirit was still active for his country's cause, still busied in the direction of his fleet. Assured of victory and of the capture and destruction of the foe, his dying words were : ' Then let us anchor ! ' "

The dimensions of the monument have been given as follows :

	Feet.
Steps (formerly between the Lions but now removed) . . .	7
Pedestal	37
Column	105
Tambour	7
Statue	17
Total .	173

Landseer's four lions were not placed in position until 1867. They have been criticised and admired by different judges. Richard Jefferies boldly described them as " the only noble open-air work of native art in the four-million-city."

FINIS

OUR revels now are ended : these our actors . . .
Are melted into air, into thin air :
And like the baseless fabrick of this vision,
The cloud capp'd towers, the gorgeous palaces,
The solemn temples, the great globe itself,
Yea, all that it inherit, shall dissolve ;
And like this insubstantial pageant faded,
Leave not a rack behind.
      SHAKESPEARE : *The Tempest.*

INDEX

ABEL, Karl Friedrich, i. 393
Abershaw, Jerry, highwayman, i. 453, 460, 464
  execution on Kennington Common, i. 462
Academy, the Royal. See Royal Academy
Adam and Eve Tavern. See Inns
Adam, Robert, ii. 216
Addison, at Holland House, i. 172, 173
  at Royal Exchange, i. 244
  The Campaign by, ii. 410
  Cato performed by Royal family, i. 470
  courtship of Countess of Warwick, i. 172
Adelaide, Queen, and Tom Thumb, i. 484
Adelphi Theatre, the, under Webster, ii. 170–172
Agincourt, Henry Fifth's return from, ii. 17
Aguilar, Baron d', his "Starvation Farm," ii. 82
Akerman, Governor of Newgate, i. 135, 136 ; ii. 174, 177
Albert, Prince, and Exhibition of 1851, ii. 452
  on motto for Royal Exchange, i. 68
Aldgate, Chaucer's house in, i. 381
Allen, Lord, at White's, ii. 336
Almack's, i. 432
  assemblies at, ii. 165
  Duke of Wellington at, ii. 32
  gambling at, ii. 166, 167
  Macaronis at, ii. 328
Alvanley, Lord, i. 117
  and Beau Brummell, i. 142
  at Brighton, ii. 480
  at White's, ii. 335, 336
Amen Corner, ii. 414
American Cousin, Our, by Tom Taylor, ii. 22, 280
Angelo, Domenico, i. 391
  and Peg Woffington, i. 391
  fencing-match at Dr. Key's, i. 392
  fight with Redman, i. 394
Angelo, Henry, on Academy of Fencing, i. 391
Angerstein, Mr. Julius, ii. 146
Anne, Queen, at Kensington Palace, i. 494 ;
  tea drinking by, ii. 203, 204
Anspach, Margravine of, at Brandenburgh House, i. 348
Applewoman of Hyde Park, the, i. 278
Apsley House, gifted to Duke of Wellington, ii. 27
Arbuthnot, Mrs., friendship with Wellington, ii. 33
Argyll, Duke of, interview with Wellington, ii. 30
Arundel, Earl of, inscription on walls of Tower, ii. 315
Askew, Dr. Antony, ii. 368
Astley, the painter, at Schomberg House, ii. 469
  Philip, equestrian, i. 310 ; ii. 201
  at Wilton House, i. 392

BACH, Sebastian, at Angelo's Academy, i. 393
  first performance on pianoforte, i. 474
Bacon, Lord, and Sir W. Raleigh, i. 15
  at Canonbury Tower, i. 40
  death of, i. 15
Baddeley, Robert, and Twelfth Night cakes, i. 79
Bailey, Old, ii. 119
" Bailiff's Daughter of Islington," i. 190
Baillie, Dr. Matthew, ii. 368
Baily, E. H., statue of Nelson by, ii. 495
Baker, Henry, ii. 245
Balfour, Jabez, on prison life, ii. 396, 398, 400
" Ball " Hughes, ii. 244, 424
Ballads, at Vauxhall concerts, i. 92, 93 ; ii. 152
Ballad-singers in London, i. 5
  of Seven Dials, i. 125
Ballooning at Vauxhall, i. 95 ; ii. 420
Bambridge, Thomas, i. 48
Bank Nun, the, ii. 52
Banks, and his horse Morocco, i. 345
Banks, Miss Sophia, ii. 292
Barclay, the Quaker host of kings, i. 437
Barber of Fleet Street, The, i. 53
Barnum and Tom Thumb, i. 481
Barnwell, George, the London Apprentice, i. 17
  at Adam and Eve Tavern, i. 337
Baronets, the Regency, i. 109
Barrett, Michael, Fenian, execution of, ii. 122
Barrow Hill, ii. 43
Barry, James, plea for Gallery of Old Masters, ii. 145, 146
Barrymore, the actor, i. 361
Barrymore, Lord, ii. 389
  at Brighton, ii. 480
Bartholomew Fair, i. 196, 345, 351–357
Bateman, Christopher, bookseller, ii. 25
Bathing-machines at Margate, i. 270
Battersea Fields, amusements at, i. 45, 46
  duelling on, i. 43, 499
  old Red House at, i. 43
Battersea Park, i. 46
" Bay, The," i. 444
Beaconsfield, Lord. See Disraeli
Beauchamp Tower, inscriptions by prisoners on, ii. 312
Beaumont, Sir George, ii. 146
Beckerstaff, Isaac, ii. 6
Beckford, William, ii. 390
Bed, the Celestial, Dr. Graham's, i. 339
Bedford, Duke of, and Beau Brummell, i. 140
Beefsteak Club, ii. 56, 85–88
  Captain Morris at, i. 111, 113
Beethoven, and the Broadwoods, i. 476
Beggars' Opera, i. 452 ; ii. 85, 90
  Carey's ballads in, ii. 153
Bell, Currer, Ellis and Acton, ii. 198
Bellamy, Miss, on Gunning family, i. 191

Bellenden, Miss, and George II., i. 467
Bellingham, John, assassin of Mr. Percival, i. 508
Bellington, Mrs., singer, ii. 167
Bellmen, London, ii. 38, 408
Bells of London, ii. 1
Belzoni, Giovanni B., i. 83
Benians, Mr., on South Sea Bubble, ii. 68, 72, 73
Bentley, Nathaniel, "Dirty Dick," i. 375
Berkeley Square, the Ghost of, ii. 157
Berners Street Hoax, the, ii. 221, 224
Berry, Lady, story of, i. 476
Besant, Sir W., on area and population of London, ii. 98
    on London bells, ii. 1
Best, Captain, duel with Lord Camelford, ii. 253
Betterton, the actor, at Bartholomew's Fair, i. 354
Betty, the boy actor, i. 266
Bible Society, The, ii. 425, 426
Bish, J., lottery-office keeper, i. 35, 36
Bishop, Sir Henry, ballads by, i. 92
Black, William, at Brighton, ii. 483
Blair, John, funeral sermons of, ii. 214
Blanchard, J. P., balloon voyage across Channel by, ii. 419
Blessington, Lady, ii. 401
    and Count d'Orsay, i. 252
    and Lord Byron, i. 253
Blood, Colonel, would-be assassin of Charles II., i. 43, 180
    attempted theft of crown by, i. 177
Blount, Sir John, director of South Sea Company, ii. 69
Blücher, Marshal, at Carlton House, ii. 118
Blue-Stockings, the, ii. 111
Boar's Head Tavern, ii. 438-440
Boat, ancient British, discovery of, ii. 304
Boat-racing on Thames, i. 232
Bolingbroke and Voltaire, ii. 384, 385
Boodle's Club, i. 109
Booksellers' shops at St. Dunstan's, ii. 375
Boscawen, Mrs., on Almack's, ii. 166
Boswell, at Hackman's execution, i. 122
    on Benjamin Stillingfleet, ii. 111
    on the Boar's Head Tavern, ii. 439
    on Vauxhall Gardens, i. 93
Bottle Hoax, the, i. 112
Boucicault, Dion, ii. 172
Bow Bells, ii. 1
Bow Street Patrol, i. 464
    Runners, i. 27
Boxing in eighteenth century, i. 197
    at Tottenham Fair, i. 334
Boxing Day, ii. 14
Bracegirdle, Mrs., i. 73, 448
Braham, Augustus, ii. 181
    John, the tenor, ii. 90
Bramston, James, on London Customs, i. 152
Brandenburgh House, Queen Caroline at, i. 347 ; ii. 117
    death and funeral from, ii. 317
Brandon, Richard, executioner of Charles I., i. 209, 210

Breslaw, the conjurer, i. 164
Bridgegate Tower, the Cripple of, i. 221
Brighton, George IV., at, ii. 479-483
    Chain Pier at, ii. 483
British Coffee House, the, ii. 213
British Museum, founding of, ii. 275-278
Britton, Thomas, coalman, ii. 24
Broadwood, John, piano manufacturer, i. 475
Brontë, Charlotte, in London, ii. 197
    meeting with Thackeray, ii. 199, 200
Brooks's Club, ii. 80, 431-433
    Beau Brummell at, i. 141
Brougham, Lord, and Princess Charlotte, i. 230
Broughton, Jack, prize-fighter, i. 197
    Code of, i. 198
    fight with Slack at Tottenham Fair, i. 334
    winner of Watermen's Boat Race, i. 233
Browning and Tennyson, ii. 232
Brownings, the, story of their elopement, i. 272
Brummell, Beau, i. 138
    and George IV., ii. 118
    and Lord Alvanley, at Brighton, ii. 480
    and "Poodle Byng," ii. 80
    and Scrope Davies, i. 225
    at White's, ii. 335, 336
    dress of, i. 140
Brutus, in Britain, i. 236
Buckstone, John Baldwin, comedian, ii. 21
    and Sothern, ii. 281
Bun House, Old Chelsea, i. 323
Bunhill Fields, Defoe's monument in, ii. 246
Buononcini's rivalry with Handel, i. 385
Burke, Edmund, and Lord Erskine, ii. 208
    on Gordon Riots, i. 133
Burney, Fanny, and Dr. Johnson, ii. 200
    on Mrs. Montague, i. 112
    visit to Leverian Museum, ii. 250
Butchell, Martin van, i. 130
Butchers of Smithfield, serenade parties by, i. 297
Byng, "Poodle," ii. 80
Byron, Lord, and Hobhouse, i. 226
    and Lady Blessington, i. 253
    at Harrow, i. 442
    on lights of London, ii. 212
    on menagerie at Exeter Exchange, i. 300
    pupil of Jackson, the pugilist, ii. 455
Byron, Lord William, duel at Star and Garter, i. 407

Cade's Rebellion, i. 62
Cadman, the steeple-jack, i. 99, 100
Caine, Hall, at Rossetti's, ii. 372, 373
Calcraft, the executioner, ii. 120, 124
    flogging of garrotters by, ii. 107
Camelford, Lord, duel with Capt. Best, ii. 252
Cane, gold-headed, of famous physicians, ii. 366
Canning, Mr., "Questions and Answers," by, ii. 260

Canonbury Tower, owners of, i. 40
  Goldsmith at, i. 41
Canterbury Music Hall, ii. 179
Capelli, Signor, cat-trainer, i. 156
Carey, Henry, author of "Sally in our
  Alley," ii. 152
Caricatures, political, ii. 71
Carlisle House, Angelo's Fencing Academy,
  at, i. 393
  Mrs. Cornelys' masquerades at, i. 428
Carlton Club, founded by Duke of Welling-
  ton, ii. 31
Carlton House, George IV. as Prince of
  Wales at, ii. 115
  portico transferred to National Gallery,
  ii. 148
Carlyle, Dr. Alexander, ii. 213, 214
Carlyle, Jane Welsh, ii. 76, 79, 228, 231
Carlyle, Thomas, and Emerson, ii. 78, 79
  and J. S. Mill, ii. 76
  and Turgenev, ii. 34
  at a party at Forster's, ii. 338
  friendship with Tennyson, ii. 228, 231
  life in London, ii. 75
Carol-singing, ii. 14
Caroline, Queen, wife of George II., Ken-
  sington Gardens laid out by, i. 495,
  496
Caroline, Queen, wife of George IV., at
  Brandenburgh House, i. 347 ; ii. 117
  attempted entrance to Coronation,
  ii. 168
  funeral of, ii. 317
Carriers, London, i. 187
Carter, Elizabeth, ii. 112
Casanova, at Mme. Cornelys' masquerades,
  i. 429
Castlemaine, Countess of, i. 196
Castlereagh, Lord, in Cato Street con-
  spiracy, i. 445
Catalini, Mme., ii. 90, 457, 458
Catesby, Robert, author of Gunpowder
  Plot, i. 287, 288
Catch phrases, ii. 61, 144, 170, 227
Catholic Emancipation Bill, i. 133
Catnach, James, on steam omnibuses, ii. 102
  printing press at Seven Dials, i. 124
Cato Street conspiracy, i. 144
Cats' Opera, the, i. 156
Cavanagh, John, the Fives player, ii. 95
Cavendish, Henry, i. 425
Celestial Bed, Dr. Graham's, i. 339
Cervetti, the 'cellist, i. 406
Chalk Farm, as duelling resort, ii. 299
  engines from Euston Station at, ii. 136
  Moore's duel with Jeffrey at, i. 378
Chambers, Ephraim, burial of, i. 42
  Sir William, i. 282
Chancery Lane, ii. 99
'Change Alley, ii. 67, 70, 71
Chapter Coffee-house, ii. 178
  the Brontës at, ii. 197, 198
Charing Cross, i. 263
Charles I. at sermon at Paul's Cross, ii. 163
  equestrian statue of, ii. 267
  execution at Whitehall, i. 157

Charles I., executioner of, i. 209
  farewell to his children, i. 157
  letter intercepted by Ireton, i. 96
  relations with Nell Gwynne, i. 317, 318,
  319
  Royal Gallery of, ii. 145, 146
Charles II., at Frost Fair on the Thames,
  i. 321
  attempted assassination by Colonel
  Blood, i. 43, 180
  founding of second Royal Exchange
  by, i. 244
  restoration to throne, ii. 339
  statues of, i. 492
"Charlies, The," ii. 37
Charlotte, Princess, at Warwick House, i.
  227-231
  death of, i. 231
  marriage with Prince Leopold of Saxe-
  Coburg, ii. 115, 117
Charlotte, Queen, custom of Christmas tree
  introduced by, ii. 16
Chartist Riots, ii. 217
Chateaubriand in London, ii. 300
Chatterton, ii. 197
  death of, ii. 476-478
Chaucer, as Custom House officer, i. 380
  house in Aldgate, i. 381
  on the Tabard Inn, i. 205
Cheap, Captain David, at British Coffee-
  house, ii. 216
Cheapside, Eleanor Cross at, ii. 4
  pageants, ii. 4
  procession of Henry V. at, ii. 18
Chelsea, poets and painters of, ii. 369-373
  Bun House, i. 323
  Pensioners, ii. 29, 39
  Hospital founded by Nell Gwynne,
  i. 319
Cherry, Andrew, the composer, i. 93
Cheshire Cheese Inn, i. 205 ; ii, 5
Chesterfield, Lord, and Bottle Hoax, i. 113
  and Rev. Dr. Dodd's forgery, ii. 174
  at Christie's, ii. 343
Chevalier d'Eon, sex impersonation by,
  i. 165
Cheyne Row, No. 5, Carlyle's house, ii. 75
Cheyne Walk, No. 16, Rossetti's house at;
  ii. 369
  Saltero's coffee-house in, ii. 464
Child's Bank, i. 11
Chimney-sweeps' May Day festival, i. 151, 152
Chop-house, Dolly's, ii. 178
Chopin, at Broadwood's, i. 475
Christie's, story of, ii. 342
Christmas in Old London, ii. 12
Chudleigh, Elizabeth, ii. 405
Chunee, the elephant, at Exeter Exchange
  menagerie, i. 300
Churchill, John, satirist, ii. 87
Cibber, Colley, on Doggett, the actor, i. 232
  on Italian opera, ii. 89
  on tea, ii. 204
Cider Cellars, The, ii. 351
Circus, Astley's, i. 310
Clapham sect, the, ii. 425-427

Clare Market, i. 154, 155
  butcher's serenades at, i. 297
Clarendon, Lord, on Lord Holland, i. 174, 175
Cleavers and Marrow-bones, i. 297
Clementi, Muzio, i. 474
Clerkenwell Explosion, the, ii. 122
  Sala on, ii. 378
Clifford's Inn, George Dyer, Hermit of,
  i. 409
Clubs, London, ii. 80, 85, 151
  Almack's, i. 432 ; ii. 165, 328
  Boodle's, i. 109
  Brooks's, ii. 431–433
  Carlton, ii. 31
  Crockford's, ii. 242
  Garrick, ii. 472
  Union, ii. 472
  White's, ii. 334
Coal Hole, The, ii. 353
Coalman, Britton, the, ii. 24
Coates, " Romeo," i. 143
  at Carlton House, ii. 118
" Cobs," or water-carriers, i. 214, 218
Cock and Pie Fields, i. 123
Cock Lane Ghost, The, i. 477
Cock Tavern, Tennyson at, ii. 229
Cockburn, Mrs., and Rousseau, ii. 463
" Cockney," origin of term, ii. 2
  Washington Irving on, ii. 368
Cockpit Theatre, i. 318
Cockspur Street, ii. 213
  Breslaw's performances at, i. 164
Coffee-houses, ii. 214
  The Bedford, ii. 485
  The British, ii. 213
  The Chapter, ii. 178, 197
  Don Saltero's, ii. 464
  Nando's, i. 98
  Tom's, Devereux Court, ii. 204
Cogers, the Old, ii. 142
Coining, i. 90
Colosseum, The, ii. 329
Comic Songs, i. 394 ; ii. 273
Conduit, the Great, i. 214
Congalton, Charles, ii. 214
Congreve, Voltaire's visit to, ii. 384
Conquest, B. O., i. 23, 24
Constable, John, i. 308
Cooke, Thomas, the Clerkenwell miser, i. 184
Copenhagen House, Islington, ii. 95
Coram, Captain, Foundlings' Hospital
  founded by, i. 284
Cornelys, Mrs., i. 325
  masquerades by, i. 391, 428–432
" Corner Memory " Thompson, i. 195
Cornhill, foundation of Exchange in, i. 243
  Maypole in, i. 148
  the Standard in, ii. 130, 132
Corsica, King of, bankruptcy of, ii. 331
Costa, Sir Michael, ii. 92
Cosway, Richard, i. 283
  at Schomberg House, ii. 469, 470, 471
Cottington, Jack, highwayman, ii. 295
Cotton, Sir Robert, collection of MSS. and
  books, ii. 275
  Charles I.'s treatment of, ii. 276

" Country Cousin's Commissions to her
  Cousins in London," i. 453
Coutts' Bank, story of, i. 362
Coutts, Baroness Burdett, i. 363
Coutts, Thomas, banker, i. 362–366
Covent Garden Theatre, burning of, i. 449
  " O. P." riots at, ii. 457
  Opera, ii. 91, 92
Coventry, Maria Gunning, Countess of, ii.
  190, 193
  Earl of, objection to powder and puffs,
  ii. 193
Coverley, Sir Roger, London as described
  by, ii. 363–365
Cowell, Samuel, author of " The Ratcatcher's
  Daughter," i. 88, 161
Cowley, on Cromwell's burial, ii. 209
Cowper, on Dr. Dodd, the forger, ii. 174
Cox's Museum, ii. 210
Crabbe, George, on burning of Newgate,
  i. 136
Craven, Lord, and Queen Elizabeth of Bohe-
  mia, ii. 269
Craven House, Drury Lane, ii. 270, 272
Craven Street, James Smith at, ii. 472,
  474
Crockford's, ii. 242
  Duke of Wellington at, ii. 31
Croft, Sir Herbert, " Love and Madness " by,
  i. 120
Cromartie, Lady, at Leicester House, i. 468
Cromwell, Charles I.'s letters intercepted
  by, i. 96
  disinterment at Restoration, ii. 210
  his head in possession of Mr. Wilkinson, ii. 209
Crown Jewels, attempted robbery of, i. 177
Crucifix, the Moving, ii. 162
" Cruel Knight, The," Ballad of, i. 476
Cruikshank, Bank Restriction Note by,
  ii. 119, 121
  caricature of Swearing on Horns, ii. 36
  home in Hampstead Road, ii. 319–322
  and Hone, ii. 486, 491
  illustrations by, ii. 319, 320
  on abolition of Bartholomew's Fair, i.
  357
  temperance crusade of, ii. 320–322
Crystal Palace, the, ii. 452–454
Culloden, battle of, news received in London,
  ii. 215
Cumberland, Duke of, i. 114, 193
Curfew, the, i. 69
  rung by Bow Bell, ii. 62
Curran, John Philpot, ii. 142
Custom House, The, Chaucer at, i. 380

DANDIES, The, ii. 80
Davenant, Sir Willaim, i. 155
Davies, John, the rackets player, ii. 96
Davies, Scrope, i. 225
  and Beau Brummell, i. 225
  and Lord Byron, i. 225, 226
Davy, Sir Humphrey, at Holland House,
  i. 174
  on gas-lighting of London, ii. 21

Dawson, Captain Jemmy, execution of, i. 219
  Nancy, i. 25
Day, Mr., and the Fairlop Oak, i. 81
Debating Society of The Cogers, ii. 142
Debtors at Fleet Prison, i. 48
Defoe, Daniel, in the pillory, i. 404 ; ii. 468
  life in London, ii. 245
Delany, Mrs., i. 469
  on Misses Gunning, ii. 191, 193
  on play at Almack's, ii. 166
Delpini, the Clown, i. 256
  at the Pantheon, i. 326
Derby Day, i. 471
Derwentwater, Lord, execution of, ii. 285
Desseausau, Chevalier, the dwarf, ii. 395
Devonshire, Georgiana, Duchess of, ii. 255
  and the Irish Dustman, ii. 258, 292
  introduction of Sheridan to Brooks's, ii. 259, 432
  support of Fox's candidature, ii. 258
  theft of Gainsborough's portrait of, ii. 259
  visit to Mme. de Staël, ii. 441
Devonshire House, ii. 257
Dibdin, Charles, song writer, i. 474 ; ii. 40
  "Poor Luddy," by, i. 420
  "The Watchman," by, ii. 40
Dickens at a party at Forster's, ii. 338
  on burning of Houses of Parliament, ii. 238
  on public executions, ii. 119
Digby, Sir Kenelm, ii. 150
Dimsdale, Sir Harry, mock Mayor of Garratt, i. 250
"Dirty Dick," i. 375
Disraeli, in youth, ii. 138–141
Dodd, Rev. Dr., execution for forgery, ii. 173
Dodington, Bubb, i. 347
"Dog and Duck Spaw," i. 63
Doggett, the actor, at Bartholomew's Fair, i. 355
  Coat and Badge Race for Watermen, i. 232
"Doll, Teddy," i. 152
Dolly's Chop-house, ii. 178
Donne, Dr. John, monument to, i. 8
Dowgate Dock, i. 331
Downing, Sir George, ii. 323
Downing Street, No. 10, story of, ii. 323
Drapers' Company, at Lord Mayor's Show, i. 439
Draughts-player, a famous, ii. 346
Drury Lane, Craven House in, ii. 270
Drury Lane Theatre, burning of, i. 448
  Twelfth Night performances at, i. 79
Dryden, on Great Fire, ii. 50, 51
  plays for Nell Gwynne, i. 318
Dubois, the Clown, ii. 227
Duck, Stephen, epitaph on Joe Miller, i. 154
Dudley, the brothers, inscriptions on walls of Tower, ii. 314, 315
Duelling on Battersea Fields, i. 43
  at Chalk Farm, ii. 299
Duels :
  Lord Alvanley and O'Connell, i. 118

Duels:
  Lord Camelford and Capt. Best, ii. 252
  Fox and Adams, i. 240
  Duke of Hamilton and Lord Mohun, i. 74
  Dr. Maginn and Mr. Berkeley, i. 434
  Lieut. Col. Montgomery and Capt. Macnamara, ii. 299
  Moore and Jeffrey, i. 378 ; ii. 299
  Mountford and Captain Hill, i. 74
  Sheridan and Capt. Matthew, i. 360
  Webster and Macready, ii. 170
  Wellington and Lord Winchelsea, i. 498
  Wilkes' exploits, ii. 311
  William, Lord Byron, and Mr. Chaworth, i. 407
Dulwich Hermit, The, i. 201
Dundreary, Lord, Sothern as, ii. 22 ; 280–284
Dundonald, Lord, discovery of coal-gas by, ii. 211
  inventor of torpedo-boat, ii. 135
Dunstan, Sir Jeffrey, Mock Mayor of Garratt, i. 247, 249, 250
Dustman, the Literary, by Slindon, ii. 290
Dustman, the London, ii. 289–292
Duval, Claude, highwayman, ii. 293
Dwarfs :
  Chevalier Desseausau, ii. 395
  Hudson, Jeffrey, ii. 249
  Tom Thumb, i. 481
Dyer, George, Hermit of Clifford's Inn, i. 409

"Eagle" 'buses, the, ii. 100
Eagle Tavern, i. 22
Eagles, Solomon, prophet of Plague and Fire, ii. 47
Earthquake Year, i. 372
Eastcheap, Boar's Head at, ii. 438
Eastlake, Sir Charles, ii. 149
Eddystone Lighthouse, destruction of, ii. 409
Eden Street, i. 337
Edgeworth, Maria, ii. 441
"Edgworth Bess," i. 456
Edward I., robbing of Temple by, i. 491
Edward IV., and Jane Shore, ii. 9
Edwards, Talbot, on attempted robbery of Crown, i. 177
Effingham, Lord, i. 146
Egan, Pierce, i. 127 ; ii. 474
Egland, James Sharpe, the Flying Pieman, i. 55
El Dorado, Sir W. Raleigh's search for, ii. 195
Eleanor, Queen, Memorial Crosses to, i. 263 ; ii. 4
Elections, municipal, burlesque, i. 147
Eliot, George, in London, i. 367
Elizabeth, Queen, at sermon at Paul's Cross, ii. 163
  Bishop Goodman on, i. 145
  statue in St. Dunstan's, i. 237
Elizabeth, Queen of Bohemia, i. 466
  and Lord Craven, ii. 269
Ellenborough, Lord, judge in Hone's trial, ii. 489
"Elms, The," Smithfield, i. 107

Elwes, John, the Miser, ii. 382
Emerson, friendship with Carlyle, ii. 78, 79
Eon, Chevalier d', at Angelo's, i. 393
    sex impersonation by, i. 165
Epitaph at Southwark Cathedral, ii. 463
Epsom Races, i. 471
    Wells, i. 473
Erskine, Lord, ii. 206
Estcourt, Richard, founder of Beefsteak
    Club, ii. 85
Esterhazy, Prince, at Crockford's, ii. 244
    Princess, ii. 167
Eugénie, Empress, ii. 262, 264
Euston Station, ii, 135, 136, 299
Evans, William, the Porter, ii. 249
Evans's Supper Rooms, ii. 149
Evergreen Hill, Hampstead, ii. 207
Exchange, The Royal, i. 242
Executioner of Charles I., the, i. 209
Executions, public, i. 464, 511 ; ii. 119
    at Tyburn, i. 105
    Dickens's letter to the *Times* on, ii. 119
    methods of, i. 89
Exeter Exchange, menagerie at, i. 299, 300

FAIRFAX, General, robbed by Mary Leith,
    ii. 288
Fairlop Fair, i. 81
    Oak, i. 81
Fairs, i. 156
    Bartholomew's, i. 196, 345, 351-357
    Southwark, i. 62, 196
    Tottenham Court, i. 333
Falstaff, at the Boar's Head, ii. 438, 439
"Fanny, Scratching," i. 477
Fauntleroy, Henry, trial and execution of,
    ii. 233, 236
Fawkes, Guy, i. 287, 288
    torture and death of, i. 294
Fencing Academy, Angelo's, i. 391
Fenian, Michael Barratt, execution of, ii. 122
Fenian Plot at Clerkenwell, ii. 122, 378
Ferrers, Lord, execution at Tyburn, ii. 62
"Ferryman's Daughter, The," i. 330
Fielding Club, the, ii. 151
Fielding, Henry, i. 464 ; ii. 327
    as Justice of Peace at Bow Street, ii.
    421-423
    Sir John, i. 136
Figg, James, prize-fighter, i. 334, 336
Fire, the Great, ii. 45-51
Fireworks at Primrose Hill, ii. 44
Fishmongers' Company, the, i. 438
Fitzball, E., author of "My Pretty Jane," i.
    93
Fitzgerald, Edward, ii. 228
    Percy, on Dr. Dodd, the forger, ii. 175,
    176
    Thomas, Earl of Kildare, inscription on
    walls of Tower, ii. 313
FitzHerbert, Mrs., ii. 470, 482
Fitzroy, Captain, i. 115
Fives, Cavanagh's skill at, ii. 94
Fleet marriages, i. 48 ; ii. 185
    Prison, i. 47
    demolition of, i. 52

Fleet Street, the Barber of, i. 53
    Dr. Johnson in, ii. 103
    Henry Eighth's Palace in, i. 97
    "Laughing Boy " of, i. 211
Flint's Drapery Stores, i. 450
Flogging of garrotters, ii. 107
"Flounder Breakfast," i. 44
Foote, Samuel, and Garrick, i. 38
    and Robert Baddeley, i. 80
    on punishment by pillory, i. 405
    on Rev. Dr. Dodd's forgery, ii. 173
    on Whitefield's preaching, i. 114, 116
Fops' Alley, ii. 92
Forster, on party with Carlyle and Dickens,
    ii. 338
Foster, Dr., of Eton, i. 277
Foubert, Major, Riding Academy of, ii. 202
Foubert's Passage, ii. 202
Foundling Hospital, The, i. 284
    Handel's interest in, i. 286
    Hogarth's interest in, i. 286
    pictures at, i. 286, 336
Fountain Court, ii. 353
"Fowler's Ghost," locomotive, ii. 137
Fox, Charles James, anecdotes of, i. 240
    as a macaroni, ii. 328
    at Brooks's, ii. 432
    at Holland House, i. 174
    Duchess of Devonshire and, ii. 258, 432
    on Betty, the boy actor, i. 266
    Sam House's support of, ii. 66
Fox, Henry, Lord Holland, marriage at Fleet,
    ii. 186
Francis, Sir Philip, i. 173 ; ii. 433
Franklin, Benjamin, as compositor in
    London, ii. 447
    on John Wilkes, ii. 309, 310
Franklin, Rev. Dr., verses on Royal
    Academy, i. 282
Fraser's Magazine, founded by Dr. Maginn,
    i. 433
    collaborators of, ii. 138, 352
Frederick, Prince of Wales, at Carlton House,
    ii. 115, 116
    at Leicester House, i. 468
    birthday reception of, i. 469
    verse on death of, i. 470
Frognal Priory, i. 195
Frost Fair on the Thames, i. 320

GAINSBOROUGH, at Schomberg House, i. 281 ;
    ii. 469
    domestic life of, ii. 470, 471
    meeting with Reynolds, ii. 471
    theft of portrait of Duchess of Devon-
    shire, by, ii. 259
Galton, Sir Francis, at Epsom Races, i. 471
Gaol-fever, i. 132
Gardiner, Bishop, sermons at Paul's Cross,
    ii. 163
Garibaldi in London, ii. 450-451
Garnerin, parachute ascents by, ii. 420
Garrat, burlesque municipal elections at,
    i. 247
Garrick, David, and James Christie, ii. 343
    and Samuel Foote, i. 38

Garrick, David, and Dr. Johnson, i. 38
  and J. J. Rousseau, ii. 461
  and Mrs. Siddons, ii. 348
  at Beefsteak Club, ii. 87
  characteristics of, i. 38
  farewell to the stage, i. 37
  on Whitefield's preaching, i. 116
Garrotters of the Sixties, ii. 107
Gas, introduction in London, ii. 211
Gate House, Highgate, ii. 35
Gay, John, Beggars' Opera by, i. 452 ;
  ii. 85, 90
  on Tottenham Fields, i. 337
Gaynam, Dr., chaplain of the Fleet, ii. 185
Gayner, manager of Boodle's, i. 110
George I., alterations on Kensington Palace,
  i. 494
  equestrian statue in Leicester Square,
  i. 468
  quarrel with his son, i. 465, 466
George II., as Prince of Wales at Leicester
  House, i. 465, et seq.
  at Margate, i. 269
George III., and Astley, the horse-trainer,
  i. 311
  and Coutts, the Banker, i. 364
  as Prince of Wales at Leicester House,
  i. 470
  Royal Academy opened by, i. 281
  Royal Library of, ii. 276
George IV., and Beau Brummell, i. 141, 142 ;
  ii. 118
  and Martha Gunn, the Bathing Woman,
  ii. 481, 482
  and Sheridan, i. 358
  at Brighton, ii. 479
  at Carlton House, ii. 115
  at Coronation Ball at Almack's, ii. 167
  Coronation of, i. 27, 349, 350 ; ii. 457
  Coronation robes of, ii. 167
  the Palladium monument to, ii. 407
  practical joke on Duke of Norfolk, ii.
  481
  treatment of [Queen Caroline, i. 349 ;
  ii. 117
Georgiana, Duchess of Devonshire. See
  Devonshire
Gerard, Father, on Gunpowder Plot, i. 290,
  295, 296
Ghost of Cock Lane, The, i. 477
Gibbon, Grinling, carvings of, ii. 268
  statue of James II., by, i. 492 ; ii. 302
Gibbon, Thomas, at Boodle's Club, i. 109
Gillray, i. 406 ; ii. 320
Glindon, Robert, The Literary Dustman, by,
  ii. 290
Godfrey, Captain John, on Broughton, the
  prize-fighter, i. 199
Godfrey, Sir Edmundbury, murder of, i. 341
Godolphin, Sidney, and Addison, i. 410
Gog and Magog, statues in Guildhall, i. 238
Golden Cross Inn, i. 417
Golden Head, The, Hogarth's house, ii. 60
" Golden Horseman, The," i. 468
Goldsmith, Oliver, at Cheshire Cheese, ii. 5, 6
  at Canonbury Tower, i. 41

Goldsmith, Oliver, on the Boar's Head, ii. 438
  visit to Duke of Northumberland, ii. 266
Goldsmiths' Company, the, i. 439
Goodman, Bishop, on Queen Elizabeth, i. 145
" Gooseberry Fair," i. 334
Gordon, Lord George, i. 132, 133, 137
Gordon Riots, the, i. 133
Gounod's Faust, performed at Canterbury
  Music Hall, ii. 180
Graham, Dr. James, i. 338
Granby, Marquis of, i. 276, 393
Granville, Lord, ii. 260
Gray's Inn, Lord Bacon at, i. 15
Grecian Coffee-house, ii. 204
Green Bushes, by Buckstone, ii. 144, 170
Green, Paddy, of Evans's Supper Rooms, ii.
  149, 150, 151
Greenberry Hill, i. 344 ; ii. 43
Greenwich Fair, Voltaire on, ii. 383, 384
Greenwich Railway, opening of, ii. 133-136
Gresham, Sir Thomas, foundation of Royal
  Exchange by, i. 242
Grey, Lady Jane, inscription on walls of
  Tower by, ii. 314
Griffiths, Major Arthur, on Thames Pirates,
  ii. 386, 387
Grimaldi, Joseph, i. 101
  at Sadler's Wells, ii. 226
Grisi, Queen Victoria's comments on, ii. 93
Grocers' Company, the, i. 438
Gronow, Captain R. H., at Waterloo, i. 169,
  170
Guildhall, destroyed in Great Fire, ii. 49
  Lord Mayor's Banquet, at, i. 437, 440
  statues of Gog and Magog at, i. 238
Gunn, Martha, Bathing Woman of Brighton,
  ii. 481
Gunning, Elizabeth, Duchess of Hamilton, ii.
  191, 192
  Maria, Countess of Coventry, ii. 190, 193
  Kitty, ii. 194
Gunnings, the, at Vauxhall, i. 95
Gunpowder Plot, the, i. 287-294
Gurwood, Colonel, anecdotes of Wellington
  by, ii. 27, 28
Gwynne, Nell, i. 196, 317, 318, 319
  Chelsea Pensioners' Hospital founded
  by, i. 319
  and Child's Bank, i. 11

Hackney College, ii. 247
Hairpowder tax, i. 375
Hakford, John de, in the pillory, i. 401
Hall, Jacob, rope dancer, i. 196
Hallam, Henry, ii. 230
  at Holland House, i. 175
  on Carlyle, ii. 75
Hamilton, Lady, at Dr. Graham's Bath
  establishment, i. 338
  relations with Nelson, i. 485 ; ii. 390
Hamilton, Duke of, marriage with Elizabeth
  Gunning, ii. 192
Hancock, Walter, steam omnibuses intro-
  duced by, ii. 101
Hand, Mrs., of Chelsea Bun House, i. 323,
  324

Handel, and Tschudi, i. 475
  at Britton, the coalman's concerts, ii. 24
  commemoration concert at the Pantheon, i. 326
  interest in Foundling Hospital, i. 286, 382
  life in London, i. 382
Hangmen, London, i. 209, 210
Hanway, Jonas, crusade against tea, ii. 205
Harcourt, Lord, on Mrs. Siddons, ii. 349
Harley, Earl, South Sea Company founded by, ii. 67
"Harmonious Blacksmith, The," i. 384
Harry, Old, ii. 433
Hastings, Marquis of, betting losses of, i. 473
Hawes, Nathaniel, highwayman, i. 463
Hawkers, London, i. 1
Hawkins, Sir John, i. 192
Haydn at Broadwood's, i. 475, 476
Haydon, B. R., and Thomas Coutts, i. 364
Haymarket masquerades, i. 192
  Theatre, under Buckstone, ii. 21
  Italian opera at, ii. 89
Heidegger Hoax, The, i. 192
Henrietta Maria, Queen, at Tyburn, i. 107
Henry I., and Rahere the jester, i. 351
Henry II., and Heraclius, i. 487, 489, 490
Henry III., Christmas feasts to the poor, ii. 16
  treatment of the Templars, i. 491
Henry V. and Dick Whittington, i. 387
  return to London after Agincourt, ii. 17
  tomb at Westminster Abbey, ii. 19
Henry VIII. at May Day Festival, i. 147
  at Primrose Hill, ii. 44
  Palace of, i. 97
  revels on Midsummer Eve, i. 70
Heraclius and Henry II., i. 487, 489, 491
Heraldic signs on London carriages, i. 271
Herbert, Sir Thomas, and Charles I., i. 157, 158, 160
Hermit of Dulwich, the, i. 201
Herrick, Robert, "The Bellman's Blessing," ii. 408
Hertford, Lord, Wellington on, ii. 31
Hibbert, Mr., Bill for abolition of Public Executions, ii. 122
Hicks, Ann, the Apple-woman, i. 278
Hicks's Hall, Clerkenwell, ii. 128, 132
Highflyer Hall, ii. 406
Highgate, swearing-in custom at, ii. 35
Highwaymen, London, i. 27, 28, 451 ; ii. 293-298, 484, 485
Hill, Aaron, i. 384
Hind, Captain James, highwayman, ii. 294
Hobhouse, and Lord Byron, i. 226
Hobson's Choice, i. 187
Hoby, the bootmaker, ii. 16
Hodges, William, R. A., i. 329
Hogarth, and Joe Miller, i. 155, 156
  decorations of Vauxhall, i. 92
  drawing of Heidegger, i. 192
  foundation of School of Design, i. 280
  "Golden Head, The," ii. 60
  house on London Bridge, i. 221, 224
  interest in Foundlings' Hospital, i. 286

Hogarth, life in London, ii. 55-61
  marriage with Sir James Thornhill's daughter, i. 280 ; ii. 56
  on portrait painting for the nobility, i. 174
  river trip to Kent, ii. 60
  series of paintings, ii. 55, 56, 58, 59
  Spiller's benefit ticket etched by, ii. 144
Holbein, Hans, house on London Bridge, i. 221, 222, 223
Holinshed on lotteries, i. 31
  on punishment by pressing, i. 30
  on steeple-flying, i. 100
Holland House, i. 171
Holland, Lady, i. 175, 176, 252, 253
  Lord, i. 174
  marriage with Lady Lennox in The Fleet, ii. 186
  William, director of the Canterbury Music Hall, ii. 182
Holly Lodge, the Macaulays at, ii. 41
Hone, Nathaniel, i. 283
Hone, William, three trials of, ii, 486-491
  parodies by, ii. 486
Hood, Thomas, "Midnight in London," i. 512
Hook, Theodore, i. 93
  and the Berners Street Hoax, ii. 224
  "Mrs. Muggins at Brandenburgh House," by, i. 348
  practical joke on "Romeo" Coates, ii. 118
"Hookey Walker," ii. 61
Hornor's Panorama of London, ii. 329
Horns, swearing-in on, custom at Highgate, ii. 35
Houghton, John, Prior of Charterhouse, i. 222
Hounslow Heath, i. 463 ; ii. 295
House, Sam, publican, ii. 66
Houses of Parliament, burning of, ii. 237-241
Howard, Charles, Lord Effingham, i. 146
Howe, Mr., mysterious disappearance of, i. 194
Hudson, Jeffrey, the dwarf, ii. 249
Hughes, "Ball," ii. 244, 424
  Margaret, actress, i. 347
Hume, David, and Rousseau, ii. 461, 462, 463
Humphries, Henry, on Thomas Doggett, i. 234
Hunt, Leigh, and George Dyer, i. 410
  on Kensington Palace, i. 493
Hunter, Dr. John, ii. 214
  Dr. William, i. 283

Impersonations by Chevalier d'Eon, i. 165
Inchbold, Mrs., on Betty, the boy actor, i. 268
Incledon, Charles, i. 93
Inns :
  Adam and Eve, i. 197, 333, 334, 336
  Angel, i. 190
  Bald-faced Stag, i. 462
  Black Bull, i. 187
  Blue Boar, i. 96
  Boar's Head, ii. 438-440

Inns :
  Catherine Wheel, i. 59, 60
  Cheshire Cheese, i. 205 ; ii. 5
  Cider Cellars, ii. 351
  Coal Hole, The, ii. 353
  Cock Tavern, ii. 229
  Dirty Dick's, i. 377
  Eagle, i. 22
  George, The, i. 63
  Golden Ball, The, ii. 213
  Golden Cross, The, i. 417
  Marquis of Granby, i. 276
  Mermaid, i. 205
  Old King's Head, i. 336
  Pied Bull, The, ii. 164
  Southwark, i. 59
  Star and Garter, i. 407
  Tabard, i. 205
  Three Brewers, i. 462
  Whistling Oyster, i. 181
  White Hart, i. 61, 62
Ireton, Colonel, Charles I.'s letter intercepted by, i. 96
Irving, Henry, ii. 347
  Washington, on Falstaff relics, ii. 439
Islington, i. 190 ; ii. 163
  Raleigh's house at, ii. 163
  Sir Hugh Myddelton's statue at, i. 219
  " Strong Man " of, i. 505
Ives, Miss Charlotte, and Chateaubriand, ii. 302

Jackson, " Gentleman," the pugilist, ii. 255
James I., escape from drowning in New River, i. 217
  treatment of Sir W. Raleigh, ii. 195, 196
James II., and Duke of Monmouth, ii. 402
  sinking of Great Seal, i. 64
  statue of, i. 492 ; ii. 302
Jay, Mr. Cyrus, on the " Cheshire Cheese," ii. 6
Jefferies, Richard, ii. 496
Jeffrey, duel with Moore, i. 378 ; ii. 299
Jekyll, Joseph, at Holland House, i. 176
Jephson, on Gordon Riots, i. 137
Jerrold, Douglas, on the Whistling Oyster, i. 183
Jersey, Lady, Quadrille introduced by, ii. 166
Johnson, Dr., and Fanny Burney, ii. 200
  and Garrick, i. 38
  and Mrs. Siddons, ii. 347
  and Mrs. Thrale, ii. 113
  as tea drinker, ii. 205
  at the Cheshire Cheese, ii. 6
  at St. Clement Danes, ii. 104
  in Fleet Street, ii. 103–105
  meeting with Edward, his college friend, ii. 104
  petition in aid of Dr. Dodd, ii. 175
  statue of, ii. 105
Jolliffe, Sir William, i. 233
Jones, Inigo, ii. 265, 266, 442
  Jedediah, in search of London, ii. 127
Jonson, Ben, at " Cheshire Cheese," ii. 5
  on Bartholomew's Fair, i. 352
  on the " water Cobs," i. 214

Jugglers, Indian, i. 303

Kaufmann, Angelica, i. 281, 282 ; ii. 112
Kean, Charles, at Brighton, ii. 483
  Edmund, i. 44 ; ii. 152, 353, 355
  at Sadler's Wells theatre, ii. 226
  debut as Shylock at Drury Lane, ii. 357–359
Keats, John, in London, i. 421
Keene, Laura, in Our American Cousin, ii. 280
Kemble, Charles, i. 361
  and Delpini, the Clown, i. 257
  in Macbeth, i. 448
Kemble, Fanny, ii. 150
  John, ii. 348, 357
  at " O. P." riots, ii. 457, 458
Kennington Common, Chartist meetings on; ii. 217, 218
  execution of Jacobean officers at, i. 219
Kensington Palace, Royal occupants of, i. 493
Ketch, John, executioner of Duke of Monmouth, ii. 404
Kildare, Earl of, inscription on walls of Tower, ii. 313
King, Dr. William, on Mr. Howe's disappearance, i. 194
King's College, Duke of Wellington as benefactor of, i. 498
King's College Hospital, Joe Miller's monument at, i. 155
King's Mews, ii. 146, 147
Kingston, Duchess of, ii. 405
" Kitty Crowder," i. 112
Knights Templars, the, i. 487
Köningsmark, Count, i. 398 ; ii. 132

Lade, Sir John, and Fox, i. 241
Lafitte, Jacques, omnibuses re-introduced to Paris by, ii. 97
Lamb, Charles, at Islington, i. 190
  and George Dyer, i. 409, 410
  and London chimneysweeps, i. 152
  on Margate Hoy, i. 270
  on Lord Nelson, ii. 391
  on Sheridan's elopement, i. 360
Lambert, Daniel, ii, 278
  George, founder of Beefsteak Club, ii. 56, 85, 86
Landseer, ii. 496
Latimer's Sermon of the Plough, ii. 163
" Laughing Boy " sign, i. 211
Laurie, Sir Peter, Lord Mayor, i. 441
Lawrence, Emily, professional thief, ii. 177
Lawrence, Sir Thomas, i. 282
  portrait of George IV., ii. 168
Leadenhall Street, " Dirty Warehouse " in, i. 375
Leather Lane, i. 309
Lee, Lady, Ballad of, ii. 411
Leeds, first Duke of, ii. 460
Leicester, Earl of, in the Tower, ii. 315
Leicester House, Queen Elizabeth of Bohemia at, ii. 271, 272
  residence of the Princes of Wales, i. 465
Leicester Square, Wylde's Globe at, iii, 475

Leigh, Percival, on the Cider Cellars, ii. 352
Leith, Mary, pickpocket, ii. 288
Lever, Sir Ashton, ii. 250
Leverian Museum, the, i. 32 ; ii. 250
  sold by lottery, ii. 251
Lewes, George Henry, and George Eliot, i. 369
Leybourne, George, the "Lion Comique," ii. 273
Libraries, Royal, ii. 276
Lillo, George, "Tragedy of George Barnwell," by, i. 17
Lilly, the astrologer, on Great Fire, ii. 47
Lindsay, Sir David, tournament with Lord Wells, ii. 492
Lincoln's Inn Fields, ii. 442
Linleys of Bath, the, i. 360
"Lion Comique," the, ii. 273
Lisbon earthquake, the, i. 372
Litany, Hone's parody on, ii. 489
Little Wild Street Chapel, commemoration sermons at, ii. 409
Lollards, their penances at Paul's Cross, ii. 161
Lombard Street, i. 242
London, area and population in 1831, ii. 98
  legendary kings and heroes of, i. 235
  Spectator on, ii. 363-365
  tradesman's description of, ii. 311
London Bridge, accidents at, ii. 460
  battle of, i. 21 ; ii. 411, 413
  demolition of, ii. 411
  shooting of, ii. 459
  tenants of, i. 221
  tournament on, ii. 492-493
London-by-the-Sea, ii. 479-483
"Lord of Misrule," The, ii. 13
Lord Mayor's Day, i. 437
  pageant in fifteenth century, i. 389
Lord's Prayer, Hone's parody on, ii. 488
Lotteries, i. 31
  account of last English, i. 35
  Leverian Museum sold by, ii. 251
  lucky numbers in, i. 32
  marriage portions by, i. 32
  penny, i. 32
  sales by, i. 31, 32
  Sloane collection bought by, ii. 277, 278
Louis Napoleon. See Napoleon III.
Louis Philippe in London, ii. 360
Loving Cup of St. Margaret's, i. 204
Low, Thomas, Bellman, ii. 408
Lud, King, statue of, i. 237
Ludgate, Old, i. 237
  burning of, ii. 49
"Luddy, Poor," by Dibdin, i. 420
Lunardi, Vincent, balloon ascents by, ii. 417
Luttrell, at Holland House, i. 175
Lyttelton, on haunted house in Berkeley Square, ii. 157

MACARONIS, the, ii. 174, 325
Macaulay, Lord, and Sydney Smith, ii. 415 416
  at Brighton, ii. 483
  last years at Campden Hill, ii. 41

Macaulay, Zachary, house at Clapham, ii. 424
  on abolition of slavery, ii. 426
Macdermott, George Hastings, comedian, ii. 274
MacLean, James, the highwayman, i. 452, 453, 464
Maclise, drawings by, ii. 338
  portrait of Cruikshank, ii. 320
  portrait of Disraeli, ii. 139, 141
  portrait of James Smith, ii. 433
Macnamara, Captain, duel with Col. Montgomery, ii. 299
Macready, W. C., duel with Webster of the Adelphi, ii. 170
Maginn, Dr. William, journalist, i. 433 ; ii. 352
  duel with Hon. Grantly Berkeley, i. 434
  on James Smith, ii. 473
  prose and verse writing of, i. 435, 436
  verse on Disraeli, ii. 138
Maggott, Poll, i. 456
Maid of Kent, Holy, ii. 162
Maiden Lane, ii. 351
  Turner's house in, ii. 445
Mannings, the, execution of, ii. 120
Marble Arch, The, ii. 322
Marconi apparatus, Whitehall, ii. 448
Margate Hoy, the, i. 269
Marriage portions by lottery, i. 32
Marriages, Fleet, i. 48 ; ii. 185
"Marigold, The," i. 12
Marlborough, Duchess of, and Queen Anne, i. 494
Marrowbones and Cleavers custom, i. 297
Mary, Queen, at Kensington Palace, i. 494
Marylebone, built by Elwes, the miser, ii. 383
Marwood, the executioner, ii. 120
Mason, Daniel, of Cogers' Debating Society, ii. 142
Masquerades, at Christmas, ii. 12
  prosecution of, ii. 89
Masson, Professor, and Carlyle, ii. 77
Mathews, Charles, ii. 281
  at burning of Drury Lane, i. 449
Matthews, Samuel, the Dulwich Hermit, i. 201
Maxwell, Sir Herbert, on Wellington, ii. 32, 33
May Day, i. 147
Mayfair, i. 152
Mayor of London, origin of office, i. 438
  Show, i. 389, 437
"Mayors of Garratt, The," i. 247
Maypole Alley, i. 147
Maypoles in London, i. 148
Mead, Dr. Richard, ii. 367
Melbourne, Lord, and Scrope Davies, i. 226
Mellon, Harriet, actress, marriage with Thomas Coutts, i. 365
Memory, A Remarkable, i. 195
Menagerie, at Bartholomew's Fair, i. 356, 357
  at Exeter Change, i. 299
Mercers' Company, i. 389, 390
Miagh, Thomas, verses on walls of Tower, ii. 313
Middlesex Election, the, ii. 307

"Midnight in London," by Hood, i. 512
Midsummer Eve in Old London, i. 69
Miles, Smoaker, the Brighton Bathing Man, ii. 482
Milestones, suburban, Knight on, ii. 127
Milkmaids' Dance on May-Day, i. 150, 151
Mill, J. S., and Carlyle, ii. 76
Millbank Penitentiary, buried jewels at, ii. 177
Miller, Joe, comedian, i. 153
    at Bartholomew's Fair, i. 355
    monument to, i. 154, 155
Milton, John, on Hobson, the carrier, i. 188
Miser, the Clerkenwell, i. 184
    Elwes, ii. 332
Misnomers, i. 329
"Miss J.," and Wellington, ii. 33
Mitford, Miss, on lotteries, i. 32
Mohocks, the, ii. 484-485
Mohun, Lord, i. 73, 74
"Moll Cutpurse," ii. 288
Monamy, Peter, i. 225
Monmouth, Duke of, execution of, ii. 402
    and Thomas Thynne of Longleat, i. 398, 399
Monmouth, Geoffrey, of, on foundation of London, i. 236
Montague, Duke of, and Bottle Hoax, i. 113
    and Heidegger Hoax, i. 192
Montague House, ii. 111
    site of British Museum, ii. 278
Montague, Mrs., ii. 111
    Blue-stocking parties, ii. 111-114
    and chimneysweeps' festival, i. 152
Montague, Lady Mary Wortley, on Fielding, ii. 421
Monteagle, Lord, and Gunpowder Plot, i. 292, 294, 295
Montford, Lord, at White's, ii. 337
Montgolfier, the French aeronaut, ii. 417
Montgomery, Lieut.-Col., duel with Capt. Macnamara, ii. 299
Moore, Thomas, at Holland House, i. 175, 176
    at Lady Blessington's, i. 254
    duel with Jeffrey, i. 378 ; ii. 299
More, Hannah, on the Blue-stockings, ii. 112, 113, 114
More, Sir Thomas, i. 75
    on Jane Shore, ii. 9, 10, 11
Morland, George, in London, ii. 354
Morocco, the dancing horse, i. 345
Morris, Captain, at Beefsteak Club, ii. 87, 111, 113
    ballads by, i. 111
Morris, William, at Rossetti's, ii. 369, 372
Morton, Charles, manager of the Canterbury Music Hall, ii. 179
Mottley, John, jest-book by, i. 153
Mountford, William, murder of, i. 73
Mozart, Wolfgang, performance on Tschudi's harpsichord, i. 475
    operas performed at Her Majesty's, ii. 90
"Mulled Sack," the highwayman, ii. 295
Murdock, inventor of gas-lighting, ii. 211
Murray, John, friendship with Belzoni, i. 85

Music Hall, The Canterbury, ii. 179
    favourites at, ii. 273
    Sadler's Wells, ii. 226
Myddelton, Sir Hugh, i. 216

NALDI, Signor, the singer, ii. 167
Nando's coffee-house, i. 98
Napoleon III. in London, ii. 220, 262-264
Nares on heraldic signs on London carriages, i. 271
"Nash, Jolly John," ii. 274
Nash, architect of Marble Arch, ii. 322
    of Regent Street, ii. 201
Nassau balloon, flight of, i. 95
National Gallery, architecture of, ii. 147
    foundation of, ii. 144
Nelson Column, The, ii. 494-496
Nelson, Lord, at Merton, i. 485
    funeral and burial in St. Paul's, ii. 393
    life in London, ii. 390
    meeting with Duke of Wellington, i. 86 ; ii. 391
    relations with Lady Hamilton, i. 485 ; ii. 390
    statue, by Baily, ii. 495, 496
Nevison, William, highwayman, ii. 296
New River Company, i. 216, 218, 219
Newbery, John, bookseller, i. 41
Newcastle, Duke of, ii. 442
Newcastle House, ii. 442-444
Newgate, Barratt's execution at, ii. 123
    Bellingham's execution at, i. 511
    burning of, i. 135, 136
    Cato Street conspirators executed at, i. 447
    Dr. Dodd's execution at, ii. 174-176
    Henry Fauntleroy at, ii. 236
    Jack Sheppard's escape from, i. 456
    public executions at, i. 108 ; ii. 119, 123
    rebuilt by Whittington, i. 388, 390
    state of prisoners in, ii. 174
    whipping of garrotters at, ii. 107
Newton, Sir Isaac, and the Maypole, i. 150
    funeral of, ii. 385
Nollekens, and Hogarth, ii. 56
Nonconformist families at Clapham, ii. 425-427
Nonesuch House, i. 222
Nonsuch Palace, ii. 473
Norfolk, Duke of, practical joke of George IV. upon, ii. 481
Nottingham House, Old, i. 493
    William III. at, i. 172
North Briton, No. 10, ii. 308
Northumberland House, ii. 265-268
"Nosey," i. 406
Nun of the Bank, The, ii. 52

OAK, the Fairlop, i. 83
Oates, Titus, flogging of, i. 90
    in pillory, i. 402
    murder of Sir E. Godfrey, i. 344, 341
O'Brien, Patrick, the giant, i. 189
O'Connor, Fergus, Chartist leader, ii. 217
Olaf, King, at battle of London Bridge, i. 21
    ii. 411, 413

Olympic Theatre, i. 303
Omnibuses, London, ii. 97
"O. P." Riots, the, ii. 457
Opera, Italian, ii. 89-93
Ormond, Duke of, and Colonel Blood, i. 180
Orsay, Count d', and Disraeli, ii. 139, 140
  and Lady Blessington, i. 252
  Carlyle on, ii. 78
Osborne, Edward, rescue of child at London Bridge by, ii. 460
O'Shea, Augustus, on flogging at Newgate, ii, 108, 109
Overy, St. Mary, Priory of, i. 332
Oxford, Earl of, founder of South Sea Company, ii. 67
Oyster, the Whistling, i. 181

Paddy Green, ii. 149, 150, 151
Paganini, in London, i. 501
Page, William, the highwayman, i. 453, 454
"Pall Mall, the Sweet Shady Side of," i. 111
Palladium, The, ii. 407
Palmerston, Lord, waltzing at Almack's, ii. 167
Panorama of London, at the Colosseum, ii. 329
Pantheon, The, i. 325
Pantomimes, Drury Lane, i. 101, 395
  Belzoni's, i. 84
Parachute ascents by Garnerin, ii. 420
Parodies, by William Hone, ii. 488
Parris, Mr. E., dome of St. Paul's repainted by, ii. 189
  panorama of London painted by, ii. 329
Parsons, William, highwayman, i. 455
Patrol, Bow Street, i. 464
Paul's Cross, ii. 160
Pavilion, the Brighton, ii. 479
Paxton, Sir Joseph, ii. 452, 453
Peel, Lady, ii. 424, 430
Peel, Sir Robert, death of, ii. 428-430
  Police Bill of, ii. 98
Peerless Pool, disturbed by earthquake, i. 374
Penn, William, at Holland House, i. 172
Pepys, Samuel, i. 63
  and George Downing, ii. 323
Percival, Mr. Spencer, assassination of, i. 508
Peter the Great in London, ii. 434-437
Peterborough, Earl of, and Henry Rich, ii. 86, 87
Peterloo meeting, the, i. 445
Petersham, Lord, collector of teas, ii. 206
Phillips, Sir Richard, on semaphore stations, ii. 448-449
Physicians, five famous, ii. 366
Pickpocket, Mary Leith, ii. 288
Picton, Sir Thomas, i. 170
Pidock's Wild Beast Show, i. 356
Pieman, The Flying, i. 550
Pigot Diamond, the, i. 32
Pilgrims' Way to Canterbury, The, i. 206, 208
Pillory, the, Defoe in, ii. 468
  for women, i. 401
Pindar, Peter, on Margate, i. 269
  on Mary Moses, R. A., i. 282

Pirates, the Thames, ii. 386
Pitcairn, Dr. David, ii. 368
Pitt, William, ii. 425, 443
Pitts, Johnny, the printer, i. 125
Plague, The Great, i. 390 ; ii. 45
Planché, James Robinson, i. 24
Planta, Joseph, M.P., ii. 260
Pole, Edmund and Arthur, inscriptions on walls of Tower, ii. 315
Police Force, London, ii. 98
  on the Thames, ii. 387
Poll of Wapping Stairs, i. 239
Pompadour, Mme., and Wilkes, ii. 308
"Poodle" Byng, ii. 80
Poole, J. J., ii. 275
"Pop goes the Weasel," i. 23
Pope on Voltaire, i. 385
Poplin, Irish, i. 469
Porson, Professor, marriage with Widow Lunan, ii. 351
Portland Vase, the, i. 480
Prance, Miles, murderer of Sir E. Godfrey, i. 341, 343
Pre-Raphaelite Brotherhood, the, ii. 369
Pressing to death, i. 29
Price, Charles, lottery-office keeper, i. 34
Primrose Hill, ii. 43
  Sir E. Godfrey's murder at, i. 341
Prison-breakers, i. 456
  life at Wormwood Scrubs, ii. 396-401
Pritchard, Mrs., i. 355, 448
Prize-fighter's burial in Westminster Abbey, i. 197
Prize-fighting at Tottenham Fair, i. 334, 335
  -rings, i. 197
Prynne, William, mutilations in pillory, i. 205
Puppet-shows, at Flockton, i. 356
  at Southwark Fair, i. 196

"Q," Old, i. 95 ; ii. 406
Quadrilles, introduction by Lady Jersey, ii. 166
Quack doctors, i. 338
Quakers, the, and Peter the Great, ii. 435
"Questions and Answers," played by Statesmen, ii. 260

Radcliffe, Dr. John, ii. 366
Rag Fair, at Rosemary Lane, i. 210
Ragg, Isaac, bellman of Holborn, ii. 408
Rahere, founder of St. Bartholomew's Hospital, ii. 182
Railways in London, ii. 133
Raleigh, Sir W., and Lord Bacon, i. 15
  at Islington, ii. 163-164
  imprisonment and execution, ii. 194
  on Banks and his horse, i. 345
Ranelagh, i. 325, 326 ; ii. 256
Rann, Jack, the highwayman, i. 454, 464
"Ratcatcher's Daughter, The," i. 87
Ray, Miss Martha, and James Hackman, i. 119
Red House, Old, i. 43, 238
Redmond, Frank, ii. 155
Regalia, attempted theft of, i. 177
Regicides, execution of, ii. 268

Reid, General John, i. 57
" Rejected Addresses," by H. and J. Smith, i. 450
Rennie, John, builder of Waterloo Bridge, i. 305, 306
Restoration, The, return of Charles II. at. ii. 339
Reynolds, at Cheshire Cheese, ii. 6
  Hone's satire on, ii. 469
  Marquis of Granby's portrait, i. 277
  meeting with Gainsborough, ii. 471
Rhodes, William Barnes, i. 309
Rich, Charles, at Beefsteak Club, ii. 87
  Henry, founder of Beefsteak Club, ii. 85
Rich, Lady Diana, i. 172
Richard II., at burial of his wife, ii. 127
  Christmas banquet of, ii. 12
  portrait at Westminster Abbey, ii. 124, 126
Richard III. and Jane Shore, ii. 10, 11
Richardson, on Adam and Eve tavern, i. 336
Richardson, John, the Great Showman, i. 354, 355
Riding Academy, Foubert's, ii. 202
Ridley, Archbishop, sermons at Paul's Cross, ii. 161
Ritchie, Lady, on Turgenev, ii. 33
River Police, Thames, ii. 387-389
Rivers, Lord, at White's, ii. 338
Robson, F., singer of comic songs, i. 394
Rodwell, on Old London Bridge, i. 221
Rogers, Samuel, and Dr. Johnson, ii. 247, 248
  and Duke of Wellington, ii. 29
  and Sidney Smith, ii. 415
  at Brighton, ii. 483
  at Holland House, ii. 172, 194
  home at Stoke Newington, ii. 247-249
  loan of Court suit to Wordsworth and Tennyson, ii. 365
" Romeo " Coates, the actor, i. 143
Rope dancers, Jacob Hall, i. 196
  Mme. Saqui, i. 94
Roper, Margaret, i. 75
Rosemary Lane, Rag Fair at, i. 210
Rossetti, D. G., home at Cheyne Walk, ii. 369
Rothschild, Baron, and the Bank Nun, ii. 45
  and Tom Thumb, i. 482
  at Royal Exchange, i. 244
  winner of the Derby, i. 473
Rousseau, J. J., in England, ii. 461-463
Royal Academy, foundation of, i. 279
  housed in National Gallery, ii. 148
  transferred to Burlington House, ii. 149
Royal College of Physicians, ii. 366
Royal Exchange. See Exchange
Rupert, Prince, jewels sold by lottery, i. 32
Rush, Mr., ii. 260
Rushlight, The Walking, i. 57
Ruskin, John, Carlyle on, ii. 79
  on Turner in Maiden Lane, ii. 447
Russell, Lord William, trial and execution of, ii. 132, 379-382
Rustat, Tobias, i. 492
Rye House Plot, the, ii. 379

Sadler's Wells, ii. 225
St. André, i. 196
St. Andrew Undershaft, Church of, i. 148, 149
St. Bartholomew the Great, Church of, ii. 182
St. Bartholomew's Fair. See Bartholomew Fair
St. Bartholomew's Hospital, i. 390
St. Clement Dane's Church, Johnson at, ii, 104
St. Dunstan's Church, i. 237
  clock, ii. 374
St. George's Day, ii. 492, 493
St. George's Fields, i. 63
  meeting of Protestants at, i. 134
St. Giles in the Fields, i. 123
St. Giles's Pound, ii. 131, 132
St. James's Street, ii. 474
St. Margaret's, painted window in, i. 203
St. Mary Overy, Priory of, i. 332
St. Pancras, ii. 43
  Parish Church, i. 81
St. Paul's Cathedral, building of, i. 259
  destruction by fire, ii. 49
  dome restored and repainted, ii. 188
  monument in, i. 8
St. Peter's Chapel, in Tower of London, ii. 402, 404
St. Saviour's, Ferryman's effigy at, i. 330
St. Stephen's Chapel, Bishop's body found in, ii. 239
Sala, George Augustus, ii. 376-378
Sala, Mme., the singer, ii. 376
Salisbury, Marchioness of, friendship with Wellington, ii. 33
Sally in our Alley, by Carey, ii. 152
Salmon, Mrs., waxwork show of, i. 193
Salt-box, as musical instrument, i. 298
Saltero's coffee-house, ii. 464
Sandwich, Lord, i. 119, 135 ; ii. 87
Saqui, Mme., at Vauxhall, i. 94
Savile House, residence of Princes of Wales, 466
Saville, Sir George, i. 133, 135
Scandiscope, the, i. 152
Schomberg House, ii. 469-471
  Dr. Graham at, i. 339
Scots in London, ii. 213
Scott, John, duel with Mr. Christie, ii. 299
  Samuel, the diver, i. 309
  Sir Walter, and Mrs. Siddons, ii. 348
  letter from Harriet Mellon to, i. 366
Scrope, Davies, i. 225
Seal, the Great, i. 64
Sedley, Sir Charles, quarrel with William, Lord Byron, i. 407
Selwyn, George Augustus, i. 138, 209 ; ii. 466-468
Semaphores, the Admiralty, ii. 448
Seven Dials, i. 123 ; ii. 474
  Catnach Press at, i. 124
Shaft Alley, i. 149
Shakespeare, on Bank's Dancing Horse, i. 345
  Gallery of Pictures, i. 31
Sharp, William, at Rossetti's, ii. 371, 372
Sharpe, Granville, ii. 427
Shelley, on Keats' Grave, i. 425
  on ruins of London, i. 447

Shenstone, on death of Capt. Dawson, i. 219
Sheppard, Jack, prison-breaker, i. 453, 454, 464
Sheridan, Richard Brinsley, i. 358–361
Shillibeer, George, introduction of omnibuses by, ii. 97
Shore, Jane, story of, ii. 9
  Mrs. Siddons as, ii, 347
Shoreditch, legend of, ii. 9
Siddons, Mrs., i. 266 ; ii. 347–350
Sidmouth, Lord, and Cato Street Conspiracy, i. 445
  last meeting with Nelson, ii. 391, 392
Sidneys of Leicester House, The, i. 466
" Simplers," i. 3
Simpson, C. H., at Vauxhall, i. 95
Sinecurist's Creed, by Hone, ii. 491
" Sixteen-string Jack," the highwayman, i. 453, 454, 464
Skeffington, Sir Lumley, i. 117
Slack, the prize-fighter, i. 199
  at Tottenham Fair, i. 334, 335
Slang Dictionary, ii. 474
Sloane, Sir Hans, collection bequeathed to the nation, ii. 277, 464
Smart, Christopher, at Canonbury Tower, i. 42
  " Song to David," i. 42
Smith, Adam, on lotteries, i. 31
  Elder & Company, and the Brontës, ii. 198
  " Gentleman," i. 267, 268
  Horace, ii. 483
  James, ii. 472–474
  Horace and James, " Rejected Addresses," i. 456
  visit to Lord Camelford, ii. 252
Smith, Sydney, at Holland House, i. 174, 175, 176
  life in London, ii. 414–416
Smithfield Gallows, i. 106
Smoaker Miles, ii. 482
Smollett, ii. 215
  on Dolly's chop-house, ii. 178
Soane, Sir John, on burning of Houses of Parliament, ii. 237
  Museum, ii. 59
Soho Square, i. 428
Soldini, Emily, ii. 180
Somerset, Duke of, at Northumberland House, ii. 266
Somerset House, murder of Sir E. Godfrey at, i. 343
  Royal Academy's rooms in, i. 280
Sothern, Edward, as Lord Dundreary, ii. 22, 280
South Sea Bubble, The, ii. 67–74
  caricature cards of, ii. 71, 74
Southcott, Joanna, i. 411
Southwark Fair, i. 62
  Inns at, i. 59, 60
Spaws, at St. George's Fields, i. 63
Spectator, The, London as described in, ii. 363
Spencer, Herbert, and George Eliot, i. 368
  at Epsom, i. 471
  on the Crystal Palace, ii. 454

Spencer, Lord Robert, gambling at Brooks's, ii. 432
Spitalfields silk industry, the, i. 469
Staël, Mme. de, life in London, ii. 440–441
Stafford, Capt. Philip, ii. 295
Stage Coach Act, ii. 100
Stanhope, Lord, on Duke of Newcastle, ii. 443
Stanley, Dean, on burning of Houses of Parliament, ii. 241
  on tomb of Richard II., ii. 124, 125
" Star and Garter," candlelight duel at, i. 407
Starvation Farm, ii. 82
Steam omnibuses, ii. 101
Steamships between Margate and London, i. 271
Steele on Don Saltero's coffee-house, ii. 464
  on London, ii. 363–365
  on " The Charlie and the Goose," ii. 37
  on the Mohocks, ii. 484
Steeple-flying, i. 99, 100
  jacks, i. 99
Stephen, Leslie, on Gordon Riots, i. 137
Stephen, Sir James, on Wilberforce at Clapham, ii. 425
Stepney, epitaph to Dame Berry at, i. 76
Stillingfleet, Benjamin, ii. 111
Stodart, Robert, i. 474
Stoke Newington, Defoe's estate at, ii. 245
  Samuel Rogers's home at, ii. 247
Storm, the Great, 1703, ii. 409
Strand Bridge, the, i. 306
Street Cries, i. 1, 214, 389 ; ii. 61
" Strong Man of Islington, The," i. 505
Sturges, Joshua, draughts-player, ii. 346
" Sucking-pig Dinner," i. 45
Swearing on the Horns, ii. 35
Swift, Dean, and Stephen Duck, i. 155
Swinburne, at Cheshire Cheese, ii. 6
  at Cheyne Walk, ii. 370
Swiss Cottage, ii. 155
Sword Swallowers at Olympic theatre, i. 303
Sydenham, Crystal Palace at, ii. 453

Tabard Inn, the, i. 207
Talleyrand, Prince, at Crockford's, ii. 244
  at Holland House, i. 176
Tarlton, Richard, the jester, ii. 178, 345, 475
Tattersall, Richard, ii. 405, 406
Taylor, Tom, on death of Hogarth, ii. 60, 61
  Our American Cousin by, ii. 22, 280
Tea-drinking, at Blue-stocking assemblies, ii. 113
  at the Pantheon, i. 328
  at Twining's, ii. 203
  by Dr. Johnson at Mrs. Thrale's, ii. 205
  John Wesley on, ii. 206
" Tellson's Bank," i. 11
Templars, The Knights, i. 487
  destruction of the Order, i. 491
Temple, Knights of the, i. 487
Temple Church, penitential cell in, i. 489, 490
Tennyson, and Browning, ii. 232
  life in London, ii. 228–232
Terry, Edward, ii. 221
Thackeray, and Charlotte Brontë, ii. 199
  at Vauxhall, i. 95

Thackeray, on the Crystal Palace, ii. 453
   on George IV. at Brighton, ii. 483
Thames, boat-racing on, i. 232
   Frost Fair on, i. 320
   pirates of, ii. 386–389
Theodore, King of Corsica, in London, ii. 331
Thistlewood, Arthur, i. 445
Thompson, " Corner Memory," i. 195
Thornhill, Sir James, i. 280
   Hogarth's marriage with his daughter,
      i. 280 ; ii. 56
   paintings on dome of St. Paul's, ii. 188
Thornton, Henry, ii. 425, 427
Thrale, Mrs., ii. 113, 114
   and Dr. Johnson, ii. 205
Thumb, Tom, in London, i. 481
   at court, i. 482
Thumb-screws, i. 30
Thurlow, Lord, i. 98, 174
Thurtell murder, the, i. 128
Thynne, Thomas, murder of, i. 397
Tickell, N., on Brooks's, ii. 431, 432
" Tiddy Doll," i. 152
Tidswell, Miss, and Edmund Kean, ii. 357
" Tiger," the, ii. 389
" Tiger Roach," ii. 485
Tilbury cart, of Hoby, the bootmaker, ii. 16
" Tippitywitchet," i. 102
Tite, Sir William, i. 68
Tobacco, introduction by Sir Walter Raleigh,
      ii. 164
Todd, Sweeney, i. 53
" Tom of Ten Thousand," murder of, i. 397
Tom's Coffee-house, ii. 204
Topham, Thomas, " The Strong Man," i.
      505
Torpedo, the first, ii. 134
Tottenham Court, Adam and Eve Tavern
      at, i. 333, 336–337
   Fair, i. 333
   origin of name, i. 333
   prize-fighting rings at, i. 197
Tournament on London Bridge, ii. 493
Tower, inscriptions by prisoners on walls of,
      ii. 312
   Subway, Verlaine on, ii. 106
Townsend, the Bow Street runner, i. 27 ;
      ii. 169
Trafalgar Square, Nelson Column in, ii. 494
Trevelyan, Sir George, on G. A. Selwyn, ii.
      466
Tschudi, Burckhard, founder of Broad-
      wood's, i. 474
Tucker, Crispin, i. 223
Turgenev, Ivan, in London, ii. 33
   and Carlyle, ii. 34
Turner, J. M. W., picture of the Pantheon
      i. 329
   youth in Maiden Lane, ii. 445
Turpin, Dick, i. 453
   execution of, i. 464
Twelfth Night performances, i. 79
Twining's Tea-house, ii. 203
Tyburn Tree, i. 105
   Hackman's execution at, i. 122
   Henrietta Maria at, i. 107

Tyburn Tree, Lord Fraser's execution at, ii.
      62
   mutilation of Regicides' bodies at, ii. 210
   " New Drop " scaffold at, ii. 62, 66
   public executions at, ii. 119, 177

UMBRELLA, the first, ii. 205

VALENTINI, ii. 89
Vanbrugh, Sir John, introduction of Italian
      opera by, ii. 89
Vance, Alfred G., comedian, ii. 273
Vase, the Portland, i. 480
Vauxhall, entertainments at, i. 91 ; ii. 420
Ventriloquism, ii. 25
Verlaine, in London, ii. 105
Vesey, Mrs., Blue-stocking hostess, ii. 114
Viardot, Mme., ii. 33, 34
Victoria, Queen, and Buckstone, the actor,
      ii. 23
   and Tom Thumb, i. 482
   incident of the " Eagle " Bus, ii. 100
   life at Kensington Palace, i. 496
   on Napoleon III. and Empress Eugenie,
      ii. 264
   on the Opera, ii. 93
" Villikins and his Dinah," i. 394
Vinegar Yard, i. 181
Violante, the steeple-jack, i. 99
Voltaire, life in London, ii. 383

WAITS, the Christmas, ii. 14
Waldegrave, Countess of, ii. 181, 191
Walford, on Seven Dials, i. 123
" Walker, Hookey," ii. 61
" Walking Rushlight, The," i. 57
Waller, Edmund, on tea, ii. 204
Walpole, Horace, i. 48
   at Vauxhall, i. 95
   attacked by highwaymen, i. 451
   friendship with King Theodore of Cor-
      sica, ii. 331
Walton, Sir Isaak, house at St. Dunstan's, ii.
      375
Waltz, introduced at Almack's, ii. 167
Wandsworth Carnival, i. 247
Wapping Old Stairs, " Molly's Song " of,
      i. 344
Ward, on London Highwaymen, i. 453
" Warden, The," Fleet Prison, i. 48
Warwick House, i. 227
Watch, the Marching, i. 71, 72
Watchmen, London, ii. 37, 422
Water-carriers, i. 5, 214
Water-supply of London, i. 213
Waterford, Marquis of, ii. 144
Waterloo Bridge, i. 305
Waterman, Sir George, ii. 196
Watermen, Thames, boat-race of, i. 232
   shooting London Bridge by, ii. 459
Waxworks, Mrs. Salmon's, i. 98
Webster, Benjamin, at the Adelphi, ii. 170–
      172, 227
   duel with Macready, ii. 170
Well Walk, Keats's favourite seat at, i.
      422

Wellington, Duke of, and Hoby the bootmaker, ii. 16
and Tom Thumb, i. 484
anecdotes of, ii. 27
domestic life of, ii. 32
duel with Earl of Winchelsea, i. 44, 498
Duke of Argyll on, ii. 30
friendship with women, ii. 32, 33
life in London, ii. 26-33
meeting with Lord Nelson, i. 86 ; ii. 391
on Chartist riots, ii, 220
Wells, Lord, tournament with Sir David
Lindsay, ii. 492
Welsh Copper Company, the, ii. 72
Wentworth, Lady, relations with Duke of
Monmouth, ii. 403
Place, Keats's house at, i. 424
Wesley, John, on tea-drinking, ii. 206
Rogers on death of, ii. 249
West, Benjamin, R. A., i. 282
Westminster Abbey, assassination sculpture
in, i. 397
Broughton, the prize-fighter's grave in,
i 199
Cromwell's burial in, ii. 209
portrait of Richard II. at, ii. 124, 126
Westminster Bridge, built by lottery, i. 31
echo at, i. 371
Westmoreland, Earl of, at Boodle's, i. 110
Westminster Review, George Eliot as assistant
editor of, i. 367, 368
Whipping Press, ii. 107
White Hart Inn, i. 61, 62
White's Chocolate House, ii. 334
Whitebait Dinner, i. 44
Whitefield, George, i. 337
Whitehall, excution of Charles I. at, i. 158–
163
Whitehead, Miss, the Bank Nun, ii. 52
Whittington, Dick, and Henry V., i. 387
benefits bestowed on London by, i. 390
Bow Bells' message to, ii. 2
his cat, i. 338
College founded by, i. 390
stone at Highgate, ii. 129
Whittle, Jemmy, i. 211
Wilberforce, William, home at Clapham, ii.
425, 426
Wild, Jonathan, ii. 295, 298

Wilke, Charles Wentworth, i. 424
Wilkes, John, ii. 142
and Middlesex election, ii. 307-311
duelling exploits of, ii. 311
North Briton, No. 10, i. 404
Wilkins, W., R.A., ii. 147, 148
William III., and Peter the Great, ii. 435,
437
at Kensington Palace, i. 493
Williams, the printer, in pillory, i. 404
Willis, Nathaniel Parke, on Disraeli, ii. 140
Willis's Rooms, ii. 165
Wilmot, Charles, ii. 353
Wilson, Richard, i. 281
Wimpole Street, No. 50, meeting of the
Brownings at, i. 272
Winchelsea, Earl of, duel with Wellington, i.
498
Winchester, Bishop of, and Beau Brummell,
i. 141
Window in St. Margaret's, i. 203
Winsor, Frederick Albert, Gas Company of,
ii. 212
Woffington, Peg, and Angelo, fencing-master,
i. 391
Wolsey, Cardinal, palace of, i. 97
Wombwell's menagerie, i. 357
Wordsworth at court, ii. 365
Wormwood Scrubs, a day's work at, ii. 396–
401
Wotton, Sir Henry, verses on Queen Eliza-
beth of Bohemia, ii. 272
Wren, Sir Christopher, alterations on Ken-
sington Palace, i. 493
Bow Church designed by, ii. 1
St. Paul's Cathedral designed by, i. 259
Wraxhall, Sir Nathaniel, on executioner of
Charles I., i. 209
Wyatt, Mr. James, architect of The Pantheon,
i. 326, 328
Wylde's Globe, Leicester Square, ii. 475

York Buildings, Peter the Great's house at,
ii. 435, 436

Zoffany, J., picture of Royal Academicians,
i. 282
Zoological Gardens at Tottenham Court,
i. 337